D1044110

Chambers
world factfinder

Chambers

CHAMBERS

An imprint of Chambers Harrap Publishers Ltd
7 Hopetoun Crescent
Edinburgh, EH7 4AY
www.chambers.co.uk

First published by Chambers Harrap Publishers Ltd 2007

A CIP catalogue record for this book is available from the British Library.

ISBN 978 0550 10330 7

Image credits:

Illustration of hydrological cycle (p538):
Copyright © 2005, Houghton Mifflin Company. Reproduced by permission from *The
American Heritage Science Dictionary*.

Illustration of carbon cycle (p540):
Copyright © 2002, Houghton Mifflin Company. Reproduced by permission from *The
American Heritage Student Science Dictionary*.

Cloud images (pp511–12), illustration of geological timescale (pp482–3):
Copyright © 2002, Houghton Mifflin Company. Adapted and reproduced by
permission from *The American Heritage Student Science Dictionary*.

Map of time zones (pp442–3), world political map (pp552–3), relief maps (pp554–66),
thematic maps (pp567–77), world flags (pp578–82):
Copyright © 2006, Larousse, Paris. Adapted and reproduced by permission from
Atlas Petit Larousse des pays du monde.

Map of volcanoes (p469):
Copyright © 2003, Larousse, Paris. Adapted and reproduced by permission from
Petite Encyclopédie Larousse, Phénomènes Naturels.

Designed and typeset by Chambers Harrap Publishers Ltd, Edinburgh

Printed and bound by Legoprint, Italy

CONTRIBUTORS

Editor

Katie Brooks

Contributors

Vicky Aldus
Kate Amann
Dorothea Gschwandtner
Michael Munro
Andrew Owen
Jacqui Owen
Alison Pickering
Howard Sargeant

Editorial Assistance

Vicky Aldus

Prepress

Heather Macpherson

Illustrations

Andrew Laycock

Index

Barbara Hird

Publishing Manager

Camilla Rockwood

INTRODUCTION

Chambers World Factfinder provides a rich and fascinating insight into our world, presented in an attractive and accessible manner. The book is divided into a number of sections, which are outlined below.

An A–Z glossary of useful terms is included in the 'Defining the World' section, which contains entries on geography, geology, ecology, meteorology and more. The section on 'People of the World' contains over 200 mini-biographies of people who have explored, investigated, documented, measured or protected our planet and its inhabitants.

The 'Nations of the World' section features demographic data for each nation, as well as information on its location, physical description, climate, economy, history and government. Details of individual nations are supplemented by panels covering diverse cultural aspects of selected countries.

The section on 'Connecting the World' covers various aspects of communication. Facts about languages, alphabets, time zones and transport are all to be found here. The 'Physical World' section comprises a wealth of information on physical geography, geology and meteorology, while 'World in the Balance' explores a range of environmental issues. Again, panels are used to explore specific topics in greater depth.

Finally, a full-colour supplement, 'Picturing the World', contains a range of political, relief and thematic maps to bring the world to life, as well as each country's national flag.

A detailed contents list and comprehensive index ensure that facts, figures, names and locations can be easily located for projects or homework. Eye-catching boxes containing additional facts and quotations are interspersed throughout the text, ensuring that this book is also ideal for browsing.

ABBREVIATIONS

AD	Anno Domini
Apr	April
Aug	August
b.	born
BC	Before Christ
bya	billion years ago
c	century
c.	circa
°C	degrees Celsius (Centigrade)
CFCs	chlorofluorocarbons
cm	centimetre(s)
CO_2	carbon dioxide
cu	cubic
d.	died
Dec	December
E	east
e	estimate
°F	degrees Fahrenheit
Feb	February
fl.	flourished
ft	foot (feet)
g	gram(s)
gal	gallon(s)
GMT	Greenwich Mean Time
h	hour(s)
ha	hectare(s)
ie	that is
in	inch(es)
ISO	International Organization for Standardization
Jan	January
Jul	July
Jun	June
kg	kilogram(s)

km	kilometre(s)
kph	kilometres per hour
l	litre(s)
lb	pound(s)
m	metre(s)
mi	mile(s)
min	minute(s)
ml	millilitre(s)
mm	millimetre(s)
Mar	March
mph	miles per hour
Mt	mount
mya	million years ago
N	north
NASA	National Aeronautics and Space Administration (USA)
Nov	November
Oct	October
Prot	Protestant
pt	pint(s)
RC	Roman Catholic
S	south
s	second(s)
Sep	September
SO_2	sulphur dioxide
sq km	square kilometres
sq mi	square miles
UK	United Kingdom
UN	United Nations
US	United States
USA	United States of America
USSR	Union of Soviet Socialist Republics
W	west
yd	yard(s)

CONTENTS

WORLD FACTFINDER

WORLD FACTFINDER

CONNECTING THE WORLD — 437

THE PHYSICAL WORLD — 459

DEFINING THE WORLD: AN A–Z OF TERMS

A

ablation zone
An area of ▸ **glaciation** in which ▸ **glaciers** are melting and therefore becoming smaller.

abrasion
Erosion caused when rocks and other material in a river or ▸ **glacier** scrape the surfaces with which they are in contact.

abyss or abyssal benthic zone
The very deep area of some oceans, deeper than 2000 m.

accretion zone
A gap between two ▸ **tectonic plates** into which ▸ **magma** flows, repairing the gap between the plates.

accumulation zone
An area of ▸ **glaciation** in which ▸ **glaciers** are becoming larger.

advection
The horizontal movement of an ▸ **air mass**.

aeolian deposits
Sediments carried and deposited by wind, eg desert sands.

aeon
The largest division of geological time. There are two aeons: the ▸ **Precambrian Aeon** and the ▸ **Phanerozoic Aeon**.

ageing population
A population in which the proportion of elderly people is increasing or, loosely, in which there is a high proportion of elderly people. Compare ▸ **youthful population**.

agroclimatology
The use of knowledge about the behaviour of different climates for the benefit of agriculture.

air frost
An air temperature of below 0°C. See also ▸ **ground frost**.

air mass
A vast body of air that has uniform temperature and humidity and that moves horizontally.

albedo
The ratio of the amount of ▸ **solar radiation** absorbed by a surface to the amount reflected. The albedo varies according to the angle at which the radiation strikes the surface.

allopatric speciation
The development of new species due to the geographical separation of populations. The separation is caused by natural obstacles such as rivers and mountains, and prevents the populations from interbreeding. Compare ▸ **sympatric speciation**.

alluvium	Sediment deposited by running water such as rivers or floods.
amplitude	The difference between the minimum and maximum values of a measurable quantity, eg rainfall or atmospheric pressure, within a given period.
anemometer	An instrument used to measure the speed or pressure of the wind.
angle of declination	see ▸ **declination**
angle of incidence	The angle at which radiation strikes a surface.
Antarctic convergence zone	The region of the Southern Ocean in which cold and dense water flowing away from the icy land mass of Antarctica meets warmer water from neighbouring oceans and sinks beneath it.
anthropology	The study of humans, covering their physical traits, culture and way of life.
anticyclone	A mass of sinking air that creates high pressure, and from which air rotates outwards. The air rotates clockwise in the Northern Hemisphere and anticlockwise in the Southern Hemisphere. Compare ▸ **cyclone**.
aquifer	Any rock formation containing water in quantities that can be recovered, eg from a well that it supplies.
arboreal	Used to describe animals that live in trees.
arête	A ridge between two ▸ **cirques** on a mountain.
arid	Used to describe very dry regions in which there is very little rainfall.
arroyo	see ▸ **wadi**
attrition	Erosion in which rocks scrape against each other and are worn down.
ascent	An upward movement of air.

B

bajada or bahada	A slope formed by the ▸ **deposition** of rock debris.
bar	(1) A raised area of sand, mud and stones at the mouth of a river or on a beach. (2) A unit used in expressing atmospheric pressure, equal to 10,000 newtons per square metre.
base flow	▸ **Groundwater** that discharges to a river, or that part of the discharge that is groundwater.

base level	The lowest level to which land in a riverbed or seabed can be eroded by water.
basin	The area from which water flows into a river and its ▸ **tributaries**.
Beaufort scale	A system of classifying wind speeds that divides wind into categories, each of which is given a number and a short description (eg force 5, fresh breeze). The standard scale has categories from 0 to 12 but categories 13 to 17 are used by some countries for hurricanes and typhooons.
beach nourishment or replenishment	Action taken to improve a beach by artificial means such as bringing in sand from elsewhere.
beach profile	A measurement of the height, length and steepness of a beach.
benthos	Creatures that live on or near the bottom of a sea, lake or other body of water.
berm	A ridge of sand or stones on a beach, formed by incoming tides.
billabong	see ▸ **ox-bow lake**
bioclimatology	The branch of ▸ **ecology** that studies the relationship between plants and animals and the climate in which they exist.
biodiversity	The variety of animals and plants found in a particular geographical region.
bioluminescence	The production of light by certain living organisms, eg glow-worms, some deep-sea fish, some bacteria and some fungi.
biomass	The total mass of all the living organisms in a specific ▸ **ecosystem** or population at a given moment.
biome	A major ecological community of living organisms, usually defined by the plant habitat (eg rainforest or grassland) with which it is associated.
biosphere	The part of the Earth's surface and atmosphere in which living things are known to exist.
biota	The organisms present in a particular area.
biotechnology	The use of living things, eg bacteria, or of the enzymes produced by them, in the manufacture of products or the development of processes such as energy production, waste processing and drug manufacture.
blowout	see ▸ **deflation hollow**

blowhole	(1) A hole in an area of surface ice where marine mammals, eg seals, can go to breathe. (2) A natural vent from the roof of a sea cave up to the ground surface, through which air and water are forced by breaking waves.
boreal zones	Areas of the Northern Hemisphere that have a climate with a great range of temperature. Temperatures do not exceed 3°C in the coldest period, and remain above 10°C in the warmest period. Boreal zones include parts of northern Europe and Russia, and the prairie regions of the USA.

C

Cainozoic Era	see ▸ **Cenozoic Era**
caldera	The summit of a volcano that has collapsed after a particularly violent eruption.
calm	The state represented by force 0 on the ▸ **Beaufort scale**, in which any wind blows at below 1 kph and in which smoke rises vertically.
Cambrian Period	The earliest ▸ **period** of the ▸ **Palaeozoic Era**, extending from 570 million to 510 million years ago, during which marine invertebrates developed.
canopy	The tops of tall trees, especially those in a ▸ **rainforest**, regarded as a distinct environment.
cape	A point of land that extends into the sea.
Carboniferous Period	see ▸ **Lower Carboniferous Period, Upper Carboniferous Period**
carrying capacity	The maximum number of people or animals that a given area of land can support.
cash crop	A crop that is grown for sale rather than for consumption by the farmer's household or by livestock.
cataclasis	The deformation of rocks by crushing.
catastrophe	A sudden and violent upheaval in some part of the surface of the earth.
catch crop	A secondary crop grown in the space unoccupied by a main crop.
catchment area	An area of land from which water flows into a river and its ▸ **tributaries**. Also called a **drainage basin.**
CBD	An abbreviation for ▸ **central business district**.

Cenozoic Era	The most recent ▸ **era** of the ▸ **Phanerozoic Aeon**, extending from 65 million years ago to the present day. Also called the **Cainozoic Era**.
central business district	The area in or near the centre of a town or city that contains its largest concentration of commercial premises. Abbrev *CBD*.
CFCs	Chlorofluorocarbons, synthetic compounds that are chemically inert and were once widely used in industry, eg in aerosol propellants. When released into the atmosphere, they react with ozone and have resulted in damage to the ▸ **ozone layer**, contributing therefore to ▸ **global warming**. See also ▸ **greenhouse effect**.
chemical weathering	The decomposition of rock caused by a chemical interaction with sea water or rainwater, or by a chemical change within the rock. Compare ▸ **mechanical weathering**.
chlorofluorocarbons	see ▸ **CFCs**
cirque	A steep-sided round hollow, rather like a natural amphitheatre, formed by glaciation. Also called a **corrie** (in Scotland) or **cwm** (in Wales).
cirrus	Wispy cloud at very high levels, consisting of ice crystals.
CITES	The Convention on International Trade in Endangered Species of Wild Fauna and Flora, which came into force in 1975. It regulates international trade in over 30,000 species of plants and animals.
class	In biological classification or ▸ **taxonomy**, a category of organisms that ranks below a ▸ **phylum** and above an ▸ **order**.
climate	The combination of atmospheric conditions, eg temperature, rainfall and wind, that exists in a given place.
climatic anomaly	A weather phenomenon, eg a period of extreme heat, that is completely untypical of the climate of a particular region.
climatic crisis	A ▸ **climatic anomaly** that is particularly extreme and lasts for a long time, regarded by some scientists as evidence of ▸ **global warming**
climatic zone	Any of the zones into which the world can be divided according to climate, roughly corresponding to zones of ▸ **latitude**.

climatology	The study of the world's climates, their history and their causes.
cloud forest	A mountain forest that is continuously covered by cloud.
col	A depression or pass in a mountain range.
cold front	The leading edge of a mass of cold air advancing against a mass of less dense warm air. Unstable weather conditions result, often leading to heavy rainfall. See also ▸ **occluded front**.
cold pole	The region in each hemisphere where the lowest temperatures have been recorded.
collective farming	(1) The running of a farm by a group of individuals, with profits shared by the whole group. (2) In the former Soviet Union, state-controlled farming on large farms formed by the merging of several smaller, formerly privately owned farms.
commuter village or town	A village or small town from which people commute to work in a nearby city or large town.
confluence	A place where rivers or streams join and flow together.
constructive wave	A type of wave, found in calm conditions, that carries and deposits material on the shore. Compare ▸ **destructive wave**.
continental climate	A climate that has low rainfall and is warm in summer and cool in winter, typical of the interior of a landmass. Compare ▸ **maritime climate**.
continental drift	The theory of the slow drifting apart of ▸ **landmasses**, believed by many scientists to have caused the formation of the world's continents from a single landmass.
continental ice sheet	A vast ▸ **glacier** that permanently covers a large area of a ▸ **landmass** and masks the contours of the ground beneath it.
continental shelf	The underwater ledge of land that borders the visible edge of a continent.
contour line	A line drawn on a map through points that are all at the same height above or below sea level.
convection	The upward movement of a mass of air that is heated by the sun and expands as a result, becoming less dense and creating an area of low pressure beneath it. The heated air eventually cools at higher altitudes, moves sideways away from the rising air below it, and falls, creating an area of high pressure.

convergence	The movement of separate air masses towards each other.
Coordinated Universal Time	see ▸ **GMT**
core	(1) The magnetic centre of the Earth. (2) The most economically important and prosperous part of a country or region. Compare ▸ **periphery**.
Coriolis effect	A phenomenon, produced by the rotation of the Earth, whereby falling objects and weather systems follow a curving path. This results in winds travelling clockwise around high-pressure systems in the Northern Hemisphere and anticlockwise in the Southern Hemisphere; the opposite is true of winds around low-pressure systems. Another consequence is that an object falling freely towards the Earth from a great height is slightly deviated from a straight line and will fall to a point east of that directly below its initial position.
corrie	see ▸ **cirque**
counterurbanization	The movement of people away from towns into the countryside.
crag	A rough, steep, cliff-like formation of rocks on a hillside.
crater	The bowl-shaped mouth of a volcano.
craton	A relatively rigid and stable area of rock in the Earth's ▸ **crust**.
Cretaceous Period	The most recent ▸ **period** of the ▸ **Mesozoic Era**, extending from 146 million to 65 million years ago, during which flowering plants developed and at the end of which dinosaurs are thought to have become extinct.
crust	The topmost layer of the Earth, around 10 km thick under the oceans and around 30 km thick where there are continents.
cumulonimbus	Massive, fluffy cloud that is bigger and slightly higher than ▸ **cumulus**, bringing heavy showers or thunderstorms and strong winds.
cumulus	Fluffy cloud at a slightly lower level than ▸ **cumulonimbus**, the appearance of which is a sign of the approach of moderate showers.
cwm	see ▸ **cirque**

cyclone	A rotating mass of air with very low pressure at the centre, circulating anticlockwise in the Northern Hemisphere and clockwise in the Southern Hemisphere.. Compare ▸ **anticyclone**.

D

debacle or débâcle	A sudden flood of water that leaves its path strewn with debris.
declination	The angle between true north and magnetic north. Also called the **angle of declination**.
decomposers	Organisms in soil that break down dead organic matter, eg animal carcasses and plant debris, and thereby produce nutrients for plants.
deflation	The movement of fine particles, eg sand, by the wind.
deflation hollow	A shallow depression from which fine material, eg sand, has been blown by wind. Also called a **blowout**.
delta	A flat, triangular stretch of land at the mouth of a river, where it splits into branches.
demographic transition model	A graph showing changes in a population over time.
deposition	The process by which eroded rock that has been transported by wind, rivers, glaciers and avalanches is laid down in a place where it settles.
depression	A low-pressure weather system consisting of a mass of warm air rising in the centre, surrounded by cooler air circulating round it. Circulation occurs in an anticlockwise direction in the Northern Hemisphere and a clockwise direction in the Southern Hemisphere. Depressions bring unsettled weather.
desert	An area of barren land in which evaporation exceeds rainfall.
desertification	The transformation of fertile land into desert.
destructive wave	A strong wave, found in storm conditions, that removes material from the shore and causes coastal erosion. Compare ▸ **constructive wave**.
Devonian Period	The ▸ **period** of the ▸ **Palaeozoic Era** during which the first forests were formed and the first amphibians developed, extending from 408 million to 362 million years ago.

dew	Water vapour that has condensed into droplets of water at ground level, on to the surfaces of objects. See also ▸ **fog**.
dew point	see ▸ **saturation point**
dinoturbation	The effects of trampling by dinosaurs on the formation of sedimentary rock.
discharge	The volume of water passing a specific point in a river over a specific period of time.
distributary	A branch of a river that flows from the main river. Compare ▸ **tributary**.
divergence	The movement of masses of air away from a central point.
dormitory	A small town or a suburb from which most residents commute to work elsewhere.
doubling time	The time it takes for a population to double.
drainage basin	see ▸ **catchment area**
drizzle	Rain consisting of very fine water droplets.
dust bowl	An area of land from which the topsoil has been eroded by strong winds and drought.

E

ecological footprint	A measure of the effect that something has on the environment, eg the amount of waste it produces or the amount of carbon dioxide it emits.
ecology	The scientific study of the relationships between living organisms and their environment, including the distribution and abundance of living organisms (ie exactly where they occur and precisely how many there are).
ecoregion	A region of the world with an ▸ **ecosystem** that is particularly rich in species, defined by the WWF as 'a large unit of land or water that contains a geographically distinct assemblage of species, natural communities and environmental conditions'. The Earth has 200 terrestrial and marine ecoregions.
ecosystem	A community consisting of animals, plants and their environment. The term emphasizes the interactions between living and non-living parts, and the flow of materials and energy between these parts.

El Niño
A periodic large-scale warming of the surface of the eastern Pacific Ocean, especially off the coast of Peru and Ecuador. It affects the patterns of ▸ **trade winds** and is associated with weather anomalies and extreme weather conditions in the Pacific region; for example, flooding in normally dry regions and drought in regions that normally have high rainfall. Compare ▸ **La Niña**.

employment structure
The number of people in work in a particular area, and the variety of jobs they do.

endemic
Used to describe a species of plant or animal that occurs only in a particular region and is believed to have evolved there.

Eocene Epoch
The second earliest ▸ **epoch** of the ▸ **Tertiary Period** of the ▸ **Cenozoic Era**, extending from 65 million to 56.5 million years ago, during which the first modern mammals appeared.

epicentre
The point on the surface of the Earth that lies immediately above the point of origin of an earthquake or nuclear explosion.

epigene
Acting or taking place at the Earth's surface.

epiphyte
A plant that grows on another plant for support but does not live on it as a parasite.

epoch
The smallest division of geological time, into which a ▸ **period** is divided.

erosion
The gradual wearing away of land by water, wind and ice.

equator
An imaginary line that encircles the world, equidistant from the North and South Poles. ▸ **Latitude** is measured in degrees north and south from this line.

equinox
Either of the two days of the year when the path of the Sun crosses a line drawn above the equator, making the hours of daylight and hours of darkness virtually equal. The equinoxes occur around 21 March and 23 September.

era
A division of geological time into which an ▸ **aeon** is divided, consisting of several ▸ **periods** that are themselves subdivided into ▸ **epochs**.

erosion
The gradual wearing away of land by the movement of water, wind and ice against it.

esker or eskar
A ridge of gravel and sand formed by a stream that issues from a retreating glacier, known as a subglacial stream. Also called a **kame**.

ethnography	The systematic description of a particular race, ethnic group or community, including the customs and culture of the group members.
ethology	The study of animal behaviour.
eutrophication	The process by which a body of water becomes over-enriched with nutrients, eg from sewage or agricultural fertilizers, resulting in overgrowth of algae and depleted oxygen levels, and the death of aquatic animals.
evolution	The development of organisms over time due to genetic variation and ▸ **natural selection**.

F

family	In biological classification or ▸ **taxonomy**, a category of organisms that ranks below an ▸ **order** and above a ▸ **genus**.
fault	A fracture in rocks along which some displacement has taken place. The displacement may vary from a few millimetres to thousands of metres. Movement along faults is the most common cause of earthquakes. See also ▸ **plate tectonics**.
faultline	A surface along which ▸ **faults** have occurred or are likely to occur.
fauna	The animal life present in a particular region or at a particular period in history. Compare ▸ **flora**.
field capacity	The water-retaining capacity of soil.
fjord	A deep and narrow inlet of the sea that exists where the sea has flooded a valley produced by a glacier, common in Norway and New Zealand.
flood plain	An extensive level area beside a river that becomes covered with water when the river floods.
flora	The plant life of a particular region or a particular period in history. Compare ▸ **fauna**.
fog	A cloud-like concentration of fine water droplets that occurs when water vapour condenses just above the ground. When condensation occurs at ground level, ▸ **dew** is formed. At higher levels, condensation causes clouds to be formed.
föhn or foehn	A warm dry wind that descends from the Alps into northern Europe, bringing a rise in temperature and pressure.

fold mountain	A mountain formed by part of the Earth's ▸ **crust** being pushed up by the collision of ▸ **tectonic plates.**
fossil	The remains of a living thing preserved in rock.
fossil fuel	A fuel that has been formed from the fossilized remains of living organisms. Coal, oil and natural gas are all fossil fuels.
free face	A slope at an angle of 45° or more, therefore too steep for eroded material or debris to lie on.
freeze-thaw	Erosion caused by the alternate freezing and thawing of water in cracks in rock, and the subsequent widening and contracting of the cracks.
fresh breeze	A force 5 wind on the ▸ **Beaufort scale**, blowing at between 30 and 38 kph and in which small trees sway.
front	The leading edge of a moving mass of cold or warm air. A cold front causes any warm air that it encounters to rise rapidly, creating the possibility of thunderstorms. A warm front rises above any layers of cold air that it encounters, causing cloud to form that may produce rain over a large area.
frost	(1) True frost, a layer of ice crystals that forms when moist air near the ground cools to below freezing without first condensing to form dew. Also called **hoar frost**. (2) Frozen dew.

G

gale	A force 8 wind on the ▸ **Beaufort scale**, blowing at between 62 and 74 kph and in which twigs snap off trees.
gentle breeze	A force 3 wind on the ▸ **Beaufort scale**, blowing at between 12 and 19 kph and in which leaves and twigs move.
gentrification	The movement of middle-class people into a formerly working-class area, and the consequent changes in the character of the area.
genus	In biological classification or ▸ **taxonomy**, a category of organisms that ranks below a ▸ **family** and above a ▸ **species**.
geochronology	The branch of ▸ **geology** in which the study of rocks and fossils is applied to determining the age of the Earth.
geodesy	The measurement of the Earth.

geographic pole	Either of two points on the Earth's surface (the geographic North Pole and the geographic South Pole), found at either end of the Earth's axis. Compare ▶ **magnetic pole**.
geology	The study of the structure, history and physical properties of the Earth.
geomorphology	The branch of ▶ **geology** that deals with land forms such as mountains, valleys and other plains, sometimes also encompassing the study of ocean basins and other underwater forms.
geothermal	Relating to heat produced naturally within the Earth.
glacial	Relating to ▶ **glaciers** or ▶ **glaciation**, or formed by the movement of glaciers.
glacial trough	A U-shaped river valley, caused by erosion of its sides by a moving ▶ **glacier**.
glaciation	The formation of ▶ **glaciers**.
glacier	A huge mass of ice fed by snow. Alpine glaciers cover mountains, or move slowly down valleys between high mountains. Continental glaciers are ice sheets covering flatter areas.
global positioning system	see ▶ **GPS**
global warming	The slow increase in the Earth's surface air temperature, thought to be caused by the ▶ **greenhouse effect**.
GMT	Greenwich Mean Time, the time in the UK when British Summer Time is not in force. GMT is the time standard in relation to which time is calculated in all other time zones of the world. Also called **Coordinated Universal Time** or UTC.
gorge	A deep narrow valley.
GPS	Global positioning system, a navigation system in which information from a network of satellites is fed to a handheld or vehicle-mounted device that displays the user's location with a high degree of accuracy.
graben	see ▶ **rift valley**
greenhouse effect	The phenomenon by which thermal radiation from the Sun, reflected by the Earth's surface, is trapped within the Earth's atmosphere by the presence of ▶ **greenhouse gases.** An increase in the greenhouse effect due to the production of these gases is a major cause of ▶ **global warming**.

greenhouse gas	Any gas that contributes to the ▸ **greenhouse effect**. The main greenhouse gases are carbon dioxide, methane and ▸ **CFCs**.
green revolution	Agricultural advances in developing countries, eg the introduction of new varieties of crop leading to an increase in food production.
Greenwich Mean Time	see ▸ **GMT**
Greenwich meridian	An imaginary line that encircles the world, passing through both North and South Poles via Greenwich in southern England. ▸ **Longitude** is measured in degrees east and west from this line.
ground frost	▸ **Frost** on the surface of the ground, which forms at a ground temperature of 0°C or less.
groundwater	Water beneath the surface of the earth that accumulates when rainwater filters through the soil. The ▸ **water table** is the upper surface of groundwater.
gulch	In the USA, a narrow ▸ **gorge** that may contain a stream.
Gulf Stream	An ocean current that brings relatively warm water from the Gulf of Mexico across the North Atlantic to the shores of the UK and western Europe, making the winters relatively mild compared with winters in many other countries on the same ▸ **latitude**.
gullying	A type of ▸ **erosion** of cliffs, caused by rain eroding soft rock and forming channels that allow surface material to wash away.
gyre	A swirling current on the surface of an ocean, driven by wind.

H

habitat	The natural environment in which an organism lives.
hanging valley	A ▸ **tributary** valley that enters a main valley at a much higher level because the main valley has become deeper as a result of glacial ▸ **erosion**.
HDI	see ▸ **Human Development Index**
hemisphere	Half of the globe. The equator can be thought of as dividing the globe into the Northern and Southern Hemispheres.
hoar frost	see ▸ **frost**

Holocene Epoch	The current ▸ **epoch** of the ▸ **Quaternary Period** of the ▸ **Cenozoic Era**, extending from 10,000 years ago to the present day.
hominid	In older usage, humans and their immediate ancestors who walked on two feet. Now considered to include any member of the Hominidae (great ape) family, which includes humans, gorillas, orang-utans and chimpanzees and their close ancestors.
horizon	The distant line at which the earth and the sky seem to meet.
horst	A block of the earth's ▸ **crust** that has remained in position while the ground around it has either subsided or been folded into mountains by pressure against its solid sides.
hot spot	(1) An area on the Earth's upper ▸ **mantle** from which a column of ▸ **magma** rises up, breaking through the Earth's ▸ **crust** and creating a volcano. (2) Any of the 25 regions that constitute the richest – and most threatened – reservoirs of plant and animal life on Earth.
Human Development Index	A scale used to measure the development of a country, using a number of indicators including adult literacy and infant mortality.
hurricane	A force 12 wind on the ▸ **Beaufort scale**, which blows at speeds above 120 kph and causes widespread destruction.
hydrography	The investigation of seas and other bodies of water, including surveying and the study of tides and currents.

I

ice age	Any of various geological periods during which most of the surface of the earth was covered in ice, particularly the most recent period during the ▸ **Pleistocene Epoch**, which ended around 10,000 years ago.
iceberg	A block of floating ice that has broken away from a ▸ **glacier**.
icecap	A permanent covering of ice, as found at the North and South Poles.
ice floe	A sheet of floating ice formed when seawater freezes. Ice floes are at least 2 to 3 metres thick.
ice sheet	A layer of ice covering a large area or an entire region.

igneous rock	Rock produced by volcanic activity in the Earth's ▸ **crust** and upper ▸ **mantle**. Examples are granite, basalt and pumice. Compare ▸ **metamorphic rock, sedimentary rock**.
inselberg	A steep-sided hill rising from a plain, often found in the semi-▸ **arid** regions of tropical countries.
intensive farming	A method of farming that uses large amounts of labour or capital to obtain the maximum yield from a limited area of land.
interglacial	Occurring between two periods of ▸ **glacial** action.
interglacial period	A retreat of ice between periods of ▸ **glaciation**.
intermontane	Used to describe a ▸ **basin** that lies between mountain ranges, often associated with a ▸ **rift valley**.
interstadial	A retreat of ice during a ▸ **glacial** period, shorter than an ▸ **interglacial**.
isobar	A line on a weather map that joins points of equal atmospheric pressure.
isotherm	A line on a weather map that joins points of equal temperature.
isthmus	A narrow neck of land connecting two larger portions.
IUCN	The International Union for the Conservation of Nature, whose official name was changed in 1990 to 'IUCN – The World Conservation Union'. It is an alliance of research and nature conservation organizations, states, government agencies, non-governmental organizations and scholars. Its aim is to conserve the integrity and diversity of nature, and it produces and updates a list of the world's most threatened species.
IVR	International Vehicle Registration, a system that identifies the country of registration of road vehicles travelling overseas by means of a code of representative letters.

J

jet stream	A high-speed wind that circulates at an altitude of more than 6 km.
Jurassic Period	The middle ▸ **period** of the ▸ **Mesozoic Era**, extending from 208 million to 146 million years ago, during which the earliest birds developed.

K

kame
see ▸ **esker**

karst
An area of rough limestone with underground drainage.

keystone species
A species that performs an essential role within an ▸ **ecosystem**. The species may only account for a small proportion of the ▸ **biomass** or the productivity of the ecosystem; however, its removal would have a marked negative effect on its dependent species and the ecosystem as a whole.

kingdom
In biological classification or ▸ **taxonomy**, the highest category of organisms, ranking above a ▸ **phylum**. At one time, only plant and animal kingdoms were recognized, but now five kingdoms are generally accepted: plants, animals, fungi, protists and prokaryotes.

knot
A unit of speed equal to 1 ▸ **nautical mile** per hour.

L

landmass
A large area of land unbroken by seas.

La Niña
A periodic cooling of the surface of the eastern Pacific Ocean, which causes abnormal weather conditions more or less opposite to those caused by ▸ **El Niño**.

lapse rate
The rate at which temperature changes in relation to height above sea level.

latitude
The angular distance of a point north or south relative to the ▸ **equator**, measured in degrees. A point on the equator has a latitude of 0°, while the ▸ **geographic poles** are at 90°N and 90°S respectively. Compare ▸ **longitude**.

lava
Molten rock from underground that flows to the Earth's surface. See also ▸ **magma**.

leaching
The removal of nutrients from the soil by the action of rainwater.

lee side
The side of an object, eg a mountain, that faces ▸ **leeward** and is therefore sheltered. Compare ▸ **weather side**.

leeward
The direction towards which the wind blows; downwind. Compare ▸ **windward**.

Less Economically Developed Country
A country with a low level of development, as measured by indicators such as income from trade. Abbrev *LEDC*. Compare ▸ **More Economically Developed Country**.

light air	A force 1 wind on the ▸ **Beaufort scale**, blowing at between 1 and 5 kph and in which smoke drifts slowly.
light breeze	A force 2 wind on the ▸ **Beaufort scale**, blowing at between 6 and 11 kph and in which leaves rustle and weathervanes begin to move.
lithosphere	The outermost layer of the Earth's ▸ **crust**, divided into ▸ **tectonic plates**.
longitude	The angular distance of a point east or west relative to the ▸ **Greenwich meridian**, measured in degrees. A point lying on the Greenwich meridian has a longitude of 0°, while a point directly opposite it has a longitude of 180°. Other longitudes are given in °E or °W. Compare ▸ **latitude**.
Lower Carboniferous Period	The ▸ **period** of the ▸ **Palaeozoic Era** during which widespread shallow seas were formed, extending from 362 million to 333 million years ago.

M

maar	A crater that forms when a rising mass of ▸ **magma** makes contact with a body of water.
magma	Molten rock when it is beneath the Earth's surface. When it rises to the Earth's surface, as can happen in a volcanic eruption, it becomes ▸ **lava**.
magnetic pole	Either of two points on the Earth's surface (magnetic North Pole and magnetic South Pole) at which the Earth's magnetic field is entirely vertical and the needle of a magnetic compass points in random directions. The positions of the magnetic poles vary over time and are close to, but not the same as, those of the ▸ **geographic poles**.
mangrove swamp	A forest habitat based around mangrove trees, salt-tolerant tropical and subtropical trees that can grow partially submerged in water. It is found in coastal areas of Central and South America, Southern Africa, south-east Asia and Australasia.
mantle	The rocky layer that lies between the Earth's ▸ **core** and its outer ▸ **crust**.
maritime climate	A climate that has little seasonal variation and is cool in summer and mild in winter, typical of coastal regions.
market economy	An economy in which prices are determined by competition on the open market, without government intervention. Compare ▸ **planned economy**.

massif	A mountainous plateau surrounded by lowland.
meander	A bend in a winding river.
mechanical weathering	The decomposition of rock caused by natural processes such as freeze-thaw, and not by chemical changes. Also called **physical weathering**. Compare ▸ **chemical weathering**.
MEDC	An abbreviation for ▸ **More Economically Developed Country**.
Mediterranean zones	Areas that have some rain and mild winters, with the coolest month generally having temperatures above 0°C and below 18°C.
Mercalli intensity scale	A scale used to compare the intensities of earthquakes based on their effects on people, objects and the Earth itself. The form of the scale used today, the Modified Mercalli scale, is divided into twelve categories, with 1 being barely detectable and 12 causing total destruction. Intensity scales are more subjective than magnitude scales such as the ▸ **Richter scale** but are useful for distinguishing between major earthquakes.
mesosphere	The layer of the Earth's atmosphere above the ▸ **stratosphere**, at an altitude of between 40 and 80 km.
Mesozoic Era	The middle ▸ **era** of the ▸ **Phanerozoic Aeon**, extending from 245 million to 65 million years ago.
metamorphic rock	Rock produced when pressure and heat cause changes in existing rocks. Examples are slate and marble. Compare ▸ **igneous rock**, **sedimentary rock**.
meteorology	The study of the Earth's atmosphere, especially in relation to weather and climate.
Miocene Epoch	The second most recent ▸ **epoch** of the ▸ **Tertiary Period** of the ▸ **Cenozoic Era**, extending from 23.3 million to 5.2 million years ago, during which grasses and grazing mammals developed.
mist	Light fog that reduces visibility to between 1 and 5 km.
moderate breeze	A force 4 wind on the **Beaufort scale**, blowing at between 20 and 29 kph and in which small branches move and dust is blown about.
monsoon	A seasonal wind in tropical regions that can bring heavy rainfall and flash flooding. The most dramatic monsoons occur in India, but monsoons also occur in northern Australia, Africa and the south-western United States.

moraine	An area of rocky debris deposited on a hillside by a ▸ **glacier**.
More Economically Developed Country	A country with a high level of development, as measured by indicators such as income from trade. Abbrev *MEDC*. Compare ▸ **Less Economically Developed Country**.

N

natural selection	A widely accepted theory of ▸ **evolution** stating that the organisms that are best adapted to their environment have the best chances of reproducing and passing on their genes.
nautical mile	A unit of distance used in navigation at sea, equal to one minute (1/60 degree) of ▸ **latitude** measured along the ▸ **equator**. Equivalent to 1.85 km or 1.15 mi. See also ▸ **knot**.
near gale	A force 7 wind on the ▸ **Beaufort scale**, blowing at between 51 and 61 kph, in which trees sway and against which people find it difficult to walk.
nekton	A collective term for organisms that can swim against ocean currents. These include fish, marine reptiles, sea birds and many other organisms. Compare ▸ **plankton**.
niche	A small area of habitat providing the conditions necessary for a particular organism or species to survive.
nivation	Erosion caused by snow, eg ▸ **freeze-thaw** and the carrying of material by melting snow.
nivation hollow	A depression caused by material being eroded by the action of snow.

O

oasis	An isolated fertile area in a sandy ▸ **desert**, usually having a source of fresh water.
occluded front	An advancing ▸ **cold front** into which a mass of warm air has been driven obliquely, forming a bulge that narrows as the warm air is lifted up and the cold air flows in beneath.
oceanic trench	A very deep steep-sided channel in the sea bed, usually deeper than 5,000 m.
Oligocene Epoch	The middle ▸ **epoch** of the ▸ **Tertiary Period** of the ▸ **Cenozoic Era**, extending from 35.4 million to 23.3 million years ago, during which true carnivores developed.

ombrophilous	Used to describe plants and animals that are adapted to high levels of humidity or rainfall.
open habitat	An expanse of open land that is treeless or has very few trees, eg a ► **steppe**.
order	In biological classification or ► **taxonomy**, a category of organisms that ranks below a ► **class** and above a ► **family**.
Ordovician Period	The ► **period** of the ► **Paleozoic Era** during which primitive fish developed, extending from 510 million to 439 million years ago.
overgrazing	The significant degrading of soil and vegetation in an area where land is given over to livestock.
overpopulation	A state in which there are more individuals in a given area than can be supported by the natural resources of the area.
ox-bow lake	A shallow curved lake found alongside a meandering river, formed when one of the bends has been cut off. Also called a **billabong** (in Australia).
ozone layer	A layer of the gas ozone in the ► **stratosphere**, at altitudes between 15 and 40 km. Ozone absorbs most of the damaging ultraviolet radiation from the Sun, and the discovery of a hole in the ozone layer, created by industrial pollution of various kinds, has led to the widespread belief that industrial nations need to change their behaviour in relation to the environment.

P

pack ice	A large mass of ice floating freely on the sea, formed when smaller pieces are driven together by wind and currents.
Palaeocene Epoch	The earliest ► **epoch** of the ► **Tertiary Period** of the ► **Cenozoic Era**, extending from 65 million to 56.5 million years ago.
palaeontology	The study of fossils.
Palaeozoic Era	The oldest ► **era** of the ► **Phanerozoic Aeon** of geological time, extending from 570 million to 245 million years ago.
pampas	A huge grassy treeless plain in southern South America.
parallel	A line that marks ► **latitude**, drawn east to west across a map or round a globe at a set distance from the ► **equator**.

pelagic	Relating to or found in the deepest parts of the open sea.
peninsula	A coastal strip of land that juts out into the surrounding water.
periglacial	Used to describe a region that borders a ▸ **glacier**.
period	A division of geological time into which an ▸ **era** is divided, itself subdivided into ▸ **epochs**.
periphery	The least economically important and often poorest part of a country or region. Compare ▸ **core**.
Permian Period	The most recent ▸ **period** of the ▸ **Palaeozoic Era**, stretching from 290 million to 245 million years ago, during which the first conifers, woody plants and other gymnosperms (primitive plants) developed.
petrology	the study of the formation of rocks, their structure, and their chemical and mineral composition.
Phanerozoic Aeon	The most recent ▸ **aeon** of geological time, the aeon to which almost all our knowledge of geological time relates, covering the period from 570 million years ago to the present day. Compare ▸ **Precambrian Aeon**.
photic zone	The upper zone of the sea into which sunlight penetrates enough to allow algae and other organisms to undergo ▸ **photosynthesis**.
photosynthesis	The biochemical process in which green plants, algae and some bacteria use energy from light to produce sugars from carbon dioxide and water, releasing oxygen as a by-product. The process occurs by means of specialized pigments such as chlorophyll.
phylum	In biological classification or ▸ **taxonomy**, a category of organisms that ranks below a ▸ **kingdom** and above a ▸ **class**.
plankton	A collective term for minute animals and plants that drift in seas and rivers and constitute a major source of food for many larger animals. Plankton consists of, among other organisms, bacteria, certain algae and tiny crustaceans. Compare ▸ **nekton**.
planned economy	An economy in which the government decides levels of production, prices and wages. Compare ▸ **market economy**.

plate tectonics	The theory that the Earth's ▸ **crust** and upper ▸ **mantle** are divided into plate-like sections that move as distinct masses. This movement is regarded as being responsible for the formation of the Earth's major physical features.
playa	A ▸ **basin** that becomes a shallow lake after heavy rainfall and dries out again in hot weather.
Pleistocene Epoch	The earliest ▸ **epoch** of the ▸ **Quaternary Period** of the ▸ **Cenozoic Era**, extending from 1.64 million years ago to 10,000 years ago, during which the first humans appeared.
Pliocene Epoch	The most recent ▸ **epoch** of the ▸ **Tertiary Period** of the ▸ **Cenozoic Era**, extending from 5.2 million to 1.64 million years ago, during which the first modern animals appeared.
plucking	A type of ▸ **erosion** caused by melt water from a ▸ **glacier** freezing to ice on rocks around it, and plucking pieces from the rock as the ice moves.
pluvial	Relating to rain or formed or carried by rain.
polar caps	Regions that consist of ▸ **tundra** and ▸ **ice cap** with a snowy climate and little or no ▸ **precipitation**. Vegetation consists of lichen and moss, with some grass in summer. The polar caps take in the Arctic regions of Russia and North America, and Antarctica.
pole	see ▸ **geographical pole; magnetic pole**
population density	The number of people living in a given area, usually per square kilometre.
population pyramid	A graph showing ▸ **population structure**. It has age groups marked along a vertical axis, with horizontal bars to the right showing the number of females in that age group and horizontal bars to the left showing the number of males.
population structure	The number of males and females within each age group in a population.
prairie	A large, open, usually treeless expanse of natural grassland found in both temperate and cold regions.
Precambrian Aeon	The ▸ **aeon** about which we have very little knowledge, during which the most primitive life forms existed, extending back in time from around 570 million years ago. Compare ▸ **Phanerozoic Aeon**.

precipitation	Moisture that falls from clouds to Earth in the form of rain, snow or hail.

Q

Quaternary Period	The second and current ▸ **period** of the ▸ **Cenozoic Era**, extending from 1.64 million years ago to the present day, during which humans appeared and developed.

R

radiation	see ▸ **solar radiation**
rainforest	A tropical forest in a region that has very heavy rainfall.
raised beach	An area that used to border the sea but is now above and further inland than the present water level.
replacement level	The birth rate required for the number of people in a population to remain the same.
ria	A long, narrow, coastal inlet that gradually decreases in depth and width as it moves further inland.
ribbon lake	A long, narrow lake in a depression carved into land by a ▸ **glacier**.
Richter scale	A scale once used to compare the magnitudes of earthquakes. The scale is logarithmic, ie an earthquake measuring 5 on the Richter scale is ten times greater than one measuring 4. The highest value ever recorded is 9.5 (Chile, 1960). However, the scale becomes much less sensitive for readings in the region of 8 or above. Scales such as the ▸ **Mercalli intensity scale** are therefore prevalent nowadays.
rift valley	A valley formed where the Earth's crust has collapsed. Also called a **graben**.
river cliff	A steep cliff on the outside of a ▸ **meander** in a river, formed from the ▸ **erosion** of the riverbank by fast-flowing water.
run-off	Rainwater that drains into rivers.

S

sabkha or sabkhah
A wide, salt-encrusted coastal plain that is above the level of normal tides and is subjected to only occasional flooding, common in Arabia.

salinization or salination
The build-up of excess amounts of salt in soil because of flooding by sea water.

saltation
The movement of sand and stones transported by water along a river bed.

salt marsh
An area of land that is usually or often flooded with salt water.

sand blow
The removal of large amounts of sand from a place by the wind.

saturation
The maximum amount of water vapour that can be contained by a mass of air at a given temperature and pressure.

saturation point
The point at which water vapour in the air condenses to liquid and there is a fall of rain, snow or hail. Also called the **dew point**.

savanna
A vast expanse of flat grassland in a tropical or subtropical region, either treeless or dotted with bushes and trees.

scree
A sloping mass of loose stones at the base of a cliff or on the face of a mountain, caused by weathering of rock.

sea arch
An arch of rock formed at the meeting of two caves that have been eroded by the sea.

sea stack
A pillar of rock rising from the sea, formed by the collapse of a ▸ **sea arch**.

sediment
Material that is transported and deposited by water, wind or ice.

sedimentary rock
Rock formed by the building up of deposited ▸ **sediment**. Examples are sandstone, shale and flint. Compare ▸ **igneous rock, metamorphic rock**.

seismology
The scientific study of earthquakes.

shantytown
A town or area where the people are very poor and live in makeshift houses.

shott
In North Africa and the Middle East, a shallow watercourse or lake that tends to dry up in certain seasons.

Silurian Period
The ▸ **period** of the ▸ **Palaeozoic Era** during which early invertebrate land animals developed, extending from 439 million to 408 million years ago.

socioeconomic group	A group of people who have similar levels of education, types of job and levels of income.
soil profile	A cross-section through a type of soil, showing the characteristics of the layers between the surface and the underlying rock.
solar radiation	Energy from the Sun in the form of heat or light. Also called **radiation**.
solifluxion or solifluction	The slow movement of soil or ▸ **scree** down a slope resulting from alternate freezing and thawing.
species	In biological classification or ▸ **taxonomy**, the lowest category, ranking below a ▸ **genus**. The organisms in a species have many characteristics in common and can mate with each other to produce fertile offspring, but cannot breed with members of other species.
sphere of influence	The area from which people travel to a particular place to use its services and facilities.
spit	A long stretch of sand running into the sea from the mainland.
steppe	A vast, grassy, usually treeless plain found in both temperate and cold regions.
storm	A force 11 wind on the ▸ **Beaufort scale**, blowing at between 102 and 120 kph and in which widespread damage is caused.
storm surge	An abnormal rise in the sea level around a coast, caused by the combination of a drop in atmospheric pressure and strong onshore winds. A storm surge usually causes a rise of around 30 cm but a 100 cm rise has been recorded.
stratosphere	The layer of the Earth's atmosphere that lies between 10 and 50 km above the Earth, just below the ▸ **mesosphere**.
strong breeze	A force 6 wind on the ▸ **Beaufort scale**, blowing at between 39 and 51 kph, in which large branches sway and telephone and electricity wires whistle.
strong gale	A force 9 wind on the ▸ **Beaufort scale**, blowing at between 75 and 86 kph, in which branches break and minor structural damage is caused.
subglacial	At the base or bottom of a ▸ **glacier**.
subsistence farming	Farming in which the land yields just enough to support the farmer, leaving little or nothing to be sold.

subtropical zones	Two zones of ▸ **steppe** and ▸ **desert** climate covering the Sahara and Kalahari deserts and parts of Australia, central Asia and Mexico.
Sverdrup	A unit used to measure the volume of ocean currents, equal to one million cubic metres per second. Abbrev *Sv*.
sympatric speciation	The development of new species due to the genetic isolation of populations that are physically in contact with one another. This can occur when their reproductive cycles no longer coincide so that they are unable to interbreed. Compare ▸ **allopatric speciation**.

T

taiga	The large area of predominantly coniferous forest located south of the Arctic ▸ **tundra** regions.
talus	A type of ▸ **scree** formed from frost-shattered rocks.
taxonomy	The classification of organisms.
tectonic plate	Any of the plate-like sections into which the Earth's ▸ **crust** and upper ▸ **mantle** are divided. According to the theory of ▸ **plate tectonics**, these move as distinct masses and are responsible for the formation of the Earth's major physical features.
temperate zones	Areas that have a rainy climate and include woodland, mountain forest and some plains in which there is no dry season. The weather is influenced by seas and rain falls at all times of the year. There are relatively small changes in temperature between the seasons, with the average temperature being in the range 3 to 18°C. Areas with a temperate climate include most of Europe, New Zealand, Asia, north-west and north-east USA, and parts of Chile.
tephra	Ash and other debris ejected by a volcano.
Tertiary Period	The earliest ▸ **period** of the ▸ **Cenozoic Era**, extending from 65 million to 1.64 million years ago, during which the first apes and modern plants appeared.
thermocline	A layer of the sea within which temperature decreases most rapidly with depth, usually found at depths of between 100 and 1,000 m.
thermohaline circulation	The circulation of currents in the world's oceans, caused by differences in temperature and salinity between masses of oceanic water.

tombolo	A ▸ **bar** of sand or gravel connecting an island with another or with the mainland.
traction	The rolling of large rocks along a river bed by the movement of the water.
trade winds	Winds that blow from regions around the ▸ **latitudes** 30° north and 30° south towards the equator, in a northwesterly direction from the south and a southwesterly direction from the north.
Triassic Period	The earliest ▸ **period** of the ▸ **Mesozoic Era**, extending from 245 million to 208 million years ago, during which the first dinosaurs and earliest mammals developed.
tributary	A stream that flows into a river or larger stream. Compare ▸ **distributary**.
tropics	A zone of wet warm climate around the equator, with an average temperature above 18°C, which covers the Amazon forest and parts of Malaysia, Indonesia, Australia, India, south-east Asia and Africa.
troposphere	The lowest layer of the Earth's atmosphere, which extends from the Earth's surface to an altitude of around 10 km, below the ▸ **stratosphere**.
tsunami	A huge and usually destructive wave produced as a result of an event such as an earthquake or volcanic eruption.
tundra	Any of the vast treeless plains that exist in polar regions, where there are extremely low temperatures, low ▸ **precipitation** and low-growing plants.
typhoon	A tropical ▸ **cyclone** in the Far East.

U

underpopulation	A state in which there are fewer individuals in a given area than can fully exploit the natural resources of the area.
Upper Carboniferous Period	The ▸ **period** of the ▸ **Palaeozoic Era** during which coal-bearing rocks were formed, extending from 333 million to 290 million years ago.
UTC	see ▸ **GMT**

V

vulcanology	The study of volcanoes.

W

wadi
A dry riverbed that only contains water in times of extremely heavy rain. The term is Arabic; other terms include **arroyo** (in the USA).

warm front
The leading edge of a mass of warm air advancing against a mass of cold air. As the warm air rises and cools, clouds are formed and there is widespread ▸ **precipitation**.

watershed
The line of high ground separating two river ▸ **basins**.

water table
The upper surface of water that has accumulated underground as rainwater has filtered through the soil. See also ▸ **groundwater**.

weather side
The side of an object, eg a mountain, that faces ▸ **windward** and is therefore exposed. Compare ▸ **lee side**.

whole gale
A force 10 wind on the ▸ **Beaufort scale**, blowing at between 87 and 101 kph, in which trees are uprooted and significant structural damage is caused.

windward
The direction from which the wind blows. Compare ▸ **leeward**.

XYZ

youthful population
A population where there is a high proportion of young people. Compare ▸ **ageing population**.

zero population growth
A situation in which the population of a country or area remains static, with births and immigration roughly equalling deaths and emigration.

PEOPLE OF THE WORLD

Joy Adamson (née Gessner), 1910–80

British naturalist and writer, born in Austria. She moved to Kenya in 1937, where she married British game warden George Adamson (1906–89) in 1943. She studied wildlife, and made her name with a series of books about the lioness Elsa: *Born Free* (1960; made into a feature film in 1966), *Elsa* (1961), *Forever Free* (1962), and *Elsa and Her Cubs* (1965). She was murdered in her home by tribesmen.

Alexander Agassiz, 1835–1910

US oceanographer and marine zoologist, born in Switzerland. The son of **Louis Agassiz**, he went to the USA in 1849 to join his father, studying engineering and zoology at Harvard. He used his engineering skills to speed up dredging and deep soundings, and also invented a new double-edged dredge and a closing tow net for mid-depth sampling. Between 1877 and 1880 he sailed the Atlantic and the Pacific oceans, studying the Gulf Stream, the plankton abundance and the dependence of the bottom fauna upon it. From 1873 to 1885 he was curator of the Harvard Museum of Comparative Zoology founded by his father.

Elizabeth Agassiz (née Cary), 1822–1907

US naturalist and educator, born in Boston, Massachusetts. She married **Louis Agassiz** in 1850 and accompanied him on his expeditions to Brazil (1865–6), which inspired them to write *A Journey in Brazil* (1868). She also travelled along the Pacific and Atlantic coasts of the Americas (1871–2). She was a founder and president of Radcliffe College for Women (1894–1902). Her other publications include *Seaside Studies in Natural History* (1865).

Louis Agassiz, 1807–73

US naturalist and glaciologist, born in Switzerland. Initially a medical student, his main interest was zoology and while still studying he published *The Fishes of Brazil* (1829). In 1832 he was appointed Professor of Natural History at the University of Neuchâtel, where he became interested in glaciers, proving that they are mobile and examining their transportation of rock material. Tracing previous glacial extents in the Alps, he developed the theory of ice ages. In 1846 Agassiz was appointed Professor of Natural History at Harvard, where in 1859 he founded the Museum for Comparative Zoology. He became an oceanographer in 1851, taking an interest in coral reefs.

Sir George Airy, 1801–92

English astronomer and geophysicist, born in Alnwick, Northumberland. He graduated with distinction (1823) from Trinity College, Cambridge, and was elected a Fellow. He became Professor of Mathematics in 1826, and Professor of Astronomy and director of the Cambridge Observatory in 1828. His investigations in planetary theory earned him the Royal Astronomical Society's Gold Medal (1833). Two years later he was appointed Astronomer Royal and director of the Greenwich Observatory. He achieved worldwide acceptance of the Greenwich zero meridian, and determined the mean density of the Earth through pendulum experiments in mines. President of the Royal Society in 1871, he was knighted in 1872.

Roald Amundsen, 1872–1928

Norwegian explorer, born in Borge. From 1902 to 1906 he became the first person to navigate the Northwest Passage, a sea route between the Atlantic and Pacific oceans through Canada's islands, in both directions. In 1910 he set sail for the North Pole in the *Fram* but, hearing that **Robert Peary** had apparently beaten him to it, he switched to the Antarctic. His expedition became the first to reach the South Pole, arriving in December 1911 (one month ahead of **Robert Falcon Scott**). In 1928 he disappeared when searching by plane for a fellow explorer, Umberto Nobile. He wrote several books, including *My Life as an Explorer* (1927).

Sir David Attenborough, 1926–

English naturalist and broadcaster, born in London. He joined the BBC in 1952 and, for the series *Zoo Quest* (1954–64), made many expeditions to film rare wildlife in natural habitats. Controller of BBC 2 (1965–8) and director of programmes (1969–72), he returned to documentary-making with such series as *Life on Earth* (1979), *The Living Planet* (1984), *The Trials of Life* (1990), *The Life of Birds* (1998) and *Life in the Undergrowth* (2005). He has written many accompanying books to these series, and has narrated additional programmes including *The Blue Planet* (2001) and *Planet Earth* (2006). He remains one of the world's most respected and popular wildlife documentary makers.

William Baffin, c.1584–1622

English navigator, probably born in London. From 1612 to 1616 he was the pilot on several expeditions in search of the Northwest Passage (eventually navigated by **Roald Amundsen**), significantly those under Robert Bylot on the *Discovery*. During these expeditions they examined Hudson Strait (1615), discovered Baffin Bay (1616), and discovered the Lancaster, Smith and Jones sounds (1616), which were later shown to lead to the Arctic and Pacific oceans. Baffin was possibly the first person to determine longitude at sea by lunar observation. He later carried out extensive surveys of the Red Sea (1616–21), and was killed at the Siege of Ormuz.

Sir Samuel Baker, 1821–93

English explorer, born in London. In 1845 he went to Ceylon (now Sri Lanka), where he supervised the construction of a railway. In 1860 he undertook the exploration of the Nile sources. At Gondokoro (1863), he met **John Speke** and **James Grant**, who told Baker of a great lake described to them by the local people. In 1864 Baker reached this inland sea into which the Nile flows and named it Albert Nyanza (Lake Albert), after Queen Victoria's consort Prince Albert (who had recently died). He was knighted in 1866, and subsequently commanded an expedition, organized by the Pasha (governor) of Egypt, for the suppression of slavery and the annexation of the equatorial Nile Basin.

Vasco Núñez de Balboa, 1475–1519

Spanish explorer, born in Jeréz-de-los-Caballeros. In 1511 he joined an expedition to Central America as a stowaway. Eventually taking command, he founded a colony at Darién, Panama, and extended Spanish influence into neighbouring areas. On one expedition he climbed a peak and sighted the Pacific Ocean, the first European to do so, and took possession for Spain. In 1519 Balboa quarrelled with the governor, Pedro Ariar de Ávila, and was beheaded.

Non-existent Notes

The official unit of currency in Panama is the balboa, which is named after Vasco Núñez de Balboa. However, while centésimo coins are circulated, no balboa banknotes are ever issued, as the currency is linked to the US dollar and dollar bills are used instead. Only once have balboa notes been briefly available, when President Arnulfo Arias created a central bank in 1941.

Robert Ballard, 1942–

US underwater explorer, born in Wichita, Kansas. In 1969 he became director of the Center for Marine Exploration, Cape Cod, leaving in 1997 to found and head the Institute for Exploration in Mystic, Connecticut. His deep-sea expeditions include the location of the wrecks of the *Bismarck*, RMS *Titanic*, the *Lusitania* and USS *Yorktown*. He also explored the Mid-Atlantic Ridge (using the submersible *Alvin*) and hydrothermal vents in the Galápagos Rift; this work led to the discovery of chemosynthesis (the formation of organic molecules by bacteria). His publications include *Exploring Our Living Planet* (1983) and *The Eternal Darkness: A Personal History of Deep-Sea Exploration* (with Will Hively, 2000).

Henry Bates, 1825–92

English naturalist, born in Leicester. With his friend **Alfred Wallace** he left to explore the Amazon in 1848. He continued until 1859 when he returned with 14,700 specimens, including almost 8,000 species of insect new to science. In 1861 his *Contributions to an Insect Fauna of the Amazon Valley* described the phenomenon now known as Batesian mimicry, in which harmless, edible species of animal resemble others that are distasteful or poisonous, and thus gain protection from predators. This discovery provided strong evidence in favour of natural selection.

Sir Francis Beaufort, 1774–1857

British naval officer and hydrographer, born in Navan, County Meath, Ireland. He joined the Royal Navy in 1787 and was severely wounded near Malaga. After a period working on shore telegraphs in Ireland he held three commands, and was dangerously wounded while surveying the coast of Asia Minor and suppressing piracy. From 1829 to 1855 he was hydrographer to the navy and produced many fine charts. He devised the Beaufort scale of wind force (1805), which is still used today, and a tabulated system of weather registration.

Obituary Omission

Beaufort's obituary in the *London Daily News* ran to 16 pages when reprinted as a booklet, yet it did not contain any mention of the Beaufort scale, the work for which he is best known today.

Giovanni Belzoni, 1778–1823

Italian explorer and antiquity hunter, born in Padua. In 1815 he went to Egypt, and turned to tomb-robbing and the exploration of Egyptian antiquities. He removed the colossal bust of Rameses II from Thebes and sent it, together with other finds, to the British Museum in London. He explored the temples of Edfu and Abu Simbel, opened the Pyramid of Khephren at Giza and discovered the ruined city of Berenice. On his return to Europe he published his discoveries as *Narrative of the Operations and Recent Discoveries within the Pyramids, Temples, Tombs and Excavations in Egypt and Nubia* (1820).

> ### The Great Belzoni
> Belzoni was 2 metres (6 feet 7 inches) tall. Before he went to Egypt he performed as a circus strongman in England, and was known as 'The Great Belzoni'.

Victor Benioff, 1899–1968

US geophysicist, born in Los Angeles. From 1924, at the Carnegie Institution in Washington, he developed seismic recording drums that produced measurements of unprecedented accuracy. He went on to invent other instruments that further enabled seismologists to track and measure earthquakes. He became assistant Professor (1937), and later Professor, of Seismology at the California Institute of Technology. He worked on earthquake mechanisms and global tectonics, developed new analytical techniques and amassed evidence of earthquakes around the Pacific. In 1954 he published his records of seismically active crustal slabs beneath ocean trenches, now known as Wadati–Benioff zones.

Vitus Bering, 1681–1741

Danish navigator, born in Horsens. He joined the Russian navy in 1703, eventually being appointed to lead an expedition in the Sea of Kamchatka to determine whether Asia and America were joined. Sailing in 1728, he followed the coast northwards until he believed he had reached the north-east point of Asia. However, he failed to see land to the east. In 1733 he commanded the Great Northern expedition to explore the Siberian coast, then in 1741 he sailed towards America, and sighting land, followed the coast northwards. However, on his return he was wrecked on the island of Avatcha (Bering Island), where he died of scurvy. The Bering Strait and the Bering Sea, both in Alaska, are also named after him. Captain **James Cook** later confirmed his findings.

Colonel John Blashford-Snell, 1936–

English explorer and youth leader, born in Hereford. He was commissioned into the Royal Engineers in 1957, and his expedition to the Blue Nile (1968) was the result of an invitation to the British army from the Ethiopian emperor Haile Selassie. Blashford-Snell went on to found the Scientific Exploration Society (SES) and led expeditions to the British Trans-Americas (1972) and the Zaire River (1975). He then led two major youth projects: Operation Drake (1978–80) and Operation Raleigh, which involved young people in adventurous, scientific and community projects in over 73 countries (1984–92) before being established as Raleigh International. His books include *Operation Raleigh: Adventure Unlimited* (1990, with Ann Tweedy) and *Something Lost Behind the Ranges* (1994). He was awarded the OBE in 1996.

Pierre Savorgnan de Brazza, 1852–1905

French explorer of Italian extraction, born in Rio de Janeiro, Brazil. He joined the French navy in 1870 and served in Gabon, West Africa, where he explored the Ogowe River (1876–8). He became a French citizen in 1874 and subsequently explored the country north of the Congo, where he secured vast grants of land for France and founded stations, including that of Brazzaville on the north shore of Stanley Pool.

> ## Brazzaville Burial
>
> In 2006 the Republic of the Congo honoured de Brazza by exhuming his remains from Algiers and reburying them in Brazzaville. The Congolese government, who wanted to pay tribute to de Brazza's stand against slavery and corporate exploitation, built a marble and glass mausoleum at a cost of £1.4m, although some people felt that it was wrong to spend so much money to honour a colonialist

Alexandre Brongniart, 1770–1847

French naturalist and geologist, born in Paris. In 1822 he became Professor of Mineralogy at the Natural History Museum in Paris. Together with **Georges Cuvier**, he studied the geological strata of the Paris Basin using the nature of fossils within the beds to map out the sequence. They thereby deduced the fundamental principle that the fossil record can be related to the age of rock strata. They noted the alternation of freshwater and marine strata in the Tertiary rocks around Paris, and interpreted this as being caused by catastrophic processes. Brongniart introduced the term 'Jurassic' for the limestones and clays of the Cotswolds.

James Bruce, 1730–94

Scottish explorer, born in Stirlingshire. He became consul-general in Algiers (1763–5), and in 1768 travelled to Abyssinia (now Ethiopia) by the Nile, Aswan, the Red Sea, and Massawa. In 1770 he reached the source of the Abbai, or headstream of the Blue Nile, which he claimed was the main stream of the Nile. His *Travels to Discover the Sources of the Nile* was published in 1790, but contained such extraordinary accounts of Abyssinia that many considered them fictitious. Their truth was later confirmed by **Richard Burton** and other travellers.

Alexander Buchan, 1829–1907

Scottish meteorologist and oceanographer, born near Kinross. From 1877 he was a member of the Meteorological Council which directed the Meteorological Office. Largely through his efforts, an observatory was established at the summit of Ben Nevis (1883). In 1868 he produced the first charts of storm tracks across the Atlantic. His major work *Report on Atmospheric Circulation* (1889) contained global charts of monthly mean temperature, pressure and wind direction for the whole year. He concluded that the British climate is subject to warm and cold spells falling approximately between certain dates annually, the so-called Buchan spells, although nowadays weather patterns are thought to be more random than this. Buchan was the first person to use a weather map as a basis for forecasting.

Sir Edward Bullard, 1907–80

English geophysicist, born in Norwich, Norfolk. He used pendulums to measure gravity in the East African Rift, and accomplished the first British seismic experiment at sea under sail (1938). During World War II he worked on degaussing ships (neutralizing their magnetic fields) to protect them from magnetic mines. As Professor of Physics at Toronto University (1946–9) he worked on the dynamo theory of the Earth's magnetic field, which proposes that the field is maintained by the flow of molten metals within the Earth's core. In 1949 he became director of the National Physical Laboratory in London (1950–5). As a professor at the University of Cambridge (1955–74) he brought the department of geodesy and geophysics into world recognition. His computer fit of the continents (1965) was instrumental in bringing the theory of continental drift back into favour.

Sir Richard Francis Burton, 1821–90

English explorer, linguist and diplomat, born in Torquay, Devon. In 1842 he served in India under Sir Charles Napier and, having mastered Hindustani, Persian, and Arabic, made a pilgrimage to Mecca disguised as a Middle Eastern tribesman (1853). Commissioned by the Foreign Office to search for the sources of the Nile, in 1856 he set out with **John Hanning Speke** on the journey on which Lake Tanganyika was discovered (1858). His books include *First Footsteps in East Africa* (1851), *Personal Narrative of a Pilgrimage to Al-Madinah and Meccah* (1855) and his translation of *The Arabian Nights* (1885–8).

Richard Byrd, 1888–1957

US explorer and aviator, born in Winchester, Virginia. He graduated from the US Naval Academy, Annapolis, in 1912 and joined the navy's aviation service. With Floyd Bennett he made the first aeroplane flight over the North Pole (1926), for which they received the Congressional Medal of Honor. In 1929 Byrd established a base, 'Little America', in the Antarctic and was the first to fly over the South Pole. He made four more expeditions to the Antarctic (1933–5, 1939–41, 1946–7 and 1955–6).

John Cabot (originally Giovanni Caboto), 1425–c.1500

Italian navigator and explorer, born in Genoa. He moved to England and settled in Bristol around 1490. In 1497, under a patent from King Henry VII, he sailed from Bristol in search of a route to Asia, accompanied by his three sons. On 24 June, after 52 days at sea, he sighted land (probably Cape Breton Island, Nova Scotia), and claimed North America for England. He is thought to have made further voyages in search of the Northwest Passage (eventually navigated by **Roald Amundsen**), and after setting out in 1498, died at sea.

Pedro Álvarez Cabral (or Cabrera), c.1467–c.1520

Portuguese navigator, born in Belmonte. He sailed from Lisbon in 1500 in command of a fleet bound for the East Indies. Drifting into the South American current of the Atlantic Ocean, he was carried to the unknown coast of Brazil, which he claimed on behalf of Portugal. From there he made for India but, after losing seven of his ships, landed at Mozambique; he was the first to provide a description of that country. From there he sailed to Calicut (Kozhikode, Kerala), where he made the first commercial treaty between Portugal and India. He returned to Lisbon in 1501.

Verney Cameron, 1844–94

English explorer, born near Weymouth, Dorset. A naval officer, he was appointed in 1872 to lead an African east coast expedition to relieve **David Livingstone**. In August 1873, at Unyanyembe (now in Tanzania), he met Livingstone's followers carrying his remains to the coast. Cameron made a survey of Lake Tanganyika, then set out to follow the River Lualaba. He struck south-west, and reached Benguela (now in Angola) on 7 November 1875, the first European to cross Africa from coast to coast. In 1878 he travelled overland to India, to assess the feasibility of a Constantinople–Baghdad railway, and in 1882 he visited the Gold Coast with **Sir Richard Burton**.

Rachel Carson, 1907–64

US naturalist and science writer, born in Springdale, Pennsylvania. She studied biology at Johns Hopkins University, taught at Maryland University (1931–6) and worked as a marine biologist for the US Fish and Wildlife Service (1936–49). She became well known with *The Sea Around Us* (1951), which warned of the increasing danger of large-scale marine pollution, and the hard-hitting *Silent Spring* (1962), which directed public concern to the problems caused by synthetic pesticides and their effect on food chains. The resulting controls on their use owe much to her work, which also contributed to the growing conservationist movement.

Howard Carter, 1874–1939

English Egyptologist, born in London. He joined Flinders Petrie's archaeological survey of Egypt as a draughtsman in 1891, then subsequently served as inspector-general of the Egyptian antiquities department, from 1907 conducting his own research under the patronage of the Earl of Carnarvon. His discoveries included the tombs of Hatshepsut (1907), Tuthmosis IV and in 1922 the virtually intact burial of Tutankhamun. The work of emptying the chambers, photographing, conserving and despatching the treasures to Cairo occupied him for the rest of his life, but he failed through ill health to produce a final, detailed report.

Thomas Cavendish, c.1555–c.1592

English explorer, born near Ipswich, Suffolk. He shared in Sir Richard Grenville's expedition to Virginia (1585). In 1586, he sailed with three ships for the Pacific Ocean and became the second English circumnavigator of the globe after **Sir Francis Drake**. With a rich booty, but only his largest vessel (the *Desire*) still intact, he returned by the Cape of Good Hope to England in 1588. Queen Elizabeth I knighted him. A second expedition (1591) with **John Davis** ended in disaster, and Cavendish died off Ascension Island.

Samuel de Champlain, 1567–1635

French explorer, born in Brouage, Saintonge. He made his first voyage to Canada in 1603. From 1604 to 1607 he explored the coasts, and on his third voyage (1608) he founded Quebec. He was appointed Lieutenant of Canada in 1612. His explorations into the interior mapped many new areas. During the Anglo-French war, Quebec was seized by the English, and he successfully negotiated its return.

Jule Charney, 1917–81

US mathematician and meteorologist, born in San Francisco. While a professor at the Massachusetts Institute of Technology (1956–81) he solved the problem of how weather systems develop from a basic flow. He also devised equations that could be used in a computer to produce weather forecasts. He was one of the first to realize the important influence of different surfaces on weather and climate.

Sir Francis Chichester, 1901–72

English adventurer and yachtsman, born in Barnstaple, Devon. In 1960 he won the first solo transatlantic yacht race, with his boat *Gipsy Moth III*, sailing from Plymouth to New York in 40 days. He made a solo circumnavigation of the world (1966–7) in *Gipsy Moth IV*, sailing from Plymouth to Sydney in 107 days and from there back to Plymouth, via Cape Horn, in 119 days. He wrote *The Lonely Sea and the Sky* (1964) and *Gipsy Moth Circles the World* (1967).

> 66
>
> *I must down to the seas again, to the lonely sea and the sky,*
> *And all I ask is a tall ship and a star to steer her by,*
> *And the wheel's kick and the wind's song and the white sail's shaking,*
> *And a grey mist on the sea's face and a grey dawn breaking.*
>
> —John Masefield, from 'Sea Fever' (1902)
>
> 99

William Clark, 1770–1838

US explorer, born in Caroline County, Virginia. He joined the army in 1789 and was appointed joint leader, with **Meriwether Lewis**, of the successful transcontinental expedition to the Pacific coast and back (1804–6). Clark later became superintendent of Indian affairs in Louisiana Territory, and then Governor of Missouri Territory.

Frank Clarke, 1847–1931

US geochemist, born in Boston. As chief chemist to the US Geological Survey (1883–1925), he undertook analyses of rocks and minerals and compiled important lists of fundamental physical and chemical constants. He was the first to present a consistent theory of the chemical evolution of geological systems. His books include *The Composition of the Earth's Crust* (1924, with Henry Washington, 1867–1934).

William Clarke, 1798–1878

English geologist and clergyman, born in East Bergholt, Suffolk. He travelled widely in Europe before emigrating to New South Wales. He was active in studying geology and mineral reserves and is credited as the first to discover gold in Australia, in the alluvium of Macquarie (1841), as well as tin and diamonds. He was the first to identify Silurian rocks in Australia, and demonstrated the Carboniferous age of the coal-bearing strata of New South Wales.

Christopher Columbus, 1451–1506

Discoverer of the New World, born in Genoa (now in Italy). He settled in Portugal after being shipwrecked in about 1470. A few years later he conceived the idea of reaching India by sailing westward; he then spent years seeking backing for an expedition until his plans were accepted by Ferdinand and Isabella of Castile (now in central Spain). In August 1492 Columbus set sail in the *Santa Maria*, accompanied by the smaller *Pinta* and *Niña*. New land was sighted on Friday 12 October, probably Watling's Island in the Bahamas. He visited Cuba and then Hispaniola (now Haiti and the Dominican Republic), planting a colony in the latter before returning to Spain on 15 March 1493. In three further voyages he sighted Dominica and the South American mainland. He died at Valladolid in Spain.

> ### The Lord's Day
> The name Dominica comes from the Latin for 'The Lord's day'. It was so called because Columbus sighted the country on a Sunday.

Frederick Cook, 1865–1940

US explorer and physician, born in New York State. He was surgeon on an Arctic expedition to Greenland in 1891 led by **Robert Peary**. In 1906 he claimed to have made the first ascent of Mount McKinley, Alaska, and in 1908 to have reached the North Pole on 21 April, but the latter was questioned by Peary. An investigative committee discredited both Cook's claim to be the first man to the North Pole and his professed ascent of Mount McKinley. He insisted on the truth of his claims but the controversy continues.

James Cook, 1728–79

English navigator, born in Marton, Yorkshire. He joined the Royal Navy, and commanded the *Endeavour* for the Royal Society expedition to the Pacific to observe the transit of Venus across the Sun (1768–71). On the return voyage, New Zealand was circumnavigated and charted and the east coast of Australia was surveyed and claimed for Great Britain. Cook commanded a second voyage in the *Resolution* and *Adventure* (1772–5), to discover how far the lands of the Antarctic stretched northwards. He sailed round the edge of the ice, visited Tahiti and the New Hebrides, and discovered New Caledonia. On his last voyage (1776–9), while seeking a passage round the north coast of America from the Pacific, he was killed by hostile natives in Hawaii on 14 February 1779.

Francisco Vázquez de Coronado, 1510–54

Spanish conquistador and explorer, born in Salamanca. In 1540 he commanded the expedition to New Mexico on which the Grand Canyon of the Colorado River was discovered.

Hernan (or Hernando) Cortés (or Cortéz), 1485–1547

Spanish conquistador, born in Medellin, Spain. In 1519 he commanded an expedition against Mexico, finally capturing the Aztec capital, Tenochtitlan, in 1521. The next year, he was formally appointed Governor and Captain-General of New Spain, but his authority was later superseded. He spent the years 1530–40 in Mexico and then returned to Spain.

Jacques Cousteau, 1910–97

French naval officer and underwater explorer, born in Saint André, Gironde. He was partly responsible for the invention of the aqualung diving apparatus (1943).

In 1950 he became commander of the oceanographic research ship *Calypso* from which he made the first underwater film. He was appointed director of the Musée Océanographique de Monaco (1957–88). His other achievements include developing the bathyscaphe, an electrically powered underwater exploration vessel. He is best known for the popularization of marine biology with his many films, including *The Undersea World of Jacques Cousteau* (1968–76). His books include *The Living Sea* (1963) and *Jacques Cousteau's Calypso* (1983).

> ❝
> *The sea is the universal sewer.*
> —Jacques Cousteau, in his testimony before the House Committee on Science and Astronautics (28 January 1971). ❞

Osbert Crawford, 1886–1957

English archaeologist and aerial photographer, born in Bombay. Serving with the Royal Flying Corps in World War I, he identified the potential of aerial photography in archaeology and subsequently produced the classic album *Wessex from the Air* (1928). He served as archaeology officer of the Ordnance Survey (1920–40) and did much to develop the cartographic recording of archaeology, especially in period maps such as the *Ordnance Survey Map of Roman Britain* (1924). In 1927 he founded the journal *Antiquity*, which he edited until his death.

Allan Cunningham, 1791–1839

English botanist and explorer, born in Wimbledon, Surrey. He became plant collector for another botanist, Sir Joseph Banks, first in Brazil and then in New South Wales. While searching for new specimens, Cunningham made many valuable explorations of the hinterland of New South Wales and Queensland, and also visited New Zealand and Norfolk Island. He returned to Sydney in 1837 as Colonial Botanist for New South Wales. Many indigenous Australian trees now bear his name.

Georges, Baron Cuvier, 1769–1832

French anatomist, born in Montbéliard. His studies of the fossils of fish and other animals, through his reconstructions of the extinct vertebrates of the Paris basin, linked palaeontology to comparative anatomy. A militant anti-evolutionist, he accounted for fossils by positing 'catastrophism' – a series of extinctions due to periodic global floods after which new forms of life appeared. He extended the classification scheme developed by **Carolus Linnaeus** by grouping related classes of living and fossil animals, thus anticipating the division of the animal kingdom into phyla. Cuvier's works include *Le Règne animal distribué d'après son organisation* (1817, 'The Animal Kingdom Distributed According to its Organization').

James Dana, 1813–95

US mineralogist, crystallographer and geologist, born in Utica, New York. From 1846 until his death he co-edited the *American Journal of Science*. He was appointed Professor of Natural History (1849–64) and Professor of Geology and Mineralogy (1864–90) at Yale. He was a scientific observer on a US exploring expedition visiting the Antarctic and Pacific (1838–42). In 1837 he published the *System of Mineralogy*, the fifth edition (1868) of which remains useful today. His other publications include *Textbook of Geology* (1864) and *Hawaiian Volcanoes* (1890).

Charles Darwin, 1809–82

English naturalist, born in Shrewsbury, Shropshire. He was naturalist on HMS *Beagle*, for a scientific survey of South American waters (1831–6), captained by **Robert Fitzroy**. During this expedition he obtained an intimate knowledge of the fauna, flora and geology of many lands. The main originator of the theory of evolution by natural selection, from 1842 Darwin set about his great work, *The Origin of Species by Means of Natural Selection* (November 1859). Though not the sole originator of the theory, Darwin was the first thinker to gain for the concept a wide acceptance among biological experts.

John Davis (or Davys), c.1550–1605

English navigator, born near Dartmouth, Devon. Between 1585 and 1587 he undertook three Arctic voyages in search of the Northwest Passage (eventually navigated by **Roald Amundsen**). In the last voyage he sailed as far north as 73°, and Davis Strait in the Arctic is named after him. After fighting against the Spanish Armada in 1588, he sought to navigate the Strait of Magellan, taking part in a venture with **Thomas Cavendish** (1591). Although the expedition was largely a disaster, with most of the crew being lost, the one positive result was Davis's discovery of the Falkland Islands. He was killed by pirates off Singapore while on a voyage to the Indies. He wrote *World's Hydrographical Description* (1595) and *The Seaman's Secrets* (1594), and invented the navigational instrument Davis's quadrant.

Richard Dawkins, 1941–

British ethologist and evolutionary biologist, born in Nairobi, Kenya. His many books explain complex evolutionary ideas to the general public as well as to other scientists. In *The Selfish Gene* (1976), he shows how natural selection can act on individual genes rather than at the individual or species level. He also describes how apparently altruistic behaviour in animals can be of selective advantage by increasing the probability of survival of genes controlling this behaviour, and introduces the concept of the 'meme', a unit of cultural transmission. His other works include *The Blind Watchmaker* (1986) and *The Ancestor's Tale* (2004).

Sir John Dawson, 1820–99

Canadian geologist, born in Pictou, Nova Scotia. From 1855 to 1893 he was Principal of McGill University, Montreal. He was an authority on fossil plants and systematically opposed **Charles Darwin**'s theories. In 1851 he discovered some of the earliest known terrestrial vertebrate fossils inside carboniferous fossil tree stumps at Joggins, Nova Scotia. His publications include *The Story of Earth and Man* (1873), *Origin of the World* (1877), and *Relics of Primeval Life* (1897).

Sir George Deacon, 1906–84

English physical oceanographer, born in Leicester. His studies of the chemistry of the Southern Ocean between 1930 and 1937 revealed the Antarctic convergence, where cold water dips beneath warmer sub-Antarctic water, and that Antarctic bottom water extends northwards into all the major oceans. This report, *The Hydrology of the Southern Ocean* (1937), earned him fellowship of the Royal Society (1944). In 1949 he became director of the National Institute of Oceanography. The

Institute of Oceanographic Sciences Deacon Laboratory is named after him.

Sir Henry De la Beche, 1796–1855

English stratigrapher and geologist, born near London. In 1832 he started mapping the geology of Dorset and Devon, and in 1835 was appointed to extend the survey into Cornwall. This marked the beginning of the first national Geological Survey, of which he became the first director. His work led to the establishment of the Mining Record Office (1839), the Museum of Practical Geology (1841) and the School of Mines and Science (1853). His books include *Manual of Geology* (1831) and *Researches in Theoretical Geology* (1834).

Bartolomeu Diaz (or Dias), c.1450–1500

Portuguese navigator and explorer. In 1486 King John II of Portugal gave him the command of two vessels to follow up the discoveries already made on the west coast of Africa. Driven by a violent storm, he sailed round the southern extremity of Africa, the Cape of Good Hope, without immediately realizing the fact, so opening the route to India. In 1497 he travelled with **Vasco da Gama**'s expedition as far as the Cape Verde Islands. He established trading posts before joining the expedition of **Pedro Cabral** in 1500, but was lost in a storm after leaving Brazil.

William Dines, 1855–1927

English meteorologist, born in Oxshott, Surrey. In 1901 he designed the pressure tube anemometer which bears his name. In 1905 he was appointed director of experiments of the upper air for the Meteorological Office, and in 1907 he started regular balloon ascents, the results of which he used to calculate correlations between pressure and temperature at various heights. Dines concluded that cyclones are caused by dynamical processes in the middle atmosphere. He went on to design numerous meteorological instruments, including the Dines radiometer (1920).

Sir Francis Drake, c.1540–1596

English navigator, born near Tavistock. In 1572, with a royal privateer's licence, he plundered the Isthmus of Panama and became the first Englishman to see the Pacific. In 1577 he set out to explore the Strait of Magellan, a route between the Atlantic and Pacific oceans. Having entered the Pacific, Drake sailed north to Vancouver but, failing to find a Northwest Passage back to the Atlantic, he crossed the Pacific. After refitting in Java he rounded the Cape of Good Hope and arrived in England in 1580, the first Englishman to circumnavigate the world. Early in 1587 he pillaged Cadiz, and in 1588 took a leading part against the Spanish Armada. He died on an expedition to the West Indies.

Jules Dumont d'Urville, 1790–1842

French naval explorer, born in Calvados. Visiting the Pacific in the *Astrolabe*, he collected important information on the ethnic groups, plants and geology of the Pacific Islands, revising existing maps (1826–9). From 1837 to 1840 he sailed to the Antarctic via the Magellan Strait but was stopped by ice at 63°S. The following year he returned and discovered Adélie and Joinville islands, so giving France its claim to Antarctica.

Edrisi (or Idrisi), c.1100–1164

Arabic geographer, born in Ceuta. He studied at Córdoba, and travelled in Spain, Barbary and Asia Minor. He settled at the court of Roger II of Sicily, who invited him to write a description of the Earth. To this end, travellers were sent on journeys of exploration and asked to send him accounts of their experiences. Edrisi's 'Description of the World' (*Nuzhat-el-Mushtâk*), or 'Book of Roger', took many years to complete (1154) and is one of the principal medieval geographies.

Vagn Ekman, 1874–1954

Swedish oceanographer, born in Stockholm. He explained the variation in direction of ocean currents with depth as an effect of the Earth's rotation (Coriolis force). He also showed that the general motion of near-surface water is the result of interaction between surface wind force, the Coriolis force, and frictional effects between water layers. The resulting variation of water velocity with depth is known as the 'Ekman spiral'.

Lincoln Ellsworth, 1880–1951

US explorer, born in Chicago. He was the first person to fly over both the North Pole (in the airship *Norge* with Umberto Nobile and **Roald Amundsen** in 1926) and the South Pole (in 1935). In his Antarctic explorations (1935, 1939), he claimed vast territories for the USA, now known as Ellsworth Land. He helped survey the route for the Canadian transcontinental railway, and in 1931 financed **Sir George Wilkins**'s submarine expedition across the Arctic.

Emin Pasha (originally Eduard Schnitzer), 1840–92

German doctor, explorer and linguist, born in Neisse. While practising medicine at Scutari (Albania), he adopted the Muslim faith. After 1876, as Emin Effendi, he was in Egyptian service and General Gordon appointed him governor of the Equatorial Province. Emin Pasha added enormously to the knowledge of African languages, made important surveys and wrote valuable geographical papers. He also sent rich collections of plants and animals to Europe. He was 'rescued' by **Henry Morton Stanley** in 1889, but immediately returned. He was murdered by Arabs.

Erik the Red (properly Erik Thorvaldson), 10th century

Norwegian sailor. He explored the Greenland coast and founded the Norse colonies there (985), His son **Leif the Lucky** landed in 'Vinland', often identified as America (1000).

> ## *Scandinavian Salesmanship*
> According to the Icelandic saga *Grœnlendinga saga* ('Saga of the Greenlanders'), Erik the Red coined the name 'Greenland' to make the territory sound appealing to potential settlers.

(William) Maurice Ewing, 1906–74

US marine geologist, born in Texas. In 1944 he established the Lamont (now Lamont–Doherty) Geological Observatory north of New York City, becoming director there in 1949. He pioneered marine seismic techniques which he used to show that the ocean crust is much thinner than the continental crust. He also discovered the deep central rift in the Mid-Atlantic Ridge (1957). His discovery that ocean sediment thickness increases with distance from the mid-ocean ridges lent support to the plate tectonics theory.

Edward John Eyre, 1815–1901

English explorer and colonist, born in Hornsea, Yorkshire. He emigrated to Australia at the age of 17, settled on the Lower Murray as a sheep farmer, and was appointed a magistrate. In 1840–1 he explored the region between South and Western Australia, and discovered Lake Eyre. In 1847 he became Governor of New Zealand and in 1862 of Jamaica. In 1865 he suppressed a native rebellion with such severity that he was recalled to England and prosecuted, but was cleared.

Sir Ranulph Fiennes, 1944–

English explorer, born in Windsor, Berkshire. He led six major expeditions between 1969 and 1986, including a hovercraft journey up the White Nile (1969) and travelling over land towards the North Pole (1976–8). Between 1979 and 1982 he organized the Transglobe expedition, which traced the Greenwich Meridian crossing both Poles. In 1993 he and Dr Michael Stroud completed the first unsupported crossing of the Antarctic on foot. In 1996 illness forced him to abandon an unsupported solo crossing of the Antarctic. In 2000 a similar attempt to walk unsupported to the North Pole also ended in failure. Fiennes's books include his autobiography *Living Dangerously* (1987) and *Captain Scott* (2003).

> ### A Marathon Achievement
>
> Sir Ranulph Fiennes and Dr Michael Stroud ran seven marathons in seven days across seven different continents. This feat, known as the Land Rover 7×7×7 Challenge, raised almost £100,000 to support the work of the British Heart Foundation charity.

Wilhelm Filchner, 1877–1957

German geographer and explorer, born in Munich. In 1910 he led the second German Antarctic expedition, which travelled to Vahsel Bay in the *Deutschland*. This was the most southerly point yet reached in that sector of the Antarctic. They became stuck in the ice of the Weddell Sea and drifted northwards for 1100 km (700 miles) before escaping nine months later, having disproved the theory of a second Antarctic continent. Filchner travelled to Tibet (1903–5, 1926–8, 1934–8), traversing the length of the region. He also undertook a magnetic survey of Nepal (1939–40).

Friedrich Finsch, 1839–1917

German naturalist and traveller, born in Silesia. He travelled all over the world and published accounts of the birds encountered, particularly in East Africa and Polynesia, but is best remembered as an expert on parrots (*Die Papageien*, 1867). In 1884 he was appointed Bismarck's imperial commissioner to New Guinea, which led to the formation of the German protectorates Kaiser Wilhelm's Land and the Bismarck Archipelago.

Robert Fitzroy, 1805–65

English naval officer and meteorologist, born in Suffolk. As commander of the *Beagle*, he surveyed the coasts of South America (1828–30). In 1831 he circumnavigated the globe in the *Beagle* accompanied by **Charles Darwin**, with whom he collaborated in *Narrative of the Surveying Voyages of HMS Adventure and Beagle* (1839). In 1855 he became the first director of the Meteorological Office, setting up telegraph stations for collecting meteorological observations. He pioneered weather charts and used these in producing gale warnings for shipping and weather forecasts for the press. He wrote *The Weather Book* (1863) and invented the 'Fitzroy barometer'.

> ## Fitzroy in the Forecast
>
> The UK Finisterre shipping forecast area was renamed Fitzroy in 2002 in Robert Fitzroy's honour. The complete list of UK shipping forecast areas is now: Viking, North Utsire, South Utsire, Forties, Cromarty, Forth, Tyne, Dogger, Fisher, German Bight, Humber, Thames, Dover, Wight, Portland, Plymouth, Biscay, Fitzroy, Trafalgar, Sole, Lundy, Fastnet, Irish Sea, Shannon, Rockall, Malin, Hebrides, Bailey, Fair Isle, Faeroes, and South-east Iceland.

Robert Flaherty, 1884–1951

US documentary film-maker and explorer, born in Michigan. Brought up in Canada, he trained as a mining prospector. He took a movie camera on his expeditions to Hudson Bay in 1913, and made the silent *Nanook of the North* (1922), followed by a documentary about the South Seas, *Moana* (1926). He wrote and directed *Tabu* (1931, with F W Murnau). His last great success was *Louisiana Story* (1948). He also produced *Man of Aran* in Ireland (1932–4) and *Elephant Boy* (1937).

Matthew Flinders, 1774–1814

English explorer, born in Donington, Lincolnshire. A naval officer and hydrographer, from 1795 to 1800 he surveyed the coast of New South Wales and the strait between Australia and Tasmania with George Bass. From 1801 to 1803 he was commissioned to circumnavigate Australia but he was wrecked on the return voyage, and was detained by the French Governor of Mauritius until 1810. The Flinders River in Queensland and the Flinders Ranges in South Australia are named after him.

Steve Fossett, 1944–

American aviator, born in Jackson, Tennessee. A businessman and former Scout, he is best known for his three circumnavigations of the Earth, as a long-distance balloonist, as a sailor, and as a solo pilot. He was the first person to make a solo flight across the Pacific Ocean in a balloon, and the first person to fly around the world alone, non-stop, in the same manner (2002). In 2005 he made the first solo, non-stop, non-refuelled aerial circumnavigation of the globe, in the Virgin Atlantic GlobalFlyer jet aircraft.

Lady Jane Franklin (née Griffin), 1792–1875

English traveller and expedition benefactor, born in England. She travelled widely with her father before marrying **Sir John Franklin** in 1828. She accompanied him on his tours through Syria, Turkey and Egypt, and whilst he was Governor of Van Diemen's Land (now Tasmania) she campaigned for the rights of women prisoners. When her husband disappeared while searching for the Northwest Passage, she financed a series of search expeditions. She was awarded the Royal Geographical Society's Founder's Medal for her contribution to the exploration of the Canadian Arctic.

Sir John Franklin, 1786–1847

English explorer, born in Lincolnshire. A naval officer, from 1818 he explored in Canada, including the Mackenzie River (1819–22, 1825–7). He was Governor of Van Diemen's Land (now Tasmania) from 1834 to 1845. In 1845 he commanded the *Erebus* and *Terror* in an attempt to discover the Northwest Passage. They worked along the North American coast but were beleaguered by ice in the Victoria Strait off northern Canada (1846). Franklin died during the following year. The survivors attempted to walk south, but died of starvation and scurvy.

> *Prairie Dove*
> Franklin's Gull, which breeds in Canada, is named after **Sir John Franklin**. This small gull is also known as the 'prairie dove', because it breeds on prairieland and flies with the grace and buoyancy of a dove.

Sir Frank Fraser Darling, 1903–79

English ecologist and conservationist, born in Chesterfield, Derbyshire. In the 1930s he studied red deer, and carried out research on sea birds showing that breeding is enhanced when it occurs in a synchronized fashion (the 'Fraser Darling effect'). Convinced of the importance of living in ecological balance with the environment, he was an early champion of conservation. He was director of the West Highland Survey (1944–50), lecturer in ecology and conservation at the University of Edinburgh (1953–8) and vice-president of the Conservation Foundation, Washington DC (1959–72). He wrote many books, carried out official ecological surveys and advised government bodies.

John Frémont, 1813–90

US explorer and politician, born in Savannah, Georgia. In 1842 he crossed the Rocky Mountains (where a peak is named after him). He explored the Great Salt Lake (1843) and examined the continental watershed (1845). In 1849 he crossed over to California, where he settled and became senator of the new state; the Californian city of Fremont is named after him. In 1853 he conducted a fifth expedition. An opponent of slavery, he was twice a Republican presidential candidate (1856, 1864) but was unsuccessful on both occasions.

Sir Vivian Fuchs, 1908–99

English explorer and scientist, born in the Isle of Wight. As director of the Falkland Islands Dependencies Survey (1947) he set up scientific bases on Graham Land peninsula. He also planned an overland crossing of Antarctica, which materialized in 1955 when he was appointed leader of the Commonwealth expedition. His party set out by snow tractor from Shackleton Base, Weddell Sea, on 24 November 1957; they reached the South Pole on 19 January 1958 and then Scott Base, Victoria Land, on 2 March. His publications include his autobiography *A Time to Speak* (1990).

Vasco da Gama, c.1469–1525

Portuguese navigator, born in Alentejo. Selected by King Manoel I to discover a route to India round the Cape of Good Hope, he left Lisbon in 1497 and, after rounding the Cape, reached Malindi (now in Kenya) early the following year. Crossing the Indian Ocean, he reached Calicut (Kozhikode, Kerala) in 1498, the first westerner to sail round the Cape to Asia. He returned to Lisbon in 1499, but 40 Portuguese left behind were murdered. The king sent out an avenging squadron under da Gama (1502), which founded the colonies of Mozambique and Sofala, bombarded Calicut, and returned richly laden in 1503. In 1524 he became Viceroy of India.

Francis (properly Marie Joseph François) Garnier, 1839–73

French soldier and explorer, born in St Étienne. He was second-in-command to Doudart de Lagrée on the Mekong River Expedition (1866–8) during which he mapped over 4991 km (3100 miles) of unknown territory in Cambodia and the Chinese province of Yunnan. He aided in the defence of Paris (1870–1), and took Hanoi in the Tonkin War (1873).

Baron Gerhard de Geer, 1858–1943

Swedish Quaternary geologist, born in Stockholm. He devised a method for dating deposits by comparing sequences of varves (the annual deposits of sediment under glacial meltwater). He was thus able to decipher an annual chronology reaching back 15,000 years. Correlating the Swedish varve sequence with others from elsewhere, he demonstrated global climatic events and greatly advanced knowledge of the most recent Ice Age.

Sir Humphrey Gilbert, 1537–83

English navigator, born in Buxham. He served in Ireland (1566–70), was made Governor of Munster, and then campaigned in the Netherlands (1570–5). In 1578 he led an unsuccessful colonizing expedition to the New World. In a second attempt in 1583 he landed in Newfoundland, claiming it for the Crown, and established a colony at St John's. He was drowned on the homeward journey.

Sibling Similarity

Sir Humphrey Gilbert was the half-brother of **Sir Walter Raleigh**. Older than Raleigh, Gilbert is said to have been an important influence on him. Raleigh took part in both of Gilbert's expeditions and, when Gilbert died, was given his half-brother's patent to colonize the New World.

Ernest Giles, 1835–97

Australian explorer, born in Bristol. He emigrated to Adelaide in 1850 and, from 1861 to 1865, searched for pastures inland from the Darling River. He explored to the west between Adelaide and Darwin, first in 1872 when he discovered Lake Amadeus and again in 1874 when he penetrated the Gibson Desert. In 1875–6 he crossed from Port Augusta to Perth, a distance of 4,000 km (2,500 miles), and back along a line just south of the Tropic of Capricorn. This feat of endurance is described in his *Australia Twice Traversed* (1889).

James Glaisher, 1809–1903

English meteorologist, born in London. In 1840 he became superintendent of the magnetic and meteorological department at Greenwich Observatory, and in 1845 he produced tables for calculating dewpoints of the air. He was a founder-member in 1850 of the British Meteorological Society (later the Royal Meteorological Society). He is best known for 29 balloon ascents between 1862 and 1866, measuring temperature, dewpoint and wind at different heights; his highest ascent is believed to have been just over 9,000 metres (30,000 feet).

Jane Goodall, 1934–

English primatologist and conservationist, born in London. She worked in Kenya with the anthropologist **Louis Leakey**, and has been scientific director of the Gombe Wildlife Research Institute in Tanzania since 1967. She has carried out a study of chimpanzees that has demonstrated the complexity of primate behaviour, discovering that chimpanzees use natural objects as tools and weapons, and that they hunt animals for meat. Active in chimpanzee conservation, her books include *In the Shadow of Man* (1971), *The Chimpanzees of Gombe: Patterns of Behavior* (1986) and *Harvest for Hope: A Guide to Mindful Eating* (2005).

William Gosse, 1842–81

Australian explorer, born in Hertfordshire. His family emigrated to Adelaide, South Australia, in 1850. Gosse joined the South Australian Surveyor-General's department and in 1873 led an expedition from Alice Springs in the Northern Territory in search of an overland route to Perth. He reached the massive sandstone monolith sighted by **Ernest Giles** the previous year, and named it Ayers Rock (now known as Uluru). Although he was forced to turn back, his maps proved invaluable to a successful 1874 expedition from Perth by Sir John Forrest (who later became the first premier of Western Australia).

Stephen Jay Gould, 1941–2002

US palaeontologist, born in New York City. With palaeontologist Niles Eldgredge, he put forward the theory of 'punctuated equilibrium' or rapid evolutionary change followed by stable periods (1972). He has also championed the idea of 'hierarchical evolution'. This suggests that natural selection operates at many levels, including genes and species as well as at the traditional level of individuals. He popularized his ideas in a series of collected essays and his books have won many awards. Influenced by Marxist ideas in his scientific work, he has been a forceful speaker against pseudo-scientific racism and biological determinism.

James Grant, 1827–92

Scottish soldier and explorer, born in Nairn. He joined the Indian army and fought in the Indian Mutiny and in the Abyssinian campaign of 1868. With **John Hanning Speke** he explored the sources of the Nile (1860–3) and made important botanical collections. On Speke's death he took command of the expedition, becoming a leading African specialist. He wrote *A Walk Across Africa* (1864).

Robert Gray, 1755–1806

US explorer, born in Rhode Island. He became the first US captain to sail around the world (1787–90), carrying sea-otter skins from the north-west to China and then returning to Boston with a Chinese cargo. In doing this he established the three-cornered China trade. His explorations of the north-west coast, especially his discovery of the Columbia River (1792), became the basis for the US claim to Oregon.

Augustus Gregory, 1819–1905

Australian surveyor and explorer, born in Nottingham. He went to Australia in 1829, joining the Western Australian Survey Department in 1841. He explored north of Perth in 1846 and discovered coal on the Irwin River. In 1848 he found lead in the Murchison River. He then headed the Northern Australian expedition (1855–6), which discovered new pastures along the route of **Ludwig Leichhardt**. In 1858 his explorations showed that many rivers drained into Lake Eyre, solving the mystery of the South Australian Lakes.

Jean Guettard, 1715–86

French botanist, invertebrate palaeontologist and geologist, born in Étampes. In 1746 he published a geological map of part of northern France, and he later produced another in which he attempted to link the geology of France with that of England. He independently recognized fossils as the remains of once-living organisms and named some invertebrate genera. He also perceived the erosion and depositional roles of running water, and was the first to demonstrate conclusively the volcanic character of the Auvergne (1752).

Richard Hakluyt, c.1552–1616

English geographer, cleric and historian, born in Hertfordshire. In 1582 he published *Divers Voyages touching the Discovery of America*, commissioned by **Sir Walter Raleigh**, advocating colonization of North America as a base for exploration via the Northwest Passage to the Orient. He went on to write *Discourse concerning Western Discoveries* (1584) and *Principal Navigations, Voyages, and Discoveries of the English Nation* (three volumes, 1598–1600); the latter contained accounts of the voyages of the Cabots, Sir Francis Drake, Sir Humphrey Gilbert, Sir Martin Frobisher and many others.

Charles Hall, 1821–71

US explorer, born in Rochester, New Hampshire. He became interested in the fate of **Sir John Franklin** and made two search expeditions (1860–2, 1864–9), bringing back relics and the bones of one of Franklin's men. In 1871 he sailed in command of the *Polaris* on an expedition to the North Pole. Unsuccessful, he went into winter quarters at Thank God Harbour, Greenland, where he became ill and died.

Robin Hanbury-Tenison, 1936–

English explorer and author. He achieved the first land crossing of South America at its widest point (1958). In 1964 he travelled from the Caribbean to the South Atlantic through South America. He took part in the Amazonas and Trans-Africa British hovercraft expeditions (1968, 1969), and in the British Trans-Americas expedition of 1972, crossing the Darién gap. He went on to lead the Royal Geographical Society's Gunung Mulu (Sarawak) Expedition (1977–8). He was a founding member of Survival International, an organization that protects tribal peoples, and is currently its president. His publications include the autobiographical *Worlds Apart* (1984) and *Worlds Within* (2004).

John Harrison, 1693–1776

English inventor and horologist, born in Foulby, Yorkshire. In 1713 the British government offered prizes for the discovery of a method to determine longitude accurately. Harrison responded by developing a marine chronometer (an instrument for the accurate measurement of time). In a voyage to Jamaica (1761–2) Harrison's chronometer allowed him to determine the longitude within 29 km (18 geographical miles). After further trials, he was awarded the first prize (1765–73).

Ferdinand Hayden, 1829–87

US geologist, born in Westfield, Massachusetts. Following work on geological surveys in Dakota, the Badlands, Missouri and Yellowstone (1853–62), he became Professor of Geology at Pennsylvania University (1865–72) and head of the US Geological Survey (1867–79). He was influential in securing the establishment of Yellowstone National Park.

> ### Running with Rocks
> Hayden was given the name 'the man who picks up rocks running' by the Sioux.

Samuel Hearne, 1745–92

English explorer, born in London. The Hudson's Bay Company sent him to Canada in 1769, and in 1770 he became the first European to travel overland by canoe and sled to the Arctic Ocean. In 1774 he set up the first interior trading post for the company at Cumberland House, and then became Governor of Fort Prince of Wales (Churchill), where he was captured and taken to France in 1782. His release was negotiated on condition that he publish an account of his travels. *A Journey from Prince of Wales' Fort ... to the Northern Ocean* was published in 1795.

Sven Hedin, 1865–1952

Swedish explorer and geographer, born in Stockholm. He went to Persia (now Iran) in 1885 as a tutor, and was attached to a Swedish–Norwegian embassy to the Shah in 1890. From then until 1908 he travelled constantly, particularly in the Himalayas, the Gobi Desert, and Tibet, of which he made the first detailed map (1908). He led the Sino-Swedish scientific expedition to the north-west provinces of China (1927–33).

Henry the Navigator, 1394–1460

Portuguese prince, born at Porto, third son of John I, King of Portugal. He was made Governor of the Algarve (1419), and set up court at Sagres. He founded an observatory and school of scientific navigation at Cape St Vincent, and sponsored many voyages of exploration. These resulted in the discovery of the Madeira Islands (1418), the Azores and the Cape Verde Islands (1456). His school helped produce the caravel, a vessel especially fitted for long voyages. His pupils also explored, and established trading posts on the west coast of Africa, thereby preparing the way for the discovery of the sea route to India.

Sir Wally (Walter) Herbert, 1934–

British explorer, born in York. He joined the Falkland Islands Dependencies Survey in Antarctica (1955–7), then made expeditions to Lapland, Svalbard and Greenland. He participated in the New Zealand Antarctic expedition (1960–2) and made the first surface crossing of the Arctic Ocean (1968–9), from Alaska to Spitsbergen via the Pole, the longest sustained sledge journey in history. Between 1978 and 1982 he made several attempts to circumnavigate Greenland. His books include *The Noose of Laurels* (1989) on the controversy about whether it was **Frederick Cook** or **Robert Peary** who first reached the North Pole.

Thor Heyerdahl, 1914–2002

Norwegian anthropologist, born in Larvik. In 1947 he sailed a balsa raft, *Kon-Tiki*, from Callao, Peru, to Tuamotu Island in the South Pacific to prove that aspects of Polynesian culture originated with settlers from the Americas. In 1970, in order to establish that ancient Mediterranean people could have crossed the Atlantic, he sailed from Morocco to the West Indies in a papyrus-reed boat *Ra II*. His journey from Iraq to Djibouti (1977–8) in the reed-ship *Tigris* showed that these craft could be manoeuvred against the wind. He jointly organized a Norwegian/Chilean expedition to Easter Island (1986–8). His books include *The Tigris Expedition* (1980) and *Easter Island* (1989).

Sir Edmund Hillary, 1919–

New Zealand mountaineer and explorer, born in Auckland. He and **Tenzing Norgay** became the first people to conquer Mount Everest, reaching the summit on 29 May 1953. Hillary was deputy leader of the British Commonwealth Antarctic Expedition (1957–8), and made the first overland trip to the South Pole using tracked vehicles. He made further Everest expeditions (1960–61 and 1963–6), and led a geological expedition to Antarctica in 1967, during which he made the first ascent of Mt Herschel. He was a member of the North Pole expedition of 1985. His publications include *High Adventure* (1955) and *Nothing Venture, Nothing Win* (autobiography, 1975).

Arthur Holmes, 1890–1965

English geologist, born in Hebburn-on-Tyne. A pioneer of geochronology, he determined the ages of rocks by measuring their radioactive constituents and played a large part in gathering age data for the Precambrian. He was an early supporter of the continental drift theory and his predictions of the amount of heat generated by radioactive decay in the Earth revealed a mechanism for continental plate movement. He wrote *Principles of Physical Geology* (1944), one of the most successful textbooks ever written.

Honda Toshiaki, 1744–1821

Japanese political economist and navigator, born in Echigo Province. He learned Dutch in order to acquire western knowledge, especially of mathematics. After surveying Hokkaido in 1801, he advocated bringing about wealth and power through the manufacture of gunpowder and metals, the encouragement of shipping, and the colonization of Hokkaido. He envisaged an end to traditional isolation and the promotion of state-sponsored foreign trade, thus anticipating later developments.

Sir John Houghton, 1931–

Welsh physicist and meteorologist, born in Clwyd. He was professor at the Department of Meteorology at Oxford, and director of the Appleton Laboratory (1979). Director-general of the Meteorological Office from 1983 to 1991, he designed various instruments that greatly increased knowledge of atmospheric chemistry, radiation properties and dynamics. He chaired the influential Scientific Assessment Working Group of the Intergovernmental Panel on Climate Change (1990) and the Royal Commission on Environmental Pollution (1992–8). His publications include *Global Warming: The Complete Briefing* (2004).

Henry Hudson, c.1550–1611

English navigator. In 1607 he set sail to seek a north-east passage across the North Pole to China, reaching Spitsbergen. On his second voyage (1608) he reached Novaya Zemlya, an island group in northern Russia. On a third voyage (1609) he discovered the Hudson River, and followed it to Albany (now in New York State). In April 1610 he set out on the *Discovery* and reached Greenland in June, arriving at what are now known as Hudson Strait and Hudson Bay. In November his ship was trapped in ice and, when the ice broke up in the spring of 1611, the men mutinied. On 23 June, Hudson was cast adrift in a boat and never seen again.

Alexander, Baron von Humboldt, 1769–1859

German naturalist, born in Berlin. Between 1799 and 1804 he explored unknown territory in South America, which led to his monumental *Voyage de Humboldt et Bonpland aux Régions Equinoxiales* (1805–34; English translation *Personal Narrative of Travels to the Equinoctial Regions*, 1814–29). In 1829 he explored Central Asia, describing his experiences in *Asie Centrale* (1843). Political changes led to his employment in political services, and it was in Paris that he published his *Examen critique de l'histoire de la géographie du nouveau continent* ('Critical examination of the geographical history of the New World', 1835–8).

Hamilton Hume, 1797–1873

Australian explorer, born in Parramatta, New South Wales. He spent eight years exploring the Goulburn and Yass plains and Lake Bathurst in southern New South Wales, reaching the Clyde River. In 1824 he set out to find an overland passage from Lake George to the southern coast. The expedition discovered part of the Murray River, and made the first sighting of Australia's highest mountain, Mount Kosciusko. In 1828 Hume joined an expedition led by Charles Sturt (1795–1869) which discovered the Darling River, but poor health ended his participation.

James Hutton, 1726–97

Scottish geologist, born in Edinburgh. He presented his ideas, the fruit of many journeys throughout Britain, before the Royal Society of Edinburgh in *A Theory of the Earth* (1785). He demonstrated that the internal heat of the Earth caused intrusions into the crust of molten rock, and that granite, after cooling, was the product. He recognized that most rocks were produced by erosion, deposited on the seafloor, lithified (transformed into stone) by heat and then uplifted to form new continents. Hutton's ideas form the basis of modern geology.

Ibn Battutah (or Batuta), 1304–68

Arab traveller and geographer, born in Tangiers, North Africa. In 30 years of travelling (1325–54) he covered all the Muslim countries, visiting Mecca, Persia (now Iran), Mesopotamia and Asia Minor (now Iraq, Syria and eastern Turkey), India, China, Sumatra, southern Spain, and Timbuktu (now in Mali). He then settled in Fez (Morocco) and dictated the entertaining history of his journeys, the *Rihlah* ('Travels'), published with a French translation in 1855–9.

Donald Carl Johanson, 1943–

US palaeoanthropologist, born in Chicago. His spectacular finds of fossil hominids 3–4 million years old at Hadar in the Afar Triangle of Ethiopia (1972–7) generated worldwide interest. They include 'Lucy', a unique female specimen that is half complete, and the so-called 'first family', a scattered group containing the remains of 13 individuals. He suggested that these remains belong to a previously undiscovered species, which he named *Australopithecus afarensis* ('southern ape of Afar'). He founded the Institute of Human Origins in California (1981), which later moved to Arizona and became associated with Arizona State University (1997).

Louis Jolliet (or Joliet), 1645–1700

French explorer, born in Quebec, Canada. In 1673 he and Father Jacques Marquette were commissioned to investigate Native American accounts of a great river called the Mississippi, which was believed to empty into the Pacific. They travelled by canoe westward on the Fox and Wisconsin rivers and then down the Mississippi to the mouth of the Arkansas River. Determining that the river probably emptied into the Gulf of Mexico, and fearing to encroach on Spanish territory, they turned back, ascending the Illinois River and on to the site of present-day Chicago.

What's in a Name?

The name 'Chicago' comes from the original name of the marshlands on which the city was built: 'Checagou'. This Native American word is said to mean 'wild onion' or 'garlic', and it has been suggested that these plants grew profusely in the area.

John Joly, 1857–1933

Irish geologist and physicist, born in Offaly. His calculation of the age of the Earth (as 80 million–90 million years) by measuring the sodium content of the sea (1899) was influential. He realized that some characteristics of minerals were caused by radioactivity and could be used for dating (1907–14). His publications included *An Estimate of the Age of the Earth* (1899) and *Radium and the Geological Age of the Earth* (1903).

Frank (Francis) Kingdon-Ward, 1885–1958

English plant collector and geographer, born in Manchester. In 1911 he became a professional plant collector for the seed company Bees of Liverpool. He made many expeditions, mainly to the remote borderlands of India, Burma (Myanmar) and China. He introduced many plants into cultivation, and he developed novel theories on the geography and palaeogeography of the Himalayas. His 25 books include *On the Road to Tibet* (1910), *The Land of the Blue Poppy* (1913), and *Pilgrimage for Plants* (1960).

Alfred Lacroix, 1863–1948

French mineralogist, petrologist and structural geologist, born in Mâcon. In 1893 he became Professor of Mineralogy at the Museum of Natural History in Paris and built up a systematic collection of minerals from around the world. He carried out research on eruptive rocks, studying the eruptions of Mont Pelée in 1902, and was first to witness the 'nuée ardente', a glowing cloud type of eruption. His studies in Madagascar in 1911 resulted in *Minéralogie de Madagascar* (1922–3, 'Mineralogy of Madagascar').

Hubert Lamb, 1913–97

English climatologist, born in Bedford. While working at the Meteorological Office during World War II he produced weather forecasts for transatlantic flights, and in 1946 he had a spell of duty on whaling ships. His expertise in analysing weather charts proved crucial to his production of a daily weather classification for Great Britain for each day from 1861, and a study of major volcanic eruptions since 1500. This work has been invaluable in climate change studies. His major publication was *Climate, Present, Past and Future* (2 vols, 1972, 1977).

René, Sieur de La Salle, 1643–87

French explorer and pioneer of Canada, born in Rouen. He settled as a trader near Montreal, Canada, and descended the Ohio and Mississippi to the sea (1682), claiming lands for France that he named Louisiana after Louis XIV. In 1684 an expedition set out to establish a French settlement on the Gulf of Mexico, but La Salle failed to find the Mississippi Delta. His followers mutinied, and he was murdered.

> ### Nutcracker Man
> *Zinjanthropus* or *Australopithecus* was nicknamed 'Nutcracker Man' because of his very large teeth.

Louis Leakey, 1903–72

British archaeologist and physical anthropologist, born of British parents in Kenya. His great discoveries of early hominid fossils took place at Olduvai Gorge in East Africa where, in 1959, he and his wife **Mary Leakey** unearthed the skull of *Zinjanthropus*. This hominid has since been reclassified as *Australopithecus* and is thought to be about 1.75 million years old. In 1960–3 Leakey found remains of *Homo habilis*, a smaller species some 2 million years old, which led him to postulate that *Homo habilis* was the true ancestor of man and that *Australopithecus* became extinct. In 1967 he discovered remains of *Kenyapithecus africanus*, a Miocene ape approximately 14 million years old.

Mary Leakey (née Nicol) 1913–96

English archaeologist, born in London. She married **Louis Leakey** in 1936. In 1948, at Rusinga Island in Lake Victoria, she discovered *Proconsul africanus*, a 1.7 million-year-old primitive ape that brought the Leakeys international attention. In 1959 her discovery of the hominid *Zinjanthropus*, filmed as it happened, captured the public imagination. Perhaps most remarkable of all was her excavation in 1976 at Laetoli (Tanzania) of three trails of fossilized hominid footprints, which demonstrated unequivocally that our ancestors already walked upright 3.6 million years ago. Her books include *Olduvai Gorge: My Search for Early Man* (1979).

Richard Leakey, 1944–

Kenyan palaeoanthropologist and politician, born in Nairobi, son of **Louis** and **Mary Leakey**. In East Africa he discovered fossil skulls of *Australopithecus boisei* (1969), of *Homo habilis* dated 1.9 million years (1972), and of *Homo erectus* dated 1.5 million years (1975). As director of the Kenya Wildlife Service (1993–4, 1998–9), he organized a high-profile campaign against ivory poaching. In 1995 he co-founded the Safina Party and became an MP in 1998. He was appointed Head of the Kenyan civil service in 1999, but resigned unexpectedly in 2001. His publications include *Origins* (1977, with Roger Lewin) and *Man-Ape Ape-Man* (1993, with L Jan Slikkerveer).

Ludwig Leichhardt, 1813–c.1848

Australian naturalist and explorer, born in Prussia (now part of Germany). After moving to Sydney he successfully mounted an expedition from Brisbane to Port Essington, a settlement on the coast of Arnhem Land. The party's arrival back in Sydney in March 1846, when they had been presumed lost, caused great excitement. In December 1846 he attempted an east–west crossing of the northern part of the continent, but was forced to turn back. In February 1848 he set off on another transcontinental journey but nothing was heard of him after April 1848.

Leif the Lucky (Leifur heppni Eiríksson), fl.1000

Icelandic explorer, son of **Erik the Red**. Just before the year 1000 he set sail from Greenland to explore westwards, reaching Baffin Land, Labrador, and an area he called 'Vínland' (Wineland) because wild grapes grew there. Vínland's location is uncertain, but remains of a Norse settlement have been found on Newfoundland. Other Icelandic settlers, led by **Thorfinn**, tried to establish a colony in 'Vínland', but withdrew in the face of hostility from the natives.

Meriwether Lewis, 1774–1809

US explorer, born near Charlottesville, Virginia. In 1801 he became personal secretary to President Thomas Jefferson, and was invited with his long-time friend **William Clark** to lead an expedition (1804–6) to explore the lands to the west of the Mississippi. This became the first overland journey across North America to the Pacific. A triumph for the young nation, the Lewis and Clark expedition strengthened

US claims to the Oregon Territory and spurred settlement of the West. Lewis was appointed Governor of the Louisiana Territory in 1806, but died in a shooting incident only three years later.

William Light, 1784–1839

English soldier and surveyor, born in Malaysia. He served in the Peninsular Wars, where he prepared battle maps. In 1834 he took command of the paddle-steamer *Nile* on its voyage to join the navy of the Pasha of Egypt. Appointed as surveyor-general to South Australia, he laid out the plan for Adelaide. The city was planned with squares and wide streets, surrounded by the first 'green belt' of open spaces and parkland: an early example of town-planning.

Carolus Linnaeus (originally Carl von Linné), 1707–78

Swedish naturalist and physician, born in Råshult. He went to Holland to study medicine in 1735, and while there published his system of botanical nomenclature in *Systema Naturae* (1735). This was followed by *Critica Botanica* (1737), in which he used his so-called 'sexual system' of classification based on the number of flower parts. His major contribution was the introduction, in Sweden in 1749, of binomial nomenclature of generic and specific names for animals and plants, which permitted the hierarchical organization later known as systematics.

Li Shizen (Li Shih-chen), 1518–93

Chinese pharmaceutical naturalist and biologist. He spent 30 years producing an encyclopedia of pharmaceutical natural history. The *Ben Cao Gang Mu* ('Great Pharmacopoeia'), completed in 1578 and published in 1596, gives an exhaustive description of 1,000 plants and 1,000 animals, and includes more than 11,000 prescriptions. By categorizing diseases, it also forms a system of medicine. He recorded many instances of the sophistication of Chinese medicine, for example the use of mercury–silver amalgam for tooth fillings, not introduced to Europe until the 19th century.

David Livingstone, 1813–73

Scottish missionary and traveller, born in Blantyre, Lanarkshire. During extensive missionary work and exploration he discovered the Victoria Falls of the Zambezi river (1855). In 1858 he set out to explore the Zambezi, Shiré and Rovuma rivers and discovered Lake Nyasa. In 1867–8 he went on to discover Lakes Mweru and Bangweulu. He struck westwards as far as the River Lualaba, thinking it might be the Nile, which afterwards proved to be the Congo. On his return to Ujiji (now in Tanzania), Livingstone was found there by **Henry Morton Stanley**. After his death in what is now Zambia, his followers carried his embalmed body to the coast, from where it was taken and buried in Westminster Abbey.

James Lovelock, 1919–

English scientist and environmentalist, born in Letchworth Garden City. In 1957 he invented the electron capture detector, an instrument that is important in detecting chemicals that are harmful to the environment. He worked for NASA during the 1960s and 70s, studying the composition of the atmospheres of different planets. This inspired him, together with Lynn Margulis, to develop the Gaia Theory, the idea that living and non-living parts of the Earth interact with each other to regulate the environment. Lovelock's books include *Gaia: A New Look at Life on Earth* (1979),

Ages of Gaia (1988), his autobiography *Homage to Gaia* (2000) and *The Revenge of Gaia* (2006). He is relatively unusual among environmentalists in his support for nuclear power as a replacement for the burning of fossil fuels.

Sir Charles Lyell, 1797–1875

Scottish geologist, born in Forfarshire (now Angus). His authoritative *Principles of Geology* (1830–3) was very influential. His 'uniformitarian' principle taught that the greatest geological changes might have been produced by the forces in operation now, given sufficient time. His interest was primarily in the biological side of geology, and his work had as great a contemporary influence as **Charles Darwin**'s *Origin of Species*.

Sir Alexander Mackenzie, 1764–1820

Scottish explorer, born in Stornoway, Isle of Lewis. He joined the Northwest Fur Company in 1779, and in 1788 established Fort Chipewayan on Lake Athabasca in Canada. From there he discovered the Mackenzie River (1789), followed it to the sea, and in 1792–3 became the first European to cross the Rocky Mountains to the Pacific Ocean.

Ferdinand Magellan, c.1480–1521

Portuguese navigator, born near Villa Real. He laid before Charles I of Spain a scheme for reaching the Moluccan Islands in Indonesia by travelling west. Sailing from Seville on 10 August 1519, his expedition coasted Patagonia, passing through the strait that bears his name (21 October to 28 November), and reached the ocean that he named the Pacific. He was killed by local people in the Philippine Islands but his ship, the *Victoria*, returned to Spain on 6 September 1522 to complete the first circumnavigation of the world, captained by Juan Sebastián Elcano.

Sir Max Mallowan, 1904–78

English archaeologist, born in London. He made excavations for the British Museum at Arpachiyah near Nineveh (1932–3), and in Syria at Chagar Bazar (1935–6) and Tell Brak (1937–8). After World War II he excavated principally at Nimrud, the ancient capital of the Middle Eastern empire of Assyria (1949–60), with striking results described in detail in *Nimrud and Its Remains* (1970). His autobiography, *Mallowan's Memoirs*, appeared in 1977.

> ### Age Before Beauty?
> In 1930 Sir Max Mallowan married the novelist Agatha Christie after meeting her at an archaeological site. She remarked that 'An archaeologist is the best husband any woman can have: the older she gets, the more interested he is in her'.

Gideon Mantell, 1790–1852

English palaeontologist, born in Lewes, Sussex. He wrote *The Fossils of the South Downs* in 1822, and completed his *Geology of the South-east of England* in 1837. He discovered several dinosaur types, including the first to be fully described; noting the similarity between its teeth and those of the iguana, he named it 'iguanodon' (1825). In 1831 he introduced the notion of the 'age of reptiles'.

Kenneth Mellanby, 1908–93

Scottish entomologist and environmentalist, born in Barrhead, Renfrewshire. He was the first director of the Nature Conservancy's Monks Wood Experimental Station (1961–74). There he worked mainly on the effects of agriculture and industry on the environment, particularly the role of pesticides such as DDT. His publications on this topic include *The Biology of Pollution* (1972) and *Waste and Pollution* (1991).

Gerardus Mercator (originally Gerhard Kremer), 1512–94

Flemish geographer and map-maker, born in Rupelmonde, Flanders. In 1569 he introduced a map projection (Mercator's map projection), in which the path of a ship steering on a constant bearing is represented by a straight line; it has been used for nautical charts ever since. In 1585 he published the first part of a book of maps of Europe, completed by his son in 1595.

> ### Maps and Mythology
>
> The cover of Gerardus Mercator's book of maps was illustrated with a drawing of the Greek god Atlas holding a globe on his shoulders. As a result, 'atlas' has become the term for a book of maps.

Andrija Mohorovičić, 1857–1936

Yugoslav seismologist and meteorologist, born in Croatia. While investigating the Croatian earthquake of 1909 he observed two distinct seismic wave arrivals. He deduced that the slower wave followed the direct route from the earthquake focus to the observation point, while the faster wave was refracted from a discontinuity in the Earth's structure. He concluded that the Earth's crust must overlie a denser mantle and he calculated the depth to this transition. The discontinuity was found to exist worldwide, and became known as the Mohorovicic discontinuity or 'Moho'.

John Muir, 1838–1914

US naturalist, born in Dunbar, Scotland. He emigrated to America in 1849 and explored the western USA, especially the Yosemite area. He farmed successfully in California, and also campaigned for a national park there. It needed a decade of Muir's vigorous oratory and article-writing before the idea of wildlife conservation became widely accepted. Muir wrote a number of books, including *Our National Parks* (1901) and *My First Summer in the Sierra* (1911). He is regarded as the father of the modern environmental movement.

Sir Roderick Murchison, 1792–1871

Scottish geologist, born in Tarradale, Ross-shire. He established two geological periods of the Palaeozoic era: the Silurian system (1835) and, with **Adam Sedgwick**, the Devonian system. From 1840 to 1845, with others, he carried out a geological survey of the Russian empire. Struck with the resemblance between the Ural mountains and Australian chains, he foreshadowed the discovery of gold in Australia (1844). In 1855 he was made director-general of the Geological Survey and director of the Royal School of Mines.

Sir John Murray, 1841–1914

Canadian marine biologist, born in Cobourg, Ontario. He was one of the naturalists on the *Challenger* expedition (1872–6) which explored all of the oceans of the world. He assisted in the editing of the Challenger Reports, and among his publications are a narrative of the expedition and *The Depths of the Ocean* (1912, with J Hjort). Murray also surveyed the depths of the Scottish freshwater lakes. He is considered one of the founders of oceanography.

Fridtjof Nansen, 1861–1930

Norwegian explorer and diplomat, born in Store-Frøen. He conceived a scheme for reaching the North Pole by letting his ship become frozen in ice north of Siberia and drift with a current towards Greenland. He started in the *Fram* in August 1893, reached the New Siberian islands in September, made fast to an ice floe, and drifted north to 84°4′N in March 1895. From there he carried on on foot, reaching the highest latitude then attained, 86°14′N, on 7 April. In 1922 he was awarded the Nobel Peace Prize for Russian relief work, and he did much for the League of Nations (the forerunner of the United Nations).

> **Forward in the Fram**
>
> The name *Fram*, given by Nansen to his ship, is a Norwegian word meaning 'forward'.

Max Nicholson, 1904–2003

English conservationist, born in Ringwood, Hampshire. As director-general of Nature Conservancy (1952–66), he stimulated and established conservation work in the UK and throughout the world. He was president of the Royal Society for the Protection of Birds (1980–5) and served on the boards of the Wildfowl Trust, World Wildlife Fund, and Common Ground International. He chaired the UK Standing Committee for World Conservation Strategy Programme (1981–3). His publications range from *Birds of England* (1926) to *The New Environmental Age* (1987).

(Nils) Otto Nordenskjöld, 1869–1928

Swedish explorer and geologist, born in Småland. In 1901 he led a Swedish party in *Antarctic* to the Antarctic Peninsula. They reached the Weddell Sea and spent two winters on Snow Hill Island. *Antarctic* was crushed by ice, but they were rescued by an Argentinian gunboat. In 1920–1 he explored the Andes. He was the nephew of **Baron Nils Nordenskjöld**.

Nils Adolf Erik, Baron Nordenskjöld, 1832–1901

Swedish Arctic navigator, born in Helsingfors (now Helsinki), Finland. A naturalized Swede, he made several expeditions to Spitsbergen and mapped the south of the island. After two preliminary trips proving the navigability of the Kara Sea, he accomplished the navigation of the Northeast Passage (on the *Vega*) from the Atlantic to the Pacific along the north coast of Asia (1878–9). He later made two expeditions to Greenland.

Lawrence Oates, 1880–1912

English explorer, born in London. In 1910 he set out with Captain **Robert Scott**'s

Antarctic expedition, and was one of the party to reach the South Pole (17 January 1912). On the return journey the explorers were dangerously delayed and became weatherbound. Lamed by severe frostbite, Oates, convinced that he would fatally handicap his companions, walked out into the blizzard, deliberately sacrificing his life to enhance his comrades' chances of survival.

> *I am just going outside and may be some time.*
> —The last words of Lawrence Oates, 17 March 1912
> (his 32nd birthday).

John Ogilby, 1600–76

Scottish topographer, printer and map-maker, born in Edinburgh. He lost everything in the Civil War, but after the Restoration was appointed king's cosmographer and geographic printer. His most important publications were the maps and atlases engraved in the last decade of his life, including Africa (1670), America (1671) and Asia (1673), and an unfinished road atlas of Great Britain (1675).

Alan Grant Ogilvie, 1887–1954

Scottish geographer, born in Edinburgh. He was established at the University of Edinburgh in the first chair of geography in Scotland (1931). Other posts included president of the Royal Scottish Geographical Society (1946–50) and president of the Institute of British Geographers (1951–2). He is known for establishing the fundamental importance of physical geography to the life of humankind.

Francisco de Orellana, c.1500–1549

Spanish explorer, born in Trujillo. He went to Peru with **Francisco Pizarro** but, after crossing the Andes in 1541, he deserted Pizarro's expedition and descended the Amazon River to its mouth.

The Naming of the Amazon

The original name of the Amazon River was Rio Santa Maria de la Mar Dulce. Francisco de Orellana is said to have renamed it after an attack by a tribe in which he believed women were fighting alongside men, the Amazons being a nation of female warriors in Greek mythology.

Peter Simon Pallas, 1741–1811

German naturalist, born in Berlin. His comparative anatomical methods laid the foundation for modern taxonomy. He spent six years (1768–74) exploring the Russian interior, and on his return he wrote on the geography, ethnography, geology, flora and fauna of the regions he had visited. His observations led him to examine the relationships between animals and their environment, so that he became the first zoogeographer. His major contribution was probably to geology, as he proposed a modern view of the formation of mountain ranges.

Mungo Park, 1771–1806

Scottish explorer, born in the Scottish Borders. In 1795 he set off inland from The Gambia, reached the Niger at Sego (Ségou, now in Mali) in July 1796, and followed it westwards to Bammaku (Bamako). Park recounted his adventures in *Travels in the Interior of Africa* (1799), which at last determined the direction of flow of the Niger. In 1805 he undertook another African journey, starting from Pisania on the Gambia River, and reached Sansanding in November 1805. He reached Boussa with four others, but they were attacked by local people and drowned in the fight.

Sir William Parry, 1790–1855

English navigator, born in Bath. He took command in five expeditions to the Arctic, in 1818 (under Sir John Ross), 1819–20, 1821–3, 1824–5 and 1827. The last was an attempt to reach the North Pole on sledges from Spitsbergen, which was unsuccessful but still travelled further north than anyone had done previously. Parry was subsequently made rear-admiral (1852), and governor of Greenwich Hospital (1853).

Pausanias, 2nd century AD

Greek geographer and historian, born probably in Lydia. He travelled through almost all Greece, Macedonia and Italy, and through part of Asia and Africa. From his observations and researches he composed an *Itinerary of Greece*, describing that country and its monuments of art. Intended as a guidebook, it is an invaluable source of information.

Auguste Pavie, 1847–1925

French explorer and diplomat, born in Dinan. In 1880 he supervised the laying of the telegraph line between Phnom Penh and Bangkok, before being granted permission to explore French Indochina (now Vietnam, Laos and Cambodia). The series of expeditions that he organized (1881–95), known as the Pavie Mission, surveyed a vast area and collected important scientific data, which were published with accompanying maps (*Mission Pavie*, 1898–1919). This achievement led to the French political domination over the Laotian states.

Robert Peary, 1856–1920

US naval commander and explorer, born in Cresson Springs, Pennsylvania. He made eight Arctic expeditions from 1886, exploring Greenland and the region later called Peary Land. In 1906 he reached 87°6′ N, and on 6 April 1909 attained the North Pole. His claim to be first to reach the Pole was substantiated when Dr **Frederick Cook**'s own claim was discredited, although some doubt still exists regarding whether Peary reached the precise 90° position.

William Penn, 1644–1718

English Quaker and colonialist, born in London. In 1681 he obtained a grant of territory in North America, called 'Pensilvania' (now Pennsylvania) in honour of his father, intending to establish a home for his co-religionists. He sailed with his emigrants for the Delaware river in 1682. He planned the city of Philadelphia, and for two years governed wisely and tolerantly. Having revisited England (1684–99) to help his persecuted Quaker brethren, in 1699 he returned to Pennsylvania. He did something to mitigate the evils of slavery, but held black slaves himself. He departed for England in 1701, where his last years were embittered by legal disputes.

City of Brotherly Love

The name 'Philadelphia' comes from the Greek meaning 'brotherly love'.

Harry Philby, 1885–1960

English Arabist and explorer, born in Ceylon (now Sri Lanka). While in charge of the British Political Mission to Central Arabia (1917–18), he crossed Arabia by camel from Uqayr to Jedda, becoming the first European to visit the Nejd plateau. He wrote about his experiences in *The Heart of Arabia* (1922). In 1926 he set up in business in Jedda, advised King Ibn Saud, and became a Muslim in 1930. In 1931 he made an epic crossing of the Empty Quarter of Arabia, one of the world's largest sand deserts, from north to south. From 1932 to 1937 he mapped the Yemen highlands. He lived in Arabia until his death.

Zebulon Pike, 1779–1813

US explorer, born in Lamberton, New Jersey. As an army lieutenant he led an expedition (1806–7) from St Louis to the Arkansas River and the Rocky Mountains, and he tried but failed to scale the Colorado peak now named after him. He fought in the War of 1812 and was killed in the assault on York (now Toronto).

Francisco Pizarro, c.1478–1541

Spanish conquistador, born in Trujillo, Spain. He served in Italy, and with the expedition that discovered the Pacific (1513). In 1526 he and Diego de Almagro sailed for Peru, and in 1531 began the conquest of the Incas. Pizarro killed their King Atahualpa, then worked to consolidate the new empire, founding Lima (1535) and other cities. Dissension with Almagro led to the latter's execution; in revenge, Almagro's followers assassinated Pizarro.

Gonzalo Pizarro, c.1506–1548

Spanish conquistador, born in Trujillo, Spain. He accompanied his half-brother **Francisco Pizarro** in the conquest of Peru, and in 1539 undertook an ill-fated expedition to the east of Quito (now in Ecuador). One of his lieutenants, **Francisco de Orellana**, deserted his starving comrades, discovered the whole course of the River Amazon, and returned to Spain. Gonzalo, meanwhile, returned to Quito with his few remaining men to find that his half-brother had been assassinated in 1541. He travelled to Lima in 1544 and killed the viceroy in a revolt. For this he was eventually defeated and executed.

Marco Polo, 1254–1324

Venetian merchant, traveller and writer. At the time of his birth, his father and uncle were on an expedition to Cathay (now China). They started out again in 1271, taking the young Marco with them, arriving at the court of Kublai Khan in 1275. The emperor sent Marco as envoy to Yunnan (China), Burma (Myanmar), Karakorum (Mongolia), Cochin-China (now Vietnam) and southern India, and for three years he served as Governor of Yang Chow (now in China). The Polos eventually returned to Venice in 1295, bringing great wealth. Marco wrote an account of his travels, *Divisament dou Monde*, an important source for our knowledge of China and the East before the 19th century.

Juan Ponce de León, 1460–1521

Spanish explorer, born in San Servas. He served against the Moors and became Governor, first of part of Hispaniola, then (1510–12) of Puerto Rico. On a quest for the fountain of perpetual youth he discovered Florida in April 1513, and was made Governor. Failing to conquer his new subjects, he retired to Cuba and died there from a wound inflicted by a poisoned arrow.

Sir Jonathon Porritt, 1950–

English broadcaster, writer and environmentalist, born in London. Appointed director of Friends of the Earth (FoE) in 1984, he became well known through his work at FoE, publications and regular television appearances. He resigned from FoE in 1990 to concentrate on his freelance career. His books include *Seeing Green – the Politics of Ecology* (1984) and *Capitalism: As If the World Matters* (2006). He has been director of the charity Forum for the Future since 1996, and chairman of the Sustainable Development Commission since 2000.

Ptolemy (Latin Claudius Ptolemaeus), c.90–168 AD

Egyptian astronomer and geographer who lived in Alexandria. As a geographer, Ptolemy made corrections to work produced by his predecessor Marinus of Tyre. His *Geography* contains a catalogue of places, with latitude and longitude, general descriptions, and details regarding his mode of noting the position of places. He calculated the size of the Earth, and constructed a map of the world and other maps. His Earth-centred view of the universe (Ptolemaic system) dominated cosmological thought until the 16th century.

Sir Walter Raleigh (or Ralegh), 1552–1618

English courtier, navigator and poet, born in Devon. From 1584 to 1589 he sent an expedition to America, and despatched an abortive settlement to Roanoke Island, North Carolina (1585–6). He later made unsuccessful attempts to colonize Virginia but did introduce tobacco and potatoes into Britain. Caught up in intrigues at the end of Elizabeth I's reign, he was arrested in 1603 and sentenced to life imprisonment. In 1616 he was released to make an expedition to the Orinoco river in South America, in search of a goldmine. Raleigh lost his fleet, and his son, and broke his terms of release by razing a Spanish town. On his return in 1618 he was executed.

> 66
>
> *This is a sharp medicine, but it is a physician for all diseases.*
>
> —Sir Walter Raleigh's description of the axe that was to behead him, 29 October 1618.
>
> 99

Knud Rasmussen, 1879–1933

Danish explorer and ethnologist, born in Jacobshavn, Greenland. The son of a Danish Inuit mother, he directed several expeditions to Greenland (from 1902) in support of the theory that the Inuit and the Native North Americans were both descended from tribes from Asia. In 1910 he established Thule base on Cape York, and crossed from Greenland to the Bering Strait by dog sledge (1921–4).

Charles Richter, 1900–85

US seismologist, born in Ohio. With Beno Gutenberg he devised the Richter scale of earthquake strength (1927–35). Professor of Seismology at Caltech from 1952, he played a key role in establishing the southern California seismic array and published *Seismicity of the Earth* (1954, with Gutenberg) and *Elementary Seismology* (1958).

Sir James Ross, 1800–62

Scottish explorer and naval officer, born in London. From 1829 to 1833 he was joint leader with his uncle (Sir John Ross) of an Arctic expedition and in 1831 he located the magnetic North Pole. He led an expedition to the Antarctic (1839–43) on the *Erebus* and the *Terror*, during which he discovered Victoria Land and the volcano Mt Erebus. He wrote an account of his travels in *Voyage of Discovery* (1847). He made a last expedition in 1848–9, searching for the ill-fated Franklin expedition in Baffin Bay.

Remembering Ross

Ross Island, James Ross Island, the Ross Sea, the Ross Ice Shelf and the Ross Dependency, all in Antarctica, are all named after Sir James Ross.

Robert Falcon Scott, 1868–1912

English explorer, born near Devonport. He commanded the National Antarctic expedition (1901–4) in the *Discovery*, exploring the Ross Sea and discovering King Edward VII Land. In 1910 he embarked upon his second expedition in the *Terra Nova* and, with a sledge party consisting of **Edward Wilson, Lawrence Oates**, H R Bowers and Edgar Evans, reached the South Pole on 17 January 1912, only to discover that **Roald Amundsen** had beaten them by a month. Evans and Oates died on the return journey and the rest of the team perished short of One Ton Depot in March, where their bodies were found eight months later.

Famous Family

Robert Falcon Scott was the father of the conservationist and painter Sir Peter Scott, who founded the Wildfowl and Wetlands Trust.

Adam Sedgwick, 1785–1873

English geologist, born in Dent, Cumbria. In 1831 he began geological mapping in Wales and introduced the Cambrian period into the geological timescale in 1835. A controversy with **Roderick Murchison** was finally resolved with the introduction of the Ordovician period by Charles Lapworth. Sedgwick's best work was on *British Palaeozoic Fossils* (1854, with Sir Frederick McCoy). Sedgwick and Murchison together studied the Lake District and south-west England, where they identified the Devonian period.

Sir Ernest Shackleton, 1874–1922

British explorer, born in County Kildare. He was a junior officer under **Robert Scott**, on the *Discovery*, in the National Antarctic expedition of 1901–4. In 1909, in command of another expedition, he reached a point 156 km (97 miles) from the South Pole. During a further expedition (1914–16), his ship *Endurance* was crushed in the ice of the Weddell Sea. Using sledges and boats he and his men reached Elephant Island, from where he and five others sailed 1,300 km (800 miles) to South Georgia using dead reckoning and organized relief for those remaining on Elephant Island. He died and was buried on South Georgia while on a fourth Antarctic expedition.

Myrtle Simpson (née Emslie), 1931–

Scottish Arctic explorer and long-distance skier, born in Aldershot. She spent her early twenties climbing in New Zealand and Peru. In 1957 she married the medical researcher and explorer Dr Hugh Simpson, with whom she travelled in Suriname and the Arctic. In 1965 she became the first woman to ski across the Greenland ice cap. In 1969 she attempted unsuccessfully to ski to the North Pole unsupported, reaching the most northerly point an unsupported woman had ever attained.

Jedediah Smith, 1799–1831

US fur-trader and explorer, born in Jericho, New York. He undertook two major explorations in the Southwest of North America between 1823 and 1830. The first of these was in the Central Rockies and Columbia River areas, trapping and observing the activities of the Hudson's Bay Company. He then became the first white man to reach California overland across the Sierra Nevada and Great Basin. He was killed by Comanches (a Native American people) while leading a wagon train to Santa Fe.

John Smith, 1580–1631

English adventurer, born in Willoughby, Lincolnshire. He was captured by the Turks and sold as a slave. He escaped to Russia and in 1607 joined an expedition to colonize Virginia. He was saved from a Native American tribe by the chief's daughter Pocahontas, and was later elected President of the colony (1608–9), but he returned to England in 1609. In 1614 he was sent to New England and explored the coast. He wrote valuable accounts of his travels, including *The True Travels, Adventures, and Observations of Captaine John Smith* (1630).

Hernando (or Fernando) de Soto, c.1500–1542

Spanish explorer, born in Jeréz de los Caballeros. He sailed to Central America in 1519. After helping **Francisco Pizarro** conquer the Incas in Peru, he was appointed Governor of Cuba and Florida (1536) and in 1539 set out to explore the latter. Following illusory tales of gold and often clashing with Native American people, he and his soldiers travelled through much of present-day Georgia, North and South Carolina, Tennessee, Alabama, and Oklahoma. They became the first Europeans to see the Mississippi River (1541), before de Soto died of a fever.

John Hanning Speke, 1827–64

English explorer, born in Ilminster, Somerset. In 1854 he joined **Richard Francis Burton** in an expedition to Somaliland and in 1857 the Royal Geographical Society sent them to search for the equatorial lakes of Africa. Speke, while travelling alone, discovered the Victoria Nyanza (Lake Victoria) and saw in it the headwaters of the Nile. In 1860 he returned with **James Grant**, explored the lake, and tracked the Nile flowing out of it. He was preparing to defend the identification against Burton's doubts when he accidentally shot himself while partridge-shooting.

Sir Henry Morton Stanley (originally John Rowlands), 1841–1904

British–US explorer and journalist, born in Denbigh, Wales. In 1859 he went to New Orleans, where he was adopted by a merchant named Stanley. As a journalist he accompanied Lord Napier's Abyssinian expedition in 1868. On 10 November 1871 he 'found' **David Livingstone** at Ujiji (Tanzania) before Stanley returned alone. In 1874 he went back to Africa, determined the shape of Lake Tanganyika and traced the Congo to the sea. In 1879 he helped found the Congo Free State. In 1886, on an expedition to relieve **Emin Pasha**, he discovered Lake Edward and Mount Ruwenzori (1888–9). His books include *How I Found Livingstone* (1872).

> **"**
> *Dr Livingstone, I presume?*
> —Sir Henry Morton Stanley, on finding Livingstone at Ujiji (Tanzania), 1871.
> **"**

Vilhjalmur Stefánsson, 1879–1962

Canadian explorer, born of Icelandic parents in Manitoba. He travelled to the Arctic to live among the Inuit (1906–7) and he conducted further studies among the Mackenzie and Copper Inuit between 1908 and 1912. From 1913 to 1918 he led the Canadian Arctic expedition to map the Beaufort Sea. He wrote several popular books, including *My Life with the Eskimo* (1913) and *The Friendly Arctic* (1921).

Georg Wilhelm Steller (originally Stöhler), 1709–46

German naturalist and explorer, born near Nuremberg. A member of the Academy of Sciences at St Petersburg, he was seconded to the expedition to Kamchatka (Russia) led by **Vitus Bering** (1737–44). He explored Siberia and Kamchatka and met Bering in Okhotsk. They sailed to Alaska, landed on Kayak Island and returned via Bering Island where they were shipwrecked and where Bering died. There Steller wrote *De Bestiis Marinis* (published in 1751, 'On Marine Animals'). He died on the return journey.

> *Celebrating Steller*
> Steller's sea-cow (now extinct), Steller's sea lion and Steller's eider are all named after Georg Wilhelm Steller.

John Lloyd Stephens, 1805–52

US archaeologist and traveller, born in Shrewsbury, New Jersey. He travelled extensively in Europe before embarking with the architect and artist Frederick Catherwood (1799–1856) on an exploration of Mesoamerica in 1839–42. They rediscovered the cities of Copan (now in Honduras), Quirigua and Palenque (now in Guatemala), and Uxmal, Chichen and Itza (now in Mexico), then unknown except to the local people. Their work founded the field of Maya archaeology, helping establish American archaeology as a discipline in its own right.

Strabo, c.60 BC–c.21 AD

Greek geographer, born in Pontus. He was at Corinth in 29 BC, he explored the Nile in 24 BC and seems to have settled at Rome after AD 14. Of his great historical work, *Historical Studies* (47 vols), only a few fragments survive, but his *Geographica* (17 vols) has survived almost complete, and is of great value for his extensive observations and copious references to his predecessors Eratosthenes, Polybius, Aristotle and Thucydides.

> ### Squint-Eyed
> The name 'Strabo' means 'squint-eyed'.

John McDouall Stuart, 1815–66

Australian explorer, born in Dysart, Fife. As a draughtsman, he accompanied Captain Charles Sturt (1795–1869) on an expedition to central Australia (1844–5). Between 1855 and 1862 he made six expeditions to the interior and reached Lake Eyre. He made three attempts to cross Australia from south to north, and on the first discovered the Finke River and the MacDonnell Ranges. On his third attempt he left Adelaide in October 1861 and reached the northern coast in July 1862.

Abel Janszoon Tasman, 1603–c.1659

Dutch navigator, born near Groningen. In 1642 he discovered Tasmania (named Van Diemen's Land until 1855) and New Zealand, and in 1643 Tonga and Fiji, having been dispatched in quest of the 'Great South Land' by Antony Van Diemen (1593–1645), Governor-General of Batavia. Tasman made a second voyage (1644) to the Gulf of Carpentaria and the north-west coast of Australia.

Haroun Tazieff, 1914–98

French vulcanologist and mountaineer, born in Warsaw, Poland. In 1967 he was made head of research at the National Centre for Scientific Research (CNRS), Paris, and was subsequently made director (1971–81). He became the first French Secretary of State for the Prevention of Natural and Technological Disasters (1984–6). He investigated many of the world's volcanoes and his books include *Forecasting Volcanic Events* (1983).

Tenzing Norgay (known as Sherpa Tenzing), 1914–86

Nepalese mountaineer, born near Makalu. He climbed many of the Himalayan peaks, and on two attempts on Everest he reached 7,010 m (23,000 ft) in 1938 and 8,600 m (28,215 ft) in 1952. In 1953 he succeeded in reaching the summit of Everest with **Edmund Hillary**. He later became president of the Sherpa Association.

Sir Wilfred Thesiger, 1910–2003

English explorer, born in Addis Ababa, Ethiopia. In 1935 he travelled by camel across the Sahara to the Tibesti Mountains (Chad). From 1945 to 1950 he explored the Empty Quarter of southern Arabia, one of the world's largest sand deserts, and the borderlands of Oman. He described these explorations in his *Arabian Sands* (1959). From 1951 to 1958 he lived with the Marsh Arabs of Iraq and published *The Marsh Arabs* in 1964. He lived with tribal peoples in East Africa from 1968 until the 1990s when he returned to England.

David Thompson, 1770–1857

Canadian explorer, born in England. He spent 13 years working as a fur-trader before becoming a surveyor and mapping the Saskatchewan, Hayes, Nelson and Churchill rivers and a route to Lake Athabasca. In 1797 he set out from Lake Superior, travelling to Lake Winnipeg and across the Rockies to settle on the Columbia River (1807). He subsequently surveyed the river's entire course. He settled in Montreal in 1812 and drew an impressive map of western Canada. He took part in the US–Canada Boundary Commission of 1816.

Joseph Thomson, 1858–95

Scottish explorer, born in Dumfriesshire. He joined the Royal Geographical Society East-Central African expedition (1878–9), taking charge on the death of the leader. He was the first European to reach Lake Nyasa (Malawi) from the north and went on to Lake Tanganyika. In 1882 he set out to find a route through the Masai country from the coast via Mount Kilimanjaro to Lake Victoria. This took him across the Nijiri Desert through the Great Rift Valley. He later explored north-west Nigeria (1885) and the Upper Congo (1890).

Sir Wyville Thomson, 1830–82

Scottish oceanographer, born in Linlithgow. His book *Depths of the Sea* (1877) was the first general textbook on oceanography, and he also investigated the mechanisms of evolution, deep-sea temperatures and the Gulf Stream. He was director of the civilian staff aboard the HMS *Challenger* expedition (1872–6), and was appointed director of the Challenger Expedition Commission. The Wyville Thomson Ridge in the North Atlantic ocean floor was named after him, since he had predicted its existence from water temperature measurements.

Thorfinn (properly Thorfinnur Karesefni), fl.1000

Icelandic explorer. Around 1000 he led an expedition of colonists from Greenland. They sailed along the north-east coasts of North America, which had previously been discovered and explored by **Leif the Lucky**. Thorfinn attempted to found a Norse colony in an area called 'Vínland' (Wineland), somewhere south of Newfoundland but the venture was abandoned after three years because of hostility from the native inhabitants. The story is told in two Icelandic sagas, *Eiriks saga rauða* ('Saga of Erik') and *Grœnlendinga saga* ('Tale of the Greenlanders').

Carl Peter Thunberg, 1743–1828

Swedish botanical explorer, born in Jönköping. He was taught by **Carolus Linnaeus** and collected plants for him. After 1770 he travelled as a ship's surgeon to South Africa, Java and Japan, collecting and describing many plants new to science. His Japanese discoveries were published as *Flora Japonica* (1784), and those from South Africa as *Prodromus Plantarum Capensium* (1794–1800) and *Flora Capensis* (1807–23, with Joseph August Schultes).

John Tradescant, the Elder, 1570–c.1638

English naturalist, gardener and traveller, born probably in Suffolk. He became head gardener to King Charles I. He travelled to Arctic Russia in 1618 and to Algeria in 1620. He later established a physic garden and the first museum open to the public, the Musaeum Tradescantianum, in London. He and his son, John Tradescant, the

Younger, introduced many plants into English gardens. These include the genus *Tradescantia*, which was named after him.

Henry Tristram, 1822–1906

English clergyman, naturalist and traveller, born in Northumberland. Tuberculosis forced him to go abroad, to Algeria. His main interest was in the flora and fauna of Palestine, where he made several long journeys, and he was the author of the first ornithological surveys of the region, including *The Land of Israel* (1865) and *The Flora and Fauna of Palestine* (1884).

Tribute to Tristram

The Middle Eastern birds Tristram's Warbler, Tristram's Serin and Tristram's Grackle are all named after Henry Tristram, as is the Far Eastern bird Tristram's Woodpecker.

Naomi Uemura, 1942–84

Japanese explorer and mountaineer, born in Tajima region. He reached the summit of Everest in 1970, becoming the first to reach the highest peak on five continents. He made a solo dog-sled journey from Ellesmere Island in the Arctic to the North Pole in 1978. In February 1984 he completed the first winter ascent of the West Buttress Route of Mt McKinley and is presumed to have died during the descent, though his body has not been found.

George Vancouver, 1757–98

English navigator and explorer, born in King's Lynn, Norfolk. He sailed with Captain **James Cook** (1772–5 and 1776–9). Promoted to captain (1794), he did survey work in Australia and New Zealand. He also carried out detailed charting along the west coast of North America, sailing round Vancouver Island in 1795.

Pierre, Sieur de la Verendrye, 1685–1749

French explorer, born in Quebec. After serving with the French army he returned to Canada to become a trader, making his base at Nipigon on Lake Superior. He and his sons travelled over much of unexplored Canada, discovering the Lake of the Woods and Lake Winnipeg. He also reached the Mandan country south of the Assiniboine River, upper Missouri, Manitoba and Dakota.

Giovanni da Verrazano, c.1480–1527

Italian navigator and explorer, born in Greve, Italy. In the service of Francis I of France, he led an expedition to North America in 1524, exploring the coast from Cape Fear northward probably as far as Cape Breton and becoming the first European to enter New York Bay. He later voyaged to Brazil and the West Indies, and is thought to have been eaten by cannibals in the Lesser Antilles.

Amerigo Vespucci, 1451–1512

Spanish explorer, born in Florence, Italy. In 1499 he promoted an expedition to the New World and sailed there in his own ship, in which he explored the coast of Venezuela. In 1505 he was naturalized in Spain. His name (Latinized as 'Americus') was somewhat fortuitously given to the American continents by a German cartographer after the publication of a distorted account of Vespucci's travels, *Quattuor Americi navigationes* ('Four Voyages', 1507).

Willem de Vlamingh, fl.1690s

Dutch navigator, born probably in north-east Holland. He was master of a Dutch East India Company vessel that left Holland in 1696 to search for a Dutch ship missing off western Australia. He retrieved a pewter plate, known as the Dirck Hartog Plate, inscribed by that mariner in 1616 and recording probably the earliest European contact with the Australian continent. Vlamingh left another plate, describing his visit, and also discovered and named the Swan River.

Kiyoo Wadati, 1902–95

Japanese seismologist. His most important contributions were to advances in the detection of deep earthquakes. He located deep, sloping seismic zones similar to those being located by **Victor Benioff**, and later it was proved that these Wadati–Benioff zones show the motion of downgoing oceanic crust. Wadati also carried out fieldwork at the Showa Antarctic base (1973–4).

Alfred Wallace, 1823–1913

English zoogeographer, born in Usk, Monmouthshire. He travelled in the Amazon basin (1848–52) with **Henry Bates**. He explored the Malay Archipelago (1854–62) and observed the demarcation, now known as Wallace's Line, between the areas supporting Asian and Australasian faunas. A pioneer of the theory of natural selection, in 1855 he published a paper on new species, and his writings hastened the publication of **Charles Darwin**'s *The Origin of Species*. In his great *Geographical Distribution of Animals* (1879) and other works, Wallace contributed much to the scientific foundations of zoogeography.

Alfred Wegener, 1880–1930

German meteorologist and geophysicist, born in Berlin. *Die Entstehung der Kontinente und Ozeane* ('The Origin of Continents and Oceans') was first published in 1915, based on his observations that the continents may once have been joined into one supercontinent (Pangaea), which later broke up, the fragments drifting apart to form the continents as they are today. Wegener provided historical, geological, geomorphological, climatic and palaeontological evidence, but at that time no logical mechanism was known by which continents could drift. The hypothesis remained controversial until the 1960s, when plate tectonics provided a plausible mechanism.

> ### A Fitting Farewell
> After Sir George Wilkins's death, his ashes were scattered over the North Pole.

Sir George Wilkins, 1888–1958

Australian explorer, born in Mt Bryan East. He first travelled to the Arctic in 1913. In 1919 he flew from England to Australia, then spent from 1921 to 1922 in the Antarctic. In 1926 he returned to the Arctic, and in 1928 made a pioneer flight from Alaska to Spitsbergen, over polar ice. In 1931 an attempt to reach the North Pole under the ice with the submarine *Nautilus* was unsuccessful. He wrote *Flying the Arctic* (1928) and *Under the North Pole* (1931).

William Wills, 1834–61

Australian surveyor and explorer, born in Devon, England. In 1860 he became second-in-command of Robert O'Hara Burke's expedition to cross Australia from south to north. They set off from Melbourne and reached the Flinders River at the Gulf of Carpentaria, but ran out of food, ate their camels, and continued on foot. Wills and Burke reached their supply depot at Cooper's Creek seven hours after the support party had left, and died of starvation.

Edward Wilson, 1872–1912

English physician, naturalist and explorer, born in Cheltenham. He first went to the Antarctic with **Robert Scott** in the *Discovery* (1900–4). In 1910 he returned to the Antarctic on the *Terra Nova* as chief of the expedition's scientific staff. One of the party that reached the South Pole, he died with the others on the return journey.

(John) Tuzo Wilson, 1908–93

Canadian geophysicist, born in Ottawa. He was a promoter of Harry Hess's 1960 theory of sea-floor spreading, and his ideas about permanent hot spots in the Earth's mantle (1963), oceanic transform faults (1965) and mountain building (1966) were major steps towards plate tectonics theory. He co-authored *Physics and Geology* (1959), one of the first geophysical textbooks. The Wilson Range in Antarctica and the Wilson ocean cycle, describing the periodic opening and closing of ocean basins, are named after him.

Zheng He (Cheng Ho), 1371–1433

Chinese admiral. He led a series of maritime expeditions to South-East Asia, India, and the east coast of Africa between 1405 and 1433. He came from a Muslim family and became a close aide of Emperor Ming Yongle (1402–24), who promoted the expeditions as a means to assert the universality of the Chinese empire and expand trade. The expeditions were considered extravagant by critics at court and were ended in the 1430s. Zheng He is credited as first to establish a direct sea route between the Pacific and Indian Oceans.

NATIONS OF THE WORLD

Information in this section was correct at the time of publication but is likely to change frequently. Some notes concerning the data are given below.

Names of countries and cities

The official name of the country is given in English. Where appropriate the short form of the local name is given first, followed by the long form. English names of capital cities are given first, followed by the local name(s). Any notable names by which a country has been previously known in the 20th century are listed with relevant dates.

Area

Area figures are for land mass only and do not include territorial waters; eg Kiribati covers c.3 million sq km (1.2 million sq mi) but actual land area is only 717 sq km (277 sq mi).

Chief towns

If no chief towns are given the country is too small or sparsely populated to have major settlements.

Population

Population estimates are taken from the *CIA World Factbook* unless otherwise stated. Estimated figures are marked e.

Nationality

Nationality gives the usual adjective form; exceptions are clearly marked.

Ethnic groups and religions

Percentage distributions may not add up to precisely 100% owing to rounding of the numbers.

Time zone

No allowance is made for Daylight Saving Time.

Currency

The three-letter ISO currency code is given alongside any commonly used abbreviations.

Country codes

Country codes are from the official ISO list.

Climate

Temperature figures are given in degrees Celsius. To convert to Fahrenheit multiply by 9, divide by 5 and add 32.

Dependencies

Dependencies and other territories are listed by type, then alphabetically.

AFGHANISTAN

Official name	Islamic Republic of Afghanistan
Local name	Afqânestân (Dari), Afğânistân (Pashto)
Former name	Afghan Empire (1881–1973), Republic of Afghanistan (1973–8), Democratic Republic of Afghanistan (1978–88), Republic of Afghanistan (1988–96)
Area	647 497 sq km (249 934 sq mi)
Capital	Kabul; Kābul, Kābol
Chief towns	Herat, Jalalabad, Kandahar and Mazar-e Sharif
Population	31 057 000 (2006e)
Nationality	Afghan
Languages	Dari, Pashto
Ethnic groups	Pashtun 42%, Tajik 27%, Hazara 9%, Uzbek 9%, others 13%
Religions	Islam 99% (Sunni 84%, Shia 15%), others 1%
Time zone	GMT +4.5
Currency	1 Afghani (Af) = 100 puls
Telephone	+93
Internet	.af
Country code	AFG

Location

A landlocked, mountainous republic in south-central Asia, bounded to the north by Turkmenistan, Uzbekistan and Tajikistan; to the east and south by Pakistan; to the west by Iran; and in the extreme north-east by China and India.

Physical description

Landlocked and mountainous, centred on the Hindu Kush system which reaches over 7000 m (23 000 ft) in the centre and north-east; highest point is Nowshak (7485 m/24 557 ft); many secondary ranges; north-west of the Hindu Kush, heights decrease towards the Turkmenistan border; north-west is the fertile valley of Herat; arid uplands lie to the south of the Hindu Kush, descending into desert in the south-west.

Climate

Continental climate with winter severity increased by altitude; summers are warm everywhere except on the highest peaks; protected from summer monsoons by the southern mountains; rain mostly occurs during spring and autumn; annual rainfall averages 338 mm; lower levels have a desert or semi-arid climate.

Economy

Economy devastated by decades of civil war; based on agriculture, especially grain, rice, fruit, nuts, vegetables and livestock; small-scale industries, including textiles, carpets, handicrafts and food processing; natural gas production in the north largely for export; major source of illegally produced opium.

Government

Since 2004, governed by an executive President, a Council of Ministers, and a bicameral legislature (*Jirga*), comprising the House of the People and the House of Elders. There are no formal political parties.

History

The nation first formed in 1747 under Ahmad Shah Durrani. In the 19th and early 20th centuries Britain saw Afghanistan as a bridge between India and the Middle East, but failed to gain control during the Afghan Wars. The feudal monarchy survived until after World War II, when the constitution became more liberal under several Soviet-influenced five-year economic plans. In 1973 the king was deposed and a republic was formed. A new constitution was adopted in 1977, but a coup in 1978 installed a new government under the communist leader, Nur Muhammad Taraki; a further coup in 1979 led to invasion by Soviet forces, which was fiercely resisted by the Mujahedin. In 1989 the Soviet troops finally withdrew, and in 1992 Mujahedin groups forced the resignation of the communist government of Muhammad Najibullah and proclaimed the Islamic State of Afghanistan. Fighting between factions continued until the rise in 1994 of the Taliban, who sought to replace the factionalism with Islamic law; this included repression of women, public floggings and executions. Within two years the Taliban had taken Kabul, executed Najibullah, and the civil war had resulted in up to 45000 Afghan deaths. By 1998 the country was mainly under Taliban control, but fierce resistance from the opposition Northern Alliance meant the civil war continued. In 2001 a US-led coalition began military action against the Taliban, believing them to harbour senior members of Al Qaeda responsible for terrorist attacks on the USA. The Taliban regime was overthrown and a UN-brokered deal saw a power-sharing administration installed, led by Hamid Karzai. Presidential elections were held in 2004, and parliamentary elections in 2005. The government's control of the country is tenuous outside Kabul and dependent on the presence of international forces. In the southern provinces in particular, Taliban-inspired violence since 2001, and especially since 2005, has hindered reconstruction.

The Buddhas of Bamiyan

Until 2001, the Bamiyan valley in central Afghanistan was the site of two vast carvings of Buddha. These were probably made in around 400 AD, during the time of the Silk Road trade route that ran through the area. The carvings, which were 53 and 38 metres tall respectively, were destroyed by the Taliban; however, it is possible that they could be rebuilt in the future.

ALBANIA

Official name	Republic of Albania
Local name	Shqipëria; Republika e Shqipërisë
Former name	Kingdom of Albania (1928–39), People's Republic of Albania (1946–76), People's Socialist Republic of Albania (1976–91)
Area	28 748 sq km (11 097 sq mi)
Capital	Tirana
Chief towns	Shkodër, Durrës, Vlorë, Korçë, Elbasan
Population	3 582 000 (2006e)
Nationality	Albanian
Language	Albanian
Ethnic groups	Albanian 95%, Greek 3%, others 2%
Religions	Islam 70% (Sunni), Christianity 30% (Orthodox 20%, RC 10%)
Time zone	GMT +1
Currency	1 Lek (Lk) = 100 qindarka
Telephone	+355
Internet	.al
Country code	ALB

Location

A mountainous republic in the western part of the Balkan peninsula, bounded to the west by the Adriatic Sea; to the north-west by Montenegro; to the north-east by Serbia; to the east by Macedonia; and to the south-east by Greece.

Physical description

Mountainous and relatively inaccessible; the northern Albanian Alps rise to 2692 m (8832 ft); highest point is Maja e Korabit (Golem Korab; 2753 m/9032 ft); rivers include the Drin, Shkumbin, Seman, Vijosë; half the population is concentrated in the western low-lying area, which occupies only one quarter of the country.

Climate

Mediterranean-type climate: hot and dry on the plains in summer (average July temperature 24–5°C), with frequent thunderstorms; winters are mild, damp and cyclonic (average January temperature 8–9°C); winters in the mountains are often severe, with snow cover lasting for several months; annual mountain precipitation exceeds 1000 mm.

Economy

Completing transition from planned to market economy; dependent on remittances from expatriate workers and foreign aid; agriculture still the main employer, producing wheat, maize, sugar beet, potatoes and fruit; main industries are agricultural product processing, textiles, oil products, cement, production of crude oil, minerals and natural gas; hydroelectric power plants on several rivers.

Government

Governed by a President, a Prime Minister and Council of Ministers, with a unicameral People's Assembly.

History

The history of the Albanians dates back to the 2nd century ad, when Ptolemy referred to a tribe, the Albanoi, in the region of modern Albania. The Albanian Ghegs and Tosks speak two forms of an Indo-European language now considered a dialect of Illyrian, the Albanians being recognized as descendants of the ancient Illyrians but with Slav, Greek, Vlach and Turkish blood. In the Middle Ages they were included within the empires of Byzantium, Samuel (of Macedonia) and Stephen I Nemanja of Serbia, but from the 12th century an independent Albanian enclave developed around Krujë. Their decentralized tribal way of life was little changed under Ottoman rule (1503–1913) and was only destroyed with the establishment of the communist regime (1945). After local uprisings, the Albanian national movement formally began with the League of Prizren (1878–81). The first general uprising resulted in independence in 1912, and in 1913 the first independent Albanian state was established. Its boundaries excluded many Albanians, many of whom still live in the Serbian province of Kosovo. Albania's independence was short-lived at first, as Italian forces occupied the country from 1914 until 1920; however, it became a republic in 1925, and a monarchy, under King Zog I, in 1928. During World War II Albania was occupied by Germany and Italy and it became a new republic in 1946. After being involved in a dispute with the Union of Soviet Socialist Republics (USSR) in 1961, it withdrew from the Warsaw Pact in 1968 but maintained close links with communist China until 1978. The Socialist People's Republic was instituted in 1976. The country gradually began to move towards democratic reform and westernization, and the first free elections were held in 1991, the communists losing power in the 1992 election. In the early 1990s the economy declined and severe food shortages led to violent rioting. Further rioting broke out in early 1997 after many Albanians lost money in the collapse of investment schemes. An influx of refugees from Kosovo in 1999 was an additional economic burden. In 2003 Albania began talks with the European Union about membership.

Nearly a King

The achievements of the Englishman C B Fry (1872–1956) were so impressive that he was offered the throne of Albania. Fry excelled in various sports: he represented England in a football match, set a long jump world record and played cricket for England 26 times. He was also a journalist and writer. After World War I he acted as a delegate for the League of Nations (the forerunner of the United Nations) and was spotted as a talented but suitably neutral candidate for the throne of the newly independent Albania. However, Fry declined the offer.

ALGERIA

Official name	People's Democratic Republic of Algeria
Local name	Al-Jazā'ir; Al-Jumhūriyya al-Jazā'iriyya ad-Dimuqratiyya ash-Sha'biyya (Arabic), Algérie; République Algérienne Démocratique et Populaire (French)
Area	2460500 sq km (949753 sq mi)
Capital	Algiers
Chief towns	Constantine, Oran, Skikda, Annaba, Mostaganem, Blida, Tlemcen
Population	32930000 (2006e)
Nationality	Algerian
Languages	Arabic, Tamazight; French is also spoken
Ethnic groups	Arab-Berber 99%, European 1%
Religions	Islam 99% (Sunni), others 1%
Time zone	GMT +1
Currency	1 Algerian Dinar (AD, DA) = 100 centimes
Telephone	+213
Internet	.dz
Country code	DZA

Location

A north African republic, bounded to the west by Morocco; to the south-west by Western Sahara, Mauritania and Mali; to the south-east by Niger; to the east by Libya; to the north-east by Tunisia; and to the north by the Mediterranean Sea.

Physical description

From the Mediterranean coast, the mountains rise in a series of ridges and plateaux to the Atlas Saharien; 91% of the population is located on the narrow coastal plain; part of the Sahara Desert lies to the south of the Atlas Saharien; in the north-east of this region is a major depression, the Chott Melrhir, which extends east into Tunisia; the Hoggar Mountains in the far south rise to 2918m (9573ft) at Mount Tahat.

Climate

Typical Mediterranean climate on the north coast; average annual rainfall of 400–800mm (mostly November–March); snow on the higher ground; Algiers, representative of the coastal region, has an annual rainfall of 760mm with average maximum daily temperatures of 15–29°C; the rest of the country has an essentially rainless Saharan climate.

Economy

Large-scale 1960s nationalization reversed in 1990s, promoting economic growth; oil and natural gas production and products account for c.60% of GDP; other industries are mining, electrical goods, light industries and food processing; agriculture is mainly on the north coast (wheat, barley, oats, grapes, citrus fruits, vegetables).

Government

Governed by a President, a Prime Minister and Council of Ministers, and a bicameral Parliament, comprising a National People's Assembly and a National Council.

History

The indigenous peoples of Algeria (Berbers) have been driven back from the coast by many invaders, including the Phoenicians, Romans (Algeria became a province of the Roman Empire), Vandals, Arabs, Turks and French. Islam and Arabic were introduced by the Arabs betwen the 8th and 11th centuries, and Islam (Sunni Muslim) is now the chief religion. The Turkish invasion took place in the 16th century, and the French colonial campaign in the 19th century resulted in control by 1902. During the 20th century the National Liberation Front (FLN) engaged in guerrilla war with French forces in 1954–62, and Algeria gained independence in 1962. The first president of the republic, Ahmed Ben Bella, was replaced after a coup led by Houari Boumédienne in 1965, who governed by decree until 1976, when elections were held and a new constitution declared him president. He was succeeded in 1979 by Chadli Benjedid. In 1992 a state of emergency was declared as a result of clashes between government forces and the Islamic Salvation Front, and for the rest of the 1990s Algeria was wracked by a bloody civil war between its secular government and Islamic fundamentalist insurgents in which an estimated 100 000 people died. The level of violence fell after 1999, when the newly elected President Bouteflika instituted a policy of reconciliation with the Islamists. Recent years have also seen increased agitation for recognition of the Berber community and the Berber language Tamazight, both of which have been granted by the government.

ANDORRA

Official name	Principality of Andorra; also sometimes known as The Valleys of Andorra
Local name	Andorra; Principat d'Andorra
Area	468 sq km (81 sq mi)
Capital	Andorra la Vella; Andorra la Vieja (Spanish), Andorre la Vielle (French), Andorra la Vella (Catalan)
Population	71 200 (2006e)
Nationality	Andorran
Languages	Catalan; French and Spanish are also spoken
Ethnic groups	Spanish 43%, Andorran 33%, Portuguese 11%, French 7%, others 6%
Religions	Christianity 95% (RC 94%, Prot 1%), none/unaffiliated 5%
Time zone	GMT +1
Currency	1 Euro (€) = 100 cents
Telephone	+376
Internet	.ad
Country code	AND

Location

A small, mountainous, semi-independent, neutral state on the southern slopes of the central Pyrenees between France and Spain.

Physical description

A mountainous country, reaching 2947 m (9669 ft) at Coma Pedrosa; occupies two valleys (del Norte and del Orient) of the River Valira.

Climate

Winters are cold but dry and sunny; the lowest average monthly rainfall is 34 mm in January; the midsummer months are slightly drier than spring and autumn.

Economy

Based on banking and financial services (no direct or value-added taxes; no currency exchange restrictions) and tourism (especially skiing), which account for more than 75% of economic activity; other main industries are construction, forestry and agriculture (tobacco and livestock breeding); hydroelectric power produced on the river.

Government

The Co-Princes (titular heads of state) are the President of France and the Spanish Bishop of Urgel, represented by permanent delegates in the principality; Andorra is governed by an Executive Council and the unicameral General Council of the Valleys.

History

One of the oldest states in Europe, Andorra has been under the joint protection of France and Spain since 1278, and became an independent parliamentary democracy in 1993.

ANGOLA

Official name	Republic of Angola
Local name	Angola; República de Angola
Former name	People's Republic of Angola (until 1992)
Area	1 245 790 sq km (480 875 sq mi)
Capital	Luanda
Chief towns	Huambo, Benguela, Lobito, Namibe (Moçâmedes), Cabinda, Malanje, Lubango
Population	12 127 000 (2006e)
Nationality	Angolan
Languages	Portuguese; Bantu and other African languages are also spoken
Ethnic groups	Ovimbundu 37%, Kimbundu 25%, Bakongo 13%, others 25%
Religions	Christianity 53% (RC 38%, Prot 15%), traditional beliefs 47%
Time zone	GMT +1
Currency	1 Kwanza (Kzrl) = 100 lwei
Telephone	+244
Internet	.ao
Country code	AGO

Location

A republic in south-west Africa, bounded to the south by Namibia; to the east by Zambia; and to the north by the Democratic Republic of the Congo; the separate province of Cabinda is enclosed by Congo and the Democratic Republic of the Congo.

Physical description

A narrow coastal plain, widening in the north towards the Congo Delta; high plateau inland with an average elevation of 1200 m (3937 ft); the highest point is Serro Môco (2619 m/8592 ft); numerous rivers rise in the plateau but few are navigable for any length. The south is desert and semi-desert.

Climate

Mostly a tropical plateau climate; a single wet season in October–March and a long dry season; more temperate above 1500 m; Huambo is representative of the upland region with an average annual rainfall of 1450 mm and average daily temperatures of 24–9°C; temperatures and rainfall are much lower on the coast, which is semi-desert as far north as Luanda (eg Namibe in the south has an average annual rainfall of 55 mm; in the far north it is 600 mm).

Economy

More stable and growing economy since the end of the civil war; rich in natural resources (oil, diamonds, gold, uranium, other minerals); oil extraction and refining provides 90% of export earnings, 75% of government revenue and over 50% of GDP; other industries are mining, forestry, fishing, cement, tobacco products and ship repair; agriculture mostly at subsistence level; export crops are coffee, sisal and cotton.

Government

Governed by an executive President, a Prime Minister and Council of Ministers and a unicameral National Assembly; owing to conflict, no elections have taken place since 1992.

History

The area became a Portuguese colony after exploration in 1483; an estimated 3 million slaves were sent to Brazil during the next 300 years. Boundaries were formally defined during the Congress of Berlin in 1884–5. Angola became an Overseas Province of Portugal in 1951 and gained independence in 1975. Shortly afterwards, civil war broke out between three internal factions: the Marxist MPLA (Popular Movement for the Liberation of Angola) government, UNITA (National Union for the Total Independence of Angola) and the FNLA (National Front for the Liberation of Angola). The FNLA and UNITA received arms from the USA in 1975–6, and in 1976 Cuban combat troops arrived to back up the MPLA. South African forces occupied an area along the Angola–Namibia frontier in 1975–6, and were active again in support of UNITA in 1981–4. Meanwhile, Angola backed the Namibian independence movement SWAPO (South west Africa People's Organization), who launched attacks on Namibia from Angolan territory in the 1970s. Eventually an international agreement signed in 1988 linked arrangements for the independence of Namibia with the withdrawal of Cuban troops and the cessation of South African support for UNITA. In 1991 a peace agreement between UNITA and the government was followed by multiparty elections, but UNITA did not accept the results and fighting resumed. The conflict continued, despite another peace agreement (1994), the deployment of UN peace-keeping forces (1995–8), and UNITA's proposed inclusion in a government of national unity (1997), until 2002, when a ceasefire was agreed after the death of UNITA leader Jonas Savimbi. UNITA gradually demobilized its forces and transformed itself into a political party. Repatriation of refugees began in 2003, and in 2004 preparations began for elections in 2006, but these were delayed until 2007 as damaged infrastructure and landmines have left parts of the country inaccessible.

ANTIGUA AND BARBUDA

Official name	State of Antigua and Barbuda
Local name	Antigua and Barbuda
Former name	formerly part of the Leeward Islands Federation (until 1956)
Area	442 sq km (171 sq mi)
Capital	St John's
Chief town	Codrington (on Barbuda)
Population	69 100 (2006e)
Nationality	Antiguan, Barbudan
Language	English
Ethnic groups	African descent 92%, British 4%, others 4%
Religions	Christianity 96% (Prot 87%, RC 9%), Rastafarianism 1%, others 2%, none/unaffiliated 1%
Time zone	GMT −4
Currency	1 East Caribbean Dollar (EC$) = 100 cents
Telephone	+1 268
Internet	.ag
Country code	ATG

Location
An independent group of three tropical islands in the Leeward Islands group of the Lesser Antilles in the eastern Caribbean Sea: Antigua, Barbuda and the uninhabited Redonda.

Physical description
Antigua is flatter than the other Leeward Islands, rising to 402 m (1319 ft) at Boggy Peak; Barbuda is a flat, coral island reaching only 44 m (144 ft) at its highest point, with a large lagoon on its western side.

Climate
Tropical, with temperatures ranging from 24°C in January to 27°C in August–September, and an average annual rainfall of 1000 mm; subject to tropical storms and hurricanes between August and October.

Economy

Tourism employs 75% of workforce; offshore financial services, construction and light manufacturing are also important; agricultural production is mostly for local consumption.

Government

Governed by a Governor-General (representing the British monarch, who is head of state), a Prime Minister and Cabinet, and a bicameral Parliament, consisting of a Senate and a House of Representatives.

History

Christopher Columbus visited Antigua in 1493. It was colonized by the English in 1632 and ceded to England in 1667. Barbuda was colonized from Antigua in 1661. Administered as part of the Leeward Islands Federation from 1871 until 1956, it became an associated state of the UK in 1967. Full independence of Antigua and Barbuda was achieved in 1981. The prime minister on independence was Vere Cornwall Bird of the Antigua Labour Party, whose family continued to dominate the country's politics until 2004.

ARGENTINA

Official name	Argentine Republic
Local name	Argentina; República Argentina
Area	2 766 890 sq km (1 068 296 sq mi)
Capital	Buenos Aires
Chief towns	Córdoba, Rosario, Mendoza, La Plata, San Miguel de Tucumán
Population	39 922 000 (2006e)
Nationality	Argentine, Argentinian
Language	Spanish
Ethnic groups	European (mostly Spanish and Italian) 97%, Mestizo, Amerindian and others 3%
Religions	Christianity 94% (RC 92% (less than 20% practising), Prot 2%), others 4%, Judaism 2%
Time zone	GMT −3
Currency	1 Peso ($) = 100 centavos
Telephone	+54
Internet	.ar
Country code	ARG

Location

A republic in south-eastern South America; bounded to the east by the southern Atlantic Ocean; to the west by Chile; to the north by Bolivia and Paraguay; and to the north-east by Brazil and Uruguay.

Physical description

The Andes stretch the entire length of Argentina (north to south), forming the boundary with Chile; the mountains extend far to the east in northern Argentina, but their width decreases towards the south; high ranges, plateaux and rocky spurs are found in the north-west; the highest peak is Aconcagua (6960 m/22 835 ft); a grassy, treeless plain (the *pampa*) is to the east; uneven, arid steppes lie to the south; the island of Tierra del Fuego is situated off the southern tip; northern Argentina is drained by the Paraguay, Paraná and Uruguay rivers, which join in the River Plate estuary; several rivers flow to the Atlantic Ocean in the south; there are many lakes in the *pampa* and Patagonia regions, the largest being Lago Argentino (1415 sq km/546 sq mi).

Climate

Most of Argentina lies in the rain shadow of the Andes; dry steppe or elevated desert in the north-west corner; moderately humid subtropical climate in the north-east; the central *pampa* region and a strip along the foot of the mountains are semi-arid with temperatures ranging from tropical to moderately cool, with average annual temperature 16°C and rainfall 500–1000 mm at Buenos Aires; between these two semi-arid areas lies the rain shadow; a desert plateau extends to the coast; some rainfall prevents absolute barrenness; the southern part is directly influenced by strong prevailing westerlies.

Economy

Strong economic growth since economic collapse of 2001–2; rich in natural resources; oil and gas are extracted, chiefly off the coast of Patagonia; fertile *pampa* supports export-orientated agriculture (grain, oil-bearing seeds, fruit, tea, tobacco, livestock), wine production and meat, flour- and sugar- processing industries; other industries include vehicles, consumer goods, textiles, chemicals, petrochemicals, printing, metallurgy and steel.

Government

Governed by an executive President, a Cabinet and a bicameral National Congress, comprising a Chamber of Deputies and a Senate.

History

The majority of the population is of European origin and the remainder is of mestizo or South American Indian origin. Argentina was settled in the 16th century by the Spanish. It declared its independence in 1816, and the United Provinces of the Río de la Plata were established. Following a war with Paraguay in 1865–70, Argentina acquired the Gran Chaco plain. In the 19th and 20th centuries, power swung between powerful political factions and between civilian and military regimes. An attempt to gain control of the Falkland Islands in 1982 resulted in defeat in the Falklands War with the UK, and precipitated the downfall of the military junta in power since 1976. Civilian rule was re-established in 1983 and has endured, despite political instability in the early 21st century following an economic collapse in 2001–2. Economic recovery began in 2003, although many Argentines remain in poverty.

ARGENTINE TANGO

The form of music and dance known as the tango has spread throughout the world and many different variants have developed. However, its roots can be traced back to the slums of the Argentine capital Buenos Aires at the close of the 19th century.

The early days of the dance

The forerunner of the tango was an African song-and-dance form called the *milonga*, which was popular in rural areas of Argentina and Uruguay in the mid-to-late 19th century. Many gauchos (South American cowboys) were displaced as railways opened up the country and the land was fenced off for agriculture, and they brought their characteristic dance to the cities. The *habanera*, a slow Cuban dance, was also a notable influence.

Tango was initially widely criticized for its seedy and debauched nature. It was frequently associated with the underclass taverns and brothels of the city; early forms probably represented the interaction between prostitute and pimp. It gradually became accepted among the 'decent' working classes of the city. This was a time when men greatly outnumbered women, owing to an influx of migrant agricultural workers. They would learn at men-only gatherings, first learning the woman's part and then the man's, before finally having the chance to dance with (and court) women.

The spread to Europe and North America

South American sailors, migrants and travellers introduced the tango to Europe and North America in around 1912. Such was its overtly sexual nature, with moves such as the *boleo* (whip-like flicks of the free leg) and *gancho* (the hooking of a leg around the partner's leg or body), that the socialite Comtesse Mélanie de Pourtalès (1839–1913) famously asked 'Is one supposed to dance it standing up?'. It was quickly 'cleaned up', however, and hundreds of tango schools were established in London and New York. The dance was further popularized when Rudolph Valentino memorably danced a tango with his partner in the film *Four Horsemen of the Apocalypse* (1921).

Thus, two very different forms of tango developed: the sanitized ballroom tango and the Argentine tango that retained its earthy origins. The 'embrace', movements and music differ substantially between these forms.

Tango music

The lute, violin, harp and guitar were the first accompaniments of the tango, which initially tended to include bawdy lyrics. These instruments were followed by the *bandoneon*, a German concertina that gave the music its distinctive sorrowful sound – recalling the poverty and prostitution of the slums. The words also evolved to embrace themes of longing and loss. The songwriter Enrique Santos Discepolo (1901–51) described it thus: 'The tango is a sorrowful thought that can be danced.'

The famous baritone Carlos Gardel (c.1890–1935) recorded some 900 tango songs, and popularized the genre by appearing in a number of feature films in the 1930s. More recently, the bandleader and performer Astor Piazzolla (1921–92) began to incorporate elements of jazz and classical music into his works. He founded the Quinteto Nuevo Tango in 1960, at which point the music began to be taken seriously as an art form in its own right.

ARMENIA

Official name	Republic of Armenia
Local name	Hayastan; Hayastany Hanrapetoutyun
Former name	Transcaucasian Soviet Federated Socialist Republic (with Azerbaijan and Georgia, 1922–36), Armenian Soviet Socialist Republic (1920–2, 1936–1990), within the Union of Soviet Socialist Republics (USSR; 1922–91)
Area	29 800 sq km (11 500 sq mi)
Capital	Yerevan
Chief towns	Vanadzor, Gyumri
Population	2 976 000 (2006e)
Nationality	Armenian
Languages	Armenian; Russian is also used
Ethnic groups	Armenian 98%, Azeri 1%, Russian and others 1%
Religions	Christianity 99% (Orthodox 95%, other 4%), others 1%
Time zone	GMT +4
Currency	1 Dram (Drm) = 100 luma
Telephone	+374
Internet	.am
Country code	ARM

Location

A mountainous republic in southern Transcaucasia, bounded to the north by Georgia; to the east and south-west by Azerbaijan; to the south-east by Iran; and to the north-west by Turkey.

Physical description

Mountainous, rising to 4090 m (13 418 ft) at Mount Aragats in the west; the largest lake is the Sevan in the east; the chief river is the Araks; the country is in an earthquake zone.

Climate

Dry and hot in the summer, cold in the winter.

Economy

Emerging market economy, achieving sustained growth but dependent on foreign aid; subject to trade embargos over the conflict with Azerbaijan; main industries are mining (diamonds, other minerals), machinery, textiles, chemicals, vehicles, microelectronics, jewellery, foodstuffs; main cash crops are grain, fruit, vegetables and livestock.

Government

Governed by a President, a Prime Minister and Cabinet, and a unicameral National Assembly.

History

The Armenians are a Christian nation of Indo-European origin, speaking a language of that family with some Caucasian features. Their history goes back to the Roman period and includes years of relative independence; their highly developed ancient culture, particularly in fine art, architecture and sculpture, reached its zenith in the 14th century. Their resentment of foreign domination during the 19th century provoked their Russian and Turkish rulers, and those who were not retained under Turkish control were taken over by the Russians in 1828. During World War I, the Turks deported two-thirds of Armenians (1.75 million) to Syria and Palestine; 600 000 were either killed or died of starvation during the journey; later, many settled in Europe, the USA and the Union of Soviet Socialist Republics (USSR). Galvanized by earlier Turkish massacres and encouraged by Lenin, Armenia declared its independence in 1918; however, it lost it again on Lenin's orders in 1920 for allegedly consorting with Soviet enemies. Armenia was proclaimed a Soviet Socialist Republic in 1920, and became a constituent republic of the USSR in 1936. At this time Soviet Armenia laid claim to Turkish Armenia. In 1988 a severe earthquake harmed the country's economy, and further damage was done from 1991 by the dispute with neighbouring Azerbaijan over Nagorno-Karabakh, a mountainous autonomous region ruled by Azerbaijan since 1923 despite having a mainly Armenian population. With the disintegration of the USSR, Armenia declared its independence in 1991 as the Republic of Armenia and became a member of the Commonwealth of Independent States (CIS). The following year a state of emergency was declared as a result of the worsening economic situation, and the dispute with Azerbaijan over Nagorno-Karabakh escalated into war. A ceasefire agreement was reached in 1994 and talks to find a peaceful resolution continue. In 1999 Armenia's parliament was stormed by gunmen who killed the prime minister, parliamentary speaker and six others.

AUSTRALIA

Official name	Commonwealth of Australia
Local name	Australia
Area	7 682 300 sq km (2 966 136 sq mi)
Capital	Canberra
Chief towns	Melbourne, Brisbane, Perth, Adelaide, Sydney
Population	20 264 000 (2006e)
Nationality	Australian
Languages	English; Aboriginal languages are also spoken
Ethnic groups	European 81%, Chinese 2%, others 17%
Religions	Christianity 66% (RC 26%, Prot 20%, other 20%), none/ unaffiliated 15%, unspecified 13%, others 5%
Time zone	GMT +8/10.5
Currency	1 Australian Dollar ($A) = 100 cents
Telephone	+61
Internet	.au
Country code	AUS

Location

An independent country and the smallest continent in the world, entirely in the southern hemisphere.

Physical description

Almost 40% of its land mass is north of the Tropic of Capricorn; the Australian continent consists largely of plains and plateaux, most of which average 600 m (1968 ft) above sea level; the West Australian Plateau occupies nearly half the whole area; in the centre are the MacDonnell Ranges, in the north-west the Kimberley Plateau, and in the west the Hamersley Ranges; most of the plateau is dry and barren desert, notably the Gibson Desert in the west, the Great Sandy Desert in the north-west, the Great Victoria Desert in the south and the Simpson Desert in the central area; in the south is the Nullarbor Plain; the Eastern Highlands or Great Dividing Range lie parallel to the eastern seaboard, rising to 2228 m (7310 ft) at Mount Kosciusko (Australia's highest point), in the Australian Alps; between the Western Plateau and the Eastern Highlands lies a broad lowland belt extending south into the Murray–Darling plains; off the north-east coast, stretching for over 1900 km (1200 mi), is the Great Barrier Reef; the island of Tasmania, a southern extension of the Eastern Highlands, rises to 1617 m (5305 ft) at Mount Ossa, and is separated from the mainland by the Bass Strait; Australia's longest river is the Murray, its chief tributaries being the Darling, Murrumbidgee and Lachlan. Fertile land with a temperate climate and reliable rainfall is limited to the lowlands and valleys near the coast in the east and south-east, and to a small part of the south-west corner. The population is concentrated in these two regions.

Climate

There are four main climatic zones: a tropical zone in the north and north-east, with rainfall concentrated in the summer months; a warm-temperate zone in the south-east, with rainfall distributed throughout the year; a Mediterranean-type zone in the south and south-west, with moderate amounts of rain which fall mainly in winter; and a continental zone in interior and semi-desert areas, with wide daily variations in temperature and scanty and unreliable rainfall. Warm or hot throughout the year. More than one-third of the country receives under 260 mm average annual rainfall; less than one-third receives more than 500 mm; half the country has a rainfall variability of more than 30%, with many areas experiencing prolonged drought. Tasmania has a temperate climate, without the extremes of heat of the mainland and with more regular rainfall, although conditions vary greatly between the mountains and the coast.

Economy

Highly diversified and robust market economy; the service sector contributes most to GDP; natural resources include oil, natural gas, bauxite, nickel, lead, zinc, copper, tin, uranium, iron ore and other minerals, exploited since the 1850s; the Gippsland basin produces two-thirds of Australia's oil and most of its natural gas, but major discoveries have been made off the north-west coast; other industries include engineering, shipbuilding, car manufacture, metals, chemicals, food processing and wine; the historically important agricultural sector is still significant despite constraints of terrain and rainfall; its most important products are wheat, other cereals and cattle and sheep, raised for meat, wool and dairy products.

Government

Governed by a Governor-General (representing the British monarch, who is head of state), a Prime Minister and Cabinet, and a bicameral federal Parliament, comprising a Senate and a House of Representatives. Each of the six states and two territories has its own Governor, executive council and legislative assembly.

History

The Aboriginal people are thought to have arrived in Australia from South-East Asia around 40 000 years ago. The first European visitors were the Dutch, who explored the Gulf of Carpentaria in 1606 and landed in 1642. Captain James Cook arrived in Botany Bay in 1770, and claimed the east coast for Britain. New South Wales was established as a penal colony in 1788. In 1829 all the territory now known as Australia was constituted a dependency of Britain. It originally developed as several widely-spread colonies, relating to Britain more than to one another. Increasing numbers of settlers were attracted to Australia, especially after the introduction of Spanish Merino sheep. Gold was discovered in New South Wales and Victoria (1851), and in Western Australia (1892). Transportation of convicts to eastern Australia ended in 1840, but continued until 1853 in Tasmania and 1868 in Western Australia. During this period, the colonies drafted their own constitutions and set up governments: New South Wales (1855), Tasmania and Victoria (1856), South Australia (1857), Queensland (1860) and Western Australia (1890). In 1901 a federal Commonwealth of Australia was established by agreement between the colonies, with the new city of Canberra chosen as the site for its capital, and Australia became independent within the Commonwealth in 1931. A policy of preventing immigration by non-whites stayed in force from the end of the 19th century until 1974. In 1986, the remaining legislative, executive and judicial links with the UK were abolished, while retaining the British monarch as head of state. A growing republican movement led in 1998 to a constitutional convention voting in favour of adopting a republican system of government, but the proposal was rejected in a national referendum in November 1999. Hard-line policies on refugees and asylum seekers were adopted in 1992, and poor conditions in detention camps led to international protests in 2001 after Australia forcibly diverted boats of asylum seekers to Nauru.

Australian states and territories

Name	Population (2006e)[1]	Area	Capital
Australian Capital Territory (ACT)	328 800	2432 sq km (939 sq mi)	Canberra
New South Wales (NSW)	6 827 700	801 427 sq km (309 431 sq mi)	Sydney
Northern Territory (NT)	206 700	1 346 200 sq km (519 768 sq mi)	Darwin
Queensland (QLD)	4 053 400	1 732 700 sq km (668 995 sq mi)	Brisbane
South Australia (SA)	1 554 724	984 376 sq km (380 070 sq mi)	Adelaide

The Rainbow Colours of Australia's Natural Features

From the iconic magnificence of the monolith Uluru in the deserts of central Australia to the dazzling hues of Queensland's Great Barrier Reef, Australia is a land of remarkable natural beauty.

A land of extremes and diversity

This vast land mass of Australia is home to extremes: geological, climatic and geographical. The sparse central wilderness known as the Outback precludes settlements. It is largely arid red desert, characterized by sandhills, scattered grassland and salt marshes, and salt lakes. Australia is also a place of staggering contrasts: deserts and rainforests sometimes lie only a few hundred kilometres apart. Even within the single state of New South Wales a temperate coastal climate changes to a hot and semi-tropical climate in the north, and to a hot and dry desert in the far west.

Natural monuments

Uluru, a red sandstone rock formation formerly known as Ayers Rock, is Australia's most famous natural landmark and is a sacred site for Aboriginal people. Officially part of the Northern Territory, Uluru is located virtually in the centre of Australia and is 443 kilometres (275 miles) from the nearest town of Alice Springs. If you were to walk around the base you would cover nearly 9.5 kilometres (6 miles), while to scale its height you would need to climb nearly 350 metres (1,150 feet). Uluru undergoes spectacular colour changes according to the position of the Sun – it is most stunning at sunset, when the colours range from fiery reds and crimsons to pinks and purples.

Another unusual rock formation, this time in Western Australia, is known as the Wave Rock. This granite wall of rock, around 100 metres (330 feet) long and 15 metres (50 feet) high, has been eroded by water and wind to create an overhang. The overall effect is of a surfing breaker, ready to crash down on a beach; striking dark streaks, formed by algae that grow on the surface of the rust-coloured rock, add to the resemblance.

Awe-inspiring mountains

The Great Dividing Range is a series of mountain ranges that runs north to south from the far north of Queensland to Victoria in the south, covering a distance of over 3,000 kilometres (2,000 miles). The Blue Mountains, which form part of this series, take their name from their bluish-green appearance when viewed from a distance. The blue tinge is a result of the dense population of eucalyptus forest; a fine mist of eucalyptus oil in the air causes the scatter of blue light.

Marvels of the ocean

Offshore Queensland is the site of possibly the greatest natural wonder in the world – the Great Barrier Reef. The spectacular coral formations stretch in a chain of tracery for more than 2,000 kilometres along the coast. Their polyps provide a breathtaking display of colours: blues, reds, purples, yellows and greens. The myriad fish, too, seem more likely to be the product of a small child's paint set than of nature – every colour of the rainbow is represented, in every combination imaginable.

Name	Population (2006e)[1]	Area	Capital
Tasmania (TAS)	488 900	68 331 sq km (26 383 sq mi)	Hobart
Victoria (VIC)	5 091 700	227 600 sq km (87 876 sq mi)	Melbourne
Western Australia (WA)	2 050 900	2 525 500 sq km (975 096 sq mi)	Perth

[1] *Source: Australian Bureau of Statistics*

Overseas territories

Norfolk Island

Location	An island external territory of Australia in the western Pacific Ocean, lying 1488 km (925 mi) north-east of Sydney.		
Area	35 sq km (4 sq mi)	**Internet**	.nf
Capital	Kingston	**Country code**	NFK
Population	1828 (2006e)		

━ Numbers by Nickname ━

The Norfolk Island telephone directory has an unusual way of identifying residents – by their nicknames. The island was settled in the 19th century by a small number of Pitcairn islanders, with the result that many of the current inhabitants share a handful of surnames. With so many Quintals and Christians listed, the inclusion of nicknames such as 'Storky', 'Kik Kik' and 'Tarzan' reduces the potential for 'wrong numbers'.

Heard and McDonald Islands

Location	An island group comprising Heard Island, Shag Island and the McDonald Islands in the Southern Ocean, approximately 4000 km (2500 mi) south-west of Fremantle, Australia.		
Area	412 sq km (159 sq mi)	**Internet**	.hm
Population	Uninhabited	**Country code**	HMD

Christmas Island

Location	An island in the Indian Ocean, approximately 360 km (224 mi) south of Java (Indonesia).		
Area	135 sq km (52 sq mi)	**Internet**	.cx
Capital	The Settlement	**Country code**	CXR
Population	1 493 (2006e)		

Cocos (Keeling) Islands

Location	An Australian external territory comprising two separate groups of atolls in the Indian Ocean, 3685 km (2290 mi) west of Darwin. There are 27 small, flat, palm-covered coral islands in the territory; the main islands are West Island and Home Island.

Area	14.2 sq km (5.5 sq mi)	**Internet**	.cc
Capital	West Island	**Country code**	CCK
Population	574 (2006e)		

AUSTRIA

Official name	Republic of Austria
Local name	Österreich; Republik Österreich
Former name	formerly part of Austria–Hungary (until 1918)
Area	83 854 sq km (32 368 sq mi)
Capital	Vienna; Wien
Chief towns	Graz, Linz, Salzburg, Innsbruck, Klagenfurt
Population	8 193 000 (2006e)
Nationality	Austrian
Languages	German; Slovene, Croatian and Hungarian are also official languages in a single province each
Ethnic group	Austrian 91%, former Yugoslavs 4%, others 5%
Religions	Christianity 79% (RC 74%, Prot 5%), Islam 4%, none/unaffiliated 14%, others 3%
Time zone	GMT +1
Currency	1 Euro (€) = 100 cents
Telephone	+43
Internet	.at
Country code	AUT

Location

A mountainous republic in central Europe, bounded to the north by Germany, the Czech Republic and Slovakia; to the south by Italy and Slovenia; to the west by Switzerland and Liechtenstein; and to the east by Hungary.

Physical description

Situated at the eastern end of the Alps, the country is almost entirely mountainous; the ranges of the Ötztal, Zillertal, Hohe Tauern and Niedere Tauern stretch eastwards from the main Alpine massif; the highest point is Grossglockner, at 3797 m (12 457 ft); chief mountain passes into Italy are the Brenner and Plöcken; most of the country is in the drainage basin of the River Danube; the Neusiedler See on the Hungarian border is the largest lake in Austria.

Climate

There are three climatic regions: the Alps (often sunny in winter but cloudy in summer); the Danube valley and the Vienna basin (the driest region); and the south-east, a region of heavy thunderstorms; with often severe winters but warmer summers than north of the Alps. In general, most rain falls in the summer months; winters are cold; there is a warm, dry wind (the Föhn) in some north-to-south valleys, especially in autumn and spring, which can be responsible for fires and snow-melt leading to avalanches.

Economy

Highly diversified market economy with a large services sector; major industries include tourism, foodstuffs, luxury commodities, mechanical engineering, steel construction, machinery, forestry, mining and metal products; the principal agricultural areas along River Danube and north of the Alps produce crops, cattle, fruit and grapes for wine-making; natural resources include oil, natural gas, minerals and hydroelectric power.

Government

Governed by a federal President, a federal Chancellor and government, and a bicameral Federal Assembly, comprising a National Council and a Federal Council. Each of the nine *Länder* (states) is administered by its own government, headed by a Governor elected by the provincial legislature.

History

Austria was part of the Roman Empire until the 5th century, then was occupied by Germanic tribes and in the late 8th century became a frontier area of Charlemagne's empire. It became a duchy and passed to the Habsburg family (1282), who made it the foundation of their empire; the head of the Habsburg house was almost continually the Holy Roman Emperor, making Austria the leading German state. Habsburg defeats in the 19th century (notably the Austro–Prussian War) and Hungarian nationalism led to the Dual Monarchy of Austria-Hungary. The assassination of Archduke Franz Ferdinand by Serbian nationalists triggered World War I. Following the collapse of Austria-Hungary at the end of the war, those German-speaking lands of the Habsburg Empire not annexed by other successor states constituted themselves on 12 November 1918 as 'German Austria', renamed Austria at the insistence of the victor powers. Between the wars the republic led an uneasy existence, with most of public opinion and most politicians seeking union with Germany. Union with Hitler's Germany, which occurred when Austria was annexed by the German Reich in March 1938 (*Anschluss*), under the name *Ostmark*, was more controversial. After World War II, Austria was reconstituted as a distinct territory by the Allies and administered as four occupied zones until 1955, when the occupying powers withdrew and it became an independent, neutral, democratic state. Austria joined the European Community in 1995 and replaced the schilling with the euro in 2002. In 2000, the inclusion of the extreme right-wing Freedom Party in a coalition government led the European Union to impose diplomatic sanctions for seven months.

AZERBAIJAN

Official name	Republic of Azerbaijan
Local name	Azərbaycan; Azərbaycan Respublikası
Former name	Azerbaijan People's Republic (1918–20), Transcaucasian Soviet Federated Socialist Republic (with Armenia and Georgia, 1922–36), Azerbaijan Soviet Socialist Republic (1920–2, 1936–90), within the Union of Soviet Socialist Republics (USSR; 1922–91)
Area	86 600 sq km (33 428 sq mi)
Capital	Baku
Chief towns	Gäncä, Sumqayit
Population	7 962 000 (2006e)
Nationality	Azerbaijani
Language	Azerbaijani (Azeri)
Ethnic groups	Azeri 91%, Dagestani 2%, Russian 2%, Armenian 1%, others 4%
Religions	Islam 93% (Shia), Christianity 5% (Orthodox), others 2%
Time zone	GMT +4
Currency	1 New Manat = 100 gopik
Telephone	+994
Internet	.az
Country code	AZE

Location

A republic in eastern Transcaucasia, bounded to the east by the Caspian Sea and to the south by Iran; Armenia splits the country in the south-west and forms the western boundary; Georgia and Russia lie to the north.

Physical description

Crossed by the Greater Caucasus in the north and the Lesser Caucasus in the south-west; the ranges are separated by the plain of the River Kura, much of it below sea level; the highest peak is Mt Bazar-Dyuzi (4480 m/14 698 ft) in the north-east; 10.5% of the total area is forested.

Climate

Continental; hot in summer, with winters that are mild in the lowlands but cold and snowy in the mountains.

Economy

In transition from command to market economy; dominated by oil and natural gas extraction (90% of exports) and related industries; agriculture is the main employer; main crops are cotton, cereals, fruit, vegetables, tea, silk and livestock.

Government

Governed by an executive President, a Prime Minister and Cabinet of Ministers, and a unicameral National Assembly (*Milli Majlis*).

History

The Azeris have a long history, mainly of subjection to the neighbouring empires. A Turkish people converted to Islam, they came under Tsarist Russian rule in 1813. The development of the oil industry in and around Baku produced leaders who, encouraged by Lenin, declared independence in 1918. However, in 1920 they were reconquered on his instructions for allegedly siding with Soviet enemies, and Azerbaijan was proclaimed a Soviet Socialist Republic; it became a constituent republic of the Union of Soviet Socialist Republics (USSR) in 1936. Between December 1988 and January 1990 riots promoted by the nationalist Azerbaijan Popular Front culminated in an anti-Armenian pogrom in the capital, and Soviet troops mounted a violent assault on the city to restore order. Before emerging as an independent republic in 1991 following the disintegration of the USSR, Azerbaijan became locked in a struggle with Armenia over the autonomous region that Stalin had set up for the latter's co-nationals in Nagorno-Karabakh. This degenerated into war in 1992. A ceasefire was announced in 1994 and talks to effect a peaceful resolution continue. Azerbaijan joined the Commonwealth of Independent States (CIS) in 1993. Despite the introduction of multiparty democracy in 1995, Azerbaijan was effectively under the rule of President Heydar Aliyev from 1992 until his death in 2003, when his equally authoritarian son, Ilham Aliyev, was elected to succeed him.

THE BAHAMAS

Official name	Commonwealth of the Bahamas
Local name	The Bahamas
Area	13 934 sq km (5 379 sq mi)
Capital	Nassau
Chief town	Freeport
Population	304 000 (2006e)
Nationality	Bahamian
Language	English
Ethnic groups	black 85%, white 12%, Asian and Hispanic 3%
Religions	Christianity 96% (Prot and others 83%, RC 13%), none/unaffiliated 3%, others 1%
Time zone	GMT −5
Currency	1 Bahamian Dollar (BA$, B$) = 100 cents
Telephone	+1 242
Internet	.bs
Country code	BHS

Location

An independent archipelago of c.700 low-lying islands and over 2000 cays, forming a chain extending c.800 km (500 mi) south-east from the coast of Florida.

Physical description

The low-lying coralline limestone islands of the Bahamas comprise the two oceanic banks of Little Bahama and Great Bahama; the highest point is Mt Alvernia on Cat Island, only 63 m (207 ft) above sea level.

Climate

Subtropical, with average temperatures of 21°C in winter and 27°C in summer; the average annual rainfall is 750–1500 mm; hurricanes are frequent from June to November.

Economy

Developing country; main economic activities are tourism (60% of GDP) and offshore financial services (tax-haven status); other industries include oil transhipment and refining, fishing, rum and liqueur distilling, salt, chemicals, fruit, vegetables.

Government

Governed by a Governor-General (representing the British monarch, who is head of state), a Prime Minister and Cabinet, and a bicameral Parliament, consisting of an elected House of Assembly and an appointed Senate.

History

Christopher Columbus reached The Bahamas in 1492, but the first permanent European settlement was established in 1647 by English and Bermudan religious refugees. The Bahamas became a British Crown Colony in 1717, and were a notorious rendezvous for buccaneers and pirates. They gained independence in 1973. The prime minister on independence was Sir Lynden Pindling, who was regarded as the founding father of The Bahamas.

The Bermuda Triangle

The islands of The Bahamas are flanked by the area known as the Bermuda Triangle, in which ships and aircraft have allegedly vanished mysteriously. 'Explanations' of the disappearances proposed over the years have ranged from the sinking of craft by giant bubbles of methane gas rising from the ocean floor to abduction by aliens. However, the US Coast Guard maintains that the rate of accidents within the Triangle is no higher than in any other comparably busy region. Similarly, the nautical insurance specialists Lloyd's of London do not consider the area to be so hazardous as to warrant special consideration.

BAHRAIN

Official name	Kingdom of Bahrain
Local name	Al-Bahrayn; Mamlakat al-Bahrayn
Former name	State of Bahrain (until 2002)
Area	678 sq km (262 sq mi)
Capital	Manama, Al Manāmah
Chief town	Al Muharraq
Population	699 000 (2006e)
Nationality	Bahraini
Languages	Arabic; English, Farsi, Hindi and Urdu are also spoken
Ethnic groups	Bahraini 63%, Asian 13%, other Arab 10%, Iranian 8%, others 6%
Religions	Islam 81% (Shia 49%, Sunni 32%), Christian 9%, others 10%
Time zone	GMT +3
Currency	1 Bahraini Dinar (BD) = 1000 fils
Telephone	+973
Internet	.bh
Country code	BHR

Location

monarchy comprising a group of 35 islands in the Arabian Gulf, midway between e Qatar peninsula and mainland Saudi Arabia; a causeway (25 km/16 mi in length) nnects Bahrain to Saudi Arabia.

Physical description

ahrain comprises 35 islands; the largest, Bahrain Island, is c.48 km (30 mi) long and –16 km (8–10 mi) wide; the highest point is Jabal Dukhan (135 m/443 ft); largely bare d infertile; causeways link the four main islands, and connect Bahrain Island to audi Arabia.

Climate

ot, humid climate, with average temperatures of 30–40°C in May–October and –30°C in winter; cool north/north-east winds, with a little rain in December–March; st of the year is dominated by either a moist north-east wind (the *Shamal*) or the ot, sand-bearing *Qaws* from the south.

Economy

osperous economy based on oil (on- and offshore) but now diversified; regional nking, financial services and commercial centre; natural gas, lime, gypsum; oil fining, aluminium smelting, ship repairing.

Government

hereditary constitutional monarchy; governed by the King, a Prime Minister and ouncil of Ministers, and a bicameral National Assembly, comprising a Chamber of eputies and a Consultative Council.

History

Bahrain was a flourishing trade centre in 2000–1800 BC. It was ruled by Iran from 1602 ad until the Iranian rulers were ousted in 1783 by the al-Khalifa family, who rule to this day. Political control of Bahrain was held by Britain from 1820 to 1971, and oil was discovered during this time, in 1932. In 1971 Bahrain gained independence and Isa ibn Sulman became ruler. He dissolved the National Assembly in 1975 as a result of disputes between Sunni and Shia Muslim communities. On his death in 199 he was succeeded by his son, Hamad bin Isa. Following a referendum on political reform in 2001, the country became a constitutional monarchy with a partially electe parliament, and the Emir adopted the title of King. Elections to a new legislative assembly were held in 2002.

BANGLADESH

Official name	People's Republic of Bangladesh
Local name	Gana Prajatantri Bangladesh
Former name	Part of the Indian states of Bengal (until 1905) and East Bengal (until 1947), then part of Pakistan as East Pakistan (until 1971)
Area	143998 sq km (55583 sq mi)
Capital	Dhaka (formerly known as Dacca)
Chief towns	Chittagong, Khulna, Narayanganj
Population	147365000 (2006e)
Nationality	Bangladeshi
Languages	Bangla (Bengali); English is the second language
Ethnic group	Bengali 98%, others 2%
Religion	Islam 83% (mostly Sunni), Hinduism 16%, others 1%
Time zone	GMT +6
Currency	1 Taka (TK) = 100 poisha
Telephone	+880
Internet	.bd
Country code	BGD

Location

An Asian republic lying between the foothills of the Himalayas and the Indian Ocean bounded to the west, north-west and east by India; to the south-east by Myanmar; and to the south by the Bay of Bengal.

Physical description

Mainly a vast, low-lying alluvial plain, cut by a network of rivers and marshes; main rivers are the Ganges (Padma), Brahmaputra (Jamuna) and Meghna, joining in the south to form the largest delta in the world; subject to frequent flooding; in the east fertile valleys and peaks of Chittagong Hill Tracts rise to c.1000 m (3280 ft); highest point is Keokradong (1230 m/4035 ft); vast areas of the southern delta are covered in mangroves and hardwood forest.

Climate

Tropical monsoon climate; a hot season in March–June with heavy thunderstorms; very humid, with higher temperatures inland; the main rainy season is June–September; cyclones in the Bay of Bengal cause widespread flooding of coastal areas.

Economy

Poor country dependent on foreign aid and remittances of expatriate workers; recent growth in energy sector (natural gas) and manufacturing (garments and knitwear (73% of export earnings), jute goods, leather, processing agricultural products); 70% of workforce employed in agriculture, especially cotton, jute (supplies 80% of world's jute), tea, sugar, fish and seafood.

Government

Governed by a President, a Prime Minister and Cabinet, and a unicameral Parliament, with a number of seats reserved for women.

History

Bangladesh formed part of the State of Bengal in British India until Muslim East Bengal was created in 1905, separate from Hindu West Bengal. Reunited in 1911, East and West Bengal were again partitioned in 1947, with West Bengal remaining in India and East Bengal forming East Pakistan. Disparity in investment and development between East and West Pakistan (separated by over 1600 km/1000 mi), coupled with language differences, caused East Pakistan to seek autonomy. The suspension of democracy following a sweeping electoral victory by the Awami League in East Pakistan in 1970, the devastation of this province of Pakistan by a cyclone in the same year (it is one of the world's most densely populated areas), and the Dhaka government's ineffectual response to the disaster – which claimed 220 000 lives and countless homes and crops – triggered fighting, which developed into a full-scale civil war in 1971. Pakistan surrendered the territory only months later following a popular uprising and military intervention by India, which had accepted huge numbers of Bengali refugees; thus the independent republic of Bangladesh was created. Political unrest led to the suspension of the constitution in 1975, and the assassination of the first president. There were further coups in 1975, when the Awami League was overthrown and disbanded, as well as in 1977 and 1982. The constitution was restored in 1986. The Awami League later regrouped and rose to become a major political force, and in 1996, led by Sheikh Hasina Wazed, it defeated the Bangladesh Nationalist Party of Khaleda Zia to become the country's ruling party. Sheikh Hasina completed her term of office in 2001, the first elected prime minister to do so, and subsequent elections returned Khaleda Zia to power.

BARBADOS

Official name	Barbados
Local name	Barbados
Area	431 sq km (166 sq mi)
Capital	Bridgetown
Chief town	Speightstown
Population	280 000 (2006e)
Nationality	Barbadian or Bajan (informal)
Language	English
Ethnic groups	black 80%, white 4%, others 16%
Religions	Christianity 71% (Prot and others 67%, RC 4%), none/unaffiliated 17%, others 12%
Time zone	GMT −4
Currency	1 Barbadian Dollar (BD$) = 100 cents
Telephone	+1 246
Internet	.bb
Country code	BRB

Location

An independent state and the most easterly of the Caribbean Islands, situated in the Atlantic Ocean.

Physical description

A small, triangular island, 32 km (20 mi) long (north-west to south-east); it rises to 340 m (1115 ft) at Mt Hillaby and is ringed by a coral reef.

Climate

Tropical, with an average annual temperature of 27°C and an average annual rainfall of 1420 mm; the hurricane season is July–November.

Economy

Tourism, offshore financial services, sugar, light manufacturing, component assembly (electronic and electrical equipment), garments.

Government

Governed by a Governor-General (representing the British monarch, who is head of state), a Prime Minister and Cabinet, and a bicameral Parliament, comprising an appointed Senate and an elected House of Assembly.

History

Early inhabitants included Amerindians from South America, who arrived in around 350 ad, Arawak Indians and Caribs, but the island was uninhabited when colonized by the English in 1627. It was a Crown colony from 1652 and attained self-government in 1961, becoming independent in 1966. Since independence, power has alternated between the Barbados Labour Party and the Democratic Labour Party.

BELARUS

Official name	Republic of Belarus
Local name	Belarus; Respublika Belarus
Former name	Belorussian People's Republic (1918–19), Byelorussian or Belorussian Soviet Socialist Republic (until 1991), within the Union of Soviet Socialist Republics (USSR; 1922–91); sometimes also formerly known as Byelorussia, Belorussia, Byelarus or White Russia
Area	207 600 sq km (80 134 sq mi)
Capital	Minsk
Chief towns	Gomel, Vitebsk, Mogilev, Bobruysk, Grodno, Brest
Population	10 293 000 (2006e)
Nationality	Belarusian
Languages	Belarusian, Russian
Ethnic groups	Belarusian 81%, Russian 11%, Polish 4%, Ukrainian 3%, others 1%
Religions	Christianity 72% (Orthodox 60%, RC 8%, Prot 4%), others 28% (including Islam and Judaism)
Time zone	GMT +2
Currency	1 Belarusian Rouble (BR) = 100 kopeks
Telephone	+375
Internet	.by
Country code	BLR

Location

A republic in eastern Europe, bounded to the west by Poland; to the north-west by Lithuania; to the north by Latvia; to the east by Russia; and to the south by the Ukraine.

Physical description

It is mostly a large plain, with many lakes (c.11 000) and marshes, and low hills in the north-west rising to 345 m (1132 ft); rivers include the Dnieper, Zapadnaya Dvina and Neman; one-third of the country is covered by forests.

Climate

Continental, with cold winters and warm, humid summers.

Economy

Much of economy still under state control; dependent on Russia for energy needs and oil for industry and re-export; main industries are machine building, metalworking, chemicals, petrochemicals, textiles, food, woodworking, radio-electronics, agriculture (grain, potatoes, vegetables, sugar beet, flax, beef, milk).

Government

Governed by a President, a Prime Minister and Council of Minister, and a bicameral National Assembly (*Natsionalnoye Sobranie*) consisting of a Council of the Republic and a Chamber of Representatives.

History

The Belorussians were one of the original Slav tribes, like the Russians themselves. They remained slightly distinct because they lived in the exposed western border area and were subject to long periods of foreign, particularly Polish, rule. Under Tsarist control from 1795, they eventually developed a national movement that declared independence in 1917. However, a feeble Belorussia had a troubled existence; it declared a Belorussian Soviet Socialist Republic in 1919 and was incorporated into the Union of Soviet Socialist Republics (USSR) in 1921. In 1945 its territory was expanded at the expense of Poland and, for Soviet political reasons, it was given separate membership of the UN. Yet its sense of national identity remained comparatively undeveloped until it achieved independence in 1991 on the disintegration of the Soviet Union; also that year it became a founding member of the Commonwealth of Independent States (CIS). Alyaksandr Lukashenka, president since 1994, has resisted economic reform, precipitating economic collapse in the late 1990s, and has become increasingly authoritarian. He has pursued closer relations with Russia, committing Belarus to greater political and economic integration with Russia in 1997 and 1999 treaties, although there has been little real progress towards this.

BELGIUM

Official name	Kingdom of Belgium
Local name	Belgique; Royaume de Belgique (French), België; Koninkrijk België (Flemish), Belgien; Königreich Belgien (German)
Area	32 545 sq km (12 562 sq mi)
Capital	Brussels; Bruxelles (French), Brussel (Flemish), Brüssel (German)
Chief towns	Antwerp, Ghent, Charleroi, Liège, Bruges, Namur, Mons
Population	10 379 000 (2006e)
Nationality	Belgian
Languages	Flemish (Dutch), French, German (mainly on the eastern border); Brussels is officially a bilingual city (French and Flemish)
Ethnic groups	Fleming 58%, Walloon 31%, others 11%
Religions	Christianity 85% (RC 75%, Prot 10%), Islam 2%, none/unaffiliated 10%, others 3%
Time zone	GMT +1
Currency	1 Euro (€) = 100 cents
Telephone	+32
Internet	.be
Country code	BEL

Location

A kingdom in north-western Europe, bounded to the north by the Netherlands; to the south by France; to the east by Germany and Luxembourg; and to the west by the North Sea.

Physical description

Low-lying and fertile in the west, with some hills in the south-east region (Ardennes); highest point is Signal de Botrange (694 m/2277 ft); the main river systems, the Sambre–Meuse and the Scheldt, drain across the Dutch border and are linked by a complex network of canals.

Climate

Temperate with strong maritime influences; mild winters, warm summers and frequent rainfall.

Economy

A long-standing centre of European trade and one of the earliest countries in Europe to industrialize, Belgium is now a highly developed and diversified market economy with a large service sector owing to the location in Brussels of several major international organizations; with few natural resources apart from coal (no longer produced), industries developed based on processing raw materials for export, eg the iron and steel industry, dependent on raw materials from Luxembourg and Germany; other industries include metallurgical and engineering products, motor vehicle assembly, processed food and beverages, chemicals, textiles, glass and petroleum; there is trade in gemstones (especially diamonds); agriculture is mainly livestock, sugar beet, vegetables, fruit, grain and tobacco; in 1948 there was full economic union between Belgium, the Netherlands and Luxembourg (Benelux Economic Union); Belgium was a founder-member of the EEC.

Government

A hereditary constitutional monarchy with a King as head of state; governed by a Prime Minister and Cabinet, and a bicameral Federal Chambers, comprising a Chamber of Representatives and a Senate. There are three communities (Flemish, Francophone, Germanophone), each with its own community government and assembly. There are three regions (Flanders, Wallonia, Brussels), each with its own regional government and assembly.

History

A line drawn east to west just to the south of Brussels divides the population by race and language into two approximately equal parts; north of the line the inhabitants are Flemings of Teutonic stock who speak Flemish, while south of the line they are French-speaking Latins known as Walloons. Belgium was part of the Roman Empire until the 2nd century ad, and after being invaded by Germanic tribes it became part of the Frankish Empire. In the early Middle Ages, some semi-independent provinces and cities grew up and from 1385 were absorbed by the House of Burgundy. They were known as the Spanish Netherlands, and were ruled by the Habsburgs from 1477 until the Peace of Utrecht (1713); the Spanish provinces were then transferred to Austria as the Austrian Netherlands. The country was conquered by the French in 1794 and formed part of the First French Republic and Empire until in 1815 it united with the northern (Dutch) provinces under King William I of the Netherlands. The southern (Belgian) provinces were unhappy with the union because of William's religious, linguistic and economic policies. The Belgian Revolution began with riots in Brussels on 25 August 1830. A provisional government, called a National Convention, declared the independence of Belgium and drafted a new constitution (7 February 1831), which made Belgium a constitutional monarchy with Leopold of Saxe-Coburg as its first king (Leopold I). The Great Powers recognized Belgian independence at the Conference of London (20 January 1831). However, William I refused to co-operate; as a result an armed standoff dragged on for most of the 1830s. Finally in 1839 the Dutch government capitulated and signed a treaty that completed the independence of Belgium. During the 20th century, Belgium was occupied by Germany in both world wars, and in the post-war period political tension between Walloons and Flemings caused the collapse of several governments until federalization began in the 1980s with the creation of regional 'subgovernments' for Wallonia and Flanders. In 1989 a new federal constitution divided Belgium into three autonomous regions: the Walloon Region (Wallonia), the Flemish Region (Flanders) and the bilingual Brussels-Capital Region; constitutional amendments in 1993 completed federalization. Belgium joined with Luxembourg and the Netherlands to form the Benelux economic union in 1948. It was a founder member of the European Economic Community in 1958, and replaced the Belgian franc with the euro in 2002.

BELIZE

Official name	Belize
Local name	Belize
Former name	British Honduras (until 1973)
Area	22963 sq km (8864 sq mi)
Capital	Belmopan
Chief towns	Belize City, Dangriga, Punta Gorda, San Ignacio
Population	288000 (2006e)
Nationality	Belizean
Languages	English; Spanish and local Mayan, Carib and Creole languages are also spoken
Ethnic groups	Mestizo 49%, Creole 25%, Maya 11%, Garifuna 6%, others 9%
Religions	Christianity 77% (RC 50%, Prot 27%), others 14%, none/unaffiliated 9%
Time zone	GMT −6
Currency	1 Belizean Dollar (BZ$) = 100 cents
Telephone	+501
Internet	.bz
Country code	BLZ

Location

An independent state in Central America, bounded to the north by Mexico; to the west and south by Guatemala; and to the east by the Caribbean Sea.

Physical description

The country has an extensive coastal plain, swampy in the north, more fertile in the south; the Maya Mountains extend almost to the east coast, rising to 1120 m (3674 ft) at Victoria Peak; they are flanked by pine ridges, tropical forests, savannas and farm land; the Belize River flows west to east; inner coastal waters are protected by the world's fifth-longest barrier reef.

Climate

Generally subtropical but tempered by trade winds; coastal temperatures vary between 10 and 36°C, with a greater range in the mountains; there is variable rainfall with an average of 1295 mm in the north and 4445 mm in the south; the drier season is from February to May; hurricanes have caused severe damage.

Economy

The main industries are tourism, garment manufacturing, food processing (sugar refining, citrus processing), construction, forestry and marine products; a significant agricultural sector produces main export items, including sugar, bananas, citrus and tropical fruit, shrimp and fish; crude oil production is expected to begin in 2006–7.

Government

Governed by a Governor-General (representing the British monarch, who is head of state), a Prime Minister and Cabinet, and a bicameral National Assembly, comprising an appointed Senate and an elected House of Representatives.

History

There is evidence of early Maya settlement in Belize, and its coast was colonized in the 17th century by shipwrecked British sailors and disbanded soldiers from Jamaica, who defended the territory against the Spanish. Created a British colony in 1862, it was administered from Jamaica, but the tie with Jamaica was severed in 1884. A ministerial system of government was introduced in 1961, and in 1964 full internal self-government was achieved. The country changed its name from British Honduras to Belize in 1973 and gained full independence in 1981. Guatemalan claims over Belize territory led to a British military presence until, in the early 1990s, Guatemala established diplomatic relations with Belize. Almost all of the British presence was withdrawn in 1993. Talks sponsored by the Organization of American States (OAS) continue in search of a final resolution to the dispute with Guatemala.

Flourishing in the Shade

The national motto of Belize is *Sub Umbra Florero*, which is Latin for 'Under the shade I flourish'. The shade to which the motto refers is that of Belize's national tree, the mahogany, which features prominently on the national coat of arms. These trees are an important part of Belize's heritage, as the mahogany industry played a central part in the national economy during the 18th and 19th centuries.

BENIN

Official name	Republic of Benin
Local name	Bénin; République Bénin
Former name	Dahomey (until 1975); People's Republic of Benin (1975–90)
Area	112 622 sq km (43 472 sq mi)
Capital	Porto-Novo (administrative and constitutional) and Cotonou (economic and seat of government)
Chief towns	Ouidah, Abomey, Kandi, Parakou, Natitingou
Population	7 863 000 (2006e)
Nationality	Beninese
Languages	French; Fon, Yoruba and several other local languages are also spoken
Ethnic groups	Fon 39%, Bariba 21%, Yoruba 10%, others 30%
Religions	traditional beliefs 50%, Christianity 30% (mostly RC), Islam 20%
Time zone	GMT +1
Currency	1 CFA Franc (CFAFr) = 100 centimes
Telephone	+229
Internet	.bj
Country code	BEN

Location

A republic in west Africa, bounded to the north by Niger; to the east by Nigeria; to the south by the Bight of Benin; to the west by Togo; and to the north-west by Burkina Faso.

Physical description

Rises from a 100 km (62 mi) sandy coast with lagoons, to low-lying plains, then to a savanna plateau at c.400 m (1300 ft); the Atakora Mountains rise to more than 500 m (1640 ft) in the north-west; highest point is Mt Sokbaro (658 m/2159 ft); several rivers flow south to the Gulf of Guinea.

Climate

Tropical climate, divided into three zones; in the south, there is rain throughout the year, especially during the 'Guinea Monsoon' (May–October); in the central area there are two rainy seasons (peaks in May–June and October); in the north, there is one (July–September); the northern dry season (October–April) is hot, has low humidity, and is subject to the dry *harmattan* wind from the north-east.

Economy

Underdeveloped and dependent on foreign aid, with a massive trade deficit; main activities are cotton growing, palm products, food processing, textiles, crude oil production.

Government

Governed by an executive President, a Council of Ministers and a unicameral National Assembly.

History

As the Kingdom of Dahomey, it was based on its capital at Abomey, and in the late 17th and early 18th centuries extended its authority from the coast to the interior, to the west of the Yoruba states. In the 1720s the cavalry of the Oyo Kingdom of the Yoruba devastated Dahomey, but when the Oyo Empire collapsed in the early 19th century, Dahomey regained its power. The state was annexed by the French in 1883 and constituted a territory of French west Africa in 1904, but regained its independence in 1960. In 1972 it was declared a Marxist–Leninist state under the leadership of President Mathieu Kérékou, who renamed it Benin in 1975. The country gradually gained stability and moved towards democratic government, abandoning Marxist–Leninism in 1989. A multiparty democratic constitution was adopted in 1991. In 2004, a 40-year border dispute with neighbouring Nigeria was resolved and the border redrawn.

BHUTAN

Official name	Kingdom of Bhutan
Local name	Druk Yul
Area	46 600 sq km (18 000) sq mi
Capital	Thimphu
Chief town	Phuntsholing
Population	2 280 000 (2006e)
Nationality	Bhutanese
Language	Dzongkha
Ethnic groups	Bhote 50%, Nepalese 35%, others 15%
Religions	Buddhism 73%, Hinduism 22%, Islam 5%
Time zone	GMT +5.5
Currency	1 Ngultrum (Nu) = 100 chetrum
Telephone	+975
Internet	.bt
Country code	BTN

Location

A small state in the eastern Himalayas, bounded to the north by China and to the south by India.

Physical description

A mountainous north, with east Himalayan peaks reaching over 7000 m (22 966 ft); the highest point is Kula Kangri (7 553 m/24 780 ft); there are mountain ridges with fertile valleys in the centre that descend to low forested foothills in the south; many rivers flow to meet the River Brahmaputra.

Climate

Subtropical in the south; cool winters and hot summers in the central valleys; severe winters and cool summers in the Himalayas, with permanent snowfields and glaciers; rainfall is heavy owing to frequent violent storms.

Economy

Cautiously modernizing economy still largely based on agriculture; main crops are rice, wheat, maize, mountain barley, potatoes, vegetables, fruit (especially oranges) and cardamom (main export); small-scale industry includes forestry and wood processing, cement, chemicals, hydroelectric power and tourism.

Government

A hereditary monarchy; governed by the King, a Council of Ministers (led by a chairman who changes annually), and a unicameral legislative National Assembly (*Tshogdu*). The King's position must be confirmed by legislative vote every three years.

History

British involvement dates from 1774 with the signing of a treaty of co-operation between Bhutan and the East India Company; the southern part of the country was annexed by Britain in 1865. In 1910 Britain agreed not to interfere in internal affairs, transferring the supervision of Bhutan's external affairs to British India, and in 1949 Bhutan signed a similar treaty with India. In 1990 large numbers of ethnic Nepalese moved to Nepal and India following the introduction of strict cultural laws. Bhutan has been governed since 1907 by maharajahs, now addressed as King of Bhutan. The absolute monarchy was replaced in 1969 by a form of democratic monarchy, with the King as the head of the government. He relinquished this role in 1998, when further reforms were introduced. A constitution announced in 2005 introduced further democratization, including parliamentary elections planned for 2008.

BOLIVIA

Official name	Republic of Bolivia
Local name	Bolivia; República de Bolivia
Area	1 098 580 sq km (424 052 sq mi)
Capital	La Paz (administrative) and Sucre (official and legislative)
Chief towns	Cochabamba, El Alto, Oruro, Potosí, Santa Cruz
Population	8 989 000 (2006e)
Nationality	Bolivian
Languages	Spanish, Quechua, Aymará
Ethnic groups	Mestizo 30%, Quechua 30%, Aymará 25%, European 10%, others 5%
Religions	Christianity 97% (RC 92%, Prot 5%), Baha'i 3%
Time zone	GMT −4
Currency	1 Boliviano ($b) = 100 centavos
Telephone	+591
Internet	.bo
Country code	BOL

Location

A landlocked republic in western central South America, bounded to the north and east by Brazil; to the west by Peru; to the south-west by Chile; to the south by Argentina; and to the south-east by Paraguay.

Physical description

Bounded to the west by the Cordillera Occidental of the Andes, rising to 6542 m (21 463 ft) at Nevado Sajama, and to the east by the Cordillera Real; between the mountains lies the 400 km (250 mi) central Altiplano Plateau, at 3600 m (11 811 ft) above sea level; major lakes in this region are Titicaca and Poopó; several rivers flow from the Andes towards the Brazilian frontier.

Climate

Varies, according to altitude; humid and semi-tropical in the lowlands, cold and semi-arid in the mountains.

Economy

Poor country dependent on foreign aid; abundant mineral resources, including 20% of world's tin; main industries are mining (zinc, tin, gold) and smelting, natural gas and oil production, agriculture (soya beans, coffee, coca, cotton, cereals, sugar) and forestry; world's third-largest producer of illegal cocaine.

Government

Governed by an executive President, a Cabinet and a bicameral National Congress, comprising a Chamber of Senators and a Chamber of Deputies.

History

Bolivia formed part of the Inca Empire in the 15th century, and there is evidence of earlier civilization. It was conquered by the Spanish in the 16th century, and achieved independence after the war of liberation in 1825. Much territory was lost after wars with neighbouring countries, with the Chaco War (1932–5) in particular having a devastating effect. In 1952 the *Movimiento Nacionalista Revolucionario* (National Revolutionary Movement), an alliance of mineworkers and peasants led by Víctor Paz Estenssoro, overthrew the military dictatorship and came to power. It brought about some far-reaching social reforms during the 1950s, including universal suffrage, the nationalization of the tin mines, and the improvement in status of the South American Indians. However, Bolivia's instability continued, as evidenced by several more changes of government and military coups during the 20th century. Economic collapse in the 1980s caused many of the poor to turn to cultivation of coca, the basis of cocaine, and crop-eradication programmes, essential to obtain overseas aid, have provoked protests and strikes in recent years.

BOSNIA AND HERZEGOVINA

Official name	Republic of Bosnia and Herzegovina; sometimes also known as Bosnia–Herzegovina
Local name	Bosna i Hercegovina; Republika Bosna i Hercegovina
Former name	Formerly part of the Kingdom of Serbs, Croats and Slovenes (until 1929), Kingdom of Yugoslavia (1929–41), Federal People's Republic of Yugoslavia (1945–63), Socialist Federal People's Republic of Yugoslavia (1963–91)
Area	51 129 sq km (19 736 sq mi)
Capital	Sarajevo
Chief towns	Banja Luka, Zenica, Tuzla, Mostar
Population	4 499 000 (2006e)
Nationality	Bosnian, Herzegovinian
Languages	Bosnian, Serbian, Croatian
Ethnic groups	Bosniak 48%, Serb 37%, Croat 14%, others 1%
Religions	Christianity 46% (Orthodox 31%, RC 15%), Islam 40%, others 14%
Time zone	GMT +1
Currency	1 convertible Marka (KM) = 100 pfennige
Telephone	+387
Internet	.ba
Country code	BIH

Location

A republic in the western part of the Balkan peninsula, bounded to the west and north by Croatia; to the east by Serbia; and to the south by Montenegro.

Physical description

The mountainous centre includes part of the Dinaric Alps; the highest point is Maglic (2386 m/7828 ft); it is split by its limestone gorges; in the north the land falls to the River Sava valley; there is 20 km (12 mi) of coastline on the Adriatic Sea.

Climate

Continental, with hot summers and cold winters.

Economy

Recovery from devastation of civil war hampered by inefficiency and uneasy relations between different national and local political entities; largely dependent on foreign aid; most agricultural output is consumed domestically; mining (minerals, metals, coal), steel, textiles, assembly of domestic appliances, vehicles and military equipment are major industries; hydroelectric power is exported.

Government

Governed by a collective presidency (which rotates among the three members: Bosniac, Serb and Croat), a Prime Minister and Council of Ministers, and a bicameral Parliamentary Assembly, consisting of a House of Peoples and a House of Representatives. Each of the two self-governing entities within the republic, the Federation of Bosnia and Herzegovina (Bosniac/Croat) and the Republika Srpska (Serb), has its own President, executive council and legislature.

History

In March 1992, Bosnia and Herzegovina followed the republics of Slovenia and Croatia in declaring its independence from Yugoslavia. Civil war broke out among communist and nationalist elements from the Yugoslav National Army and extreme nationalist paramilitary groups, gradually and brutally engulfing the civilian population until all civil order dissolved. A three-sided civil war raged between the Muslims loyal to the government, and the Serbs and Croats who proclaimed themselves independent and began fighting for territory. By the end of 1992 the Serbs had besieged Sarajevo and were carrying out a brutal policy of ethnic cleansing, which UN peacekeeping forces attempted to stop. An alliance made in 1994 between Bosnian Muslims and Bosnian Croats enabled the recapture of territory during 1995, and NATO air-strikes helped to end the Sarajevo siege. The signing of the Dayton Peace Accord in December 1995 brought relative, if rather tense, peace. It created a federal multi-ethnic Bosnian government with a rotating presidency and two separate administrations divided along ethnic and geographic lines into the Republic Srpska (Bosnian Serb) and the Bosniac/Croat Federation. Civilian aspects of the Accord are overseen by the Office of the UN High Representative. Military aspects of the Accord have been overseen by peacekeeping and stabilizing forces of the UN (1995), NATO (1995–2005) and the European Union (since 2005). The Hague war crimes tribunal has convicted a number of people for the atrocities committed between 1992 and 1995.

BOTSWANA

Official name	Republic of Botswana
Local name	Botswana
Former name	Bechuanaland (until 1966)
Area	582 096 sq km (24 689 sq mi)
Capital	Gaborone
Chief towns	Francistown, Lobatse, Selebi-Phikwe, Orapa, Jwaneng
Population	1 640 000 (2006e)
Nationality	Motswana (singular), Batswana (plural)
Languages	English, Setswana, Kalanga, Sekgalagadi
Ethnic groups	Tswana (Setswana) 79%, Kalanga 11%, Basarwa 3%, others 7%
Religions	Christianity 72%, traditional beliefs 6%, other 1%, none/unaffiliated 21%
Time zone	GMT +2
Currency	1 Pula (P) = 100 thebe
Telephone	+267
Internet	.bw
Country code	BWA

Location

A landlocked republic in southern Africa, bounded to the south by South Africa; to the west and north by Namibia; and to the east by Zimbabwe.

Physical description

The Kalahari Desert covers 84% of the land, at an average elevation of c.1100 m (3609 ft); most people live in the fertile east, bordered by the River Limpopo; the highest point is Mt Otse (1491 m/4892 ft); the terrain in the south and west progresses through savanna and dry scrubland to the aridity of the Kalahari Desert; to the north and north-west are the swamps of the Okavango Delta and deciduous forests.

Climate

Subtropical in the north, increasingly arid in the south and west, and more temperate in the east; rainfall in the north and east is low in summer (October–April) with an average annual measure of 450 mm; average maximum daily temperatures range between 23 and 32°C; annual rainfall is erratic in the Kalahari Desert, decreasing south and west to below 200 mm.

Economy

Relatively prosperous owing to mineral resources, chiefly diamonds (30% of GDP), copper, nickel (second-largest African producer), salt, soda ash, potash and coal; agriculture is mainly at subsistence level, except cattle-rearing (80% of the sector output; beef is a major export); diversifying into safari tourism and financial services.

Government

Governed by an executive President, a Cabinet and a unicameral National Assembly; a House of Chiefs acts as an advisory council on tribal matters and constitutional changes.

History

The area was visited by missionaries in the 19th century and came under British protection in 1885. The southern part became a British Crown Colony, then part of Cape Colony in 1895, while the northern part became the Bechuanaland Protectorate. In 1964 it achieved self-government, and in 1966 it gained independence and changed its name to Botswana. Although stable and relatively prosperous since independence, it faces serious demographic and social problems owing to the high level of HIV/AIDS infection, which the government has developed programmes to counter.

Botswana's Baskets

The women in Northern Botswana are traditionally highly skilled basket weavers, particularly in the villages of Etsha and Gumare. Baskets are crafted from Mokola Palm, which is dyed using roots, shrubs and fungus and then coiled and woven creating intricate geometric designs.

BRAZIL

Official name	Federative Republic of Brazil
Local name	Brasil; República Federativa do Brasil
Area	8 511 965 sq km (3 285 618 sq mi)
Capital	Brasília
Chief towns	São Paulo, Rio de Janeiro, Belo Horizonte, Recife, Salvador
Population	188 078 000 (2006e)
Nationality	Brazilian
Languages	Portuguese; Spanish and English are widely spoken
Ethnic groups	white 54%, mulatto 38%, black 6%, others 2%
Religions	Christianity 89% (RC 74% (nominal), Prot 15%), Spiritualism 1%, others 2%, none/unaffiliated 8%
Time zone	GMT −2/5
Currency	1 Real (R$) = 100 centavos
Telephone	+55
Internet	.br
Country code	BRA

Location

A republic in eastern and central South America, bounded to the north by French Guiana (a French département), Suriname, Guyana and Venezuela; to the north-west by Colombia; to the west by Peru, Bolivia and Paraguay; to the south-west by Argentina; to the south by Uruguay; and to the east by the Atlantic Ocean.

Physical description

Nearly 60% of the country is taken up by the low-lying Amazon basin in the north, drained by rivers that carry 20% of the Earth's running water; north of the Amazon are the Guiana Highlands, including the country's highest peak, Pico da Neblina (3014 m/9888 ft); south of the Amazon and occupying Brazil's centre is the Brazilian Plateau, with vegetation varying from thorny scrub forest to wooded savanna (campo cerrado); between the plateau and the east coast lie the Brazilian Highlands, rising to 2890 m (9482 ft) at Pico da Bandeira; on the Atlantic coast a thin strip of land, 100 km (62 mi) wide, contains 30% of the population; there are eight river systems, notably the Amazon in the north, the São Francisco in the centre, and the Paraguay, Paraná and Uruguay in the south; Brazil contains the world's biggest rainforest; where forest canopy has been cleared, soils are susceptible to erosion.

Climate

Almost entirely tropical; the equator passes through the northern region, and the Tropic of Capricorn through the south-eastern; in the Amazon basin the annual rainfall is 1500–2000 mm, with no dry season; the average midday temperatures are 27–32°C; there are more distinct wet and dry seasons on the Brazilian Plateau; the dry region in the north-east is susceptible to long droughts, with daily temperatures in the region of 21–36°C, and monthly rainfall as little as 3 mm in August, rising to 85 mm in March; on the narrow coastal strip, the climate is hot and tropical, with

BRAZILIAN CAPOEIRA

Capoeira, a distinctive fusion of dance and martial arts, has become a popular pastime all over the world. However, it has its roots in the dark days of the Atlantic slave trade.

The emergence of capoeira

From the 16th to the 19th centuries, traders of the Portuguese Empire shipped slaves into South America from western Africa, especially from countries such as Angola that were part of Portugal's African empire. Roughly 40 per cent of all African slaves were intended for the sugar plantations of northern Brazil. Displaced from their homeland, the slaves fought hard to retain their cultural traditions in the New World. Capoeira developed as a reaction to imprisonment and as a form of defence against the oppressors.

Capoeira was prohibited and banished from the senzalas (slave barracks). However, the banning of capoeira served only to relegate it to the status of a clandestine art. It also served to unite slaves from different parts of Africa in their common cause of rebellion. As a means of disguising their practice sessions, the slaves developed capoeira as a dance form complete with participatory clapping and musical accompaniment. Special rhythms, called *cavalaria*, were added to the music to warn the slaves that they were on the verge of being discovered; participants also adopted multiple *apelidos* (nicknames) to throw the authorities off their scent.

In 1888 Brazil became the final country to abolish slavery. Freed slaves moved to the cities and continued to practise capoeira, which swiftly became associated with criminal activity and was banned by the Brazilian authorities in 1890. Punishment was severe, including practitioners having the tendons on the backs of their feet cut, and the martial art went underground.

Modern-day capoeira

Today, the essence of capoeira is to marry martial art training, physical fitness and fluid dance movements to the accompaniment of clapping and the beats of musical instruments. Capoeira practitioners (*capoeiristas*) perform within a circle of spectators, the *roda*, who take turns playing instruments, singing, and sparring in pairs in the centre of the circle. The martial art itself is acrobatic and uses feints, sweeps, turns, leaps, kicks and head-butts. The action is led by a *mestre* (or master practitioner). Modern-day capoeira has developed two main styles, known as 'Angola' and 'regional'. The former, more traditional, form is slower and more flowing while the latter is more combat-orientated and often uses faster movements. Mestre Bimba (properly Manuel dos Reis Machado, 1900–74), the father of capoeira regional, opened the first legal capoeira school in Salvador, Bahia, Brazil, in 1932. Mestre Vicente Ferreira Pastinha (1889–1981), who was a central figure in the promotion of capoeira Angola, followed in 1942.

The music of capoeira

The songs performed talk of the history of the capoeira and can be written or improvised; call-and-response singing is another notable feature. Instruments include the *berimbau*, a stringed musical instrument shaped like an archer's bow with an attached gourd for resonance, the *pandeiros* (tambourines), a *reco-reco* (rasp), an *agogô* (double gong bell), *atabaque* (conga-like drum) and *caxixi* (rounded wicker baskets filled with beans or stones).

rainfall varying greatly north to south; the southern states lie outside the tropics, with a seasonal, temperate climate.

Economy

A diversified middle-income economy stabilized by recent reforms; one of the world's largest farming countries, especially in coffee (the world's largest exporter), cocoa and soya beans (the second-largest exporter), maize, rice, wheat, sugar, citrus fruit and beef; exploits its rich natural resources, including iron ore (reserves possibly the world's largest), manganese, bauxite, beryllium, chrome, nickel, gold, gemstones; oil and natural gas; steel, chemicals, petrochemicals, food processing, wood products, footwear, textiles, motor and aerospace vehicles, financial services, electronics, tourism; large investments in hydroelectric power, alcohol fuel, coal and nuclear power; timber reserves are the third largest in the world but expansion of agriculture and forestry hastens continuing destruction of the Amazon rainforest, to worldwide concern; a road network is being extended through the rainforest.

Government

A federal republic governed by an executive President, a Cabinet and a bicameral National Congress, consisting of the Federal Senate and the Chamber of Deputies. Each of the 26 states has a governor and legislative assembly.

History

The territory was claimed for the Portuguese after a fortuitous landfall by Pedro Cabral in 1500, and the first settlement was at Salvador da Bahia. There were 13 feudal grants, which were replaced in 1572 by a viceroyalty. The country was divided into north and south, with capitals at Salvador and Rio de Janeiro. During the Napoleonic Wars, the Portuguese court transferred to Brazil. Brazilian independence was declared in 1822, and a monarchy was established. In 1889 there was a coup, which was followed in 1891 by the declaration of a republic. Large numbers of European immigrants arrived in the early 20th century. A revolution, headed by Getúlio Vargas, established a dictatorship in 1930–45, but a liberal republic was restored in 1946. Another coup in 1964 led to a military-backed presidential regime, and a military junta was established in 1969. Under President Figueiredo (1979–85) the military government began a process of liberalization, allowing the return of political exiles to stand for state and federal offices, and in 1985 elections restored civilian government. Subsequent governments and leaders have faced a particularly difficult economic situation, but plans to develop the Amazon basin have attracted controversy because of the threat posed to environmentally important rainforest.

BRUNEI DARUSSALAM

Official name	State of Brunei, Abode of Peace
Local name	Brunei; Negara Brunei Darussalam
Area	5765 sq km (2225 sq mi)
Capital	Bandar Seri Begawan
Chief towns	Kuala Belait, Seria, Bangar
Population	379 000 (2006e)
Nationality	Bruneian
Languages	Malay; English and Chinese are widely spoken
Ethnic groups	Malay 67%, Chinese 15%, indigenous 6%, others 12%
Religions	Islam 67%, Buddhism 13%, Christianity 10%, traditional beliefs and others 10%
Time zone	GMT +8
Currency	1 Brunei Dollar (B$) = 100 sen
Telephone	+673
Internet	.bn
Country code	BRN

Location

A state on the north-west coast of Borneo, south-eastern Asia, bounded by the South China Sea in the north-west, and on all other sides by Malaysia's Sarawak state.

Physical description

The country is divided in two by the Limbang River valley in Sarawak (Malaysia); a swampy coastal plain rises through foothills to a mountainous region on the Malaysian border; the highest point is Bukit Pagon (1850 m/6098 ft); equatorial rainforest covers 75% of the land area.

Climate

Tropical climate, with high temperatures and humidity, and no marked seasons; average daily temperature ranges between 24 and 30°C; average annual rainfall is 2540 mm on the coast, doubling in the interior.

Economy

Largely dependent on oil and gas (nearly 50% of GDP) and income from overseas investments; now diversifying into financial services and tourism; main crops are rice, vegetables, and fruit; also poultry farming.

Government

A hereditary monarchy; governed by the Sultan, advised by a Privy Council, a Council of Cabinet Ministers and a Religious Council. The unicameral Legislative Council was reconvened in 2004 (for the first time in 20 years) and passed constitutional changes enlarging it and making it partially elected in future.

History

Formerly a powerful Muslim sultanate, it came under British protection in 1888, achieved internal self-government in 1971, and gained independence in 1984. In 2004 the Sultan reopened the Legislative Council, which had been disbanded 20 years earlier.

BULGARIA

Official name	Republic of Bulgaria
Local name	Bălgarija; Republika Bălgarija
Former name	People's Republic of Bulgaria (1946–90)
Area	110 912 sq km (42 812 sq mi)
Capital	Sofia, Sofija
Chief towns	Plovdiv, Varna, Ruse, Burgas, Stara Zagora, Pleven
Population	7 385 000 (2006e)
Nationality	Bulgarian
Languages	Bulgarian; Turkish and Roma are also spoken
Ethnic groups	Bulgarian 84%, Turkish 9%, Roma 5%, others 2%
Religions	Christianity 84% (Orthodox 83%, other 1%), Islam 12%, others 4%
Time zone	GMT +2
Currency	1 Lev (Lv) = 100 stotinki
Telephone	+359
Internet	.bg
Country code	BGR

Location

A republic in the east of the Balkan peninsula, south-eastern Europe, bounded to the north by Romania; to the west by Serbia and Macedonia; to the south-east by Turkey; to the south by Greece; and to the east by the Black Sea.

Physical description

The centre is traversed west to east by the Balkan Mountains, rising to over 2000 m (6562 ft); the Rhodope Mountains in the south-west rise to nearly 3000 m (9842 ft); the highest point is Musala (2925 m/9596 ft); the lowland plains are in the basins of the main rivers, the Danube in the north and the Maritsa in the south-east; other rivers are the Iskur, Yantra and Struma.

Climate

Largely continental, with hot summers and cold winters, but to the south the climate is increasingly Mediterranean; winters are slightly warmer on the Black Sea coast.

Economy

Completing transition to industrialized market economy; industries include power generation (including nuclear power), machine building, metal working, oil refining and petrochemicals, food processing, chemicals, construction materials, metals, textiles and garments; fertile agricultural land produces fruit, vegetables, tobacco, grapes for wine-making, wheat, barley, sunflower seeds and livestock; tourism is expanding.

Government
Governed by a President, a Prime Minister and Cabinet, and a unicameral National Assembly.

History
In the 7th century Bulgars crossed the Danube and gradually merged in with the Slavonic population and established the Kingdom of Bulgaria, which was continually at war with the Byzantine Empire until it was destroyed by the Turks in the 14th century. It was under Turkish rule until 1878, when a principality was created, but full independence was only achieved in 1908, when it became a kingdom. It was aligned with Germany in both world wars and in 1944 was occupied by the Union of Soviet Socialist Republics (USSR). The monarchy was abolished in 1946 and it was proclaimed a Socialist People's Republic. In the early 1990s a multiparty government introduced political and economic reforms, which initially caused some difficulties. Political stability was achieved in the late 1990s, and Bulgaria made sufficient progress to join the European Union in 2007.

BURKINA FASO

Official name	Burkina Faso
Local name	Burkina Faso
Former name	Upper Volta (until 1984)
Area	274 540 sq km (105 972 sq mi)
Capital	Ouagadougou
Chief towns	Bobo-Dioulasso, Koudougou, Ouahigouya, Tenkodogo
Population	13 903 000 (2006e)
Nationality	Burkinabé
Languages	French; many local languages are also spoken
Ethnic groups	Mossi 45%, Mande 10%, Fulani 9%, Bobo 7%, others 29%
Religions	Islam 50%, traditional beliefs 40%, Christianity 10% (mainly RC)
Time zone	GMT
Currency	1 CFA Franc (CFAFr) = 100 centimes
Telephone	+226
Internet	.bf
Country code	BFA

Location
A landlocked republic in west Africa, bounded to the north and west by Mali; to the east by Niger; to the south-east by Benin; to the south by Togo and Ghana; and to the south-west by Côte d'Ivoire.

Physical description

A low-lying plateau, falling away to the south; highest point is Tena Kourou 749 m/2457 ft); many rivers (tributaries of the Volta or Niger) are unnavigable in the dry season; wooded savannas in the south; semi-desert in the north.

Climate

Tropical climate, with average temperature of 27°C in the dry season (December–May); rainy season (June–October), with violent storms (August); the *harmattan* wind blows from the north-east (December–March); rainfall decreases from south to north.

Economy

Very poor country, dependent on foreign aid; agriculture, mostly at subsistence level and subject to drought; main cash crops are cotton (world's third-largest producer) and livestock; industries include gold mining (third-largest export), cotton processing, and agricultural products and light manufacturing (soap, cigarettes, textiles).

Government

Governed by a President, a Prime Minister and Council of Ministers, and a unicameral National Assembly.

History

The area was part of the Mossi Empire in the 18th and 19th centuries before becoming a French protectorate in 1898. At first it was part of French Sudan (now Mali), then in 1919 it was made into Upper Volta. This was abolished in 1932, with most land joined to Côte d'Ivoire. In 1947 its original borders were reconstituted, and in 1958 it gained autonomy within the French community, followed by independence as Upper Volta in 1960. It was renamed Burkina Faso in 1984. In the three decades following independence there were several military coups, the last by Blaise Compaoré in 1987; military rule ended in 1991 with multiparty elections, which were won by Compaoré and the Popular Front.

Land of Honest Men

Previously known as Upper Volta, after the upper reaches of the River Volta, Burkina Faso was renamed in 1984 by the politician Thomas Sankara (1950–87). The new name came from the local languages and means 'Land of Honest Men' or 'Land of Upright Men'.

BURUNDI

Official name	Republic of Burundi
Local name	Burundi; République du Burundi (French), Republika y'UBurundi (Kirundi)
Former name	Urundi, as part of Ruanda-Urundi (with Rwanda, until 1962), Kingdom of Burundi (1962–6)
Area	27 834 sq km (10 744 sq mi)
Capital	Bujumbura
Chief towns	Bubanza, Ngozi, Muyinga, Muramvya, Gitega, Bururi, Rutana
Population	8 090 000 (2006e)
Nationality	Burundian
Languages	French, Kirundi
Ethnic groups	Hutu 85%, Tutsi 14%, others 1%
Religions	Christianity 67% (RC 62%, Prot 5%), traditional beliefs 23%, Islam 10%
Time zone	GMT +2
Currency	1 Burundi Franc (BuFr, FBu) = 100 centimes
Telephone	+257
Internet	.bi
Country code	BDI

Location

A small landlocked republic in central Africa, bounded to the north by Rwanda; to the east and south by Tanzania; to the south-west by Lake Tanganyika; and to the west by the Democratic Republic of the Congo.

Physical description

Mostly a plateau with an average height of c.1500 m (4 921 ft), lying across the Nile–Congo watershed and sloping eastwards towards Tanzania; bounded to the west by Lake Tanganyika and to the north-west by the narrow River Ruizi plain; the River Akanyaru forms the northern border; the highest point is at Mount Heha (2670 m/8760 ft).

Climate

Equatorial climate, varying with altitude and season; moderately wet, except during the dry season (June–September); the average annual rainfall at Bujumbura is 850 mm.

Economy

A very poor country, dependent on foreign aid; the economic mainstay is agriculture, mostly subsistence level but with coffee, tea, sugar, cotton and hides the main cash crops; small-scale industry includes light manufacturing, food processing, assembly of imported components and public sector construction; reserves of oil, nickel, copper and other resources not exploited.

Government

Governed by an executive President, a Council of Ministers and a bicameral Parliament, consisting of a National Assembly and a Senate. The 2005 constitution specifies the proportions of Hutu and Tutsi and of women members in each chamber and in the Council of Ministers.

History

From the 16th century the country was ruled by Tutsi kings who dominated a Hutu population. Germany annexed the area in 1890, and included it in German East Africa. After World War I it became a League of Nations mandated territory, being administered by the Belgians from 1919. In 1946 it joined with Rwanda to become the UN Trust Territory of Ruanda–Urundi, but broke this union on gaining independence in 1962; it became a republic in 1966. Civil war broke out in 1972 and there were military coups in 1976 and 1987. A multiparty constitution was adopted in 1992 and the following year saw the end of Tutsi dominance with the election of a Hutu head of state and a Hutu majority in the National Assembly. Soon after the election, however, the Tutsi-dominated army staged a coup in which the president was killed, and his successor was killed with the Rwandan president when their plane was shot down. These deaths sparked off fierce ethnic conflict and led to the loss of hundreds of thousands of lives during the ensuing decade. In 1996 the incumbent Hutu president was ousted by another coup and a multi-ethnic government was formed. Talks from 1999 resulted in 2001 in the inauguration of a transitional power-sharing government, although a peace agreement was not signed until 2003; rebel forces began to demobilize in 2004. Presidential and legislative elections were held in 2005.

CAMBODIA

Official name	Kingdom of Cambodia
Local name	Kâmpuchéa; Preăh Réaché 'Anachâkr Kâmpuchéa
Former name	Formerly part of Indochina (until 1953), Kingdom of Cambodia (1953–70), Khmer Republic (1970–6), Democratic Kampuchea (1976–9), People's Republic of Kampuchea (1979–89), State of Cambodia (1989–93)
Area	181 035 sq km (69 880 sq mi)
Capital	Phnom Penh; Phnum Pénh
Chief towns	Battambang, Kâmpŏng Som, Kâmpŏng Chhnăng
Population	13 881 000 (2006e)
Nationality	Cambodian
Languages	Khmer; French and English are also widely spoken
Ethnic groups	Khmer 90%, Vietnamese 5%, Chinese 1%, others 4%
Religions	Buddhism 95%, Islam 2%, others 3%
Time zone	GMT +7
Currency	1 Riel (CRI) = 100 sen
Telephone	+855
Internet	.kh
Country code	KHM

Location

A republic in south-east Asia, bounded to the north-west by Thailand; to the north by Laos; to the east by Vietnam; and to the south and south-west by the Gulf of Thailand.

Physical description

Occupies a plain surrounding the Tonlé Sap (lake), a freshwater depression on the Cambodian Plain, which is crossed by the flood plain of the Mekong River; the highest land lies in the south-west, where the Cardamom Mountains run for 160 km (100 mi) across the Thailand border, rising to 1813 m (5948 ft) at Phnom Aôral.

Climate

Tropical monsoon climate, with a wet season in May–November; heavy rainfall in the south-western mountains; high temperatures in the lowland region throughout the year; the average monthly rainfall at Phnom Penh is 257 mm in October, 7 mm in January.

Economy

Very poor country, dependent on foreign aid; agriculture is the main activity, largely at subsistence level; main crops are rice, rubber, livestock, maize, tobacco and vegetables; a growing industrial sector includes fishing, forestry, mining (gemstones), construction, manufacturing (garments, footwear), tourism; offshore oil and gas deposits have been discovered.

Government

A hereditary constitutional monarchy with a King as head of state; governed by a Prime Minister and government ministers, and a bicameral legislature, comprising the National Assembly and a Senate.

History

Originally part of the Kingdom of Funan, it was taken over by the Khmers in the 6th century. From the 15th century it was in dispute with the Vietnamese and the Thais. In 1863 it was established as a French protectorate, and it became part of Indochina in 1887. It gained independence from France in 1953, with Prince Sihanouk as prime minister. From the late 1960s there was growing insurgency led by the Khmer Rouge, a communist guerrilla force, and in 1970 the monarchy was overthrown in a right-wing coup and the country was renamed the Khmer Republic. Fighting throughout the country between communist and nationalist factions also involved troops from North and South Vietnam and the USA. In 1975 Phnom Penh surrendered to the Khmer Rouge, and the following year the republic of Democratic Kampuchea was proclaimed. An attempt to reform the economy on co-operative lines and the introduction of an extreme and brutal regime by Pol Pot in 1975–8 caused the deaths of an estimated 2.5 million people. There was further fighting in 1977–8, and Phnom Penh was captured by the Vietnamese in 1979, causing the Khmer Rouge to flee. The Vietnamese immediately established a government in Cambodia led by Heng Samrin, but fighting with the Khmer Rouge guerrillas and Sihanouk's nationalist forces did not stop until the Vietnamese withdrawal in 1987–9. In 1983 an anti-Vietnamese government-in-exile (the Coalition Government of Democratic Kampuchea) was recognized by the UN. In 1989 the name of Cambodia was restored. Under a UN peace plan agreed in 1991 and after a period of transitional government under the UN, in 1993 a new constitution was adopted and multiparty elections took place. In the new democratic monarchy, Prince Sihanouk became king, his son Prince Norodom Ranariddh was appointed prime minister, and Hun Sen, a former leader of the Vietnamese-backed government, became second prime minister. The Khmer Rouge continued guerrilla warfare until 1996, when internal divisions caused it to weaken; Pol Pot died in 1998 and the remaining Khmer Rouge surrendered in 1999. Meanwhile the ruling coalition suffered divisions; in 1997 Hun Sen and his armed supporters ousted Prince Ranariddh, but in the 1998 election Hun Sen's party failed to win a large enough majority to form a government and the coalition with the royalist party has continued since. King Sihanouk abdicated in 2004 in favour of his son Norodom Sihamoni.

CAMEROON

Official name	Republic of Cameroon
Local name	Cameroun; République du Cameroun
Former name	Kamerun (until 1919), French Cameroon (until 1960) and British Cameroon (until 1961, when southern part joined new Republic of Cameroon, northern part joined Nigeria), Federal Republic of Cameroon (1961–72), United Republic of Cameroon (1972–84)
Area	475 439 sq km (183 519 sq mi)
Capital	Yaoundé
Chief town	Douala
Population	17 341 000 (2006e)
Nationality	Cameroonian
Languages	French, English; many local languages are also spoken
Ethnic groups	Fang 21%, Bamileke and Bamum 19%, Douala, Luanda and Bassa 15%, Fulani 10%, others 35%
Religions	Christianity 40%, traditional beliefs 40%, Islam 20%
Time zone	GMT +1
Currency	1 CFA Franc (CFAFr) = 100 centimes
Telephone	+237
Internet	.cm
Country code	CMR

Location

A republic in west Africa, bounded to the south-west by Equatorial Guinea; to the south by Gabon; to the south-east by Congo; to the east by the Central African Republic; to the north-east by Chad; and to the north-west by Nigeria.

Physical description

Equatorial rainforest on the low coastal plain rising to a central plateau of over 1300 m (4265 ft); the western region is forested and mountainous, rising to 4070 m 13 352 ft) at Mount Cameroon, an active volcano and the highest peak in west Africa; the north-central land rises towards the Massif d'Adamaoua; low savanna and semi-desert plains in the north towards Lake Chad; rivers flowing from the central plateau to the Gulf of Guinea include the River Sanaga.

Climate

The north has a wet season in April–September, with the remainder of the year being dry; annual rainfall in the north is 1000–1750 mm; the equatorial south experiences rain throughout the year, with two wet seasons and two dry seasons; Yaoundé, in the south, has an average annual rainfall of 4030 mm and maximum daily temperatures ranging between 27 and 30°C; a small part of Mount Cameroon receives over 10 000 mm of rain annually.

Economy

Poor country, dependent on foreign aid; main industries based on natural resources, including oil and petroleum products (40% of export earnings), timber, aluminium and agricultural products; agriculture employs c.70% of the workforce; cash crops are cocoa (world's fifth-largest producer), coffee, cotton and rubber; tourism is growing, especially to national parks and reserves.

Government

Governed by a President, a Prime Minister and government ministers, and a unicameral National Assembly; a 1996 constitutional amendment providing for a second legislative chamber has not been implemented.

History

The country was first explored by the Portuguese navigator Fernando Po, and later by traders from Spain, the Netherlands and Britain. It became a German protectorate, Kamerun, in 1884, and after World War I was divided into French and British Cameroon in 1919, which was confirmed by the League of Nations mandate in 1922. The UN turned mandates into trusteeships in 1946. French Cameroon became independent as the Republic of Cameroon in 1960, while the northern sector of British Cameroon voted to become part of Nigeria, and the southern sector part of Cameroon; the Federal Republic of Cameroon was established, with separate parliaments, in 1961. The federal system was abolished in 1972, and the country's name was changed to the United Republic of Cameroon; the word 'United' was dropped from the name after a constitutional amendment in 1984. From 1972 to 1992 it was ruled by one party, the Cameroon People's Democratic Movement, with Paul Biya as president from 1982. Political pluralism was restored in 1992, and in multiparty elections Biya was re-elected president and the ruling party was returned to power. Both have continued to hold power since, in elections whose fairness has been disputed by the opposition. Cameroon joined the Commonwealth of Nations in 1995, the first country to do so that has never been fully under British rule at any point in its history.

CANADA

Official name	Canada
Local name	Canada
Area	9 970 610 sq km (3 848 655 sq mi)
Capital	Ottawa
Chief towns	Calgary, Edmonton, Montréal, Québec, Toronto, Vancouver, Victoria, Winnipeg
Population	33 099 000 (2006e)
Nationality	Canadian
Languages	English, French
Ethnic groups	British origin 28%, mixed 26%, French origin 23%, other European 15%, Amerindian 2%, others 6%
Religions	Christianity 70% (RC 43%, Prot 23%, other 4%), Islam 2%, others/unaffiliated 12%, none 16%
Time zone	GMT −3.5/8
Currency	1 Canadian Dollar (C$, Can$) = 100 cents
Telephone	+1
Internet	.ca
Country code	CAN

Location

An independent country in North America, bounded to the south by the United States of America; to the west by the Pacific Ocean; to the north-west by Alaska; to the north by the Arctic Ocean and Baffin Bay; to the north-east by the Davis Strait; and to the east by the Labrador Sea and the Atlantic Ocean.

Physical description

The main topographical divisions are: the mountainous Appalachian–Acadian region (Nova Scotia, New Brunswick); the Canadian Shield, which comprises more than half the country, in the north and east; the St Lawrence–Great Lakes lowlands (south Québec, Ontario); the interior plains (prairies) south and west of the Shield; the western mountains, including the Rocky, Cassiar, Mackenzie and Coast ranges; and the Arctic archipelago (Nunavut); the Coast Mountains flank a rugged, heavily indented Pacific coastline, rising to 5950 m (19 520 ft) at Mount Logan, the highest peak in Canada; the Arctic coast is permanently ice-bound or obstructed by ice floes, except for Hudson Bay (frozen for c.9 months each year); major rivers include the Yukon and Mackenzie in the west, North Saskatchewan, South Saskatchewan, Saskatchewan and Athabasca in the centre, and Ottawa and St Lawrence in the east; the Great Lakes occupy the south-east of Ontario; 44% of land area is forested.

Climate

Varies, from Arctic and sub-Arctic in the north to temperate in the south; cold air from the Arctic sweeps south and east in winter and spring; mild winters and warm summers on the west coast and some inland valleys of British Columbia; winter temperatures on the Atlantic shores are warmer than those of the interior, but summer temperatures are lower; much of the southern interior has warm summers and long, cold winters; tornadoes occur in the southern interior in May–September.

Economy

Highly developed industrialized and diversified market economy, with services (finance, real estate, tourism) the largest sector; abundant natural resources are the basis of major industries, including timber, pulp and newsprint (world's largest exporter), minerals, especially uranium (world's largest producer), diamonds (world's third-largest producer), asbestos, zinc, silver, nickel, potash, gypsum, molybdenum, sulphur, oil (especially Alberta), natural gas and fisheries; manufacturing industries produce motor vehicles and parts, iron and steel, industrial machinery, aircraft and telecommunications equipment, chemicals and plastics; leading agricultural producer, particularly of wheat (world's second-largest exporter), barley, oilseed, fruit, vegetables and dairy products.

Government

Governed by a Governor-General (representing the British monarch, who is head of state), a Prime Minister and Cabinet, and a bicameral federal Parliament, comprising a Senate and a House of Commons. Each of the ten provinces and three territories has its own Lieutenant-Governor (Commissioner in the territories), executive council and legislative assembly.

History

There is evidence of Viking settlement in around 1000. The country was visited by John Cabot in 1497, and in 1528 St John's, Newfoundland, was established as the shore base for the English fisheries. The Gulf of St Lawrence was explored for France by Jacques Cartier in 1534; Newfoundland was claimed for England in 1583, making it England's first overseas colony. Samuel de Champlain founded the city of Quebec in 1608. The Hudson's Bay Company was founded in 1670, and in the late 17th century there was conflict between the British and the colonists of New France. Britain gained large areas from the 1713 Treaty of Utrecht. After the Seven Years' War, during which General James Wolfe captured Quebec (1759), the Treaty of Paris gave Britain almost all of France's possessions in North America. The province of Quebec was created in 1774, and migration of loyalists from the USA after the American Revolution led to the division of Quebec into Upper and Lower Canada, reunited as Canada in 1841. The Dominion of Canada was created in 1867 by a confederation of Quebec, Ontario, Nova Scotia and New Brunswick. Rupert's Land and Northwest Territories were bought from the Hudson's Bay Company in 1869–70, and were later joined by Manitoba (1870), British Columbia (1871, after promise of a transcontinental railroad), Prince Edward Island (1873), Yukon (1898, following the Klondike Gold Rush), Alberta and Saskatchewan (1905) and Newfoundland (1949). In 1982 the Canada Act gave Canada full responsibility for its constitution. There was recurring political tension in the latter part of the 20th century arising from the French-Canadian separatist movement in Quebec, and from the desire for autonomy of the Native American and Inuit populations; a 1992 referendum approved the creation of the vast autonomous territory of Nunavut for the Inuit people, and this was implemented in 1999. Although independence for Quebec was rejected in a 1995 referendum in the province, in 2006 the parliament agreed that the Quebecois should be considered a 'nation' within Canada.

Provinces of Canada

Name	Population (2006e)[1]	Area	Capital
Alberta (AB)	3375800	661848 sq km (255472 sq mi)	Edmonton
British Columbia (BC)	4310500	944735 sq km (364667 sq mi)	Victoria
Manitoba (MB)	1177800	647797 sq km (250050 sq mi)	Winnipeg
New Brunswick (NB)	749200	72908 sq km (28142 sq mi)	Fredericton
Newfoundland and Labrador (NL)	509700	405212 sq km (156412 sq mi)	St John's
Northwest Territories (NT)	41900	1346106 sq km (519597 sq mi)	Yellowknife
Nova Scotia (NS)	934400	55284 sq km (21340 sq mi)	Halifax
Nunavut (NU)	30800	2093190 sq km (807971 sq mi)	Iqaluit
Ontario (ON)	12687000	1076395 sq km (415488 sq mi)	Toronto
Prince Edward Island (PE)	138500	5660 sq km (2185 sq mi)	Charlottetown
Québec (QC)	7651500	1542056 sq km (595234 sq mi)	Québec City
Saskatchewan (SK)	985400	651036 sq km (251300 sq mi)	Regina
Yukon Territory (YT)	31200	482443 sq km (186223 sq mi)	Whitehorse

[1] Source: Statistics Canada

CAPE VERDE

Official name	Republic of Cape Verde
Local name	Cabo Verde; República de Cabo Verde
Area	4033 sq km (1557 sq mi)
Capital	Praia
Chief town	Mindelo
Population	421 700 (2006e)
Nationality	Cape Verdean
Languages	Portuguese; Crioulo, a Creole language blending Portuguese and west African words, is widely spoken
Ethnic groups	Mestizo 71%, African 28%, European 1%
Religions	Christianity 98% (RC), others 1%, none/unaffiliated 1%
Time zone	GMT −1
Currency	1 Escudo Caboverdiano (CVEsc) = 100 centavos
Telephone	+238
Internet	.cv
Country code	CPV

Location
An island group in the Atlantic Ocean, lying off the west coast of Africa.

Physical description
The islands are of volcanic origin and are mostly mountainous; the highest peak is Pico do Cano at 2829 m (9281 ft), an active volcano on Fogo Island; coastal plains are semi-desert; savanna or thin forest lies on the mountains; fine, sandy beaches are found on most islands.

Climate
Located at the northern limit of the tropical rain belt; low and unreliable rainfall mainly in August–September; cooler and damper in the uplands; severe drought can occur; the tropical heat is subject to only a small temperature range during the year.

Economy
Poor country, dependent on foreign aid and remittances from expatriate workers; recent growth was based on service sector (tourism, shipping, transport); industry includes food processing, beverages, garments, footwear, fishing and fish processing, salt mining; agriculture constrained by aridity and drought, causing periodic food shortages; irrigated land produces bananas, sweet potatoes, sugar cane, coffee and peanuts.

Government
Governed by a President, a Prime Minister and Council of Ministers, and a unicameral National Assembly.

History

The islands were colonized by the Portuguese in the 15th century and used as a penal colony. Administered with Portuguese Guinea until 1879, the group became an overseas province of Portugal in 1951. It gained independence in 1975 after a campaign by the African Party for the Independence of Cape Verde and Guinea-Bissau (PAICV), which remained the only legal party (dropping Guinea-Bissau from its name in 1980) until multiparty elections took place in 1991. That year the new Movement for Democracy came to power. The PAICV returned to power in the 2001 elections.

CENTRAL AFRICAN REPUBLIC

Official name	Central African Republic (CAR)
Local name	République Centrafricaine (French), Ködörösêse tî Bêafrîka (Sango)
Former name	Ubangi Shari (until 1958), Central African Republic (1958–76), Central African Empire (1976–9)
Area	626 780 sq km (241 937 sq mi)
Capital	Bangui
Chief towns	Berbérati, Bouar, Bossangoa
Population	4 303 000 (2006e)
Nationality	Central African
Languages	French; Sango is also widely spoken
Ethnic groups	Baya 33%, Banda 27%, Mandjia 13%, Sara 10%, Mboum 7%, others 10%
Religions	Christianity 50% (Prot 25%, RC 25%), traditional beliefs 35%, Islam 15%
Time zone	GMT +1
Currency	1 CFA Franc (CFAFr) = 100 centimes
Telephone	+236
Internet	.cf
Country code	CAF

Location

A republic in central Africa, bounded to the north by Chad; to the north-east by Sudan; to the south by the Democratic Republic of the Congo and Congo; and to the west by Cameroon.

Physical description

Occupies a plateau forming the watershed between the Chad and Congo river basins; most northern rivers drain towards Lake Chad, and southbound rivers flow towards the River Ubangi; the highest ground is in the north-east (Massif des Bongos) and north-west; highest point is Mont Ngaoui (1420 m/4659 ft).

Climate

Tropical, with a rainy season in the north between May and September; average annual rainfall is between 875 and 1000 mm; there is a more equatorial climate in the south.

Economy

Very poor country, dependent on foreign aid; rich natural resources, much unexploited, although diamond-mining and forestry are major industries; economic mainstay is agriculture, accounting for more than 50% of GDP; c.85% of the workforce is engaged in subsistence agriculture; cash crops are cotton, coffee and tobacco.

Government

Governed by a President, a Prime Minister and government minister, and a unicameral National Assembly.

History

For a time it was part of French Equatorial Africa (known as Ubangi Shari). It became an autonomous republic within the French community in 1958 and gained independence in 1960 with David Dacko as president. He was overthrown in 1966 in a coup led by Colonel Bokassa, who established a monarchy known as the Central African Empire in 1976 with himself as emperor. Bokassa was deposed and fled in 1979 (he returned in 1986 for trial and was found guilty of murder and other crimes in 1987). The country reverted to a republic and David Dacko became president until he was ousted by a military coup in 1981. Civilian rule returned in 1986, and in 1992 the constitution was amended to allow for opposition parties and to reduce the powers of the president. Elections the following year brought in a coalition government. The political situation remained unstable, with several coup attempts in recent years, culminating in a successful coup in 2003 which installed General François Bozize as president. A new constitution was approved in 2004 and in 2005 Bozize was elected president.

Heart of Africa

In the Sango language, the Central African Republic is known as *Beafrika*, which means 'Heart of Africa'.

CHAD

Official name	Republic of Chad
Local name	Tchad; République du Tchad
Area	1 284 640 sq km (495 871 sq mi)
Capital	N'Djamena; Ndjamena
Chief towns	Moundou, Sarh, Abéché
Population	9 944 000 (2006e)
Nationality	Chadian
Languages	French, Arabic; many local languages are also spoken of which the most widely used is Sara
Ethnic groups	Arab 26%, Sara 25%, Teda 18%, others 31%
Religions	Islam 51%, Christianity 35%, traditional beliefs 7%, others 7%
Time zone	GMT +1
Currency	1 CFA Franc (CFAFr) = 100 centimes
Telephone	+235
Internet	.td
Country code	TCD

Location

A landlocked republic in north central Africa, bounded to the north by Libya; to the east by Sudan; to the south by the Central African Republic; and to the west by Cameroon, Nigeria and Niger.

Physical description

A mostly arid, semi-desert plateau at the edge of the Sahara Desert with an average altitude of 200–500 m (656–1640 ft); isolated massifs along the eastern border with Sudan rise to 1500 m (4921 ft); the Tibesti Mountains in the north rise to 3415 m (11 204 ft) at Emi Koussi; vegetation is generally desert scrub or steppe; the Logone and Chari rivers drain from the southern hills into Lake Chad; most people live in the fertile south.

Climate

The south is tropical, with moderate rainfall in May–October, but dry for the rest of the year; the hot and arid north is almost rainless; the central plain is hot and dry, with a brief rainy season in June–September.

Economy

Poor country, formerly dependent on international aid and agriculture but starting to experience an oil boom since fields in the Doba basin began production in 2003; subsistence agriculture, herding and fishing employ 80% of the workforce; main cash crops are cotton and livestock; salt is mined around Lake Chad.

Government

Governed by a President, a Prime Minister and Cabinet, and a unicameral National Assembly.

History

Chad was part of French Equatorial Africa in the 19th century, became a French colony in 1920, and gained independence in 1960. Since independence it has been politically unstable, arising from tension between the Muslim Arab north and the Christian and animist African south, different factions attracting support from Libya and France. After a number of coups in the 1960s and 1970s, factional fighting led to civil war until 1987, when Libya was forced to withdraw. In 1990 another Libyan-backed coup brought to power Idriss Déby. Under Déby, there was gradual democratization and a new constitution was introduced in 1996. A rebellion by the Movement for Democracy and Justice in Chad led to civil war in 1998 and, despite several peace agreements, violence continues; by late 2006 Déby's regime was looking vulnerable. Chad has also experienced an influx of thousands of Sudanese refugees from Darfur since early 2004, and its forces have clashed with Sudanese militia on the border.

CHILE

Official name	Republic of Chile
Local name	Chile; República de Chile
Area	756 626 sq km (292 058 sq mi)
Capital	Santiago
Chief towns	Valparaíso, Concepción, Talcahuano, Antofagasta, Viña del Mar
Population	16 134 000 (2006e)
Nationality	Chilean
Language	Spanish
Ethnic groups	Mestizo 95%, Amerindian 3%, others 2%
Religions	Christianity 99% (RC 89%, Prot 10%), others 1%
Time zone	GMT −4
Currency	1 Chilean Peso (Ch$) = 100 centavos
Telephone	+56
Internet	.cl
Country code	CHL

Location

A republic in south-western South America, bounded to the west by the Pacific Ocean; to the east by Argentina; to the north-east by Bolivia; and to the north-west by Peru.

Physical description

A long narrow country lying between the Andes and the South Pacific Ocean; highest point is Ojos del Salado (6910 m/22 660 ft); the Andes rise in the north to 6732 m (22 057 ft) at Llullaillaco, declining in height in the centre and south; Chile extends from the arid Atacama Desert in the north through a fertile central valley, 40–60 km (25–40 mi) wide at 1200 m (3937 ft) in altitude, lying between the Andes and the coastal range, to the heavily indented coastline, sea channels, ice-fields and glaciers of Chilean Patagonia.

Climate

Generally temperate but highly varied climate (spans 37° of latitude); extreme aridity in the north desert (the world's driest desert); a Mediterranean climate with warm, wet winters and dry summers in the central zone; and cool, wet and windy in the far south; the average temperature at Valparaíso on the coast varies from below 12°C in July to nearly 18°C in January, with an average annual rainfall of 505 mm; at Santiago (high altitude), the rainfall is below 375 mm; at Antofagasta, in the north, it is just over 12 mm.

Economy

Emerging market economy based on its natural resources and agriculture; mining produces copper (40% of exports; Chile is world's largest producer), gold, iron ore, nitrates (world's only commercial producer of nitrate of soda), molybdenum, iron, silver; oil and gas production is declining; other major industries are forestry and wood products, fishing and fish products, agriculture (fruit, vegetables, cereals, meat, wool) and wine-making.

Government

Governed by an executive President, a Cabinet and a bicameral National Congress, comprising a Chamber of Deputies and a Senate.

History

Originally occupied by South American Indians, the arrival of the Spanish in the 16th century made Chile part of the Viceroyalty of Peru. In 1810 it declared its independence from Spain, which resulted in war until the Spanish were defeated in 1818. Border disputes with Bolivia, Peru and Argentina brought a Chilean victory in the War of the Pacific (1879–84). In the late 1920s economic unrest led to a military dictatorship until 1931. The Marxist coalition government of President Allende was ousted in 1973 and replaced by a military junta led by General Pinochet, who banned all political activity; this resulted in considerable political opposition, both at home and abroad. A constitution providing for an eventual return to democracy came into effect in 1981, and after 1988 there were limited political reforms. Free elections were held in late 1989, and in 1990 the National Congress was restored and Pinochet's rule ended. Various attempts were made to bring Pinochet to trial for human rights atrocities committed during his time in office, but none had been successful by the time of his death in 2006. Since the return to democracy, the military's influence on government has been reduced and the country has been relatively stable.

Navel of the World

Rapa Nui (or Easter Island) is an island belonging to Chile. Its earliest settlers named it 'Te Pito O Te Henua' meaning 'Navel of the World', possibly referring to its extreme isolation – at over 2,000 miles from the South American mainland and 2,000 miles from Tahiti, it is considered one of the most secluded places in the world.

CHINA

Official name	People's Republic of China (PRC)
Local name	Zhong Guo; Zhonghua Renmin Gongheguo
Area	9597000 sq km (3704000 sq mi)
Capital	Beijing (formerly known as Peking)
Chief towns	Shanghai, Tianjin, Shenyang, Wuhan, Guangzhou
Population	1313974000 (2006e)
Nationality	Chinese
Languages	standard Chinese (Putonghua) or Mandarin, also Yue (Cantonese), Wu, Minbei, Minnan, Xiang, Gan, Hakka and minority languages
Ethnic groups	Han 92%, others (includes Zhuang, Uygur, Hui, Yi, Tibetan, Miao, Manchu, Mongol, Buyi, Korean) 8%
Religions	Chinese folk religion 20%, Buddhism 8%, Christianity 5% (Prot 4%, RC 1%), Islam 2%, others 6%, none/unaffiliated 59%
Time zone	GMT +8
Currency	1 Renminbi Yuan (RMBY, $, Y) = 10 jiao = 100 fen
Telephone	+86
Internet	.cn
Country code	CHN

Location

A socialist state in central and eastern Asia, bounded to the north-west by Kyrgyzstan and Kazakhstan; to the north by Mongolia; to the north-east by Russia; to the east by North Korea, the Yellow Sea and the East China Sea; to the south by the South China Sea, Vietnam, Laos, Myanmar (Burma), India, Bhutan and Nepal; and to the west by India, Pakistan, Afghanistan and Tajikistan.

Physical description

Over two-thirds of the country comprise upland hills, mountains and plateaux; the highest mountains are in the west, where the Tibetan Plateau rises to an average altitude of 4000m (13123ft) ('the roof of the world'); the highest point is Mount Everest (8850m/29035ft); the land descends to the desert or semi-desert of Sinkiang and Inner Mongolia north and east of the Tibetan Plateau; the broad and fertile plains of Manchuria lie in the north-east, separated from North Korea by the densely forested Changpai Shan uplands; further east and south, the prosperous Sichuan Basin is drained by the Yangtze River; the southern plains and east coast, with rich, fertile soils, are heavily populated.

Climate

Varied, with seven zones: (1) north-east China has cold winters, with strong north winds and warm, humid summers, but unreliable rainfall; in Manchuria, the rivers are frozen for four to six months each year, and snow lies for 100–150 days; (2) central China has warm and humid summers, sometimes typhoons or tropical cyclones on the coast; (3) south China, partly within the tropics, is the wettest area in summer; frequent typhoons (especially during July–October); (4) south-west China has summer temperatures moderated by altitude, winters are mild with little rain; summers are wet in the mountains; (5) Tibet autonomous region, a high plateau surrounded by mountains, has severe winters with frequent light snow and hard frost, summers are warm, but nights are cold; (6) Xinjiang and the western interior has an arid desert climate, cold winters, and well-distributed rainfall throughout the year; (7) Inner Mongolia has an extreme continental-type climate, with cold winters and warm summers, and strong winds in winter and spring.

Economy

Centrally planned economy liberalized since 1980s to give a quasi-market economy with large private sector and strong international trade; industrial sector is now highly diversified and includes heavy industry (iron, steel, minerals, machinery, armaments, textiles), manufacturing (garments, household goods, consumables) and construction; coal, oil and increasing amounts of hydroelectric power from the Three Gorges Dam (construction completed 2006); agriculture still employs about 50% of the workforce, producing cotton, tea, hemp, jute, flax, silk, cereals, peas, beans, rice, sugar and livestock; financial sector and tourism of growing economic importance.

Government

Governed by an elected National People's Congress of around 3000 deputies, who appoint a State Council (led by a Prime Minister) and elect a President. The Chinese Communist Party is the ruling party and its leadership is formally elected by the party congress, held every five years.

History

Chinese civilization is believed to date from the Xia Dynasty of approximately 2200–1767 BC. The Shang Dynasty (c.1766–1122 BC) saw the introduction of bronze, and was presided over by a chariot-riding warrior aristocracy. The Western Zhou Dynasty ruled over a prosperous feudal agricultural society (c.1066–771 BC); the Eastern Zhou Dynasty (770–256 BC) was the era of Confucius and Lao Zi (Lao-tzu). The Qin Dynasty (221–206 BC) unified the warring states and provided a system of centralized control; there was expansion west during the Western and Eastern Han dynasties (206 BC–AD 220). From the 4th century, a series of northern dynasties was set up by invaders, with several dynasties in the south; these were gradually reunited during the Sui (581–618) and Tang (618–907) dynasties. After a period of partition into Five Dynasties (907–60) there emerged the Song Dynasty (960–1279), remembered for literature, philosophy and inventions (eg movable type, gunpowder); Genghis Khan established the Mongol Yuan Dynasty (1279–1368). There followed visits by Europeans, such as Marco Polo, in the 13th and 14th centuries, and the Ming Dynasty (1368–1644) increased contacts with the West. It was overthrown by the Manchu people, who ruled until 1911, and enlarged the empire to include Manchuria, Mongolia, Tibet, Taiwan and parts of Turkestan. Opposition to foreign penetration led to the Opium Wars (1839–42, 1858–60), in which defeat compelled China to open ports to foreign trade. The Sino–Japanese War (1895) gave control of Taiwan and Korea to Japan. The Boxer Rising (1898–1900) was a massive protest against foreign influence. The Republic of China was founded by Sun Yat-sen (1912) after the fall of the Qing Dynasty, but was followed by chaos and an era of regional warlords. Unification came under Jiang Jieshi (Chiang Kai-shek), who made Nanjing the capital in 1928. Conflict between nationalists and communists led to the Long March (1934–5), with

THE SYMBOLISM OF CHINA

Chinese history and culture are full of emblematic meaning, with many symbols such as animals, birds, flowers and colours being derived from the natural world.

The Chinese calendar and Chinese astrology

One of the most widely known examples of Chinese symbolism is the Chinese calendar. The traditional Chinese year is based on a complex 12-month lunar calendar. Each month is associated with a particular animal that gives positive and negative attributes or characteristics, such as good fortune, wealth, justice or sorrow: the animals in question are the tiger, rabbit, dragon, snake (or serpent), horse, sheep (or ram), monkey, chicken (or cockerel), dog, pig, rat and ox. These animals are also associated with particular years in a 12-year pattern, and a person's year and month of birth are said to influence their external and internal personality traits respectively.

In Chinese astrology there are five elements – water, fire, wood, metal and earth – and each of these is associated with a colour: black, red, blue-green, white and yellow respectively. They are further associated with compass points (north, south, east, west, and centre), and with the seasons (winter, spring, summer and autumn, with the earth being represented by all seasons). The 12-year cycle based on animals links with these elements to form a great 60-year cycle in which each animal can occur in conjunction with each of the elements.

Sacred animals

The paramount animal in Chinese symbolism is the dragon, which features frequently in literature and art. It symbolizes celestial and terrestrial power, strength, and wisdom. The five-clawed dragon became the Chinese imperial emblem associated with the greatest emperors, the four-clawed version being considered more common. China also celebrates other sacred animals, including the unicorn, phoenix, tiger and tortoise.

The importance of colour

The colour red features heavily in Chinese life, as it symbolizes all things fortunate. At New Year small red packages are distributed containing money, and brides traditionally wear red at their weddings. Yellow or gold is the imperial colour, and the emperors wore yellow robes emblazoned with dragons.

Yin and Yang

Chinese philosophy talks of two fundamental energies: yin (literally 'shaded') and yang ('sunlit'). They are opposites but complementary, with yin being associated with a female passive force and yang a masculine active force. The interplay and balance between the two is responsible for the seasons, the elements and other facets of life.

Symbolism in writing

Even the Chinese writing system makes use of symbolism. Chinese characters are not simply letters but represent meaningful units of language that are combined to form words. Some characters are pictographs – graphic symbols or pictures that directly represent their meaning. Although these have become stylized beyond recognition, their early forms were drawings of items in nature, such as the sun, the moon, water, mountain and rain.

communists moving to north-west China under Mao Zedong (Mao Tse-tung). The deeply corrupt nationalist regime was defeated in 1950 and withdrew to Taiwan. The People's Republic of China was proclaimed in 1949, with its capital at Beijing (Peking). The first Five-Year Plan (1953–7) was a period of nationalization and collectivization; the Great Leap Forward (1958–9) emphasized local authority and the establishment of rural communes, but this attempt to accelerate industrial and agricultural progress resulted in a famine in which between 30 million and 40 million died. The Cultural Revolution was initiated by Mao Zedong in 1966 and plunged the country into ten years of political and social turmoil ended only by Mao's death in 1976. Many policies were reversed after Mao's death, and with the return to power of Deng Xiaoping there began a drive towards rapid industrialization and wider trade relations with the West. The killing of student-led pro-democracy protesters in Tiananmen Square, Beijing, in 1989 provoked international outrage and the introduction of economic sanctions, but these had no effect and were relaxed after 1990. Gradual steps towards a controlled market economy continued throughout the 1990s and by the early 21st century China was emerging as a major economic power. In 1997 China entered a new era with the death of Deng Xiaoping, who was succeeded as leader by Jiang Zemin, and the handover in July of former British Crown Colony Hong Kong.

Special Administrative Regions

Hong Kong (HK)

Local name	Xianggang; Xianggang Tebie Xingzhengqu		
Location	A Special Administrative Region of China, comprising the Kowloon/New Territories peninsula and more than 200 islands in the South China Sea; highest point is Tai Mo Shan (958m/3143ft).		
Area	16 sq km (6 sq mi)	Internet	.hk
Population	6 940 000 (2006e)	Country code	HGK

History

Britain first occupied Hong Kong during the first Opium War in 1841, and it was officially ceded 'in perpetuity' to Britain by China under the terms of the Treaty of Nanjing in 1842. Under British rule, Hong Kong became a free-trade port and attracted migrants from the nearby province of Guangdong. The Kowloon Peninsula on the adjoining mainland was added to Britain's colony of Hong Kong in 1860, following the second of the Opium Wars (1856–60). Hong Kong was occupied by the Japanese in World War II, but re-occupied by the British in 1945. The New Territories had been leased to Britain for 99 years in 1898, and, under the Sino–British Declaration initialled in 1984 by which Britain agreed to cede the whole of Hong Kong at the end of the lease, the region was restored to China in 1997. Tung Chee-Hwa was appointed the first chief executive of the new Hong Kong Special Administrative Region and pledged to abide by the 'one country, two systems' plan, also outlined in the 1984 declaration, to preserve the existing way of life.

Macao

Local name	Aomen; Aomen Tebie Xingzhengqu; Macau (Portuguese)
Location	A Special Administrative Region of China, the Macao peninsula is linked by bridge and causeway to two islands in the South China Sea; highest point is Coloane Alto (172 m/565 ft)
Area	1067 sq km (412 sq mi) **Internet** .mo
Population	435 200 (2006e) **Country code** MAC

History

Macao was used as a base for Catholic missionaries in the 17th and 18th centuries as well as being a port of call for British traders on their way to Canton in the early 19th century. Until the 19th century, Macao was a flourishing trade centre, but the silting of its harbour and increasing competition from Hong Kong led to its decline. With the overthrow of the Salazar dictatorship in Portugal in 1975 and the new government's commitment to decolonization, China exercised greater influence in the colony. In 1987 it was agreed that Macao would be formally returned to Chinese control in 1999 under the same arrangements applying to the British return of Hong Kong to China in 1997 (ie that the capitalist system should remain in place).

CHINA, REPUBLIC OF ▸ TAIWAN

CHINESE TAIPEI ▸ TAIWAN

CIS ▸ ARMENIA, AZERBAIJAN, BELARUS, GEORGIA, KAZAKHSTAN, KYRGYZSTAN, MOLDOVA, RUSSIA, TAJIKISTAN, TURKMENISTAN, UKRAINE, UZBEKISTAN

COLOMBIA

Official name	Republic of Colombia
Local name	Colombia; República de Colombia
Area	1 140 105 sq km (440 080 sq mi)
Capital	Bogotá; Santa Fé de Bogotá
Chief towns	Medellín, Cali, Barranquilla
Population	43 953 000 (2006e)
Nationality	Colombian
Language	Spanish
Ethnic groups	Mestizo 58%, white 20%, Mulatto 14%, black 4%, mixed black and Amerindian 3%, Amerindian 1%
Religions	Christianity 95% (RC), others 5%
Time zone	GMT −5
Currency	1 Colombian Peso (Col$) = 100 centavos
Telephone	+57
Internet	.co
Country code	COL

Location

A republic in the north-west of South America. It is bounded to the north by Panama and the Caribbean Sea; to the west by the Pacific Ocean; to the east by Venezuela; to the south-east by Brazil; and to the south by Ecuador and Peru.

Physical description

Caribbean and Pacific coastlines, with several island possessions; on the mainland, the Andes run north to south, branching into three ranges dividing narrow coastal plains in the north and west from the extensive forested lowlands of the Amazon basin; the highest peaks are Pico Cristóbal Colón and Pico Simón Bolívar, both 5775m (18947ft) high; the Cordillera Oriental in the east surrounds large areas of plateau; rivers flow to the Pacific Ocean, Caribbean Sea and Amazon River.

Climate

A mostly tropical climate, modified by altitude; hot and humid in the north-west and west, with annual rainfall over 2500mm; the Caribbean coast has less rainfall and a dry period (December–April); the annual rainfall of the Andes is 1000–2500mm, falling evenly throughout the year; there are hot and humid tropical lowlands in the east, with annual rainfall of 2000–2500mm.

Economy

Growing and diversifying economy; development of the interior is hampered by a lack of transport infrastructure; coal, oil, natural gas and hydroelectric resources are exploited; gold, platinum, silver, emeralds, iron ore and other minerals are mined; major cash crops are coffee, sugar, rice, bananas, cut flowers, cotton, livestock products; manufactures comprise textiles, paper products and leather goods. There is widespread illegal drug trafficking (especially cocaine), which the government has been attempting to eradicate with help from the USA since mid-1989.

Government

Governed by an executive President, a Cabinet and a bicameral Congress, comprising a Senate and a Chamber of Representatives).

History

From the early 16th century the country was conquered by the Spanish, who dominated the Amerindian peoples. Governed by Spain within the Viceroyalty of Peru, it later became the Viceroyalty of New Granada. After the campaigns of Simón Bolívar, it gained independence in 1819, and formed a union with Ecuador, Venezuela and Panama as Gran Colombia; the union ended with the secession of Venezuela in 1829 and Ecuador in 1830, leaving New Granada to adopt the name Colombia. Colombia suffered civil war (known as La Violencia) in the 1950s, and there has been considerable political unrest since the 1980s because of left-wing insurgency and the activities of drugs cartels. There is widespread illegal cocaine trafficking, which successive governments have been attempting to eradicate with help from the USA since 1989. A new constitution was adopted in 1991, but a state of emergency was declared in 1992 because of violence by the drugs traffickers, insurgents and paramilitaries. These have presented less of a threat to civil order in recent years, but the government has been unable to suppress or reach a negotiated settlement with the insurgents, although paramilitary groups are being disarmed.

COMOROS

Official name	Union of the Comoros
Local name	Comores; Union des Comores
Former name	Federal Islamic Republic of the Comoros (until 2001)
Area	1862 sq km (719 sq mi)
Capital	Moroni; Môrônî
Population	691 000 (2006e)
Nationality	Comoran
Languages	French, Arabic; Shikomoro, or Comoran, a local Arabic–Swahili dialect is also spoken
Ethnic groups	Comorian 97%, others 3%
Religions	Islam 98% (Sunni), Christianity 2% (RC)
Time zone	GMT +3
Currency	1 Comoran Franc (KMF) = 100 centimes
Telephone	+269
Internet	.km
Country code	COM

Location

A group of three volcanic islands (Njazidja (formerly Grand Comore), Anjouan and Mohéli) located at the northern end of the Mozambique Channel between Mozambique and Madagascar.

Physical description

Interiors vary from steep mountains to low hills; the highest point is the active volcano Le Karthala (2360 m/7743 ft) on Njazidja.

Climate

Tropical; May–October is the dry season and November–April is the hot, humid season; average temperatures are 20°C in July and 28°C in November.

Economy

Very poor country, dependent on foreign aid and remittances from expatriate workers; main activities are agriculture (vanilla, copra, cloves, coconuts, bananas, cassava), tourism and perfume distillation.

Government

Governed by an executive President of the Union (the post rotates among the elected presidents of the three main islands), a Cabinet and a unicameral Assembly of the Union. Each of the three main islands has its own President, government and legislative assembly.

History

Under French control from 1843 to 1912, it became a French Overseas Territory in 1947. Internal political autonomy was achieved in 1961, and unilateral independence was declared in 1975 by the Comorian President Ahmed Abdallah, who was deposed later that year. The island of Mayotte, however, decided to remain under French administration. Political instability has dogged the republic since independence, with a number of coups between 1976 and 1999, some supported by European mercenaries, and demands for greater autonomy by the three main islands. In 1997, Anjouan and Mohéli demanded to secede from the Comoros and return to French rule. Following a coup in 1999, the military took control and reunited the country. A new constitution in 2002 created a federal Union of the Comoros, with greater autonomy and individual presidents for the three islands.

CONGO

Official name	Republic of Congo; also sometimes known as Congo (Brazzaville)
Local name	Congo; République du Congo
Former name	Middle Congo (until 1960), Republic of Congo (1960–70), People's Republic of the Congo (1970–92)
Area	341 945 sq km (131 990 sq mi)
Capital	Brazzaville
Chief towns	Pointe-Noire, Loubomo, Nkayi
Population	3 702 000 (2006e)
Nationality	Congolese, Congo
Languages	French, Kikongo, Lingala, Monokutuba
Ethnic groups	Kongo 49%, Sangha 20%, Teke 17%, Mbosi 11%, others 3%
Religions	Christianity 50% (RC), traditional beliefs 48%, Islam 2%
Time zone	GMT +1
Currency	1 CFA Franc (CFAFr) = 100 centimes
Telephone	+242
Internet	.cg
Country code	COG

Location

A west central African republic, bounded to the west by Gabon; to the north-west by Cameroon; to the north by the Central African Republic; to the east and south by the Democratic Republic of the Congo; and to the south-west by the Atlantic Ocean.

Physical description

A short Atlantic coastline fringes a broad mangrove plain that rises inland to mountains reaching 900 m (2953 ft); the inland mountain ridge is deeply cut by the River Congo flowing south-west to the coast; beyond this ridge, the Niari Valley rises up through terraced hills to reach 1040 m (3412 ft) at Mont de la Lékéti on the Gabon frontier; mainly covered by dense grassland, mangrove and rainforest; several rivers flow east and south to meet the Oubangui and Congo rivers, which form the eastern and southern borders.

Climate

Hot, humid, equatorial climate; annual rainfall is 1250–1750 mm, decreasing near the Atlantic coast and in the south; temperatures vary little, with average daily maximum temperatures at Brazzaville between 28 and 33°C; the dry season is June–September.

Economy

Poor country, with high external debt; dependent on oil; also produces phosphates, natural gas, lead, zinc, gold, diamonds; main industries are oil refining, forestry and wood processing, and agriculture; the main cash crops are sugar cane, cocoa and coffee.

Government

Governed by an executive President, a Cabinet and a bicameral Parliament consisting of a National Assembly and a Senate.

History

The first European visitors to the area were the Portuguese in the 15th century. The French established a colonial presence there in the late 19th century, and from 1908 to 1958 it was part of French Equatorial Africa, known as the 'Middle Congo'. It gained independence as the Republic of Congo in 1960, and in 1968 a military coup created the first Marxist state in Africa, renaming the country the People's Republic of the Congo. Marxism was renounced in 1990 and opposition parties were permitted. Elections took place in 1993 but the results were disputed and fighting between opposing ethnic and political groups ensued. A military coup in 1997 initiated a civil war that lasted until 2003. The subsequent peace is fragile; some rebels remain active in the south, where many have turned to banditry.

Shaking to the Soukous

Congo and the Democratic Republic of Congo share much of their popular music culture. The form known as *soukous* originated in the area in the 1940s as a fusion of African and South American music. It spread firstly through Africa in the 1970s and then to Europe in the 1980s. The term probably comes from the French word *secouer*, meaning 'to shake', a reference to the accompanying dance styles. These days *soukous ndombolo* is the most popular form; the accelerating beats and provocative movements have led to attempts to band the genre in parts of Africa, although this only seems to have increased its popularity.

CONGO, DEMOCRATIC REPUBLIC OF THE

Official name	Democratic Republic of the Congo (DR Congo, DRC or DROC); also sometimes known as Congo (Kinshasa)
Local name	Congo; République Démocratique du Congo
Former name	Congo Free State (until 1908), Belgian Congo (1908–60), Republic of the Congo (1960–4), Democratic Republic of the Congo (1964–71), Zaïre (1971–97)
Area	2 343 950 sq km (904 765 sq mi)
Capital	Kinshasa
Chief towns	Lubumbashi, Kisangani, Mbuji-Mayi, Kananga
Population	62 660 000 (2006e)
Nationality	Congolese, Congo
Languages	French, Kikongo, Lingala, Tshiluba
Ethnic groups	Bantu and Hamitic 44%, others 56%
Religions	Christianity 70% (RC 50%, Prot 20%), Islam 10%, others and traditional beliefs 20%
Time zone	GMT +1/2
Currency	1 Congolese Franc (CF) = 100 centimes
Telephone	+243
Internet	.cd
Country code	COD

Location

A central African republic, bounded to the west by Congo and the Atlantic Ocean; to the south-west by Angola; to the south-east by Zambia; to the east by Tanzania, Burundi, Rwanda and Uganda; to the north-east by Sudan; and to the north and north-west by the Central African Republic.

Physical description

The country lies mostly in the low-lying basin of the River Congo and its principal tributaries, the Lualaba and the Kasai; it rises in the east to a densely forested plateau, which is bounded to the east by a chain of lakes (Alberts, Edward, Kivu and Tanganyika) and volcanic mountains; the Ruwenzori Mountains in the north-east rise to 5110 m (16 765 ft) at Pic Marguerite on Mt Ngaliema (Mt Stanley); the Mitumbar Mountains lie further south; a narrow strip of land follows the River Congo to the Atlantic Ocean and a short 43 km (27 mi) coastline.

Climate

Equatorial, with high temperatures, humidity and rainfall; the equator crosses the north of the country, creating different climatic cycles either side of it, with the dry season falling in December–February in the north and May–September in the south; the average annual rainfall at Kisangani is 1700 mm; the average maximum daily temperatures range between 28 and 31°C.

Economy

Devastated after decades of mismanagement and civil war; renewed activity since 2002; rich natural resources (copper, cobalt, diamonds, tin, manganese, zinc, gold, silver, iron ore, rare-earth metals, offshore oil, hydroelectric power, timber); main industries are mining (diamonds, cobalt, copper, zinc), mineral processing, oil production, manufacturing (textiles, footwear, food processing, beverages, cigarettes), cement, forestry, ship repair; most of the population is involved in subsistence farming; cash crops include coffee, sugar, palm oil, rubber, tea, quinine.

Government

Governed by a President, a Prime Minister and Cabinet, and a bicameral Parliament, comprising a National Assembly and a Senate.

History

The Bantu had settled most of the country by AD 1000, and the first Europeans to visit were the Portuguese, in 1482. There were expeditions by Henry Morton Stanley in 1874–7, and the country was claimed by King Leopold II of Belgium and recognized in 1885 at the Congress of Berlin as the Congo Free State. In 1908 it became a Belgian colony and was renamed the Belgian Congo. On gaining independence in 1960 it was renamed the Democratic Republic of the Congo, and the mineral-rich Katanga (later, Shaba) province claimed independence; this resulted in civil war which destroyed the new government of Patrice Lumumba. A UN peacekeeping force entered the country and remained until 1964. The following year President Mobutu Sese Seko seized power in a coup. He renamed the country Zaire in 1971 and at first was credited with introducing a hitherto unknown degree of stability; however, his regime became increasingly corrupt and unpopular. Further conflict erupted in 1977–8, and there were power struggles in the early 1990s with violent ethnic unrest in Shaba, Kivu and Kasai provinces in 1993. In addition, over 1 million refugees from the civil war in Rwanda entered Zaire in 1994. In 1996 Zaire was invaded by a rebel army led by Laurent Kabila, an ethnic Tutsi, who succeeded the following year in overthrowing the government and forcing Mobutu into exile. Kabila was installed as head of state and the country was renamed the Democratic Republic of the Congo, but civil war with extensive foreign intervention continued. Kabila was assassinated in 2001 and was succeeded by his son Joseph. Following disengagement in 2001 and peace talks in 2002, an interim government of national unity was formed in 2003, and a new constitution in 2005 provided for elections in 2006. The presidential election was won by Joseph Kabila. UN peacekeeping troops remain in the country to disarm rebel forces and because of continuing fighting with renegade rebels.

Rainy Days

The annual rainfall in the Democratic Republic of the Congo has been known to surpass 200 cm (80 in) and sustains the second largest rainforest in the world. The area also experiences the highest frequency of thunderstorms on Earth.

COSTA RICA

Official name	Republic of Costa Rica
Local name	Costa Rica; República de Costa Rica
Area	51 022 sq km (19 694 sq mi)
Capital	San José
Chief towns	Cartago, Heredia, Liberia, Puntarenas, Limón
Population	4 075 000 (2006e)
Nationality	Costa Rican
Language	Spanish
Ethnic groups	white and Mestizo 94%, black and Mulatto 3%, Amerindian 1%, Chinese 1%, others 1%
Religions	Christianity 85% (RC), others 15%
Time zone	GMT −6
Currency	1 Costa Rican Colón (CR¢) = 100 céntimos
Telephone	+506
Internet	.cr
Country code	CRI

Location

The second smallest republic in Central America, bounded to the west by the Pacific Ocean; to the north by Nicaragua; to the east by the Caribbean; and to the south-east by Panama.

Physical description

A chain of volcanic mountain ranges runs the length of Costa Rica (some volcanoes are active); the highest peak is Chirripó Grande (3819m/12 529ft) in the Cordillera de Talamanca; between the mountain, the central plateau, the Meseta Central, covers an area of 5200 sq km (2000 sq mi) at an altitude of 800–1400m (2600–4600ft); it is drained in the west by the Rio Grande into the Pacific and in the north-east by the River Reventazón into the Caribbean; between the mountains and the coast the land is low and swampy, with tropical forest as the land rises and lowland savanna in the north-west.

Climate

Tropical climate, with a small temperature range and abundant rainfall; more temperate in the central uplands; dry season is December–May; average annual rainfall is 3300mm, with much local variation; the average annual temperature is 26–28°C.

Economy

Prosperous, diversifying market economy; main industry is tourism, especially 'eco-tourism' (one-third of the country is national parkland or nature reserve); manufacturing produces computer components, medical supplies, textiles, foodstuffs, garments, construction materials, plastic goods; agriculture produces coffee, bananas, sugar, pineapples, beef and timber.

Government

Governed by an executive President, a Cabinet and a unicameral Legislative Assembly.

History

Visited by Christopher Columbus in 1502, it was named Costa Rica ('rich coast') in the belief that vast gold treasures existed. It was under Spanish rule from 1530 until it gained its independence in 1821, and was a member of the Central American Federation in 1824–39. During the 20th century there was political unrest, with civil war in 1948, following which the army was disbanded. Since the civil war, power has alternated between the two main political parties. The 2006 presidential election was won by Arias Sánchez, president in 1986–90 and winner of the 1987 Nobel Peace Prize for devising a peace plan that ended the civil wars in neighbouring Nicaragua and in El Salvador.

CÔTE D'IVOIRE

Official name	Republic of Côte d'Ivoire
Local name	Côte d'Ivoire; République de la Côte d'Ivoire
Former name	Ivory Coast (until 1986)
Area	320 633 sq km (123 764 sq mi)
Capitals	Yamoussoukro (official) and Abidjan (administrative and economic)
Chief towns	Bouaké, Daloa, Man, Korhogo, Gagnoa
Population	17 655 000 (2006e)
Nationality	Ivorian
Languages	French; many local languages are also spoken
Ethnic groups	Akan 40%, Kru 17%, Voltaic 15%, Malinke 15%, Southern Mande 11%, others 2%
Religions	Christianity 38%, Islam 35%, traditional beliefs 27%
Time zone	GMT
Currency	1 CFA Franc (CFAFr) = 100 centimes
Telephone	+225
Internet	.ci
Country code	CIV

Location

A republic in west Africa, bounded to the south-west by Liberia; to the north-west by Guinea; to the north by Mali and Burkina Faso; to the east by Ghana; and to the south by the Gulf of Guinea.

Physical description

Sandy beaches and lagoons, backed by a broad rainforest-covered coastal plain; the land rises towards savanna at 300–350 m (980–1150 ft); Mount Nimba massif in the north-west reaches 1752 m (5748 ft) at the highest point; rivers generally flow north to south.

Climate

Tropical, varying with distance from the coast; rainfall decreases towards the north; the average annual rainfall at Abidjan is 2100 mm; average temperatures are 25–7°C.

Economy

In decline owing to civil war; largely based on agriculture, which employs c.68% of the population; main cash crops are cocoa (world's largest producer), coffee (fifth-largest robusta coffee producer), bananas, palm oil, rice, sugar, cotton, pineapples, rubber; industries include food processing, textiles, forestry, fishing, production of oil and hydroelectric power, oil refining and vehicle assembly.

Government

Governed by an executive President, a Prime Minister and Cabinet, and a unicameral National Assembly.

History

Explored by the Portuguese in the 15th century and the centre of the ivory trade from the 16th century, the area came under French influence from 1842. Declared a French protectorate in 1889 and a French colony in 1893, it became a territory within French west Africa in 1904. It gained independence in 1960 as a one-party republic, with Felix Houphouët-Boigny as president. He introduced a multiparty system for the first time in 1990, when the elections were won by his Democratic Party of the Côte d'Ivoire (PDCI). He was succeeded on his death in 1993 by Henri Konan-Bédié, who ruled until overthrown in a 1999 coup by Robert Guëi. Guëi fled in 2000 after popular protests against rigged elections and Laurent Gbagbo, believed to be the winning candidate, became president. Political turmoil continued, leading to civil war from 2002 until 2003, when a ceasefire left the country divided between the government-controlled south and the rebel-held north, with international peacekeeping troops deployed in a buffer zone. Clashes have continued, however, and the peace agreement has not been fully implemented. A transitional power-sharing government was formed in 2005 but the 2005 elections have been delayed indefinitely.

Boigny's Basilica

Yamoussoukro, Côte d'Ivoire's capital city, is home to the largest church in Africa and possibly even in the world (although its rival, St Peter's Basilica in the Vatican City, can hold more people). The Basilica of Our Lady of Peace was built by Felix Houphouët-Boigny when he was president, after he decided to turn the sparsely populated Yamoussoukro into the country's new capital city. The church features a large stained-glass image of him, and also boasts 7,000 individually air-conditioned seats.

CROATIA

Official name	Republic of Croatia
Local name	Hrvatska; Republika Hrvatska
Former name	Formerly part of Kingdom of Serbs, Croats and Slovenes (until 1929), Kingdom of Yugoslavia (1929–41), Independent State of Croatia (1941–45), Federal People's Republic of Yugoslavia (1945–63), Socialist Federal Republic of Yugoslavia (1963–91)
Area	56 538 sq km (21 824 sq mi)
Capital	Zagreb
Chief towns	Rijeka, Cakovec, Split, Zadar
Population	4 495 000 (2006e)
Nationality	Croat, Croatian
Language	Croatian
Ethnic groups	Croat 90%, Serb 4%, others 6%
Religions	Christianity 93% (RC 88%, Orthodox 5%), Islam 1%, others 6%
Time zone	GMT +1
Currency	1 Kuna (Kn) = 100 lipa
Telephone	+385
Internet	.hr
Country code	HRV

Location

A mountainous republic in eastern Europe, bounded to the south-west and west by the Adriatic Sea; to the north by Slovenia; to the north-east by Hungary; to the east by Serbia; and to the south-east by Bosnia and Herzegovina and Montenegro.

Physical description

The Adriatic coastline, 1778 km (1105 mi) in length with more than 1180 islands and islets, is backed by long mountain ranges dividing the coast from the fertile plains of the north-east; the highest point is Dinara (1830 m/6004 ft); the main river is the Sava, flowing across the northern plain.

Climate

Continental; hot summers and cold winters; milder on the coast.

Economy

Industrialized market economy; main activities are shipbuilding, manufacturing (textiles, food processing, wood processing, cement, chemicals, fertilizers, pharmaceuticals), tourism, fishing, mining, production of oil and hydroelectric power; agriculture produces grains, fruit, vegetables, livestock and tobacco.

Government

Governed by a President, a Prime Minister and Cabinet, and a unicameral Assembly.

History

Croatia includes the region lying between Bosnia and Hungary, called Slavonia, which was recorded as a kingdom in its own right in 1240 and was administered by the Hungarian King Béla IV as a *banovina* with its own *ban* (viceroy) within the Kingdom of Croatia in 1260. Slavonia was ruled by members of the ruling dynasty in Hungary during the 13th and 14th centuries, but was returned to the Croatian *ban* in 1476. The Slavonian *sabor* (parliament) was joined to that of Croatia in the mid-16th century but Slavonia was then occupied by the Ottomans until the Treaty of Karlowitz (1699), when it passed to the Habsburg Emperor and was absorbed into the Military Frontier. The Croatian people were originally Slav settlers who migrated during the 6th and 7th centuries from White Croatia in the Ukraine to the old Roman provinces of Pannonia and Dalmatia. Their independent kingdom, ruled by Croatian kings, existed from 910 until 1102, when the Croatian crown passed to the Hungarian Árpád Dynasty. From 1526 to 1918 the Croatian and Hungarian crowns were joined under the Habsburg Dynasty, but during the 15th and 16th centuries the Croats became divided between three empires: the Croats in Croatia and Slavonia were subject to the Habsburgs; those in Dalmatia were subject to Venice; and those in Bosnia and Herzegovina to the Ottomans. In 1868 Croatia and Slavonia were made a joint crown land under Hungarian rule. Not until 1918 and the creation of the Kingdom of Serbs, Croats and Slovenes (later Yugoslavia) were the Croats all subject to one government. During occupation by the Axis powers in 1941–5, after the disintegration of Yugoslavia, part of Croatia and Bosnia and Herzegovina formed the Independent State of Croatia, a satellite state of the Axis powers. Benito Mussolini chose Prince Aimone of Saxony, the Duke of Spoleto, to be King, but the Prince never took over his kingdom. The state was, instead, subject to the brutal regime of Ante Pavelić, the leader of the Ustaša fascist movement. In 1945 Croatia became one of the constituent republics of the Federal People's Republic of Yugoslavia. In 1991 the Croatian president Franjo Tudjman declared Croatia's independence from the Yugoslav Federation, which was followed by confrontation with the National Army and civil war; an official ceasefire was declared in 1992 but fighting restarted in 1993. From 1992 Croatian forces were involved in the war in Bosnia and Herzegovina, where there is a large Croat population. Since the death of the authoritarian Tudjman in 1999, Croatia has been more outward looking. It has joined the World Trade Organization, and is expected to join the European Union in 2010.

Dubrovnik, Pearl of the Adriatic

A UNESCO World Heritage Site, the heart of Dubrovnik's old town remains virtually unchanged since the 13th century. Its legendary beauty inspired the writer George Bernard Shaw to comment in 1929 'If you want to see heaven on earth, come to Dubzrovnik.'

CUBA

Official name	Republic of Cuba
Local name	Cuba; República de Cuba
Area	110 860 sq km (42 792 sq mi)
Capital	Havana; La Habana
Chief towns	Santiago de Cuba, Camagüey, Holguín, Santa Clara, Guantánamo
Population	11 383 000 (2006e)
Nationality	Cuban
Language	Spanish
Ethnic groups	Mulatto 51%, white 37%, black 11%, Chinese 1%
Religions	traditional beliefs 54%, Christianity 46% (RC 40%, Prot 6%)
Time zone	GMT −5
Currency	1 Cuban Peso (Cub$) = 100 centavos
Telephone	+53
Internet	.cu
Country code	CUB

Location

An island republic in the Caribbean Sea.

Physical description

An archipelago, comprising the island of Cuba, Isla de la Juventud, and c.1600 islets and cays; the main island is 1250 km (777 mi) long, varying in width from 191 km (119 mi) in the east to 31 km (19 mi) in the west; heavily indented coastline; the south coast is generally low and marshy and the north coast is steep and rocky, with some fine harbours; the main ranges are the Sierra del Escambray in the centre, the Sierra de los Organos in the west, and the Sierra Maestra in the east; the highest peak is Pico Turquino (2005 m/6578 ft); the island is mostly flat, with wide, fertile valleys and plains.

Climate

Subtropical, warm and humid; the average annual temperature is 25°C; the dry season is November–April; the average annual rainfall is 1375 mm; hurricanes usually occur between June and November.

Economy

Nationalized and centrally planned economy since 1959; crisis caused by collapse of communism in Europe led to limited privatization and market reforms in the 1990s; now attracting foreign investment; main cash crops are sugar (world's second-largest producer) and tobacco; chief industries are tourism, sugar refining, oil production, tobacco processing, nickel mining (world's fifth-largest producer) and biotechnology.

Government

Governed by an executive President, a Council of Ministers and a unicameral National

Assembly of the People's Power; a Council of State, appointed by the National Assembly, represents it between sessions. The Cuban Communist Party is the only legal political party.

History

The island was visited by Christopher Columbus in 1492, and was a Spanish colony until 1898. Spain relinquished its rights over Cuba following a US-supported revolution led by José Martí. Cuba gained independence in 1902, with the USA retaining naval bases and reserving the right of intervention in domestic affairs. The struggle against the dictatorship of General Batista led by Fidel Castro, unsuccessful in 1953, was finally successful in 1959, and a communist state was established. In 1961 an invasion by US-supported Cuban exiles was defeated at the Bay of Pigs, and in 1962 the discovery of the installation of Soviet missile bases in Cuba prompted a US naval blockade. The collapse of the Soviet Union in 1991 meant that Cuba lost the commercial, military and economic support that it had enjoyed since 1960, and Castro was forced to reduce public services and introduce food rationing. After emigration was permitted (1980), many Cubans settled in Florida, leading to the need for an agreement between Cuba and the USA (1994) to regulate the flow of asylum seekers. For over 30 years the USA maintained a continually tightening economic and political blockade of Castro's Cuba, cemented by the Helms–Burton Act of 1996. However, this has failed to destroy the economy, which has benefited in recent years from the relaxation of state controls and increased overseas investment and tourism. Fidel Castro stood down temporarily in July 2006 to undergo surgery, leaving his brother Raul in charge of the government.

CYPRUS

Official name	Republic of Cyprus
Local name	Kipros; Kypriaki Demokratía (Greek), Kibris; Kibris Çumhuriyeti (Turkish)
Area	9251 sq km (3571 sq mi)
Capital	Nicosia; Lefkosía (Greek), Lefkoşa (Turkish)
Chief towns	Larnaca, Limassol, Kyrenia; Famagusta (formerly the chief port) is under Turkish occupation and has been declared closed by the Cyprus government
Population	784 000 (2006e)
Nationality	Cypriot
Languages	Greek, Turkish, with English widely spoken
Ethnic groups	Greek 77%, Turkish 18%, others 5%
Religions	Christianity 78% (Orthodox), Islam 18%, others 4%
Time zone	GMT +2
Currency	1 Cyprus Pound (C£) = 100 cents; Turkish lira are used in the northern part under Turkish occupation
Telephone	+357
Internet	.cy
Country code	CYP

Location

An island republic in the north-east Mediterranean Sea.

Physical description

The Kyrenia Mountains extend 150 km (90 mi) along the north coast, rising to 1024 m (3360 ft) at Mount Kyparissovouno; the forest-covered Troödos Mountains are in the centre and south-west, rising to 1951 m (6401 ft) at Mount Olympus; the fertile Mesaoria plain extends across the island's centre; the coastline is indented, with several long, sandy beaches.

Climate

Typical Mediterranean climate, with hot, dry summers and warm, wet winters; average annual rainfall is 500 mm, with great local variation; average daily temperatures (July–August) range from 22°C on the Troödos Mountains to 29°C on the central plain; winters are mild, with an average temperature of 4°C in higher parts of the mountains, and 10°C on the plain; there is snow on higher land in winter.

Economy

The Greek Cypriot area has a diverse market economy dominated by the services sector; main industries are tourism (20% of GDP), financial services, shipping services, food and wine, textiles and garments, chemicals, pharmaceuticals, metal products, wood products; main agricultural products are citrus fruits, potatoes, grapes, vegetables; the Turkish Cypriot economy is internationally isolated and heavily dependent on Turkish financial support; largely agricultural, exporting citrus fruits, potatoes and textiles; small tourist industry.

Government

Governed by an executive President, a Council of Ministers and a unicameral House of Representatives; Turkish members ceased to attend in 1983, when the Turkish community declared itself independent (as the 'Turkish Republic of Northern Cyprus', recognized only by Turkey).

History

Cyprus has a recorded history of 4000 years, with its rulers having included the Greeks, Ptolemaic Egyptians, Persians, Romans, Byzantines, Arabs, Franks, Venetians, Turks and British. Byzantine control of the island ended at the time of the Third Crusade when Richard I, the Lionheart, conquered Cyprus on his way to Palestine and established Guy of Lusignan as King of Cyprus. This marked the beginning of a long period in which aspiring Crusaders could look on Cyprus as a relatively safe haven. In the 15th century, because the piracy out of the island had remained a constant threat to Muslim seaborne trade in the eastern Mediterranean, the Circassian Mamluk, Sultan al-Ashraf Barsbay, mounted an attack and established Mamluk influence. Later, when Cyprus became effectively a protectorate of the Venetian empire, it still paid tribute to the Mamluk Sultan. The last vestige of Frankish influence in the eastern Mediterranean, the island fell to the Ottoman Sultan, Selim II, in 1571 and remained under Ottoman control until ceded to the British in 1878. It became a British Crown Colony in 1925. Greek Cypriot demands for union with Greece (*enosis*) led in the 1950s to guerrilla warfare waged against the British administration by EOKA, and a four-year state of emergency (1955–9). Cyprus achieved independence in 1960, with

Britain retaining sovereignty over the military bases at Akrotiri and Dhekelia. Despite a constitution providing for power-sharing between the Greek and Turkish Cypriots, there were intercommunal clashes throughout the 1960s and in 1971; a UN peacekeeping force was deployed in 1964. The 1974 Turkish invasion led to occupation of the northern third of the island, causing the displacement of over 160 000 Greek Cypriots; the island was partitioned into two parts, from the north-west coast above Pomos to Famagusta in the east, cutting through Nicosia where it is called the Green Line. Famagusta (the chief port prior to the 1974 Turkish invasion) remains under Turkish occupation, and has been declared closed by the Cyprus government. Turkish government members ceased to attend government in 1983, when the Turkish community declared itself independent (as the 'Turkish Republic of Northern Cyprus'). Reunification talks in the 1980s and 1990s were inconclusive, but the impetus provided by Cyprus's approaching admission to the European Union led to UN-sponsored talks from 1999 onwards that resulted in 2004 in the Annan plan for a united republic with a two-state federal structure. This was accepted in a referendum by the Turkish Cypriots but rejected by the Greek Cypriots, and only the southern part of the island joined the European Union in 2004.

CZECH REPUBLIC

Official name	Czech Republic
Local name	České Republiky, Česká Republika, Cesko
Former name	formerly part of Czechoslovakia (until 1993)
Area	78 864 sq km (30 441 sq mi)
Capital	Prague; Praha
Chief towns	Brno, Plzen, Ostrava, Olomouc
Population	10 235 000 (2006e)
Nationality	Czech
Language	Czech
Ethnic groups	Czech 90%, Moravian 4%, Slovak 2%, others 4%
Religions	Christianity 29% (RC 27%, Prot 2%), others 3%, unspecified 9%, none/unaffiliated 59%
Time zone	GMT +1
Currency	1 Koruna (KZK) = 100 halérů
Telephone	+420
Internet	.cz
Country code	CZE

Location

A landlocked republic in eastern Europe, bounded to the west by Germany; to the north and east by Poland; to the south-east by Slovakia; and to the south by Austria.

Physical description

Bohemia (west and centre) comprises rolling fertile plains and plateaux surrounded by low mountains; Moravia (east) is mostly hilly, rising to the western range of the Carpathian mountains in the east, and divided by the River Morava valley; the highest point is Sněžka (1602 m/5256 ft) in the north; drained by the Morava, Vltava, Elbe and Oder rivers; there are many lakes; forests and woods cover one-third of the land.

Climate
Continental, with warm, humid summers and cold, dry winters.

Economy
Has become a prosperous market economy since 1990; industrialized in 19c; major industries produce iron, steel, machinery, motor vehicles, chemicals, glass, armaments, hydroelectric power, timber and wood products; main crops are wheat, potatoes, sugar beets, hops, fruit, pigs and poultry.

Government
Governed by a President, a Prime Minister and Council of Ministers, and a bicameral Parliament consisting of a Chamber of Deputies and a Senate.

History
The republic comprises the former provinces of Bohemia, Silesia and Moravia, and from 1918 to 1993 it formed part of Czechoslovakia. It became an independent republic on 1 January 1993 following the dissolution of Czechoslovakia, and Václav Havel, formerly president of Czechoslovakia, became president. In 1999 the Czech Republic was admitted to NATO and in 2004 it joined the European Union.

DENMARK

Official name	Kingdom of Denmark
Local name	Danmark; Kongeriget Danmark; also sometimes known as Rigsfællesskabet, the United Kingdom of Denmark, including the Faroe Islands and Greenland
Area	43 076 sq km (16 627 sq mi)
Capital	Copenhagen; København
Chief towns	Århus, Odense, Ålborg, Esbjerg, Randers, Kolding
Population	5 451 000 (2006e)
Nationality	Dane, Danish
Language	Danish
Ethnic groups	Danish 96%, Faroese and Inuit 1%, others 3%
Religions	Christianity 84% (Prot 83%, RC 1%), Islam 4%, unaffiliated 7%, unspecified/others 1%, none 4%
Time zone	GMT +1
Currency	1 Danish Krone (Dkr) = 100 øre
Telephone	+45
Internet	.dk
Country code	DNK

Location

A kingdom in northern Europe, the smallest of the Scandinavian countries, comprising most of the Jutland peninsula and 406 islands, including several in the Baltic Sea (the largest are Zealand, Fyn, Lolland, Falster and Bornholm), and some of the northern Frisian Islands in the North Sea.

Physical description

Uniformly low-lying; the highest point (Ejer Bavnehøj in east Jylland) is only 173 m (567 ft) high; there are no large rivers and few lakes; the shoreline is indented by many lagoons and fjords, the largest of which is Lim Fjord, which cut off the northern extremity of Denmark in 1825.

Climate

Cool maritime climate, giving cold and cloudy winters and warm, sunny summers; the average annual rainfall is usually below 675 mm.

Economy

Highly industrialized and diversified market economy based on intensive agriculture, forestry, energy and processing industries; agricultural exports include grains, meat, dairy products, fish; industry produces electronic appliances, foodstuffs, beer, chemicals, furniture, ships, windmills; oil, natural gas and electricity are exported.

Government

A hereditary constitutional monarchy with a Queen as head of state; governed by a Prime Minister and Cabinet and a unicameral Parliament, at which the Faeroe Islands and Greenland each have two representatives.

History

Denmark formed part of Viking kingdoms between the 8th and 10th centuries and was the centre of the Danish Empire under Canute in the 11th century. In 1397 the Union of Kalmar brought Sweden and Norway under Danish rule; Sweden separated from the union in the 16th century, and Norway was ceded to Sweden in 1814. Schleswig-Holstein was lost to Germany in 1864, but northern Schleswig was returned after a referendum in 1920. Denmark was occupied by Germany during World War II. Iceland became independent of Danish rule in 1944; the Faroe Islands and Greenland remain dependencies but were granted internal self-government in 1948 and 1979 respectively. Denmark joined the European Community in 1973. A referendum in 2000 rejected a proposal to replace the krone with the euro.

Danish self-governing territories

Faroe Islands

Location	The group of islands lying between the Shetland Islands and Iceland, and subject to the Danish crown.		
Area	1399 sq km (540 sq mi)	**Internet**	.fo
Capital	Torshavn	**Country code**	FRO
Population	47 200 (2006e)		

Greenland

Location	The second-largest island in the world (after Australia), lying north-east of North America in the North Atlantic and Arctic oceans, and subject to the Danish crown.		
Area	2 175 600 sq km (839 780 sq mi)	**Internet**	.gl
Capital	Nuuk (Godthåb)	**Country code**	GRL
Population	56 800 (2006e)		

DJIBOUTI

Official name	Republic of Djibouti
Local name	Djibouti; République de Djibouti (French), Jibūti; Jumhūriyah Jibūti (Arabic)
Former name	French Somaliland (until 1967), French Territory of the Afars and Issas (1967–77)
Area	23 310 sq km (8 998 sq mi)
Capital	Djibouti; Djīboûtî
Chief towns	Tadjoura, Dikhil, Obock, Ali-Sabieh
Population	486 400 (2006e)
Nationality	Djiboutian
Languages	Arabic, French
Ethnic groups	Issa 60%, Afar 35%, Arab and others 5%
Religions	Islam 94% (Sunni), Christianity 6% (RC 4%, Prot 2%)
Time zone	GMT +3
Currency	1 Djibouti Franc (DF, DjFr) = 100 centimes
Telephone	+253
Internet	.dj
Country code	DJI

Location

A republic in north-east Africa, bounded to the north-west, west and south by Ethiopia; to the south-east by Somalia; to the north by Eritrea and to the east by the Gulf of Aden.

Physical description

A series of plateaux dropping down from the mountains to a flat, low-lying rocky desert; there is a 350 km (220 mi) fertile coastal strip around the Gulf of Tadjoura, which juts deep into the country; the highest point, Moussa Ali, rises to 2020 m (6627 ft) in the north; the lowest point, Lake Abbé, is 155 m (508 ft) below sea level.

Climate

Semi-arid, with a hot season in May–September; very high temperatures on coastal plains all year round, maximum average daily temperature dropping below 30°C for only three months (December–February); slightly lower humidity and temperatures in the interior highlands (more than 600m); rainfall averages 130mm annually at Djibouti.

Economy

Poor, and dependent on foreign aid; large service sector (80% of GDP) based on its strategic location as a military base for European forces and the port of Djibouti's role as a transit port for landlocked neighbouring countries and commercial hub of free trade zone in north-east Africa; aridity restricts agriculture to irrigated areas (date palms, fruit, vegetables) and livestock-rearing by nomads; some fishing and tourism.

Government

Governed by a President, a Prime Minister and Council of Ministers, and a unicameral National Assembly.

History

Settled by the Afars and Issas about 2000 years ago, the area was the object of French colonial interest in the mid-19th century and became the capital of French Somaliland in 1892. Following World War II it became a French Overseas Territory, and from 1967 was called the French Territory of the Afars and the Issas. It became independent as Djibouti in 1977, under President Hassan Gouled Aptidon and the Popular Rally for Progress Party, which became the only legal political party in 1981. In 1991 fighting broke out in protest at Issa domination of the government; introduction of a limited multiparty system in 1992 failed to resolve matters and the civil war continued until power-sharing was agreed in 1994. Some factions continued to fight until 2000, when a peace agreement was signed. Free and unrestricted multiparty elections were held for the first time in 2003.

DOMINICA

Official name	Commonwealth of Dominica
Local name	Dominica
Area	751 sq km (290 sq mi)
Capital	Roseau
Chief towns	Portsmouth, Grand Bay
Population	69 000 (2006e)
Nationality	Dominican
Languages	English; French Creole is also spoken
Ethnic groups	African/mixed African-European 97%, Amerindian 2%, others 1%
Religions	Christianity 92% (RC 77%, Prot 15%), others 6%, none 2%
Time zone	GMT –4
Currency	1 East Caribbean Dollar (EC$) = 100 cents
Telephone	+1 767
Internet	.dm
Country code	DMA

Location

An independent republic located in the Windward Islands, in the east Caribbean Sea.

Physical description

Roughly rectangular in shape, with a deeply indented coastline; the island is c.50 km (30 mi) long and 26 km (16 mi) wide, rising to 1447 m (4747 ft) at Morne Diablotin; it is of volcanic origin, with many fumaroles and sulphur springs; it has a central ridge, with lateral spurs and deep valleys, with several rivers; forests covers 67% of the land area.

Climate

Tropical; warm and humid; average monthly temperatures are 26–32°C; average annual rainfall is 1750 mm on the coast and 6250 mm in the mountains; subject to hurricanes in July–November.

Economy

Largely agriculture and produce processing; tourism is growing; economy is diversifying into fishing, forestry and light industry; main products are bananas, fruit juices, soap, coconut oil, lime oil, bay oil, copra, rum, vegetables and citrus fruits.

Government

Governed by a President, a Prime Minister and Cabinet, and a unicameral House of Assembly.

History

Christopher Columbus reached the island in 1493, and there were attempts at colonization by the French and British in the 18th century. It became a British Crown Colony in 1805. It was part of the Federation of the West Indies from 1958 to 1962, and gained independence in 1978. Edison James became prime minister in 1995, ending the 15-year tenure of Dame Eugenia Charles, the Caribbean's first woman prime minister. However, James's United Workers' Party lost the 2000 election to the Dominica Labour Party.

The Valley of Desolation

In an island where geothermal activity is a visible and ever-present part of daily life, one of the most popular tourist excursions involves a six-hour round trek through the steam-filled springs and colourful mineral deposits of the Valley of Desolation to the Boiling Lake – a flooded fumarole filled with water heated to boiling point by the molten lava below.

DOMINICAN REPUBLIC

Official name	Dominican Republic (DR)
Local name	República Dominicana; La Dominicana
Area	48 442 sq km (18 699 sq mi)
Capital	Santo Domingo
Chief towns	Santiago, La Vega, San Juan, San Francisco de Macorís, La Romana
Population	9 184 000 (2006e)
Nationality	Dominican
Language	Spanish
Ethnic groups	Mulatto 73%, white 16%, black 11%
Religions	Christianity 95% (RC), others 5%
Time zone	GMT −4
Currency	1 Dominican Republic Peso (RD$, DR$) = 100 centavos
Telephone	+1 809
Internet	.do
Country code	DOM

Location

A republic of the West Indies, comprising the eastern two-thirds of the island of Hispaniola, and bordering Haiti to the west.

Physical description

Crossed by the Cordillera Central, a heavily wooded range with many peaks over 3000 m (9840 ft); the Pico Duarte (3175 m/10 417 ft) is the highest peak in the Caribbean; Lake Enriquillo lies in a broad valley cutting east to west; there is a wide coastal plain to the east.

Climate

Tropical maritime, with a rainy season from May to November; the average temperature at Santo Domingo ranges between 24°C (January) and 27°C (July); average annual rainfall is 1400 mm; hurricanes may occur in June–November.

Economy

There is a developing economy based on tourism, free trade zones and agriculture (sugar, coffee, cocoa, bananas, tobacco, beef); dependent on foreign aid and remittances from expatriate workers; industries include sugar refining, pharmaceuticals, cement, mining (ferronickel, gold, silver), light manufacturing and textiles.

Government

Governed by an executive President, a Cabinet and a bicameral National Congress consisting of a Senate and a Chamber of Deputies.

History

Christopher Columbus reached the island in 1492 and it became a Spanish colony in the 16th and 17th centuries; the eastern province of Santo Domingo remained Spanish after the partition of Hispaniola in 1697. Taken over by Haiti on several occasions, it gained independence in 1844 under its modern name, but was reoccupied by Spain in 1861–5. A long dictatorship at the end of the 19th century was followed by revolution and bankruptcy. The dictatorship of General Rafael Trujillo (1930–61) was followed by a period of instability and then from the mid-1960s by a succession of right-wing and centre-right governments. Political crises and allegations of fraud and corruption dominated the 1980s and 1990s. In 2003–4, protests against the government's economic policies were widespread.

EAST TIMOR

Official name	Democratic Republic of East Timor
Local name	Timor-Leste; República Democrática de Timor-Leste (Portuguese), Timor Lorosa'e; Republika Demokratika Timor Lorosa'e (Tetum)
Former names	Portuguese Timor (until 1975), part of Indonesia (1976–2002)
Area	14874 sq km (5743 sq mi)
Capital	Dili
Chief towns	Baucau, Pante Macassar
Population	1063000 (2006e)
Nationality	Timorese
Languages	Portuguese, Tetum; English and Indonesian are also spoken
Ethnic groups	Malay-Polynesian, Papuan
Religions	Christianity 93% (RC 90%, Prot 3%), Islam 4%, others 3%
Time zone	GMT +8
Currency	1 US Dollar ($) = 100 cents
Telephone	+670
Internet	.tp
Country code	TLS

Location

A republic in South-East Asia occupying the eastern half of the island of Timor and the enclave of Oecusse in the west of the island.

Physical description

Mountainous and forested, with numerous rivers; the highest peak is Tata Mailau at 2950m (9678ft); the state also includes the smaller islands of Pulau Atauro and Jaco.

Climate

Hot and humid equatorial climate; dry season (June–September), rainy season (December–March); the average temperature is 27°C on the coast, falling inland and with altitude.

Economy

Very poor country, dependent on foreign aid; largely agrarian; main products are coffee, sandalwood, marble and vanilla; oil and natural gas exploitation generates revenue but few jobs.

Government

Governed by a President, a Prime Minister and Council of Ministers, and a unicameral National Parliament.

History

Colonized by the Portuguese in the 16th century, it remained an overseas territory of Portugal after World War II when the western part of Timor became part of Indonesia. Colonial administration withdrew following the 1974 coup in Portugal, and in 1975 it declared itself independent as the Democratic Republic of East Timor. After a civil war between supporters of independence and those advocating integration into Indonesia, East Timor was annexed by Indonesia in 1976. The annexation was not recognized by the UN. Resistance to Indonesian rule was met with severe repression. In a 1999 referendum, 78 per cent of the population voted for independence; the vote was ratified by Indonesia but provoked violence by pro-Indonesian factions. UN peacekeeping forces were deployed and a UN Transitional Administration in East Timor (UNTAET) was created. East Timor became independent in 2002. UN deployment ended in 2005 but peacekeeping troops returned in 2006 after clashes with sacked army personnel developed into widespread factional violence.

ECUADOR

Official name	Republic of Ecuador
Local name	Ecuador; República del Ecuador
Area	270 699 sq km (104 490 sq mi)
Capital	Quito
Chief towns	Guayaquil, Cuenca, Riobamba, Esmeraldas
Population	13 547 000 (2006e)
Nationality	Ecuadorean, Ecuadorian
Languages	Spanish; Quechua is also spoken
Ethnic groups	Mestizo 65%, Amerindian 25%, white 7%, black 3%
Religions	Christianity 96% (RC 94%, Prot 2%), others 4%
Time zone	GMT −5
Currency	1 US Dollar ($) = 100 cents
Telephone	+593
Internet	.ec
Country code	ECU

Location

A republic straddling the equator in the north-west of South America. It is bounded to the north by Colombia; to the south and east by Peru; and to the west by the Pacific Ocean, and its territory includes the Galápagos Islands in the Pacific Ocean.

Physical description

The Andes run north to south down the centre of the country; three main ranges rise to peaks which include Cotopaxi (5896 m/19 344 ft); the highest point is Mount Chimborazo (6267 m/20 560 ft) and its enclosing high plateaus (*Sierra*); the Andes divide the broad coastal plain (*Costa*) of the west from the eastern alluvial plains (*Oriente*), covered with rainforest and dissected by rivers flowing from the Andes towards the Amazon; frequent serious earthquakes; the Galápagos Islands comprise six main volcanic islands.

Climate

Tropical climate in coastal regions, with hot, humid weather and rain throughout the year (especially December–April); varies from 2000 mm in the north to 200 mm in the south; central Andes temperatures are much reduced by altitude; Quito has warm days and chilly nights, with frequent heavy rain in the afternoon; hot and wet equatorial climate in the east.

Economy

Based on oil (40% of export earnings) and agriculture; main cash crops are bananas (world's leading exporter), coffee, cocoa, fish (tuna), shrimps, vegetables and cut flowers; industries process food and timber products; oil is piped from the *Oriente* to refineries at Esmeraldas.

Government

Governed by an executive President, a Cabinet and a unicameral National Congress.

History

Formerly part of the Inca Empire, it was conquered by the Spanish in 1527 and included in the Viceroyalty of New Granada. On gaining independence in 1822, it joined with Panama, Colombia and Venezuela to form Gran Colombia, but left the union to become an independent republic in 1830. The country was politically unstable throughout the 20th century (there were 22 presidents between 1925 and 1948, none completing a term in office), and the volatility has continued owing to economic difficulties since the 1980s and popular protests at economic reforms. Ecuador adopted the US dollar in 2000 in an attempt to stabilize the economy.

Darwin's Legacy

The Galápagos islands, situated 600 miles west of Ecuador, are renowned for their immense variety of rare and unusual species. However, human habitation, tourism and the introduction of non-indigenous species has contributed to the decline of local habitats and species. Some of the species most at risk are the so-called 'Darwin finches' that inspired Charles Darwin (1809–82) to write *The Origin of Species by Means of Natural Selection* (1859).

EGYPT

Official name	Arab Republic of Egypt
Local name	Misr; Al Jumhūriyya al-Miṣryya al-'Arabiyya
Former name	formerly part of the United Arab Republic (1958–61; name retained until 1971)
Area	1 001 449 sq km (386 559 sq mi)
Capital	Cairo; El Qāhirah
Chief towns	Alexandria, Port Said, Aswan, Suez, El Gîza
Population	78 887 000 (2006e)
Nationality	Egyptian
Language	Arabic
Ethnic groups	Eastern Hamitic 91%, others 9%
Religions	Islam 90% (mostly Sunni), Christianity 10% (mostly Coptic)
Time zone	GMT +2
Currency	1 Egyptian Pound (£E, LE) = 100 piastres
Telephone	+20
Internet	.eg
Country code	EGY

Location

A republic in north-east Africa, bounded to the west by Libya; to the south by Sudan; to the east by the Red Sea; to the north-east by Israel; and to the north by the Mediterranean Sea.

Physical description

The River Nile flows north from Sudan, dammed south of Aswan to create Lake Nasser, to its huge delta, 250 km (160 mi) across and 160 km (100 mi) north to south, on the Mediterranean coast; it divides the mainly flat and arid country into the narrow, sparsely inhabited Eastern Desert between the Nile valley and the Red Sea and the broad Western Desert, which covers over two-thirds of the country and contains seven major depressions; the largest and lowest of these is the Qattara Depression (133 m/436 ft below sea level); the Sinai Peninsula to the east of the Red Sea is a desert region with mountains rising to 2637 m (8651 ft) at Gebel Katherîna, Egypt's highest point; 90% of the population lives on the Nile flood plain (c.3% of the country's area).

Climate

Mainly desert, except for an 80 km (50 mi)-wide Mediterranean coastal fringe, where annual rainfall is 100–200 mm; very hot on the coast when the dust-laden *khamsin* wind blows north from the Sahara (March–June); Alexandria, on the coast, has an average annual rainfall of 180 mm; elsewhere, rainfall is less than 50 mm.

Economy

Based on services (tourism (over 50% of GDP), Suez Canal revenues), oil and agriculture; land under cultivation increased by irrigation; main crops are cotton, rice, maize, wheat, vegetables, fruit and livestock; chief industries produce crude oil and petroleum products, natural gas, textiles, processed food, chemicals, pharmaceuticals, metals (iron ore, manganese), metal products, phosphates and gypsum.

Government

Governed by an executive President, a Prime Minister and Council of Ministers, and a unicameral People's Assembly; the Consultative Council has an advisory role. Political parties based on religious adherence are banned.

History

The history of Egypt can be traced as far back as around 6000 BC, to Neolithic cultures on the River Nile. A unified kingdom embracing lower and upper Egypt was first created in around 3100 BC, ruled by Pharaoh dynasties; the pyramids at El Gîza were constructed during the Fourth Dynasty. Egyptian power was greatest during the New Empire period (1567–1085 BC). The area became a Persian province in the 6th century bc and was conquered by Alexander the Great in the 4th century bc. Ptolemaic Pharaohs ruled Egypt until 30 BC, when it was conquered and ruled by the Roman Empire (30 BC to AD 324) and the Byzantine Empire. It was conquered by Arabs in AD 672. From 1798 until 1801, it was occupied by France under Napoleon. The Suez Canal was constructed in 1869. A revolt in 1879 against the ruling Khedive was put down by British intervention in 1882. Egypt became a formal British protectorate in 1914, but declared its independence in 1922. It was used as a base for Allied forces during World War II. King Farouk was deposed by the army in 1952, and Egypt was declared a republic in 1953. Nationalization of the Suez Canal in 1956 provoked a joint Anglo-French and Israeli invasion, the forces being obliged to withdraw by international pressure. An attack on Israel, followed by Israeli invasion in 1967, resulted in the loss of the Sinai Peninsula and control of part of the Suez Canal (regained following negotiations in the 1970s). In 1981 President Sadat was assassinated, and relations with Arab nations were strained by Egypt's recognition of Israel, but they improved again during the 1980s. Sadat's successor, President Hosni Mubarak, has followed a policy of moderation and reconciliation, playing an active role in the Middle East peace process to resolve the Arab–Israeli conflict in the 1990s, but has been unable to stem terrorism at home. During the 1990s there were violent clashes between Muslims and Coptic Christians. The Islamic fundamentalists (mainly the Islamic Group and al-Jihad organizations) grew increasingly violent in their campaign against the government, and by the end of the decade foreign tourists as well as Egyptians were among their targets. Although Mubarak's presidency has been approved by national referendum every six years since 1981 and there are direct legislative elections, lack of general political freedom has aroused increasing frustration and resentment, expressed in public demonstrations in recent years.

ÉIRE ▶ IRELAND, REPUBLIC OF

THE PYRAMIDS: EGYPTIAN WONDER OF THE WORLD

The oldest of the Seven Wonders of the World, and the only one still in existence today, is the Great Pyramid in the complex at Giza, Egypt. Located on the banks of the River Nile opposite Cairo, the pyramids were built during the 26th century BC.

The Great Pyramid

The largest of the pyramids is variously known as the Great Pyramid, the Pyramid of Khufu and the Pyramid of Cheops. It housed the remains of the pharaoh known as Khufu in Egyptian (Cheops in Greek), the second king of the 4th dynasty. It is 137 m (450 ft) tall and is believed to be built from more than 2 million blocks of stone, each weighing about 2.5 tonnes. It took about 23 years to complete, under the direction of the pharaoh himself; contrary to the ideas of the Greek historian Herodotus, the work was carried out by hand and was done by farmers and labourers rather than slaves. The Great Pyramid was the tallest structure on earth for around 4,000 years, until it was surpassed by the Gothic spires of Lincoln Cathedral.

The Great Pyramid is part of a complex with two others: Khafre and Menkaure (Chephren and Mycerinos in Greek), tombs named after Khufu's son and grandson respectively.

Structure of the pyramids

Originally, the surface of the pyramids was made from polished limestone and covered with ancient inscriptions. The earliest Egyptian pyramids were stepped, such as the pyramid of Zoser at Saqqara. By the time of construction at Giza, however, the stepped construction was filled in to give a smooth appearance.

The interiors of Egyptian pyramids consisted of a series of passageways and rooms, with the pharaoh's tomb hidden deep within. The pharaoh was provided with jewels and precious metals for his journey to the afterlife, so that his life might be more comfortable there. The passageways were designed to protect the tomb by confusing potential grave robbers, leading up and down or sometimes being built as deliberate dead ends. The builders blocked the passageways behind them, and it is reputed that they even cast bad luck charms on anyone who dared to break in. (This idea is most familiar today in the famous Tutankhamun Curse, rumoured to have affected those associated with the discovery of the tomb of the 18th-dynasty boy pharaoh in 1922.)

The Great Sphinx

Presiding over the Giza complex is the 'Great Sphinx' Sesheps. Built from limestone in the form of lion's body and human head, this magnificent statue faces due east, looking at the rising sun. The Sphinx was a guardian deity and it is likely that such statues were often given the facial features of the pharaoh they honoured. Unfortunately the face now lacks its nose; for a long time, French troops were accused of breaking it off with a cannonball during the Battle of the Pyramids in 1798. However, it is now known that the nose was missing earlier than this, and their general Napoleon certainly seems to have had a lot of respect for the site; speaking to his troops before the battle he said: 'Think of it, soldier; from the summit of these pyramids, forty centuries look down upon you.'

EL SALVADOR

Official name	Republic of El Salvador
Local name	El Salvador; República de El Salvador
Area	21 476 sq km (8290 sq mi)
Capital	San Salvador
Chief towns	Santa Ana, San Miguel, Mejicanos
Population	6 822 000 (2006e)
Nationality	Salvadoran
Language	Spanish
Ethnic groups	Mestizo 90%, white 9%, Amerindian 1%
Religions	Christianity 82% (RC 57%, Prot 25%), unaffiliated 17%, others 1%
Time zone	GMT −6
Currency	1 US Dollar ($) = 100 cents
Telephone	+503
Internet	.sv
Country code	SLV

Location

The smallest of the Central American republics, bounded to the north and east by Honduras; to the west by Guatemala; and to the south by the Pacific Ocean.

Physical description

Two volcanic ranges running east to west divide El Salvador into three geographical regions, ranging from a narrow coastal belt in the south through upland valleys and plateaux to mountains in the north (the highest point, Cerro El Pital, is 2730 m/8957 ft); the River Lempa, dammed for hydroelectricity, flows south to the Pacific; there are many volcanic lakes; earthquakes are common.

Climate

Varies greatly with altitude; hot and tropical on the coastal lowlands; single rainy season (May–October); temperate uplands; average annual temperature at San Salvador is 23°C; average annual rainfall is 1775 mm.

Economy

Largely based on the service sector (commerce, financial services), manufacturing and agriculture (coffee, sugar, shrimps); main industries are offshore assembly for re-export, food processing, beverages, petroleum products, chemicals; fertilizers; textiles, furniture, metals.

Government

Governed by an executive President, a Council of State and a unicameral Legislative Assembly.

History

Originally part of the Aztec kingdom, it was conquered by the Spanish in 1526 and achieved independence from Spain in 1821. A member of the Central American Federation until its dissolution in 1839, it became an independent republic in 1841. In the mid-20th century it was ruled by dictatorships, suffered political unrest, and waged war with Honduras in 1965 and 1969. There was also considerable political unrest in the 1970s, with guerrilla activity against the US-supported government intensifying from 1977 into a civil war in which 75 000 died and many became refugees. A peace agreement was signed in 1992 in which the left-wing guerrilla group Frente Farabundo Marti de Liberación Nacional (FMLN) was recognized as a political party; it won a few seats in the 1994 elections in which the right-wing Alianza Republicana Nacionalista (ARENA) came to power. Since then, FMLN has increased its share of the vote, often being the largest party in parliament, but it has never held office, as ARENA has always formed coalition governments with smaller right-wing parties. Severe earthquakes in early 2001 and a volcanic eruption and a tropical storm in late 2005 caused widespread devastation.

ENGLAND ▸UNITED KINGDOM

EQUATORIAL GUINEA

Official name	Republic of Equatorial Guinea
Local name	Guinea Ecuatorial; República de Guinea Ecuatorial
Former name	Spanish Guinea (until 1968)
Area	26 016 sq km (10 042 sq mi)
Capital	Malabo, on Bioko
Chief towns	Bata and Evinayong on the mainland, Luba and Riaba on Bioko
Population	540 000 (2006e)
Nationality	Equatorial Guinean or Equatoguinean
Languages	Spanish, French; pidgin English and Fang and other local languages are also spoken
Ethnic groups	Fang 82%, Bubi 11%, Ndowe 4%, others 3%
Religions	Christianity 93% (RC 87%, Prot 6%), traditional beliefs 5%, Islam 1%, none/unspecified 1%
Time zone	GMT +1
Currency	1 CFA Franc (CFAFr) = 100 centimes
Telephone	+240
Internet	.gq
Country code	GNQ

Location

A republic in western central Africa, comprising a mainland area (Río Muni) and several islands (notably Bioko and Annabón) in the Gulf of Guinea.

Physical description

The mainland rises sharply from a narrow coastal plain of mangrove swamps towards a heavily forested mountainous plateau; deeply cut by several rivers; the islands are volcanic; Bioko Island, about 160 km (100 mi) north-west of the mainland, rises to 3007 m (9865 ft) at Pico de Basilé.

Climate

Hot and humid equatorial; average annual rainfall is c.2000 mm; average maximum daily temperature is 29–32°C.

Economy

Transformed by discovery of oil and natural gas off Bioko in the 1990s; other activities are agriculture (mostly subsistence level except for cocoa production), fishing, forestry and wood processing.

Government

Governed by a President, a Prime Minister and Council of Ministers, and a unicameral House of Representatives of the People.

History

Equatorial Guinea was first visited by Europeans in the 15th century. The island of Fernando Po (Bioko) was claimed by Portugal in 1494 and held until 1788. The area was occupied by Britain from 1781 until 1843; the rights to it were subsequently acquired by Spain in 1844. It gained independence in 1968 and was ruled by President Macias Nguema until a military coup in 1979 led by his nephew, Obiang Nguema, ended his repressive regime. A new constitution was approved in 1991 and multiparty democracy was legalized in 1992. Even so, Nguema's Equatorial Guinea Democratic Party (PDGE) has maintained its grip on power; most of the elections since 1992 have been boycotted because of irregularities by the opposition parties, some of which have been banned. Opposition leaders were imprisoned in 2002 for allegedly taking part in an attempted coup, and another alleged coup by foreign nationals was suppressed in 2004.

> ### ¡Aquí Se Habla Español!
> Equatorial Guinea is the only fully independent country in Africa to have Spanish as an official language. It is also the smallest Spanish-speaking country in the world.

ERITREA

Official name	State of Eritrea
Local name	Eritrea; Hagere Eretra, al-Dawla al-Iritra
Former name	formerly part of Ethiopia (until 1993)
Area	121 320 sq km (46 841 sq mi)
Capital	Asmara; Asmera
Chief towns	Assab, Massawa, Keren, Tessenai
Population	4 787 000 (2006e)
Nationality	Eritrean
Languages	Arabic, Tigrinya; several local languages are also spoken
Ethnic groups	Tigrinya 50%, Tigrean 35%, Afar 4%, Saho 3%, Kunama 3%, others 5%
Religions	Islam 60% (Sunni), Christianity 37% (Coptic 32%, RC 5%), others 3%
Time zone	GMT +3
Currency	1 Nakfa (Nfa) = 100 cents
Telephone	+291
Internet	.er
Country code	ERI

Location

A country in north-east Africa, bounded to the north and north-west by Sudan; to the west and south-west by Ethiopia; to the south by Djibouti; and to the east by the Red Sea.

Physical description

Low-lying coastal plain stretching 1000 km (620 mi) along the Red Sea, rising to an inland plateau; highest point is Soira (3018 m/9901 ft).

Climate

Hot and dry along the Red Sea desert coast; cooler and wetter in the central highlands; semi-arid in the western hills and lowlands.

Economy

Reconstructing after war; dependent on foreign aid and expatriates' remittances; subsistence agriculture supports 80% of the population, but subject to drought and famine; industries include food processing, beverages, textiles, garments and ship repair.

Government

Governed by an executive President, a State Council and a unicameral National Assembly; transitional arrangements put in place at independence remain in operation, and elections under the constitution approved in 1997 have been postponed indefinitely.

History

The area was under the control of the Ottoman Empire from the mid-16th century. Occupied by Italy in 1884, it became an Italian colony in 1890. It was used as a base for the Italian invasion of Abyssinia in 1935, and became part of Italian East Africa in 1936. It was then taken by the British in 1941, federated with Ethiopia at the request of the UN in 1952, and made a province of Ethiopia in 1962. This galvanized into action the Eritrean Liberation Front (ELF), which had been founded as the Eritrean Liberation Movement in 1958, and it waged guerrilla warfare against the government throughout the 1960s and 1970s. In 1970 a communist faction broke away to form the Eritrean People's Liberation Front (EPLF), which emerged during the 1980s as the dominant rebel group. Despite this division and much fighting between rebel groups, it managed, through support from the Eastern bloc and some Arab countries, to prevent its destruction both while Haile Selassie was Emperor and when Mengistu Haile Mariam was president. When Soviet support waned, the EPLF joined with other Ethiopian rebel groups, including the Tigray People's Liberation Front, and overthrew the Mengistu regime in 1991. The EPLF immediately formed a separate provisional Eritrean government. A referendum on independence in April 1993 recorded a massive vote in favour, and Eritrea's independence was declared the following month. The EPLF became the ruling political party, renaming itself the People's Front for Democracy and Justice. The post-independence regime has become increasingly authoritarian; elections scheduled for 2001 did not take place and have not been rescheduled, and the transitional government remains in power. Since 1998, Eritrea and Ethiopia have clashed frequently over border territory, especially in Tigray, and international arbitration has been unable to resolve the dispute so far.

ESTONIA

Official name	Republic of Estonia
Local name	Eesti; Eesti Vabariik (Estonian), Estonskaya (Russia)
Former name	Estonian Soviet Socialist Republic (1940–90), within the Union of Soviet Socialist Republics (USSR; 1940–91)
Area	45 100 sq km (17 409 sq mi)
Capital	Tallinn
Chief towns	Tartu, Narva, Kohtla-Järve, Pärnu
Population	1 324 000 (2006e)
Nationality	Estonian
Language	Estonian
Ethnic groups	Estonian 68%, Russian 26%, Ukrainian 2%, Belarusian 1%, Finnish 1%, others 2%
Religions	Christianity 28% (Lutheran Prot 14%, Orthodox 13%, other Christian 1%), unaffiliated 34%, other and unspecified 32%, none 6%
Time zone	GMT +2
Currency	1 Kroon (KR) = 100 sents
Telephone	+372
Internet	.ee
Country code	EST

Location

A republic in eastern Europe, bounded to the west by the Baltic Sea; to the north by the Gulf of Finland; to the east by Russia; and to the south by Latvia.

Physical description

Mostly a plain of marshes, over 1500 lakes and forests (36% of land area); the highest point is Suur Munamagi (318m/1043ft); there are many islands on the coast, notably Saaremaa, Hiiumaa and Muhu.

Climate

Cool summers, wet winters.

Economy

Industrialized market economy; main agricultural products are potatoes, vegetables, livestock, dairy products and fish; industries include forestry, food processing, engineering, electronics, textiles, information technology and telecommunications equipment.

Government

Governed by a President, a Prime Minister and Council of Ministers, and a unicameral Parliament (*Riigikogu*).

History

Occupied by Vikings in the 9th century, during its history it has been owned by Denmark, Sweden, Poland, Russia and the Teutonic Knights of Germany. For a time it was divided into two areas: northern Estonia and Livonia (southern Estonia and Latvia), but it was ceded to Russia in its entirety by Sweden in the Treaty of Nystadt in 1721. It achieved independence in 1918, was annexed by the Soviet Union and declared a Soviet Socialist Republic in 1940, and was occupied by Germany during World War II. Soviet forces re-annexed the country in 1944 and it remained part of the Soviet Union until 1991 when, following a resurgence of the nationalist movement in the 1980s, it declared its independence. A new constitution was agreed in 1992, and the last Russian troops were withdrawn in 1994. Since independence, Estonia has pursued pro-western policies, joining the European Union and NATO in 2004.

Peace at Christmas

Christmas is the most important festival on the Estonian calendar, and many traditions are associated with it. One such custom is the declaration of Christmas Peace. On Christmas Eve each year, the President of Estonia declares Christmas Peace and attends a special service. The practice was started by the order of Queen Kristina of Sweden in the 17th century, while Estonia was still under Swedish control.

ETHIOPIA

Official name	Federal Democratic Republic of Ethiopia (FDRE)
Local name	Ityopiya; Ya'Ityopya Federalawi Dimokrasyawi Repeblik
Former name	Abyssinia (until 1936), part of Italian East Africa (1936–41), People's Democratic Republic of Ethiopia (1987–91)
Area	1 128 497 sq km (435 600 sq mi)
Capital	Addis Ababa; Ādīs Ābeba, Addis Abeba
Chief towns	Dire Dawa, Harer
Population	74 778 000 (2006e)
Nationality	Ethiopian
Languages	Amharic; 70 local languages are also spoken
Ethnic groups	Oromo 40%, Amhara and Tigrean 32%, Sidamo 9%, Shankella 6%, Somali 6%, others 7%
Religions	Islam 47%, Christianity 36% (Coptic), traditional beliefs 12%, others 5%
Time zone	GMT +3
Currency	1 Ethiopian Birr (EB) = 100 cents
Telephone	+251
Internet	.et
Country code	ETH

Location

A landlocked republic in north-east Africa, bounded to the west and south-west by Sudan; to the south by Kenya; to the east and north-east by Somalia; and to the north by Djibouti and Eritrea; the country is landlocked, having lost about 10% of its territory and all of its Red Sea coastline when the former province of Eritrea gained its independence in 1993.

Physical description

Dominated by a mountainous central plateau; split diagonally by the Great Rift Valley the highest point is Ras Dashen (4620 m/15 157 ft); the plateau is crossed east to west by the Blue Nile, which has its source in Lake Tana; the north and east are relatively low-lying; in the north-east the Danakil Depression dips to 116 m (381 ft) below sea level; the state became landlocked when its former province of Eritrea became independent.

Climate

Tropical, moderated by higher altitudes; distinct wet season (April–September); temperatures warm, but rarely hot all year round; annual rainfall generally more than 1000 mm; hot, semi-arid north-east and south-east lowlands receive less than 500 mm annually; subject to severe droughts since the 1980s.

Economy

One of the world's poorest countries, dependent on foreign aid; progress often reversed by severe drought and resulting famine, deaths and resettlement;

agriculture employs more than 80% of the population, especially subsistence farming and herding; small food processing industry; some natural resources but little exploited; exports mainly coffee, qat, gold, leather goods, livestock and oil seeds.

Government

Governed by a President, a Prime Minister and Council of Ministers, and a bicameral Parliament, consisting of a House of Federation and a House of People's Representatives.

History

Ethiopia, formerly Abyssinia, is the oldest independent country in sub-Saharan Africa, and the first African country to be Christianized. Abyssinian independence was recognized by the League of Nations in 1923, but after the invasion of Italy in 1935 the country was annexed as Italian East Africa from 1936 to its liberation in 1941, when Emperor Haile Selassie returned from exile. A military coup in 1974 led to the establishment of the Marxist Provisional Military Administrative Council (PMAC) or Dergue, and opposition was met by mass arrests and executions in 1977–8. In addition to war with Somalia over the Ogaden district during the 1970s and 1980s, there was internal conflict with separatist Eritrean and Tigrean forces, who secured victories over government troops in the early 1980s while the country suffered severe famine. The PMAC dissolved in 1987 and its power was transferred to the People's Democratic Republic, but an attempted coup in 1989 was followed by the complete collapse of the regime in 1991 and renewed famine in 1992. Eritrea secured its independence in 1993. A transitional government ruled until a new federal system, the Federal Democratic Republic of Ethiopia, was established in 1995. Relative stability and economic growth slowly returned; however, since 1998 there have been frequent clashes with Eritrea over border territory, especially in Tigray, and international arbitration has been unable to resolve the dispute so far. In late 2006, Ethiopian forces entered Somalia in support of its transitional government against the Islamic militia that took control of much of central and southern Somalia in 2006.

> 66
>
> *Throughout history it has been the inaction of those who could have acted, the indifference of those who should have known better, the silence of the voice of justice when it mattered most, that has made it possible for evil to triumph.*
>
> —Haile Selassie (1891–1975), Emperor of Ethiopia, in an address to a special session of the UN General Assembly, 4 October 1963. This made him the first head of state to address both that organization and the League of Nations.
>
> 99

FALKLAND ISLANDS ▸ UNITED KINGDOM
FAROE ISLANDS ▸ DENMARK

FIJI

Official name	Republic of the Fiji Islands
Local name	Viti; Matanitu Ko Viti
Area	18 333 sq km (7 076 sq mi)
Capital	Suva
Chief towns	Lautoka, Ba, Labasa, Nadi, Nausori
Population	846 000 (2006e)
Nationality	Fijian
Languages	Fijian, English, Hindi
Ethnic groups	Fijian 55%, Indian 37%, others 8%
Religions	Hinduism 38%, Christianity 46% (Prot 37%, mainly Methodist, RC 9%), Islam 8%, Sikhism 1%, others 7%
Time zone	GMT +12
Currency	1 Fiji Dollar (F$) = 100 cents
Telephone	+679
Internet	.fj
Country code	FJI

Location

A Melanesian island group of around 332 islands (c.100 permanently inhabited) and more than 500 islets in the south-west Pacific Ocean, forming an independent republic.

Physical description

The larger islands are generally mountainous and rugged; there are areas of flat land suitable for cultivation in the coastal plains, river deltas and valleys; the highest peak, Tomaniivi, is on Viti Levu (1324 m/4348 ft); there are hot springs in isolated places; most smaller islands consist of limestone, with little vegetation; there is an extensive coral reef (Great Sea Reef) stretching for 500 km (300 mi) along the western fringe; dense, tropical forest lies on the wet, windward side in the south-east; it is mainly treeless on the dry, leeward side.

Climate

Tropical maritime climate, with hot, humid weather; temperatures average 20–29°C; winds are variable in the wet season (November–April), when tropical cyclones can occur; the average annual rainfall varies from 1900 to 3050 mm, the higher rainfall occurring in the east and south-east.

Economy

Developed and diversified economy but dependent on foreign aid and expatriates' remittances after political instability and stagnation; agriculture employs 70% of the workforce; main industries are tourism, which is growing, sugar production and milling, garment manufacturing and gold mining (all in decline), fishing and forestry.

Government

Governed by a President (appointed by the Great Council of Chiefs), a Prime Minister and Cabinet, and a bicameral Parliament consisting of an appointed Senate and an elected House of Representatives.

History

Fiji was visited by Abel Tasman in 1643, and by Captain James Cook in 1774. It became a British colony in 1874. It gained independence in 1970 as a constitutional monarchy, and became a republic after the 1987 coup. Initially stable, the country became politically volatile in the 1980s owing to tensions between the native Melanesians and the growing ethnic Indian population. The 1987 election brought to power an Indian-dominated coalition, which led to military coups in May and September; a civilian government was restored in December. A new constitution upholding ethnic Melanesian political power was effected in 1990, but was attacked by opposition parties as racist and the racist elements were removed in 1997. The 1999 election brought to power a multiracial coalition government headed by an Indian prime minister. He and most of the Cabinet were held hostage for several weeks in 2000 by ethnic Fijians; the military intervened and imposed military government. Elections restored civilian government in 2001, but in 2006 attempts by the government to reduce the military's influence in politics resulted in another military coup.

FINLAND

Official name	Republic of Finland
Local name	Suomi; Suomen Tasavalta (Finnish), Finland; Republiken Finland (Swedish)
Area	338 145 sq km (130 524 sq mi)
Capital	Helsinki (Finnish), Helsingfors (Swedish)
Chief towns	Tampere, Turku, Espoo, Vantaa
Population	5 231 000 (2006e)
Nationality	Finn, Finnish
Languages	Finnish, Swedish; Sami and Russian are spoken by minorities
Ethnic groups	Finnish 93%, Swedish 6%, others 1%
Religions	Christianity 86% (Prot 84%, Orthodox 1%, other Christian 1%), none/unaffiliated 14%
Time zone	GMT +2
Currency	1 Euro (€) = 100 cents
Telephone	+358
Internet	.fi
Country code	FIN

Location

A republic in northern Europe, bounded to the east by Russia; to the south by the Gulf of Finland; to the west by the Gulf of Bothnia and Sweden; and to the north by Norway.

Physical description

A low-lying glaciated plateau, with an average height of 150 m (492 ft); the highest peak is a spur of Halti Fell (1328 m/4356 ft) on the north-western border; there are more than 60 000 shallow lakes in the south-east, providing a system of inland navigation; with land still rising from the sea, the country's area is increasing by 7 sq km (2.7 sq mi) each year; more than one quarter of the country lies north of the Arctic Circle; chief rivers are the Tornio, Kemi and Oulu; the archipelago of Saaristomeri is in the south-west, with more than 17 000 islands and skerries; the Ahvenanmaa islands are in the west; forest land covers 65% of the country, and water 10%.

Climate

The country's northern climes are ameliorated by the Baltic Sea; western winds bring warm air currents in summer; Eurasian winds bring cold spells in winter and heatwaves in summer; average annual precipitation in the south is 600–700 mm, and 500–600 mm in the north, with half of it falling as snow; during the summer the sun stays above the horizon for more than 70 days

Economy

Highly industrialized market economy; traditional timber and metals industries now supplemented by cutting-edge telecommunications and electronics manufacturing; main exports are electronic and electrical goods, chemicals, metals, timber, paper, wood pulp; agriculture and foodstuffs (especially grain) and energy are major imports.

Government

Governed by a President, a Prime Minister and Council of State, and a unicameral Parliament (*Eduskunta*).

History

Finland was ruled by Sweden from 1157 until it was ceded to Russia in 1809 and became an autonomous grand duchy of the Russian Empire. A nationalist movement developed in the 19th century and Finland declared its independence after the Bolshevik Revolution in 1917. It resisted invasion by the Union of Soviet Socialist Republics (USSR) in 1939 but was defeated in 1940 and forced to cede territory; in the hope of recovering this territory it joined Germany's attack on the Soviet Union in 1941, and lost territory to the USSR under the treaty concluded after the 1944 armistice. Under a 1948 treaty with the USSR, Finland was obliged to demilitarize its Soviet border and to adopt a neutral stance in international affairs; these terms lasted until the Soviet Union collapsed in 1991. Finland joined the European Union in 1995, and replaced the markka with the euro in 2002.

FINLAND: LAND OF THE FAINTLY UNUSUAL

Finland is not a run-of-the mill country – after all, it has come up with both the home of Father Christmas and the children's books *The Moomins*. Maybe it has something to do with the long winter nights and summer days, but when people gather over a cup or two of coffee (of which the Finns are the world's biggest consumers) and a newspaper (most European newspapers are printed on Finnish newsprint), they seem to be able to dream up countless unusual pastimes.

Fun with phones and sprinting with spouses

A town named Nokia gave its name to Finland's most recognizable export, the mobile phone. Another Finnish town, Savonlinna, gave *its* name to one of the country's wackiest competitions – the Mobile Phone Throwing World Championships. Inaugurated in 2000, this annual event sees competitors launch a mobile phone from a throwing circle to see who can propel it the furthest. The competition is open to all, even the very youngest, and special awards are given for 'artistic performance' as well as distance. The rules are rudimentary, but 'a contestant can be excluded from the Championships if he/she is considered to be a danger for himself/herself, to other contestants or to the public'.

For an all-round show of strength there are always the Wife-Carrying World Championships, held in the town of Sonkajärvi since 1992. The roots of the competition date from a time when it was common practice to steal women from neighbouring villages. Every 'wife' must weigh at least 49 kg (or be weighted down); as well as a trophy, the winner receives the equivalent weight of his wife in beer. It is clearly stipulated in the rules that 'all the participants must have fun'.

From marshes to music

More surreal yet are the World Mosquito Killing Championships, held every year in Pelkosenniemi where the appropriate insects are plentiful. The object is to kill as many as possible in five minutes using only your hand – the world record is 21! While in the swamps, we shouldn't forget two further events: the three-day World Swamp Football Championships, where players of both sexes compete up to their knees in a muddy field, and the Swamp Volleyball World Championships.

On a musical note, Oulu hosts the outlandish Air Guitar World Championships, where contestants can use the services of a personal 'air roadie' and compete to win an actual guitar. Not to be outdone, Heinola has been hosting the World Karaoke Championships since 2003. Music of a more rural sort is on offer at the Cattle Calling Championships, in which the cows are serenaded with songs and shouting.

Extreme events

All in all, it doesn't seem to take much for the Finns to want to get competitive, and there is an event for everyone. Those who like it cold can compete in the International Ice Swimming Championships in Oulu; for those who favour the other extreme there are the World Sauna Endurance Championships, again at Heinola, where competitors try to endure 110°C (230°F) temperatures. Finally, and only for the massively foolhardy, there is the Ant-Hill Competition: the sport is to see who can sit for longest on an ant-hill – naked!

FRANCE

Official name	French Republic
Local name	France; République Française
Area	551 000 sq km (213 000 sq mi)
Capital	Paris
Chief towns	Marseilles, Lyons, Toulouse, Nice, Strasbourg
Population	60 876 000 (2006e)
Nationality	French
Language	French
Ethnic groups	European, with North African, German, Indochinese and Basque minorities
Religions	Christianity 88% (RC 86%, Prot 2%), Islam 7%, Judaism 1%, unaffiliated 4%
Time zone	GMT +1
Currency	1 Euro (€) = 100 cents
Telephone	+33
Internet	.fr
Country code	FRA

Location

A republic in western Europe, bounded to the north and north-east by the English Channel, Belgium, Luxembourg; to the east by Germany, Switzerland, Italy and Monaco; to the south by the Mediterranean Sea, Spain and Andorra; and to the west by the Bay of Biscay.

Physical description

A country of low and medium-sized hills and plateaux deeply cut by rivers; bounded to the south and east by large mountain ranges, notably (in the interior) the Armorican Massif, the Massif Central, the Cévennes, the Vosges and the Ardennes; in the east the Jura and the Alps rise to 4807 m (15 771 ft) at Mont Blanc, the highest point; in the south are the Pyrenees; the chief rivers include the Loire, Rhône, Seine and Garonne; also includes the island of Corsica in the Mediterranean Sea.

Climate

The south has a Mediterranean climate, with warm, moist winters and hot, dry summers; in the north-west the climate is maritime, with an average annual rainfall of 573 mm; the east has a continental climate with an average annual rainfall of 786 mm.

Economy

Highly industrialized and diversified economy with strong services sector; currently in transition from extensive state ownership to greater market orientation; western Europe's foremost producer of agricultural products, chiefly cereals, beef, sugar beet, potatoes, wine, grapes and dairy products; metal and chemical industries are based on reserves of iron ore, bauxite, potash, salt and sulphur; heavy industry (steel, machinery, textiles, clothing, chemicals, vehicles) is based around the northern coalfields; other industry includes aircraft, motor vehicles, electronic goods, textiles, plastics, pharmaceuticals, food processing; several nuclear power sites, providing 75 per cent of all electricity; hydroelectric power comes from the Alps; tourism and fishing are also important.

Government

Governed by a President, a Prime Minister and Council of Ministers, and a bicameral legislature consisting of a National Assembly and a Senate.

History

There is evidence of prehistoric settlement in France, as revealed in Paleolithic carvings and rock paintings (eg at Lascaux) and in Neolithic megaliths (eg at Carnac). Celtic-speaking Gauls were dominant by the 5th century bc. The country was part of the Roman Empire from 125 bc to the 5th century ad, and was invaded by several Germanic tribes between the 3rd and 5th centuries. The Franks inaugurated the Merovingian epoch in the 5th century. Clovis I was the first Merovingian king to control large parts of Gaul; the last to hold significant power was Dagobert I (died 638), though the royal dynasty survived until Childeric III's deposition in 751. The Carolingian ruling dynasty ultimately replaced the Merovingians when Pepin III, the Short, became King of the Franks in 751. The power of the Carolingian kings came to a peak in the 8th century, with the succession of Charlemagne. A feudal monarchy was founded in 987 by Hugh Capet; this was the third Frankish royal dynasty (the Capetian Dynasty), which ruled France until 1328. The Plantagenets of England acquired several French territories in the 12th century, but lands were gradually recovered during the Hundred Years' War (1337–1453), apart from Calais (regained in 1558). The Capetian dynasty was followed by the Valois and Bourbon dynasties, from 1328 and 1589 respectively. In the 16th century there was ongoing rivalry between Francis I and Emperor Charles V, then the Wars of Religion took place from 1562 until 1598. In the 17th century the power of the monarchy was restored, reaching its peak under Louis XIV. However, the French Revolution of 1789 dismantled the *ancien régime* (old order) in the name of liberty, equality and fraternity, and the First Republic was declared in 1792. The First Empire (1804–14) was ruled by Napoleon I, before the restoration of the Bourbon monarchy for a period between 1814 and 1848. The Second Republic (1848–52) was followed by the Second Empire (1852–70), ruled by Louis Napoleon (Napoleon III), and the Third Republic lasted from 1870 to 1940. There was great political instability between the world wars, with several governments holding office for short periods. The country was occupied by Germany from 1940 until 1944, with the pro-German government at Vichy and the Free French in London under the conservative and nationalist de Gaulle. The Fourth Republic began in 1946; shortly afterwards there was war in Indochina (1946–54), and conflict in Algeria (1954–62). Most of France's colonies were granted independence between 1954 and 1962. The Fifth Republic began in 1958; that same year, France became a founding member of the European Economic Community, and in 2002 it replaced the French franc with the euro. In 2003 the constitution was amended to decentralize power, devolving some economic, education and transport powers to the regions and departments. Proposals to give a degree of autonomy to Corsica were defeated in 2003, however, and separatists resumed the campaign of violence begun in the 1970s.

Overseas Departments

French Guiana

Location	Situated on the north-eastern coast of South America, it is bounded to the west by Suriname; to the east and south by Brazil; and to the north by the Atlantic Ocean.
Area	90 909 sq km (35 091 sq mi)	**Internet**	.gf
Capital	Cayenne	**Country code**	GUF
Population	199 500 (2006e)		

Guadeloupe

Location	A group of seven islands in the central Lesser Antilles, in the east Caribbean Sea.
Area	1779 sq km (687 sq mi)	**Internet**	.gp
Capital	Basse-Terre	**Country code**	GLP
Population	452 700 (2006e)		

Martinique

Location	An island in the Windward group of the Lesser Antilles, east Caribbean Sea, between Dominica and St Lucia.
Area	1079 sq km (416 sq mi)	**Internet**	.mq
Capital	Fort-de-France	**Country code**	MTQ
Population	436 100 (2006e)		

Réunion

Location	An island in the Indian Ocean, to the east of Madagascar.
Area	2510 sq km (969 sq mi)	**Internet**	.re
Capital	St-Denis	**Country code**	REU
Population	787 500 (2006e)		

Overseas territories

French Polynesia

Location	An island grouping of five scattered archipelagoes in the south-east Pacific Ocean, between the Cook Islands in the west and the Pitcairn Islands in the east.
Area	3941 sq km (1521 sq mi)	**Internet**	.pf
Capital	Papeete	**Country code**	PYF
Population	247 600 (2006e)		

New Caledonia

Location	A large island with a group of small islands as dependencies in the south-west Pacific Ocean, 1100 km (680 mi) east of Australia.		
Area	18 575 sq km (7170 sq mi)	**Internet**	.nc
Capital	Nouméa	**Country code**	NCL
Population	219 200 (2006e)		

French Southern and Antarctic Territories

Location	A group of islands in the southern Indian Ocean, and Adélie Land in Antarctica.		
Area	507 781 sq km (196 003 sq mi)	**Internet**	.tf
Population	Scientific staff only	**Country code**	ATF

Wallis and Futuna Islands

Location	Two groups of islands in the south-central Pacific Ocean, lying north-east of Fiji		
Area	274 sq km (106 sq mi)	**Internet**	.wf
Capital	Matu-Utu	**Country code**	WLF
Population	16 100 (2006e)		

Territorial collectivities

Mayotte

Location	A small island group of volcanic origin, east of Comoros, in the west Indian Ocean.		
Area	374 sq km (144 sq mi)	**Internet**	.yt
Capital	Mamoudzou	**Country code**	MYT
Population	201 200 (2006e)		

St Pierre and Miquelon

Location	Two small groups of islands in the North Atlantic Ocean, south of Newfoundland (Canada).		
Area	240 sq km (93 sq mi)	**Internet**	.pm
Capital	St Pierre	**Country code**	SPM
Population	7000 (2006e)		

GABON

Official name	Gabonese Republic
Local name	Gabon; République Gabonaise
Former name	French west Africa (1910–60)
Area	267 667 sq km (103 319 sq mi)
Capital	Libreville
Chief towns	Lambaréné, Franceville, Port Gentil
Population	1 425 000 (2006e)
Nationality	Gabonese
Language	French
Ethnic groups	Bantu tribes (Fang, Bapounou, Nzebi and Obamba are the main groupings) 89%, other Africans and Europeans 11%
Religions	Christianity 73%, traditional beliefs 10%, Islam 12%, unaffiliated 5%
Time zone	GMT +1
Currency	1 CFA Franc (CFAFr) = 100 centimes
Telephone	+241
Internet	.ga
Country code	GAB

Location

A republic in west equatorial Africa, bounded to the south, east and north-east by Congo; to the north by Cameroon; to the north-west by Equatorial Guinea; and to the west by the Atlantic Ocean.

Physical description

On the equator for 880 km (550 mi) west to east; the land rises from a narrow coastal plain with lagoons and estuaries towards the African central plateau, cut by several rivers, notably the Ogooué; the highest point is Mont Ibounji (1575 m/5167 ft); c.85% of the land is rainforest, with savanna in the east and south.

Climate

Equatorial climate, hot, wet and humid; average annual rainfall is 1250–2000 mm, rising to 2500 mm near the coast and at altitude; dry season in June–August; average maximum daily temperatures at Libreville are 33–7°C.

Economy

Prosperous economy based on oil (51% of GDP), natural gas, minerals (manganese, iron ore, uranium) and forestry; industries mostly process the energy, mineral, timber and agricultural products; agriculture, largely at subsistence level, employs 60% of the workforce; main products are cocoa, coffee, sugar, palm oil, rubber, cattle and fish.

Government

Governed by a President, a Prime Minister and Council of Ministers, and a bicameral legislature consisting of a Senate and a National Assembly.

History

Gabon was visited by the Portuguese in the 15th century and was under French control from the mid-19th century. A slave ship was captured by the French and the liberated slaves formed the settlement of Libreville in 1849. The country was occupied by France in 1885, and became one of four territories of French west Africa in 1910. It gained independence in 1960. President Bongo assumed power in 1967 and in 1968 a one-party state was established. Unrest in the late 1980s led to the introduction in 1991 of a new constitution allowing a multiparty system. The president's party has remained the ruling party under the multiparty system (amid allegations of electoral fraud), although it has formed coalition governments that include opposition party members since 1994.

THE GAMBIA

Official name	Republic of the Gambia
Local name	Gambia
Former name	Senegambia (with Senegal, 1982–9)
Area	11 295 sq km (4015 sq mi)
Capital	Banjul
Chief towns	Serrekunda, Brikama, Bakau, Georgetown
Population	1 641 000 (2006e)
Nationality	Gambian
Languages	English; Mandinka, Fula and Wolof and other local languages are also spoken
Ethnic groups	Mandinka 42%, Fulani 18%, Wolof 16%, Dyola 10%, Serahuli 9%, non-African 1%, others 4%
Religions	Islam 90%, Christianity 9%, traditional beliefs 1%
Time zone	GMT
Currency	1 Dalasi (GMD) = 100 butut
Telephone	+220
Internet	.gm
Country code	GMB

Location

A republic situated in west Africa, bounded on all sides by Senegal except for the Atlantic Ocean coastline in the west.

Physical description

The Gambia is a strip of land stretching 322 km (200 mi) east to west along the River Gambia; mostly a flood plain flanked by savanna and low hills, not rising above 90 m (295 ft).

Climate

Tropical, with a hot rainy season in June–September; there is high humidity in the wet season with high night temperatures; the average annual rainfall at Banjul is 1295 mm, average temperatures range from 23°C in January to 27°C in July; inland, average temperatures rise to more than 40°C and rainfall decreases.

Economy

The economic mainstays are agriculture, re-export trade with neighbouring countries and tourism; agriculture, largely at subsistence level, employs 75% of the workforce; groundnuts are the chief crop and groundnut processing is the main industry; small-scale manufacturing also includes the processing of fish and hides, agricultural machinery assembly, metalworking, woodworking, beverages and clothing.

Government

Governed by an executive President, a Cabinet and a unicameral National Assembly.

History

Visited by the Portuguese in 1455, it was settled by the English in the 17th century and became a British Crown Colony in 1843. It gained its independence in 1965, and became a republic in 1970 under the presidency of Sir Dawda Jawara, who was president until overthrown in a 1994 military coup. The country has enjoyed relative stability, but the regime is authoritarian and, although multiparty elections have been held since 2001, opposition parties regularly boycott polls and there is intimidation of the opposition and the media.

The Voyage of No Return

The Gambia, the smallest country on the African mainland, is a narrow strip of land that follows the snaking River Gambia to Africa's Atlantic coast. The river was the first major trade route into the African interior, and as such became a focus of the African slave trade. It is estimated that as many as 3 million slaves were taken from the Gambia region during the period of the transatlantic slave trade.

GEORGIA

Official name	Republic of Georgia
Local name	Sak'art'velo; Sak'art'velos Respublikis
Former name	Georgian Democratic Republic (1918–21), Transcaucasian Soviet Federated Republic (with Armenia and Azerbaijan, 1922–36), Georgian Soviet Socialist Republic (1936–90), within the Union of Soviet Socialist Republics (USSR; 1922–91)
Area	69 700 sq km (26 900 sq mi)
Capital	T'bilisi or Tbilisi; also sometimes called Tiflis
Chief towns	Kutaisi, Rustavi, Batumi, Sukhumi, Poti
Population	4 661 000 (2006e)
Nationality	Georgian
Languages	Georgian; Russian, Armenian and Azeri are also spoken
Ethnic groups	Georgian 84%, Azeri 6%, Armenian 6%, Russian 1%, others 3%
Religions	Christianity 84% (Georgian Orthodox 65%, Russian Orthodox 10%, Armenian Orthodox 8%, RC 1%), Islam 10%, others 1%, none 5%
Time zone	GMT +3
Currency	1 Lari (GEL) = 100 tetri
Telephone	+995
Internet	.ge
Country code	GEO

Location

A republic in eastern Europe, occupying central and western Transcaucasia. It is bounded to the south-east by Azerbaijan; to the south by Armenia; to the south-west by Turkey; to the west by the Black Sea; and to the north by Russia.

Physical description

Mostly mountainous, with the Greater Caucasus in the north and the Lesser Caucasus in the south; the highest point is Mount Shkhara (5201 m/17 063 ft); chief rivers are the Kura and Rioni; forest covers c.39% of the republic.

Climate

Subtropical, warm and humid in the west; continental in the east with hot summers and cold winters.

Economy

Recovering from near collapse of the 1990s; agriculture is the largest sector, employing 40% of the workforce, producing wines, tea, tobacco and citrus fruits; main industries are steel, aircraft, machine tools, vehicles, textiles, footwear, chemicals, wood products, financial services, re-export of oil and gas (transit state for pipelines from landlocked eastern neighbours to the Black Sea).

Government

Governed by a President, a Prime Minister and Council of Ministers, and a unicameral Parliament.

History

Founded in the 4th century bc, it was later ruled by the Romans and then the Arabs. An independent empire in the 11th century later fell to Persia and Turkey. Part of the Russian empire from the early 19th century, it declared independence in 1918 but was occupied by Soviet troops in 1921 and proclaimed a Soviet Socialist Republic. It formed the Transcaucasian Republic with Armenia and Azerbaijan before becoming a separate republic of the Union of Soviet Socialist Republics (USSR) in 1936. In the 1980s growing demands for autonomy or independence were brutally suppressed, but nevertheless led to independence being declared in 1991. Clashes between supporters of President Zviad Gamsakhurdia and the National Guard developed into a civil war that resulted in the deposition of the president and the suspension of parliament. Gamsakhurdia was replaced in 1992 by Eduard Shevardnadze, who set about restoring stability to the nation. In addition to the civil conflict, which continued throughout 1993, there was fighting by secessionists in the regions of Abkhazia, to whom Shevardnadze agreed in 1994 to give a measure of autonomy, and South Ossetia. Georgia joined the Commonwealth of Independent States (CIS) in 1993. Shevardnadze was forced to resign in November 2003 after massive demonstrations over alleged electoral fraud, and the presidential election in 2004 was won by Mikhail Saakashvili.

GERMANY

Official name	Federal Republic of Germany
Local name	Deutschland; Bundesrepublik Deutschland
Former name	German Empire (1871–1918), German Republic (1919–33), Third Reich (1933–45), German Democratic Republic (East Germany) and German Federal Republic (West Germany) (1945–90)
Area	357 868 sq km (138 137 sq mi)
Capital	Berlin
Chief towns	Bonn, Hamburg, Munich, Cologne, Essen, Leipzig, Frankfurt (am Main)
Population	82 422 000 (2006e)
Nationality	German
Languages	German; Sorbian (a Slavic language) is spoken by a few
Ethnic groups	German 92%, Turkish 2%, others 6%
Religions	Christianity 68% (Prot 34%, RC 34%), Islam 4%, others/ unaffiliated 28%
Time zone	GMT +1
Currency	1 Euro (€) = 100 cents
Telephone	+49
Internet	.de
Country code	DEU

Location

It is bounded to the east by Poland and the Czech Republic; to the south-east and south by Austria; to the south-west by Switzerland; to the west by France, Luxembourg, Belgium and the Netherlands; and to the north by the North Sea, Denmark and the Baltic Sea.

Physical description

The Baltic coastline is backed by a fertile low-lying plain, low hills and many glacial lakes; the central uplands include the Rhenish Slate Mountains, the Black Forest and the Odenwald and Spessart; the land rises in the south in several ranges, notably the Bavarian Alps (highest peak is the Zugspitze, 2962 m (9717 ft), and the Harz Mountains of the Thüringian Forest; major rivers include the Rhine (running south to north), Elbe, Ems, Weser, Ruhr, Danube, Oder and Neisse; a complex canal system links the chief rivers.

Climate

Temperate in the north-west, with mild but stormy winters; elsewhere, the climate is continental (more temperate in the east); the east and south have lower winter temperatures, with considerable snowfall and some freezing of canals; the average winter temperature in the north is 2°C, and in the south it is −3°C; average summer temperature in the north is 16°C, and slightly higher in the south; the average annual rainfall on the plains is 600–700 mm, increasing in parts of the Alps to 2000 mm.

Economy

A diverse, highly industrialized and technologically advanced economy, although reunification in the 1990s caused recession and stagnation of the economy; in the north and the centre there is substantial heavy industry, especially iron and steel (in the Ruhr Valley), coal mining, cement, metal products, chemicals, textiles, machinery, electrical goods, food processing, precision and optical equipment, motor vehicles, shipbuilding and textiles; coal, iron ore, zinc, lead and potash are mined; agriculture includes arable and livestock farming, fruit, wheat, barley, potatoes, sugar beet and forestry; the Rhine and Mosel valleys are major wine-producing areas; tourism is increasing, especially in the south.

Government

Governed by a federal President, a federal Chancellor and government, and a bicameral legislature, comprising the Federal Assembly (*Bundestag*) and the Federal Council (*Bundesrat*). Each of the 16 states (*Länder*) has its own government and legislature.

History

A central European state formed by the political unification of West Germany and East Germany in 1990. It was the location of the union of the ancient Germanic tribes within the Frankish Empire of Charlemagne in the 8th century and of an elective monarchy after 918 under Otto I, with the Holy Roman Empire divided into several hundred states. Many reforms and territorial changes took place during the Napoleonic era, and after the Congress of Vienna (1814–15) a German Confederation of 39 states under Austria was formed. Under Otto von Bismarck, Prussia succeeded Austria as the leading German power and excluded her from the North German

Confederation. The union of Germany and foundation of the Second Reich (1871), with the King of Prussia as hereditary German Emperor, gave rise, from around 1900, to an aggressive foreign policy that eventually led to World War I. After the German defeat, the Second Reich was replaced by the democratic Weimar Republic and, in 1933, political power passed to the Nazi Party. Adolf Hitler's acts of aggression as Chancellor and Leader (*Führer*) of the totalitarian Third Reich eventually led to World War II and a second defeat for Germany, with the collapse of the German political regime. The area of Germany was subsequently reduced, and occupied by the UK, USA, France, Union of Soviet Socialist Republics (USSR) and Poland, whose zone is now recognized as sovereign Polish territory. This Western occupation softened with the creation of the Federal Republic of Germany (1949) out of the three western zones, and a socialist German Democratic Republic (East Germany) out of the Soviet-occupied zone. Western forces continued to occupy West Berlin, which became a province of West Germany, while East Germany was governed on the communist Soviet model, with the Socialist Unity Party (SED) guaranteed a pre-eminent role. Anti-Soviet demonstrations in East Germany were put down in 1953, and both republics were recognized as sovereign states the following year. In 1958 West Germany was a founder-member of the European Economic Community, and in 2002 it replaced the Deutschmark with the euro. The flow of refugees from East to West Germany continued until 1961, but was largely stopped by the building of the Berlin Wall. East Germany was accorded diplomatic recognition and membership of the UN after signing a treaty with West Germany in 1973. In East Germany the movement for democratic reform, as well as mounting economic crisis, culminated (November 1989) in the opening of the Berlin Wall and other border crossings to the West, and a more open government policy. Free elections (March 1990) led first to economic union with West Germany (July) and then full political unification (October), in which West Germany's federal system of government, built around 10 states (*Länder*) with considerable powers, absorbed East Germany as five additional states. Germany is a leading industrial and trading nation, and a dominant force in the European Union, but since reunification has experienced economic problems and outbreaks of racial violence by the far right. Chancellor Helmut Kohl and the Christian Democratic Union (CDU) held power for 16 years from 1982, and were defeated in 1998 by the Social Democratic Party (SPD) led by Gerhard Schröder. Schröder lost a vote of confidence in 2005 and called an early election that resulted in a narrow victory for the opposition; the three main political parties formed a 'grand coalition' under the opposition leader Angela Merkel, who became Germany's first female Chancellor.

Canine Luxury Tax

German dog owners have to pay an annual tax for their pooches. The tax is known as *Hundesteuer* – literally 'dog licence fee' – and started in Germany around 1810 under the assumption that someone who could afford to own an animal as a pet could also afford to pay a tax on it. The tax amount varies throughout the country; in Berlin the cost is €150 per year.

THE WEIMAR ERA IN GERMANY

Weimar, a city in central Germany, was the capital of German intellectual and literary culture during the 18th and 19th centuries. It was home to the writers Johann Wolfgang von Goethe (1749–1832) and Friedrich Schiller (1759–1805); Franz Liszt (1811–86) was the musical director at the state theatre; and Johann Sebastian Bach (1685–1750) also lived in the city. Following World War I, the German National Assembly met in Weimar to draft a democratic constitution. The German Republic known as the Weimar Republic (1919–33) was thus established, and the city saw a second burst of creative activity.

Design and architecture

Possibly the most significant figure of the era was the architect Walter Gropius (1883–1969), who in 1919 founded the Bauhaus architectural and design school. This revolutionized modern design in both those fields as well as in industry, fine and graphic arts, and theatre design. The core concern of the movement was the marrying of artistry and function.

The arts

The Swiss painter Paul Klee (1879–1940) and the Russian artist Wassily Kandinsky (1866–1944) were both teachers at the Bauhaus. At the start of the century Kandinsky was one of the founders of the Expressionist group known as Der Blaue Reiter (The Blue Rider), whose artists were concerned with abstract elements and vivid colours. By the 1920s, however, he was indulging in intricate works that emphasized geometric shapes and designs, such as realized in *Composition VIII No. 260*. Klee too declared himself 'possessed by colour' and produced strikingly angular images such as *Temple Gardens* (1920).

Fritz Lang (1890–1976) was the leading film-maker of the period. His films were visually powerful and designed to provoke shocking emotions in their audiences. They also dealt with big themes: *Metropolis* (1927) envisaged cities of the future and M (1931) was concerned with the actions of a child killer. Lang sought exile in 1933, as did the Expressionist dramatist Bertolt Brecht (1898–1956), famous for *The Threepenny Opera* (*Die Dreigroschenoper*, 1928) and *The Mother* (*Die Mutter*, 1930), and the theatre director Max Reinhardt (1873–1943). During this period the composer Arnold Schoenberg (1874–1951) began to write a new type of music that was not rooted in a particular key. His 12-tone music system was introduced in his *Five Piano Pieces*, completed in 1923.

The sciences

The German theoretical physicist Albert Einstein (1879–1955) was an established world figure by the time of Weimar. His lead encouraged a number of German physicists in the inter-war years, including Max Planck (1858–1947), Gustav Hertz (1887–1975), Wernher von Braun (1912–77), who was responsible for the V-2 rockets, and Edward Teller (b.1908), the principal architect of the hydrogen bomb. Further afield, the period produced the pioneers of psychoanalysis: Carl Jung (Swiss, 1875–1961) and Sigmund Freud (Austrian, 1856–1939).

The end of an era

When Hitler came to power in 1933, establishments such as the Bauhaus were closed down by the Nazis. The majority of the great minds nurtured under the Weimar Republic emigrated or were exiled, and the Weimar Era came to an end.

GHANA

Official name	Republic of Ghana
Local name	Ghana
Former name	British Gold Coast and British Togoland (until 1957)
Area	238 686 sq km (92 133 sq mi)
Capital	Accra
Chief towns	Sekondi-Takoradi, Kumasi, Tamale
Population	22 410 000 (2006e)
Nationality	Ghanaian
Languages	English; several African languages are also spoken
Ethnic groups	African 98% (Including Akan 44%, Mossi 16%, Ewe 13%, Ga-Adangame 8%, Gurma 3%, Yoruba 1%), others 2%
Religions	Christianity 63%, traditional beliefs 21%, Islam 16%
Time zone	GMT
Currency	1 Cedi (¢) = 100 pesewas
Telephone	+233
Internet	.gh
Country code	GHA

Location
A republic in west Africa, bounded to the west by the Côte d'Ivoire; to the north by Burkina Faso; to the east by Togo; and to the south by the Gulf of Guinea.

Physical description
Coastline of sand bars and lagoons; low-lying plains inland, leading to the Ashanti plateau in the west and the River Volta basin in the east, dammed to form Lake Volta; mountains rise in the east to 885 m (2904 ft) at Afadjato.

Climate
Tropical climate, including a warm, dry coastal belt in the south-east, a hot, humid south-west corner, and hot, dry savanna in the north; Kumasi has an average annual rainfall of 1400 mm.

Economy
Poor country, dependent on international aid; economy based on gold, cocoa (world's second-largest producer), forestry and tuna fishing; diamonds, manganese and bauxite are also mined; agriculture is largely at subsistence level; industries include light manufacturing, aluminium smelting and food processing.

Government
Governed by an executive President, a Council of Ministers and a unicameral Parliament.

History

Ghana was discovered by Europeans in the 15th century, and became the centre of the slave trade in the 18th century. The modern state was created in 1957 by the union of two former British territories, British Gold Coast (Crown Colony in 1874) and British Togoland, and the name was taken from the ancient Kingdom of Ghana. It became independent in 1957 and a republic in 1960, the first British colony in Africa to achieve independence. The country was mostly under military rule, interspersed with short-lived civilian governments, from 1966 until 1992, when a multiparty constitution was approved. In 2002–4, a reconciliation commission investigated human rights abuses during military rule. Since the mid-1990s there have been clashes between different ethnic groups in the north, mostly over land ownership.

GREECE

Official name	Hellenic Republic
Local name	Ellas, Ellada; Elliniki Dimokratia
Former name	Kingdom of Greece (until 1924 and 1935–73), Republic of Greece (1924–35)
Area	131 957 sq km (50 935 sq mi)
Capital	Athens
Chief towns	Thessaloniki, Patras, Heraklion, Volos, Larisa, Piraieus
Population	10 688 000 (2006e)
Nationality	Greek
Language	Greek
Ethnic groups	Greek 98%, others 2%
Religions	Christianity 98% (Orthodox), Islam 1%, others 1%
Time zone	GMT +2
Currency	1 Euro (€) = 100 cents
Telephone	+30
Internet	.gr
Country code	GRC

Location

A republic in south-eastern Europe, occupying the southern part of the Balkan Peninsula and numerous islands in the Aegean and Ionian seas.

Physical description

The country consists of a large area of mainland at the end of the Balkan Peninsula, including the Peloponnese in the south, which is linked to the rest of the mainland by the narrow Corinth Isthmus; nearly 80% of the country is mountainous or hilly; the main ranges are the Pindhos Mountains in the north, the Rhodope Mountains in the north-east, and the east coast range, which includes Mount Olympus (2917 m/9570 ft), the highest point in Greece; there are several rivers and small lakes; there are over 1400 islands, notably Crete, Euboea, Lesbos, Rhodes, Chios, Cephalonia, Corfu, Lemnos, Samos and Naxos, also with hilly or mountainous interiors.

Climate

Mediterranean on the coast and islands, with mild, rainy winters and hot, dry summers; rainfall occurs almost entirely in the winter months; average annual rainfall in Athens is 414 mm.

Economy

Market economy with a large public sector; the service sector accounts for 72% of GDP and employs 68% of the workforce, mainly in tourism and shipping; agriculture is based on cereals, vegetables, fruit, tobacco, beef and dairy products; industries include food and tobacco processing, textiles, metal products, chemicals, mining (iron, magnesite, bauxite and lignite), oil refining and petroleum products.

Government

Governed by a President, a Prime Minister and Cabinet, and a unicameral Parliament; Mount Athos, in Macedonia region, is a self-governing community of 20 monasteries.

History

Greece has been inhabited since Palaeolithic times, and its prehistoric civilization culminated in the remarkable Minoan culture of Crete (3400–1100 BC). The Dorians (a sub-group of Hellenic peoples) invaded from the north in the 12th century bc, and Greek colonies were established along the north and south Mediterranean coasts and on the shores of the Black Sea. Between the 8th and 6th centuries bc the Greeks settled throughout the eastern Mediterranean, establishing colonies along the shores of Asia Minor and the adjoining islands. There were many city states on the mainland, notably Sparta and Athens. In the southern part of the Balkan Peninsula, a distinctive Greek culture has persisted unbroken since antiquity; the Slav and Avar invaders who arrived in waves in the 6th century and later settled in the southern part of the Balkan Peninsula were accepted as Greeks and assimilated into the original population. In the 5th century bc Persian invasions were repelled at Marathon, Salamis, Plataea and Mycale, and Greek literature and art flourished. Conflict between Sparta and Athens (the Peloponnesian War, 431–404 BC) weakened the country, which was overwhelmed by the Macedonians (4th century bc) under Philip II of Macedon, who unified the Greek city states under their leadership. Military expeditions under his son, Alexander III, the Great, penetrated Asia and Africa. Macedonian power was broken by the Romans in 197 BC. After the fall of the western Roman Empire, Greece and Crete formed part of the Greek-speaking Byzantine Empire that stretched deep into Asia Minor and the Middle East. The Byzantine Age (330–1204) was a period of political and cultural influence for the Greeks in the Balkans and eastern Mediterranean. After the sack of Constantinople (1204), the Balkan Greeks fell prey to the ambitions of the Franks and Venetians, and finally to the Turks who occupied Greece from 1460 to 1830. Crete was purchased by the Venetian Republic in 1210 and enjoyed an artistic renaissance, but it too fell to the Ottomans (1669) and went into a long decline. The Greek national revival began in the late 18th century, and led to the Greek War of Independence (1821–8) against the Turks. By the end of the war Greece, though ravaged, was a free state, and it gained formal recognition of its independence from the Ottoman Empire in 1832. During the war, the Cretans joined the insurgents but were quickly crushed and made subject to the Egyptian Viceroy, Ali Pasha. Once again under Ottoman control from 1840, Cretan demands for *enosis* (union with Greece) grew apace, with several revolts (1858, 1866–9 and

GREECE: HOME OF THE OLYMPIC GAMES

The true origins of the Olympic Games are much debated and various legends have descended from Greek mythology. The most popular are those surrounding Hercules (Heracles), the ancient hero of strength and courage who, as a penance for the murder of his wife and children, was forced into 12 'labours' or trials of skill and strength.

The early Olympics

The ancient Games were held by the Greeks at Olympia in Elis, the location of Zeus's shrine. They took place every fourth year in the month of July; the four-yearly interval came to be known as an Olympiad in Greek chronology. The first historical records describing the ancient Olympic Games date from 776 BC, when a list of victors was published, but many historians believe that the earliest event was several hundred years earlier.

The 776 BC Games lasted just one day and featured a single race. The track was one stade (stadium-length) long: this measure was reputedly 60 times the length of Hercules's foot, and corresponds to 192 m (210 yd). Athletes from around the Greek world were invited to compete and an Olympic truce ensured that the athletes were not molested on their way to the Games. All competitors were to be honourable and of Greek descent. Slaves and women were not allowed to compete; indeed, married women were not even allowed to spectate (and not wholly because the competitors were naked!) The prizes were modest – victors were presented with a crown or a garland of olive leaves. However, they became national heroes, had verses written in their honour and statues created in their likeness.

Development of the Games

A range of events was added to the programme over the next few centuries: longer races, running in armour; chariot racing, wrestling, boxing, the pankration (a no-holds-barred mixture of wrestling and boxing), and the event most synonymous with Olympic ideals: the pentathlon. The pentathlon comprised different events during its history but most commonly featured running, jumping, throwing the discus and javelin, and wrestling. The Games flourished until AD 393, when the emperor Theodosius abolished them because he thought they were not religious enough. The Olympian site fell into disuse and was destroyed in an earthquake in the 6th century AD.

The modern Olympics

A revival of interest in the ancient Games occurred in the 18th century. In 1894 an international conference was called by the French educator Baron Pierre de Coubertin, who believed that the greatness of the ancient Greek empire could in part be explained by the Greeks' devotion to physical fitness and competitive events. Within two years the first Olympics of the modern world were held in Greece, in Athens. As before, the Games excluded women; 241 competitors from 14 countries attended. In contrast, the August 2004 Games, also in Athens, were attended by more than 11,000 athletes from 202 countries. Baron de Coubertin died in 1937 before seeing such rapid expansion of participation; he was laid to rest in Lausanne, the Swiss town that is the home of the International Olympic Committee but his heart is interred in a marble monument at Olympia.

1895), but these were handled cautiously by the Greek government lest it antagonize the Ottoman Empire. After a brief military campaign, Crete was declared independent under a High Commissioner appointed by the Great Powers (1898). The Cretan assembly declared its *enosis* in 1908, but not until the Treaties of London (1913) was it joined to the Kingdom of Greece. After gaining independence, Greek society was riddled with divisions, with the 19th century seeing continuous arguments over the constitution and form of government. In the 20th century the Greeks were at war from 1912 to 1922, and from 1940 to 1949. The Balkan Wars and World War I both brought substantial territorial gains. These were followed by a disastrous war against the Turks in Anatolia (1919–22) during which around 30 000 Christians were killed in İzmir (Smyrna) in September 1922, and over a million Greeks were forced to leave Asia Minor. The Greek Republic was established in 1924 and the monarchy restored in 1935. Meanwhile, Crete became a stronghold of support for its native son, Eleuthérios Venizélos, and rebelled against Ioannis Metaxas (1938). During World War II, Greece and Crete were occupied by the Germans, and Greece was afterwards ravaged by a bloody civil war (1944–9) between monarchists and communists. Following a tentative period of democracy, a military coup in 1967 led to the right-wing dictatorship of the Greek Colonels (1967–74). The monarchy was formally abolished and democracy restored in 1974, since when there has been relative peace and stability. Greece joined the European Community in 1981 and replaced the drachma with the euro in 2002.

GREENLAND ▶DENMARK

GRENADA

Official name	Grenada
Local name	Grenada
Area	344 sq km (133 sq mi)
Capital	St George's
Chief towns	Gouyave, Victoria, Grenville
Population	89 700 (2006e)
Nationality	Grenadian or Grenadan
Language	English
Ethnic groups	African descent 82%, mixed 13%, European and East Indian 5%
Religion	Christianity 100% (RC 53%, Prot 47%)
Time zone	GMT −4
Currency	1 East Caribbean Dollar (EC$) = 100 cents
Telephone	+1 473
Internet	.gd
Country code	GRD

Location
An independent constitutional monarchy of the West Indies and the most southerly of the Windward Islands, in the eastern Caribbean Sea.

Physical description

Comprises the main island of Grenada (34 km/21 mi long and 19 km/12 mi wide) and the South Grenadines (including Carriacou), an arc of small islands extending from Grenada north to St Vincent; Grenada is of volcanic origin, with a ridge of mountains along its entire length; the highest point is Mount St Catherine, which rises to 843 m (2766 ft).

Climate

Subtropical; the average annual temperature is 23°C; the average annual rainfall varies from 1270 mm on the coast to 5000 mm in the interior; the rainy season is June–December.

Economy

Poor country, dependent on international aid; main activities are tourism, financial services, agriculture (chiefly nutmeg, bananas, cocoa, fruit, vegetables, mace and fish), processing agricultural products, textiles and light assembly industries.

Government

Governed by a Governor-General (representing the British monarch, who is head of state), a Prime Minister and Cabinet, and a bicameral legislature comprising an appointed Senate and an elected House of Representatives.

History

Christopher Columbus discovered the island in 1498. Settled by the French in the mid-17th century, it was ceded to Britain in 1763 by the Treaty of Paris. It was retaken by France in 1779, and ceded again to Britain in 1783. It became a British Crown Colony in 1877 and gained its independence in 1974 under Prime Minister Eric Gairy. The government was overthrown in 1979 by Maurice Bishop, who became prime minister but was deposed and killed in a further uprising in 1983. These events prompted an invasion by US and Caribbean troops to restore stable government, which has been maintained since elections in 1984, with power alternating between the two main political parties.

Spice Island

Sometimes called 'Spice Island', Grenada has long been an important source of cocoa and spices, including cloves, ginger, cinnamon and turmeric. The island's most important export, however, is the nutmeg. So central is this small fruit to the island's economy that it is depicted on the country's flag.

GUADELOUPE ▸ FRANCE

GUAM ▸ UNITED STATES OF AMERICA

GUATEMALA

Official name	Republic of Guatemala
Local name	Guatemala; República de Guatemala
Area	108 889 sq km (42 031 sq mi)
Capital	Guatemala City; La Ciudad de Guatemala
Chief towns	Quetzaltenango, Escuintla, Antigua, Mazatenango
Population	12 293 000 (2006e)
Nationality	Guatemalan
Languages	Spanish; several Indian languages are also spoken
Ethnic groups	Amerindian 40%, Mestizo (Ladino) and European 59%, others 1%
Religions	Christianity 95% (RC 73%, Prot 22%), traditional beliefs (Mayan) 5%
Time zone	GMT −6
Currency	1 Quetzal (Q) = 100 centavos
Telephone	+502
Internet	.gt
Country code	GTM

Location

The northernmost of the Central American republics, bounded to the north and west by Mexico; to the south-west by the Pacific Ocean; to the east by Belize and the Caribbean Sea; and to the south-east by Honduras and El Salvador.

Physical description

Over two-thirds is mountainous with extensive forests; from the narrow Pacific coastal plain, the highlands rise steeply to heights of 2500–3000 m (8200–9840 ft); there are many volcanoes on the southern edge of the highlands; rivers flow to both the Pacific Ocean and the Caribbean Sea; the highest point is Tajumulco (4220 m/13 845 ft).

Climate

Tropical in the lowlands and on the Caribbean coast, cooler at altitude; rainy season in May–October; Guatemala City's average temperatures are 17°C in January and 21°C in July; average annual rainfall is 1316 mm; there is much higher rainfall on exposed slopes; subject to severe hurricanes and earthquakes.

Economy

Developing country, still dependent on international aid; agriculture is the most important sector, accounting for c.43% of exports, chiefly coffee, sugar, bananas, cardamom, fruit, vegetables, cut flowers; industries include textiles, garments, ceramics; tourism is growing.

Government

Governed by an executive President, a Cabinet, and a unicameral Congress of the Republic.

History

Mayan and Aztec civilizations flourished before the Spanish conquest of 1523–4. Guatemala gained independence from Spain as part of the Central American Federation in 1821. The Federation was officially dissolved in 1840, following which the country has had a series of dictatorships broken by short periods of representative government. In 1985 civilian rule was restored and has survived attempted coups in 1989 and 1993. In 1996, after 35 years of fighting between left-wing Guatemalan National Revolutionary Unity guerrillas and the government, a peace agreement was finally reached, ending Latin America's longest civil war. Guatemala's long-standing dispute regarding its claim to Belize edged closer to resolution in 1991, when Guatemala recognized Belize's independence. Talks in 2002 led to agreement on a draft settlement to the border dispute.

GUIANA, FRENCH ▸FRANCE

GUINEA

Official name	Republic of Guinea
Local name	Guinée; République de Guinée
Former name	French west Africa (1904–46), French Guinea (1946–58), Republic of Guinea (1958–79), People's Revolutionary Republic of Guinea (1979–84)
Area	246 048 sq km (94 974 sq mi)
Capital	Conakry
Chief towns	Kankan, Kindia, Labé
Population	9 690 000 (2006e)
Nationality	Guinean
Languages	French; eight local languages are also spoken widely
Ethnic groups	Peulh 40%, Malinke 30%, Soussou 20%, others 10%
Religions	Islam 85%, Christianity 8%, traditional beliefs 7%
Time zone	GMT
Currency	1 Guinea Franc (GFr) = 100 centimes
Telephone	+224
Internet	.gn
Country code	GIN

Location

A republic in west Africa, bounded to the north-west by Guinea-Bissau; to the north by Senegal and Mali; to the east by Côte d'Ivoire; to the south by Liberia and Sierra Leone; and to the south-west by the Atlantic Ocean.

Physical description

The coast is characterized by mangrove forests, rising to a forested and widely cultivated narrow coastal plain; the Fouta Djallon massif in the north-west lies c.900 m (2952 ft) above the coastal plain; the highest point is Mount Nimba (1752 m/5748 ft); savanna plains in the east are cut by rivers flowing towards the upper basin of the River Niger; the Guinea Highlands in the south-east are forested and generally rise above 1000 m (3280 ft).

Climate

Tropical climate (wet season May–October); the average temperature in the dry season on the coast is 32°C, dropping to 23°C in the wet season; cooler inland and drier in the east; the average annual rainfall at Conakry is 4923 mm.

Economy

Undeveloped and dependent on international aid; agriculture, mostly at subsistence level, employs 80% of the workforce; chief cash crops are coffee, tropical fruits and fish; main industries are mining (bauxite, iron ore, gold and diamonds), alumina refining, processing agricultural produce and light manufacturing.

Government

Governed by an executive President, a Council of Ministers and a unicameral National Assembly.

History

Part of the Mali Empire in the 16th century, it became a French protectorate in 1849 and was governed with Senegal as Rivières du Sud. It became a separate colony in 1893, and a constituent territory within French west Africa in 1904. It reverted to separate colonial status as an Overseas Territory in 1946, and became independent in 1958. The first president, Ahmed Sékou Touré, established a one-party state pursuing Marxist policies and remained in power until his death in 1984. Shortly after his death a coup established a Military Committee for National Recovery under Lansana Conté, who introduced economic liberalization and in 1993 reintroduced a multiparty system. Conté was elected president and has retained office in subsequent elections. Since 2000, an influx of refugees from conflicts in neighbouring countries has created an additional economic burden, and increasing ethnic tension.

Guinean by Name ...

A variety of African flora and fauna are named after Guinea. The guinea fowl, genus *Numida*, is a ground-dwelling bird belonging to the pheasant family. Guinea grass, genus *Panicum*, is a tall grass that is related to millet. The guinea worm, *Dracunculus medinensis*, is a nematode worm that is parasitic to humans. Despite their name, however, guinea pigs are not from Guinea, or indeed from any part of Africa, but from South America. Neither are they pigs, but rodents.

GUINEA-BISSAU

Official name	Republic of Guinea-Bissau
Local name	Guiné-Bissau; República da Guiné-Bissau
Former name	Portuguese Guinea (1952–74)
Area	36 260 sq km (14 000 sq mi)
Capital	Bissau
Chief towns	Bafatá, Bolama, Mansôa
Population	1 442 000 (2006e)
Nationality	Guinea-Bissauan
Languages	Portuguese, Guinean Creole (Crioulo); many African languages are also spoken
Ethnic groups	Balante 30%, Fulani 20%, Malinke 14%, Mandyako 13%, Pepel 7%, other African 15%, others 1%
Religions	traditional beliefs 50%, Islam 45%, Christianity 5%
Time zone	GMT
Currency	1 CFA Franc (CFAFr) = 100 centimes
Telephone	+245
Internet	.gw
Country code	GNB

Location

A republic in west Africa, bounded to the south-east by Guinea; to the north by Senegal; and to the south-west by the Atlantic Ocean.

Physical description

An indented coast typified by islands and mangrove-lined estuaries, backed by forested coastal plains; a low-lying country with savanna-covered plateaux in the south and east, rising to 310 m (1017 ft) on the Guinea border; chief rivers are the Cacheu, Geba and Corubal; includes the heavily forested Bijagos Archipelago.

Climate

Tropical climate with a wet season (June–October); average annual rainfall at Bissau is 1950 mm and the temperature range is 24–7°C.

Economy

Very poor, and dependent on international aid; based on agriculture, mostly at subsistence level, and fishing; chief cash crops are groundnuts, palm kernels, cashew nuts, rice, fish and timber; small-scale industry processes agricultural produce and produces beer and soft drinks; unexploited mineral reserves.

Government

Governed by an executive President, a Prime Minister and Council of Ministers, and a unicameral National People's Assembly.

History

Discovered by the Portuguese in 1446, Guinea-Bissau was administered as part of the Cape Verde islands until 1879 when it became a separate Portuguese colony. After becoming an Overseas Territory of Portugal in 1952, it gained independence in 1973; Luís Cabral was president from 1974. He was deposed by a military coup led by João Vieira in 1980, and the constitution was changed in 1984 to make Vieira president. A multiparty system was introduced in 1990, and the first multiparty elections were held in 1994; they were won by the ruling party and Vieira was re-elected. An army mutiny in 1998 developed into a civil war until Vieira was ousted in 1999 but the president elected in 2000, Kumba Yalla, was deposed in a military coup in 2003. Constitutional government was reintroduced with a legislative election in 2004 and a presidential election in 2005 that was won by Vieira.

GUYANA

Official name	Co-operative Republic of Guyana
Local name	Guyana
Former name	British Guiana (until 1966)
Area	214 969 sq km (82 978 sq mi)
Capital	Georgetown
Chief towns	Linden, New Amsterdam
Population	767 200 (2006e)
Nationality	Guyanese
Languages	English; Creole, Hindi, Urdu and local dialects are also spoken
Ethnic groups	East Indian 50%, black 36%, Amerindian 7%, white, Chinese and mixed 7%
Religions	Christianity 57% (Prot 49%, RC 8%), Hinduism 28%, Islam 7%, unaffiliated 4%, others 2%, none 2%
Time zone	GMT −3.5
Currency	1 Guyana Dollar (G$) = 100 cents
Telephone	+592
Internet	.gy
Country code	GUY

Location

A republic on the northern coast of South America, bounded to the east by Suriname; to the west by Venezuela; to the south by Brazil; and to the north by the Atlantic Ocean.

Physical description

Narrow coastal plains rise to the highlands in the west and savanna in the south; the highest peak is Mount Roraima (2810 m/9219 ft) in the Pakaraima Mountains; much of the interior (c.85%) is covered with rainforest; the coastal plain, below sea level at high tide, is protected by sea defences, dams and canals; the main rivers are the Essequibo, Demerara and Berbice, with many rapids and waterfalls in the upper courses.

Climate

Equatorial climate, moderated by north-eastern trade winds; the lowlands are hot and wet, with high humidity; Georgetown, in the coastal lowland area, has average temperatures of 22–31°C and two seasons of high rainfall (May–July, November–January); there are lower temperatures and less rainfall on the high inland plateau.

Economy

Slow recovery from 1990s problems; dependent on international aid; main activities are agriculture (sugar and rice), processing agricultural products, mining (bauxite, gold and diamonds), forestry, fishing (shrimps); some tourism.

Government

Governed by an executive President, a Prime Minister and Cabinet, and a unicameral National Assembly.

History

The coast of Guyana was sighted by Christopher Columbus in 1498 and settled by the Dutch from the late 16th century. Several areas were ceded to Britain in 1815, and the country formally came under British rule when these were consolidated as British Guiana in 1831. Guyana gained independence in 1966 and became a republic in 1970. The first two decades of independence were dominated by the autocratic Forbes Burnham, prime minister 1966–80 and president 1980–5. His death in 1985 ended his party's monopoly of power, and power has alternated since between the two main political parties. Party affiliations reflect the racial divisions between those of African descent and those of Indian descent, and the persistent tension between the two has a destabilizing effect on politics.

Land of Many Waters

The name Guyana is derived from an Amerindian word meaning 'land of many waters'. The table-top mountain Monte Roraima, the highest point in Guyana, is the source of many of the country's rivers. It is also believed to have provided the inspiration for the adventure novel *The Lost World* (1912) by Sir Arthur Conan Doyle (1859–1930).

HAITI

Official name	Republic of Haiti
Local name	Haïti; République d'Haïti
Area	27750 sq km (10712 sq mi)
Capital	Port-au-Prince
Chief towns	Port-de-Paix, Cap-Haïtien, Gonaïves, Les Cayes, Jacmel, Jérémie
Population	8308000 (2006e)
Nationality	Haitian
Languages	French, Creole
Ethnic groups	black 95%, Mulatto and white 5%
Religions	Christianity 96% (RC 80%, Prot 16%), others 3%, none/ unaffiliated 1% *note: around half the population practises voodoo*
Time zone	GMT −5
Currency	1 Gourde (G, Gde) = 100 centimes
Telephone	+509
Internet	.ht
Country code	HTI

Location

A republic in the West Indies, occupying the western third of the island of Hispaniola in the Caribbean Sea.

Physical description

Consists of two mountainous peninsulas (the Massif du Nord in the north and the Massif de la Hotte in the south), separated by a deep structural depression, the Plaine du Cul-de-Sac; to the east is the Massif de la Selle, with Haiti's highest peak, La Selle (2680 m/8792 ft); Haiti includes the islands of Gonâve off the west coast and Tortue off the north coast.

Climate

Tropical maritime; average monthly temperatures range from 24 to 29°C; average annual rainfall for the north coast and mountains is 1475–1950 mm, but only 500 mm in the west; the wet season is May–September; hurricanes are common.

Economy

Poorest country in the western hemisphere; heavily dependent on international aid and expatriates' remittances; nearly 70% of the population depends on subsistence agriculture; the chief activities are agriculture (coffee, cocoa, mangoes and sugar), fishing, manufacturing (garments, leather goods, electronic components, food processing, beverages and tobacco products).

Government

Governed by a President, a Prime Minister and Cabinet, and a bicameral National Assembly comprising a Chamber of Deputies and a Senate.

History

Christopher Columbus reached Hispaniola in 1492, and Haiti was created when the western third of the island was ceded to France in 1697. The Haitian Revolution, the only successful slave revolution in the New World, took place in 1791–1804 and culminated in the independence of Haiti (1804). From 1822 to 1844 Haiti was united with Santo Domingo (Dominican Republic). In the late 19th century it experienced great instability; there were 22 changes of government between 1843 and 1915, when it came under US occupation for 19 years until 1934. From 1957 to 1986 the Duvalier family had absolute power, their rule being enforced by a civilian militia known as the Tonton Macoute. After Jean-Claude Duvalier fled the country in 1986, it came under military rule until Jean-Bertrand Aristide was elected president in 1990. Aristide was deposed in 1991 in a military coup that instigated a period of repressive rule during which the Tonton Macoute were revived under the name *attachés*. Following US-led negotiations with the military leaders, and amid fears of a US invasion, Aristide was restored to power in 1994. He was voted out of office in the elections the following year and René Préval became president in 1996. Aristide was re-elected in 2000, but in 2004 he went into exile after mounting protests at government corruption developed into an armed rebellion. René Préval was elected president again in 2006.

HONDURAS

Official name	Republic of Honduras
Local name	Honduras; República de Honduras
Area	112088 sq km (43266 sq mi)
Capital	Tegucigalpa
Chief towns	San Pedro Sula, Choluteca, La Ceiba, El Progreso
Population	7326000 (2006e)
Nationality	Honduran
Languages	Spanish; Amerindian dialects and English are also spoken
Ethnic groups	Mestizo 90%, Amerindian 7%, black 2%, white 1%
Religions	Christianity 100% (RC 80%, Prot 20%)
Time zone	GMT −6
Currency	1 Lempira (L, La) = 100 centavos
Telephone	+504
Internet	.hn
Country code	HND

Location

A republic in Central America, bounded to the south-west by El Salvador; to the west by Guatemala; to the east and south-east by Nicaragua; to the north by the Caribbean Sea; and to the south by the Pacific Ocean.

Physical description

The interior is mountainous (c.75% of the land area), with lower-lying land only along the Caribbean and Pacific coasts; the southern plateau rises to 2870m (9416ft) at

Cerro Las Minas; the Laguna Caratasca lies in the extreme north-east; the Bay Islands in the Caribbean Sea and a group of nearly 300 islands in the Gulf of Fonseca also belong to Honduras.

Climate

Tropical climate in coastal areas, temperate in the centre and west; two wet seasons in upland areas (May–July, September–October); variable temperatures in the interior, 15–24°C; on the coastal plains the average temperature is 30°C.

Economy

Poor country, dependent on international aid; agriculture, fishing and forestry are the main activities and basis of most industry; chief products are coffee, shrimps, bananas, gold, palm oil, fruit, lobster, timber, textiles, garments; offshore assembly for re-export and tourism are growing.

Government

Governed by an executive President, a Cabinet and a unicameral National Congress.

History

The centre of Maya culture between the 4th and 9th centuries, it was settled by the Spanish in the early 16th century and became a province of Guatemala. Honduras gained independence from Spain in 1821 and joined the Central American Federation. It became an independent sovereign state in 1838. The country experienced periods of instability interspersed with military rule until 1981, when a civilian government was elected. During the 1980s it became embroiled in the civil wars in El Salvador and Nicaragua, providing training bases for the counter-insurgents supported by the USA. This provoked internal unrest, which continued after the external wars ended; it lasted throughout the 1990s and raised concerns about human rights abuses. In 1998–9 the police and armed forces were brought under civilian control, but the problem of gang warfare continues.

Football War

In July 1969 a war was fought between Honduras and El Salvador, provoked by the wave of migration from overpopulated El Salvador to the unoccupied territories of Western Honduras. The war has come to be known as the Football War, because recriminations between the two Central American states came to a head during the qualifying matches for the 1970 World Cup. As it only lasted a few days, it is also referred to as the 100-Hours War.

HONG KONG ►CHINA

HUNGARY

Official name	Republic of Hungary
Local name	Magyarorszag; Magyar Köztársaság
Former name	Part of Austria-Hungary (until 1918), Hungarian People's Republic (1918, 1919, 1949–89), Hungarian Soviet Republic (1919), Hungarian State (1919–20, 1944–6), Hungarian Kingdom (1920–44), Hungarian Republic (1946–9)
Area	93 030 sq km (35 910 sq mi)
Capital	Budapest
Chief towns	Debrecen, Miskolc, Szeged, Pécs, Györ
Population	9 981 000 (2006e)
Nationality	Hungarian
Language	Magyar (Hungarian)
Ethnic groups	Magyar 92%, Roma 2%, others 6%
Religions	Christianity 75% (RC 52%, Prot 19%, other Christian 4%), others 11%, none/unaffiliated 14%
Time zone	GMT +1
Currency	1 Forint (Ft) = 100 fillér
Telephone	+36
Internet	.hu
Country code	HUN

Location

A landlocked republic in the Danube basin, central Europe, bounded to the north by Slovakia; to the north-east by the Ukraine; to the east by Romania; to the south by Serbia; to the south-west by Croatia; and to the west by Slovenia and Austria.

Physical description

Mostly low-lying, with low mountains in the north, north-east and north-west; the highest peak is Kékes (1014 m/3327 ft); the north-west highlands are a spur of the Alps and separate the Little Hungarian Plain from Lake Balaton and the central plains; drained by the River Danube and its tributaries (flowing north to south); frequent flooding, especially in the Great Plains, east of the Danube.

Climate

Extreme continental climate with a marked difference between summer and winter; wettest in spring and early summer; winters are cold with snow lying for 30–40 days and the River Danube is sometimes frozen over for long periods; fog is frequent during settled winter weather.

Economy

Transformed since 1989 into a market economy with strong growth; nearly half of the land is cultivated; agricultural products include cereals, sunflower seeds, vegetables, livestock and grapes for wine-making; large industrial sector includes mining, metallurgy, construction materials, food processing, textiles, chemicals, pharmaceuticals and motor vehicles, logistics and business services.

Government

Governed by a President, a Prime Minister and Cabinet, and a unicameral National Assembly.

History

The Magyars probably settled the Hungarian plain in the 9th century and a kingdom was formed under St Stephen I in the 11th century. This was conquered by Turks in 1526 and became part of the Habsburg Empire in the 17th century. Austria and Hungary were reconstituted as the Dual Monarchy of Austria-Hungary in 1867. The year 1869 was declared the Hungarian Millennium to celebrate the 1000th anniversary of the Magyars' original settlement; it was used by the Hungarian government within Austria-Hungary not only to celebrate the political and economic achievements of the previous half century, but also as an anti-Habsburg demonstration, and it marked an intensification of the attempt to Magyarize Hungary's subject nationalities. Protests were made by the Magyar poor, as well as by Slavs and Romanians. After World War I Hungary became a republic, but a communist revolt introduced a new regime in 1919. A nominally monarchical constitution under a regent, Admiral Miklós Horthy, was restored in 1920 but, after the failure of its policy of alliance with Germany in World War II, a new republic under communist government was formed in 1949. In 1956 there was a national insurrection known as the Hungarian Uprising, which followed the denunciation of Stalin at the 20th Congress of the Soviet Communist Party for his oppressive rule. Rioting students and workers demanded radical reform. When the new Prime Minister Imre Nagy announced plans for Hungary's withdrawal from the Warsaw Pact, among other things, Soviet troops and tanks crushed the uprising. Many were killed, thousands fled abroad, and Nagy was executed. Reform was set back for more than a decade, but in the 1960s János Kádár introduced limited liberalization that encouraged the development of the most prosperous and liberal regime in the Soviet bloc. In 1989 pressure for political change was led from within the Communist Party; Hungary was declared a democratic state in the same year and multiparty elections were held in 1990. Since the elections of 1994, when the Hungarian Democratic Forum (MDF) were ousted by a Hungarian Socialist Party-led coalition under Prime Minister Gyula Horn, Hungary has experienced gradual economic growth. Hungary joined NATO in 1999 and the European Union in 2004.

The Biro Brothers

In the 1930s, the Hungarian newspaper editor Ladislao (László) Bíró (1899–1985) produced the first commercially successful ballpoint pen with assistance from his brother George, a chemist. The secrets behind the pen were fast-drying printing ink, familiar to László through his work, and a tiny rotating ball that allowed the highly viscous ink to flow even though it was too thick for a conventional nib. Even today, this type of pen is still known as a 'biro'.

ICELAND

Official name	Republic of Iceland
Local name	Ísland; Lyðveldið Ísland
Former name	formerly part of Denmark (until 1918), Kingdom of Iceland (1918–44)
Area	103 000 sq km (40 000 sq mi)
Capital	Reykjavík
Chief towns	Akureyri, Húsavík, Akranes, Keflavík, Ísafjördur
Population	299 400 (2006e)
Nationality	Icelander, Icelandic
Language	Icelandic
Ethnic groups	Icelandic 94%, Danish 1%, others 5%
Religions	Christianity 94% (Prot 90%, RC 2%, other Christian 2%), none/unaffiliated 6%
Time zone	GMT
Currency	1 Króna (IKr, ISK) = 100 aurar
Telephone	+354
Internet	.is
Country code	ISL

Location

An island state lying between the northern Atlantic Ocean and the Arctic Ocean, south-east of Greenland and 900 km (550 mi) west of Norway.

Physical description

A volcanic island of relatively recent geological origin, at the northern end of the mid-Atlantic Ridge, with several active volcanoes (eg Hekla); the coastline is heavily indented, with many long fjords; an inland plateau of glaciers, lakes and lava fields covers 80% of the interior, rising to mountainous ridges in the north, centre and south; the highest point is Hvannadalshnúkur (2119 m/6952 ft) in the south-east; famous for its hot springs and geysers, notably *Geysir* from which the term is derived; subterranean hot water provides geothermal power.

Climate

Temperate, owing to influence of Gulf Stream, but changeable, with relatively mild winters; average daily temperatures are −2°C (January) to 14°C (July–August); Reykjavík is generally ice-free throughout the year; summers are cool and cloudy; average monthly rainfall reaches 94 mm (October).

Economy

Prosperous market economy based largely on inshore and deep-water fishing (70% of the export earnings); stock farming, dairy farming, horse-breeding and tourism are important; diversifying into aluminium and diatomite production, information technology and biogenetics.

Government

Governed by a President, a Prime Minister and Cabinet, and a unicameral legislature (*Althing*).

History

The island was settled by the Norse in the 9th century, and in the 10th century it was the seat of the world's oldest parliament, the *Althing*. It united with Norway in 1262, and with Norway came under Danish rule in 1397. When Norway was ceded to Sweden in 1814, Iceland remained Danish. In 1918 Iceland became an independent kingdom with the same sovereign as Denmark, and since 1944 it has been a fully independent republic. The extension of the fishing limit around Iceland in 1958, 1972 and 1975 precipitated the 'Cod War' disputes with the UK. Subsequent attempts to restrict fishing in Icelandic waters have allowed stocks to recover from the overfishing of the 1980s, and economic dependence on fisheries is being reduced by diversification. However, concerns about the economy led the prime minister, Halldór Ásgrímsson, to resign in 2006.

INDIA

Official name	Republic of India
Local name	Bhārat (Hindi)
Area	3 287 950 sq km (1 269 338 sq mi)
Capital	New Delhi
Chief towns[1]	Ahmadabad, Bangalore, Chennai, Hyderabad, Jaipur, Kanpur, Kolkata, Lucknow, Mumbai, Nagpur, Poona
Population	1 095 352 000 (2006e)
Nationality	Indian
Languages	Hindi, English and 14 other official languages
Ethnic groups	Indo-Aryan 72%, Dravidian 25%, others 3%
Religions	Hinduism 81%, Islam 13%, Christianity 2%, Sikhism 2%, others and unspecified 2%
Time zone	GMT +5.5
Currency	1 Indian Rupee (Re, Rs) = 100 paise
Telephone	+91
Internet	.in
Country code	IND

[1] *India has renamed several of its cities and states in recent years, reverting to pre-colonial names. Thus, Bombay is now known as Mumbai, Calcutta as Kolkata, and Madras as Chennai. Other such changes may follow.*

Location

A federal republic in southern Asia, bounded to the north-west by Pakistan; to the north by China, Nepal and Bhutan; to the east by Myanmar (Burma) and Bangladesh; to the south-east by the Bay of Bengal; and to the south-west by the Arabian Sea; the disputed area of Jammu and Kashmir lies to the north.

Physical description

The second largest state in Asia, bordered to the north by the mountain ridges and valleys of the Himalayas; the highest peaks are over 7000 m (22 966 ft) in the Karakoram Range and the Ladakh Plateau; Kanchenjunga (8598 m/28 298 ft) is the highest point; east of Bangladesh lie the plains and mountainous uplands of Assam; the central river plains formed by the basins of the Indus, Ganges and Brahmaputra rivers rise to low hills; south of these is the Deccan Peninsula, with coastal plains rising to a central plateau bounded by the Western and Eastern Ghats hills; the Thar Desert north-west of Rajasthan is bordered by semi-desert areas.

Climate

Dominated by the Asiatic monsoon; rains come from the south-west (June–October); rainfall decreases (December–February) as winds blow in from the north, followed by drought until March or May; temperatures in the northern mountains vary greatly with altitude; rainfall decreases east to west on the northern plains, with desert conditions in the extreme west; temperatures vary with altitude on the Deccan Plateau, although towards the south of the plateau region the climate is tropical, even in the cool season; the west coast is subject to rain throughout the year, particularly in the south, where humidity is high; cyclones and storms on the south-east coast (especially October–December), with high temperatures and humidity during the monsoon season; Assam has a similar climate to the northern plains and Himalayas but such heavy rainfall in June–October that Cherrapunji is one of the three wettest places on Earth, with average annual rainfall measuring 10 800 mm (425 in).

Economy

The closed economy opened in the 1990s, initiating sustained growth and transformation from a largely agricultural economy to one based on services (information technology, telecommunications and tourism) and manufacturing (textiles, garments, chemicals, pharmaceuticals, food processing, steel, transport equipment, cement, machinery, software, jewellery and leather goods); other industries include mining (coal, iron ore, diamonds and other gems), oil and natural gas production; agriculture, fishing and forestry support 60% of the population; main crops are rice, cereals and pulses for subsistence and sugar, jute, cotton and tea as cash crops.

Government

A federal democratic republic; governed by the President of the Union, a Prime Minister and Cabinet, and a bicameral Houses of Parliament (*Sansad*), consisting of a Council of States (*Rajya Sabha*) and a House of the People (*Lok Sabha*). There are 28 states, six union territories and the national capital territory. Each state has a Governor, Council of Ministers and legislative assembly. Each territory is administered by an Administrator or Lieutenant-Governor.

History

The Indus civilization, which emerged in around 2500 BC, was destroyed in 1500 BC by the Aryans, who developed the Brahminic caste system. The Mauryan Emperor Asoka unified most of India, and established Buddhism as the state religion in the 3rd century bc. Hinduism spread in the 2nd century bc, and there were Muslim influences during the 7th and 8th centuries, with a sultanate established at Delhi.

Delhi was captured by Timur in 1398 and the Mughal Empire was established by Babur in 1526, and extended by Akbar and Aurangzeb. The Portuguese, French, Dutch and British had footholds in India in the 18th century, which led to conflict between France and Britain in 1746–63. The development of British interests was represented by the British East India Company, and British power was established after the Indian Uprising (1857) was crushed. A movement for independence arose in the late 19th century, and the Government of India Act in 1919 allowed the election of Indian ministers to share power with appointed British governors; a further Act in 1935 allowed the election of independent provincial governments. Passive resistance campaigns led by Mahatma Gandhi began in the 1920s, and independence was granted in 1947, on the basis of partition establishing a separate Muslim state (Pakistan). Indian states were later reorganized on a linguistic basis. There was a Pakistan–India war over the disputed territory of Kashmir and Jammu in 1948; this still unresolved issue underlay further India–Pakistan conflict in 1965 and 1971 (the Indo–Pakistan Wars), as well as periods of tension in 1999 and 2000–2 that were heightened by the fact that both countries now possessed nuclear weapons. There has been sporadic Hindu–Muslim hostility internally too – notably in 1978, but also in 1992 and 2002, when the mosque at Ayodhya was the focus of violent rioting that claimed many lives. Separatist movements continue, especially that of the Sikhs' demand for an independent Sikh state in the Punjab. The suppression of the militant Sikh movement in 1984 led to the assassination of Indira Gandhi. Also in 1984, a major gas leak in the city of Bhopal caused around 2500 deaths. Rajiv Gandhi, leader of the Congress (I) Party, was assassinated in 1991 during the general election. Increasing tension generally resulted in inter-communal violence and the declaration in 1993 of a national state of emergency; in recent years, the main security threats have been from Kashmiri separatists and Islamic extremists. The Congress (I) Party were heavily defeated in 1996, and a period of political instability followed in which there were several general elections and allegations of widespread corruption in public life. Economic reforms, begun in the early 1990s, continued and India is emerging as a major world economy with a growing middle class. The Congress (I) Party, eclipsed by the Hindu nationalist Bharatiya Janata Party (BJP) in the 1990s, won a surprise victory in the 2004 general election under Sonia Gandhi; she refused the premiership and Manmohan Singh became prime minister, the first Sikh to hold the office.

Symbolic Colours

The national flag of India has three horizontal stripes, of deep saffron, white and green, and a navy-blue wheel, the *Ashoka Chakra*, in the centre. India's first vice-president declared that the saffron stripe represented impartiality, white represented truth, green represented the relationship between the people and their natural environment, and the wheel represented virtue and peaceful progress. A common modern interpretation is that saffron is for courage and sacrifice, white is for truth and peace, green for faith and prosperity, and the wheel for justice.

TRADITIONAL INDIAN DRESS

India is a country with a population of more than a billion and is home to many diverse religions, languages and cultures. Traditional Indian dress signifies many aspects of a person and can be indicative of status, age, location or religion; although many people wear Western clothing nowadays, the various forms of traditional dress are still popular.

The sari

The most recognizable piece of everyday female dress is the sari, a word believed to derive from the Sanskrit word *sati* meaning a strip of cloth. The sari, also spelt saree, was traditionally 5–6 m (16–20 ft) long and made from a piece of cotton fabric – cotton has been grown in that part of the world for around 5,000 years. While essentially a long piece of cloth, the borders and one end are highly decorated. Silk and chiffon saris also feature on more special occasions and are embellished with embroidery of gold and silver thread or silks in many brilliant colours. The sari can be worn in many different ways, depending on the occasion or the region of the country.

The sari is worn over a petticoat or thin skirt. The draping of the sari is an art form in itself and there are many regional variations. A common style is to wrap the sari around the waist, then create pleated folds that are tucked into the top of the petticoat; the decorative end, known as the *pallu* or *pallav*, is draped over the shoulder and sometimes secured with a pin or a decorative brooch. This is known as the Nivi style. In Bengal the pleating is traditionally omitted, and in some regions such as Maharashtra and Tamil Nadu the sari is 8 or 9 m (26–30 ft) long.

A woman's modesty is protected by wearing a *choli* – a cropped top that reveals the midriff. Jewellery makes an important addition to the overall look, with gold items being favoured. Toe rings, anklets, ear piercings (infant girls routinely have their ears pierced), bangles, nose rings, rings and necklaces all feature, as does hair ornamentation.

Other styles of dress for women

The *choli* can be worn with a long flowing skirt called a *lehenga*, rather than with a sari. This outfit is a tradition of Rajasthan and Gujarat in north-western India. An alternative style of dress is the salwar kameez, an outfit that originated in the Kashmir and Punjab regions. It comes in three parts: the *salwar* (or *shalwar*), loosely tied wide-legged trousers that taper to the ankle; the *kameez* (or *kurta*), a loose tunic that covers the top half; and the *duppata*, or scarf. A *churidar* is similar to the *salwar* but the trousers fit more tightly at the hips, thighs and ankles.

Male dress

The typical image of male dress is of the *dhoti* (also spelt *dhooti* or *dhuti*), as worn by Mohandas Gandhi. It is a rectangular piece of cloth, resembling a loin cloth, wrapped around the waist and legs. It goes by many other local names including *mundu*, veshti, *pancha* and *panche*. An alternative is the *lungi*, a large piece of cloth that is worn in much the same manner as a sarong. Men can also wear salwar kameez, which are usually white.

INDONESIA

Official name	Republic of Indonesia
Local name	Indonesia
Former name	Netherlands East Indies, Dutch East Indies (until 1949), Republic of the United States of Indonesia (1949–50)
Area	1 906 240 sq km (735 809 sq mi)
Capital	Jakarta
Chief towns	Jayapura, Bandung, Semarang, Surabaya, Medan, Palembang
Population	245 453 000 (2006e)
Nationality	Indonesian
Languages	Bahasa Indonesia; English, Dutch and Javanese and other local dialects are widely spoken; 300 regional languages
Ethnic groups	Javanese 45%, Sundanese 14%, Madurese 7%, Coastal Malays 7%, others 27%
Religions	Islam 88%, Christianity 8% (Prot 5%, RC 3%), Hinduism 2%, Buddhism 1%, others 1%
Time zone	GMT +7/9
Currency	1 Rupiah (Rp) = 100 sen
Telephone	+62
Internet	.id
Country code	IDN

Location

A republic in South-East Asia comprising the world's largest island group.

Physical description

Five main islands and 30 smaller archipelagos totalling 13 677 islands and islets, of which c.6000 are inhabited; most have narrow coastal plains with hilly or mountainous interiors; more than 100 volcanic peaks on Java, of which 15 are active; the highest point is Puncak Jaya (5030 m/16 503 ft); over 50% of the country is covered with rainforest.

Climate

Equatorial climate (hot and humid), affected alternately by the north monsoon (November–March) and the south monsoon (May–September) and often particularly wet in April and October; annual rainfall of 1500–4000 mm (60–160 in); the average temperature is 27°C on island coasts, falling inland and with altitude.

Economy

Largely state-controlled economy, based on exploitation of oil (80% of export earnings) and natural gas and production of petrochemicals; other activities include mining (iron ore, copper, manganese, chromium and coal), agriculture (sugar, fruit, nuts and silk), manufacturing (chemicals, textiles, carpets, construction materials, food processing, metal fabrication and armaments) and forestry.

overnment

overned by an executive President, a Cabinet and a bicameral People's Consultative ssembly, comprising a House of Representatives and a House of Representatives of e Regions.

istory

donesia comprises the island group of the Moluccas, also called the Spice Islands; alimantan, four provinces in the Indonesian part of Borneo; Sumatra, which is e fifth-largest island in the world and was the centre of the Buddhist kingdom of ri Vijaya between the 7th and 13th centuries, and was discovered by Marco Polo the 13th century; and the western half of the mountainous island of Timor. The donesian islands were settled in early times by Hindus and Buddhists, whose ower lasted until the 14th century. Islam was introduced during the 14th and 15th enturies. Portuguese settlers arrived in the early 16th century, and the Dutch East dia Company was established in 1602. Indonesia was occupied by the Japanese in Vorld War II; it then declared its independence in 1945 under Dr Sukarno, although is was not recognized by the Dutch until 1949. The expulsion of Dutch citizens led a breakdown of the economy, causing hardship and unrest. Sukarno's rule became creasingly authoritarian; in the disarray following an unsuccessful military coup 1965, General Suharto deposed Sukarno in 1967 and made himself president. uharto's period in office was dogged by Islamic fundamentalist uprisings, ethnic olence, and the long-running separatist war in East Timor. Following an economic ollapse and calls for political reform, Suharto was replaced in 1998 by his deputy, J Habibie. Habibie's caution and the debacle in East Timor further damaged overnment prestige; in 1999, in the first democratically held elections for 44 years, abibie was succeeded by Abdurrahman Wahid. Allegations of corruption persisted nd Wahid was impeached in 2001 and replaced by the vice-president, Megawati ukarnoputri. She was defeated in the 2004 presidential election by Susilo Bambang udhoyono. Since independence in 1945, several islands have developed separatist novements: the Moluccas fought an unsuccessful separatist war in the 1950s; ast Timor, a Portuguese colony until 1975, was illegally annexed by Indonesia om 1976 until 1999, when it regained its independence after a long and violent eparatist campaign; Irian Jaya (now Papua) was granted a degree of autonomy in 002 but separatist agitation continues; and Aceh province in Sumatra was granted degree of autonomy in 2005. Since the mid-1990s, ethnic and religious tensions ave emerged, resulting in intercommunal violence in Kalimantan, Sulawesi and the 1oluccas; and Islamic extremists linked to al-Qaeda have been held responsible r bombings in Bali in 2002, 2003 and 2005. Sumatra, and in particular Aceh, was evastated in 2004 by the Indian Ocean tsunami, which killed over 200 000 people in donesia.

> ### *Vociferous Volcano*
> The explosive volcanic eruption of Krakatoa in 1883 generated the loudest sound in recorded history. It was heard clearly as far away as Perth, Australia, as well as on the island of Rodrigues near Mauritius.

IRAN

Official name	Islamic Republic of Iran
Local name	Îrân; Jomhûri-ye-Eslâmi-ye-Îrân
Former name	Persia (until 1935)
Area	1648000 sq km (636128 sq mi)
Capital	Tehran
Chief towns	Mashhad, Isfahan, Tabriz, Shiraz, Abadan
Population	68688000 (2006e)
Nationality	Iranian
Languages	Farsi (Persian); Turkic and several minority languages are also spoken
Ethnic groups	Persian 51%, Azeri 24%, Gilaki and Mazandarani 8%, Kurdish 7%, others 10%
Religions	Islam 98% (Shia 89%, Sunni 9%), others 2%
Time zone	GMT +3.5
Currency	1 Iranian Rial (Rls, RI) = 100 dinars
Telephone	+98
Internet	.ir
Country code	IRN

Location

A republic in south-west Asia, bounded to the north by Armenia, Azerbaijan, Turkmenistan and the Caspian Sea; to the east by Afghanistan and Pakistan; to the south by the Gulf of Oman and the Arabian Gulf; to the south-west by Iraq; and to the north-west by Turkey.

Physical description

Largely composed of a vast arid central plateau, with an average elevation of 1200 m (3936 ft), and with many salt and sand basins; rimmed by mountain ranges that drop down to narrow coastal lowlands; bordered to the north by the Elburz Mountains, rising to 5670 m (18602 ft) at Mount Damavend; the Zagros Mountains in the west and south rise to 3000–4600 m (9843–15092 ft); prone to earthquakes.

Climate

Mainly a desert climate, with annual rainfall below 300 mm; average temperatures at Tehran are 2°C (January) and 29°C (July); average annual rainfall is 246 mm; the Caspian coastal strip is much wetter (800–2000 mm) than the interior and rain is more widely distributed throughout the year; hot and humid on the shores of the Arabian Gulf.

Economy

Largely state-controlled economy, based on exploitation of oil (80% of export earnings) and natural gas and production of petrochemicals; other activities include mining (iron ore, copper, manganese, chromium and coal), agriculture (sugar, fruit, uts and silk), manufacturing (chemicals, textiles, carpets, construction materials, ood processing, metal fabrication and armaments) and forestry.

Government

Governed by an executive President, a Council of Ministers and a unicameral Consultative Council (*Majlis al-Shoura*); legislation passed by the Majlis must be approved by the Council of Guardians of the Constitution; the Assembly of Experts elects the Spiritual Leader of the Revolution (*Wali-e Faqih*), who exercises overall authority.

History

Iran was an early centre of civilization; its dynasties include its first royal house, the Achaemenids (from the 7th century BC) and the aggressive Sassanids (from the 3rd century). It was ruled by the Arabs, Turks and Mongols until the Safavid Dynasty between the 16th and 18th centuries and the Qajar Dynasty in the 19th and 20th centuries. The Qajar monarchy was overthrown in 1921 in a military coup led by Reza Shah Pahlavi, who was elected Shah in 1925. He was deposed in 1941 and succeeded as Shah by his son Muhammad Reza Shah Pahlavi. Protests against the Shah's regime in the 1970s led to a revolution in 1978. The Shah went into exile and an Islamic Republic was proclaimed under Ayatollah Khomeini in 1979. Since Khomeini's death in 1989, there has been a struggle for political ascendency between conservatives and more liberal reformers; although liberalization has generally been blocked by the religious authorities and the judiciary, there is a vocal popular pro-democracy movement. The Iran–Iraq War took place in 1980–8, claiming possibly one million Iranian lives. During the Gulf War (1991) and the Iraq War (2003) Iran remained neutral, although it is suspected of supporting Shia insurgents in Iraq since 2003. During the 1990s relations between Iran and the West, particularly the USA, became strained over Iran's alleged abuses of human rights, its hostility to the Middle East peace process and its rumoured involvement in both international terrorism and the development of nuclear weapons. In the aftermath of the Iraq War there were concerns that Iran might become the next target of the USA's War on Terror because it had started to build a nuclear reactor in 2002. The International Atomic Energy Agency (IAEA) reported in 2003 that there was no evidence that Iran was developing nuclear weapons, but Iran's resumption of its uranium enrichment programme in 2005 was condemned by the IAEA and led to the UN Security Council imposing trade sanctions.

Persian Paradise

An important feature of life in ancient Persia (now Iran) was the walled garden. These gardens were places of deep tranquillity, with plenty of shade and cooling water features. Although some had a relaxed natural layout, many were formal and were divided and sub-divided into geometrical patterns, often incorporating architectural elements. The gardens were used for spiritual as well as relaxation purposes; the Persian term for such a garden, *pairi-daeza* ('walled enclosure'), is the origin of the English word 'paradise'.

IRAQ

Official name	Republic of Iraq
Local name	Al Iraq; Al-Jumhūryya al 'Iraqiyya
Former name	part of the Ottoman Empire (until 1916), State of Iraq (1920–1), Iraqi Kingdom (1921–32), Kingdom of Iraq (1932–58)
Area	434 925 sq km (67 881 sq mi)
Capital	Baghdad
Chief towns	Basra, Kirkuk, Mosul
Population	26 783 000 (2006e)
Nationality	Iraqi
Languages	Arabic; Kurdish is also spoken
Ethnic groups	Arab 77%, Kurdish 18%, Turkmen, Assyrian and others 5%
Religions	Islam 97% (Shia 62%, Sunni 35%), Christianity and others 3%
Time zone	GMT +3
Currency	1 Iraqi Dinar (ID) = 1000 fils
Telephone	+964
Internet	.iq
Country code	IRQ

Location

A republic in south-west Asia, bounded to the east by Iran; to the north by Turkey; t the north-west by Syria; to the west by Jordan; to the south-west and south by Sau Arabia; and to the south-east by Kuwait and the Arabian Gulf.

Physical description

Largely comprises the vast alluvial tract of the Tigris–Euphrates lowland (which is equal to ancient Mesopotamia); the two rivers are separated in their upper courses by the plain of Al Jazirah, which rises to 1547 m (5075 ft), and join about 190 km (118 mi) from the Arabian Gulf; the lowland here has swamp vegetation; mountains in the north-east rise to more than 3000 m (9843 ft); the highest point is Haji Ibrahim (3600 m/11 810 ft); desert in other areas.

Climate

Mainly arid; summers are very hot and dry; winters are often cold; average temperatures at Baghdad are 10°C in January and 35°C in July, with an average annual rainfall of 140 mm; rainfall is highest in the north-east, where the annual average is 400–600 mm.

Economy

Impoverished by three decades of under-investment, war, trade sanctions and the current security problems undermining reconstruction; the economy is based on oil and natural gas production, now returning to pre-war levels; other industries include textiles, chemicals, construction materials, food processing and metals; main agricultural products are grains, rice, vegetables, dates, cotton and livestock.

overnment

overned by a President, a Prime Minister and Council of Ministers, and a unicameral
ouncil of Representatives in which 69 seats are set aside for women.

istory

q was part of the Ottoman Empire from the 16th century until World War I. It was
ptured by British forces in 1916 and became a British-mandated territory in 1921.
gained independence under the Hashemite Dynasty in 1932, but the monarchy
as overthrown and replaced by military rule in 1958. Since the 1960s, Kurdish
tionalists in the north-east have been fighting to establish a separate state. Saddam
ussein came to power as president in 1979. His invasion of Iran in 1980 led to the
in–Iraq War, which lasted until 1988. The invasion of Kuwait in 1990 led to UN
nctions, the Gulf War in 1991, and Iraqi withdrawal. Tension in the area remained,
d Iraqi attacks on Kurdish settlements and Shiite refugees continued. UN sanctions
mained in place owing to Iraq's refusal to co-operate with proposed UN inspections
d verification of the destruction of its weapons of mass destruction. In 2003 a US-
d military force invaded and occupied the country, toppling Saddam Hussein, who
as captured in December 2003, tried for crimes against humanity and executed
December 2006. From May 2003 onwards, an insurgency developed with the
parent aim of destabilizing the country. Despite deteriorating internal security,
vereignty was handed over to an interim government in 2004. This was replaced
April 2006 by a multi-ethnic and multi-racial coalition, following elections in
ecember 2005 to a permanent legislature. The brutal sectarian violence raises fears
civil war.

RELAND

Official name	Republic of Ireland
Local name	Éire; Poblacht na hÉireann
Area	70 282 sq km (27 129 sq mi)
Capital	Dublin; Baile Átha Cliath
Chief towns	Cork, Limerick, Waterford, Galway, Drogheda, Dundalk, Sligo
Population	4 062 000 (2006e)
Nationality	Irish
Languages	English, Irish Gaelic; the Gaelic-speaking areas, mostly in the west, are known as the *Gaeltacht*
Ethnic groups	Irish 95%, others 5%
Religions	Christianity 93% (RC 88%, Prot 3%, other Christian 2%), others and unspecified 4%, none 3%
Time zone	GMT
Currency	1 Euro (€) = 100 cents
Telephone	+353
Internet	.ie
Country code	IRL

Location

A republic occupying southern, central and north-western Ireland, separated from Great Britain by the Irish Sea and St George's Channel, and bounded to the north-east by Northern Ireland, part of the UK.

Physical description

Much of the interior comprises a central plain surrounded by hills and low mountains and containing expanses of bog and many lakes; it is drained by slow-moving rivers such as the Shannon, Liffey and Slaney; there are long east-to-west valleys in the south; the mountains on the west coast are part of the Caledonian system of Scandinavia and Scotland, with quartzite peaks weathered into conical mountains such as Croagh Patrick (765 m/2510 ft); a younger mountain system in the south creates a landscape of ridges and valleys; the highest point is Carrauntoohil (1041 m/3415 ft).

Climate

Mild and changeable, with few extremes of temperature; rainfall is heaviest in the west, often over 3000 mm; it is drier in the east and south, the Dublin annual average being 785 mm.

Economy

Transformed since the 1980s from a mainly agricultural economy to one based on services (information technology and tourism) and industry; major industries are metals and minerals extraction and processing, production of food and drink, clothing, chemicals, pharmaceuticals, machinery, transport equipment and vehicles, and computer software and hardware; agriculture, fishing and forestry are less significant than previously, although livestock and livestock products are a major export; there is some natural gas and hydroelectric power production.

Government

Governed by a President, a Prime Minister (*Taoiseach*) and Cabinet, and a bicameral National Parliament (*Oireachtas*) comprising a House of Representatives (*Dáil Éireann*) and a Senate (*Seanad Éireann*).

History

Ireland was occupied by Goidelic-speaking Celts during the Iron Age, and a high kingship was established in around 200 ad, with its capital at Tara (Meath). Following conversion to Christianity by St Patrick in the 5th century, Ireland became a centre of learning and missionary activity. The south-east was attacked by Vikings from around 800. Henry I of England declared himself Lord of Ireland in 1171, and Anglo-Norman expansion created a Lordship of Ireland which at one point dominated much of the island before being pushed back into Munster and Leinster by a Gaelic revival in the 14th and 15th centuries. Henry VIII took the title 'King of Ireland' in 1541 but direct Crown rule was confined to the area around Dublin known as the Pale, though the Anglo-Norman vassals of the Crown ruled over much more. Elizabethan conquest unified the island under English control, which was shaken by a Catholic rebellion during the War of the Three Kingdoms in the 1640s. Parliamentary forces under Oliver Cromwell reconquered Catholic Ireland in 1649–50. The Protestant communities in Ulster continued to survive this turmoil, as they did later on when upporters of the deposed Catholic King James VII and II were defeated by William III t the Battle of the Boyne (1690). Following a century of suppression, the struggle for ish freedom developed in the 18th and 19th centuries, including such revolutionary ovements as Wolfe Tone's United Irishmen (1796–8), and later Young Ireland (1848) nd the Fenians (1866–7). The Act of Union, uniting Ireland and Britain, came into ffect in 1801; the Catholic Relief Act (1829) enacted Catholic emancipation and nabled Catholics to sit in Parliament; and Land Acts (1870–1903) attacked Irish overty (prior to these acts, the Irish Famine in 1845–7 had drastically reduced the opulation). Two Home Rule Bills were introduced by Gladstone (1886, 1893), and third Home Rule Bill was passed in 1914 but never came into effect because of Vorld War I. In 1916 there was an armed rebellion against British rule (the Easter ising), and in 1919 a republic was proclaimed by Sinn Féin. A partition proposed y Britain in 1920 was largely ignored by the Irish Republic. In 1921 a treaty gave eland dominion status as the Irish Free State, subject to the right of Northern Ireland o opt out; this right was exercised, and a frontier was agreed in 1925. The Irish onstitution of 1937 renamed the country Éire and declared the country a sovereign, dependent and democratic state with a directly elected president. All constitutional nks between the Irish Republic and the UK were severed with the declaration of e republic in 1948, although under the Republic of Ireland Act 1949 (Ireland) and e Ireland Act 1949 (UK), the republic retained special citizenship arrangements and ade preference with Britain. Since 1973 the Irish Republic has been a member of the uropean Community, and replaced the Irish pound or punt with the euro in 2002. ince the 1990s Irish prime ministers Albert Reynolds (1992–4), John Bruton (1994–7) nd Bertie Ahern (b.1997) have been involved in the Northern Ireland peace process. he president of Ireland from 1990 was Mary Robinson; she was succeeded in 1997 y Mary McAleese.

> **"**
>
> *For the great Gaels of Ireland*
> *Are the men that God made mad,*
> *For all their wars are merry,*
> *And all their songs are sad.*
>
> —English critic, novelist and poet G K Chesterton
> (1874–1936), from *Ballad of the White Horse* (1911).
>
> **"**

IRELAND, NORTHERN ▸ UNITED KINGDOM

ISLE OF MAN ▸ UNITED KINGDOM

ISRAEL

Official name	State of Israel
Local name	Medinat Yisra'el (Hebrew), Dawlat Isrā'īl (Arabic)
Area	20770 sq km (8017 sq mi)
Capital[1]	Tel Aviv-Jaffa
Chief towns	Jerusalem, Haifa, Beersheba, Acre, Holon
Population	6352000 (2006e)
Nationality	Israeli
Languages	Hebrew, Arabic
Ethnic groups	Jewish 76% (Israeli-born 51%, born elsewhere 25%), Arab and others 24%
Religions	Judaism 76%, Islam 16%, Christianity 2%, Druze 2%, unspecified 4%
Time zone	GMT +2
Currency	1 New Israeli Shekel (NIS/ILS) = 100 agora
Telephone	+972
Internet	.il
Country code	ISR

[1] *Israel claims Jerusalem as its capital, but this is not recognized internationally.*

Location

A democratic republic in the Middle East, bounded to the north by Lebanon; to the north-east by Syria; to the east by Jordan (the River Jordan forms part of the border); to the south-west by Egypt; and to the west by the Mediterranean Sea.

Physical description

Extends 420 km (260 mi) north to south; width varies from 20 km (12 mi) to 116 km (72 mi); the narrow coastal plain is crossed by several rivers; the mountainous interior rises to 1208 m (3963 ft) at Mount Meron; the mountains in Galilee and Samaria, dissected by faults, drop eastwards to below sea level in the Jordan–Red Sea rift valley; the Negev Desert in the south occupies c.60% of the country's area.

Climate

Typically Mediterranean in the north and centre, with hot, dry summers and mild, wet winters; average temperatures at Tel Aviv-Jaffa are 14°C in January and 27°C in July; average annual rainfall is 550 mm; rainfall is heavier inland, with occasional snow; low rainfall in the Negev, decreasing in the south.

Economy

Highly developed and diversified economy, based on technically advanced industry and agriculture developed intensively since the 1970s; major industries are technology (aviation, electronics, biotechnology, computer software, telecommunications and alternative energy sources), manufacturing (wood and paper products, food, drink, tobacco products, metal goods, chemicals, plastics, cement, textiles and footwear), oil refining, potash, phosphates, construction, diamond-cutting, agriculture (citrus and other fruits, vegetables, cotton, tobacco, meat and dairy products) and tourism, primarily to religious centres; irrigation schemes have greatly extended the area under cultivation.

Government

Governed by a President, a Prime Minister and Cabinet, and a unicameral legislature (*Knesset*).

History

Zionists settled in Palestine in the 1880s when it was under Ottoman rule, and the British declared support for a Jewish 'national home' there in 1917. However, Zionist ambitions were never satisfied under the League of Nations mandate given to Britain (1918–47), although Jewish immigration in the 1930s and 1940s increased greatly due to Nazi persecution. The British evacuated Palestine after World War II, unable to control a new flood of Jewish immigration strongly supported by the USA. Tension between Arabs and Jews led the UN in 1947 to support the formation of two states in Palestine, one Jewish and the other Arab. When the Arab side rejected this, David Ben-Gurion announced the creation of the independent State of Israel on 14 May 1948. Military conflict with surrounding countries ensued in which Israeli forces were victorious. Further wars took place in 1956 (Suez Crisis) and 1967 (Six-Day War), when Israel gained control of the Gaza Strip, the Sinai Peninsula as far as the Suez Canal, the West Bank of the River Jordan (including the eastern sector of Jerusalem), and the Golan Heights in Syria; these areas have since been referred to as the 'occupied territories'. Wars also broke out in 1973 (Yom Kippur War) and in 1982 (Lebanon War), which forced the Palestine Liberation Organization (PLO) to leave Beirut in 1982–5. In contrast, a peace agreement was reached with Egypt in 1979 (under which Sinai was returned) and with Jordan in 1994. During the 1990s there were several attempts to launch peace talks to resolve the Israeli–Palestinian conflict. The Oslo Accords (1993) led to the establishment of the Palestinian Autonomous Areas in Jericho and the Gaza Strip (1994–5), Hebron (1997) and six West Bank towns (1998). However, violence continued, with suicide bombings in Israeli cities, an armed struggle in south Lebanon (until Israeli troops withdrew in 1999), and more fighting between West Bank Palestinians and Israeli forces. Efforts to negotiate a final settlement have been hindered since 2001 by the election of Israeli governments critical of the peace process, the outbreak of a second intifada in 2000, the Israeli refusal to negotiate with Yasser Arafat because of the Palestinian authorities' failure to rein in the violence of extremists, and Israel's construction of a wall between Israeli and Palestinian areas despite international protests. Negotiations with the Palestinians resumed in 2005 after the death of Yasser Arafat in 2004 and the election of his moderate successor, Mahmoud Abbas, and were boosted by the evacuation of Israeli settlements and withdrawal of Israeli forces from the Gaza Strip in 2005. However, they stalled again in early 2006 with the victory of the extremist Hamas movement in the Palestinian legislative elections. The situation deteriorated dramatically in summer 2006 when the kidnapping of Israeli soldiers in the Gaza Strip and on the Lebanon border prompted Israeli military invasions of Gaza and southern Lebanon.

ITALY

Official name	Italian Republic
Local name	Italia
Former name	Kingdom of Italy (until 1946)
Area	301 225 sq km (116 273 sq mi)
Capital	Rome; Roma
Chief towns	Milan, Turin, Genoa, Naples, Bologna, Palermo, Florence, Venice
Population	58 133 000 (2006e)
Nationality	Italian
Languages	Italian; German is also spoken in the Trentino-Alto Adige, French in Valle d'Aosta, and Slovene in Trieste-Gorizia
Ethnic groups	Italian 94%, others 6%
Religions	Christianity 83% (RC), Islam 1%, unaffiliated 14%, others 2%
Time zone	GMT +1
Currency	1 Euro (€) = 100 cents
Telephone	+39
Internet	.it
Country code	ITA

Location

A republic in southern Europe, comprising the boot-shaped peninsula extending south into the Mediterranean Sea, as well as Sicily, Sardinia and some 70 smaller islands. It is bounded to the north-west by France; to the north by Switzerland and Austria; and to the north-east by Slovenia.

Physical description

The Italian peninsula extends c.800 km (500 mi) south-east from the Lombardy plains; it is mostly mountainous, the Apennine range forming a spine along its length that rises to peaks of more than 2000 m (6562 ft); to the north of the range lies the broad, fertile Lombardo–Venetian plain in the basin of the River Po and to its east are the plains of Emilia-Romagna in the north and Apulia in the south; the Alps and Dolomite mountains divide Italy from France, Switzerland, Austria and Slovenia; at the foot of the Alps lie lakes Maggiore, Como and Garda; the chief rivers include the Po, Tiber, Arno, Volturno, Liri and Adige; Sicily includes the limestone massifs of Monti Nebrodi and the volcanic cone of Mount Etna (3323 m/10 902 ft), one of three active volcanos in the country, the others being Vesuvius (1277 m/4190 ft) and Stromboli (926 m/3038 ft); Sardinia rises to 1835 m (6020 ft) at Monti del Gennargentu.

Climate

The climate is predominantly Mediterranean (mild, wet winters and hot, dry summers), but with Alpine conditions in the north and colder, wetter and often snowy winters in the higher areas of peninsular Italy; the west coast is warmer than the Adriatic coast and receives more rainfall.

Economy

A diversified market economy, with industry largely concentrated in the north and agriculture in the south; the main industry is tourism; other industries are based on processing imported raw materials and manufacturing goods (precision machinery, motor vehicles, chemicals, pharmaceuticals, electrical goods, textiles, fashion, clothing and footwear); agricultural products, including wine, minerals and non-ferrous metals are also exported.

Government

Governed by a President, a Prime Minister and Cabinet, and a bicameral legislature consisting of a Chamber of Deputies and a Senate.

History

In pre-Roman times, Italy, which did not at that time include the Po Valley, was inhabited by Etruscans in the north, Latins in the centre of the country and Greeks in the south. Most regions were part of the Roman Empire by the 3rd century BC; barbarian tribes invaded in the 4th century AD, and the last Roman emperor was deposed in AD 476. Italy was later ruled by the Lombards and by the Franks under Charlemagne, who was crowned Emperor of the Romans in 800. It became part of the Holy Roman Empire under Otto I, the Great, in 962, and popes and emperors were in conflict throughout the Middle Ages. There were disputes between Guelfs and Ghibellines in the 12th century. Italy was divided amongst five main powers during the 14th and 15th centuries (Kingdom of Naples, Duchy of Milan, republics of Florence and Venice, and the papacy). The country made a major contribution to European culture through the Renaissance. Four satellite republics were set up after a successful French invasion during the wars of the French Revolution, and Napoleon I was crowned King of Italy in 1805. The 19th century saw the upsurge of liberalism and nationalism (the Risorgimento); unification was achieved by 1870 under Victor Emmanuel II of Sardinia, aided by Cavour and Garibaldi. Colonies were established in Eritrea (1870–89) and Somaliland (1889), but the attempt to secure a protectorate over Abyssinia was defeated at the Battle of Adowa (1896). During World War I, Italy fought alongside the Allies. The Fascist movement brought Mussolini to power in 1922, and he led the conquest of Abyssinia (1935–6) and occupation of Albania (1939). The alliance with Hitler in World War II led to the end of the Italian Empire. Italy became a democratic republic in 1946, but political instability resulted in 45 governments in 47 years until partial reform of the voting system in 1993 produced longer-lasting governments. Italy was a founding member of the European Economic Community in 1958, and in 2002 replaced the lira with the euro. Following corruption scandals, there was a drive in the early 1990s to reform the political establishment; Silvio Berlusconi (prime minister 1994, 2001–6) was dogged by accusations of corruption, of which he was acquitted in 2004 following a four-year trial. His centre-right coalition government was replaced after the 2006 election by a centre-left coalition headed by Romano Prodi.

IVORY COAST ►CÔTE D'IVOIRE

THE ITALIAN RENAISSANCE

The Renaissance, literally 'a rebirth', was an era of great cultural activity that spanned the period from the 14th to the 16th century. During this time there was renewed interest in the arts, literature and philosophy of the classical period, reflected by the contemporary flowering of these disciplines. Although the influence of the Renaissance spread throughout Europe, its emergence took place in Italy. Renaissance artists received their patronage from the Church, the wealthy city-states, and rich families such as the Medici in Florence and the Visconti and the Sforza in Milan.

Art and architecture

Some of the most famous artistic treasures of the period are to be found in Florence, the city often considered to be the focus of the Italian Renaissance. These include the bronze relief doors of the Baptistery by Lorenzo Ghiberti (1378–1455), which depict biblical scenes.

Two of the greatest Florentine artists of the era were Giotto (c.1265–1337) and Michelangelo Buonarroti (1475–1564). Giotto broke away from the stylized forms of the medieval period and painted religious works that were lifelike in their execution. His most important images form the fresco cycle in the Scrovegni Chapel in Padua. Michelangelo's fame rests with the re-painting of the ceiling of the Sistine Chapel in the Vatican between 1508 and 1512; the nine central panels illustrate stories from the Book of Genesis. The walls are also highly decorated, and demonstrate the work of a number of other Italian artists including Sandro Botticelli (1445–1510), Perugino (c.1450–1523) and Luca Signorelli (c.1441–1523).

The Renaissance also saw the important development of perspective in painting. The goldsmith, architect and sculptor Filippo Brunelleschi (1377–1446) mastered the principles of this revolutionary technique. Brunelleschi also designed and built the technically challenging octagonal dome of the Basilica di Santa Maria del Fiore, the cathedral church in Florence.

Written works

Italian writing of the period was dominated by three majestic writers. The poet Petrarch (1304–74) is most famous for his *Canzoniere* (c.1327, 'Songbook'), an anthology of passionate sonnets addressed to Laura, a real woman he glimpsed at the church of Sainte Claire d'Avignon. Poet and humanist Giovanni Boccaccio (1313–75) is noted for his masterpiece *Il Decamerone* (1353, 'Ten Days'), a collection of stories told during a period of ten days by a group of Florentine people who fled the plague and stayed at a country villa. The statesman and political philosopher Niccolò Machiavelli (1469–1527) wrote his treatise *Il Principe* (1532, *The Prince*) on acquiring and retaining political power.

Music

One of the most remarkable religious composers of the period was Giovanni Pierluigi da Palestrina (c.1525–94), a choirmaster at St Peter's in Rome who composed hundreds of masses and motets. Secular music was popular and was regularly accompanied by the lute. The spinettino (a small harpsichord), the psaltery (a plucked, stringed instrument) and the lira da braccho (a violin-like instrument) were also popular. The late Italian Renaissance saw the origins of the operatic form, championed by Claudio Monteverdi (1567–1643); the première of his *Orfeo,* based on the Greek myth, took place in 1607.

JAMAICA

Official name	Jamaica
Local name	Jamaica
Area	10 957 sq km (4 229 sq mi)
Capital	Kingston
Chief towns	Montego Bay, Spanish Town
Population	2 758 000 (2006e)
Nationality	Jamaican
Languages	English; Jamaican Creole is also spoken
Ethnic groups	black 91%, mixed 7%, East Indian 1%, others 1%
Religions	Christianity 66% (Prot 64% (about half Church of God), RC 2%), Rastafarianism 1%, unaffiliated 21%, others 12%
Time zone	GMT −5
Currency	1 Jamaican Dollar (J$) = 100 cents
Telephone	+1 876
Internet	.jm
Country code	JAM

Location

An island nation of the West Indies in the Caribbean Sea.

Physical description

The third largest island in the Caribbean Sea, with a maximum length of 234 km (145 mi) and width varying from 35 km (22 mi) to 82 km (51 mi); mountainous and rugged, particularly in the east where the Blue Mountains rise to 2256 m (7401 ft) at Blue Mountain Peak; there are more than 100 small rivers.

Climate

Tropical climate at sea level, more temperate at higher altitudes; coastal temperatures range from 21 to 34°C, with an average annual rainfall of 1980 mm; there is virtually no rainfall on the south and south-west plains; the island lies within the hurricane belt.

Economy

Weak economy, dependent on international aid and expatriates' remittances; main activities are tourism, bauxite and alumina production, agriculture (sugar, bananas, coffee and yams), textiles, food processing, rum, metal, paper and chemicals.

Government

Governed by a Governor-General (representing the British monarch, who is head of state), a Prime Minister and Cabinet, and a bicameral Parliament consisting of an elected House of Representatives and an appointed Senate.

History

The island was visited by Christopher Columbus in 1494 and settled by the Spanish in 1509. From 1640, west African slave labour was imported for work on the sugar plantations. Jamaica was occupied by the British in 1655. Self-government was introduced in 1944, and independence was achieved in 1962. Post-independence politics has been dominated by the Jamaican Labour Party and the People's National Party. Fraught relations between the two deteriorated into violence in the 1970s. Despite greater political stability in recent years, there are high levels of crime and violence, largely connected with drugs.

JAPAN

Official name	Japan
Local name	Nihon/Nippon
Area	381 945 sq km (147 431 sq mi)
Capital	Tokyo; Tōkyō, Tôkyô
Chief towns	Yokohama, Osaka, Nagoya, Sapporo, Kyoto, Kobe
Population	127 484 000 (2006e)
Nationality	Japanese
Language	Japanese
Ethnic groups	Japanese 99%, others 1%
Religions	Shintoism and Buddhism 84%, Christian 1%, others 15%
Time zone	GMT +9
Currency	1 Yen (Y, ¥) = 100 sen
Telephone	+81
Internet	.jp
Country code	JPN

Location

An island state off the east coast of Asia. It comprises the four large islands of Hokkaido (the northernmost island), Honshu (the largest island), Kyushu and Shikoku (in the south-west), and many small islands.

Physical description

The islands have narrow coastal plains rising to wooded, mountainous interiors, so less than 20% of the land can be cultivated; on Hokkaido the central range rises to more than 2000 m (6562 ft); Honshu includes Japan's highest point, Mount Fuji (3776 m/12 388 ft); there are many volcanoes, mainly extinct or dormant; the more southerly islands of Shikoku and Kyushu have low cones and rolling hills; further south is the Ryukyu chain of volcanic islands, of which Okinawa is the largest; Japan lies on the boundaries of three tectonic plates and 20% of the world's earthquakes occur there.

Climate

An oceanic climate, influenced by the Asian monsoon, with temperatures reduced by altitude; in the north there are short, warm summers and severe winters with heavy snow, and heavy rainfall on western coasts; in the south there are mild, almost subtropical winters with light rainfall, and very warm summers whose heat is often oppressive, especially in the cities; typhoons occur in summer and early autumn; Akita in north Honshu has an average daily temperature of $-5-+2°C$ in January, 19–28°C in August, and rainfall in this area is a minimum of 104mm in February–March and a maximum of 211mm in September.

Economy

There is a highly industrialized market economy, now recovering from 14 years of stagnation; the main activities are financial services and banking, and industries producing high-technology electronic products, motor vehicles, office machinery, chemicals, machine tools, steel and other metals, ships, textiles and processed food; intensive agriculture, rice being the principal crop; fishing; and forestry.

Government

A hereditary constitutional monarchy with an Emperor as head of state; governed by a Prime Minister and Cabinet, and a bicameral Diet (*Kokkai*), comprising a House of Representatives (*Shugiin*) and a House of Councillors (*Sangiin*).

History

Originally occupied by the Ainu, in the 4th century the country developed from individual communities into small states; by the 5th century, the Yamato Dynasty was the most dominant. Its culture was strongly influenced by China between the 8th and 12th centuries. From 1603 it was united and ruled by the Tokugawa Dynasty of military dictators, who tamed the feudal lords. Contact with the West was severely restricted until the visit of the US Commodore Matthew Perry in 1853 opened Japan up to foreign trade and industrialization. After the Meiji Restoration in 1868, successful wars were waged with imperial China (1894–5), and Russia (1904–5), and Korea was annexed in 1910. Intense nationalism in the 1920s was accompanied by a rise in militarism, leading to the occupation of Manchuria in 1931–2 and a pact with the Axis powers in 1940. Japan entered World War II with a surprise attack on the US fleet at Pearl Harbor, Hawaii, in 1941, and occupied British, Dutch and French possessions in South-East Asia (1941–2). It was pushed back during 1943–5 and surrendered after atomic bombs were dropped on Hiroshima and Nagasaki in 1945. There was strong economic growth from the 1960s until the 1990s, when Japan suffered a marked economic contraction from which it started to emerge only in 2001. The Liberal Democrat Party has dominated post-war politics, holding power continuously from 1955 to 1993 and forming part of the coalition governments since 1995. During the premiership of Junichiro Koizumi (2001–6) relations deteriorated with some neighbouring countries, especially China and North Korea. Koizumi was succeeded by Shinzo Abe in 2006.

JAPANESE GIANTS OF SUMO WRESTLING

Sumo wrestling is an ancient martial art – the oldest written records date from the 8th century but it is believed to be more than 1,500 years old. It has its roots in the Shinto religion and has many specialized rituals.

Size matters

The most notable feature of the sport is the immense size of the wrestlers, who are known as *sumotori* or *rikishi*. They rarely weigh less than 130 kg (285 lb) and often grow to 200 kg (440 lb) or more, thanks to prodigious quantities of food including a high-protein stew called *chanko nabe*. Their great weight makes them immovable and ensures a low centre of gravity so that their opponents cannot push them to the floor or out of the ring.

Sumo traditions

Sumo fights take place in a wrestling ring known as a *dohyo*, which has a diameter of 4.55 m (15 ft) and is laid with earth. A *yakata*, a roof-shaped canopy modelled on a Shinto sanctuary, is erected above the ring. Red, green, white and black tassels hang from each corner of the *yakata* to represent the seasons.

A sumo fight is accompanied by much ritual and ceremony. Before each bout the *dohyo* is purified by throwing salt upon it, and the *rikishi* make a number of ritual moves and stances before fighting. The *rikishi* fight barefoot and naked save for a loincloth (*mae-tate-mitsu*) and a thick silk belt (*mawashi*). Their hair is grown long and worn in a topknot known as a *chon-mage*.

Fights are supervised by a *gyoji* (referee) who wears a silk kimono and a special court hat. He traditionally bears a fan as a symbol of authority, and a dagger, said to have been originally supplied so that a referee might disembowel himself if he gave an incorrect decision.

The fights

Opponents settle into a crouched position known as *tachiai* before fighting starts. A *rikishi* wins a bout by knocking his opponent out of the ring or off his feet. There are about 80 movements or *kimarite* in sumo wrestling: throws, twists, lifts, and throws across the back. Bouts generally last around 90 seconds but can be over more quickly – there are usually no weight categories, so the largest wrestlers tend to have an advantage even though nimble wrestlers can catch their opponents unawares.

Training

The training of *rikishi* takes place in 'stables' (there are currently 54 in Japan), run by retired champions who pass on their knowledge. Young boys are apprenticed at 15. The discipline in the stables is strict and regimented and the hierarchy well observed, with six different divisions: *Makuuchi*, *Juryo*, *Makushita*, *Sandanme*, *Jonidan* and *Jonokuchi*. Only the latter two levels are salaried; members of these are known as *sekitori*. Members of the lower levels receive only a small allowance and have to endure harsher living conditions. At the top of the tree are *Yokozuna*, grand champions who are greatly revered.

Every year there are six major tournaments, called *basho*, each of which lasts about two weeks. Wrestlers move up and down the divisions according to their wins, so previously earned privileges can be lost through poor performance. However, once a wrestler reaches the Yokozuna he cannot be displaced except by retirement.

JORDAN

Official name	Hashemite Kingdom of Jordan
Local name	Al'Urdunn; Al-Mamlaka al-Urdunniyya al-Hashimiyya
Former name	Emirate of Transjordan (until 1946), Hashemite Kingdom of Transjordan (1946–9)
Area	89 213 sq km (34 445 sq mi)
Capital	Amman; 'Ammān
Chief towns	Irbid, Zarqa, Salt, Karak, Aqaba
Population	5 907 000 (2006e)
Nationality	Jordanian
Language	Arabic
Ethnic groups	Arab 98%, others 2%
Religions	Islam 92% (Sunni), Christianity 6%, others 2%
Time zone	GMT +2
Currency	1 Jordanian Dinar (JD) = 1000 fils
Telephone	+962
Internet	.jo
Country code	JOR

Location

A kingdom in the Middle East, bounded to the north by Syria; to the north-east by Iraq; to the east and south by Saudi Arabia; and to the west by Israel.

Physical description

The Red Sea–Jordan rift valley forms the western border; much of it lies below sea level, the lowest point being −400 m (−1312 ft) at the Dead Sea; the sides of the rift rise steeply through undulating hill country to heights above 1000 m; the land levels out into a desert plateau that extends eastwards over the rest of the country, so only 25% of the land is suitable for cultivation; the desert is sandy in the south, hard and rocky further north; the highest point is Jabal Rum (1754 m/5755 ft).

Climate

The desert plateau and Jordan valley (90% of the country) have very hot summers and cold winters, with annual rainfall below 200 mm; there is a Mediterranean climate elsewhere, with hot, dry summers and cool, wet winters; temperatures at Amman are 7°C (January), 25°C (July); average annual rainfall is 290 mm.

Economy

There is a growing economy, although the country is still dependent on international aid; few natural resources; main activities are tourism, mining (potash and phosphates), oil refining, manufacturing (textiles, garments, pharmaceuticals and machinery), agriculture (vegetables, fruit and nuts); there are developing irrigation schemes in the Jordan valley.

Government

A hereditary monarchy; governed by the King, a Prime Minister and Council of Ministers, and a bicameral National Assembly consisting of a Senate and a House of Deputies.

History

Jordan was part of the Roman Empire, and came under Arab control in the 7th century. It was the centre of Crusader activity in the 11th and 12th centuries, and part of the Turkish Ottoman Empire from the 16th century until World War I. With the collapse of the empire in 1918, the area was divided into Palestine (west of the River Jordan) and Transjordan (east of the River Jordan), both administered by Britain. Transjordan gained independence in 1946, changing its name to Jordan. After the British mandate over Palestine ended in 1948, the newly created State of Israel fought to control the West Bank area. An armistice in 1949 left Jordan in control of the West Bank, and the West and East Banks united within Jordan in 1951. However, Israel took control of the West Bank after the Six-Day War in 1967. Following attempts by the Jordanian army to expel Palestinian guerrillas from the West Bank in 1970–1, civil war erupted; an amnesty was declared in 1973, and claims to the West Bank were ceded to the Palestine Liberation Organization (PLO) in 1974. Legal and administrative links with the West Bank were cut in 1988, and Jordan formally renounced sovereignty over the West Bank and East Jerusalem in 1999. Following internal unrest in 1989, political, social and economic reforms were initiated and the first elections since 1967 took place. A ban on political parties ended in 1991 and the first multiparty elections since 1956 took place in 1993. King Hussein, who ruled from 1952 to 1998, was succeeded on his death by his son, Abdullah II, who has instituted economic reforms in association with the International Monetary Fund. Since 2003, Jordan has experienced a number of terrorist attacks that appear to be the work of Islamic extremists, possibly linked to al-Qaeda.

Winston's Hiccup

The border between Jordan and Saudi Arabia is largely a straight line, but it has an odd kink at the southern end. This is known as 'Winston's hiccup', ostensibly because it resulted from Winston Churchill hiccuping as he drew the boundaries of Transjordan (as Jordan was then known) after drinking too much wine at lunch. Disappointingly, though, the story is not true.

KAZAKHSTAN

Official name	Republic of Kazakhstan
Local name	Qazaqstan; Qazaqstan Respūblīkasy
Former name	Kazakh Soviet Socialist Republic (until 1991), within the Union of Soviet Socialist Republics (USSR; 1922–91)
Area	2 717 300 sq km (1 048 878 sq mi)
Capital	Astana
Chief towns	Karaganda, Semipalatinsk, Chimkent, Petropavlovsk
Population	15 233 000 (2006e)
Nationality	Kazakhstani
Languages	Kazakh, Russian
Ethnic groups	Kazakh 53%, Russian 30%, Ukrainian 4%, Uzbek 3%, German 2%, others 8%
Religions	Islam 47%, Christianity 46% (Orthodox 44%, Prot 2%), others 7%
Time zone	GMT +4/6
Currency	1 Tenge = 100 tiyn
Telephone	+7
Internet	.kz
Country code	KAZ

Location

A republic in western Asia, bounded to the north by Russia; to the south by Turkmenistan, Uzbekistan and Kyrgyzstan; to the east by China; and to the west by the Caspian Sea.

Physical description

Steppeland in the north gives way to desert in the south; the lowest elevation is near the eastern shore of the Caspian Sea (−132 m/−433 ft); there are mountain ranges in the east and south-east; the highest point is Khan Tengri (6995 m/22 949 ft); the chief rivers are the Irtysh, Syrdarya, Ural, Emba and Ili; the largest lake is Lake Balkhash; the Aral Sea lies on the southern border with Uzbekistan.

Climate

Continental; hot summers and cold winters.

Economy

Fast-growing economy owing to the oil boom; other industries include mining (coal, phosphorus, chrome, lead, zinc, silver and ferrous metals), mineral processing, agriculture (grain, wool, cotton and livestock), machine-building (construction equipment, tractors, agricultural machinery and electric motors) and chemicals.

Government
Governed by a President, a Prime Minister and Cabinet, and a bicameral Parliament consisting of the Senate and the Assembly (*Majilis*).

History
Formerly the home of nomadic Kazakhs and ruled by Mongol khans, it was taken over by Tsarist Russia during the 19th century. In the early 20th century a nationalist movement was violently suppressed; it became an autonomous republic of the Soviet Union in 1920 and a full republic in 1936. In 1991 it became an independent republic, and was a founding member of the Commonwealth of Independent States (CIS). Economic reform began in 1993, but the country has serious economic and environmental problems. Nursultan Nazarbayev, head of state since 1990, presides over an authoritarian regime with poor human rights and civil liberties records.

KENYA

Official name	Republic of Kenya
Local name	Kenya; Jamhuri ya Kenya
Former name	British East Africa Protectorate (until 1920)
Area	580 370 sq km (224 080 sq mi)
Capital	Nairobi
Chief towns	Mombasa, Kisumu, Nakuru, Malindi
Population	34 708 000 (2006e)
Nationality	Kenyan
Languages	English and Swahili, with many tribal languages spoken
Ethnic groups	Kikuyu 22%, Luhya 14%, Luo 13%, Kalenjin 12%, Kamba 11%, other African 27%, others 1%
Religions	Christianity 78% (Prot 45%, RC 33%), traditional beliefs 10%, Islam 10%, others 2%
Time zone	GMT +3
Currency	1 Kenyan Shilling (Ksh) = 100 cents
Telephone	+254
Internet	.ke
Country code	KEN

Location
A republic in east Africa, bounded to the south by Tanzania; to the west by Uganda; to the north-west by Sudan; to the north by Ethiopia; to the north-east by Somalia; and to the east by the Indian Ocean.

Physical description
Crossed by the equator; the Great Rift Valley in the west runs north to south; the south-west plateau includes the highest point, Mount Kenya (5200 m/17 060 ft), and the Aberdare range; arid semi-desert in the north, generally under 600 m (1969 ft); numerous lakes, including part of Lake Victoria in south-west and Lake Turkana, the largest body of water, in the north; the Chalbi Desert lies south-east of Lake Turkana;

the coastal strip south of the River Tana is typified by coral reefs, mangrove swamps and small island groups.

Climate

Tropical climate on the coast, with high temperatures and humidity; more temperate at altitude; in Mombasa the average annual rainfall is 1200mm, the average daily temperatures are 27–31°C; average annual rainfall decreases from 500mm in the south to 250mm in the far north; frost and snow lie in the high mountains.

Economy

Very poor country, dependent on international aid; agriculture and horticulture employ 75% of the workforce; chief cash crops are tea (world's fourth-largest producer), coffee and vegetables; other activities include food processing, small-scale manufacturing (consumer goods and textiles), tourism, oil refining and fishing.

Government

Governed by an executive President, a Cabinet and a unicameral National Assembly.

History

Anthropologists have found very early fossil hominids in the region. The coast was settled by Arabs in the 7th century; the country came under Portuguese control in the 16th and 17th centuries, and under British control as an East African Protectorate in 1895. After it became a British colony in 1920, an independence movement led to the Mau Mau rebellion in 1952–60. Led by the Kenya African National Union (KANU), it gained independence in 1963 under Prime Minister Jomo Kenyatta, who became president when Kenya became a republic in 1964. He was succeeded on his death in 1978 by Daniel Arap Moi. In 1991 a multiparty system was legalized. Moi won the elections of 1992 and 1998 amid allegations of electoral fraud, and during the 1990s there were sporadic outbreaks of violent unrest fuelled by demands for constitutional change. Moi's long rule came to an end in 2001, when KANU lost elections to opposition parties and the National Rainbow Coalition's Mwai Kibaki was elected president. A corruption scandal in 2006 implicating serving and former government ministers put overseas aid at risk of suspension.

The Earliest Kenyans

The Rift Valley and Lake Victoria regions of Kenya are home to some of the most important fossil sites in the world. Fossils of some of our early hominid ancestors have been found there, including *Homo erectus* ('Upright Man') and *Homo habilis* ('Handy Man'). Recent fossil evidence has shown for the first time that chimpanzees were present during the same period. Much older inhabitants have also been found in the area – over 200 dinosaur specimens dating from the Mesozoic era more than 200 million years ago.

KIRIBATI

Official name	Republic of Kiribati
Local name	Kiribati; Ribaberikin Kiribati
Former name	Gilbert Islands, as part of the Gilbert and Ellice Islands (until 1979)
Area	717 sq km (277 sq mi)
Capital	Tarawa
Population	105 400 (2006e)
Nationality	I-Kiribati
Languages	English, I-Kiribati
Ethnic groups	Micronesian 99%, others 1%
Religions	Christianity 92% (RC 52%, Prot 40%), others 8%
Time zone	GMT +12/14
Currency	1 Australian Dollar ($A) = 100 cents
Telephone	+686
Internet	.ki
Country code	KIR

Location

A group of 33 low-lying coral islands scattered over c.3 million sq km (1.2 million sq mi) of the central Pacific Ocean.

Physical description

The islands seldom rise to more than 4 m (13 ft) and usually consist of a reef enclosing a lagoon; Banaba, a solid coral outcrop with a fringing reef, rises to 87 m (285 ft).

Climate

There is a maritime equatorial climate in the central islands; the islands further north and south are tropical; the average annual temperature is 27°C; the average annual rainfall varies from 500 mm south of the equator to 3000 mm in the north; the rainy season is June–November north of the equator and November–April south of it; some islands suffer from periodic drought.

Economy

A weak economy since phosphate deposits ran out in 1979; dependent on international aid, expatriates' remittances, copra, coconuts, seaweed, fish and tourism.

Government

Governed by an executive President, a Cabinet and a unicameral House of Parliament.

History

The Gilbert and Ellice Islands were visited by British seafarers in the 18th century, proclaimed a British protectorate in 1892, and annexed in 1916. The two island groups separated in 1975, and the Gilbert Islands achieved independence in 1979 under the name of Kiribati. In 1999, Kiribati joined the UN. Kiribati is threatened by rising sea levels; two atolls were reported submerged in 1999. In 2002 Kiribati, with Tuvalu and the Maldives, announced its attention to take legal action against the USA over its refusal to sign the Kyoto Protocol.

> ## A Matter of Pronunciation
>
> It might look as though Kiribati would be a straightforward name to say. However, it is actually pronounced 'keer-ree-bahss'.

KOREA, NORTH

Official name	Democratic People's Republic of Korea (DPRK)
Local name	Chosun; Chosun Mincu-chui In'min Kongwa-guk
Area	122 098 sq km (47 130 sq mi)
Capital	Pyongyang; P'yŏngyang
Chief towns	Chongjin, Sinuiju, Wonsan, Kaesong
Population	23 113 000 (2006e)
Nationality	North Korean
Languages	Korean
Ethnic group	Korean 100%
Religions	traditional beliefs 16%, Chondogyo 14%, Buddhism 2%, Christianity 1%, none/unaffiliated 67%
Time zone	GMT +9
Currency	1 Won (NKW) = 100 chon
Telephone	+850
Internet	.kp
Country code	PRK

Location

A socialist state in eastern Asia, in the northern half of the Korean Peninsula, bounded to the north by China; to the north-east by Russia; to the west by Korea Bay and the Yellow Sea; to the east by the Sea of Japan; and to the south by South Korea, from which it is separated by a demilitarized zone.

Physical description

Lies on a high plateau occupying the northern part of a mountainous peninsula; many areas rise to more than 2000 m (6562 ft); the highest point is Mount Paektu (2744 m/9003 ft); lower mountains and foothills in the south descend to narrow coastal plains in the east and wider coastal plains in the west.

Climate

Temperate, with warm summers and severely cold winters; rivers freeze for 3–4 months, and ice blocks harbours; daily temperatures at Pyongyang in the west range from $-3°C$ to $-13°C$ in January, and from 20 to 29°C in July–August; average rainfall in Pyongyang ranges between a minimum of 11 mm in February and a maximum of 237 mm in July.

Economy

In a desperate condition after decades of under-investment, high foreign debt and shortages, especially of fuel; reliant on massive amounts of international food aid; main activities are heavy industry (steel, cement and machinery), mining (coal, minerals and metals), manufacturing (machine tools, military equipment and textiles), fishing; agriculture accounts for over 25% of economic activity but inefficiencies and natural disasters brought famine in the 1990s and malnutrition is still widespread.

Government

A totalitarian republic, nominally Communist (Korean Workers' Party) but with political control maintained through the personality cult created by the late Kim Il-sung (died 1994; declared 'Eternal President' in 1998) and continued by his son, Kim Jong-il, the Chairman of the the National Defence Committee (de facto head of state); there is a Premier and Cabinet, and a unicameral Supreme People's Assembly.

History

The peninsula was united in the 7th century by the Silla Dynasty, which was succeeded by the Koryo Dynasty in 935 and then by the Yi Dynasty, which ruled (1392–1910) as a vassal of China. In 1910 it was formally annexed by Japan; after Japan's defeat in World War II it was partitioned along the 38th parallel (latitude 38°N), the north being occupied by Soviet troops and the south by US troops. The Korean War (1950–3) was fought between these communist and non-communist forces. Reunification talks have taken place intermittently since 1980. Power in North Korea lies in the hands of the Korean Workers' (Communist) Party, whose leader was the president. Kim Il Sung was president from 1972 until his death in 1994, and in 1998 was declared 'Eternal President'; since 1998, as the Chairman of the National Defence Committee, his son Kim Jong Il has held power.A combination of natural disasters and economic mismanagement led to acute food shortages in the 1990s and the country is still dependent on international food and fuel aid. International concerns in the 1990s over North Korea's attempts to develop a nuclear capacity were heightened by its decision to reactivate its nuclear programme in 2002 and its withdrawal from the Nuclear Non-Proliferation Treaty in 2003. Diplomatic efforts to resolve the nuclear issue began in 2003, and in 2005 North Korea agreed to give up its weapons for aid and security guarantees. However, in 2006 it claimed to have tested a nuclear weapon.

KOREA, SOUTH

Official name	Republic of Korea (ROK)
Local name	Han'guk; Dae-han-min-guk
Area	98 913 sq km (38 180 sq mi)
Capital	Seoul; Sŏul
Chief towns	Inchon, Pusan, Taegu
Population	48 847 000 (2006e)
Nationality	South Korean
Language	Korean
Ethnic group	Korean 100%
Religions	Christianity 29% (Prot 18%, RC 11%), Buddhism 23%, unaffiliated 47%, others 1%
Time zone	GMT +9
Currency	1 Won (W) = 100 jeon
Telephone	+82
Internet	.kr
Country code	KOR

Location

A republic in eastern Asia occupying the southern half of the Korean Peninsula and comprising about 3000 islands off its west and south coasts; bounded to the west by the Yellow Sea; to the east by the Sea of Japan; to the south by the Korean Strait; and to the north by North Korea, from which it is separated by a demilitarized zone.

Physical description

The Taebaek Sanmaek Range runs north to south along the east coast, reaching heights of more than 900 m (2953 ft); it descends through a series of ridges to broad, undulating coastal lowlands; c.3000 islands off the west and south coasts, the largest of which is Cheju-do, on which is situated the highest peak, Halla-san (1950 m/6398 ft).

Climate

Extreme continental climate, with cold winters and hot summers; typhoons possible in the wettest months (June–September); average daily temperatures at Seoul range from −9 to 0°C in January and 22 to 31°C in August.

Economy

Transformed since 1960s from a largely agrarian into a highly industrialized economy; initially based on heavy industry (steel, motor vehicles, shipbuilding and petrochemicals) and electrical goods but widened from the 1980s to include electronics, telecommunications equipment, computers, textiles, clothing, leather goods and chemicals; tourism is growing.

Government

Governed by a President, a Prime Minister and State Council, and a unicameral National Assembly.

History

The peninsula was united in the 7th century by the Silla Dynasty, which was succeeded by the Koryo Dynasty in 935 and then by the Yi Dynasty, which ruled (1392–1910) as a vassal of China. In 1910 it was formally annexed by Japan; after Japan's defeat in World War II it was partitioned along the 38th parallel (latitude 38°N), the north being occupied by Soviet troops and the south by US troops. In a bid to unite the country, North Korean forces invaded in 1950, sparking off the Korean War (1950–3) between communist and non-communist forces. After 1948, the country experienced mostly authoritarian, often military, rule. There was a military coup in 1961, led by Park Chung-hee, whose repressive regime introduced military law in 1972; he was assassinated in 1979. Pro-democracy agitation led to the first multiparty elections in 1988 but politics continued to be dogged by allegations of corruption and electoral fraud and by military influence. Reunification talks with North Korea have taken place intermittently since 1980, but tensions remain because of the North's nuclear programme and concern over its weak economy, as well as the prospect of US troop withdrawals from the demilitarized zone.

KUWAIT

Official name	State of Kuwait
Local name	Dawlat al-Kuwayt
Area	17818 sq km (6878 sq mi)
Capital	Kuwait City; Al Kuwayt
Chief towns	Shuwaikh, Mina al Ahmadi
Population	2418000 (2006e)
Nationality	Kuwaiti
Languages	Arabic; English is also widely spoken
Ethnic groups	Kuwaiti 45%, other Arab 35%, South Asian 9%, Iranian 4%, others 7%
Religions	Islam 85% (Sunni 60%, Shia 25%), others 15%
Time zone	GMT +3
Currency	1 Kuwaiti Dinar (KD) = 1000 fils
Telephone	+965
Internet	.kw
Country code	KWT

Location

An independent state at the head of the Arabian Gulf, bounded to the north and west by Iraq; to the south by Saudi Arabia; and to the east by the Arabian Gulf.

Physical description

Consists of the mainland and nine islands; the terrain is flat or gently undulating, rising in the south-west to 271 m (889 ft); the Wadi al Batin runs along the western border with Iraq; the terrain is generally stony with sparse vegetation.

Climate

Hot, dry climate, with an average annual rainfall of 111 mm; summer temperatures are very high, often above 45°C (July–August); winter daytime temperatures often exceed 20°C; humidity is generally high; sandstorms are common throughout the year.

Economy

The economy prospered after the oil industry was developed in the 1940s; now recovered from the ravages of the 1991 Gulf War; main products are oil (95% of export earnings), petrochemicals, processed food, textiles, furniture, fertilizers, construction materials; other revenue from foreign reserves and investments, shipbuilding and repair.

Government

A hereditary constitutional monarchy; governed by the Amir, a Prime Minister and Council of Minister, and a unicameral National Assembly.

History

The port was founded in the 18th century, and the state has been ruled since 1756 by the Sabah family. Britain became responsible for Kuwait's foreign affairs in 1899. It became a British protectorate in 1914, and independent in 1961. The invasion and annexation of Kuwait by Iraq in August 1990 led to the Gulf War in January–February 1991, with severe damage to Kuwait City and the infrastructure of the country. Major post-war problems included large-scale refugee emigration, the burning of oil wells by Iraq (all capped by November 1991) and the pollution of Gulf waters by oil. In 1992 the port of Umm Quasr and part of an oilfield were passed to Kuwait when the boundary between Iraq and Kuwait was moved by 600 m (1970 ft). In 2003 Kuwait was a base for the build-up of forces for the Iraq War and it remains an important transit route for military and civilian traffic into and out of Iraq.

Kuwaiti Hospitality

An ancient tradition of Kuwaiti hospitality is the *diwanyiah*, a reception at which a man entertains his male acquaintances. The original meaning of the term was the section of a Bedouin tent in which the men would entertain visitors away from the rest of the family. Today, however, the word refers to the gathering itself as well as to the meeting place, which is usually a room set apart from the rest of the house. Gatherings are held in the evening; guests can come and go, and are served tea, coffee and snacks by the host as they sit on cushions and chat. Most *diwaniyahs* are relaxed affairs but are nonetheless imporant occasions for networking. More formal *diwaniyahs* are also held on topics such as politics or science, and are an important part of Kuwait's political system.

KYRGYZSTAN

Official name	Kyrgyz Republic
Local name	Kyrgyz Respublikasy
Former name	Kyrgyz Soviet Socialist Republic (until 1990), within the Union of Soviet Socialist Republics (USSR; 1922–91)
Area	198 500 sq km (76 621 sq mi)
Capital	Bishkek; Biškek
Chief towns	Osh, Przhevalsk, Kyzyl-Kiya
Population	5 214 000 (2006e)
Nationality	Kyrgyz or Kirghiz
Languages	Kyrgyz, Russian
Ethnic groups	Kyrgyz 67%, Uzbek 14%, Russian 11%, Ukrainian 1%, others 7%
Religions	Islam 75%, Christianity 20% (Orthodox), others 5%
Time zone	GMT +6
Currency	1 Som (Kgs) = 100 tyiyn
Telephone	+996
Internet	.kg
Country code	KGZ

Location

A landlocked mountainous republic in north-east Central Asia, bounded to the north by Kazakhstan; to the west by Uzbekistan; to the south and south-west by Tajikistan; and to the south-east and east by China.

Physical description

Lies in the Tien Shan Mountains with the Pamirs to the south; c.75% of land is mountainous; the highest point is at Pik Pobedy (7439 m/24 406 ft); the chief river is the Naryn and Lake Issyk-Kul is the largest lake.

Climate

Varies according to location; subtropical in the south-west, dry in the north and west, continental to polar in the mountainous east.

Economy

Transformed into market economy since 1991 but struggling; main activities are agriculture (55% of employment and 35% of GDP; cash crops are cotton, wool, meat and tobacco), mining (coal, gold, mercury, tin and uranium), hydroelectric power generation and light manufacturing (machinery and footwear).

Government

Governed by a President, a Prime Minister and Cabinet, and a unicameral Supreme Council.

History

Russian forces conquered the area in the late 19th century and it was incorporated into the Russian Empire. The Russian Revolution in 1917 led to a short civil war but the area became part of the Union of Soviet Socialist Republics (USSR) in 1921. In 1991 it gained its independence and became a member of the Commonwealth of Independent States (CIS). The first multiparty elections were held in 1995. The country has implemented economic reforms but with some difficulties, including inflation of over 700 per cent in 1993, high levels of unemployment and widespread malnutrition. President Askar Akayev, first elected in 1990, was deposed in 2005 in a popular uprising in protest at alleged government interference in the 2005 election. Kurmanbek Bakiyev became acting president and was subsequently elected to the post. His government's failure to address corruption or the rising level of political violence led to its resignation in December 2006 and the calling of early elections.

LAOS

Official name	Lao People's Democratic Republic
Local name	Lao; Sathalanalat Paxathipatai Paxaxôn Lao
Former name	Kingdom of Laos (1945–75)
Area	236800 sq km (91405 sq mi)
Capital	Vientiane
Chief towns	Luang Prabang, Pakse, Savannakhét
Population	6368000 (2006e)
Nationality	Lao or Laotian
Language	Lao
Ethnic groups	Lao 52%, Khmu 11%, Phuthai 10%, Hmong 7%, ethnic Vietnamese/Chinese 1%, others 19%
Religions	Buddhism 60%, traditional beliefs and other faiths 40%
Time zone	GMT +7
Currency	1 Kip (Kp) = 100 at
Telephone	+856
Internet	.la
Country code	LAO

Location

A landlocked republic in south-east Asia, bounded to the east by Vietnam; to the south by Cambodia; to the west by Thailand and Myanmar (Burma); and to the north by China.

Physical description

The land rises from the fertile valley of the Mekong River, which follows much of the border with Thailand in the west, to rugged hills and mountains covered with dense jungle in the east; the highest point is Phn Bia (2820m/9252ft).

Climate

Monsoonal with heavy rain in May–September; hot and dry February–April; average annual temperatures in Vientiane are 14–34°C, but it is cooler in the mountains.

Economy

Very poor, and dependent on international aid; agriculture, mostly at subsistence level, employs more than 75% of the workforce; the main cash crop is coffee; other activities include infrastructure construction projects, food processing, garment manufacture, low-tech assembly, forestry, mining (tin, copper and gypsum) and hydroelectric power.

Government

Governed by a President, a Prime Minister and Council of Ministers, and a unicameral National Assembly; the Lao People's Revolutionary Party is the only legal political party.

History

Small principalities were united in the 14th century into the kingdom of Lan Xang, which dominated until 1713. It then split into three kingdoms that became tributaries of Siam (Thailand) in the late 18th century and then a French protectorate in 1893. Occupied by the Japanese in World War II, it gained independence from France as a constitutional monarchy in 1954; however, much of the next 20 years was spent in civil war between the pro-Western and royalist parties and the communist-supported Pathet Lao (now the Lao People's Revolutionary Party, LPRP). The country was partitioned between the two sides in 1973 but in 1975 the Pathet Lao seized power and established a communist republic. Although still officially a communist state, Laos initiated economic liberalization in 1986 and joined the Association of South East Asian Nations (ASEAN) in 1997. Civil disturbances, including bombings and armed attacks on buses, in 2000 and 2003 were attributed to insurgents from the Hmong people or anti-government groups.

Lao Mouth Organs

The most distinctive Lao musical instrument is the *khaen*, a type of bamboo mouth organ. It has two rows of bamboo pipes, reminiscent of those in Pan-pipes, each of which contains a small metal reed traditionally made by hammering a small coin on an elephant's thigh bone. The pipes are bound together with thick grass; they are held in a carved wooden windchest using *kissoot*, black wax obtained from insects. The *khaen* is played by blowing through the windchest; fingerholes in the pipes allow control of which notes are sounded.

LATVIA

Official name	Republic of Latvia
Local name	Latvija; Latvijas Republika
Former name	Latvian Soviet Socialist Republic (1940–90), within the Union of Soviet Socialist Republics (USSR; 1940–91)
Area	64 100 sq km (24 749 sq mi)
Capital	Riga; Rīga
Chief towns	Daugavpils, Liepaja
Population	2 290 000 (2005e)
Nationality	Latvian
Languages	Latvian; Russian is also spoken
Ethnic groups	Latvian 57%, Russian 30%, Belarusian 4%, Ukrainian 3%, others 6%
Religions	Christianity 58% (Prot 36% (Lutheran), RC 22%), other, unaffiliated and none 42%
Time zone	GMT +2
Currency	1 Lat (Ls) = 100 santims
Telephone	+371
Internet	.lv
Country code	LVA

Location

A republic in north-eastern Europe, bounded to the west by the Baltic Sea; to the north-west by the Gulf of Riga; to the north by Estonia; to the east by Russia; to the south-east by Belarus; and to the south by Lithuania.

Physical description

Flat and low-lying; more than 40% of the land is forested; the north-west coast is indented by the Gulf of Riga; the chief river is the Daugava; the highest point is Gaizinkalns (312 m/1024 ft).

Climate

Moderate winters; cool, rainy summers.

Economy

Transformed into a market economy since 1991, although some enterprises are still state-owned; services (transit and banking) are now the largest sector; other activities include forestry and manufacturing (vehicles, textiles, machinery, fertilizers, domestic appliances, electronics, pharmaceuticals and food processing).

Government

Governed by a President, a Prime Minister and Cabinet of Ministers, and a unicameral legislature (*Saeima*).

History

Incorporated into Russia in 1721, it became an independent state in 1918 but was annexed by the Soviet Union in 1940. It was occupied by Germany during World War II and re-annexed by the Union of Soviet Socialist Republics (USSR) on liberation. Nationalism grew in the 1980s, and in 1990 independence talks began with the USSR. Independence was declared in 1991 and the last Russian troops left Latvia in 1994, but tensions remain between the Russian and Latvian communities. Since the restoration of democracy in 1993, Latvia has had a succession of centre-right coalition governments. It joined NATO and the European Union in 2004.

LEBANON

Official name	Lebanese Republic
Local name	Al-Lubnān; Al-Jumhūriyya al-Lubnaniyya (Arabic), Liban; République Libanaise (French)
Area	10452 sq km (4034 sq mi)
Capital	Beirut; Bayrūt
Chief towns	Tripoli, Saida, Zahle
Population	3874000 (2006e)
Nationality	Lebanese
Languages	Arabic; French, English and Armenian are also spoken
Ethnic groups	Arab 95%, Armenian 4%, others 1%
Religions	Islam 60%, Christianity 39%, others 1%
Time zone	GMT +2
Currency	1 Lebanese Pound (LL, L£) = 100 piastres
Telephone	+961
Internet	.lb
Country code	LBN

Location

A republic on the eastern coast of the Mediterranean Sea, south-west Asia, bounded to the north and east by Syria, and to the south by Israel.

Physical description

The narrow Mediterranean coastal plain rises gradually east to the Lebanon Mountains, which extend along most of the country; peaks include the Qornet es-Sauda (3087m/10137ft); the arid eastern slopes fall abruptly to the fertile El Beqaa plateau (c.1000m/3280ft); the Anti-Lebanon range lies in the east; the River Litani flows south between the ranges.

Climate

Mediterranean, varying with altitude, with hot, dry summers and warm, moist winters, except in the mountains, where heavy snow is usual; average rainfall at Beirut is 920mm and average temperatures are 13–27°C. It is much cooler and drier in the Beqaa Valley and irrigation is essential.

Economy

successfully reconstructed after the civil war, restoring position as regional entrepôt and financial service centre; recovery devastated by Israeli attacks on Hezbollah summer 2006; services (banking and tourism) form the largest sector; main industries are food processing, jewellery, cement, textiles, mineral and chemical products, timber, furniture, oil refining, metals; agriculture produces fruit, vegetables, tobacco and livestock.

Government

Governed by a President (who must be a Maronite Christian), a Prime Minister (who must be a Sunni Muslim) and Cabinet, and a unicameral National Assembly (divided equally between Christians and Muslims).

History

The area was part of the Phoenician Empire from the 5th century bc until the 1st century ad, when it came under Roman rule. It was contested between Christians and Muslims during the Crusades before becoming part of the Ottoman Empire from the 16th century until the empire's collapse after World War I. In 1920 the state of Greater Lebanon was created, based upon the autonomous Maronite Christian area around Jabal Lubnan and incorporating the Muslim coastal regions to the north and south and the Beqaa valley. This was administered by France under a League of Nations mandate until 1941, when it declared its independence. The 1943 constitution enshrined power-sharing by all the country's religions but tensions between Christians and Muslims erupted in 1975 into a civil war between a coalition of Christian groups and Druze and Muslim militias. Conflict continued for 15 years, drawing in the Palestinian Liberation Organization (based in Beirut until forced to withdraw from Lebanon by Israel in 1982), Syrian troops (in support of Muslim factions), and Israeli forces, which invaded in 1978 and 1982 in reprisal for Palestinian guerrilla raids on Israel. A ceasefire sponsored by the Arab League came into effect in 1989, and a peace plan – the Ta'if Accord – proposed constitution changes that would reduce the domination of Maronite Christians in government. Resistance to this by a few factions was crushed by Syria and a fragile peace was achieved in 1991. Government elections took place in 1992, though they were boycotted by many Maronite Christian parties. Syria exerted a strong influence on Lebanese politics after the civil war, with pro-Syrian governments in office and Syrian troops remaining in the country. However, popular opposition to Syria was inflamed by the assassination of a leading politician in 2005; huge rallies brought down the pro-Syrian government and obliged Syria to withdraw its remaining troops and intelligence agents. Despite the withdrawal of Syria, the government's control of the country remained weak. Clashes in southern Lebanon between Israeli troops (or the Israel-backed South Lebanon Army between 1985 and 2000) and Hizbullah guerrillas had continued since the end of the civil war, and in summer 2006 Hizbullah activities provoked massive Israeli air, sea and land strikes that left over 1000 Lebanese civilians dead and devastated the country's infrastructure.

LESOTHO

Official name	Kingdom of Lesotho
Local name	Lesotho; Mmuso wa Lesotho
Former name	Basutoland (until 1966)
Area	30 460 sq km (11 758 sq mi)
Capital	Maseru
Chief towns	Mafeteng, Quthing
Population	2 022 000 (2006e)
Nationality	Mosotho (singular), Basotho (plural)
Languages	Sesotho and English; Zulu and Xhosa are also spoken
Ethnic groups	Sotho 99%, others 1%
Religions	Christianity 90% (RC 45%, Prot 45%), others 10%
Time zone	GMT +2
Currency	1 Loti (plural Maloti) (M, LSM) = 100 lisente
Telephone	+266
Internet	.ls
Country code	LSO

Location
An African kingdom completely surrounded by South Africa.

Physical description
A small country, 230 km (140 mi) east to west and 200 km (120 mi) north to south; the Drakensberg Mountains lie in the north-east and east and include Lesotho's highest peak, Thabana-Ntlenyana (3482 m/11 424 ft); the Mulati Mountains run south to west from the north-east border forming a steep escarpment; only 13% of the land, most in the west, is cultivable; the population mainly lives west of the highlands at an altitude of 1500–1800 m (4920–5900 ft); there is serious soil erosion, especially in the west; the main rivers are the Orange and the Caledon.

Climate
Mild, dry winters at lower altitudes but snow is frequent in the mountains; the warm summer season runs October–April; the lowland summer maximum temperature is 32°C, the winter minimum is 7°C; average annual rainfall is 725mm.

Economy
Very poor; revenues derive from customs dues, expatriates' remittances and exporting water and hydroelectric power to South Africa; the small manufacturing base (processing agricultural products) and tourism are developing; agriculture, mostly at subsistence level, employs 86% of the workforce, but productivity is declining owing to drought, soil erosion and loss of labour force to HIV/AIDS; recent slump in garment manufacturing.

Government

A hereditary constitutional monarchy with a King as head of state; governed by a Prime Minister and Cabinet, and a bicameral Parliament consisting of a National Assembly and a Senate.

History

Lesotho was originally inhabited by hunting and gathering San (Bushmen). Bantu peoples arrived in the 16th century, and the nation of the Basotho was organized in 1824 by Moshoeshoe I. After fighting both the Afrikaners and the British, Moshoeshoe put his country under British protection as Basutoland in 1868, and it was administered until 1880 from the Cape Colony. In 1884 it came under direct control of the British government as a British High Commission Territory. The Kingdom gained independence as a hereditary monarchy in 1966. Chief Jonathan, prime minister since 1966 and effectively a dictator since 1970, was overthrown in a military coup in 1986. Military rule ended after another coup in 1991 led to the restoration of democracy in 1993. Protests after the 1998 election led to the revision of the constitution before the 2002 election. Lesotho faces serious problems owing to the high level of HIV/AIDS infection (among the highest in the world) and food shortages caused by successive years of drought.

LIBERIA

Official name	Republic of Liberia
Local name	Liberia
Area	111 370 sq km (42 999 sq mi)
Capital	Monrovia
Chief towns	Harper, Greenville, Buchanan, Robertsport
Population	3 042 000 (2006e)
Nationality	Liberian
Languages	English; many local languages are also spoken
Ethnic groups	African 95% (includes Kpelle, Bassa, Grebo, Gio, Kru, Mano), Americo-Liberian 2.5%, Congo People 2.5%
Religions	Christianity 40%, traditional beliefs 40%, Islam 20%
Time zone	GMT
Currency	1 Liberian Dollar (L$) = 100 cents
Telephone	+231
Internet	.lr
Country code	LBR

Location

A tropical republic in west Africa, bounded to the north-west by Sierra Leone; to the north by Guinea; to the east by the Côte d'Ivoire; and to the south by the Atlantic Ocean.

Physical description

Low coastal belt with lagoons, beaches and mangrove marshes; a rolling plateau

(500–800 m/1640–2624 ft) with grasslands and rainforest; land rises inland to mountains; the highest point is Mount Wateve (1380 m/4528 ft); rivers cut south-west through the plateau.

Climate

Equatorial climate, with high temperatures and abundant rainfall; rainfall declines from south to north; high humidity during the rainy season (April–September), especially on the coast; the average annual rainfall at Monrovia is 4150 mm.

Economy

Devastated by civil war; rich in natural resources; main activities are agriculture (cocoa, coffee and palm oil), forestry (timber and rubber), mining (iron, diamonds and gold), processing rubber and palm oil; the largest merchant fleet in the world, including the registration of many foreign ships.

Government

Governed by an executive President, a Cabinet, and a bicameral National Assembly consisting of a House of Representatives and a Senate.

History

Mapped by the Portuguese in the 15th century, it originated as a result of the activities of the philanthropic American Colonization Society wishing to establish a homeland for former slaves. The country was first settled in 1822, and constituted as the Free and Independent Republic of Liberia in 1847. A military coup in 1980 established a military government called a People's Redemption Council, with a chairman (Samuel Doe) and a cabinet. Doe's National Democratic Party of Liberia formed the government in the mid-1980s under a new constitution, and Doe became president in 1986. Dissatisfaction with Doe's autocratic and corrupt rule resulted in civil war in 1990. Despite the intervention of an Economic Community of west African States (ECOWAS) peacekeeping force, and numerous ceasefires and peace agreements, fighting continued until 2003 when all factions signed the Comprehensive Peace Agreement and the UN Mission in Liberia (UNMIL) was established to supervise the peace process. Disarming of militia was completed in 2004, and a new president and legislature were elected in 2005. In 2006 a commission was set up to investigate human rights abuses between 1979 and 2003.

> ### Love of Liberty
> The name 'Liberia' means 'Land of the Free', and was chosen because the country was established for freed slaves. The importance of freedom is also reflected in the national motto: 'The love of liberty brought us here'.

BYA

fficial name	Great Socialist People's Libyan Arab Jamahiriya
ocal name	Lībyā; Al-Jamāhīriyya Al-'Arabiyya Al-Lībiyya Ash-Sha'biyya Al-Ishtirākiyya
ormer name	United Libyan Kingdom (1951–63), Libyan Kingdom (1963–9), Libyan Arab Republic (1969–77)
rea	1758610 sq km (678823 sq mi)
apital	Tripoli; Tarābulus
hief towns	Misratah, Benghazi, Tobruk
opulation	5901000 (2006e)
ationality	Libyan
anguage	Arabic
thnic groups	Arab and Berber 97%, others 3%
eligions	Islam 97% (Sunni), others 3%
ime zone	GMT +2
urrency	1 Libyan Dinar (LD) = 1000 dirhams
elephone	+218
iternet	.ly
ountry code	LBY

cation

north African state, bounded to the north-west by Tunisia; to the west by Algeria; the south-west by Niger; to the south by Chad; to the south-east by Sudan; to the st by Egypt; and to the north by the Mediterranean Sea.

ysical description

ainly low-lying Saharan desert or semi-desert; the land rises in the south to ore than 2000 m (6561 ft) in the Tibesti Massif; the highest point, Pic Bette 286 m/7500 ft), lies on the Chad frontier; surface water is limited to infrequent ses.

imate

editerranean climate on the coast; the coastal city of Tripoli has an average annual nfall of 385 mm with average maximum daily temperatures of 16–30°C; average nual rainfall in the desert seldom exceeds 100 mm; temperatures in the south are ore than 40° for three months of the year.

onomy

rgely state-controlled economy, dominated by oil (95% of total exports) and natural s; diversifying into production of petrochemicals, iron, steel and aluminium as well processing agricultural products; agricultural sector is small and 75% of food is ported.

Government

In principle, the state is governed by the masses, through the appointed, unicameral General People's Congress, which appoints the General People's Committee; in practice, power rests in the hands of the 'Leader of the Revolution', Colonel Gaddafi.

History

Controlled at various times by Phoenicians, Carthaginians, Greeks, Vandals and Byzantines, Libya came under Arab domination during the 7th century. It was under Turkish rule from the 16th century until the Italians gained control in 1911, and was named Libya by them in 1934. It suffered heavy fighting during World War II, then came under British and French control. It became the independent Kingdom of Libya in 1951. A military coup established a republic under Muammar Gaddafi in 1969, and it was governed by a Revolutionary Command Council. Government policy since the revolution has been based on the promotion of Arab unity and the furtherance of Islam. Relations with other countries were strained from the 1970s until 2003 by controversial activities, including the alleged organization of international terrorism: diplomatic relations were severed by the UK after the murder of a policewoman in London in 1984; Tripoli and Benghazi were bombed by the US Air Force in response to alleged terrorist activity in 1986; two Libyan fighter planes were shot down by aircraft operating with the US Navy off the north African coast in 1989; and sanctions were imposed by the UN Security Council against Libya in 1992 following its refusal to extradite for trial two men suspected of organizing the bombing of a PanAm aircraft over Lockerbie in 1988. Sanctions were suspended in 1999 after the suspects were handed over for trial under Scottish law in the Netherlands, and lifted in 2003 after Libya admitted responsibility for the bombing and paid compensation. Since 2003, Gaddafi has sought to end Libya's international isolation, abandoning its programmes for developing weapons of mass destruction and promising in 2004 to allow UN nuclear weapons inspections.

> **Well, Well ...**
>
> There are no permanent natural rivers in Libya, only wadis that fill during flash floods and quickly dry out again, and the occasional oasis. Fresh water is instead mainly obtained from a large aquifer underneath the country, which is accessed via artesian wells.

LIECHTENSTEIN

Official name	Principality of Liechtenstein
Local name	Liechtenstein; Fürstentum Liechtenstein
Area	160 sq km (62 sq mi)
Capital	Vaduz
Chief towns	Schaan, Triesen, Balzers
Population	34 000 (2006e)
Nationality	Liechtensteiner
Language	German, spoken in the form of an Alemannic dialect
Ethnic groups	Liechtensteiner 86%, Italian, Turkish and others 14%
Religions	Christianity 83% (RC 76%, Prot 7%), others 6%, unknown 11%
Time zone	GMT +1
Currency	1 Swiss Franc (SFr, SwF) = 100 centimes = 100 rappen
Telephone	+423
Internet	.li
Country code	LIE

Location

A small landlocked independent principality in central Europe, lying between the Austrian state of Voralberg to the east and the Swiss cantons of St Gallen and Graubünden to the west.

Physical description

Situated in the Alps, bounded to the west by the River Rhine, its valley occupying 40% of the country; much of the rest consists of forested mountains, rising to 2599 m/8527 ft in the Grauspitz.

Climate

Alpine, moderated by a warm south wind (the *Föhn*); average high temperature of 20–28°C in summer; average annual rainfall is 1050–1200 mm.

Economy

Highly industrialized and diversified economy; largest sectors are services (banking, financial services, tourism and postage stamps) and specialized and high-technology industries such as dental products, electronics, metal manufacturing, textiles, ceramics, pharmaceuticals, food products, precision and optical instruments.

Government

A hereditary constitutional monarchy; governed by the Prince, a Cabinet and a unicameral legislature (*Landtag*).

History

Originally the medieval counties of Vaduz and Schellenberg, this small territory came into the hands of the princes of Liechtenstein between 1699 and 1712. A principality of the Holy Roman Empire from 1719, Liechtenstein became a member of the Confederation of the Rhine in 1806 and of the German Confederation from 1815 until 1866, when it became fully independent. Its neutrality, declared in 1868, was respected in both world wars. Close economic and political ties have existed at different times with Austria and Switzerland.

LITHUANIA

Official name	Republic of Lithuania
Local name	Lietuva; Lietuvos Respublika
Former name	Lithuanian Soviet Socialist Republic (1940–90), within the Union of Soviet Socialist Republics (USSR; 1940–91)
Area	65 200 sq km (25 167) sq mi
Capital	Vilnius
Chief towns	Kaunas, Klaipėda, Šiauliai
Population	3 586 000 (2006e)
Nationality	Lithuanian
Languages	Lithuanian; Russian and Polish are also spoken
Ethnic groups	Lithuanian 83%, Polish 7%, Russian 6%, others 4%
Religions	Christianity 85% (RC 79%, Russian Orthodox 4%, Prot 2%), others and unspecified 5%, none 10%
Time zone	GMT +2
Currency	1 Litas (Lt) = 100 centas
Telephone	+370
Internet	.lt
Country code	LTU

Location

A republic in north-eastern Europe, bounded to the north by Latvia; to the east and south by Belarus; to the south-west by Poland and the Kaliningrad region of Russia; and to the west by the Baltic Sea

Physical description

Rolling plains with low hills in the west and south-east and more than 2800 lakes; the highest point is Juozapine Hill (294 m/965 ft); the chief river is the Neman.

Climate

Varies between maritime and continental; wet, with moderate winters and summers.

Economy

Transformed since 1991 into a diverse, largely private-sector market economy; main industries are textiles and clothing, oil processing, forestry, food processing, manufacturing (machinery, machine tools, electric and electronic equipment and components, chemicals and furniture), shipbuilding, amber extraction and jewellery-making.

Government

Governed by a President, a Prime Minister and Cabinet, and a unicameral legislature (*Seimas*).

History

The last part of Europe to become fully Christian (15th century), by the 14th century Lithuania formed a large grand duchy in central and eastern Europe. It was confederated with Poland from the 16th century until 1795, when it came under imperial Russian control following the partition of Poland. Intensive Russification led to revolts in the 19th and early 20th centuries. Occupied by Germany in World War I, it became an independent republic in 1918 but was annexed by the Union of Soviet Socialist Republics (USSR) in 1940 before a second German occupation in 1941. Soviet control was re-established in 1944. Nationalism in the 1980s led to a unilateral declaration of independence in 1990; independence was recognized internationally in 1991 and the last Russian troops left the country in 1993. Since independence there has been a succession of short-lived governments, mostly centre-right coalitions. Lithuania joined NATO and the European Union in 2004.

LUXEMBOURG

Official name	Grand Duchy of Luxembourg
Local name	Luxembourg; Grand-Duché de Luxembourg (French), Luxemburg; Grossherzogtum Luxemburg (German), Lëtzebuerg; Groussherzogtom Lëtzebuerg (Luxembourgish)
Area	2586 sq km (998 sq mi)
Capital	Luxembourg
Chief towns	Esch-sur-Alzette, Dudelange, Differdange
Population	459 000 (2006e)
Nationality	Luxembourger, Luxembourg
Languages	French, German, Luxembourgish
Ethnic groups	Luxembourger 60%, Portuguese 15%, French 5%, Italian 4%, Belgian 4%, German 2%, others 10%
Religions	Christianity 90% (RC), Islam 2%, others and none 8%
Time zone	GMT +1
Currency	1 Euro (€) = 100 cents
Telephone	+352
Internet	.lu
Country code	LUX

Location

An independent constitutional monarchy in north-western Europe, bounded to the east by Germany; to the west by Belgium; and to the south by France.

Physical description

Divides into the wooded hilly region of Ösling in the north and the flatter, more fertile Gutland; the highest point is Buurgplaatz (559 m/1833 ft); water resources have been developed by canalization of the River Mosel, by hydroelectric dams on the River Our and by reservoirs on the River Süre.

Climate

It is drier and sunnier in the south, but winters can be severe; in the sheltered Mosel Valley, summers and autumns are warm enough for cultivation of vines.

Economy

Very prosperous economy based on service sector (banking, financial services and tourism); industry still dominated by iron and steel (25% of export earnings) but diversifying into information technology, telecommunications, freight transport, food processing, chemicals, metal products, engineering, rubber and glass.

Government

A hereditary constitutional monarchy with a Grand Duke as head of state; governed by a Prime Minister and Council of Ministers, and a unicameral Chamber of Deputies; a State Council has an advisory role.

History

After being occupied by the Romans and then the Franks (in the 5th century), Luxembourg came under the control of the House of Luxembourg in the 11th century. The first Count of Luxembourg was created in 1060; the family, which owned lands in the area between the Maas and the Mosel from the 13th century, took its name from the Castle of Lützelburg, and came to prominence when Henry VII was elected to the throne in 1308. Although the family lost the throne after Henry's death, Henry's son John gained control of Bohemia and the Luxemburgers' power grew comparable with that of the Habsburgs. Their most important representative was Emperor Charles IV, who elevated Luxembourg to a duchy in 1354. From 1346 until 1437 (when the dynasty died out in the male line with the death of Sigismund), all but one of the German kings came from the House of Luxembourg. The country of Luxembourg was controlled by various European powers (Burgundy 1443–77, Habsburgs 1477–1555, Spain 1555–1684, France 1684–97) before returning to Habsburg control after the War of the Spanish Succession. It was made a Grand Duchy and passed to the Netherlands following the Congress of Vienna in 1815. In 1830 much of Luxembourg joined the Belgians in the revolt against William I; this resulted in the division of the country, with the western, French-speaking region joining Belgium. The remaining Grand Duchy was granted political autonomy in 1838, and recognized as a neutral independent state in 1867. Occupied by Germany in both world wars, it entered into economic union with Belgium in 1921, joined the Benelux economic union in 1948, and abandoned neutrality on joining NATO in 1949. Luxembourg was a founding member of the European Economic Community in 1958, and the Luxembourg franc was replaced by the euro in 2002.

MACAO ▸CHINA

MACEDONIA

Official name	Former Yugoslav Republic of Macedonia (FYROM or FYR Macedonia)
Local name	Makedonija; Republika Makedonija, Poranesna Jugoslovenska Republika Makedonija
Former name	Formerly part of Kingdom of Serbs, Croats and Slovenes (until 1929), Kingdom of Yugoslavia (1929–41), Federal People's Republic of Yugoslavia (1945–63), Socialist Federal People's Republic of Yugoslavia (1963–91)
Area	25 713 sq km (9925 sq mi)
Capital	Skopje
Chief towns	Bitola, Gostivar, Tetovo, Kumanovo
Population	2 050 000 (2006e)
Nationality	Macedonian
Languages	Macedonian, Albanian
Ethnic groups	Macedonian 64%, Albanian 25%, Turkish 4%, others 7%
Religions	Christianity 65% (Orthodox), Islam 33%, others 2%
Time zone	GMT +1
Currency	1 Denar (D, den) = 100 deni
Telephone	+389
Internet	.mk
Country code	MKD

Location

A landlocked republic in the Balkan Peninsula in southern Europe; bounded to the west by Albania; to the south by Greece; to the east by Bulgaria; and to the north by Serbia.

Physical description

Mountainous, with deep basins and valleys and two large lakes, Ohrid and Prespa, on the south-west border with Albania; bisected by the River Vardar; the highest point is Golem Korab (Maja e Korabit at 2753 m/9032 ft).

Climate

Mediterranean, with cold winters and warm summers.

Economy

Made a slow transition to a market economy after 1991 and remains poor; main activities are agriculture (tobacco, vegetables and dairy products), wine-making, food processing, textiles, chemicals, mining (iron), steel-making, cement and pharmaceuticals.

Government

Governed by a President, a Prime Minister and government ministers (who are elected by, but not members of, the legislature), and a unicameral Assembly (*Sobranje*). Ethnic Albanians have considerable local autonomy in areas where they predominate.

History

The area of ancient Macedonia (consisting of the present region of Macedonia in northern Greece and the Former Yugoslav Republic of Macedonia) was inhabited by Macedonians who spoke a Slav language closer to Bulgarian than Serbo-Croat. Through the centuries, many tribes and nations settled in Macedonia and its ethnic composition is accordingly complex; the French *macédoine* is a synonym for 'medley' or 'mixture'. Slav tribes arrived in the 7th century and mixed with the Greek and romanized Illyrians and Thracians, while the Byzantine rulers established settlements of Scythians and christianized Turks. In the 9th century the Bulgars conquered Macedonia but the region returned to Byzantine rule until the Ottoman conquest (1355). Under the Turks, Sasi, Tartars, Cerkezi, Gypsies and Jews all settled and mixed with the local population. A nationalist movement emerged at the end of the 19th century, its members insisting that the Macedonians were neither Bulgars nor Serbs but a distinct Slav nation with its own language; this was a claim that the neighbouring Serbs, Bulgars and Greeks, nations all bent on territorial expansion, were determined to discount. After the Balkan Wars in 1913, Macedonia was divided between Greece and Serbia. It is the Serbian part that was given to Yugoslavia by the Treaty of Neuilly in 1919, an act confirmed by the treaties signed at the Paris Peace Conference in 1947 when the region was named the Republic of Macedonia within the Federal Republic of Yugoslavia. Despite claims to parts of it by Albania and Bulgaria, and deteriorating relations with Greece (which claims that its region called Macedonia is the only one entitled to the name), Macedonia formally seceded from Yugoslavia in 1991 and was admitted to the UN in 1993 as the Former Yugoslav Republic of Macedonia. UN and US peacekeeping forces arrived in 1992 and 1993 to maintain borders and prevent the conflict in Bosnia and Herzegovina spreading to Macedonia; the UN force was withdrawn in 1998. There was ongoing tension and sporadic violence between ethnic Albanians and Macedonians throughout the 1990s. Violence intensified in 2001, with a short-lived uprising by ethnic Albanian rebel groups demanding more rights. A peace deal in August led to constitutional changes that improved the status and rights of ethnic Albanians; ethnic Albanian areas were given greater autonomy in 2004. NATO forces oversaw disarmament of the rebels in 2001; it handed over peacekeeping duties to the European Union in 2003. Branko Crvenkovski was elected president in 2004 after President Trajkovski was killed in an air crash. Macedonia is formally a candidate for membership of NATO and the European Union.

MADAGASCAR

Official name	Republic of Madagascar
Local name	Madagasikara; Repoblikan'I Madagasikara (Malagasy), Madagascar; République du Madagascar (French)
Former name	Malagasy Republic (1958–75), Democratic Republic of Madagascar (until 1992)
Area	587 040 sq km (226 656 sq mi)
Capital	Antananarivo
Chief towns	Toamasina, Mahajanga, Fianarantsoa, Antsiranana, Toliara
Population	18 595 000 (2006e)
Nationality	Malagasy
Languages	Malagasy, French
Ethnic groups	Merina 26%, Betsimisaraka 16%, Betsileo 12%, Tsimihety 7%, Sakalava 7%, others 32%
Religions	Christianity 50%, traditional beliefs 40%, Islam 10%
Time zone	GMT +3
Currency	1 Ariary (A) = 5 iraimbilanja
Telephone	+261
Internet	.mg
Country code	MDG

Location

An island republic in the Indian Ocean, separated from east Africa by the Mozambique Channel.

Physical description

Bisected north to south by a ridge of mountains rising to 2876 m (9436 ft) at Maromokotra; cliffs to the east drop down to a coastal plain through tropical forest; a terraced descent to the west through savanna to the coast, which is heavily indented in the north; great biodiversity, with high proportion of species unique to the island.

Climate

Temperate climate in the highlands; the average annual rainfall is 1000–1500 mm; tropical coastal region with an annual rainfall at Toamasina in the east of 3500 mm; cyclones occur regularly.

Economy

Poor country, dependent on agriculture and fishing; chief cash crops are coffee, vanilla, fish, sugar, cloves, pepper, cotton, prawns; other activities are mining (chromite, graphite and sapphires), manufacturing (garments, soap, beverages and glassware), food processing, chemicals, oil refining, cement, metalworking and car assembly.

Government

Governed by a President, a Prime Minister and Council of Ministers, and a bicameral Parliament comprising a National Assembly and a Senate.

History

Madagascar was settled by Indonesians in the 1st century ad and by African traders in the 8th century. The French established trading posts in the late 18th century and claimed the island as a protectorate in 1885. After becoming an autonomous overseas French territory (the Malagasy Republic) in 1958, it gained independence in 1960 and was named Madagascar again in 1975. Following anti-government riots, in 1992 a new constitution was approved. This reduced the powers of the president, Didier Ratsiraka, who had held office since 1975. He was defeated in 1993 but returned to office in 1997 after winning the 1996 elections. Disputed elections in 2001 led to several months of political confusion and unrest that brought the country close to civil war; Marc Ravalomanana emerged as the winner, and Ratsiraka then fled into exile. Ravalomanana was re-elected in the 2006 presidential election.

MADEIRA ▶PORTUGAL

MALAWI

Official name	Republic of Malawi
Local name	Dziko la Malaŵi
Former name	Nyasaland (until 1964), part of the Federation of Rhodesia and Nyasaland (1953–63)
Area	118 484 sq km (45 735 sq mi)
Capital	Lilongwe
Chief towns	Blantyre, Zomba, Limbe, Salima
Population	13 014 000 (2006e)
Nationality	Malawian
Languages	English, Chichewa
Ethnic groups	Maravi 59%, Lomwe 20%, Yao 13%, Ngoni 6%, others 2%
Religions	Christianity 70%, Islam 20% (Sunni), others 10%
Time zone	GMT +2
Currency	1 Kwacha (MK) = 100 tambala
Telephone	+265
Internet	.mw
Country code	MWI

Location

A landlocked republic in south-eastern Africa, bounded to the south-west and south-east by Mozambique; to the east by Lake Nyasa (Lake Malawi); to the north by Tanzania; and to the west by Zambia.

Physical description

Crossed north to south by the Great Rift Valley in which lies Africa's third-largest lake, Lake Nyasa (Lake Malawi); high plateaux on either side; Shire highlands in the south rise to nearly 3000 m (9840 ft) at Sapitwa Peak on Mount Mulanje.

Climate

Tropical climate in the south, with high year-round temperatures (28–37°C); average annual rainfall is 740 mm; more moderate temperatures in centre; higher rainfall in the mountains overlooking Lake Nyasa (1500–2000 mm).

Economy

Very poor country, dependent on international aid; agriculture, mostly at subsistence level, employs 85% of the workforce but is susceptible to drought, flooding and soil degradation; chief cash crops are tobacco (60% of export earnings), tea, sugar, coffee, cotton and groundnuts; manufacturing (agricultural processing, textiles, garments, consumer products), forestry and sawmill products.

Government

Governed by an executive President, a Cabinet and a unicameral National Assembly.

History

The area was explored by the Portuguese in the 17th century, and European contact was established by David Livingstone in 1859. Scottish church missions were established in the area; it was claimed as the British Nyasaland Districts Protectorate in 1891, and then called the British Central Africa Protectorate in 1893. It was established as the British colony of Nyasaland in 1907, and in the 1950s it joined with Northern and Southern Rhodesia (now Zambia and Zimbabwe) to form the Federation of Rhodesia and Nyasaland. After gaining independence in 1964 with Hastings Banda as prime minister, it became a republic in 1966 and a one-party state with Banda as president. As a result of international pressure and growing unrest within the country, a referendum was held in 1993 in which the population voted for a multiparty system. Bakili Muluzi was elected president in 1994 and served until 2004, when Bingu wa Mutharika took office and launched an anti-corruption campaign. Malawi faces serious problems because of the high level of HIV/AIDS infection among the population and recent crop failures owing to drought.

Lake of Stars

Lake Nyasa, or Lake Malawi as it is also called, was referred to by the explorer David Livingstone as the 'Lake of Stars' because of its glittering surface.

MALAYSIA

Official name	Federation of Malaysia
Local name	Malaysia
Area	329 749 sq km (127 283 sq mi)
Capital	Kuala Lumpur; Putrajayais the administrative centre
Chief towns	George Town, Ipoh, Malacca, Johor Baharu, Kuching, Kota Kinabalu
Population	24 386 000 (2006e)
Nationality	Malaysian
Languages	Bahasa Malaysia (Malay); Chinese, English, Tamil and local languages are also spoken
Ethnic groups	Malay and indigenous 50%, Chinese 24%, indigenous people 11%, Indian 7%, others 8%
Religions	Islam 60%, Buddhism 19%, Christianity 9%, Hinduism 6%, traditional Chinese religions 3%, others 3%
Time zone	GMT +8
Currency	1 Malaysian Dollar/Ringgit (M$) = 100 cents
Telephone	+60
Internet	.my
Country code	MYS

Location

An independent federation of states in South-East Asia, comprising most of the lower part of the Malay Peninsula (bounded by Thailand to the north and linked by a causeway to Singapore in the south) and part of the island of Borneo (bounded by Indonesia to the south and Brunei in the north).

Physical description

Peninsular Malaysia consists of a mountain chain running north to south, rising to Mount Tahan (2189 m/7182 ft); there are narrow eastern and broader western coastal plains; mostly tropical rainforest and mangrove swamp; a coastline of long, narrow beaches; the chief river is the Pahang (456 km/283 mi long); Sarawak, on the north-western coast of Borneo, has a narrow, swampy coastal belt backed by foothills rising sharply towards mountain ranges on the Indonesian frontier; Sabah, in the north-eastern corner of Borneo, has a deeply indented coastline and a narrow western coastal plain, rising sharply into the Crocker Range, reaching 4094 m (13 432 ft) at Mount Kinabalu, Malaysia's highest peak.

Climate

Tropical, with little variation in temperature and high humidity; the climate is strongly influenced by the monsoon winds (April–September and November–February); the wet seasons are March–May and September–November; it is cooler and wetter in the mountains.

Economy

Diversified emerging economy driven by exports; agriculture, forestry and mining produce raw materials (rubber, palm oil, metals and timber) for processing and manufacturing industries; electronic equipment, textiles and chemicals are also produced; oil and natural gas production and processing, especially in Sarawak and Sabah; tourism is a major industry.

Government

Governed by a supreme head of state, a Prime Minister and Cabinet, and a bicameral Parliament, consisting of a Senate and a House of Representatives; the supreme head of state is elected by the rulers of the nine states of peninsular Malaysia from among their number. Each of the eleven states is a hereditary constitutional monarchy governed by its sultan or raja, an executive council and a legislative assembly.

History

Malaysia formed part of the Srivijaya Empire between the 9th and 14th centuries and experienced Hindu and Muslim influences in the 14th and 15th centuries. From the 16th century, Portugal, the Netherlands and Britain vied for control. Singapore, Malacca and Penang were formally incorporated into the British Colony of the Straits Settlements in 1826. British protection was extended over Perak, Selangor, Negeri Sembilan and Pahang, constituted into the Federated Malay States, in 1895, and protection treaties with several other states (Unfederated Malay States) were agreed in 1885–1930. The region was occupied by the Japanese in World War II, after which Sarawak became a British colony, Singapore became a separate colony, the colony of North Borneo was formed, and the Malay Union was established, uniting the Malay states and the Straits Settlements of Malacca and Penang. In 1948 the nine peninsular states were federated as the Federation of Malaya. Growing resentment by the Chinese-dominated Malayan Communist Party (MCP) of Malay dominance within the Federation led to an insurrection led by the MCP against British rule. The insurrection and the campaign to crush it, the Malayan Emergency, lasted from 1948 until 1960, although the insurrection was effectively broken by the mid-1950s. Malaya gained independence in 1957, and in 1963 it combined with Singapore, Sarawak and Sabah to form the Federation of Malaysia; Singapore withdrew from the Federation in 1965. Post-independence politics has been dominated by the United Malay National Organization, initially as the governing party and since 1971 as the dominant partner in coalition governments. Mahathir bin Muhammad served as prime minister for 22 years (1981–2003), a period which saw increasingly authoritarian rule and considerable tension between ethnic groups because of policies favouring Malays. Parts of the country were devastated by the 2004 Indian Ocean tsunami.

> 66
>
> *If you can't be famous, at least you can be notorious.*
>
> —Malaysian politician Mohamad Mahathir (b.1925), the country's longest serving Prime Minister (1981 to 2003), in 1990. (Quoted in the *Eastern Express*, 24 April 1995.)
>
> 99

MALDIVES

Official name	Republic of Maldives
Local name	Dhivehi Raajje
Former name	Maldive Islands
Area	300 sq km (120 sq mi)
Capital	Malé
Population	359 000 (2006e)
Nationality	Maldivian
Languages	Dhivehi; English is spoken widely
Ethnic groups	Maldivian (mixture of South Indian, Sinhalese and Arab) with African minorities
Religion	Islam 100% (Sunni)
Time zone	GMT +5
Currency	1 Rufiyaa (MRf, Rf) = 100 laarees
Telephone	+960
Internet	.mv
Country code	MDV

Location

A republic consisting of an island archipelago in the Indian Ocean. Fua Mulaku Island is the largest island, while Huvadhoo Atoll is the largest atoll.

Physical description

Small, low-lying islands, no more than 2.4 m (8 ft) above sea level, with sandy beaches fringed with coconut palms. Of the 1190 islands, spread over 26 coral atolls, fewer than 200 are inhabited.

Climate

Generally warm and humid; affected by south-west monsoons (April–October); the average annual rainfall is 2100 mm and the average daily temperature is 22°C.

Economy

Undeveloped, but experienced steady growth until devastated by the 2004 tsunami; main industry is tourism (33% of GDP); other activities are shipping, fishing, manufacturing (garments and accessories), boat-building, coconut processing and handicrafts; agriculture is constrained by lack of cultivable land, so most food is imported.

Government

Governed by an executive President, a Ministers' Cabinet and a unicameral People's Assembly.

History

A former dependency of Ceylon (now Sri Lanka), it was a British protectorate from 1887 until 1965, when it gained independence. Its sultanate was abolished in 1968 when it became a republic under President Ibrahim Masir. He was succeeded in 1978 by Maumoon Abdul Gayoom, who was re-elected for a sixth term in 2003. His tenure has allowed economic development, although his regime is accused of repression and human rights abuses. Pro-democracy demonstrations in 2003–4 led to the legalization of political parties in 2005. In recent years, the Maldivian authorities have expressed concern over the impact of global warming and rising sea levels, as 80 per cent of the land is one metre or less above sea level. Most of the islands were devastated by the Indian Ocean tsunami in 2004.

MALI

Official name	Republic of Mali
Local name	Mali; République du Mali
Former name	French Sudan (until 1959), Mali Federation (until 1960)
Area	1 240 192 sq km (478 714 sq mi)
Capital	Bamako
Chief towns	Ségou, Mopti, Sikasso, Kayes, Gao, Timbuktu
Population	13 717 000 (2006e)
Nationality	Malian
Languages	French; local languages are spoken widely
Ethnic groups	Mande 50% (includes Bambara, Malinke, Soninke), Peul 17%, Voltaic 12%, Songhai 6%, Tuareg and Moor 10%, others 5%
Religions	Islam 90% (mostly Sunni), traditional beliefs 9%, Christianity 1%
Time zone	GMT
Currency	1 CFA Franc (CFAFr) = 100 centimes
Telephone	+223
Internet	.ml
Country code	MLI

Location

A landlocked republic in west Africa, bounded to the north-east by Algeria; to the north-west by Mauritania; to the west by Senegal; to the south-west by Guinea; to the south by the Côte d'Ivoire; to the south-east by Burkina Faso; and to the east by Niger.

Physical description

On the fringe of the Sahara; the lower part of the Hoggar massif is located in the north; arid plains lie between 300 m (984 ft) and 500 m (1640 ft); there is arid desert in the north with sand dunes; largely savanna in the south; the main rivers are the Niger and Sénégal; the highest point is Hombori Tondo (1155 m/3789 ft).

Climate

Subtropical in south to arid in north; in the south the rainy season lasts for five months (June–October); the average annual rainfall is c.1000 mm in the south, decreasing to almost zero in the Saharan north.

Economy

Very poor; dependent on international aid and expatriates' remittances; agriculture and herding, mainly at subsistence level, employs 80 per cent of the workforce; usual self-sufficiency in food recently undermined by drought and locust attacks; cash crops are cotton (35% of export earnings) and livestock; other activities include mining (gold (50% of export earnings) and phosphates), food and cotton processing and construction.

Government

Governed by a President, a Prime Minister and Council of Ministers, and a unicameral National Assembly.

History

Between the 13th and 15th centuries the medieval Kingdom of Mali flourished in the Western Sudan, dominating the trade routes of the Sahara with North Africa. The kingdom reached its peak in the 14th century and declined in the 15th century. Although it had a quasi-Islamic ruling group, it was dominated by Muslim merchants, and it became an important factor in the Islamicization of west Africa. Mali was governed by France from 1881 to 1895 and was a territory of French Sudan (part of French west Africa) until 1959, when it entered a partnership with Senegal as the Federation of Mali. It achieved independence as a separate nation in 1960. Its first president, Modibo Keita, was overthrown in 1968 in a military coup led by Moussa Traoré, who held power until ousted by the military in 1991 following pro-democracy rioting. In 1992 a new multiparty constitution was introduced and the elections were won by the Alliance for Democracy in Mali Party and President Alpha Oumar Konaré. Konaré soon faced a rebellion by Tuareg tribesmen (the Tuareg Unified Movements and Fronts of Azawad) in the north of the country; a peace agreement was signed in 1994, and greater autonomy was granted in 2006. Konaré was replaced as president by Amadou Toumani Touré in 2002.

> "
>
> *Then I rais'd*
> *My voice and cried, 'Wide Afric, doth thy Sun*
> *Lighten, thy hills enfold a City as fair*
> *As those which starr'd the night o' the elder World?*
> *Or is the rumour of thy Timbuctoo*
> *A dream as frail as those of ancient Time?'*
>
> —English poet Alfred, Lord Tennyson (1809–92), from his blank-verse poem 'Timbuctoo' (1829). The poem was written during his time at the University of Cambridge, and led to his being awarded the Chancellor's medal for English verse.
>
> "

MALTA

Official name	Republic of Malta
Local name	Malta; Repubblika ta' Malta
Area	316 sq km (122 sq mi)
Capital	Valletta
Chief towns	Sliema, Birkirkara, Qormi, Rabat, Victoria
Population	400 200 (2006e)
Nationality	Maltese
Languages	English, Maltese; there are many Arabic words in the local vocabulary
Ethnic groups	Maltese 98%, British 2%
Religions	Christianity 98% (RC), others 1%, none/unaffiliated 1%
Time zone	GMT +1
Currency	1 Maltese Lira (LM) = 100 cents = 1000 mils
Telephone	+356
Internet	.mt
Country code	MLT

Location

An archipelago republic in the central Mediterranean Sea.

Physical description

The islands are generally low-lying, rising to 253 m (830 ft); there are no rivers or mountains; well-indented coastline.

Climate

Dry summers and mild winters; average annual rainfall is c.400 mm; average daily winter temperature is 13°C.

Economy

Market economy now dominated by service sector (tourism, financial services, freight transhipment and retailing); main industries are manufacturing (electronics, textiles and beverages), ship repair (the former naval dockyards having been converted to commercial use) and food processing; agricultural sector produces only 20% of food requirements.

Government

Governed by a President, a Prime Minister and Cabinet, and a unicameral House of Representatives.

History

Malta has at various times been controlled by Phoenicians, Greeks, Carthaginians and Romans. It was conquered by Arabs in the 9th century, and later by Spain. Under Emperor Charles V it was given to the Knights Hospitallers in 1530. Captured by the British during the Napoleonic Wars, and a Crown Colony from 1815, it was an important strategic base in both world wars. It was particularly important in World War II when it was blockaded and subject to aerial bombardment for five months; its resistance led to the people of Malta being awarded the George Cross in 1942. It achieved independence in 1964 and became a republic in 1974, developing links with communist and Arab countries from the early 1970s. It became more pro-European from the late 1980s, and joined the European Union in 2004.

MAN, ISLE OF ▸ UNITED KINGDOM

MARIANA ISLANDS, NORTH ▸ UNITED STATES OF AMERICA

MARSHALL ISLANDS

Official name	Republic of the Marshall Islands (RMI)
Local name	Majol (Marshallese), Marshall Islands (English)
Former name	Formerly part of the Trust Territory of the Pacific Islands (1947–79)
Area	c.180 sq km (70 sq mi)
Capital	Majuro
Population	66 600 (2006e)
Nationality	Marshallese
Languages	Marshallese, English
Ethnic groups	Micronesian 97%, others 3%
Religions	Christianity 93% (Prot 85%, RC 8%), Baha'i 1%, unaffiliated 2%, others 4%
Time zone	GMT +12
Currency	1 US Dollar ($, US$) = 100 cents
Telephone	+692
Internet	.mh
Country code	MHL

Location
An independent archipelago republic in the central Pacific Ocean.

Physical description
Low-lying coral, limestone and sand islands, atolls and reefs, with few natural resources.

Climate
Hot and humid; the wet season is from May to November; occasional typhoons.

Economy
Subsistence economy based on copra and other coconut products, and dependent on US aid; government is largest employer (64%); activities include farming, fishing, tourism, and services to US military bases.

Government
Governed by an executive President, a Cabinet and a unicameral Parliament. A Council of Chiefs has a consultative role on land and customs.

History

Originally settled by Micronesians, the islands were explored by the Spanish in 1529 and became a German protectorate in 1886. After World War I they came under Japanese control, and after World War II the group became a UN Trust Territory 1947–78), administered by the USA. US nuclear weapons tests were held on the Bikini and Enewetak atolls between 1946 and 1962. After the Marshall Islands became a self-governing republic in 1979, a compact of free association with the USA was signed in 1982. This came into force in 1986, giving the republic its independence; under this compact the USA retained control of external security and defence and gave financial help. The UN trusteeship ended in 1990. A renegotiated compact came into force in 2004.

MARTINIQUE ▶FRANCE

MAURITANIA

Official name	Islamic Republic of Mauritania
Local name	Mauritanie; République Islamique de Mauritanie (French), Mūrītāniyā; Al-Jumhūriyya al-Islāmiyya al-Mawrītāniyyā (Arabic)
Area	1 029 920 sq km (397 549 sq mi)
Capital	Nouakchott
Chief towns	Nouadhibou, Atar
Population	3 177 000 (2006e)
Nationality	Mauritanian
Languages	Arabic; French is also widely spoken
Ethnic groups	mixed Arab and black 40%, Arab 30%, black 30%
Religion	Islam 100%
Time zone	GMT
Currency	1 Ouguiya (U, UM) = 5 khoums
Telephone	+222
Internet	.mr
Country code	MRT

Location

A republic in north-west Africa, bounded to the south-west by Senegal; to the south and east by Mali; to the north-east by Algeria; to the north by Western Sahara; and to the west by the Atlantic Ocean.

Physical description

The Saharan zone in the north covers two-thirds of the country with sand dunes, mountainous plateaux and occasional oases; the coastal area has minimal rainfall and little vegetation; savanna grasslands lie in the Sahelian zone; the Sénégal River valley is the chief agricultural region; the highest point is Kediet Idjill (915 m/3002 ft) in the north-west.

Climate

Dry and tropical with sparse rainfall; temperatures can rise to more than 49°C in the Sahara.

Economy

Very poor country; agriculture and animal husbandry, mostly at subsistence level, employ 50% of the workforce; susceptible to drought and affected recently by locusts; main industries are mining (iron ore (40% of export earnings) and gold), fishing and fish processing; oil refining; offshore oil and gas to be exploited.

Government

Governed by an executive President, a Prime Minister and Council of Ministers, and a bicameral Parliament comprising a Senate and a National Assembly.

History

The coast was sighted by the Portuguese in the 15th century, and European trading settlements were established from the 16th century. In the mid-19th century, France gained control of the territory and it became a French protectorate within French west Africa in 1903 and a French colony in 1920. It gained independence in 1960. When the Spanish withdrew from Western Sahara in 1976, Mauritania and Morocco divided the territory between them. After conflict with the Polisario Front guerrillas, however, Mauritania renounced all rights to the region in 1979 and left Morocco to annex it. There were military coups in 1978 and 1984, the latter bringing to power Colonel Maaouya ould Sid Ahmed Taya. Civilian rule was restored with multiparty elections in 1992. During the 1990s there was ethnic tension between the Arab north and African south, and internal unrest by opposition groups, exacerbated by food shortages resulting from several years of drought and a locust infestation in 2004. There were civil disturbances and several attempted coups before President Taya was deposed in a military coup in 2005 led by Colonel Ely ould Mohamed Vall. A military council ruled until elections were held in 2006 and 2007.

Place of the Winds

Nouakchott, the capital of Mauritania, probably takes its name from a Berber phrase meaning 'Place of the Winds'. Being on the coast, it is affected by oceanic trade winds as well as by a hot, dry wind known as the harmattan.

MAURITIUS

Official name	Republic of Mauritius
Local name	Mauritius
Area	1865 sq km (720 sq mi)
Capital	Port Louis
Population	1 241 000 (2006e)
Nationality	Mauritian
Languages	English; French is also spoken
Ethnic groups	Indo-Mauritian 68%, Creole 27%, others 5%
Religions	Hinduism 48%, Christianity 32% (RC 24%), Islam 17%, others 3%
Time zone	GMT +4
Currency	1 Mauritian Rupee (MR, MauRe) = 100 cents
Telephone	+230
Internet	.mu
Country code	MUS

Location

A small island nation in the Indian Ocean.

Physical description

A volcanic island, with a central plateau; it falls steeply to narrow coastlands in the south and south-west; the highest peak is Piton de la Petite Rivière Noire (828 m/2717 ft); dry, lowland coast, with wooded savanna, mangrove swamp and bamboo in the east; surrounded by coral reefs enclosing lagoons and sandy beaches.

Climate

Tropical-maritime, with temperatures averaging between 22 and 26°C; there is a wide variation in rainfall, with most rain falling in the central plateau; the country lies in the cyclone belt (November–April).

Economy

Traditional industries of sugar (25% of export earnings) and textiles and garment manufacture are supplemented by tourism and other manufacturing (chemicals, metal products and transport equipment); diversifying into financial services, information technology and telecommunications as sugar and textile exports decline.

Government

Governed by a President, a Prime Minister and Council of Ministers, and a unicameral National Assembly.

History

The island was visited by Arabs in the 10th century and discovered by the Portuguese in the 16th century. The Dutch took possession in 1598–1710, followed by the French in 1710–1810 and the British in 1810. It was formally ceded to Britain by the Treaty of Paris in 1814, and governed jointly with the Seychelles as a single colony until 1903. It became an independent state in 1968 and a republic in 1992. The Mauritian Socialist Party held power from 1982 to 1995, returning to power in 2000 in coalition with the Mouvement Militant Mauricien. The coalition lost the 2005 election to the Socialist Alliance.

MAYOTTE ▸FRANCE

MEXICO

Official name	United Mexican States
Local name	México, Estados Unidos Méxicanos
Area	1 978 800 sq km (763 817 sq mi)
Capital	Mexico City
Chief towns	Guadalajara, Léon, Monterrey, Ciudad Juárez
Population	107 449 000 (2006e)
Nationality	Mexican
Languages	Spanish; Mayan and other indigenous languages are also spoken
Ethnic groups	Mestizo 60%, Amerindian 30%, white 9%, others 1%
Religions	Christianity 95% (RC 89%, Prot 6%), others 5%
Time zone	GMT −6/8
Currency	1 Mexican Peso (Mex$) = 100 centavos
Telephone	+52
Internet	.mx
Country code	MEX

Location
A federal republic in the south of North America, bounded to the north by the United States of America; to the west by the Gulf of California; to the west and south-west by the Pacific Ocean; to the south by Guatemala and Belize; and to the east by the Gulf of Mexico.

Physical description
Bisected by the tropic of Cancer; situated at the southern end of the North American Western Cordillera; narrow coastal plains border the Pacific Ocean and the Gulf of Mexico; land rises steeply to a central plateau, reaching a height of c.2400 m (7874 ft) around Mexico City; the plateau is bounded by the Sierra Madre Occidental in the west and Sierra Madre Oriental in the east; volcanic peaks lie to the south, notably Citlaltépetl (5699 m/18 697 ft); limestone lowlands of the Yucatán peninsula stretch into the Gulf of Mexico in the south-east; the country is subject to earthquakes.

Climate
Great climatic variation between the coastlands and mountains; desert or semi-desert conditions in the north-west; typically tropical climate on the east coast; generally

wetter on the south coast; extreme temperature variations in the north, very cold in winter, very warm in summer.

Economy

Diverse market economy closely linked to the United States of America; main activities are oil and natural gas extraction, petrochemicals, iron and steel production, manufacturing (food, beverages, textiles, garments, tobacco, chemicals, motor vehicles and consumer durables), offshore assembly for US market, mining (especially silver), tourism and financial services; agriculture produces maize, wheat, soya beans, rice, beans, cotton, coffee, fruit, tomatoes, beef, poultry and dairy products.

Government

Governed by an executive President, a Cabinet and a bicameral Congress of the Union comprising a Senate and a Chamber of Deputies. Each of the 31 states has its own constitution, a Governor and a Chamber of Deputies.

History

Mexico was at the centre of Mesoamerican civilizations for over 3000 years: the Gulf Coast Olmecs; the Zapotecs at Monte Albán near Oaxaca; the Mixtecs at Mitla; the Toltecs at Tula; the Mayas in the Yucatán; and the Aztecs at Tenochtitlán. These peoples were subjugated from the 14th century by the Aztecs, who were destroyed by the Spanish under Hernan Cortés in 1519–21. As the Viceroyalty of New Spain, Mexico came under Spanish rule until the 19th century. The struggle for independence began in 1810; this was finally achieved in 1821 and Mexico became a federal republic in 1824. It lost nearly a third of its territory in all to the USA in 1836 and after the Mexican War (1846–8). There was civil war in 1858–61, and another Mexican War in 1862–7 during which French forces occupied Mexico City in 1863, declaring Archduke Maximilian of Austria to be Emperor of Mexico. The French withdrew and Maximilian was executed in 1867. The presidency of Porfirio Díaz (1876–80, 1884–1911) saw material progress but his dictatorial regime provoked the Mexican Revolution, which began in 1910 and did not end until 1920 and the establishment of a constitutional republic. Lázaro Cárdenas, president from 1934 to 1940, nationalized foreign-owned oil and railway companies, and carried out massive land reforms. After his presidency, however, the radicalism of the Institutional Revolutionary Party (PRI), which came to dominate political life, increasingly became more rhetoric than reality. It formed a succession of authoritarian governments until it lost its parliamentary majority in 1997 (for the first time since 1929); National Action Party (PAN) candidates have won the presidential elections since 2000. The second half of the 20th century was rendered difficult due to economic problems, only partially relieved by mass emigration to the USA. Mexico became part of the North American Free Trade Agreement in 1994. Armed revolts by the Zapatista National Liberation Army (EZLN) in the southern state of Chiapas in 1994–5 caused a political crisis but talks were broken off in 1998. The Zapatistas' campaign resumed in 2001 with a march from Chiapas to Mexico City in support of a bill of indigenous rights, which was enacted in May 2001. However, the Zapatistas broke off negotiations with the government, claiming that the bill's provisions had been watered down.

ANCIENT MEXICAN CIVILIZATIONS

For over 3,000 years, Mexico and its surrounding area was home to several advanced civilizations, generally referred to as the Mesoamerican cultures.

The Olmec civilization

The earliest known civilization in the area, the Olmec, flourished between c.1500 and 300 BC and is considered the ancestor of subsequent Mesoamerican civilizations. The first great Olmec city was at San Lorenzo in modern-day Veracruz, which prospered between 1200 and 900 BC. Later, a second centre developed at La Venta in Tabasco (800 to 400 BC).

The Olmecs left evidence of a rudimentary writing system, the forerunner of Mayan hieroglyphics. They worshipped a number of deities: the 'were-jaguar', a half-man, half-jaguar beast; the feathered serpent; and gods of fire, sun and maize. The Olmecs are renowned for their artistic as well as their architectural acheivements, in particular their massive carved basalt heads, distinguished by rounded faces, flattened-nose features and close-fitting helmets.

The Teotihuacán and Zapotec civilizations

The decline of the Olmec civilization was matched by the rise of that of the city of Teotihuacán. The Teotihuacán city was around 40 km (25 mi) to the north-east of present-day Mexico City, and had grown into a major city by the second century AD. At its centre was the Pyramid of the Sun, a stone structure standing 61 m (200 ft) high with a long flight of steps leading to a temple at the summit. Also part of the complex is the Pyramid of the Moon, linked to the Pyramid of the Sun by the mile-long Avenue of the Dead.

Meanwhile in Oaxaca, to the south, the Zapotecs were flourishing. They were famous for their stone structures and for devising a bar-and-dot number system.

The Toltec and Aztec civilizations

The Toltecs established a military state at Tula in the 10th century AD. They built serpent columns, gigantic warrior statues known as the *Atlantes*, and the *tzompantli*, a wallrack on which they displayed the heads of their sacrificial victims. They were displaced by the Aztecs at the end of the 12th century.

The Aztecs dominated Mexico between the 14th and 16th centuries. Like the Toltecs, they were a military people and performed human and animal sacrifices. Their great legacy was their reclamation of land – shallow and swampy lakes in the central valley were transformed into islands for growing maize and vegetables. The Aztec capital, Tenochtitlán, was built there.

The downfall of the Aztecs began when their Emperor Montezuma naively welcomed the Spanish *conquistador* Hernán Cortés into his palace as a god, an act that would eventually lead to the Spanish conquest of Mexico.

The Maya

The Mayan civilization extended through southern Mexico and deep into Central America from c.250 AD. The Maya built temples and pyramids, carved inscriptions on *stelae* (stone pillars), and developed an advanced system of hieroglyphics and a solar calendar system. They worshipped nature gods: Chac (rain and thunder), Kinich Ahau (the Sun god), and Yumil Kaxob (maize) were important in agriculture. A supreme deity, Kukulcán, was related to the Aztec god Quetzalcoatl, 'the feathered snake'.

MICRONESIA, FEDERATED STATES OF

Official name	Federated States of Micronesia (FSM)
Local name	Micronesia
Former name	Formerly part of the Trust Territory of the Pacific Islands (1947–79)
Area	702 sq km (271 sq mi)
Capital	Palikir (on Pohnpei)
Chief towns	Kolonia (Colonia), Weno, Lelu
Population	108 000 (2006e)
Nationality	Micronesian; also Chuukese, Kosraen, Pohnpeian, Yapese
Languages	English; eight major indigenous languages are also spoken
Ethnic groups	Chuukese 42%, Pohnpeian 27%, others 31%
Religions	Christianity 97% (RC 50%, Prot 47%), others 3%
Time zone	GMT +10/11
Currency	1 US Dollar (US$) = 100 cents
Telephone	+691
Internet	.fm
Country code	FSM

Location

A federal republic consisting of a group of 607 islands divided into four states – Yap, Chuuk (formerly Truk), Pohnpei (formerly Ponape) and Kosrae (formerly Kosaie) – in the western Pacific Ocean.

Physical description

Islands vary geologically, from low, coral atolls to high mountainous islands; Pohnpei, Kosrae and Chuuk have volcanic outcroppings; highest point is Totolom (791 m/2595 ft).

Climate

Tropical; heavy rainfall all year round, especially in the eastern islands; subject to typhoons.

Economy

Subsistence economy based on farming and fishing; dependent on US aid; tourism is growing but constrained by remoteness; other activities are construction, fish processing, specialized aquaculture and handicrafts.

Government

Governed by an executive President, a Cabinet and a unicameral Congress. Each of the four states has its own government and traditional leadership council. There are no political parties.

History

The islands were probably first settled by eastern Melanesians in 1500 BC. The Spanish colonized them in the 17th century and sold them to Germany in 1898. Japan occupied the islands for the Allies in World War I and administered them as a mandated territory from 1920 until ousted in 1944 by US forces. In 1947 the islands became part of the UN Trust Territory of the Pacific Islands, administered by the USA. From 1965 there was a growing campaign for independence, and Micronesia became a self-governing federation in 1979. A compact of free association with the USA came into force in 1986, when Micronesia became independent, with the USA responsible for its security and defence. A renegotiated compact came into force in 2004. Micronesia was admitted to the UN in 1991.

MOLDOVA

Official name	Republic of Moldova
Local name	Moldova; Republica Moldova
Former name	Formerly part of Romania (1918–40), Moldavia or Moldavian Soviet Socialist Republic (until 1991), within the Union of Soviet Socialist Republics (USSR; 1922–91)
Area	33 843 sq km (13 066 sq mi)
Capital	Chisinau
Chief towns	Tiraspol, Bendery, Beltsy
Population	4 467 000 (2006e)
Nationality	Moldovan
Language	Moldovan
Ethnic groups	Moldovan/Romanian 78%, Ukrainian 8%, Russian 6%, Gagauzi 4%, Bulgarian 2%, others 2%
Religions	Christianity 98% (Orthodox), Judaism 2%
Time zone	GMT +2
Currency	1 Leu (Mld) = 100 bani
Telephone	+373
Internet	.md
Country code	MDA

Location

A landlocked republic in eastern Europe, bounded to the west by Romania, and to the north, east and south by the Ukraine.

Physical description

The terrain consists of a hilly plain, reaching a height of 429 m (1407 ft) at Mount Balanestiin; chief rivers are the Dniester and Prut.

Climate

Continental, with cold to moderate winters and warm summers.

Economy

Poorest country in Europe, dependent on remittances from expatriates working abroad (c.30% of workforce); most industry lies in breakaway Transdniestria region; agriculture contributes 23% of GDP, producing grains, tobacco, sugar beet, vegetables, fruit, beef and dairy products; other activities are wine-making and manufacturing (food processing, agricultural machinery, foundry equipment, domestic appliances, hosiery, footwear and garments).

Government

Governed by a President, a Prime Minister and Cabinet, and a unicameral Parliament.

History

Between the 15th century and 1812, the area known as Moldavia also included the region to the east called Bessarabia, the ownership of which was disputed between Russia and the Ottoman Turks. In 1812 Bessarabia, together with the eastern part of Moldavia, was ceded to Russia and thereafter came under Russian rule. Meanwhile, the Danubian Principalities joined together to form the Principality of Romania in 1862. Following a nationalist movement, Bessarabia declared its independence from Russia in 1918 and united with Romania, but in 1940 Romania was forced to cede Bessarabia to the Union of Soviet Socialist Republics (USSR) and it was incorporated with another small strip of land as the Moldavian Soviet Socialist Republic. Moldavia achieved independence from the USSR as the Republic of Moldova in 1991 and became a member of the Commonwealth of Independent States (CIS). The ineffectualness of the moderate reformist governments of the 1990s led to a resurgence of support for the Communist Party, which has won all the elections since 1998. Ethnic tensions led the Russian and Ukrainian ethnic minorities in the Dniestr region (east of the River Dniestr) and the Gagauz (Turkic-speaking) minority in the south-west to declare independence in 1990, although this was not recognized. There was fierce fighting in Dniestr in 1991–2, where Russian troops have been stationed since in order to maintain the 1992 ceasefire while talks continue. Both regions were granted special autonomy status in the 1994 constitution; however, this has not satisfied the Dniestr region, which has reasserted its demand for independence. The failure to achieve a settlement has left the region in a state of limbo, prey to corruption, organized crime and smuggling.

The Little Ewe

The *Miorița* ('Little Ewe') is a folk tale in the form of a ballad, which originates from the historic region of Moldavia and is still widely respected in modern Moldovan culture. It tells of three shepherds, from Moldavia, Transylvania and Vrancea (now a county in Romania), who meet while looking after their sheep. Miorița, a favourite ewe belonging to the Moldavian, warns him that the other shepherds are plotting to kill him and steal his possessions. However, the Moldavian does not try to evade his apparent fate. Instead, he tells the ewe to ask the killers to bury his body near his flock, and to tell his mother that he went away to marry a princess so that she will not be upset by his failure to return.

MONACO

Official name	Principality of Monaco
Local name	Monaco; Principauté de Monaco
Area	1.9 sq km (0.75 sq mi)
Capital	Monaco
Chief town	Monte Carlo
Population	32 500 (2006e)
Nationality	Monégasque or Monacan
Language	French
Ethnic groups	French 47%, Monégasque 16%, Italian 16%, others 21%
Religions	Christianity 95% (RC 90%, Prot 5%), others 5%
Time zone	GMT +1
Currency	1 Euro (€) = 100 cents
Telephone	+377
Internet	.mc
Country code	MCO

Location

A small principality on the Mediterranean Riviera, close to the Italian frontier with France.

Physical description

Hilly, rugged and rocky, rising to 63 m (206 ft); expanded into the sea by infilling; almost entirely urban.

Climate

Warm, dry summers and mild winters.

Economy

Prosperous economy based on services (tourism, gambling, financial services, real estate) and light industry manufacturing consumer products.

Government

A hereditary constitutional monarchy; governed by the Prince, a Council of Government and a unicameral National Council; close political ties with France.

History

In 1297 the Grimaldi family won Monaco from the Genoese, who had held it since 1191, but they did not secure full possession until 1419. Though the Grimaldis were allies of France (except when they were under Spanish protection in 1524–1641), Monaco was formally annexed by France in 1793 during the French Revolutionary regime. It has been under French protection ever since, apart from a period under Sardinia in 1815–61. In 2002 the French franc was replaced by the euro as the official currency.

MONGOLIA

Official name	State of Mongolia
Local name	Mongol Uls
Former name	Outer Mongolia (until 1924); People's Republic of Mongolia (1924–91)
Area	1 564 619 sq km (604 099 sq mi)
Capital	Ulan Bator; Ulaanbaatar
Chief towns	Darhan, Erdenet
Population	2 832 000 (2006e)
Nationality	Mongolian
Language	Khalkha Mongolian
Ethnic groups	Mongol 94%, Kazakh 5%, others, Chinese and Russian 1%
Religions	Buddhist Lamaism 50%, Shamanism and Christianity 6%, Islam 4%, none 40%
Time zone	GMT +7/8
Currency	1 Tugrug (Tug) = 100 möngö
Telephone	+976
Internet	.mn
Country code	MNG

Location

A landlocked republic in eastern central Asia, bounded to the north by Russia and on other sides by China.

Physical description

One of the highest countries in the world, with an average height of 1580 m (5184 ft); the highest point is Tavan Bogd at 4373 m (14 350 ft); terrain ranges from desert in the south (the Gobi Desert covers the southern third of the country) through grassy steppes to the Mongolian Altai and Hangai mountains in the west, and taiga; the largest lakes are found in the north-west; the major rivers flow north and north-east.

Climate

Climatic conditions are extreme, with long, severe winters and short, warm summers; the average temperature at Ulan Bator is −27° in January and 11–22°C in July; rainfall is generally low; arid desert conditions prevail in the south.

Economy

Difficult transition from planned to market economy; main activities are mining (copper, gold, tin, coal, uranium and tungsten), cashmere production, agriculture (livestock, wool and hides), processing animal products, manufacturing (construction materials, food, beverages and textiles) and construction.

Government

Governed by a President, a Prime Minister and Cabinet, and a unicameral legislature (State Great Hural).

History

Originally the homeland of nomadic tribes, which united under Genghis Khan in the 13th century to become part of the great Mongol Empire, Mongolia was assimilated into China and divided into Inner and Outer Mongolia. Inner Mongolia remains an autonomous region of China, but Outer Mongolia declared itself an independent monarchy in 1911 when China's imperial regime collapsed. Although Chinese rule was reasserted in 1915, Mongolian revolutionaries, with Soviet support, overthrew the Chinese in 1921 and formed a government. When the king died in 1924, the Mongolian People's Republic was formed and aligned itself with the Union of Soviet Socialist Republics (USSR), following similar policies. With Soviet support it resisted Japanese attacks in the late 1930s, but in a 1946 referendum it voted for independence from Soviet control. A pro-democracy campaign led to multiparty elections in 1990, and economic liberalization followed. The former communist party has continued to dominate politics since 1990, although it lost power to an alliance of nationalists and social democrats in 1996–2001.

MONTENEGRO

Official name	Republic of Montenegro
Local name	Crna Gora
Former names	Formerly part of Kingdom of Serbs, Croats and Slovenes (until 1929), Kingdom of Yugoslavia (1929–41), Federal Republic of Yugoslavia (1945–2003); Federal Republic of Serbia and Montenegro (2003–6)
Area	13812 sq km (5333 sq mi)
Capitals	Podgorica (administrative centre); Cetinje (historic and cultural capital)
Chief towns	Priština, Subotica
Population	640000 (2004)
Nationality	Montenegrin
Languages	Montenegrin (the Ijekavian dialect of Serbian), Serbian and Albanian
Ethnic groups	Montenegrin 43%, Serb 32%, Bosniak 8%, Albanian 5%, others 12%
Religions	Christianity 74% (Orthodox 70%, RC 4%), Islam 21%, others 5%
Time zone	GMT +1
Currency	1 Euro (€) = 100 cents
Telephone	+382
Internet	.me
Country code	MNE

┌───┐
Black Mountain
The names 'Crna Gora' and 'Montenegro' both mean
'black mountain', referring to the dark forests on the
slopes of Montenegro's mountains.
└───┘

Location

A republic in the Balkan Peninsula, bounded to the north-west by Bosnia and
Herzegovina; to the north-east by Serbia; to the east by the Serbian province of
Kosovo; to the south by Albania; to the south-west by Croatia; and to the west by
the Adriatic Sea.

Physical description

Densely forested mountains in the interior are cut by river valleys and canyons; the
highest point is Bobotov Kuk (2522 m/8274 ft); fertile lowlands lie alongside lakes and
in river valleys; the low-lying, 293 km-long Adriatic coastline is highly indented; the
main river is the Tara.

Climate

Mediterranean, with hot dry summers and autumns; there is a colder upland climate
inland, with heavy winter snow.

Economy

Economic and fiscal autonomy since 1990s; reform has stimulated some recovery
from effects on former federal economy of wars with Croatia and Bosnia and
Herzegovina; main activities are tourism, aluminium production, steel-making,
processing agricultural products and manufacturing (consumer goods); agriculture
produces cereals, tobacco, potatoes, fruit, livestock products; wine-making.

Government

Governed by a President, a Prime Minister and Cabinet, and the unicameral Assembly
of Montenegro.

History

The area was part of the Roman province of Illyria, settled by Slavs in the 7th century
and established as the independent province of Zeta. In the late 12th century it was
incorporated into the Serbian empire. Montenegrin independence was recognized
at the Congress of Berlin in 1878; it retained its independent monarchy until 1918,
when King Nicholas was deposed and Montenegro was absorbed into Serbia. With
Serbia and territories of the former Austro-Hungarian empire, it formed the Kingdom
of Serbs, Croats and Slovenes (renamed Yugoslavia in 1929), which was united
under the Serbian monarch, Peter I. Yugoslavia was occupied by Axis forces in 1941
and re-established in 1945 as the communist Federal People's Republic (comprising
Croatia, Slovenia, Bosnia and Herzegovina, Macedonia, Montenegro and Serbia)
under President Josip Tito. After Tito's death in 1980, nationalisms resurfaced; the
federation eventually disintegrated when Croatia and Slovenia seceded in 1991 and
Bosnia and Herzegovina and Macedonia followed in 1992. Serbia and Montenegro
remained as the Federal Republic of Yugoslavia, which was declared on 27 April
1992. Montenegrin desire for independence led to a restructuring in 2003 into a

looser federation of the two republics, called Serbia and Montenegro. Following a referendum in May, Montenegro declared its independence in June 2006.

MOROCCO

Official name	Kingdom of Morocco
Local name	Al Maghrib; Al Mamlaka Al-Maghribiyya
Area	446 550 sq km (172 412 sq mi)
Capital	Rabat; Ar Ribāt, Er Ribât
Chief towns	Casablanca, Fez, Marrakesh, Tangier, Meknès, Kenitra, Tétouan, Oujda, Agadir
Population	33 241 000 (2006e)
Nationality	Moroccan
Languages	Arabic; Berber and French are also spoken
Ethnic groups	Arab and Berber 99%, others 1%
Religions	Islam 99% (mostly Sunni), Christianity 1%
Time zone	GMT
Currency	1 Dirham (DH) = 100 centimes
Telephone	+212
Internet	.ma
Country code	MAR

The Western Kingdom

The local name for Morocco, Al Mamlaka Al-Maghribiyya, means 'The Western Kingdom'. The short form, Al Maghrib, simply means 'The West'.

Location
A kingdom in north Africa, bounded to the south-west by Western Sahara, over which Morocco claims sovereignty; to the south-east and east by Algeria; to the north-east by the Mediterranean Sea; and to the west by the Atlantic Ocean.

Physical description
Dominated by a series of mountain ranges, rising in the High Atlas in the south to 4165 m (13 665 ft) at Mount Toubkal; the Atlas Mountains descend south-east to the north-west edge of the Sahara Desert; the broad coastal plain is bounded to the west by the Atlantic Ocean.

Climate
Mediterranean climate on the north coast; it is settled and hot in May–September; the average annual rainfall is 400–800 mm, decreasing towards the Sahara, which is virtually rainless; Rabat, on the Atlantic coast, has average maximum daily temperatures of 17–28°C; heavy winter snowfall in the High Atlas; the desert region experiences extreme heat in summer, with chilly winter nights.

Economy

Poor country; many dependent on remittances from expatriate workers; large public sector; main sector is agriculture, which employs 40% of the workforce and produces cereals, citrus fruits, vegetables, wine, olives, livestock; other activities are mining (especially phosphate) and mineral processing, food processing, fishing, manufacturing (leather goods, garments, transistors and telecommunications equipment), oil refining, chemicals, construction and tourism.

Government

A hereditary constitutional monarchy; governed by the King, a Prime Minister and a Cabinet, and a bicameral Parliament consisting of a House of Representatives and a House of Councillors.

History

From the 12th century bc the northern coast was occupied by Phoenicians, Carthaginians and Romans. Arabs invaded in the 7th century ad, and Europeans began to establish an interest in the region in the 19th century. The Treaty of Fez in 1912 established Spanish Morocco (capital, Tétouan) and French Morocco (capital, Rabat), and the international zone of Tangier was created in 1923. The protectorates gained independence in 1956 as a monarchy under the Alawite Dynasty, still the ruling house, although the coastal towns of Ceuta and Melilla remain Spanish. Since the accession of Muhammad VI in 1999, Morocco has started to move away from absolute monarchy. In 1975 the former Spanish Sahara (Western Sahara) was annexed and partitioned by Morocco and Mauritania; Mauritania withdrew in 1979 in the face of conflict with the Polisario Front independence movement and Morocco annexed the rest of the territory. Fighting continued until 1991, when a ceasefire came into effect, but an impasse over a proposed referendum on the territory's future status has prevented progress towards a resolution.

Non-self-governing territory

Western Sahara

Location	A disputed territory in north-west Africa, which is administered by Morocco but claims independence. It is bounded by Morocco in the north; Algeria in the north-east; to the east and south by Mauritania; and to the west by the Atlantic Ocean.		
Area	252 126 sq km (97 321 sq mi)	**Nationality**	Sahrawi, Sahraoui; Sahrawian, Sahraouian
Capital	El Aaiún; Laâyoune, La 'Youn	**Internet**	.eh
Population	261 794 (2003e)	**Country code**	ESH

MOROCCAN CUISINE

The north African country of Morocco faces both the Mediterranean Sea and the inner continent of Africa. Its culture and cuisine have been influenced by the indigenous Berbers, and by waves of invaders and traders including Romans, Arabs, and European powers such as the Portuguese, Spanish and French.

Ingredients

Moroccan cooking is typically highly spiced and flavoured, and is infused with ingredients such as garlic, chillis, cinnamon, saffron, lemons (especially preserved lemons), coriander, olives, dates, almonds, cumin, turmeric, ginger, cayenne, sesame, paprika, anise, mint and sugar. Fittingly for a coastal nation, Moroccan cuisine uses fish, generally simply prepared but marinated beforehand with *charmoula* – a mix of garlic, pepper, paprika, cumin, coriander, lemon juice and olive oil. Islam prohibits the eating of pork, so the most popular meats are chicken, lamb, mutton and goat. The Moroccan staple is couscous, a semolina dish of Berber origin that is served with meats and fish. A 'couscous of seven vegetables' is common in Fez and may comprise onions, pumpkin, courgettes, turnips, chilli peppers, carrots and tomatoes.

Starters and soups

A typical Moroccan meal might start with hummus, a chickpea pâté; *falafel,* fried patties of ground, spiced chickpeas; or *tabbouleh,* a salad of cracked wheat flavoured with mint, parsley and cucumber. *Harira,* a national dish traditionally served to end the fast of Ramadan, is a soup made from tomatoes, beef or mutton and chickpeas or lentils and is hearty enough to be a meal in itself. Another popular soup is *chorba fassia,* a meat and vegetable soup from Fez.

Meat dishes

Mechoui is a Berber dish of roast lamb, generally prepared on special occasions when an entire animal is cooked on a spit. The crispy skin is flavoured with salt, garlic and cumin. A dish familiar to many who are not otherwise well versed in Moroccan cuisine is the tagine, a thick meat stew that uses a range of ingredients but is often flavoured with almonds. Tagine is the name given to both the dish and the conical earthenware pot in which it is cooked. The dish is served with flat bread called *khubz*. Also familiar are the kebab, and the *kefta,* a spiced lamb or beef sausage that is grilled on a skewer.

A touch of sugar

A distinctive Moroccan tradition is that of marrying sweet and savoury flavours. *Bisteeya,* also known variously as *bsteeya, bastilla, bstilla* or *pastille,* is a creative pastry construction built in three layers: spicy chicken or pigeon covered with eggs in a lemony onion sauce topped with sweetened almonds. The pie is wrapped in a thin filo pastry called *warka* and finished with cinnamon and sugar. Another sweet/savoury cross is *briouates* (or *brioats*), triangular pasties of mutton or goat spiced with cinnamon and sugar and fried in hot oil.

Dessert is not ubiquitous in Moroccan cuisine. However, a meal may be rounded off with *Kaab el ghazal* ('gazelles' horns'), crescent-shaped sweet almond pastries with fluted edges, or with *m'hanncha,* a Moroccan 'serpent cake' of coiled sweet pastry. Another typical dish is *rozz bel hleeb*, a traditional rice pudding. Such desserts are likely to be washed down with an even sweeter confection – mint tea, a green syrupy drink laced with sugar.

MOZAMBIQUE

Official name	Republic of Mozambique
Local name	Moçambique; República de Moçambique
Former name	People's Republic of Mozambique (1975–90)
Area	799 390 sq km (306 644 sq mi)
Capital	Maputo
Chief towns	Nampula, Beira, Pemba
Population	19 889 000 (2006e)
Nationality	Mozambican
Languages	Portuguese; more than 30 local languages are also spoken
Ethnic groups	Makua 47%, Tsonga 23%, Malawi 12%, Shona 11%, Yao 4%, others 3%
Religions	Christianity 41% (RC 24%, others 17%), Islam 18%, others 18%, none 23%; some aspects of traditional beliefs are widespread
Time zone	GMT +2
Currency	1 Metical (Mt, MZM) = 100 centavos
Telephone	+258
Internet	.mz
Country code	MOZ

Location

A republic in south-eastern Africa, bounded to the south by Swaziland; to the south and south-west by South Africa; to the west by Zimbabwe; to the north-west by Zambia and Malawi; to the north by Tanzania; and to the east by the Mozambique Channel and the Indian Ocean.

Physical description

The main rivers are the Zambezi and Limpopo, providing irrigation and hydroelectricity; south of the Zambezi, the coast is low-lying, with sandy beaches and mangroves; low hills of volcanic origin are found inland; the Zimbabwe Plateau lies further north; the coast north of the Zambezi is more rugged and is backed by a narrower coastal plain, with a savanna plateau inland; the highest peak, Mount Binga, is 2436 m (7992 ft).

Climate

Tropical, with relatively low rainfall in the coastal lowlands; average annual rainfall at Beira, in the central coast zone, is 1520 mm, with maximum daily temperatures of 25–32°C; in the drier areas of the interior lowlands, rainfall decreases to 500–750 mm; Mozambique has one rainy season in December–March.

Economy

Very poor, and dependent on international aid; recovery from civil war (1977–92) hindered by natural disasters (2000–3) and high rates of HIV/AIDS infection; main sector is agriculture and fishing, which employ 83% of the workforce; chief cash crops are prawns, fish, cotton, cashew nuts, sugar, citrus fruits; growing industrial base, especially minerals (aluminium processing), natural gas, hydroelectric power, forestry, garment manufacturing and food processing.

Government

Governed by an executive President, a Prime Minister and Council of Ministers, and a unicameral Assembly of the Republic.

History

The country was originally inhabited by Bantu peoples from the north between the 1st and 4th centuries. By the late 15th century the coast had been settled by Arab traders and discovered by Portuguese explorers. Administered as part of Portuguese India from 1751, Mozambique acquired separate colonial status as Portuguese East Africa in the late 19th century and became an overseas province of Portugal in 1951. An independence movement, the Frente de Libertação de Moçambique (Frelimo), formed in 1962 and began a guerrilla war against the Portuguese in 1964. Independence was gained in 1975 and Mozambique became a socialist one-party state. A brutal civil war erupted between the ruling party Frelimo and the opposition group Renamo until in 1992 a peace agreement was signed and Renamo became a political party. A new constitution under a multiparty system was implemented in 1990, and in 1994 the first multiparty elections were won by Frelimo. Reconstruction was slowed by natural catastrophes in 2000–3; the legacy of landmines and resulting amputees, and a high level of HIV/AIDS infection, are also serious problems.

MYANMAR (BURMA)

Official name	Union of Myanmar; still often referred to internationally as Burma
Local name	Myanmar; Pyidaungsu Myanmar Naingngandaw
Former name	Union of Burma (1948–73), Socialist Republic of the Union of Burma (1973–88), Union of Burma (1988–9)
Area	678 576 sq km (261 930 sq mi)
Capitals	Rangoon; Yangon (historic capital), Naypyidaw (administrative capital since 2005)
Chief towns	Mandalay, Henzada, Pegu, Myingyan
Population	52 000 000 (2006e)
Nationality	Burmese or Myanmarese
Languages	Burmese; several minority languages are also spoken
Ethnic groups	Burman 68%, Shan 9%, Karen 7%, Rakhine 4%, Chinese 3%, Indian 2%, Mon 2%, others 5%
Religions	Buddhism 89%, Christianity 4%, Islam 4%, Animism 1%, others 2%
Time zone	GMT +6.5
Currency	1 Kyat (K) = 100 pyas
Telephone	+95
Internet	.mm
Country code	MMR

> ## The Seat of Kings
> Myanmar's new administrative capital, Naypyidaw,
> has been built just outside the small town of
> Pyinmana in the centre of the country. The name
> Naypyidaw translates as 'Seat of Kings'.

Location

A republic in South-East Asia, bounded to the north and north-east by China; to the
east by Laos and Thailand; to the north-west by India; to the west by Bangladesh;
and to the south and west by the Bay of Bengal and the Andaman Sea.

Physical description

Rimmed in the north, east and west by mountains rising in the north to Hkakabo Razi
(5881 m/19 294 ft) and descending in a series of ridges and valleys to central lowlands
drained by the Irrawaddy and the Chindwin; the Salween and Sittang rivers drain
the eastern mountains; the Irrawaddy River delta extends across more than 240 km
(150 mi) of tidal forest.

Climate

Tropical monsoon climate, with a marked change between the cooler, dry season of
the north-east monsoon (November–April) and the hotter, wet season of the south-
west monsoon (May–September); coastal areas and higher mountains in the east
and north have heavy annual rainfall (2500–5000 mm); sheltered interior lowlands are
often as low as 1000 mm; lowland temperatures are high all year round (especially
March to May); there is high humidity on the coast.

Economy

Very poor; international aid withdrawn owing to military regime's human rights
abuses; agriculture employs 70% of the workforce and contributes 55% of GDP;
chief cash crops are rice, beans, pulses and fish; other activities include forestry,
mining (minerals and gemstones), oil and gas production; manufacturing and
services are struggling; tourism is growing; major producer of illegal drugs.

Under military rule; a State Peace and Development Council (formerly the State Law
and Order Restoration Council) of senior generals appoints the Cabinet and the SPDC
chairman is de facto head of state. The unicameral Constituent Assembly elected in
1990 has not been allowed to convene. Political parties are banned.

History

The country was first unified in the 11th century by King Anawrahta. Kublai Khan
invaded in 1287. A second dynasty was established in 1486, but it was plagued by
internal disunity and wars with Siam from the 16th century. A new dynasty under
King Alaunghpaya was founded in 1752. Burma was annexed to British India in
1886 following the Anglo–Burmese Wars of 1824–85. It was separated from India in
1937, becoming a Crown colony, and was occupied by the Japanese in World War
II. It gained independence as the Union of Burma in 1948. The government was
overthrown in 1962 in a military coup led by General Ne Win, who introduced a
single-party socialist state, and the country has remained under military rule since.
Following pro-democracy demonstrations in 1987–8, martial law was imposed, the

country's name was changed to Myanmar, and Aung San Suu Kyi, the leader of the opposition National League for Democracy (NLD) party, was placed under house arrest. The 1990 election, the country's first multiparty election for 30 years, was won by the NLD but the result was ignored by the military rulers; persecution of pro-democracy demonstrators has continued despite international protests. Aung San Suu Kyi took part in UN-brokered talks with the government in 2000, but the NLD boycotted a constitutional convention held in 2004 and their leader remained under house arrest. There has been fighting since independence with armed insurgent groups, mostly derived from ethnic groups. Since 1992, 15 ethnic groups have signed ceasefire agreements following offensives against them by the government, and the largest, the Kayin (Karen), began talks in 2004 about a ceasefire. The UN and the European Union have expressed concern about human rights abuses against the country's ethnic minorities.

NAMIBIA

Official name	Republic of Namibia
Local name	Namibia
Former name	South west Africa (until 1968)
Area	823 144 sq km (317 734 sq mi)
Capital	Windhoek
Chief towns	Lüderitz, Keetmanshoop, Grootfontein
Population	2 044 000 (2006e)
Nationality	Namibian
Languages	English; Afrikaans, German and local languages are also widely spoken
Ethnic groups	Ovambo 50%, Kavango 9%, Damara 7%, Herero 7%, white 6%, mixed 6%, Nama 5%, others 10%
Religions	Christianity 90%, traditional beliefs 10%
Time zone	GMT +1
Currency	1 Namibian Dollar (N$) = 100 cents
Telephone	+264
Internet	.na
Country code	NAM

Location

A republic in south-western Africa, bounded to the north by Angola; to the north-east by Zambia; to the east by Botswana; to the south by South Africa; and to the west by the Atlantic Ocean; the narrow Caprivi Strip in the north-east connects Namibia with Zambia and Zimbabwe.

Physical description

The Namib Desert runs along the Atlantic Ocean coast; the inland plateau has a mean elevation of 1500 m (4921 ft); the highest point is Königstein peak on Brandberg (2574 m/8445 ft); the Kalahari Desert lies to the east and south; the Orange River forms the southern frontier with South Africa.

Climate

Arid with low rainfall and cooler temperatures on the coast; higher temperatures and rainfall in the interior; the average annual rainfall at Windhoek, in the interior, is 360 mm and the average maximum daily temperature range is 20–30°C.

Economy

Main industrial activity is the exploitation of rich mineral deposits (diamonds (over 50% of export earnings), copper, gold, zinc, lead and uranium); the agricultural sector employs over half the workforce, mostly at subsistence level, but cattle-ranching and fishing produce exports; diversifying into tourism and manufacturing.

Government

Governed by an executive President, a Prime Minister and Cabinet, and a bicameral Parliament consisting of a National Assembly and a National Council.

History

Pre-colonial Namibia was inhabited by Bantu tribes and San (Bushmen). It became the German protectorate of South west Africa in 1884, and from 1904 the Germans waged near-genocidal wars to crush the Herero and Nama peoples. Occupied by South African troops in 1914, it was mandated to South Africa by the League of Nations in 1920. After World War II, South Africa continued to administer the area as South west Africa, and refused the UN's demand in 1961 that it terminate the mandate. The South west Africa People's Organization (SWAPO) began a guerrilla war against South Africa in 1966, and the UN challenged South African rule, changing the country's name to Namibia in 1968 and recognizing SWAPO as representative of the Namibian people in 1972. In 1988 South Africa agreed to Namibian independence in exchange for the withdrawal of Cuban troops from Angola, and Namibia gained its independence in 1990 under President Sam Nujoma. In 1994 the Walvis Bay area, a major port and South African enclave, was returned to Namibia. The country has enjoyed stability since 1990, apart from a brief secessionist campaign in the Caprivi Strip in 1998–9.

Petrified Forest

The 'Petrified Forest' in northern Namibia is home to a large number of fossilized tree trunks, some of which are over 30 metres long. The trees were the forerunners of modern conifers and their fossilized remains are around 280 million years old. Despite the name, there was never actually a forest in the area; the trees were probably washed away from their original location by floods caused by glaciers melting at the end of a long ice age.

NAURU

Official name	Republic of Nauru
Local name	Naoero (Nauruan), Nauru (English)
Area	21 sq km (8 sq mi)
Capital	There is no capital as such, but government offices are situated in Yaren District
Population	13 300 (2006e)
Nationality	Nauruan
Languages	Nauruan; English is also widely understood
Ethnic groups	Nauruan 58%, other Pacific Islanders 26%, Chinese and Vietnamese 8%, European 8%
Religions	Christianity (predominantly Prot, with RC minority); also Buddhism
Time zone	GMT +12
Currency	1 Australian Dollar ($A) = 100 cents
Telephone	+674
Internet	.nr
Country code	NRU

Location

An independent republic formed by a small, isolated island in the west-central Pacific Ocean, 42 km (26 mi) to the south of the equator and 4000 km (2500 mi) north-east of Sydney, Australia.

Physical description

The ground rises from sandy beaches to form a fertile coastal belt c.100–300 m (330–980 ft) wide, the only cultivable soil; a central plateau inland, which reaches 65 m (213 ft) at its highest point, is composed largely of phosphate-bearing rocks.

Climate

Tropical, with average daily temperatures of 24–34°C, and average humidity between 70 and 80 per cent; annual rainfall averages 1524 mm and falls mainly in the monsoon season (November–February), with marked yearly deviations; experiences occasional cyclones.

Economy

Dependent on revenue from phosphate mining, but reserves are now close to exhaustion; trust funds created with past revenue were bankrupted in 2004 through mismanagement; limited subsistence agriculture and fishing; diversifying into offshore banking and small-scale tourism.

Government

Governed by an executive President, a Cabinet and a unicameral Parliament.

History

The island was annexed by Germany in 1888 as part of the Marshall Islands Protectorate. Occupied by Allied troops in 1914, it was administered by Australia as a League of Nations mandate after World War I, and as a UN trust territory after World War II. It gained independence in 1968. Nauru's future is uncertain as phosphate reserves are running out, the economy has been in crisis since 2004, and it faces environmental problems caused by mining and the threat of rising sea levels as a result of global warming.

NEPAL

Official name	Kingdom of Nepal
Local name	Nepāl; Nepāl Adhirājya
Area	145 391 sq km (56 121 sq mi)
Capital	Kathmandu
Chief towns	Patan, Bhadgaon
Population	28 287 000 (2006e)
Nationality	Nepalese
Languages	Nepali; around 70 local dialects and languages are also spoken
Ethnic groups	Nepali 59%, Bihari 20%, Tamang 3%, Tharu 3%, Newar 3%, others 12%
Religions	Hinduism 81%, Buddhism 11%, Islam 4%, others 4%
Time zone	GMT +5.75
Currency	1 Nepalese Rupee (NRp, NRs) = 100 paise/pice
Telephone	+977
Internet	.np
Country code	NPL

Location

A landlocked independent kingdom lying along the southern slopes of the Himalayas in central Asia, bounded to the north by the Tibet region of China, and to the east, south and west by India.

Physical description

Rises steeply from the plains of the Ganges basin; high fertile valleys in the hill country at c.1300 m (4265 ft), such as the Vale of Kathmandu, are enclosed by mountain ranges; the country is dominated by the glaciated peaks of the Himalayas, the highest of which is Mount Everest at 8848 m (29 035 ft).

Climate

Varies from subtropical lowland, with hot, humid summers and mild winters, to an alpine climate over 3300 m, where peaks are permanently snow-covered; temperatures at Kathmandu vary from 40°C in May to 2°C in December; the monsoon season occurs during the summer (June–September); average annual rainfall decreases from 1778 mm in the east to 889 mm in the west.

Economy

One of the least developed countries in Asia; dependent on international aid, trade with India and expatriates' remittances; agriculture employs 80% of the people and generates 38% of GDP; the main industry is tourism; other activities include construction, finance, manufacturing (especially carpets, garments and leather goods), processing of agricultural products (rice, jute, sugar and oilseed).

Government

A hereditary constitutional monarchy; governed by the King, a Prime Minister and a Council of Ministers, and a bicameral legislature (*Sansad*) consisting of a House of Representatives and a National Council. The King assumed direct power in 2005–6 in an attempt to overcome a Marxist insurgency; democracy was restored in April 2006 and the Sansad voted to curtail further the King's powers.

History

Nepal was ruled between about the 4th and 10th centuries by the Licchavi Dynasty, then from the 10th to the 18th centuries by the Malla Dynasty under which Hinduism became the dominant religion. Modern Nepal was formed from a group of independent hill states that were united in the 18th century. In 1769 the current ruling dynasty came to power following an invasion by Gurkhas, who moved the capital to Kathmandu. War with the British in 1815–16 curtailed Nepal's expansion; its independence was formally recognized by Britain in 1923. The Rana family held power as hereditary chief ministers from 1846 until 1950–1, when the monarchy was restored to power. Apart from 1959–60, when a parliamentary system of government was in place, the kings ruled as absolute monarchs until 1990. A new constitution then introduced a multiparty parliamentary system and a reduction in the king's powers, following pro-democracy riots. But the factionalized nature of the country's politics led to frequent changes of government, and the instability was exacerbated by a Maoist insurrection that began in 1996 and spread from the remote west to the rest of the country. The government attempted to suppress the insurgents, often by brutal methods, but with little success. King Gyanendra succeeded to the throne in 2001 after the murder of his brother, King Birendra, by Crown Prince Dipendra (who committed suicide). He assumed direct power in 2005–6 in an attempt to defeat the insurgents but found himself isolated as the political class allied itself with the insurgents to demand the restoration of democracy. The legislature, reinstated in April 2006, voted to reduce the king's political powers and in November the government signed a peace agreement with the insurgents that ended the insurgency, included insurgents in a transitional government and allowed the UN to supervise disarmament.

Funny Flags

Nepal is the only country in the world that has a non-rectangular national flag. It represents a combination of two individual pennants, which were used by previous rulers of the country. The only other non-rectangular official flag is that of the US state of Ohio.

THE NETHERLANDS

Official name	Kingdom of the Netherlands; often known as Holland
Local name	Nederlanden; Koninkrijk der Nederlanden
Area	41 526 sq km (16 033 sq mi)
Capitals	Amsterdam; The Hague (Den Haag) is the seat of government
Chief towns	Rotterdam, Utrecht, Haarlem, Eindhoven, Arnhem, Groningen
Population	16 491 000 (2006e)
Nationality	Netherlander, Dutch
Languages	Dutch; Frisian is spoken in Friesland, and English is widely spoken
Ethnic groups	Dutch 83%, Turks, Moroccans, Antilleans, Surinamese, Indonesians and others 17%
Religions	Christianity 51% (RC 31%, Prot 20%), Islam 6%, others 2%, none/unaffiliated 41%
Time zone	GMT +1
Currency	1 Euro (€) = 100 cents
Telephone	+31
Internet	.nl
Country code	NLD

Location

A maritime kingdom in north-western Europe, bounded to the west and north by the North Sea; to the east by Germany; and to the south by Belgium.

Physical description

Generally low and flat, except in the south-east where hills rise to 321 m (1053 ft); around 27% of the land area is below sea level, an area inhabited by c.60% of the population, and is protected from submersion by coastal dunes and artificial dykes; the country is largely a delta comprising silt from the mouths of the Rhine, Waal, Maas, IJssel and Schelde rivers; the many canals connecting the rivers total 6340 km (3940 mi) in length; land reclamation from the sea by polder dykes has been carried out for centuries; reclamation of the Zuiderzee (the remnant of which now forms the IJsselmeer) began in 1920.

Climate

Temperate maritime climate; average temperatures are 1.7°C (January) and 17°C (July); annual rainfall, distributed fairly evenly throughout the year, exceeds 700 mm.

Economy

Highly developed and diversified market economy based on foreign trade through its role as a European transhipment hub (Rotterdam and the Europoort); main industrial activities are food processing, oil refining and production of electrical machinery and equipment, metal and engineering products, chemicals and microelectronics, and fishing; highly intensive agricultural sector includes animal husbandry, horticulture, potatoes, sugar beet and cereals; the Netherlands is the world's third-largest exporter of agricultural produce; Amsterdam is a world diamond centre.

Government

A hereditary constitutional monarchy with a Queen as head of state; governed by a Prime Minister and Council of Ministers, and a bicameral States-General (*Staten-Generaal*), which consists of a First Chamber and a Second Chamber.

History

The Netherlands was part of the Roman Empire until the 4th century ad, and part of the Frankish Empire by the 8th century. It was then incorporated into the Holy Roman Empire. The Netherlands passed to the Dukes of Burgundy in the 15th century and then to Philip II, who succeeded to Spain and the Netherlands in 1555. Attempts to stamp out Protestantism led to rebellion in 1572, and the seven northern provinces united against Spain in 1579. These United Provinces of the Netherlands achieved independence, which was finally recognized by Spain in 1648 at the end of the Eighty Years' War, and so founded the modern Dutch state. Between 1795 and 1813 it was overrun by the French, who established the Batavian Republic. Thereafter, it was united with Belgium as the Kingdom of the United Netherlands, until Belgium broke away to form a separate kingdom in 1830. The country was neutral in World War I, but there was strong Dutch resistance to German occupation during World War II. In the late 1940s there were conflicts over the independence of Dutch colonies in South-East Asia, particularly Indonesia. The Netherlands joined with Belgium and Luxembourg to form the Benelux economic union in 1948. It was a founding member of the European Economic Community in 1958, and in 2002 replaced the guilder with the euro.

Netherlands overseas territories

Netherlands Antilles (Dutch Antilles)

Local name	Nederlandse Antillen		
Location	A group of islands in the Caribbean Sea, comprising the southern group of Curaçao and Bonaire north of the Venezuelan coast, and the northern group of St Maarten, St Eustatius and Saba, lying east of Puerto Rico (USA).		
Area	960 sq km (371 sq mi)	**Internet**	.an
Capital	Willemstad	**Country code**	ANT
Population	221 700 (2006e)		

Aruba

Location	An island in the Caribbean Sea, about 30 km (19 mi) north of Venezuela, and 79 km (44 mi) west of Curaçao.		
Area	193 sq km (75 sq mi)	**Internet**	.aw
Capital	Oranjestad	**Country code**	ABW
Population	71 900 (2006e)		

NEW CALEDONIA ▸FRANCE

NEW ZEALAND

Official name	New Zealand (NZ)
Local name	New Zealand (English), Aotearoa (Maori)
Area	268 812 sq km (103 761 sq mi)
Capital	Wellington; Re Wahnganui-a-Tara
Chief towns	Auckland, Christchurch, Dunedin, Hamilton
Population	4 076 000 (2006e)
Nationality	New Zealander or Kiwi (informal)
Languages	English, Maori
Ethnic groups	European 70%, Maori 8%, mixed 8%, Asian 6%, Pacific Islanders 4%, others 4%
Religions	Christianity 53% (Prot 32%, RC 12%, other Christian 9%), others 3%, none/unaffiliated 44%
Time zone	GMT +12
Currency	1 New Zealand Dollar (NZ$) = 100 cents
Telephone	+64
Internet	.nz
Country code	NZL

Location

An independent state comprising a group of islands in the Pacific Ocean to the south-east of Australia.

Physical description

The two principal islands, North and South, are separated by the Cook Strait; there is also Stewart Island, and several minor islands; North Island is mountainous in the centre, with many hot springs; peaks rise to 2797 m (9176 ft) at Mount Ruapehu and there are several volcanoes; South Island is mountainous for its whole length, rising in the Southern Alps to 3753 m (12 312 ft) at Mount Cook (Aoraki); there are many glaciers and mountain lakes; the largest area of level lowland is the Canterbury Plain on the eastern side of South Island.

Climate

Temperate, and highly changeable, with all months moderately wet; it is almost subtropical in the north and on the east coast, with mild winters and warm, humid summers; Auckland daily temperatures are 8–13°C (July), 16–23°C (January), average monthly rainfall 145 mm (July), 79 mm (December–January); the temperatures in South Island are generally lower.

Economy

Mixed market economy with strong trade orientation; highly efficient agricultural sector provides the majority of exports, chiefly dairy products, meat, fish, wool (world's third-largest exporter), fruit and wine; main industries are food processing, wood and paper products, textiles, iron and steel, machinery, transport equipment, banking and insurance, tourism and mining (gold, iron, coal and non-metallic minerals); natural gas and hydroelectric power generation.

Government

Governed by a Governor-General (representing the British monarch, who is head of state), a Prime Minister and Cabinet, and a unicameral House of Representatives.

History

The islands are thought to have been settled by Polynesian explorers about 1000 years ago. The first European sighting was in 1642 by Abel Tasman, who named it Staten Landt; it later became known as Nieuw Zeeland, after the Dutch province. Captain Cook sighted it in 1769, and British settlement began in 1792. The country remained a dependency of New South Wales until 1841. Outbreaks of war in the 1840s and 1860s between immigrants and Maori, known as the Maori Wars, were disastrous for the Maori, much of whose land was taken. The country became the self-governing Dominion of New Zealand in 1907, and its independence was formally acknowledged in 1947. During the 1990s Maori activists demanded compensation for the land that the European settlers had taken from their people, and the government agreed either to pay compensation to certain tribes or to give them areas of land.

Self-governing territories

Cook Islands

Location	A widely scattered group of 15 volcanic and coral islands in the South Pacific Ocean, c.3200 km (2000 mi) north-east of New Zealand.		
Area	238 sq km (92 sq mi)	Internet	.ck
Chief town	Avarua	Country code	COK
Population	21 400 (2006e)		

Niue

Location	A self-governing territory of New Zealand, located in the South Pacific Ocean, 2140 km (1330 mi) north-east of New Zealand.		
Area	263 sq km (101 sq mi)	Internet	.nu
Chief town	Alofi	Country code	NIU
Population	2 200 (2006e)		

Non-self-governing territories

Tokelau

Location	A non-self-governing island territory under New Zealand administration, comprising three small atolls (Atafu, Nukunonu and Fakaofo) in the South Pacific Ocean, c.3500 km (2200 mi) north-east of New Zealand.		
Area	10.1 sq km (3.9 sq mi)	Internet	.tk
Population	1 400 (2006e)	Country code	TKL

Ross Dependency

Location	An Antarctic territory administered by New Zealand.
Area	Land: 413540 sq km (159626 sq mi); permanent shelf ice: 336770 sq km (129993 sq mi)
Population	Populated solely by scientists.

NICARAGUA

Official name	Republic of Nicaragua
Local name	Nicaragua; República de Nicaragua
Area	130668 sq km (57128 sq mi)
Capital	Managua
Chief towns	León, Granada, Masaya, Chinandega, Matagalpa, Corinto
Population	5570000 (2006e)
Nationality	Nicaraguan
Languages	Spanish; English and local languages are also spoken
Ethnic groups	Mestizo 69%, white 17%, black 9%, Amerindian 5%
Religions	Christianity 90% (RC 73%, Prot 17%), others 2%, none 8%
Time zone	GMT −6
Currency	1 Córdoba (C$) = 100 centavos = 10 reales
Telephone	+505
Internet	.ni
Country code	NIC

Location

The largest of the Central American republics, bounded to the north by Honduras; to the east by the Caribbean Sea; to the south by Costa Rica; and to the west by the Pacific Ocean.

Physical description

Mountainous western half with volcanic ranges rising to more than 2000 m (6562 ft) in the north-west; highest point is the Dipilto-Jalapa ridge (2107 m/6913 ft); two large lakes, Lake Nicaragua and Lake Managua, lie between the central mountains and the coastal mountain range; rolling uplands and forested plains lie to the east; many short rivers flow into the Pacific Ocean and the lakes.

Climate

Tropical, with average annual temperatures in the range 15–35°C according to altitude; there is a rainy season from May–November when humidity is high; the average annual rainfall at Managua is 1140 mm; subject to devastating hurricanes.

Economy

Poorest Latin American country; agriculture and fisheries account for largest share of export earnings; main cash crops are coffee, shellfish, cotton, tobacco, bananas, beef and sugar; other activities include food processing, forestry, gold-mining, oil refining, manufacturing (chemicals, machinery, metal products, textiles, garments, beverages and footwear).

Government

Governed by an executive President, a Cabinet and a unicameral National Assembly.

History

The Pacific coast was colonized by the Spanish in the early 16th century. Nicaragua gained independence from Spain in 1821 and left the Central American Federation in 1838. The plains of eastern Nicaragua, the Mosquito Coast, remained largely undeveloped and were under British protection until 1860. In the late 19th and early 20th centuries the country was ruled by the dictatorial José Santos Zelaya, who was overthrown in 1909 by a coup supported by the USA. The USA continued to exert its influence until the 1930s, when another dictator, Anastasio Somoza (García) came to power in 1938; he ruled until his assassination in 1956. He was succeeded by first one son, Luis Somoza Debayle, and then another, Anastasio Somoza Debayle, the latter ruling from 1967 until the Sandinista National Liberation Front (FSLN) seized power in 1979 and established a socialist junta of national reconstruction. The former supporters of the Somoza government (the Contras), based in Honduras and supported by the USA until 1989, carried on a guerrilla war against the junta from 1979. Ceasefires and disarmament were agreed in 1990 and 1994. The ceasefires were the result of the Sandinistas' unexpected defeat in the 1990 elections by the National Opposition Union. Since the late 1990s, governments have been liberal or liberal-dominated coalitions, keeping the FSLN from power even though it is often the largest party in the National Assembly. In 2006 the FSLN candidate Daniel Ortega (president 1985–1990) was elected president.

NIGER

Official name	Republic of Niger
Local name	Niger; République du Niger
Area	1 267 000 sq km (489 189 sq mi)
Capital	Niamey
Chief towns	Agadès, Diffa, Dosso, Maradi, Tahoua, Zinder
Population	12 525 000 (2006e)
Nationality	Nigerien
Languages	French; Hausa and Djerma are spoken widely
Ethnic groups	Hausa 56%, Djerma 22%, Fulani 9%, Tuareg 8%, others 5%
Religions	Islam 80%, Christianity and traditional beliefs 20%
Time zone	GMT +1
Currency	1 CFA Franc (CFAFr) = 100 centimes
Telephone	+227
Internet	.ne
Country code	NER

Location

A landlocked republic in west Africa, bounded to the north-east by Libya; to the north-west by Algeria; to the west by Mali; to the south-west by Burkina Faso; to the south by Benin and Nigeria; and to the east by Chad.

Physical description

Niger lies on the southern fringe of the Sahara Desert, on a high plateau; the Hamada Manguene Plateau lies in the far north; the Aïr Massif is in the centre; the Ténéré du Tafassasset Desert is in the east; the Western Talk Desert occupies the centre and north; water in quantity is found only in the south-west around the River Niger and in the south-east around Lake Chad; the highest point is Mt Greboun (2310m/7580ft).

Climate

One of the hottest countries in the world; marked rainy season in the south from June to October; rainfall decreases in the north to almost negligible levels in desert areas; the annual rainfall at Niamey is 554mm; droughts can occur.

Economy

The poorest country in the world, dependent on international economic and food aid; agriculture and herding, mostly at subsistence level, engage 90% of the workforce; production is affected by recurrent droughts, locusts and desertification; the main commercial crops are cotton, livestock and vegetables; the other main activity is the mining of uranium ore (30% of export earnings).

Government

Governed by a President, a Prime Minister and Council of Ministers, and a unicameral National Assembly.

History

According to archaeological evidence the region was inhabited during the Palaeolithic period. It was ruled by the Tuaregs from the 11th century, the Zerma from the 17th century, and the Hausa from the 14th century. The Hausa ousted the Tuaregs in the 18th century, but were themselves ousted by the Fulani. The first European occupiers were the French from 1883. Niger became a territory within French west Africa in 1904, and gained independence in 1960. A military coup in 1974 heralded a military dictatorship until 1989, when civilian government was restored but under a one-party system. Civil unrest in 1990 led to the approval of a multiparty constitution in 1992. The government elected in 1993 was ousted in 1996 by a military coup led by Ibrahim Baré Maïnassara; he was assassinated in 1999, and Daouda Wanke became president. Constitution changes later in 1999 restored democracy and Mamadou Tandja was elected president; he was re-elected in 2004 and his party remained the largest parliamentary party. Locust infestations in 2004 and drought since 2005 caused severe food shortages from 2005 and the UN appealed for food aid several times in 2005–6.

NIGERIA

Official name	Federal Republic of Nigeria
Local name	Nigeria
Area	923 768 sq km (356 574 sq mi)
Capital	Abuja
Chief towns	Lagos, Ibadan, Ogbomosho, Kano, Oshogbo, Ilorin, Abeokuta, Port Harcourt
Population	139 900 000 (2006e)
Nationality	Nigerian
Languages	English; Hausa, Yoruba and Igbo are also spoken
Ethnic groups	Hausa/Fulani 29%, Yoruba 21%, Igbo 18%, Ijaw 10%, Kanuri 4%, Ibibio 3%, Tiv 2%, others 13%
Religions	Islam 50% (Sunni), Christianity 50%
Time zone	GMT +1
Currency	1 Naira (N, N) = 100 kobo
Telephone	+234
Internet	.ng
Country code	NGA

Location

A republic in west Africa, bounded to the west by Benin; to the north by Niger; to the north-east by Chad; to the east by Cameroon; and to the south by the Gulf of Guinea and the Bight of Benin.

Physical description

The coastal strip has a long, sandy shoreline with mangrove swamp, dominated by the River Niger delta; an undulating area of tropical rainforest and oil palm bush lie north of the coastal strip; the relatively dry central plateau is characterized by open woodland and savanna; the far north of the country is on the edge of the Sahara Desert and is largely a gently undulating savanna with tall grasses; there are numerous rivers in Nigeria, notably the Niger and Benue; the Gotel Mountains are on the south-eastern frontier and the highest point is at Mount Vogel (2024 m/6640 ft).

Climate

There are two rainy seasons in the coastal areas; the wettest part is the Niger delta and the mountainous south-eastern border, with an average annual rainfall above 2500 mm, decreasing towards the west; Ibadan, in the south-east, has an average daily maximum temperature of 31°C and an average annual rainfall of 1120 mm; there is only one rainy season in the north; the dry season extends from October to April, when little rain falls.

Economy

Low-income country, heavily dependent on oil (95% of export earnings) and liquefied natural gas; reforms introduced to stimulate non-oil sector; agriculture, mostly at subsistence level, engages 70% of the workforce but Nigeria is a net food importer;

cash crops include cocoa and rubber; other major activities are mining (coal, tin and columbite), processing agricultural products, manufacturing, printing, shipbuilding and repair.

Government

Governed by an executive President, a Federal Executive Council and a bicameral National Assembly consisting of a Senate and a House of Representatives. Each of the 36 states has a Governor and a legislative assembly.

History

There are over 250 tribal groups, notably the Hausa and Fulani in the north, Yoruba in the south, and Igbo in the east. Nigeria was at the centre of the Nok culture between 500 BC and AD 200. Several African kingdoms developed throughout the area in the Middle Ages (eg the Hausa and Yoruba), and Muslim immigrants arrived in the 15th and 16th centuries. European settlers arrived and participated in the gold and slave trades. A British colony was established at Lagos in 1861, and protectorates of North and South Nigeria were created in 1900. These were amalgamated as the Colony and Protectorate of Nigeria in 1914, which became a federation in 1954 and gained independence in 1960. Nigeria was declared a federal republic in 1963 under President Azikiwe. A military coup took place in 1966, and the Igbo people in the east formed the Republic of Biafra in 1967, resulting in the Biafran War and eventually the surrender of Biafra in 1970. There were further military coups in 1983 and 1985, after which governments were military or military-dominated until 1999. In 1999, civilian rule was reintroduced and the first civilian-run elections in 20 years were held in 2003. Ethnic and religious tensions and violence have increased since 1999; the main division is between the mainly Muslim north and the predominantly Christian south, but there are also groups calling for secession or greater autonomy.

Tribal Masquerades

Many of Nigeria's tribal groups perform masquerades, which may be for entertainment or spiritual purposes. They also play an important part in the passing down of tribal history and culture to future generations. A notable feature of many of these masquerades is the wearing of elaborately carved wooden masks. As well as having spiritual and cultural significance, these also ensure that the identities of the participants remain secret.

POST-COLONIAL LITERATURE OF NIGERIA

The African nation of Nigeria has produced some of the greatest literary works of the past 50 years. Traditional oral literature, passed from generation to generation, has influenced modern writers, who have also grappled with themes of colonialism, protest, and the conflict between tradition and modernity.

Wole Soyinka

The Nobel laureate Wole Soyinka (b.1934) is a playwright, poet and novelist who studied in both Nigeria and Britain. Soyinka draws on tribal myths in much of his work. His 1960 play *A Dance of the Forests* marked Nigerian independence but warned of the ability of newly found power to corrupt. A fierce and long-time critic of Nigerian political forces, he was imprisoned from 1967 to 1969; *Poems From Prison* (1969) tells of his captivity. In the 1990s he was sentenced to death for treason by the military regime of Sani Abacha, after which he wrote his satirical play *King Baabu* (2001) about a fictional African despot.

Chinua Achebe

The first and most famous work of the novelist and poet Chinua Achebe (b.1930) is *Things Fall Apart* (1958), which explores the impact of the modern world on traditional African culture. Two follow-up novels, *No Longer at Ease* (1960) and *Arrow of God* (1964), continue Achebe's concerns about the collision between traditional practices and colonial government.

Cyprian Ekwensi

The work of Cyprian Ekwensi (b.1921) is concerned with the experiences of urban Nigerians. *People of the City* (1954) is a collection of short stories about life in Lagos; *Jagua Nana* (1961) is the tale of a prostitute who shifts between her early rural beginnings and a dissolute and corrupt city existence. Like many of his contemporaries, Ekwensi was a commentator of the Biafran War of the late 1960s, producing such works as *Survive the Peace* (1976) and *Divided We Stand* (1980).

Ken Saro-Wiwa

Author and environmentalist Ken Saro-Wiwa (1941–95) was also involved in the Biafran War. He wrote about his experiences in his poetry collection *Songs in a Time of War* (1985), which he followed with a satirical novel, *Sozaboy: a Novel in Rotten English* (1985). An ardent environmentalist, and leader of the Movement for the Survival of the Ogoni People, Saro-Wiwa fought against the Western exploitation of the Ogoni region for oil resources and the displacement of the region's people because of environmental contamination. His works on the issue include *Nigeria, The Brink of Disaster* (1991) and *Genocide in Nigeria: The Ogoni Tragedy* (1992). He was charged by the Abacha government of incitement to murder (widely considered as falsified charges) and was executed in 1995.

Other notable writers

Acclaimed female writers from Nigeria include Flora Nwapa (1931–93), who was the first African woman to have a book in English published internationally, and the novelist Buchi Emecheta (b.1944). Notable poets were Christopher Okigbo (1930–67), killed in the Biafran War, and John Pepper Clark (b.1935). Novelists have included Biyi Bandele-Thomas (b.1967), Amos Tutuola (1920–97), and Ben Okri (b.1959), winner of the Booker Prize for *The Famished Road* (1991).

NORWAY

Official name	Kingdom of Norway
Local name	Norge; Kongeriket Norge
Area	323895 sq km (125023 sq mi)
Capital	Oslo
Chief towns	Bergen, Trondheim, Stavanger, Kristiansand
Population	4611000 (2006e)
Nationality	Norwegian
Languages	Norwegian, in the varieties of Bokmål and Nynorsk; Sami and Finnish are spoken by minorities
Ethnic groups	Norwegian 96%, Sami (Lapp) 1%, others 3%
Religions	Christianity 90% (Prot 87%, RC 1%, other Christian 2%), Islam 2%, others and none/unaffiliated 8%
Time zone	GMT +1
Currency	1 Norwegian Krone (NKr) = 100 øre
Telephone	+47
Internet	.no
Country code	NOR

Location

A kingdom in north-west Europe, bounded to the north by the Arctic Ocean; to the east by Sweden, Finland and Russia; to the west by the North Sea and Norwegian Sea; and to the south by the Skagerrak; includes the dependencies of Svalbard and Jan Mayen (Arctic) and Bouvet Island, Peter I Island and Queen Maud Land (Antarctica).

Physical description

The interior is covered by mountains and elevated, barren tablelands (especially in the south-west and centre) separated by deep, narrow valleys; much of the interior rises above 1500 m (4921 ft); the highest point is Galdhøpiggen (2469 m/8100 ft); there are numerous lakes, the largest of which is Lake Mjøsa, and some of the highest waterfalls in the world; major rivers include the Glåma, Dramselv and Lågen; the coastline is irregular with many long deep fjords and fringed by small islands; the two largest island groups, off the north-west coast, are Lofoten and Vesterålen; half the country lies inside the Arctic Circle; c.25% is forested.

Climate

An Arctic winter climate in the interior highlands, with snow, strong winds and severe frosts; comparatively mild winter conditions exist on the coast; rainfall is heavy on the west coast; average annual rainfall at Bergen is 1958 mm; there are colder winters and warmer, drier summers in the southern lowlands.

Economy

The prosperous market economy is based primarily on oil and gas extraction and processing and on fisheries; the other main activities are engineering (shipping, telecommunications and hydroelectric power equipment), shipping freight services, food processing, forestry, pulp and paper products, metals, chemicals, mining, textiles and tourism; less than 3% of the land is under cultivation.

Government

A hereditary constitutional monarchy with a King as head of state; governed by a Prime Minister and Council of State, and a unicameral Parliament (*Storting*) which divides into an Upper House (*Lagting*) and a Lower House (*Odelsting*) to debate legislative matters.

History

A noble family from Sweden settled in southern Norway in the 7th century, and the establishment of Norway as a united kingdom was achieved in around 900 by Harald the Fair-Haired. Canute brought Norway under Danish rule in 1029 but after his death the throne reverted to Magnus I. When the royal house died out in the 14th century, the Danish monarch was the nearest heir; in 1397 Norway, Sweden and Denmark were united under a single monarch. Sweden seceded in 1523 but Norway remained Danish until 1814, when it was ceded to Sweden; it continued to have its own legislature although the government was appointed by the Swedish monarch. Growing nationalism resulted in the dissolution of the union and independence in 1905. Norway declared neutrality in both world wars, but was occupied by Germany in 1940–4. The Labour Party has dominated post-war political life, governing on its own or in coalitions for most of the period since 1945. Norway joined NATO in 1949 but has rejected membership of the European Community/European Union in referenda in 1972 and 1994.

Norwegian dependencies

Bouvet Island

Location	An inaccessible and uninhabited ice-covered island of volcanic origin in the South Atlantic ocean, lying approximately 1370 km (850 mi) to the south-west of the Cape of Good Hope, South Africa.		
Local name	Bouvetøya	Internet	.bv
Area	59 sq km (23 sq mi)	Country code	BVT

Svalbard and Jan Meyen Islands

Location	Svalbard Islands lie to the north of Norway and to the east of Greenland (Denmark) at the eastern edges of the Barents Sea, south of the Arctic Ocean; Jan Meyen Island lies to the north-east of Iceland and east of Greenland between the Norwegian Sea and the Greenland sea.		
Area	Svalbard: 62 049 sq km (23 957 sq mi); Jan Meyen: 373 sq km (144 sq mi)	Capital	Longyearbyen
		Internet	.sj
		Country code	SJM

OMAN

Official name	Sultanate of Oman
Local name	'Umān; Saltanat 'Umān
Former name	Sultanate of Muscat and Oman (until 1970)
Area	300 000 sq km (115 800) sq mi
Capital	Muscat
Chief towns	Matrah, Nazwa, Salalah
Population	3 102 000 (2006e)
Nationality	Omani
Language	Arabic
Ethnic groups	Arab 74%, Pakistani 22%, others 4%
Religions	Islam 86% (Ibadhi 75%), Hinduism 13%, others 1%
Time zone	GMT +4
Currency	1 Omani Rial (RO) = 1000 baisa
Telephone	+968
Internet	.om
Country code	OMN

Location

An independent state in the extreme south-eastern corner of the Arabian Peninsula. It is bounded to the north-west by the United Arab Emirates; to the west by Saudi Arabia; to the south-west by Yemen; to the north-east by the Gulf of Oman; and to the south-east and east by the Arabian Sea.

Physical description

The tip of the Musandam peninsula in the Strait of Hormuz is separated from the rest of the country by an 80 km (50 mi) strip belonging to the United Arab Emirates; over 80% of the country is desert, with mountains in the north and south-west; the highest point is Jebel Shams (3075 m/10 088 ft); the alluvial plain of the Batinah lies east and north of the Hajar mountains, along the Gulf coast.

Climate

A desert climate with much regional variation; hot and humid coast from April to October with a maximum temperature of 47°C; hot and dry interior during this summer period; relatively temperate in mountains; light monsoon rains in the south from June to September.

Economy

Prosperity is based on oil and gas extraction; other main activities are oil refining, construction, agriculture (dates, limes, bananas, alfalfa and vegetables), fishing and production of cement, copper, steel, chemicals and optic fibre; diversifying by developing liquefied natural gas production and transhipment ports, metal manufacturing, petrochemicals, information and communication technology, fisheries, manufacturing and tourism.

THE FRANKINCENSE OF OMAN

Frankincense is the name given to gum resins used in perfume and incense. It was one of the three gifts, along with gold and myrrh, said to have been presented to the infant Jesus by the Maji, and it is especially associated with religious rites and ceremonies as well as embalming.

Production of frankincense

Frankincense is tapped from the tree *Boswellia thurifera* (also known as *B. sacra* and *B. carterii*), from the Burseraceae (Torchwood) family. This tree has traditionally been grown in north-eastern Africa and more specifically in southern Arabia, Ethiopia and Somalia, lands abutting the Arabian and Red Seas and Persian Gulf. The alternative term for frankincense, olibanum, comes from the Arabic *al-luban*, meaning 'milk' or 'white', and refers to the initial milky appearance of the sap after the incision is made. However, the good quality frankincense comes from the clear yellowish material that later emerges. It is gathered from May to September; it hardens on exposure to the air and contains volatile oils that are fragrant when burnt. Its constituent ingredients include terpene, sesquiterpene and diterpene.

The Incense Route

Omani frankincense has traditionally been the most prized variety, and in antiquity it commanded similar prices to gold. It became an important product for merchant traders as the incense was carried from the desert lands to the African shores of the Mediterranean and beyond to Europe. The route was named the Incense Route, a partner of the Silk Route that traversed China and the Middle East as far as the eastern Mediterranean. The Incense Route is believed to have started at Shabwah in the south of the Arabian peninsula, then crossing the Rub' al Khali or 'Empty Quarter' desert before ending at Gaza, a port north of the Sinai Peninsula on the Mediterranean Sea.

According to the Roman historian Pliny the Elder, the camel caravans took more than 60 days to make the journey. It is thought that 3,000 tonnes of incense were carried every year. Associated items traded at the same time included precious gems, ivory, textiles and spices. The frankincense trade prospered between the 3rd century BC and the 2nd century AD before coming to an end because of dangerous nomadic raiding parties.

Uses of incense in modern times

Frankincense was re-introduced to Europe by the Franks (Germanic tribes) during the time of the Crusades several hundred years later – the name frankincense is believed to derive from 'incense of the Franks' – and has been widely used ever since. Even today in Oman the spicy, fruity and woody scent of frankincense hangs in the air, emanating from the incense burners in public places. As well as being fragrant, the burning of frankincense can also ward off insects. There are many other uses besides burning, too. The resin is steam-distilled to draw off the essential oils, which are used in aromatherapy, perfumes, soaps and lotions. The oils are used as anti-inflammatories; they are said to have disinfecting properties and are used to help with skin conditions. These treatments follow in a long tradition – frankincense cure-all remedies appear in Islamic and ancient Chinese texts.

Government

A hereditary absolute monarchy; ruled by the Sultan, who legislates by decree, implemented by a Cabinet. An elected Consultative Council and appointed Council of State have advisory roles. There are no political parties. Women have participated in politics since 1997.

History

Oman was a dominant maritime power of the western Indian Ocean in the 16th century. A sultanate ruled by the present dynasty was established in 1749, and came under British influence in the 19th century. It suffered internal dissension in 1913–20 between supporters of the Sultanate and members of the Ibadhi sect who wanted to be ruled exclusively by their religious leader. This flared up again in the 1950s but by 1959 the sultan had established control over the whole country. An insurrection in the south from the mid-1960s was defeated with external military assistance in 1975. In 1970 Sultan Qaboos bin Said overthrew his father in a bloodless coup and initiated a modernization programme.

PAKISTAN

Official name	Islamic Republic of Pakistan
Local name	Pākistān; Islāmī Jamhūriya e Pākistān
Former name	formerly part of India (until 1947); Dominion of Pakistan (1947–56); known as West Pakistan (until 1971)
Area	803 943 sq km (310 322 sq mi)
Capital	Islamabad; Islāmabād
Chief towns	Karachi, Lahore, Faisalabad, Rawalpindi
Population	165 803 000 (2006e)
Nationality	Pakistani
Languages	Urdu; English and several local languages are also spoken
Ethnic groups	Punjabi 66%, Sindhi 13%, Pashtun 11%, Muhajir 8%, Balochi 2%
Religions	Islam 97% (Sunni 77%, Shia 20%), Christianity, Hinduism and others 3%
Time zone	GMT +5
Currency	1 Pakistan Rupee (PRs, Rp) = 100 paisa
Telephone	+92
Internet	.pk
Country code	PAK

Location

An Asian state, bounded to the east by India; to the west by Afghanistan and Iran; and to the north by China; the disputed area of Jammu and Kashmir lies to the north-east.

Physical description

Mostly lying on the alluvial flood plain of the River Indus; bounded to the north and west by mountains rising to 8611 m (28254 ft) at K2; largely flat plateau, low-lying plains and arid desert to the south of the Karakoram range.

Climate

Dominated by the Asiatic monsoon; in the mountains and foothills of the north and west, the climate is cool with summer rain and winter snow; in the upland plateaux, summers are hot and winters are cool, with the possibility of some winter rain; in summer the Indus Valley is extremely hot and is fanned by dry winds, often carrying sand; throughout the country, the hottest season lasts from March to June, with the highest temperatures occurring in the south; the rainy season lasts from late June to early October and coincides with the south-western monsoon.

Economy

Poor country, developing with international assistance; agriculture employs 42% of the workforce, producing cotton, wheat, rice, sugar and livestock products; cotton supports the major industries of cotton processing (spinning and weaving) and textile manufacturing (cotton yarn and fabrics, garments and bedlinen); other activities are food processing, pharmaceuticals, construction materials, paper products, fertilizer, leather goods, carpets and rugs.

Government

Governed by a President, a Prime Minister and Cabinet, and a bicameral Parliament consisting of a National Assembly and a Senate. Four of the six provinces have a Governor, an executive and a legislative assembly; the Federal Capital Territory and the Tribal Areas are administered by the federal government.

History

Pakistan's walled cities at Mohenjo-Daro, Harappa and Kalibangan are evidence of civilization in the Indus Valley over 4000 years ago. Muslims ruled the region under the Mughal Empire from 1526 to 1761, and the British ruled most areas from the 1840s. The predominantly Muslim areas of British India were partitioned at independence in 1947 to form the state of Pakistan, consisting of West Pakistan (Baluchistan, North-West Frontier, West Punjab, Sind) and East Pakistan (East Bengal), which were physically separated by 1600 km (1000 mi). Pakistan was proclaimed an Islamic republic in 1956. Differences between East and West Pakistan developed into civil war in 1971, resulting in East Pakistan becoming an independent state (Bangladesh). A coup in 1958 led to military rule until civilian government was restored in 1971 with Zulfikar Ali Bhutto as prime minister. This government was overthrown in a military coup led by General Zia ul-Haq in 1977, and Bhutto was executed in 1979 despite international appeals for clemency. Civilian government was restored following Zia's death in 1988 but proved unstable, with several changes of government amid allegations of corruption. When the democratically elected Premier Nawaz Sharif developed into an elected dictator, there was another military coup in 1999. This was led by General Pervez Musharraf, who became head of government and, in 2001, president; after elections in 2002 a civilian government took office, led by a civilian prime minister. There was a Pakistan–India war over the disputed territory of Kashmir and Jammu in 1948; this still unresolved issue underlay further

India–Pakistan conflict in 1965 and 1971 (the Indo–Pakistan Wars), as well as periods of tension in 1999 and 2000–2 that were heightened by the fact that both countries now possessed nuclear weapons. Since September 2001, Pakistan has aligned itself with Western countries and provided support to the allies in the Afghan War. This policy angered the government's opponents, who used procedural disruptions to prevent the National Assembly from functioning properly in 2002–3. The policy also exacerbated the sectarian violence between Shia and Sunni extremists, which had begun in the 1980s, and provoked attacks on the federal government, Christians and Westerners. In addition, it led to unrest on the Afghan border, where many al-Qaeda- and Taliban-linked militants have established bases. International concerns were raised in 2004 by disclosures about Pakistan's sale of its nuclear technology to other countries.

PALAU

Official name	Republic of Palau
Local name	Belau; Belu'u era Belau
Former name	Formerly part of the Trust Territory of the Pacific Islands (1917–79)
Area	494 sq km (191 sq mi)
Capital	Melekeok
Population	20 600 (2006e)
Nationality	Palauan
Languages	Palauan; in certain islands, Sonsoralese, Tobi, Angaur, English and Japanese are also official languages
Ethnic groups	Palauan (Micronesian with Malaysian and Melanesian admixtures) 70%, Filipino 15%, Chinese 5%, other Asian 2%, white 2%, others 6%
Religions	Christianity 65% (RC 42%, Prot 23%), traditional beliefs (Modekngei) 9%, others 10%, none/unaffiliated 16%
Time zone	GMT +9
Currency	1 US Dollar ($, US$) = 100 cents
Telephone	+680
Internet	.pw
Country code	PLW

Location

A group of c.350 small islands and islets in the west Pacific Ocean, 960 km (600 mi) east of the Philippines.

Physical description

Varies from the mountainous main island of Babelthuap to low-lying coral islands, often surrounded by coral reefs; highest point is Mount Ngerchelchauus (242 m/794 ft).

Climate

Tropical; hot all year, with high humidity; the wet season is in May–November; the average annual temperature is 27°C and the average annual rainfall is 3810 mm; typhoons are common.

Economy

Dependent on US aid; main activities are tourism, subsistence agriculture (coconuts, copra, cassava and sweet potatoes) and fishing.

Government

Governed by an executive President, a Cabinet and a bicameral National Congress consisting of a House of Delegates and a Senate.

History

The islands were nominally Spanish until 1899, when control passed to Germany. Japan occupied the islands on behalf of the Allies in 1914 and administered them as a League of Nations mandate from 1920 until ousted by US forces in 1944. In 1947 the islands became part of a UN trust territory administered by the USA. They became a self-governing republic in 1981; independence was achieved in 1994 under a compact of free association with the USA, by which the USA retained responsibility for Palau's defence.

PANAMA

Official name	Republic of Panama
Local name	Panamá; República de Panamá
Former name	Part of Colombia (until 1903)
Area	77 381 sq km (29 762 sq mi)
Capital	Panama City; La Ciudad de Panamá
Chief towns	David, Colón, Santiago
Population	3 191 000 (2006e)
Nationality	Panamanian
Language	Spanish
Ethnic groups	Mestizo 70%, Amerindian and mixed (West Indian) 14%, white 10%, Amerindian 6%
Religion	Christianity 100% (RC 85%, Prot 15%)
Time zone	GMT −5
Currency	1 Balboa (B, Ba) = 100 centésimos; the US Dollar is also in use
Telephone	+507
Internet	.pa
Country code	PAN

Location

A republic occupying the south-eastern end of the isthmus of Central America, bounded to the north by the Caribbean Sea; to the south by the Pacific Ocean; to the west by Costa Rica; and to the east by Colombia.

ysical description

stly mountainous, with coastal plains either side of the central range; the Serranía Tabasará in the west rises to more than 2000 m (6562 ft); the highest point is Barú cano in Chiriqui (3475 m/11 400 ft); the Azuero peninsula lies to the south; lake-dded lowland cuts across the isthmus; dense tropical forests lie on the Caribbean ast.

mate

pical, with a mean annual temperature of 32°C; the rainy season is May–cember; average annual rainfall at Colón, on the Caribbean coast, is 3280 mm, ile in Panama City it is 1780 mm.

onomy

sed on a large services sector (80% of GDP) centred on operation of the ama Canal, the Colón free-trade zone, financial services and ship registration; pansion of the canal approved in 2006; other activities are construction, brewing, nufacturing (construction materials and textiles), sugar refining, agriculture ananas, rice, coffee and sugar cane), which employs 21% of the workforce, and hing.

vernment

verned by an executive President, a Cabinet and a unicameral Legislative sembly.

story

e area was visited by Christopher Columbus in 1502 and quickly gained strategic portance as a centre of Spanish trade movement, a vital link between the ribbean and Pacific. It remained under Spanish colonial rule until 1821, when it ined its independence and joined the union known as Gran Colombia. After this paration in 1830, Panama became part of Colombia until 1903 when it achieved independence after a US-inspired revolution. Panama was under military rule nost constantly between 1968, when General Omar Torrijos established a military tatorship, and 1989, when General Manuel Noriega was ousted by US forces after egations of corruption and drugs trafficking; Panama abolished its standing army 1991. Panama assumed sovereignty of the Panama Canal, previously administered the USA, in 1999, and in 2006 a plan to double its capacity was approved by erendum.

Race to the Sky

Panama City has recently played host to a race to build the tallest building in Latin America. Palacio de la Bahía, scheduled for completion in 2009, was to stand 350 m (1,150 ft) high with 97 floors. When the height of the building was unveiled, 24 floors were added to the plans for its competitor, the Ice Tower, making its final height 381 m (1,250 ft) with 104 floors. The Palacio de la Bahía project was cancelled in 2006 owing to financial and technical problems, leaving the Ice Tower to claim the crown of tallest building when it is completed in 2010.

PAPUA NEW GUINEA

Official name	Independent State of Papua New Guinea (PNG)
Local name	Papuaniugini; Gau Hedinarai ai Papua–Matamata Guinea
Area	462 840 sq km (178 656 sq mi)
Capital	Port Moresby
Chief towns	Lae, Madang, Rabaul
Population	5 670 000 (2006e)
Nationality	Papua New Guinean
Languages	Pidgin English; English, Motu and more than 800 other languages are spoken
Ethnic groups	Papuan 85%, Melanesian 1%, others 14%
Religions	Christianity 66% (Prot and others 44%, RC 22%), traditional beliefs 34%
Time zone	GMT +10
Currency	1 Kina (K) = 100 toea
Telephone	+675
Internet	.pg
Country code	PNG

Location

An independent island group in the south-west Pacific Ocean, comprising the eastern half of the island of New Guinea, bordering Indonesia to the west, and many smaller islands.

Physical description

On the island of New Guinea, the mountains are densely covered with tropical rainforest and run across the centre, with snow-covered peaks rising more than 4000 m (13 123 ft); the highest point is Mount Wilhelm (4509 m/14 793 ft); large rivers flow to the south, north and east; vast mangrove swamps lie along the coast; the archipelago islands are mountainous, mostly volcanic, and fringed with coral reefs.

Climate

Tropical monsoon climate, with temperatures and humidity constantly high; the average temperature range is 22–33°C; high rainfall, which averages 2000–3000 mm but can be 5000 mm in the mountains.

Economy

Poor, underdeveloped and dependent on international aid; agriculture, mainly at subsistence level, employs more than 80% of the workforce; the chief cash crops are coffee, palm oil, copra, cocoa and vanilla; the main industries are mining (gold, silver, copper and nickel), oil and natural gas production, forestry, fishing and processing agricultural products.

Government

overned by a Governor-General (representing the British monarch, who is head of ate), a Prime Minister and National Executive Council, and a unicameral National arliament. Bougainville has had internal autonomy since 2005, with its own resident, government and legislative assembly.

History

ossibly inhabited by South-East Asians who came to Papua New Guinea via ndonesia many thousands of years ago, it was visited by the Portuguese and the panish in the 16th century before being colonized by the British and Dutch in the te 18th century. In 1884 Britain proclaimed a protectorate in the south-east, while ermany proclaimed the north-east quadrant to be a German protectorate. German ew Guinea was established in the north-east in 1899. The German colony ccupied by Australia in World War I; Australia administered the British and German reas as mandated territories from 1920 until independence, except during the apanese occupation of 1942–5. The territories were combined in 1949 as the UN rust Territory of Papua and New Guinea. In 1963 the UN transferred the western art of New Guinea to Indonesia. The remaining territory was renamed Papua New uinea in 1971 and gained its independence in 1975. The island of Bougainville ttempted to secede at independence; the separatist campaign became an armed onflict in 1989, with fighting between separatists and government forces continuing ntil a ceasefire in 1998. A peace agreement signed in 2001 provided autonomy for ougainville and guaranteed a referendum on the island's status in 10 to 15 years; e first autonomous government was elected in 2005. Papua New Guinea suffers om rampant crime, and in 2004 an Australian study judged it to be on the brink of ocial and economic collapse.

PARAGUAY

Official name	Republic of Paraguay
Local name	Paraguay; República del Paraguay
Area	406 750 sq km (157 000 sq mi)
Capital	Asunción
Chief towns	Villarrica, Concepción
Population	6 506 000 (2006e)
Nationality	Paraguayan
Languages	Spanish, Guaraní
Ethnic groups	Mestizo 95%, others 5%
Religions	Christianity 99% (RC 90%, Prot 9%, mostly Mennonite), others 1%
Time zone	GMT −4
Currency	1 Guaraní (Gs) = 100 céntimos
Telephone	+595
Internet	.py
Country code	PRY

Location

A landlocked country in central South America, bounded to the north-west by Bolivia; to the north and east by Brazil; to the south-west by Argentina.

Physical description

Divided into two regions by the River Paraguay, lying mostly at altitudes below 450m (1476ft); bordered to the south and east by the River Paraná; the Gran Chaco in the west is mostly grassy plains or scrub forest; more fertile land lies in the east; the Paraná Plateau is mainly wet, treeless savanna; the highest point is Cerro Pero (842m/2762ft).

Climate

Tropical in the north-west, with hot summers, warm winters, and rainfall up to 1250mm; lower temperatures in the south-east, with rainfall up to 1750mm; the temperature at Asunción ranges from 12°C in winter to 35°C in summer.

Economy

Poor country; agriculture, mostly at subsistence level, employs 45% of the workforce; chief cash crops are soya beans, cassava, cotton, sugar, cereals, vegetables, fruit and meat; other activities include hydroelectric power generation, forestry and manufacturing (processing agricultural and forestry products, basic consumer goods, textiles and chemicals).

Government

Governed by an executive President, a Council of Ministers and a bicameral Congress consisting of a Chamber of Deputies and a Senate.

History

Originally inhabited by Guaranís, the area was settled by the Spanish after 1537 and by Jesuit missionaries who arrived in 1609. It gained independence from Spain in 1811. During the disastrous War of the Triple Alliance (1864–70) against Brazil, Argentina and Uruguay, Paraguay lost over half of its population. In 1935 it regained territory disputed with Bolivia after the three-year Chaco War. Civil war broke out in 1947, and in 1954 General Alfredo Stroessner seized power and became president. His autocratic and increasingly repressive regime was ousted in a coup in 1989. The first multiparty elections were held in 1993, but political instability has persisted since the 1990s, with assassinations, a coup attempt, widespread corruption and organized crime.

A River of Power

The Paraná River is the second longest river in South America. It runs through Paraguay as well as Brazil and Argentina and produces more hydroelectric power than any other river in the world. Fittingly, Paraguay's name comes from the Guaraní word *pararaguay,* which means 'from a great river'.

PERU

Official name	Republic of Peru
Local name	Perú; República del Perú
Area	1 284 640 sq km (495 871 sq mi)
Capital	Lima
Chief towns	Arequipa, Chiclayo, Cuzco, Trujillo
Population	28 303 000 (2006e)
Nationality	Peruvian
Languages	Spanish, Quechua; Aymara is also widely spoken
Ethnic groups	Amerindian 45% (principally Quechua), Mestizo 37%, white 15%, black, Japanese, Chinese and others 3%
Religions	Christianity 83% (RC 81%, Prot 2%), others 1%, none/ unaffiliated 16%
Time zone	GMT −5
Currency	1 Nuevo Sol (Pes) = 100 cénts
Telephone	+51
Internet	.pe
Country code	PER

Location

A republic on the west coast of South America, bounded to the north by Ecuador; to the north-east by Colombia; to the east by Brazil and Bolivia; and to the south by Chile.

Physical description

Arid plains and foothills on the coast, with areas of desert and fertile river valleys; the central sierra, with an average altitude of 3000 m (9842 ft), contains 50% of the population; the highest point is Huascarán (6768 m/22 204 ft); rivers cut through the plateau, forming deep canyons; the forested Andes and the Amazon basin lie to the east; the major rivers flow to the Amazon.

Climate

Mild temperatures all year on the coast; dry, arid desert in the south; in the north, the coastal region has bursts of torrential rain every ten years or so with rising sea temperatures and the cold current retreats south: this phenomenon is known as El Niño. Andean temperatures never rise above 23°C, with a large daily temperature range and night frost in the dry season; in the Peruvian portion of the Amazon basin in the east, the climate is typically wet and tropical.

Economy

Poor but developing market economy; the main industries are mining (copper, gold, zinc and, silver), oil and natural gas extraction and oil refining; other activities include steel and metal fabrication, fishing and fish processing, manufacturing (textiles and garments), food processing, tourism; agricultural products include coffee, cotton, sugar and rice.

Government
Governed by an executive President, a Council of Ministers and a unicameral Congress.

History
Peru had a highly developed Inca civilization by the 15th century, but this empire fell to the Spanish in 1531–3 and the Viceroyalty of Peru was established. Its gold and silver mines made Peru the principal source of wealth in Spain's American empire. After declaring its independence in 1821, Peru entered into several border disputes during the 19th century (eg the War of the Pacific in 1879–83); disputes with Ecuador and Chile were only resolved in 1998 and 1999. Following independence, military dictatorships alternated with periods of democratic rule until 1980, since when democratic civilian rule has prevailed. Terrorist activities, principally by the Maoist *Sendero Luminoso* (Shining Path) guerrilla movement, and drug-related violence destabilized the government and the economy in the 1980s and 1990s; the violence and the retaliation by the authorities led to over 60 000 deaths and widespread human rights abuses. The legacy of criminal violence and lawlessness, much of it related to drug-trafficking, remains. In 2001 Alejandro Toledo became Peru's first president of native Peruvian Indian descent.

PHILIPPINES

Official name	Republic of the Philippines
Local name	Pilipinas; República Ñg Pilipinas
Area	299 679 sq km (115 676 sq mi)
Capital	Manila
Chief towns	Quezon City, Basilan, Cebu, Bacolod, Davao, Iloilo
Population	89 469 000 (2006e)
Nationality	Filipino, Philippine
Languages	Filipino (based on Tagalog), English; eight major dialects and many local dialects are also spoken
Ethnic groups	Tagalog 28%, Cebuano 13%, Ilocano 9%, Bisaya/Binisaya 8%, Ilongo 8%, Bicol 6%, Waray 3% others 25%
Religions	Christianity 92% (RC 81%, Prot 11%), Islam 5%, others 3%
Time zone	GMT +8
Currency	1 Philippine Peso (PHP) = 100 centavos
Telephone	+63
Internet	.ph
Country code	PHL

Location
A republic consisting of an archipelago of more than 7100 islands and islets, situated to the north-east of Borneo (Indonesia) and to the south of Taiwan.

Physical description

Largely mountainous, with north to south ridges rising to more than 2500m (8200ft); the highest point is Mount Apo (2954m/9691ft); there are narrow coastal plains and broad interior plateaux; forests cover half the land area; some islands are ringed by coral reefs.

Climate

The lowlands have a warm and humid tropical climate throughout the year, with an average temperature of 27°C; lying astride the typhoon belt, the Philippines are affected by c.15 cyclonic storms annually.

Economy

Poor but developing; remittances of c.9 million expatriate workers are vital to the economy; the main industries are electronics assembly, garments, footwear, pharmaceuticals, chemicals, wood products, oil refining, mining (copper) and fishing; growing services sector (tourism, information technology and other call centre operations, finance); agriculture and fisheries employ 20% of the workforce.

Government

Governed by an executive President, a Cabinet and a bicameral Congress, comprising a Senate and a House of Representatives. The Mindanao region has autonomy, with its own governor and legislative assembly.

History

The Philippines was claimed for Spain by Magellan in 1521 but ceded to the USA after the Spanish–American War of 1898. It became self-governing in 1935, was occupied by the Japanese during World War II, and achieved independence in 1946. During the period 1945–53 the communist-dominated Huk rebellion was suppressed. Ferdinand Marcos seized power in 1965 and imposed martial law in 1972–81. His regime became increasingly repressive and corrupt, and was believed responsible for the assassination of the exiled political leader Benigno Aquino on his return to Manila in 1983. Marcos was ousted by mass protests after he falsified results to deny Corazon Aquino's victory in the 1986 presidential election. President Aquino survived political unrest and several attempted coups to introduce a new constitution and entrench democracy. Her successor, Fidel Ramos, instigated peace talks with the communist and Muslim rebels responsible for long-running insurgencies. The Moro National Liberation Front, Muslim separatists in the southern islands, ended its activities after a 1996 agreement created an autonomous Muslim region in Mindanao and three other islands. This agreement was not accepted by the Moro Islamic Liberation Front, which has been in talks with the government since 2003, although the ceasefire was breached in 2005. Clashes with communist insurgents have continued despite peace talks in 2004. After September 2001, Abu Sayyaf, an Islamic group suspected of links with al-Qaeda, emerged on the island of Jolo.

PITCAIRN ISLANDS ▶UNITED KINGDOM

POLAND

Official name	Republic of Poland
Local name	Polska; Rzeczpospolita Polska
Former name	People's Republic of Poland (1952–89)
Area	312 612 sq km (120 668 sq mi)
Capital	Warsaw
Chief towns	Łódz, Kraków, Wrocław, Poznań, Gdańsk, Katowice, Lublin
Population	38 537 000 (2006e)
Nationality	Pole, Polish
Language	Polish
Ethnic groups	Polish 97%, German, Belarusian, Ukrainian and others 3%
Religions	Christianity 92% (RC 90%, Orthodox and Prot 2%), none/unaffiliated 8%
Time zone	GMT +1
Currency	1 Złoty (Zl) = 100 groszy
Telephone	+48
Internet	.pl
Country code	POL

Location

A republic in central Europe, bounded to the north by the Kaliningrad region of Russia and the Baltic Sea; to the west by Germany; to the south-west by the Czech Republic; to the south by Slovakia; to the south-east by the Ukraine; and to the north-east by Belarus and Lithuania.

Physical description

Mostly part of the great European plain, lying at less than 200 m (650 ft) above sea level; the Carpathian and Sudetes Mountains in the south rise in the High Tatra to 2499 m (8199 ft) at Mount Rysy; the Polish plateau to the north of the Tatra is cut by the Bug, San and Vistula rivers; Europe's richest coal basin lies in the west (Silesia); north of the plateau there are lowlands with many lakes; the Baltic coastal area is flat, with sandy heathland and numerous lagoons (coastline length is 491 km/305 mi); the main Polish rivers are the Vistula and Oder; rivers are often frozen in winter and liable to flood; forests cover one-fifth of the land.

Climate

Continental climate, with severe winters and hot summers; rain falls chiefly in summer and seldom exceeds 650 mm annually.

Economy

Transformed from planned to market economy in 1990s; the main industries are machine building, iron and steel, mining (coal, sulphur, copper, silver and lead), chemicals, shipbuilding, food processing, glass, beverages and textiles; modernized but inefficient agricultural sector employs 16% of workforce, producing vegetables, fruit, cereals, meat and dairy products.

Government

Governed by a President, a Prime Minister and Council of Ministers, and a bicameral National Assembly comprising a Diet (*Sejm*) and a Senate.

History

Poland was inhabited from 2000 BC or earlier and became an independent kingdom in the 9th century AD. Under the Piast Dynasty the Poles emerged as the most powerful of a number of Slavic groups in 1025. Towards the end of Jagiełłon rule Poland formed a union with Lithuania (1569), at which point it stretched from the Baltic to the Black Sea. This Commonwealth was weakened by attacks from Russia, Brandenburg, Turkey and Sweden, and eventually in 1772, 1793 and 1795 Poland was deprived of its independent statehood. Its territories were divided between Prussia, Russia and Austria, with Russia gaining the lion's share. Following the 1815 Congress of Vienna, Poland became a semi-independent state called the Congress Kingdom of Poland and was incorporated into the Russian Empire under Alexander I. The Poles constantly struggled for national liberation; there were uprisings in 1830, 1846–9 and 1863, which led to the kingdom being fully absorbed and subjected to a repressive campaign of Russification. However, the struggle was eventually won at the end of World War I in 1918 when an independent Polish state emerged. Germany invaded Poland in 1939, precipitating World War II, and Poland was partitioned between Germany and the Union of Soviet Socialist Republics (USSR) in the same year. The country was liberated by Soviet forces in 1944, when a People's Democracy was established under Soviet influence; by 1947 communists controlled the government. In 1980 a mass movement for civil and national rights coalesced around the independent trade union Solidarity. Its leaders were detained in 1981–3, and a state of martial law was imposed. The economic situation worsened and there was continuing unrest in the 1980s, resulting in talks between the government, Solidarity and the Roman Catholic Church in 1989. The communist government lost power in multiparty elections later that year and Solidarity helped to form a coalition government, its leader, Lech Wałesa, becoming president in 1990. The transition to a market economy in the 1990s was accompanied by popular discontent, political difficulties and recession, but nevertheless a private sector developed within the economy and democratic government is entrenched. Poland joined NATO in 1999 and the European Union in 2004.

Modern Exodus

Since Poland joined the European Union in 2004, fifteen years after the end of communist rule, it is estimated that as many as 1,000,000 young Poles have migrated to western Europe in search of work. In escaping the EU's highest unemployment levels, migrating workers are creating a pronounced shortage of skilled workers in their home country.

POLYNESIA, FRENCH ►FRANCE

POLISH CUISINE

'Warming', 'hearty', 'rich' and 'filling', even sometimes 'stodgy', are just some of the descriptions all too frequently applied to Polish food. Think dumplings and soup, potatoes and cream, and sausages and stews ... One description that cannot be levelled, however, is 'boring'. Polish food uses all kinds of ingredients ranging from fish, meat, game and offal to fruits, vegetables and cereals. Its cuisine has been influenced by its historic neighbours: Russia, Germany and the Austro-Hungarian and Lithuanian empires.

Soups

A typical Polish main meal consists of three courses, most likely starting with a soup. The most famous Polish soup (*zupa*), in fact one of the most famous soups Europe-wide in all its various guises, is a beetroot soup. The Polish equivalent of the more famous borscht is called *barszcz* and is sometimes served with dumplings. A chilled summer variant is made with soured milk, beets and dill and is called *chłodnik*. Another favourite is *żurek*, a soured rye soup that can be further flavoured with egg, mushroom and/or sausage. *Zupa grzybowa* is a mushroom soup with cream; *rosó*, a clear chicken consommé; *grochówka*, a thick pea soup; and *kapuśniak* or *kwaśnica*, a sour cabbage soup.

Cabbage-based dishes

Cabbage features heavily in traditional Polish cuisine. *Kapusta*, a pickled cabbage that is the Polish equivalent of the German sauerkraut, appears in many recipes, including two that are considered national dishes: *bigos* and *pierogi*. *Bigos* is a 'hunter's stew' with cabbage, pieces of meat, sausage and mushroom. It is commonly eaten with rye bread or potatoes. *Pierogi* are semi-circular dumplings made with a variety of fillings including cabbage, meat, cottage cheese or mushrooms, or even potatoes for those who enjoy their carbohydrates. *Pierogi* also come in sweet berry varieties. Concluding the cabbage theme is *golabki:* cabbage parcels stuffed with meat and sometimes rice.

Other savouries

Freshwater fish are highlights of the Polish cuisine. These include pike, perch and a Christmas favourite, the carp. Salmon and pickled herring are also popular. Pork is the most widely used meat and is the main ingredient in *golonka* (pork knuckles cooked with vegetables) and *flaki* (pork tripe stew). *Kotlet schabowy* is a breaded pork cutlet that is similar to the Austrian Wiener schnitzel. *Kiełbasa*, Polish sausage that comes in many different types, is usually also made from pork.

Other dishes include steak tartare, raw minced beef with chopped onion and raw egg. This dish, which originated in Mongolia and reached Poland via Russia, is popular in restaurants. Potatoes are another staple and feature in dumplings and potato pancakes, the latter often served with cream. *Kasza* is a buckwheat cereal served as an accompaniment or with lard and onions (*gryczna ze skwarkami*).

Desserts – and beyond

The most famous Polish dessert is a poppyseed cake called *makowiec*, but ice cream and doughnuts (*pączki*) are equally popular. *Sernik* is a cheesecake made with a quark-type cheese. Most meals are finished with (and even punctuated by) Polish vodka, renowned for its multitude of flavours including orange, vanilla, cherry, walnut, bison grass and rose petal.

PORTUGAL

Official name	Portuguese Republic
Local name	Portugal; República Portuguesa
Former name	Kingdom of Portugal (until 1910)
Area	91 982 sq km (34 142 sq mi)
Capital	Lisbon
Chief towns	Oporto, Setúbal, Coimbra
Population	10 606 000 (2006e)
Nationality	Portuguese
Language	Portuguese
Ethnic groups	Portuguese 95%, others 5%
Religions	Christianity 96% (RC 94%, Prot 2%), others 1%, none/unaffiliated 3%
Time zone	GMT
Currency	1 Euro (€) = 100 cents
Telephone	+351
Internet	.pt
Country code	PRT

Location

A country in south-western Europe on the western side of the Iberian Peninsula, bounded to the north and east by Spain; and to the south and west by the Atlantic Ocean; also includes the islands of the Azores and Madeira.

Physical description

There are several mountain ranges formed by the west spurs of the Spanish mountain system; the chief range is the Serra da Estrêla in the north, rising to 1991 m (6532 ft); the highest point in Portuguese territory is Mount Pico on Ilha do Pico (Pico Island) in the Azores (2351 m/7713 ft); the coast and the areas south of the Tagus are lower-lying; the four main rivers (the Douro, Minho, Tagus and Guadiana) are the lower courses of rivers beginning in Spain; large forests of pine, oak, cork-oak, eucalyptus and chestnut cover about 20% of the country.

Climate

Temperate maritime, with increased variation between summer and winter temperatures inland; the west coast is relatively cool in summer; there is most rainfall in winter.

Economy

Diversified and increasingly service-based economy; main activities are tourism, manufacturing (vehicle components, textiles, footwear, pulp and paper, cork, ceramics, chemicals and food processing), metals and metalworking, oil refining, wine-making, shipbuilding, forestry, fishing and agriculture; hydroelectric power and other sustainable energy sources are increasingly exploited.

Government

Governed by a President, a Prime Minister and Council of Ministers, and a unicameral Assembly of the Republic.

History

Portugal became a kingdom under Alphonso I in 1139. The Portuguese Empire began in the 15th century, a time of world exploration by the Portuguese. Portugal came under Spanish domination from 1580 to 1640, and was invaded by the French in 1807. The monarchy was overthrown and the First Republic established in 1910. A military coup took place in 1926; in the early 1930s the country came under the Estado Novo regime of Dr Antonio Salazar, whose dictatorship lasted over 35 years (1932–68). His successor was overthrown in 1974 in a military coup that caused great turmoil until elections in 1976 began to stabilize the situation. Civilian government was formally restored in 1982. Portugal joined the European Community in 1986, and replaced the escudo with the euro in 2002.

Autonomous regions

Azores

Location	An island archipelago of volcanic origin in the North Atlantic ocean, lying 1400–1800 km (870–1100 mi) to the west of the Cabo da Roca on mainland Portugal.		
Local name	Açores	Capital	Ponta Delgada
Area	2300 sq km (900 sq mi)	Population[1]	242 200 (2005e)

Madeira

Location	The main island in a Portuguese archipelago off the coast of North Africa, 990 km (615 mi) south-west of Lisbon.		
Area	796 sq km (307 sq mi)	Population[1]	245 000 (2005e)
Capital	Funchal		

[1] *Source: Instituto Nacional de Estatística (Portuguese National Institue of Statistics)*

Do you know the Bishop of Norwich?

Perhaps the most famous Portuguese export is the fortified wine known as Port, grown exclusively in the picturesque Douro Valley. The valley forms the world's oldest *appellation contrôlée* area, defined in 1756. Port was particularly favoured in eighteenth-century Britain, and a wealth of ritual and etiquette surrounding the wine's consumption grew with its popularity. As it was considered bad form to ask directly to be passed the port bottle, one would enquire 'Do you know the Bishop of Norwich?'.

PUERTO RICO ▸ **UNITED STATES OF AMERICA**

QATAR

Official name	State of Qatar
Local name	Qatar; Dawlat Qatar
Area	11 437 sq km (4415 sq mi)
Capital	Doha; Ad Dawhah
Chief towns	Dukhan, Al Khawr, Umm Sai'd, Al Wakrah
Population	885 300 (2006e)
Nationality	Qatari
Languages	Arabic; English is also spoken
Ethnic groups	Arab 40%, Pakistani 18%, Indian 18%, Iranian 10%, others 14%
Religions	Islam 95%, others 5%
Time zone	GMT +3
Currency	1 Qatar Riyal (QR) = 100 dirhams
Telephone	+974
Internet	.qa
Country code	QAT

Location

A low-lying state on the east coast of the Arabian Peninsula, comprising the Qatar Peninsula and numerous small offshore islands. It is bounded to the south by Saudi Arabia and the United Arab Emirates, and elsewhere by the Arabian Gulf.

Physical description

The peninsula, 160 km (100 mi) long and 55–80 km (34–50 mi) wide, slopes gently from the Dukhan Heights (98 m/322 ft) to the east shore; the highest point is Qurayn Abu al Bawl (103 m/338 ft); barren terrain, mainly sand and gravel; coral reefs offshore.

Climate

Desert climate with average temperatures of 23°C in the winter and 35°C in the summer; high humidity; sparse annual rainfall not exceeding 75 mm per annum.

Economy

Prosperity based on oil and liquefied natural gas (85% of export earnings); diversified into oil refining, petrochemicals and fertilizers; other activities are steel-making, cement, ship repair, fishing; agriculture is constrained by terrain and climate and contributes less than 1% of GDP.

Government

A hereditary absolute monarchy; ruled by the Emir, assisted by a Council of Ministers and advised by an appointed Advisory Council. A constitution announced in 2004 will introduce a partially elected legislative council.

History

Under the suzerainty of Bahrain for most of the 19th century, Qatar was then ruled by the Ottoman Empire before becoming a British protectorate after the Turkish withdrawal in 1916. It declared its independence in 1971. Sheikh Khalifa bin Hamad al-Thani ruled from 1972 until 1995, when he was deposed by his son, Sheikh Hamad bin Khalifa al-Thani. The latter has introduced liberal reforms, including extending voting rights to women (1999) and announcing a new constitution (2004) that provides for a partially elected consultative council.

REPUBLIC OF CHINA ▸TAIWAN

ROMANIA

Official name	Romania
Local name	Romănia
Former name	Kingdom of Romania (until 1947), People's Republic of Romania (1947–65), Socialist Republic of Romania (1965–89); known as Rumania in English until 1966
Area	237 500 sq km (91 675 sq mi)
Capital	Bucharest; Bucureşti
Chief towns	Braşov, Constanţa, Iaşi, Timişoara, Cluj-Napoca
Population	22 303 000 (2006e)
Nationality	Romanian
Language	Romanian
Ethnic groups	Romanian 89%, Magyar 7%, Romany 2%, others 2%
Religions	Christianity 99% (Orthodox 87%, Prot 7%, RC 5%), Islam and others 1%
Time zone	GMT +2
Currency	1 New Leu (L, plural Lei) = 100 bani
Telephone	+40
Internet	.ro
Country code	ROU

Location

A republic in south-eastern Europe, bounded to the south by Bulgaria; to the west by Serbia and Hungary; to the east by Moldova and the Black Sea; and to the north and east by the Ukraine.

Physical description

The Carpathian Mountains separate Old Romania from Transylvania, and form the heart of the country; the Eastern Carpathians, between the northern frontier and the Prahova Valley, constitute an area of extensive forest cut by many passes; the higher Southern Carpathians are situated between the Prahova Valley and the Timis-Cerna gorges; the Western Carpathians lie between the River Danube and the River Somes; the highest peak is Mount Moldoveanu (2544 m/8349 ft); the Romanian Plain in the south includes the Baragan Plain (to the east), the richest arable area, and the Oltenian Plain (to the west), crossed by many rivers; there are c.3500 glacial ponds, lakes and coastal lagoons; over one-quarter of the land is forested.

Climate

Continental, with cold, snowy winters and hot, dry summers; the mildest area in winter is along the Black Sea coast; the plains of the north and east can suffer from drought; average annual rainfall is 1000 mm (in the mountains) and 400 mm (in the Danube delta).

Economy

Still in transition from planned to market economy; main industries are textiles and footwear, light machinery, vehicle assembly, mining (especially coal and iron ore), forestry, metals and metal products, chemicals, food processing, oil and gas extraction, oil refining, wine-making; agriculture contributes 13% of GDP but is largely at subsistence level and inefficient; chief crops are cereals, sugar beet, vegetables, sunflower seeds, fruit and livestock.

Government

Governed by a President, a Prime Minister and Cabinet, and a bicameral Parliament comprising a Senate and a Chamber of Deputies.

History

The Romanian people are descended from the Dacians, Romans, Vlachs, Slavs and the other settlers in Moldavia and Wallachia (modern Romania) who speak Romanian. While the culture of the Slav settlers came to dominate elsewhere in the north Balkans, the Romanians' ancestors assimilated to the Latin culture of the earlier Romanized inhabitants. Under the Ottoman Empire (between the 15th and 19th centuries), the Romanians began their movement for national independence in the 1820s, aspiring to the unification of Moldavia, Wallachia and Transylvania. In 1862 Moldavia and Wallachia merged to form the unitary Principality of Romania; a monarchy was created in 1866 and independence achieved in 1878. Romania joined the Allies in World War I, and acquired Transylvania, Bessarabia and Bukovina in the post-war settlement. Romania supported Germany in World War II and Soviet forces occupied the country in 1944. After the war it lost territories to Russia, Hungary and Bulgaria. The monarchy was abolished and a communist People's Republic established in 1947. Under the autocratic President Nicolae Ceauşescu, leader of the Romanian Communist Party from 1965, Romania became increasingly independent of the Union of Soviet Socialist Republics (USSR), forming relationships with China and several Western countries. In 1989 violent repression of protests, resulting in the deaths of thousands of demonstrators, sparked a popular uprising and the overthrow of the Ceauşescu regime; the president and his wife were executed. Although Romania became a multiparty democracy in 1991, governments were dominated by former communists until 1996 when Ion Iliescu was defeated in the presidential election by Emil Constantinescu. Iliescu was re-elected president in 2000 but lost the 2004 election to Traian Basescu. Romania joined NATO in 2004 and the European Union in 2007.

RUSSIA

Official name	Russian Federation
Local name	Rossiya; Rossiiskaya Federatsiya
Former name	Russian Empire (until 1917), Russian Republic (1917), Russian Socialist Federal Soviet Republic (until 1991), within the Union of Soviet Socialist Republics (USSR; 1922–91)
Area	17 075 400 sq km (6 591 104 sq mi)
Capital	Moscow; Moskva
Chief towns	St Petersburg, Nizhniy Novgorod, Rostov-on-Don, Volgograd, Yekaterinburg, Novosibirsk, Chelyabinsk, Kazan, Samara, Omsk
Population	142 893 000 (2006e)
Nationality	Russian
Languages	Russian; many minority languages are also spoken
Ethnic groups	Russian 80%, Tatar 4%, Ukrainian 2%, Bashkir 1%, Chuvash 1%, others 12%
Religions	Christianity 22% (Russian Orthodox 20%, other Christian 2%), Islam 15%, none/unaffiliated 63%
Time zone	GMT +2/12
Currency	1 Rouble (R) = 100 kopeks
Telephone	+7
Internet	.ru
Country code	RUS

Location

A republic occupying much of eastern Europe and northern Asia, bounded to the north by the Arctic Ocean; to the north-west by Norway, Finland, Estonia, Latvia, Belarus and Ukraine; to the west by the Black Sea, Georgia and Azerbaijan; to the south-west by the Caspian Sea and Kazakhstan; to the south-east by China, Mongolia and North Korea; and to the east by the Sea of Okhotsk and the Bering Sea. The Kaliningrad enclave borders Lithuania and Poland.

Physical description

Vast plains dominate the western half of the country; the Ural Mountains separate the East European Plain in the west from the West Siberian Lowlands in the east; the Central Siberian Plateau lies east of the River Yenisei; further east lies the North Siberian Plain; the Caucasus, Tien Shan and Pamir ranges lie along the southern frontier; the Lena, Ob, Severnaya Dvina, Pechora, Yenisey, Indigirka and Kolyma rivers flow to the Arctic Ocean; the Amur and Amgun rivers of the Kamchatka Peninsula flow to the Pacific Ocean; the Caspian Sea basin includes the Volga and Ural rivers; there are more than 20 000 lakes, the largest being the Caspian Sea, Lake Taymyr and Lake Baikal, the highest point is Mount Elbrus (5642 m/18 510 ft).

Climate

There are several different climate regions; variable weather in the north and the centre; throughout the country, winters are cold, with temperatures increasingly severe in the east and north, and summers are hot in the south and warm elsewhere; the average temperature in Moscow is 9°C in January and 18°C in July; average annual rainfall is 630mm; Siberia has a continental climate, with very cold and prolonged winters, and short, often warm summers.

Economy

Post-Communist transition from a planned to a market economy partially reversed by renationalization of key industries after 2000; main industries are oil, natural gas, forestry, mining (coal, iron ore, non-ferrous metals and gemstones) and metallurgy; machine-building (including aircraft, space vehicles and defence, transport, communications, agricultural and construction equipment), shipbuilding, power generation and transmission equipment, medical and scientific instruments, consumer durables, textiles, food processing; agricultural production reflects the highly varied terrain and climate, including cereals, cotton, vines, tobacco and stock-breeding.

Government

Governed by a President, a Prime Minister and Council of Ministers, and a bicameral Federal Assembly consisting of the Council of the Federation and the State (*Duma*). The regime has become increasingly authoritarian and centralized since 2000.

History

Russia was settled by many ethnic groups, initially Slavs, Turks and Bulgars (between the 3rd and 7th centuries ad). In the 13th century it came under the overlordship of the Mongols. Moscow was established as a centre of political power in the north during the 14th century; the grand duchy of Moscovy threw off Mongol overlordship, beginning a process of unification and expansion. Internal disorder and constant warfare with neighbouring countries (eg Poland and Sweden) retarded Russian development until the reign of Tsar Peter I, the Great. Under Catherine II, the Great, Russia became a great power, extending its territory into southern and eastern Asia. Defeat in the Russo-Japanese War (1904–5) precipitated a revolution that, although unsuccessful, brought Russia's first constitution and parliament. The Russian Revolution in 1917 later ended the monarchy. Within the communist Union of Soviet Socialist Republics (USSR, formed in 1920), Russia was the dominant political force. It covered 75 per cent of the Soviet area and contained 50 per cent of its population. With the disbandment of the Union in 1991, Russia became an independent republic and assumed the Soviet Union's permanent seat on the UN Security Council. It also became a founding member of the Commonwealth of Independent States (CIS). Relations with some former Soviet republics deteriorated in the early 1990s, and the process of transition to a market economy caused a severe economic crisis in 1993. Boris Yeltsin was succeeded in 2000 by Vladimir Putin, whose presidency has seen increasing centralization, the re-assertion of state control over the media and parts of the economy, and a more authoritarian attitude towards democratic processes. The federal government's authority has been challenged by separatist movements in some constituent republics. Chechnya's assertion of independence has led to two wars, in 1994–6 and since 1999; direct rule from Moscow was imposed in 2000.

THE MUSIC AND LITERATURE OF NINETEENTH-CENTURY RUSSIA

The 19th century was a time of great change for Russia and its citizens. The Napoleonic invasion of Russia, the abolition of serfdom and the spread of revolutionary thinking were all taken as themes by the great writers and composers of the time.

Nineteenth-century Russian literature

Aleksandr Pushkin (1799–1837) is seen as the founder of Russian literature in the vernacular. His *Ruslan and Lyudmila* (1820) is a long romantic poem based on Russian folklore; in *Eugene Onegin* (1823–31) he created a novel in verse form that inspired writers and composers. His liberal views led to his exile and house arrest; publication of his drama *Boris Godunov* (1825) was delayed by the authorities for several years.

Nikolai Gogol (1809–52), another writer who fell foul of the authorities, was widely recognized for his unfinished novel *Dead Souls* (1842), a satirical exposition of serfdom. His play *The Government Inspector* (1836), another satire, describes the immense corruption in tsarist Russia.

The 1860s were a particularly productive time. The novelist Ivan Turgenev (1818–83) wrote his most important work, *Fathers and Sons*, in 1862, describing the growing divide between traditionalists and modern thinkers. The epic *War and Peace* (1863–9) by Leo Tolstoy (1828–1910) depicts the lives of two aristocratic families against the backdrop of the Napoleonic invasion; Tolstoy's criticism of aristocratic society in general can be seen in *Anna Karenina* (1874–6). In *Crime and Punishment* (1866) by Fyodor Dostoevsky (1821–81) the protagonist Raskolnikov commits murder to escape poverty, and is haunted by the consequences; the question of whether the end can justify the means in such crimes was as relevant for Russian revolutionaries of the time as it is today.

The end of the 19th century saw the publication of four renowned plays by Anton Chekhov (1860–1904). His last, *The Cherry Orchard* (1904), addresses the changes faced by the upper and lower classes in adjusting to life after the abolition of serfdom in 1861. Chekhov's short stories are also acclaimed.

Russian nationalist music

In 1812 Napoleon led a French invasion of Russia, the swift defeat of which fuelled the fires of nationalism. The composer Mikhail Glinka (1804–57) is regarded as the founder of this trend within music. His two major works were the operas *A Life for the Tsar* (1836) and *Ruslan and Lyudmila* (1842); the latter was based on Pushkin's poem.

Glinka strongly influenced a group of composers, nicknamed The Five or The Mighty Handful, who advocated nationalist feelings in their work: Aleksandr Borodin (1833–87), Modest Mussorgsky (1839–81), Nikolai Rimsky-Korsakov (1844–1908), César Cui (1835–1918) and their leader Mily Balakirev (1837–1910). They worked closely together: Rimsky-Korsakov completed the opera *Prince Igor* that Borodin had started in 1869 and he also re-orchestrated Mussorgsky's opera *Boris Godunov* (the libretto of which was based on Pushkin's play).

The foremost composer of the age, however, was Pyotr Tchaikovsky (1840–93). One of his most popular and recognizable pieces of music is the 70th-anniversary celebration of the Russian defeat of Napoleon, *The 1812 Overture*.

RWANDA

Official name	Republic of Rwanda
Local name	Rwanda; République Rwandaise, Republika y'u Rwanda
Former name	Ruanda, as part of Ruanda-Urundi (with Burundi, until 1962)
Area	26 338 sq km (10 166 sq mi)
Capital	Kigali
Chief towns	Butare, Ruhengeri
Population	8 648 000 (2006e)
Nationality	Rwandan
Languages	English, French, Kinyarwanda; Swahili is widely used in commerce
Ethnic groups	Hutu 84%, Tutsi 15%, Twa 1%
Religions	Christianity 82% (RC 56%, Prot 26%), Islam 5%, traditional beliefs and others 13%
Time zone	GMT +2
Currency	1 Rwanda Franc (RF, RWFr) = 100 centimes
Telephone	+250
Internet	.rw
Country code	RWA

Location

A landlocked republic in central Africa, bounded to the north by Uganda; to the east by Tanzania; to the south by Burundi; and to the west by the Democratic Republic of the Congo and Lake Kivu.

Physical description

The country is situated at a relatively high altitude, the highest point being Karisimbi volcano (4507 m/14 787 ft) in the Virunga range; the western third of the country drains into Lake Kivu and then the River Congo, the remainder drains towards the River Nile; there are many lakes.

Climate

Tropical highland climate; two wet seasons (October–December and March–May), with the highest rainfall in the west, decreasing in the central uplands and to the north and east; the average annual rainfall at Kigali is 1000 mm.

Economy

Poor country, dependent on international aid; agriculture, mostly at subsistence level, engages c.90% of the population; chief cash crops are coffee, tea and livestock products; small-scale industries include mining (coltan, cassiterite and tin), processing of agricultural products, light manufacturing and small-scale tourism.

Government

Governed by a President, a Prime Minister and Council of Ministers, and a bicameral Parliament consisting of a Chamber of Deputies and a Senate.

History

The Hutu peoples who settled the country came under the dominance of Tutsi peoples, who migrated into the area and established a monarchy in the 15th century. The country became a German protectorate in 1899, and was mandated with Burundi to Belgium as the Territory of Ruanda–Urundi after World War I. It became a UN Trust Territory administered by Belgium after World War II. Unrest in 1959 led to a Hutu revolt and the overthrow of Tutsi rule, and in 1962 the union with Burundi was broken when both nations gained independence. A military coup took place in 1973, and there was a gradual return to stability under the new Hutu president Juvénal Habyarimana, whose party, the National Revolutionary Movement for Development (MRND), was the only legal party until 1991. Successive incursions by Tutsi rebels from the 1960s onwards were defeated by the army until 1990, when the advance of the Rwandan Patriotic Front (FPR) forced the government to negotiate a power-sharing accord, signed in 1993. Ethnic unrest continued unabated during this period, and was exacerbated by massacres of Tutsis by the Hutu-dominated army. President Habyarimana's death in an air crash in 1994 reignited ethnic conflict, resulting in the loss of around 800 000 lives in three months (often in large-scale massacres of Tutsis and moderate Hutus by the army and Hutu militias) until the killing was ended by the FPR, which established its control over the whole country and set up a multi-ethnic government of national unity. Hundreds of thousands of refugees fled to Burundi and Tanzania to escape either the massacres or the FPR advance; most of the refugees were repatriated in the late 1990s. Since 1994, political reforms and reconciliation measures have been introduced in an effort to stabilize the country, although areas bordering the Democratic Republic of the Congo experienced great suffering and tension in 1998–2002 because of the Rwandan army's involvement in the civil war there.

ST HELENA ▸UNITED KINGDOM

ST KITTS AND NEVIS

Official name	Federation of St Kitts and Nevis; also known as St Christopher and Nevis
Local name	St Kitts and Nevis
Area	269 sq km (104 sq mi)
Capital	Basseterre
Population	39 100 (2006e)
Nationality	Kittitian, Nevisian
Language	English
Ethnic groups	black 93%, Mulatto 4%, white 1%, others 2%
Religions	Christianity 75% (Prot 50%, RC 25%), others 25%
Time zone	GMT −4
Currency	1 East Caribbean Dollar (EC$) = 100 cents
Telephone	+1 869
Internet	.kn
Country code	KNA

Location

An independent state in the North Leeward Islands in the eastern Caribbean Sea. It comprises the islands of St Christopher (St Kitts), Nevis and Sombrero.

Physical description

St Kitts is 37 km (23 mi) long and has an area of 168 sq km (65 sq mi); a mountain range rises to 1156 m (3793 ft) at Mount Liamuiga; Nevis, 3 km (2 mi) south-east, has an area of 93 sq km (36 sq mi) and is dominated by a central peak rising to 985 m (3232 ft).

Climate

Tropical, influenced by the north-east trade winds; warm, with an average annual temperature of 26°C and an average annual rainfall of 1375 mm; low humidity; subject to hurricanes.

Economy

The sugar industry, historically the economic mainstay, closed down in 2005 as unviable; current main activities are tourism, offshore financial services and light manufacturing (distilling, food processing, garments and electronics); Nevis is developing a sea-cotton industry.

Government

Governed by a Governor-General (representing the British monarch, who is head of state), a Prime Minister and Cabinet, and a unicameral National Assembly.

History

Originally inhabited by Caribs, the islands were visited by Christopher Columbus in 1493, who named the larger one Saint Christopher. The name was shortened to St Kitts by English settlers in 1623 when the island became the first British colony in the West Indies. Control was disputed between France and Britain in the 17th and 18th centuries, and the island was ceded to Britain in 1783. St Kitts and Nevis were united in 1882, along with Anguilla (which became a separate British dependency in 1980). They became internally self-governing in 1967 and gained independence in 1983. In 1997 the government of Nevis voted to secede from St Kitts but in 1998 a referendum on the issue failed to secure the necessary two-thirds majority.

Mount Misery

Mount Liamuiga on St Kitts is a dormant volcano and is named after the original Carib name for the whole island. In the Carib language, *liamuiga* means 'fertile land' – a reference to the island's rich volcanic soil. However, the mountain has not always had such a positive image; it was originally called Mount Misery, and was only awarded its new title when St Kitts and Nevis gained independence in 1983.

ST LUCIA

Official name	St Lucia
Local name	St Lucia
Area	616 sq km (238 sq mi)
Capital	Castries
Chief towns	Vieux Fort, Soufrière
Population	168 000 (2006e)
Nationality	St Lucian
Languages	English; French patois is also spoken
Ethnic groups	black 90%, mixed 6%, East Indian 3%, white 1%
Religions	Christianity 82% (RC 67%, Prot 10%, other Christian 5%), Rastafarian 2%, other 10%, none/unaffiliated 6%
Time zone	GMT −4
Currency	1 East Caribbean Dollar (EC$) = 100 cents
Telephone	+1 758
Internet	.lc
Country code	LCA

Location

An independent constitutional monarchy and the second-largest of the Windward Islands, situated in the eastern Caribbean Sea.

Physical description

The island is 43 km (27 mi) long and 23 km (14 mi) wide; mountainous centre, rising to 950 m (3117 ft) at Mount Gimie; twin volcanic peaks of Gros and Petit Piton rise steeply from the sea on the south-west coast of the island.

Climate

Tropical; annual temperatures range from 18 to 34°C; the wet season is June–December; average annual rainfall is 1500 mm on the north coast and 4000 mm in the interior.

Economy

Services (tourism and offshore financial services) form the largest sector of the economy; other activities include agriculture (bananas, cocoa, vegetables, fruit and coconuts), light manufacturing (garments, beverages, corrugated cardboard boxes and food processing) and assembling electronic components.

Government

Governed by a Governor-General (representing the British monarch, who is head of state), a Prime Minister and Cabinet, and a bicameral Parliament consisting of a House of Assembly and a Senate.

History

Originally inhabited by Arawak Indians who were displaced by Caribs, the island was reputedly sighted by Christopher Columbus in 1502. It was settled by the French in the 17th century, but ownership was disputed between Britain and France from 1659 until it was ceded to Britain in 1814. It became internally self-governing in 1967 and gained independence in 1979.

ST PIERRE AND MIQUELON ▸FRANCE

ST VINCENT AND THE GRENADINES

Official name	St Vincent and the Grenadines
Local name	St Vincent and the Grenadines
Area	390 sq km (150 sq mi)
Capital	Kingstown
Population	118 000 (2006e)
Nationality	St Vincentian or Vincentian
Languages	English; French patois is also spoken
Ethnic groups	black 66%, mixed 19%, East Indian 6%, Carib Amerindian 2%, others 7%
Religions	Christianity 88% (Prot 75%, RC 13%), others 12%
Time zone	GMT −4
Currency	1 East Caribbean Dollar (EC$) = 100 cents
Telephone	+1 784
Internet	.vc
Country code	VCT

Location

An independent state in the Windward Islands, situated in the eastern Caribbean Sea.

Physical description

Comprises the island of St Vincent (length 29 km/18 mi; width 16 km/10 mi) and the northern Grenadine Islands; St Vincent is volcanic in origin and hilly; the highest peak is Soufrière, an active volcano rising to a height of 1234 m (4049 ft).

Climate

Tropical, with an average annual temperature of 25°C, and an average annual rainfall of 1500 mm.

Economy

Based on services (tourism and offshore financial services), manufacturing (food processing, furniture, garments and starch) and agriculture (bananas, arrowroot (world's largest producer) and coconuts).

Government

Governed by a Governor-General (representing the British monarch, who is head of state), a Prime Minister and Cabinet, and a unicameral House of Assembly.

History

St Vincent was visited by Christopher Columbus in 1498. The first European settlement was in 1762 by British settlers, who were resisted by the native Caribs and the French but defeated both. Most of the Caribs were deported in 1797 following an uprising, and black Africans were imported as slave labour. St Vincent and the Grenadines was part of the Windward Islands Colony (1880–1958) and then joined the West Indies Federation in 1958–62. It became internally self-governing in 1969, and gained its independence in 1979.

SAMOA

Official name	Independent State of Samoa
Local name	Samoa; 'O la Malo Tu To'atasi o Samoa
Former name	Western Samoa (until 1997)
Area	2842 sq km (1097 sq mi)
Capital	Apia
Population	177 000 (2006e)
Nationality	Samoan
Languages	Samoan, English
Ethnic groups	Samoan 93%, mixed 6%, European 1%
Religions	Christianity 81% (Prot 57%, RC 20%, other Christian 4%), others 19%
Time zone	GMT −11
Currency	1 Tala (ST$) = 100 sene
Telephone	+685
Internet	.ws
Country code	WSM

Location

An island nation in the south-west Pacific Ocean, 2600 km (1600 mi) north-east of Auckland, New Zealand.

Physical description

The islands are formed from ranges of extinct volcanoes, rising to 1829 m (6000 ft) on Savai'i; many dormant volcanoes; highest point is Mount Silisili (1857 m/6092 ft); thick tropical vegetation; several coral reefs.

Climate

Tropical; rainy season is November–April; average annual temperatures are 22–30°C; average annual rainfall is 2775 mm; cyclones occur.

Economy

Poor country dependent on international aid, expatriates' remittances, fishing and largely subsistence agriculture; chief cash crops are fish, coconuts, copra, taro; diversifying into tourism, offshore financial services and light manufacturing (vehicle parts, garments and beer).

Government

Governed by an elected monarch as head of state, a Prime Minister and Cabinet, and a unicameral Legislative Assembly.

History

Inhabited since around 1000 BC, Samoa was visited by the Dutch in 1772; in 1889 it was divided between Germany (which acquired Western Samoa) and the USA (which acquired Tutuila and adjacent small islands, now known as American Samoa). After 1914 Western Samoa was administered by New Zealand, firstly under a League of Nations mandate from 1919 to 1946 and then as a UN Trust Territory, until it gained independence in 1962. Malietoa Tanumafili II became head of state for life in 1963. The legislative assembly voted to change the country's name to Samoa in 1997.

SAMOA, AMERICAN ▸ UNITED STATES OF AMERICA

SAN MARINO

Official name	Republic of San Marino
Local name	San Marino; Repubblica di San Marino
Area	61 sq km (24 sq mi)
Capital	San Marino
Chief town	Serravalle
Population	29 000 (2006e)
Nationality	Sammarinese
Language	Italian
Ethnic groups	Sammarinese 88%, Italian 11%, others 1%
Religions	Christianity 95% (RC), unaffiliated, others and none 5%
Time zone	GMT +1
Currency	1 Euro (€) = 100 cents
Telephone	+378
Internet	.sm
Country code	SMR

Location

A very small landlocked republic completely surrounded by central Italy, lying 12 mi (20 km) from the Adriatic Sea.

Physical description

Ruggedly mountainous, centred on the limestone ridges of Mount Titano (755 m/2477 ft) and the valley of the River Ausa.

Climate

Mediterranean climate modified by altitude, with cold, often snowy, winters and warm summers (20–30°C); rainfall is moderate, with an annual average of 880 mm.

Economy

Based on tourism (over 50% of GDP), sale of postage stamps and coins, agriculture (wine and cheeses), banking and manufacturing (garments, electronics and ceramics).

Government

Governed by two *capitani reggenti* ('Captains Regent') elected for six-month terms as joint heads of state, a Congress of State (cabinet) and the unicameral Great and General Council.

History

Reputedly founded in the 4th century by a Christian stonecutter as a refuge against religious persecution, its independence was recognized by the pope in 1631; in 1862 a treaty of friendship with Italy preserved San Marino's independence. The San Marino lira was replaced by the euro in 2002 as the official currency.

SÃO TOMÉ AND PRÍNCIPE

Official name	Democratic Republic of São Tomé e Príncipe
Local name	São Tomé e Príncipe; República Democrática de São Tomé e Príncipe
Area	1001 sq km (386 sq mi)
Capital	São Tomé
Chief town	Santo António
Population	193 000 (2006e)
Nationality	São Toméan
Language	Portuguese
Ethnic groups	black 90%, Portuguese and Creole 10%
Religions	Christianity 75% (RC 70%, Prot 5%), others 5%, none 19%
Time zone	GMT
Currency	1 Dobra (Db) = 100 centavos
Telephone	+239
Internet	.st
Country code	STP

Location

An equatorial island republic in the Gulf of Guinea, off the coast of west Africa.

Physical description

Volcanic, densely forested islands; São Tomé lies c.440 km (275 mi) off the north coast of Gabon, has an area of 860 sq km (332 sq mi) and reaches a height of 2024 m (6640 ft) at Pico de São Tomé; Príncipe, the smaller of the two islands, lies c.200 km (125 mi) off the north coast of Gabon, covers 140 sq km (54 sq mi) and has similar terrain.

Climate

Tropical; the average annual temperature is 27°C on the coast, 20°C in the mountains; there is a rainy season from October to May; the average annual rainfall varies from 500 mm to 1000 mm.

Economy

Poor country, dependent on international aid; economy based on agriculture (cocoa (95% of export earnings), copra, coffee and palm oil); diversifying into tourism and (from c.2010) offshore oil and gas production.

Government

Governed by a President, a Prime Minister and Cabinet, and a unicameral National Assembly.

History

The islands were discovered by the Portuguese between 1469 and 1472, and became a Portuguese colony in 1522. From 1641 to 1740 it was held by the Dutch, then was recovered by Portugal. It later became a port of call en route to the East Indies. Resistance to Portuguese rule led to riots in 1953, and the formation of a liberation movement based in Gabon. It gained independence in 1975, and was a one-party state until a new constitution was introduced in 1990 and multiparty elections were held in 1991. Príncipe was granted autonomy in 1995. Democracy has brought a degree of instability, with short-lived coups in 1995 and 2003, and tensions have been heightened recently by political disagreement over control of the expected revenues from the country's offshore oil reserves.

SAUDI ARABIA

Official name	Kingdom of Saudi Arabia
Local name	Al-Mamlaka al-'Arabiyya as-Sa'ūdiyyah
Area	2 331 000 sq km (899 766 sq mi)
Capital	Riyadh; Ar Riyād
Chief towns	Jeddah, Mecca, Medina, Ta'if, Ad Dammam, Abha
Population	27 020 000 (2006e)
Nationality	Saudi or Saudi Arabian
Language	Arabic
Ethnic groups	Arab 90%, Afro-Asian 10%
Religion	Islam 100% (Sunni 90%, Shia 10%); public practice of any religion other than Islam is forbidden
Time zone	GMT +3
Currency	1 Saudi Arabian Riyal (SR, SRIs) = 20 qursh = 100 halala
Telephone	+966
Internet	.sa
Country code	SAU

Location

An Arabic kingdom comprising about four-fifths of the Arabian Peninsula, bounded to the west by the Red Sea; to the north-west by Jordan; to the north by Iraq; to the north-east by Kuwait; to the east by the Arabian Gulf, Qatar and the United Arab Emirates; to the south-east and south by Oman; and to the south and south-west by Yemen.

Physical description

The Red Sea coastal plain is bounded to the east by mountains; the highlands in the south-west include Jabal Sawda', Saudi Arabia's highest peak (3133 m/10 278 ft); the Arabian Peninsula slopes gently northwards and eastwards towards the oil-rich Al Hasa plain on the Arabian Gulf; the interior comprises two extensive areas of sand desert, the Nafud in the north and the Great Sandy Desert in the south; the central Najd has some large oases; salt flats are numerous in the eastern lowlands; a large network of wadis drains north to east.

Climate

Hot and dry, with average temperatures varying from 21°C in the north, to 26°C in the south; day temperatures may rise to 50°C in the interior sand deserts; night frosts are common in the north and highlands; the Red Sea coast is hot and humid; average rainfall is low.

Economy

Prosperity based on oil (world's leading oil exporter and largest proven reserves) and gas; diversified since 1970s so non-oil sector now contributes 60% of GDP, through petrochemicals, financial services, construction, building materials, mining (gold, iron ore and copper) and metal fabrication, ship and aircraft repair, and services for the pilgrimage trade; agricultural productivity increased by irrigation, desalination and aquifers; main products are cereals, fruit, meat and dairy products.

Government

A hereditary absolute monarchy based on Islamic teachings and Arab Bedouin tradition; ruled by the King, assisted by a Council of Ministers and advised by an appointed Consultative Council. There are no political parties.

History

Saudi Arabia is famed as the birthplace of Islam and contains the holy cities of Mecca, Medina and Jedda. The modern state was founded by Saudi Arabia's first king, Ibn Saud. He was the leader of the fundamentalist Wahhabi sect, and by 1932 he had united the four tribal provinces of Hejaz, Asir, Najd and Al Hasa. The ruling family has preserved stability by suppressing dissent, and has resisted calls for greater democracy for many years, although it made limited concessions in 2005. Internal tension also grew in the 1990s because of the continuing presence of foreign, especially US, troops in the country after the 1991 Gulf War; these troops and other foreign nationals became terrorist targets. Despite redeployment of foreign troops to Qatar, attacks increased after the start of the war with Iraq in 2003 and include Saudi as well as foreign victims. Some dissident groups are believed to have links to al-Qaeda.

SENEGAL

Official name	Republic of Senegal
Local name	Sénégal; République du Sénégal
Former name	part of the Federation of Mali (1959–60); Senegambia (with The Gambia, 1982–9)
Area	196 840 sq km (75 980 sq mi)
Capital	Dakar
Chief towns	Thiès, Kaolack, St Louis, Ziguinchor
Population	11 987 000 (2006e)
Nationality	Senegalese
Languages	French, Wolof; several other local languages are spoken
Ethnic groups	Wolof 43%, Pular 24%, Serer 15%, Jola 4%, others 14%
Religions	Islam 94% (Sunni), Christianity 5% (mostly RC), traditional beliefs 1%
Time zone	GMT
Currency	1 CFA Franc (CFAFr) = 100 centimes
Telephone	+221
Internet	.sn
Country code	SEN

Location

A country in west Africa, bounded to the north by Mauritania; to the east by Mali; to the south by Guinea and Guinea-Bissau; and to the west by the Atlantic Ocean. It surrounds The Gambia on three sides.

Physical description

The most westerly country in mainland Africa; the coast is characterized by dunes, mangrove forests and mudbanks; an extensive low-lying basin of savanna and semi-desert vegetation lies to the north; seasonal streams drain to the River Sénégal; the south rises to c.500 m (1640 ft).

Climate

Tropical, with a rainy season between June and September; high humidity levels and high night-time temperatures, especially on the coast; rainfall decreases from the south (1000–1500 m) to the north (300–350 mm); the average annual rainfall at Dakar is 541 mm and the average temperature ranges from 22 to 28°C.

Economy

Poor country, dependent on international aid; agriculture and fishing employ c.60% of the workforce; main cash crops are fish, groundnuts and cotton; main industries are food and fish processing, phosphate mining, oil refining, production of fertilizer and construction materials, and tourism.

Government

Governed by an executive President, a Prime Minister and Council of Ministers, and a unicameral National Assembly.

History

Senegal was part of the Mali Empire in the 14th and 15th centuries. The French established a fort at Saint-Louis in 1659, and it was incorporated as a territory within French west Africa in 1902. It became an autonomous state in 1958, and joined with French Sudan as the independent Federation of Mali in June 1960, but withdrew in August to become a separate independent republic. It became a one-party state in 1966 and the Socialist Party dominated political life for 40 years until Abdoulaye Wade was elected president in 2000 and his Senegalese Democratic Party won the 2001 legislative election. In 1989 a violent dispute with neighbouring Mauritania developed into a virtual war; peace was restored in 1991–2. A separatist uprising led by the Movement of Democratic Forces of Casamance began in southern Senegal in 1993 and continued sporadically throughout the 1990s; a peace deal with the rebels was signed in 2004, although a rebel faction continues to fight.

SERBIA

Official name	Republic of Serbia
Local name	Srbija
Former name	Formerly part of Kingdom of Serbs, Croats and Slovenes (until 1929), Kingdom of Yugoslavia (1929–41), Federal Republic of Yugoslavia (1945–2003); Federal Republic of Serbia and Montenegro (2003–6)
Area	88 361 sq km (34 116 sq mi)
Capital	Belgrade; Beograd
Chief towns	Kragujevac, Nis, Novi Sad, Priština (in Kosovo), Subotica
Population	9 396 000 (2002)
Nationality	Serb, Serbian
Languages	Serbian; Romanian, Hungarian, Slovak, Ukrainian and Croatian are also spoken in Vojvodina, and Albanian in Kosovo
Ethnic groups	Serb 66%, Albanian 17%, Magyar 3%, others 14%
Religions	Christianity 83% (Orthodox 79%, RC 4%), Islam 5%, others 12%
Time zone	GMT +1
Currency	1 Dinar (D, Din) = 100 paras
Telephone	+381
Internet	.yu
Country code	YUG

Location

A republic in the Balkan Peninsula of south-eastern Europe, bounded to the south-west by Montenegro; to the west by Bosnia and Herzegovina and Croatia; to the north by Hungary; to the north-east by Romania; to the east by Bulgaria; and to the south by Macedonia and Albania; includes the province of Kosovo, which has been under UN administration since 1999.

Physical description

Dominated in the north by the Danube, Tisza and Sava rivers, with fertile plains in the north-east; drained in the centre by the River Morava; mountain ranges in the south are cut by deep river valleys; there are several great lakes in the south; highest point is Daravica (2656 m/8714 ft).

Climate

A Mediterranean climate on the Adriatic coast; a continental climate in the north and north-east; rain falls throughout the year; there is a colder upland climate, with winter snow.

Economy

Fragile recovery from 1990s war with Bosnia, insurgencies and economic sanctions; still requires international aid; economic mainstay is agriculture, which employs 30% of the workforce and produces cereals, sugar beet, sunflowers, meat and dairy products; industries include processing agricultural and forestry products (sugar, pulp and paper), machine building, mining (lead), metallurgy, manufacturing (consumer goods, electronics and pharmaceuticals), petroleum products and chemicals.

Government

Governed by a President, a Prime Minister and Council of Ministers, and the unicameral Assembly of Serbia.

History

The medieval kingdom of Serbia, originally a vassal state of the Byzantine Empire, grew to form a large and prosperous state in the Balkans until it fell to the Turks in 1389. It gained autonomy within the Ottoman Empire in 1815 and achieved independence in 1878, becoming a kingdom in 1881. After World War I Serbia joined with Montenegro and territories of the former Austro-Hungarian Empire to form the Kingdom of Serbs, Croats and Slovenes (renamed Yugoslavia in 1929), which was united under the Serbian monarch, Peter I. Yugoslavia was occupied by Axis forces in 1941 and re-established in 1945 as the communist Federal People's Republic (comprising Croatia, Slovenia, Bosnia and Herzegovina, Macedonia, Montenegro and Serbia) under President Josip Tito. After Tito's death in 1980, nationalisms resurfaced; the federation eventually disintegrated when Croatia and Slovenia seceded in 1991 and Bosnia and Herzegovina and Macedonia followed in 1992. Serbia and Montenegro remained as the Federal Republic of Yugoslavia, which was declared on 27 April 1992. Slobodan Milosevic, president of Serbia from 1989, became president of Yugoslavia in 1997. In 1999, Serbian violence in suppressing secessionism in Kosovo, and the ethnic cleansing of the province's Albanian population, led to the bombing of Serbia by NATO between March and June. Milosevic was indicted by the UN war crimes tribunal during the conflict for his part in the atrocities carried out in the province; his trial at the Hague tribunal began in 2002 and ended with his death in 2006. Kosovo is now a UN-administered autonomous province within Serbia, with its own parliament and the euro as its currency. Milosevic was defeated in the 2000 presidential election by Vojislav Kostunica. The federation was restructured in 2003 into a looser union of the two republics, called Serbia and Montenegro. In June 2006, the union was dissolved following Montenegro's vote in favour of independence, and Serbia succeeded to the union's membership of international bodies.

SEYCHELLES

Official name	Republic of Seychelles
Local name	Seychelles; République des Seychelles (French); Repiblik Sesel (Creole)
Area	453 sq km (175 sq mi)
Capital	Victoria
Population	81 500 (2006e)
Nationality	Seychellois
Languages	Creole; English is also spoken
Ethnic groups	Mulatto 94%, Malagasy 3%, Chinese 2%, English 1%
Religions	Christianity 92% (RC 82%, Prot and other Christian 10%), Hinduism 2%, Islam 1%, others 5%
Time zone	GMT +4
Currency	1 Seychelles Rupee (SR) = 100 cents
Telephone	+248
Internet	.sc
Country code	SYC

Location

An island group in the south-west Indian Ocean, north of Madagascar, comprising 115 islands.

Physical description

The islands fall into two main groups: the first, a compact group of 41 steep granitic islands, are mountainous, rising to 906 m (2969 ft) at Morne Seychellois on Mahé; the steep forest-clad slopes drop down to coastal lowlands with a vegetation of grass and dense scrub; the second is a group of low-lying coralline islands and atolls which are situated to the south-west.

Climate

Tropical, with a rainfall that varies with altitude and is higher on the southern sides of the islands; the wettest months are November to March; rarely affected by tropical storms.

Economy

Developing country; economy based on tourism and fishing; diversified into agriculture (coconuts and cinnamon), manufacturing (processing fish and agricultural products, consumer goods).

overnment

overned by an executive President, a Council of Ministers and a unicameral National ssembly.

story

e islands were visited by Vasco da Gama in 1502, and colonized by the French 1768. The population is largely descended from 18th-century French colonists d their freed African slaves. Captured by Britain in 1794, it was incorporated as dependency of Mauritius in 1814 and became a separate British Crown Colony 1903. It became an independent republic in 1976. Following a coup in 1977, it came a one-party state under President France-Albert René. Opposition parties ve been permitted since 1991, however, and multiparty elections have been held nce 1993. The Seychelles People's Progressive Front has remained the ruling party t opposition parties are increasing their share of the vote in elections. President né retired in 2004 and was replaced by Vice-President James Michel, who was ected president in 2006. Widespread damage was caused by the Indian Ocean unami in 2004.

Sea Coconut

The Seychellois islands of Praslin and Curieuse are home to the palm tree *Lodoicea seychellarum*, commonly known as the coco-de-mer or 'sea coconut'. The coconuts from these palms are the largest seeds in the world; their diameter can be as large as 50 cm (20 in) and they can weigh up to 25 kg (50 lb). Their common name stems from the fact that sailors first saw the nuts floating in the sea; it was many years before the parent plants were discovered.

The coco-de mer is also known as the double coconut, as it has a distinctive two-lobed appearance. Sailors who saw the floating coconuts likened their appearance to that of a woman's buttocks. This piece of imagery gave rise to the species' early botanical name *Lodoicea callipyge*: the term 'callipygous' means 'beautiful buttocks'.

SIERRA LEONE

Official name	Republic of Sierra Leone
Local name	Sierra Leone
Area	72 325 sq km (27 917 sq mi)
Capital	Freetown
Chief towns	Bo, Sefadu, Makeni, Kenema, Lunsar
Population	6 005 000 (2006e)
Nationality	Sierra Leonean
Languages	English, Mende, Temne; Krio (a Creole language) is also widely spoken
Ethnic groups	African 90% (20 ethnic groups, including Mende 30%, Temne 30%), others 10%
Religions	Islam 60% (Sunni), traditional beliefs 30%, Christianity 10%
Time zone	GMT
Currency	1 Leone (Le) = 100 cents
Telephone	+232
Internet	.sl
Country code	SLE

Location

A coastal republic in west Africa, bounded to the north by Guinea; to the south-east by Liberia; and to the south and south-west by the Atlantic Ocean.

Physical description

A low narrow coastal plain with mangrove swamps and beaches; behind this is low-lying wooded land, rising in the west to an average height of 500 m (1640 ft) in the Loma Mountains; the highest point is Loma Mansa (also called Bintimani; 1948 m/6391 ft); the Tingi Mountains in the south-east rise to 1853 m/6079 ft.

Climate

Tropical, with a rainy season from May to November; the highest rainfall is on the coast; temperatures are uniformly high throughout the year, c.27°C; the average annual rainfall at Freetown is 3436 mm.

Economy

Very poor country, dependent on international aid; slow recovery from civil war; main activities are mining (diamonds, rutile), agriculture, which is mostly at subsistence level but through cash crops (coffee and cocoa) provides c.50% of GDP, fishing, oil refining, ship repair, processing agricultural products and light manufacturing.

Government

Governed by an executive President, a Cabinet and a unicameral Parliament.

History

he area was visited by Portuguese navigators in the 15th century and British
lave traders in the 16th and 17th centuries. In the 1780s coastal land was bought
om local chiefs by English philanthropists who established settlements, including
reetown, for freed slaves. Sierra Leone became a British Crown Colony in 1808,
nd the hinterland was declared a British protectorate in 1896. The country gained
ndependence in 1961 and became a republic in 1971 under the one-party regime
f President Siaka Stevens, who retired in 1985 and was succeeded as president
y Joseph Momoh. Transition to multiparty democracy under a new constitution
dopted in 1991 was aborted by a military coup in 1992 led by Captain Valentine
trasser. The country returned to civilian rule in 1996 but the government was ousted
y another coup in 1997, although it was restored to power the following year with
he help of a Nigerian-led coalition of west African forces. The return to multiparty
nd civilian rule was complicated by a civil war that had begun in 1991. A 1999 peace
ccord could not be implemented at first, as the ceasefire collapsed in 2000 despite
he presence of UN peacekeeping forces, who were drawn into the fighting. A 2001
easefire was more effective and disarmament of rebel forces was completed by
004. President Ahmad Kabbah, first elected in 1996, was re-elected in 2002, and
rogress began towards restoring stability to the country. A war crimes tribunal was
et up in 2004.

SINGAPORE

Official name	Republic of Singapore
Local name	Singapore; Repablik Singapura (Malay), Singapur Kuṭiyara'su (Tamil), Xinjiapo Gongheguo (Chinese)
Former name	Part of Straits Settlement (until 1942), State of Singapore (1959–63), part of the Federation of Malaysia (1963–5)
Area	647 sq km (250 sq mi)
Capital	Singapore; Singapura (Malay), Singapur (Tamil), Xinjiapo (Chinese)
Population	4 492 000 (2006e)
Nationality	Singaporean
Languages	English, Chinese (Mandarin), Tamil, Malay; other Chinese dialects are also spoken
Ethnic groups	Chinese 77%, Malay 14%, Indian 8%, others 1%
Religions	Buddhism 42%, Islam 15%, Christianity 15% (RC 5%, other Christian 10%), Taoism 9%, Hinduism 4%, none/unaffiliated 15%
Time zone	GMT +8
Currency	1 Singapore Dollar (S$) = 1 Ringgit = 100 cents
Telephone	+65
Internet	.sg
Country code	SGP

Location

A republic at the southern tip of the Malay Peninsula, in South-East Asia. It consists of the island of Singapore (linked to Malaysia by a causeway) and about 50 adjacent islets.

Physical description

The highest point of low-lying Singapore Island is at Bukit Timah (177 m/581 ft); the island measures c.42 km (26 mi) by 22 km (14 mi) at its widest; an important deep-water harbour lies to the south-east.

Climate

Equatorial, with high humidity, an average annual rainfall of 2438 mm, and a daily temperature range from 21 to 34°C.

Economy

Highly industrialized and diverse economy based on the service sector (entrepôt trade, banking, financial and business services, tourism, retail and consumer services); major transhipment centre; main industries are manufacturing (electronics, engineering, biomedical sciences, chemicals), oil refining, rubber processing, food processing and ship repair.

Government

Governed by a President, a Prime Minister and Cabinet, and a unicameral Parliament. The People's Action Party has dominated politics since 1959.

History

Originally part of the Sumatran Sri Vijaya kingdom, in 1819 it was leased by the British East India Company from the Sultan of Johore. Singapore, Malacca and Penang were incorporated as the Straits Settlements in 1826; they became a British Crown Colony in 1867, and were occupied by the Japanese during World War II. Self-governing from 1959, Singapore was part of the Federation of Malaya from 1963 until it withdrew and became an independent republic in 1965. Although Singapore is a multiparty state, the People's Action Party (PAP) has dominated political life since 1959; opposition candidates were elected for the first time in 1984. The PAP leader Lee Kuan Yew was prime minister from 1959 until he retired in 1990. His son Lee Hsien Loong became prime minister in 2004.

> **"**
>
> *In Singapore you don't volunteer to go into politics – you are invited to enter.*
>
> — Singaporean politician Lee Hsien Loong (b.1952), 1984. (Quoted in *Goh Tok Chong* by Alan Chong, 1991.)
>
> **"**

LOVAKIA

Official name	Republic of Slovakia or the Slovak Republic
Local name	Slovensko; Slovenská Republika
Former name	formerly part of Czechoslovakia (until 1993)
Area	49 035 sq km (18 927 sq mi)
Capital	Bratislava
Chief towns	Košice, Banská Bystrica, Prešov
Population	5 439 000 (2006e)
Nationality	Slovak
Language	Slovak
Ethnic groups	Slovak 86%, Magyar 10%, Romany 2%, others 2%
Religions	Christianity 84% (RC 69%, Prot 11%, Orthodox 4%), other/unaffiliated 3%, none 13%
Time zone	GMT +1
Currency	1 Slovak Koruna (Sk) = 100 halierov
Telephone	+421
Internet	.sk
Country code	SVK

Location

landlocked republic in eastern Europe, bounded to the north by Poland; to the east by Ukraine; to the south by Hungary; to the south-west by Austria; and to the west by the Czech Republic.

Physical description

owlands in the south; Tatra Mountains in the north rise to 2655 m (8710 ft) at erlachovsky Stit.

Climate

ontinental; hot in summer, cold in winter.

Economy

ndustrialized and diverse economy; completing transition to market economy; main activities are mining (coal, iron ore, metals and minerals) and metal products, griculture (cereals, sugar beet, hops, fruit and livestock), beverages (wine and beer), uels and energy (natural gas, coke, oil and nuclear), chemicals, synthetic fibres, machinery, paper, printing, ceramics, transport vehicles; textiles, electrical and optical quipment and rubber products.

Government

overned by a President, a Prime Minister and Cabinet, and a unicameral National ouncil.

History

The area formed part of Great Moravia in the 9th century, belonged to the Magyar Empire from the 10th century, and came under Habsburg rule from the 16th century. A Slovak national movement gradually grew during the 19th century and broke away from Hungarian rule when the Austro-Hungarian Empire collapsed after World War I. Slovakia became a province of Czechoslovakia in 1918, but many Slovaks objected to the centralized nature of the state established in 1918 and the greater prosperity of the Czech lands. In 1939, on Hitler's instructions, a supposedly independent republic under German protection was carved out of Czechoslovakia. After liberation by Soviet forces in 1945, Slovakia was returned to Czechoslovakia, where a communist regime assumed power in 1948. Little was done by the communists to meet Slovak aspirations, but nationalist demands intensified again with the collapse of communism in 1989; the federation was dissolved into two separate states, with Slovakia becoming an independent republic in January 1993. The Movement for a Democratic Slovakia dominated the coalition governments of the early 1990s, but a centre-right coalition came to power in 1998 and was re-elected in 2002. The coalition introduced the constitutional and economic reforms required for NATO and European Union membership; Slovakia joined both in 2004.

SLOVENIA

Official name	Republic of Slovenia
Local name	Slovenija; Republika Slovenija
Former name	formerly part of Kingdom of Serbs, Croats and Slovenes (until 1929), Kingdom of Yugoslavia (1929–41), Federal People's Republic of Yugoslavia (1945–63), Socialist Federal People's Republic of Yugoslavia (1963–91)
Area	20251 sq km (7817 sq mi)
Capital	Ljubljana
Chief towns	Maribor, Kranj, Celje, Koper
Population	2010000 (2006e)
Nationality	Slovene, Slovenian
Language	Slovene
Ethnic groups	Slovene 83%, Serb 2%, Croat 2%, Bosniak 1%, others 12%
Religions	Christianity 61% (RC 58%, Orthodox 2%, other Christian 1%), Islam 2%, others 23%, none/unaffiliated 14%
Time zone	GMT +1
Currency	1 Euro (€) = 100 cents
Telephone	+386
Internet	.si
Country code	SVN

Location

A mountainous republic in central Europe, bounded to the north by Austria; to the west by Italy; to the south by Croatia; to the east by Hungary; and with a short coastline on the Adriatic Sea.

Physical description

The land is mountainous, with Mount Triglav (2864 m/9396 ft) as its highest point; it drops down towards the Adriatic coastline and the valleys of the chief rivers, the Sava and Drava; over 50% is forested.

Climate

Continental, with hot summers and cold winters, in the plateaux and valleys in the east; Mediterranean climate on the Adriatic coast.

Economy

Smooth transition to market economy in 1990s, though much still in state ownership; main industries are mining (coal, iron ore, lead and zinc), metal processing, electronic and optical equipment, vehicles, electric power equipment, forestry and timber processing, textiles, chemicals, rubber, plastics, machinery production, tourism; agriculture produces potatoes, hops, cereals, sugar beet and grapes.

Government

Governed by a President, a Prime Minister and Cabinet, and a unicameral National Assembly. A National Council has an advisory role.

History

Settled by Slovenians in the 6th century, it was later controlled by Slavs and Franks. It was part of the Austro-Hungarian Empire until 1918 when it joined with Croatia, Montenegro, Serbia, and Bosnia and Herzegovina to form the Kingdom of Serbs, Croats and Slovenes. This was renamed Yugoslavia in 1929 and became a communist republic after World War II. In July 1991, President Milan Kucan declared Slovenia's independence from the Yugoslav Federation. The Yugoslav National Army intervened, leading to the so-called 'Ten-Day War' with Slovenian forces, but the federal forces withdrew under an European Union-brokered ceasefire. Elections in 1992 saw Milan Kucan re-elected as president, an office he held until 2002. All the governments since 1991 have been coalitions; the Liberal Democracy of Slovenia party was the major party in every coalition from 1991 until 2004. Slovenia joined the European Union and NATO in 2004, and in 2007 replaced the tolar with the euro.

Europe's Oldest Musical Instrument

In 1980, archaeologists excavating the palaeolithic cave site Divje Babe I in north-western Slovenia uncovered the bone of a cave bear with four artificial holes in it. Radiocarbon dating and comparison with similar artefacts suggest that this may be the oldest musical instrument in Europe – it was probably made by Neanderthals around 43,000 years ago.

SOLOMON ISLANDS

Official name	Solomon Islands
Local name	Solomon Islands
Former name	British Solomon Islands (until 1975)
Area	27 556 sq km (10 637 sq mi)
Capital	Honiara
Chief towns	Gizo, Auki, Kirakira
Population	552 400 (2006e)
Nationality	Solomon Islander
Languages	English; Melanesian pidgin and 90 local languages are also spoken
Ethnic groups	Melanesian 94%, Polynesian 3%, Micronesian 1%, others 2%
Religions	Christianity 97% (Prot 62%, RC 19%, others 16%), others 3%
Time zone	GMT +11
Currency	1 Solomon Islands Dollar (SI$) = 100 cents
Telephone	+677
Internet	.sb
Country code	SLB

Location

An independent country consisting of an archipelago of 400 islands in the south-west Pacific Ocean; the six main islands are Choiseul, Guadalcanal, Malaita, New Georgia, Makira and Santa Isabel.

Physical description

The six larger islands (Choiseul, Guadalcanal, Malaita, New Georgia, Makira and Santa Isabel) have densely forested mountain ranges of mainly volcanic origin, deep, narrow valleys, and coastal belts lined with coconut palms; they are ringed by reefs; the highest point is Mount Makarakomburu (2477 m/8127 ft) on Guadalcanal.

Climate

Equatorial; average temperature is 27°C; high humidity; rainfall averages c.3500 mm per year.

Economy

Poor country, dependent on international aid; still recovering from ethnic unrest and lawlessness (1998–2003); agriculture, mainly at subsistence level, provides over 40% of GDP; main activities are forestry, fishing, mining (gold production currently suspended), production of copra and palm oil.

Government

Governed by a Governor-General (representing the British monarch, who is head of state), a Prime Minister and Cabinet, and a unicameral National Parliament.

History

Inhabited since 1500 BC or earlier, the islands were discovered by the Spanish in 1568. The southern Solomon Islands were placed under British protection in 1893, and the outer islands were added to the protectorate in 1899. The islands were captured by the Japanese in 1942 and recaptured by US forces in 1943 after fierce fighting, especially on the island of Guadalcanal. The islands gained their independence in 1978. Tension between different ethnic groups on Guadalcanal in the late 1990s led to conflict between two rival militias from 1998 and an attempted coup in 2000. A fragile peace was brokered in 2000 but worsening economic and social problems in 2002 led to growing lawlessness. In mid-2003 the government requested assistance from neighbouring countries; order was restored and the militias disarmed.

SOMALIA

Official name	Somalia
Local name	Soomaaliya; Jamhuuriyadda Dimoqraadiya Soomaaliya
Former name	British Somaliland (until 1960); Italian Somalia (until 1936), Italian East Africa (1936–50); United Republic of Somalia (1960–69), Somali Democratic Republic (1969–91)
Area	637 657 sq km (246 199 sq mi)
Capital	Mogadishu; Muqdisho (Somali), Muqdishu (Arabic)
Chief towns	Hargeysa, Berbera, Kismayu, Baidoa
Population	10 312 000 (2006e)
Nationality	Somali
Languages	Somali, Arabic; English and Italian are also spoken widely
Ethnic groups	Somali 85%, Bantu, Arab and others 15%
Religions	Islam 98% (Sunni), Christianity 2%
Time zone	GMT +3
Currency	1 Somali Shilling (SoSh) = 100 cents
Telephone	+252
Internet	.so
Country code	SOM

Location

A north-east African republic, bounded to the north-west by Djibouti; to the west by Ethiopia; to the south-west by Kenya; to the east by the Indian Ocean; and to the north by the Gulf of Aden.

Physical description

Occupies the eastern Horn of Africa where an arid coastal plain broadens to the south and rises inland to a plateau at nearly 1000 m (3280 ft); forested mountains on the Gulf of Aden coast rise to 2416 m (7926 ft) at Mount Shimbiris.

Climate

Considerable variation in climate between the north coast (hot, humid, low rainfall), the east coast (cooler with less variation in temperature, humid, higher rainfall) and inland (very hot, low humidity, very little rain); serious and persistent threat of drought.

Economy

Very poor country, with many dependent on remittances from emigrant workers; political situation prevents economic development or delivery of international aid; thriving entrepreneurial informal economy in some sectors (telecommunications, trade); main activity is agriculture, primarily livestock-raising by nomads and semi-nomads but also cultivation of bananas and fishing, which provides 40% of GDP and 65% of export earnings.

Government

A transitional federal government was created in 2004, comprising a President, a Prime Minister and Cabinet, and a unicameral National Assembly; it controls little of the country.

History

The country was settled by Arabs between the 7th and 10th centuries, and was the object of Italian, French and British interest after the opening of the Suez Canal in 1869. Modern Somalia was formed by the amalgamation of the Italian and British protectorates upon independence in 1960. In 1969 a military coup led by Muhammad Siad Barre established a socialist Islamic regime that became a one-party state in 1979. Civil war began in 1988, with fighting between government forces and rebel groups, particularly the Somali National Movement (SNM); Barre was forced to flee in 1991. Attempts to establish a new central government were unsuccessful as political and clan rivalries split the former rebels. The SNM declared the north-west region independent as the Somaliland Republic in 1991, and in 1998 the north-east declared its autonomy as the region of Puntland; neither has received international recognition but each has a functioning government and relative stability. Elsewhere, the state effectively disintegrated amid clan-based factional conflict between rival 'warlords'. Agriculture was disrupted by severe drought as well as the fighting in the south in the early 1990s; UN relief convoys and the multinational forces sent to protect them came under attack and were withdrawn in 1995. The fighting, famines and disease caused an estimated one million deaths. Talks in 2002–4 resulted in an agreement to establish a federal government and transitional institutions to govern until elections in 2007. Members of the transitional government and legislature only began to return to Somalia in 2005; they were based in Baidoa, 250 km (155 mi) from the capital because of the security situation. Muslim militias loyal to the Union of Islamic Courts (UIC) took control of Mogadishu and other parts of the south in July 2006 after defeating local warlords. The UIC advanced on Baidoa in December but was driven back, and then out of all the territory it held, by government troops supported by Ethiopian forces.

SOUTH AFRICA

Official name	Republic of South Africa (RSA)
Local name	South Africa; Republiek van Suid-Afrika
Area	1 228 376 sq km (474 275 sq mi)
Capitals	Pretoria (administrative), Bloemfontein (judicial) and Cape Town (Kaapstad) (legislative)
Chief towns	Durban, Johannesburg, Port Elizabeth
Population	44 188 000 (2006e)
Nationality	South African
Languages	IsiZulu, IsiXosa, Afrikaans, Sepedi, English, Setswana, Sosetho, Xitsonga are the main languages; other local languages are also spoken
Ethnic groups	black African 79%, white 10%, coloured 9%, Indian/Asian 2%
Religions	Christianity 80% (Prot 37%, RC 7%, other Christian 36%), Islam 1%, other 2%, none/unaffiliated 17%
Time zone	GMT +2
Currency	1 Rand (R) = 100 cents
Telephone	+27
Internet	.za
Country code	ZAF

Location

A republic in the south of the African continent. It is bounded to the north-west by Namibia; to the north by Botswana; to the north-east by Zimbabwe, Mozambique and Swaziland; to the east and south-east by the Indian Ocean; and to the south-west and west by the southern Atlantic Ocean; Lesotho is landlocked within its borders.

Physical description

Occupies the southern extremity of the African plateau, fringed by mountains and a lowland coastal margin to the west, east and south; the northern interior comprises the Kalahari Basin, scrub grassland and arid desert, at an altitude 650–1250 m (2133–4101 ft); the peripheral highlands rise to over 1200 m (3937 ft); the Great Escarpment rises east to 3482 m (11 424 ft) at Thabana Ntlenyana; the highest point is Mafadi (3451 m/11 322 ft); the Orange River flows west to meet the Atlantic; its chief tributaries are the Vaal and Caledon rivers.

Climate

Subtropical in the east, with lush vegetation; the average monthly rainfall at Durban is 28 mm in July, 130 mm in March, the annual average is 1101 mm; dry moistureless climate on the west coast; Mediterranean climate in southern tip; the annual average rainfall at Cape Town is 510 mm, with minimum daily temperatures of 7°C in July, to an average maximum of 26°C in January–February; desert region further north, with an annual average rainfall of less than 30 mm.

Economy

Developed, diversified industrial economy but wide wealth disparity so subsistence agriculture supports very poor; main activities are mining (platinum, gold, chromium, diamonds, other metals and non-metallic minerals), vehicle assembly, metalworking, iron and steel, manufacturing (machinery, textiles, chemicals and fertilizers), fuels and energy (coal, natural gas and nuclear), financial services, tourism, agriculture (cotton, cereals, sugar, fruits, vegetables and livestock), wine-making, fishing, forestry; inadequate water resources supplemented by imports.

Government

Governed by an executive President, a Cabinet and a bicameral Parliament consisting of a National Assembly and a National Council of Provinces. Each of the nine provinces has its own constitution, executive and legislature.

History

South Africa was originally inhabited by Khoisan tribes, and many Bantu tribes arrived from the north around 1000. The Portuguese reached the Cape of Good Hope in the late 15th century, and it was settled by the Dutch in 1652. The British arrived in 1795 and annexed the Cape in 1814. In 1836 the Boers (descendants of Dutch colonists) undertook the Great Trek north-east across the Orange River to Natal, where the first Boer republic was founded in 1839. Natal was annexed by the British in 1846, but the Boer republics of Transvaal (founded 1852) and Orange Free State (1854) received recognition. The discovery of diamonds in 1866 and gold in 1886 led to rivalry between the British and the Boers, which resulted in the Boer Wars of 1880–1 and 1899–1902. In 1910 Transvaal, Natal, Orange Free State and Cape Province were united to form the Union of South Africa, a dominion of the British Empire. It became a sovereign state within the Commonwealth of Nations in 1931, but left the Commonwealth and became a republic in 1961. Post-war, South African politics became dominated by the treatment of the non-white majority. Between 1948 and 1991 the apartheid policy resulted in the development of separate political institutions for different racial groups; eg Africans were considered permanent citizens of the 'homelands' to which each tribal group was assigned and were given no representation in the South African parliament. Continuing racial violence and strikes led to the declaration of a state of emergency in 1986. Several countries imposed economic and cultural sanctions in protest at the apartheid system. The progressive dismantling of apartheid by the government of F W de Klerk took place from 1990, but negotiations towards a non-racial democracy were marked by continuing violent clashes. In 1993 a new constitution gave the vote to all South African adults, and in 1994 free democratic elections resulted in the formation of a multiracial government led by the African National Congress (ANC), and Nelson Mandela became president. In the same year, South Africa rejoined the Commonwealth and took its UN seat again. The ANC has remained in power since 1994. President Mandela was succeeded in 1999 by Thabo Mbeki, who was re-elected in 2004. A Truth and Reconciliation Commission began hearings in 1996 on human rights abuses committed by the former government and liberation movements during the apartheid era.

SOUTH GEORGIA ▸UNITED KINGDOM
SOUTH KOREA ▸KOREA, SOUTH
SOUTH SANDWICH ISLANDS ▸UNITED KINGDOM

SOUTH AFRICA'S PRECIOUS RESOURCES

South Africa is home to literally a wealth of natural resources. From diamonds and gold to platinum and uranium, its mines have contributed significantly to the economy over the last 150 years.

The lure of diamonds

The chance find of a large diamond on the banks of the Orange River in 1866, in the region of South Africa then known as the Natal, prompted a feverish era of prospecting in the country for precious gems and minerals. Around 30,000 people descended on the region, armed only with pickaxes and shovels but determined to seek a fortune.

In the same decade diamonds were first found on the farm of Nicolaas and Diederick de Beers, near what would become the town of Kimberley. The De Beers sold their farm shortly after the discovery but the names of De Beers and Kimberley have been bywords for diamond mining ever since. Cecil Rhodes (1853–1902), who later colonized Rhodesia (now Zambia and Zimbabwe), bought out the property's mines in 1873 and rapidly expanded the business. He and fellow diamond magnate Alfred Beit (1853–1906) founded De Beers Consolidated Mines in 1888; within ten years the company had secured most of the rights to mining in southern Africa.

Exploitation of gold – and humans

Hand in hand with the first discoveries of diamonds came the beginnings of the gold-mining industry. In 1889 rich deposits of gold were discovered in the Witwatersrand, a rocky uplift that stretches 100 km (60 mi) from east to west, leading to a gold-mining boom. The gold in the Witwatersrand occurs in tiny specks in pebble beds called *bankets* (Afrikaans for 'almond toffee'). Deeper and deeper mines were sunk into the beds until, by the 1930s, the ore was being mined at a depth of about 3,300 m (12,000 ft).

The city of Johannesburg was established in 1886 to service the needs of the thousands of workers who flocked to the Witwatersrand, many of them white British migrants. Over time the white workers were displaced by black workers who were paid less and could therefore be employed more profitably. In his 1914 text *Native Life in South Africa*, Sol Plaatje, first Secretary of the African National Congress, describes the lives of black miners thus:

> 200,000 subterranean heroes who by day and by night, for a mere pittance, lay down their limbs and their lives to the familiar 'fall of rock' and who, at deep levels ranging from 1,000 feet to 1,000 yards in the bowels of the earth, sacrifice their lungs to the rock dust which develops miners' phthisis and pneumonia ...

South African mining in modern times

Nowadays, South Africa is the world's leading producer of platinum, a grey-white metal that is even more valuable than gold. With deposits located mainly north of Pretoria, platinum ores were first discovered in the country in 1924. The metal is used in chemical experiments, electrical apparatus and fine jewellery.

The Witwatersrand region is still an important source of gold, producing about 600 tonnes each year. In addition, another lucrative resource is extracted as a by-product of gold mining: uranium. Traditionally, this radioactive metal was not deemed useful and was simply left in the tailings (waste). These days, however, it is utilized in nuclear power plants.

SPAIN

Official name	Kingdom of Spain
Local name	España; Reino de España
Former name	Spanish Republic (1931–9), Spanish State (1936–78)
Area	504 782 sq km (190 078 sq mi)
Capital	Madrid
Chief towns	Barcelona, Valencia, Seville, Zaragoza, Málaga
Population	40 398 000 (2006e)
Nationality	Spaniard, Spanish
Languages	Spanish (Castilian); Catalan, Galician (Gallego) and Basque (Euskera) are also spoken in certain regions
Ethnic groups	Castilian Spanish 72%, Catalan 17%, Galician 7%, Basque (Euskera) 2%, others 3%
Religions	Christianity 94% (RC), others 6%
Time zone	GMT +1
Currency	1 Euro (€) = 100 cents
Telephone	+34
Internet	.es
Country code	ESP

Location

A country in south-western Europe, bordered to the north-east by France and Andorra; to the west by Portugal; to the north-west and north by the Atlantic Ocean; and to the east by the Mediterranean Sea.

Physical description

The country consists mainly of a central plateau (the Meseta, average height 700 m/2297 ft) crossed and surrounded by mountains; the Andalusian or Baetic Mountains in the south-east rise to 3478 m (11 410 ft) at Mulhacén; the Pyrenees in the north rise to 3404 m (11 168 ft) at Pico de Aneto; the main rivers are the Duero, Tajo (Tagus), Guadiana, Guadalquivir, Ebro and Miño; the highest point is Pico de Teide (3718 m/12 198 ft) on the island of Tenerife in the Canary Islands.

Climate

The Meseta has a continental climate, with hot summers, cold winters and low rainfall; there is high rainfall in the mountains, with deep winter snow; the south Mediterranean coast has the warmest winter temperatures on the European mainland.

Economy

Industrialized and diversified market economy; main activities are tourism, mining (coal, iron ore, copper, zinc, lead, uranium and tungsten), steel-making, fishing (one of Europe's largest fleets), manufacturing (metal products, textiles, garments and footwear, chemicals, vehicles, machine tools, ceramics, pharmaceuticals, medical equipment and food processing), shipbuilding, agriculture and wine-making.

Government

A hereditary constitutional monarchy with a King as head of state; governed by a Prime Minister and Council of Ministers, and a bicameral National Assembly (*Cortes Generales*) comprising a Congress of Deputies and a Senate. Each of the 19 autonomous regions has its own executive and legislature.

History

Early inhabitants included Iberians, Celts, Phoenicians, Greeks and Romans. From the 8th century there was Muslim domination; this was followed by Christian reconquest, which was completed by 1492. Spain assumed its modern form with the dynastic union of the crowns of Aragon and Castile, a union that was effective by 1479. In the 16th century the Spanish exploration of the New World led to the growth of the Spanish Empire. There was a period of decline after the Revolt of the Netherlands in 1581. Significant set-backs included the defeat of the Spanish Armada in 1588; defeat by France, acknowledged in the Treaty of the Pyrenees (1659); the War of the Spanish Succession in 1702–13; Spain's involvement in the Peninsular War against Napoleon I in 1808–14; and the Spanish–American War in 1898 that led to the loss of Cuba, Puerto Rico and the remaining Pacific possessions. The dictatorship of Miguel Primo de Rivera (1923–30) was followed by the exile of the King and the establishment of the Second Republic in 1931. A military revolt headed by General Franco in 1936 led to the Spanish Civil War and a Fascist dictatorship until Franco's death in 1975. At this point Spain became a constitutional monarchy, with Prince Juan Carlos of Bourbon, nominated as Franco's successor in 1969, acceding to the throne. The transition to democracy began with free elections in 1977 and the introduction of a democratic constitution in 1978, and survived attempted military coups in 1978 and 1981. Spain joined the European Community in 1986, and replaced the peseta with the euro in 2002. From the 1960s onwards, the Basque separatist movement, ETA, has carried out a terrorist campaign of bombings, assassinations and kidnappings in an attempt to win independence for the Basque country; numerous ceasefires, the most recent in 2006, have been broken, and attempts to negotiate a settlement have failed. Increasing degrees of autonomy have been granted to 19 regions, including the Basque country, since 1978.

Spanish archipelagoes[1]

Balearic Islands

Location	An archipelago of five major islands (Majorca, Minorca, Ibiza, Formentera and Cabrera) and eleven islets in the west Mediterranean Sea, situated near the east coast of Spain.
Area	5014 sq km (1935 sq mi) **Population**[2] 1 001 000 (2006e)
Capital	Palma de Mallorca

SPANISH ARCHITECTURE

From the Romans to Richard Rogers, and from the Moors to Modernismo, the architecture of Spain has been shaped by invasion and foreign influences.

Roman legacies

Evidence of the 700-year Roman occupation of Spain is seen today in the spectacular granite double-tiered arches of the Aqueduct of Segovia in central Spain, built c.50 AD. There are also extensive Roman remains at Mérida in western Spain, which include a theatre and amphitheatre, the 64-arch Puente Romano, the Temple of Diana, the Arch of Trajan, the Circus Maximus and the Los Milagros Aqueduct.

Moorish invasion

In the early 8th century the Moorish invaders from north Africa conquered parts of Spain. Their architectural heritage is most evident in southern Spain. The interior of the Moorish Great Mosque of Córdoba, now a Christian church, is filled with double-tiered red-and-white striped arches mounted on columns, forming numerous arcades. The Alhambra complex at Granada was a citadel, the palace of the last Moorish rulers of Spain. The unassuming external appearance of the red-brick buildings (*al Hamra* meaning 'the red one' in Arabic) belies the ornate decoration of the interiors, which feature stucco lacework tracery, marble and coloured tiles.

Mudéjar style

Moorish style was followed by Mudéjar. This term is from the Arabic *mudajjan* meaning 'allowed to remain' and originally referred to Muslims living in Christian-ruled areas of Spain. Architecturally it refers to a cosmopolitan blend of Christian, Islamic and Jewish influences. It was epitomized by the use of glazed tiles and decorative brickwork and peaked between the 12th and 16th centuries. Notable buildings in this style include the Alcázar (castle) of Seville.

Romanesque and Gothic influences

The rounded arches and vaults of the 10th- and 11th-century Romanesque style can be seen in the cathedral at Santiago de Compostela. The Gothic style was introduced from France in the 12th century. Its pointed arches, clustered columns, sculptural detail and stained-glass windows are best seen in the cathedrals of northern and central Spain, such as Burgos, Toledo and León.

Modernismo and beyond

The form of art and architecture known as Art Nouveau in France and Britain was known in Spain as Modernismo. It reached the peak of its expression in Barcelona in Catalunya and its greatest exponent was the Catalan architect Antoni Gaudí (1852–1926). Gaudí's unfinished masterpiece, the church of La Sagrada Familia, is famous for its elongated openwork spires. Also representative of his work is the Casa Batlló apartment block, with its undulating and intricate wavelike façade, and Parc Güell, with its fantastical mosaics.

Postmodern masterpieces include the titanium-enwreathed Museo Guggenheim in Bilbao, designed by Frank Gehry (b.1929). The architectural practice of Richard Rogers (b.1933) won the Stirling Prize for Architecture in 2006 for the new glass-enclosed terminal at Barajas Madrid Airport. It has a wave-form roof, a bamboo-lined interior, and a colour-coded decorative scheme to aid the throughflow of passengers.

Canary Islands

Location	An archipelago of seven major islands (Gran Canaria, Fuerteventura, Lanzarote, Tenerife, La Palma, Hierro and Gomera) in the Atlantic Ocean, lying 100 km (62 mi) off the north-west coast of Africa.
Area	7273 sq km (2807 sq mi) **Population**[2] 1 995 800 (2006e)
Capital	Las Palmas

[1] *Each archipelago forms one of the 17 autonomous communities of Spain, the other 15 being on the mainland*

[2] *Source: Instituto Nacional de Estadística (National Statistics Institute of Spain)*

SRI LANKA

Official name	Democratic Socialist Republic of Sri Lanka
Local name	Sri Lanka; Sri Lanka Prajatantrika Samajavadi Janarajaya
Former name	Ceylon (until 1972)
Area	65 610 sq km (25 325 sq mi)
Capitals	Colombo (commercial) and Sri Jayawardenepura Kotte (legislative)
Chief towns	Jaffna, Kandy, Galle, Trincomalee
Population	20 222 000 (2006e)
Nationality	Sri Lankan
Languages	Sinhala, Tamil; English and other local languages are spoken
Ethnic groups	Sinhalese 74%, Sri Lankan Moor 7%, Indian Tamil 5%, Sri Lankan Tamil 4%, others 10%
Religions	Buddhism 69%, Islam 8%, Hinduism 7%, Christianity 6%, unspecified 10%
Time zone	GMT +5.5
Currency	1 Sri Lankan Rupee (SLR, SLRs) = 100 cents
Telephone	+94
Internet	.lk
Country code	LKA

Location

An island state in the Indian Ocean situated off the south-east coast of India.

Physical description

A pear-shaped island, lying off the southern tip of India; low-lying areas in the north and south, and along the coasts; the coastal plain is fringed by sandy beaches and lagoons; the centre is a massif more than 1500 m (4921 ft) above sea level; the highest peak is Pidurutalagala at 2524 m (8281 ft); the northern region is generally arid in the dry season; nearly half the country is forest, jungle or scrubland.

Climate

High temperatures and humidity in the northern plains; temperatures in the interior are reduced by altitude; affected by the south-west monsoon (May–September) and the north-east monsoon (November–March); the average daily temperatures at Trincomalee are 24–33°C; rainfall is heavy, particularly on the south-west coast and in the mountains.

Economy

Poor country, with economy damaged by decades of civil war and 2004 tsunami; largest sector is services (tourism, telecommunications, banking and insurance); agriculture employs c.33% of the workforce; chief cash crops are tea, spices, coconut, rubber, tobacco; main industries are forestry, fishing, mining (coal, diamonds, emeralds and rubies), oil refining and manufacturing (textiles, garments and processing agricultural products).

Government

Governed by an executive President, a Prime Minister and Cabinet, and a unicameral Parliament.

History

The Sinhalese (from northern India) colonized part of the island in the 5th century bc and dominated the northern plain until around AD 1200, when they gradually moved south-westwards due to the many Tamil invasions from southern India. Buddhism spread amongst the Sinhalese from about 200 BC. Some coastal areas of the country were conquered by the Portuguese in the 15th century; it was then taken over by the Dutch in 1658. British occupation began in 1796, and the island became a British colony in 1802. The whole island was united for the first time in 1815 and was named Ceylon. Tamil labourers were brought in from southern India during colonial rule, to work on coffee and tea plantations. Ceylon gained independence as a dominion within the Commonwealth in 1948; it became a republic in 1972, when it adopted the name Sri Lanka. Acute tension exists between the Buddhist Sinhalese majority and the Hindu Tamil minority, who live predominantly in the north and east of the island. Separatist movements began to campaign for an independent Tamil state in the Tamil majority areas in the 1970s, and in the early 1980s the Liberation Tigers of Tamil Eelam (LTTE) began a guerrilla war against government forces for control of these areas. The fighting has remained mainly in the Jaffna Peninsula, though sporadic terrorist attacks have taken place elsewhere. Attempts to negotiate a settlement in the 1980s and 1990s were unsuccessful. A number of normalization measures resulted from talks in 2002–3 but these stalled owing to disagreement within the government over concessions made to the Tamils, who withdrew because of the slow progress; an attempt to reopen the talks in 2006 failed. The 2002 ceasefire held until early 2006, since when violence has escalated. The 2004 Indian Ocean tsunami killed over 30 000 people and caused widespread devastation in Sri Lanka.

SUDAN

Official name	Republic of Sudan
Local name	As-Sūdān; Al-Jumhūriyya As-Sūdān
Former name	Anglo-Egyptian Sudan (until 1956), Democratic Republic of The Sudan (1969–85)
Area	2 504 530 sq km (966 749 sq mi)
Capital	Khartoum; Al Khartūm, Al Khurtūm
Chief towns	Port Sudan, Wad Medani, Omdurman
Population	41 236 000 (2006e)
Nationality	Sudanese
Languages	Arabic; a number of local languages and dialects are also spoken
Ethnic groups	African 52%, Arab 39%, Beja 6%, others 3%
Religions	Islam 70% (mostly Sunni), traditional beliefs 25%, Christianity 5%
Time zone	GMT +3
Currency	1 Sudanese Dinar (SD) = 10 pounds
Telephone	+249
Internet	.sd
Country code	SDN

Location

A north-east African republic, bounded to the north by Egypt; to the north-west by Libya; to the west by Chad; to the south-west by the Central African Republic; to the south by the Democratic Republic of the Congo; to the south-east by Uganda and Kenya; to the east by Ethiopia; and to the north by the Red Sea.

Physical description

The largest country in Africa; largely desert, except where crossed by the middle reaches of the River Nile; the eastern edge is formed by the Nubian Highlands and an escarpment rising to more than 2000 m (6562 ft) on the Red Sea; the Imatong Mountains in the south rise to 3187 m (10 456 ft) at Kinyeti, the country's highest point; the Darfur Massif is located in the west; the White Nile flows north to meet the Blue Nile at Khartoum.

Climate

Desert conditions in the north, with minimal annual rainfall of 160 mm at Port Sudan, increasing in the tropical south to 1000 mm; in the hottest months (July–August), the temperature rarely falls below 24°C in the north.

Economy

Very poor; oil production began in 1999 and oil and petroleum products are now the main exports; agriculture, mostly at subsistence level, employs c.80% of workforce and provides 39% of GDP; cultivable area has been extended by irrigation schemes; chief cash crops are cotton, sesame, livestock, groundnuts, gum arabic, sugar cane;

industries are oil refining, processing of cotton, edible oils and sugar, manufacturing (textiles, cement, soap, footwear, pharmaceuticals and armaments) and vehicle assembly.

Government

Transitional; the 2005 constitution established an executive President, a Cabinet and a National Legislature consisting of the National Assembly and the Council of States; elections are to be held by 2008. The south has a largely autonomous government with a president who also serves as the national vice-president.

History

Sudan was Christianized in the 6th century. Islam was introduced in the 7th century, but only became widespread from the 13th century. Egypt established control of northern Sudan in the early 19th century but the Mahdi Revolt in the 1880s led to a combined British–Egyptian campaign to subdue the country, resulting in a jointly administered condominium under a British governor between 1899 and 1955. Sudan gained its independence in 1956; the post-independence period has been dominated by conflict arising from tensions between the Arab Muslim north and the African Christian and animist south. The first civil war in the south (1955–72) resulted in greater autonomy for the south. The second civil war (1983–2004) ended with an agreement creating a largely autonomous administration (installed in 2005) and a power-sharing national government; under the agreement, a referendum on independence for the south will be held after six years. The civil wars caused political instability in the whole country, resulting in several coups, and Sudan was under military rule for most of the period from 1955 to 1996. An estimated 1.5 million died in the conflicts and famines caused by war and drought. There has been a separate conflict in the western region of Darfur since 2003, arising from intercommunal violence between Arab nomads and African farmers. The severe reprisals against African rebels by government-backed Arab militias, and government obstruction of aid agencies' relief work, have left thousands dead and over two million people displaced. The government has failed to disarm the militias, and until late 2006 resisted international pressure to extend the limited mandate of African Union peacekeeping troops or allow their replacement by UN peacekeepers.

Water Power

The Merowe High Dam project, situated on the Nile in northern Sudan, is the largest contemporary hydroelectric power project in Africa. Usage rights to the waters of the Nile, which, along with its tributaries, covers much of Sudan, are controlled by the Nile Waters Treaty negotiated by the British in 1959. The treaty allots 82 per cent of the water volume of the Nile to Egypt and the remaining 18 per cent to Sudan, with no allocation for any of the countries further upstream. Ethiopia, Uganda, Rwanda, Burundi, Kenya and Tanzania are not entitled to significant use of the water, including irrigation and hydropower; these countries are now calling for a revision of the treaty made under colonial rule.

SURINAME

Official name	Republic of Suriname
Local name	Suriname; Republiek Suriname
Former name	Netherlands Guiana, Dutch Guiana (1954–75)
Area	163 265 sq km (63 020 sq mi)
Capital	Paramaribo
Chief towns	Brokopondo, Nieuw Amsterdam
Population	439 000 (2006e)
Nationality	Surinamer, Surinamese
Languages	Dutch; English, Hindi, Javanese and Sranang Tongo (Surinamese) are also spoken
Ethnic groups	Hindustani 37%, Creole 31%, Javanese 15%, black 10%, Amerindian 2%, Chinese 2%, others 3%
Religions	Christianity 48% (Prot 25%, RC 23%), Hinduism 27%, Islam 20%, traditional beliefs 5%
Time zone	GMT −3
Currency	1 Surinamese Dollar (SRD, $) = 100 cents
Telephone	+597
Internet	.sr
Country code	SUR

Location

A republic in north-eastern South America, bounded to the west by Guyana; to the south by Brazil; to the east by French Guiana; and to the north by the Atlantic Ocean.

Physical description

Diverse natural regions, ranging from coastal lowland through savanna to mountainous upland; the coastal strip is mostly covered by swamp; the highland interior in the south is covered with dense tropical rainforest; the highest point is Juliana Top (1230 m/4035 ft).

Climate

Tropical, moderated by trade winds; hot and humid, with two rainy seasons (March–July and December–January); Paramaribo temperatures range from 22 to 33°C; the average monthly rainfall is 310 mm in the north and 67 mm in the south.

Economy

Developing country, still in receipt of international aid; economy dominated by mining (bauxite and gold) and alumina production; other activities are oil extraction, forestry, fishing, agriculture (rice and bananas) and food processing

Government

Governed by an executive President, a Council of Ministers and a unicameral National Assembly.

History

Sighted by Christopher Columbus in 1498, Suriname was first settled by the Dutch in 1602 and the British in 1651. The British part was taken by the Dutch in 1667, captured by the British in 1799, and restored to the Netherlands in 1818. Suriname became an independent republic in 1975, after which around 40 per cent of the population emigrated to the Netherlands. There were military coups in 1980 and 1982. A guerrilla campaign for a return to democracy began in 1986; civilian government was restored in 1988 but another coup was staged in 1990. Democracy was restored with elections in 1991, which brought to power the New Front for Democracy and Development coalition. This was led by Ronald Venetiaan, who served as president until 1996 and again from 2000. In 2004, the Surinamese dollar replaced the guilder as the official currency.

SWAZILAND

Official name	Kingdom of Swaziland
Local name	Umbuso we Swatini
Area	17 363 sq km (6 702 sq mi)
Capitals	Mbabane (administrative) and Lobamba (legislative)
Population	1 136 000 (2006)
Nationality	Swazi
Languages	English, SiSwati
Ethnic groups	Swazi 97%, European 3%
Religions	Christianity 60% (Prot 35%, RC 25%), traditional beliefs 30%, Islam 1%, others 9%
Time zone	GMT +2
Currency	1 Lilangeni (plural Emalangeni) (Li, E) = 100 cents
Telephone	+268
Internet	.sz
Country code	SWZ

Location

A small landlocked monarchy in south-east Africa, bounded to the north, west, south and south-east by South Africa, and to the north-east and east by Mozambique.

Physical description

A small country, with mountainous Highveld in the west; the highest point is Emblembe at 1862 m (6109 ft); the more populated Middleveld in the centre descends to 600–700 m (1970–2300 ft); the rolling, bush-covered Lowveld in the centre is irrigated by river systems; the Lubombo runs along the east of the Lowveld.

Climate

The Highveld is humid and near temperate, with an average annual rainfall of 1000–2280 mm; the Middleveld and Lubombo are subtropical and drier; the Lowveld is tropical, with relatively little rain (500–890 mm, susceptible to drought); the average annual temperature is 16°C in the west and 22°C in the east.

Economy

Poor, and dependent on customs union revenues and expatriates' remittances; agriculture, mostly at subsistence level, employs 80% of the workforce; chief cash crops are sugar cane, cotton, citrus fruits and pineapples; main activities are mining (coal and asbestos), wood pulp, processing agricultural products (sugar and soft drink concentrate) and manufacturing (textiles, garments and consumer durables).

Government

A hereditary monarchy; governed by the King, a Prime Minister and Cabinet, and a bicameral Parliament comprising a Senate and a House of Assembly.

History

The Swazi people probably arrived in the area in the 16th century. Boundaries with the Transvaal were decided in the 19th century; independence was guaranteed in 1881 and again in 1884, when the country became a South African protectorate. The British agreed to the Transvaal administration of Swaziland in 1894; however, after the Second Boer War, Swaziland, though retaining its monarchy, came under British rule as a British High Commission territory in 1903. It gained independence in 1968 under King Sobhuza II, who assumed absolute power in 1973. Mswati III acceded to the throne in 1986 and has faced increasingly strong demands for democratization, reinforced by demonstrations and strikes; a new constitution introduced in 2006 maintains the ban on political parties.

SWEDEN

Official name	Kingdom of Sweden
Local name	Sverige; Konungariket Sverige
Area	411479 sq km (158830 sq mi)
Capital	Stockholm
Chief towns	Gothenburg, Malmö, Uppsala, Norrköping, Västerås, Örebro, Linköping
Population	9016000 (2006e)
Nationality	Swede, Swedish
Languages	Swedish; Sami and Finnish are spoken by minorities
Ethnic groups	Swedish 90%, Finnish and Lapp 3%, others 7%
Religions	Christianity 85% (Prot 83%, RC 2%), unaffiliated 14%, others 1%
Time zone	GMT +1
Currency	1 Swedish Krona (Skr) = 100 øre
Telephone	+46
Internet	.se
Country code	SWE

Location

A constitutional monarchy in northern Europe, occupying the eastern side of the Scandinavian peninsula, bounded to the east by Finland, the Gulf of Bothnia and the Baltic Sea; to the south-west by the Skagerrak and Kattegat; and to the west and north-west by Norway.

Physical description

The terrain is mostly flat or undulating lowlands in the south and east, with mountains in the west; the Kjölen Mountains form much of the boundary with Norway; the highest peak is Kebnekaise (2111 m/6926 ft); there are a number of lakes (9% of the area), the chief being Vänern, Vättern and Mälaren; there are numerous coastal islands, notably Gotland and Öland; several rivers flow south-east towards the Gulf of Bothnia; there are many waterfalls; c.57% of the country is forested.

Climate

Continental, with a considerable range of temperatures between the summer and winter, except in the south-west, where winters are warmer; enclosed parts of the Baltic Sea often freeze in winter; the average number of days with a mean temperature below freezing increases from 71 in Malmö to 184 at Haparanda near the Arctic Circle.

Economy

Highly industrialized and diversified economy; industries such as forestry (wood products, pulp and paper), mining (iron ore, copper and uranium), steel-making and hydroelectric power generation supplemented in the latter part of 20c by engineering and high-technology manufacturing (specialized machinery and systems, motor vehicles, aircraft, electrical and electronic equipment, pharmaceuticals, plastics and chemicals) and telecommunications.

Government

A hereditary constitutional monarchy with a King as head of state; governed by a Prime Minister and Cabinet, and a unicameral legislature (*Riksdag*).

History

Sweden was formed from the union of the kingdoms of the Goths and Svears in the 7th century. It did not, however, include the southern parts of the peninsula (Skåne, Halland and Blekinge), which were part of Denmark, until they were conquered in 1658. Sweden established sovereignty over Finland in the 13th century. With Norway, Sweden was brought under Danish rule in 1397, but it regained its independence after a rebellion in 1521 and the election to the throne of Gustav I Vasa. Sweden's power reached its height in the 17th century but later waned; Finland was lost to Russia in 1809. Norway was ceded to Sweden in 1814, but the union was dissolved in 1905 when Norway became independent. Sweden has been a neutral country since 1814. It became a member of the European Union in 1995, but in 2003 decided to replace the krona with the euro.

SWITZERLAND

Official name	Swiss Confederation
Local name	Schweiz; Schweizerische Eidgenossenschaft (German), Suisse; Confédération Suisse (French), Svizzera; Confederazione Svizzera (Italian), Svizra; Confederaziun Svizra (Romansch)
Area	41 228 sq km (15 914 sq mi)
Capital	Berne; Bern, Berna
Chief towns	Zurich, Lucerne, St Gallen, Lausanne, Basle, Geneva
Population	7 524 000 (2006e)
Nationality	Swiss
Languages	German 64%, French 20%, Italian 7%, Romansch 1%, other 9%; many Swiss speak more than one of these
Ethnic groups	German 65%, French 18%, Italian 10%, Romansch 1%, others 6%
Religions	Christianity 79% (RC 42%, Prot 35%, other Christian 2%), Islam 4%, others 1%, none/unaffiliated 16%
Time zone	GMT +1
Currency	1 Swiss Franc (SFr, SwF) = 100 centimes = 100 rappen
Telephone	+41
Internet	.ch
Country code	CHE

Location

A landlocked European republic, bounded to the east by Liechtenstein and Austria; to the south by Italy; to the west by France; and to the north by Germany.

Physical description

The most mountainous country in Europe, with the Alps occupying about two-thirds of the country in the south and east; the highest peak is Dufourspitze (4634 m/15 203 ft); the average height of the Pre-Alps in the north-west is 2000 m (6562 ft); the Jura Mountains run along the western border with France; the central plateau, at an average altitude of 580 m (1903 ft), is fringed by large lakes; major lakes include Constance, Zurich, Lucerne, Neuchâtel and Geneva; chief rivers are the Rhine, Rhône, Adige, Inn, and the tributaries of the Po; there are c.3000 sq km (1160 sq mi) of glaciers, notably the Aletsch; the country is densely forested.

Climate

Temperate, varying greatly with relief and altitude; there are warm summers, with considerable rainfall; winter temperatures average 0°C; average annual rainfall in the central plateau is c.1000 mm; average annual temperature is 7–9°C; the *Föhn*, a warm wind, is noticeable in the Alps during late winter and spring.

Economy

Highly industrialized and diversified economy with large service sector (banking, insurance, financial and corporate services, tourism); main industries are precision engineering, pharmaceuticals, chemicals, telecommunications, food processing and packaging, graphic machinery, electrical and mechanical engineering, metalworking.

Government
Governed by a President (elected annually), who chairs the Federal Council, and a bicameral Federal Assembly comprising a Council of States and a National Council. Each of the 20 cantons and six half-cantons has its own government and considerable autonomy.

History
The area was part of the Holy Roman Empire in the 10th century. The Swiss Confederation was created in 1291, when the cantons of Uri, Schwyz and Unterwalden formed a defensive league. The Confederation expanded during the 14th century and was the centre of the Reformation in the 16th century. Swiss independence and neutrality were recognized under the Treaty of Westphalia in 1648. The country was conquered by Napoleon I, who in 1798 instituted the Helvetian Republic. In 1815 it was organized as a confederation of 22 cantons, and in 1848 a federal constitution was adopted. Switzerland has been neutral for two centuries, including during both world wars, but joined the UN in 2002. Many policy decisions are made by national referenda.

SYRIA

Official name	Syrian Arab Republic
Local name	As-Sūriyya; Al-Jumhūriyya Al-'Arabiyya as-Sūriyya
Former name	formerly part of the United Arab Republic, with Egypt (1958–61)
Area	185 180 sq km (71 479 sq mi)
Capital	Damascus; Dimashq
Chief towns	Halab (Aleppo), Homs, Hama, Latakia
Population	18 881 000 (2006e)
Nationality	Syrian
Languages	Arabic; Kurdish, Armenian, Aramaic and Circassian are also spoken
Ethnic groups	Arab 90%, Kurds, Armenian and others 10%
Religions	Islam 90% (Sunni 74%, others 16%), Christianity 10%
Time zone	GMT +2
Currency	1 Syrian Pound (LS, S$) = 100 piastres
Telephone	+963
Internet	.sy
Country code	SYR

Location
A republic in the Middle East, bounded to the west by the Mediterranean Sea and Lebanon; to the south-west by Israel and Jordan; to the east by Iraq; and to the north by Turkey.

Physical description

Behind a narrow Mediterranean coastal plain, the Jabal al Nusayriyah mountain range rises to c.1500 m (4921 ft); steep drop in the east to the Euphrates River valley; the Anti-Lebanon range in the south-west rises to 2814 m (9232 ft) at Mount Hermon; open steppe and desert to the east.

Climate

Mediterranean on the coast, with hot, dry summers and mild, wet winters; desert or semi-desert climate in 60% of the country, with an annual rainfall below 200 mm; the *khamsin* wind causes temperatures to rise to 43–9°C; in Damascus the average annual rainfall is 225 mm, and average temperatures range from 7°C in January to 27°C in July.

Economy

Moving slowly away from state control and state ownership of the economy; main industries are oil (55–60% of export earnings), gas, mining (phosphate) and manufacturing (petroleum products, textiles, garments, food processing, beverages and tobacco); agricultural sector produces cotton, fruit, vegetables, wheat, meat and livestock.

Government

Governed by an executive President, a Council of Ministers and a unicameral People's Assembly. The Ba'ath Party has dominated politics since 1963.

History

The country was part of the Phoenician, Persian, Roman and Byzantine empires. It was conquered by Muslim Arabs in the 7th century, when Damascus became the capital of the Umayyad Dynasty. It was subsequently ruled by foreign dynasties, including the Egyptian Fatimids and Mamluks, before being conquered by Turks in the 11th century. The scene of many battles during the Crusades in the Middle Ages, it was part of the Ottoman Empire in 1517. It enjoyed a brief period of independence in 1920 before being made a French mandate. Syria regained its independence in 1946. It merged with Egypt and Yemen to form the United Arab Republic in 1958, but re-established itself as an independent state under its present name in 1961. Syria was involved in the Arab–Israeli wars in 1948, 1967 and 1973, losing the Golan Heights region to Israel in 1967. Syrian intervention in Lebanon began in 1976, when Syrian troops were sent to restore order during the civil war; its military presence influenced politics there after the civil war ended, until the troops were withdrawn in 2005. Many Western states continue to accuse Syria of supporting militants in Lebanon and Iraq, and relations with the USA deteriorated further in 2006 over the conflict between Lebanon and Israel. President Hafez al-Asad seized power in a coup in 1970, formally taking office in 1971. On his death in 2000, he was succeeded by his son, Bashar. Bashar al-Asad introduced some openness into political life but the results alarmed the establishment and restrictions have been reimposed.

TAIWAN

Official name	Republic of China; also sometimes known as Chinese Taipei
Local name	T'ai-wan; Chung-hua Min-kuo
Former name	Formosa (until 1949)
Area	36 000 sq km (13 896 sq mi)
Capital	T'aipei
Chief towns	Chilung, Kaohsiung, Taichung
Population	23 036 000 (2006e)
Nationality	Taiwanese, Chinese
Languages	Chinese (Mandarin); Taiwanese and Hakka are also spoken
Ethnic groups	Taiwanese Chinese (including Hakka) 84%, mainland Chinese 14%, Ainu 2%
Religions	Buddhism and Taoism 93%, Christianity 4%, Islam and others 3%
Time zone	GMT +8
Currency	1 New Taiwan Dollar (NT$) = 100 cents
Telephone	+886
Internet	.tw
Country code	TWN

Location

An island republic consisting of Taiwan Island and several smaller islands, lying c.130 km (80 mi) off the south-east coast of China.

Physical description

The island is c.395 km (245 mi) long, 100–145 km (60–90 mi) wide; a mountain range runs north to south, covering over half of the island; the highest peak is Yu Shan (3997 m/13 113 ft); the low-lying land is mainly on the west; the island is crossed by the tropic of Cancer.

Climate

Subtropical, except in the far south, where it is tropical; affected by the monsoon (May–November); high rainfall, averaging more than 2000 mm per annum in the lowlands and much more in the mountains; especially heavy rain in the typhoon season (July–September); summers are hot and humid; mild and short winters; the average daily temperature at T'aipei is 12–19°C in January, and 24–33°C in July–August; the monthly rainfall is 71 mm in December and 290 mm in June.

Economy

Highly industrialized and diverse market economy; main industries are high-technology manufacturing (electronics and computer products), oil refining, chemicals, textiles, iron and steel, machinery, cement and food processing.

Government

Governed by a President, a Premier and Executive Yuan, and a unicameral Legislative Yuan. The National Assembly, a largely ad hoc ceremonial body, was disbanded in 2005.

History

Taiwan was discovered by the Portuguese in 1590 and conquered by the Chinese in the 17th century. Ceded to Japan in 1895, it was returned to China in 1945. The Nationalist government (the Guomindang) withdrew to Taiwan after being defeated by the communists in mainland China in 1949. Emergency measures adopted in 1949 froze political life on the island until the late 1980s, when demands grew for democratization of the authoritarian one-party state. Martial law was lifted in 1987; Taiwan ended its state of war with China in 1991, officially recognizing the communist People's Republic of China for the first time. The first multiparty elections were held in 1992. Since then, power has shifted from the mainlanders to the native Taiwanese, and 50 years of Guomindang rule ended when the Democratic Progressive Party won the presidency in 2000 and the 2001 legislative election. China regards Taiwan as a province of the People's Republic and has sanctioned the use of force to prevent Taiwan declaring itself independent.

TAJIKISTAN

Official name	Republic of Tajikistan
Local name	Toçikiston; Cumhurii Toçikiston
Former name	Tajik Soviet Socialist Republic (until 1991), within the Union of Soviet Socialist Republics (USSR; 1929–91)
Area	143 100 sq km (55 200 sq mi)
Capital	Dushanbe; Dušanbe
Chief towns	Khudzand, Kulyab, Kurgan-Tyube
Population	7 321 000 (2006e)
Nationality	Tajik or Tadzhik, Tajikistani
Languages	Tajik, Uzbek, Russian
Ethnic groups	Tajik 80%, Uzbek 15%, Russian 1%, Kyrgyz 1%, others 3%
Religions	Islam 90% (Sunni 85%, Shia 5%), others 10%
Time zone	GMT +5
Currency	1 Somoni (S) = 100 dirams
Telephone	+992
Internet	.tj
Country code	TJK

Location

A landlocked republic in south-eastern Central Asia, bounded to the west and north by Uzbekistan; to the north by Kyrgyzstan; to the east by China; and to the south by Afghanistan.

Physical description

Largely mountainous; the Tien Shan, Gissar-Alai and Pamir ranges cover more than 90% of the area; Peak Ismoili Somoni, formerly Communism Peak, reaches 7495 m (24 590 ft); the lower-lying areas are the Fergana Valley in the north, the Gissar and Vakhsh valleys near Tashkent and the Khatlon region in the south; the River Syrdarya flows through the north and the River Amudarya through the south of the country.

Climate

Continental; hot, dry summers and very cold winters.

Economy

Poor, with a fragile economy; dependent on expatriates' remittances and international aid; large agricultural sector employs 67% of workforce, producing cotton, fruit and livestock as cash crops; main industries are aluminium production (40% of export earnings), hydroelectric power generation, mining (zinc and lead), food processing (vegetable oil) and manufacturing (textiles, fertilizers, cement, machine tools and domestic appliances).

Government

Governed by an executive President, a Prime Minister and Council of Ministers, and a bicameral Supreme Assembly (*Majlisi Oli*) comprising an Assembly of Representatives and a National Assembly.

History

Inhabited by Tajiks, who originated in Iran, it was conquered by Arabs in the 7th and 8th centuries and then by the Mongol Empire in the 13th century. It remained under the control of various khanates until the 19th century. In 1868 the north was subsumed into the Russian Empire, while the south was annexed by the Emirate of Bukhara. At the time of the Russian Revolution in 1917, the central Asian emirates attempted to assert their independence but Bolshevik control was established in northern Tajikistan in 1918 and in the Bukhara emirate in 1920. Tajikistan was given full republic status within the Union of Soviet Socialist Republics (USSR) in 1929. It became independent in 1991, and joined the Commonwealth of Independent States (CIS). In 1992 anti-government demonstrations escalated into civil war between pro-government forces and Muslim and pro-democracy groups. A peace treaty signed in 1997 was implemented by 2000, although assassinations and bombings targeting government ministers and buildings have continued. Former communists have dominated the presidency and governments since 1991. The regime is authoritarian, stifling dissent, and recent elections have been deemed neither free nor fair.

The Outermost Alexandria

Khudzand, the second largest city in Tajikistan, sits at the edge of the Fergana Valley on the ancient route from China to the Mediterranean known as the Silk Road. Khudzand was famous for marking the farthest eastward expansion of Alexander the Great (356–323 BC). Alexander built a fortress there called Alexandria Eskhat ('the Outermost Alexandria'), but it was destroyed in 1220 by Genghis Khan (c.1162–1227).

TANZANIA

Official name	United Republic of Tanzania
Local name	Tanzania
Former name	Republic of Tanganyika (1962–4), United Republic of Tanganyika and Zanzibar (1964)
Area	945 087 sq km (364 898 sq mi)
Capitals	Dodoma (political) and Dar es Salaam (commercial)
Chief towns	Zanzibar, Mwanza, Tanga, Arusha
Population	37 445 000 (2006e)
Nationality	Tanzanian
Languages	Kiswahili, English; Arabic is also spoken in Zanzibar, and there are many local languages
Ethnic groups	Tanganyika: Bantu 95% (includes over 120 tribes, none more than 10% of population), other African 4%, Asian, European, Arab and others 1%; Zanzibar: Arab, African, mixed
Religions	Tanganyika: Islam 35%, traditional beliefs 35%, Christianity 30%; Zanzibar: Islam 99%, others 1%
Time zone	GMT +3
Currency	1 Tanzanian Shilling (Tsh) = 100 cents
Telephone	+255
Internet	.tz
Country code	TZA

Location

An east African republic, consisting of the mainland region of Tanganyika, and Zanzibar, just off the coast in the Indian Ocean, which includes Zanzibar Island, Pemba Island and some small islets.

Physical description

The largest east African country, just south of the equator; the coast is fringed by long sandy beaches protected by coral reefs; the coastal plain rises towards a central plateau with an average elevation of 1000 m (3280 ft); high grasslands and mountain ranges lie to the centre and south; the Great Rift Valley branches around Lake Victoria in the north, where there are several high volcanic peaks, notably Mount Kilimanjaro (5895 m/19 340 ft); the extensive Serengeti plain lies to the west; the eastern branch of the Rift Valley runs through central Tanzania from north to east of Lake Victoria, containing several lakes; the western branch runs south down the west side of Lake Victoria, and includes Lake Tanganyika and Lake Rukwa.

Climate

Tropical, modified by altitude; hot and humid on the coast and offshore islands; the average temperatures are c.23°C in June–September and 27°C in December–March; average annual rainfall is more than 1100 mm; hot and dry on the central plateau, with an average annual rainfall of 250 mm; semi-temperate at altitudes above 1500 m; permanent snow on high peaks.

Economy

Very poor, and dependent on international aid; agriculture contributes 43% of GDP and employs c.80% of the workforce; main commercial crops are coffee, cashew nuts, cotton, tea, sugar cane, beer, tobacco and, on Zanzibar, cloves and coconuts; main industries are tourism, mining (gold, diamonds and iron) and manufacturing (processing agricultural products, cement, petroleum products, footwear, garments, wood products and fertilizer).

Government

Governed by an executive President, a Cabinet and a unicameral National Assembly.

History

Inhabited by Caucasoid peoples and then in the 5th century by Bantus from western Africa, the area had early links with Arab, Indian and Persian traders. The Swahili culture developed between the 10th and 15th centuries, and Portuguese explorers arrived in the 15th century. The island of Zanzibar was the capital of the Omani empire in the 1840s. Penetration of the interior by German missionaries and British explorers took place in the mid-19th century, and Zanzibar became a British protectorate in 1890. German East Africa was established in 1891 and by 1907 Germany controlled the whole country. After World War I, Tanganyika (mainland Tanzania) became a mandated territory under British administration (1919) and in 1961 it gained independence; it became a republic in 1962. Zanzibar was given independence as a constitutional monarchy, with the Sultan as head of state; the Sultan was overthrown in 1964, and Zanzibar united with Tanganyika to form the United Republic of Tanzania. The country was a one-party state under the Revolutionary Party of Tanzania (CCM) from 1977 to 1992, when a multiparty system was approved. The first multiparty elections were held in 1995 and were won by the CCM, which continues to dominate politics. Zanzibar is semi-autonomous, with its own president and legislature.

Dr Livingstone, I presume?

Dr David Livingstone (1813–73) travelled widely in Africa, working to open trade routes and campaigning to bring an end to the slave trade. In 1866 he was asked by the Royal Geographical Society to settle a disputed question regarding the watershed of central Africa and the sources of the Nile. He started in Zanzibar (now part of Tanzania) and pressed westwards until he discovered Lakes Mweru and Bangweulu; he later went as far as the River Lualaba, which proved to be the Congo. After severe illness Livingstone returned to Ujiji, where he was found in 1971 by Henry Morton Stanley (1841–1904) and greeted with the famous words, 'Dr Livingstone, I presume?'

THAILAND

Official name	Kingdom of Thailand
Local name	Prathet Thai
Former name	Siam (until 1939 and 1945–9)
Area	513 115 sq km (198 062 sq mi)
Capital	Bangkok; Krung Thep
Chief towns	Chiang Mai, Nakhon Ratchasima
Population	64 631 000 (2006e)
Nationality	Thai
Language	Thai
Ethnic groups	Thai 75%, Chinese 14%, others 11%
Religions	Buddhism 95%, Islam 4%, others 1%
Time zone	GMT +7
Currency	1 Baht (B) = 100 satang
Telephone	+66
Internet	.th
Country code	THA

Location

A kingdom in South-East Asia, bounded to the west by the Andaman Sea; to the west and north-west by Myanmar (Burma); to the north-east and east by Laos; to the east by Cambodia; and to the south by Malaysia.

Physical description

The centre is dominated by the fertile flood plain of the Chao Phraya River; a north-eastern plateau rises above 300 m (984 ft) and covers one-third of the country; a mountainous northern region rises to 2595 m (8514 ft) at Doi Inthanon; a narrow, low-lying southern isthmus with a spine of mountains separates the Andaman Sea from the Gulf of Thailand and is covered in tropical rainforest; there are mangrove-forested islands off the coast.

Climate

Equatorial climate in the south; tropical monsoon climate in the north and centre; rainfall mostly during the south-west monsoon (May–October) except in Kra Isthmus, which is wetter during the north-east monsoon (November–April), when the rest of the country has less rainfall.

Economy

Developing economy; main industry is tourism; agriculture employs nearly half the workforce and produces rice, cassava, rubber, maize, sugar cane, coconuts, soy beans and livestock; other activities include fishing, mining (tin, tungsten), processing agricultural products, manufacturing (textiles, footwear, computers and parts, furniture, plastics, vehicles and parts, electronics, jewellery and electrical appliances).

Government

A hereditary constitutional monarchy with a King as head of state; governed by a Prime Minister and Cabinet, and a legislature; following the 2006 coup, the bicameral National Assembly was replaced by an interim National Legislative Assembly and a National Assembly.

History

There is evidence that Thailand had Bronze Age communities in around 4000 BC. By the 7th century AD, Buddhism had spread to the country from India; Thailand's successful nationalist and reform movements have often had Buddhist leaders, and the work of the monastic order or *sangha* remains highly regarded in social terms. The Thai nation was founded in the 13th century, and is the only country in south and south-east Asia to have escaped colonization by a European power. It was occupied by the Japanese during World War II and had a military or military-controlled government for most of the time from 1945, until mass demonstrations in 1992 resulted in a return to civilian government and a reduction in the power of the military. After months of political turmoil, the military staged a coup in 2006 and established an interim government to rule until elections in 2007. Thailand was struck by the 2004 Indian Ocean tsunami, which killed thousands of people and caused widespread devastation.

TOGO

Official name	Togolese Republic
Local name	Togo; République Togolaise
Former name	French Togoland (until 1956)
Area	56 600 sq km (21 848 sq mi)
Capital	Lomé
Chief towns	Sokodé, Kpalimé, Atakpamé
Population	5 549 000 (2006e)
Nationality	Togolese
Languages	French; many local languages are also spoken
Ethnic groups	African 99% (mainly Ewe, Dagomba, Mina and Kabye), others 1%
Religions	traditional beliefs 51%, Christianity 29%, Islam 20%
Time zone	GMT
Currency	1 CFA Franc (CFAFr) = 100 centimes
Telephone	+228
Internet	.tg
Country code	TGO

Location

A republic in west Africa, bounded to the west by Ghana; to the north by Burkina Faso; to the east by Benin; and to the south by the Gulf of Guinea.

Physical description

Togo rises from the lagoon coast of the Gulf of Guinea, through low-lying plains to the Atakora Mountains, which run north-east to south-west across the centre of the country; the highest peak is Pic Baumann (Mount Agou; 986m/3235 ft); semi-arid savanna lies north of the mountains.

Climate

Tropical; one rainy season in the north (May–September) and two on the coast (April–June, October); the average annual rainfall at Lomé on the coast is 875 mm.

Economy

Very poor, dependent on international aid; agriculture employs 65% of the workforce and contributes 39% of GDP; chief cash crops are cotton, coffee and cocoa; industries are phosphate mining, processing agricultural products and light manufacturing; regional transhipment point and re-exports now generate highest export earnings.

Government

Governed by a President, a Prime Minister and Council of Ministers, and a unicameral National Assembly.

History

Formerly part of the Kingdom of Togoland, it was a German protectorate from 1884 to 1914. After World War I, it was divided between France (French Togo) and Britain (part of British Gold Coast) by mandate of the League of Nations (1922). In 1946 the British and French governments placed their territories under UN trusteeships. British Togoland integrated with Ghana when it became independent in 1957. French Togo gained its independence as Togo in 1960. There were military coups in Togo in 1963 and 1967, the latter bringing General Gnassingbé Eyadéma to power. In 1979 a new constitution was adopted, making the country a one-party state. Eyadéma was forced by violent demonstrations to legalize other political parties in 1992, but he and his party won the first multiparty elections in 1993 and all subsequent elections. They maintained their brutal suppression of opposition, particularly at the time of the 1998 elections. When Eyadéma died in 2005, his son Faure Gnassingbé was elected president. Reconciliation talks in 2006 agreed to the participation of opposition parties in a government of national unity pending credible elections.

The Slave Coast

The coast of Togo, along with that of Benin, was a busy area in the slave trade from the 16th to the early 19th century. The trade declined once the Abolition of the Slave Trade Act (1807) prohibited new slaves within the British Empire.

TONGA

Official name	Kingdom of Tonga
Local name	Tonga; Pule'anga Fakatu'l 'O Tonga (also sometimes known as the Friendly Islands)
Area	748 sq km (289 sq mi)
Capital	Nuku'alofa, on Tongatapu
Population	114 700 (2006e)
Nationality	Tongan
Languages	English, Tongan
Ethnic groups	Tongan 98%, others 2%
Religions	Christianity 79% (Prot 63%, RC 16%), others 21%
Time zone	GMT +13
Currency	1 Pa'anga/Tongan Dollar (T$) = 100 seniti
Telephone	+676
Internet	.to
Country code	TON

Location

An independent island group of c.170 islands in the south-west Pacific Ocean.

Physical description

Tonga consists of c.170 islands, 36 of which are inhabited, divided into three main groups (coral formations of Ha'apai and Tongatapu-Eua, mountainous Vava'u); the largest island is Tongatapu, with two-thirds of the population and an area of 260 sq km (100 sq mi); the western islands are mainly volcanic and some are still active; they rise to a height of 500–1000 m (1640–3280 ft); the highest point is the extinct volcano Kao (1046 m/3432 ft).

Climate

Semi-tropical; the average annual temperature at Tongatapu is 23°C and the average annual rainfall is 1750 mm; occasional cyclones (November–April), earthquakes and offshore volcanic activity.

Economy

Poor country, dependent on international aid and expatriates' remittances; main activities are agriculture (squashes, coconuts, bananas, vanilla beans, cocoa, coffee, ginger and black pepper), fishing and tourism.

Government

A hereditary monarchy; governed by the King, a Prime Minister and Privy Council (cabinet), and a unicameral Legislative Assembly (*Fale Alea*) dominated by hereditary chiefs.

istory

habited from as early as 1000 BC, the islands were visited by Captain James
ook in 1773 and named the Friendly Islands. They received missionaries and
ere established as a nation under King George Tupou I. Tonga became a British
rotectorate in 1899, under its own monarchy, and gained independence in 1970. A
ro-democracy movement started in 1992, Tonga's first political party was formed
1994, and elected MPs were appointed to the cabinet for the first time in 2005.
urther reform was promised after demonstrations, some violent, in 2005 and 2006.

RINIDAD AND TOBAGO

Official name	Republic of Trinidad and Tobago
Local name	Trinidad and Tobago
Area	5128 sq km (1979 sq mi)
Capital	Port of Spain
Chief towns	San Fernando, Arima, Scarborough
Population	1 100 000 (2006e)
Nationality	Trinidadian, Tobagonian
Language	English
Ethnic groups	East Indian 40%, black 37%, mixed 20%, others 3%
Religions	Christianity 54% (RC 26%, Prot 22%, other Christian 6%), Hinduism 22%, Islam 6%, others 15%, none/unaffiliated 3%
Time zone	GMT −4
Currency	1 Trinidad and Tobago Dollar (TT$) = 100 cents
Telephone	+1 868
Internet	.tt
Country code	TTO

ocation

republic comprising the southernmost islands of the Lesser Antilles chain in the
outh-east Caribbean Sea, just north of the South American mainland.

hysical description

he island of Trinidad is roughly rectangular in shape; separated from Venezuela in
e south by the 11 km (7 mi) Gulf of Paria; the island is crossed by three mountain
anges; the highest point is El Cerro del Aripo (940 m/3084 ft); the remainder of the
nd is low-lying, with large coastal mangrove swamps; Pitch Lake in the south-west
the world's largest reservoir of natural asphalt; Tobago lies 30 km (19 mi) to the
orth-east; the Main Ridge extends along most of the island, rising to 576 m (1890 ft).

limate

ropical, with an annual average temperature of 29°C; the average annual rainfall is
270 mm in the west, 3048 mm in the north-east.

conomy

lost prosperous country in the Caribbean owing to oil and natural gas production;

other activities include tourism, oil refining, food processing, petroleum products, chemicals (ammonia and methanol), steel products, cement, beverages, cotton textiles, car and appliance assembly, agriculture (cocoa, coffee, citrus fruits and flowers).

Government

Governed by a President, a Prime Minister and Cabinet, and a bicameral Parliament comprising a Senate and a House of Representatives.

History

Originally inhabited by Arawak and Carib Indians, the islands were visited by Christopher Columbus in 1498. Trinidad was settled by Spain in the 16th century; it was raided by the Dutch and French in the 17th century, when tobacco and sugar plantations worked by imported African slaves were established, and ceded to Britain in 1802 under the Treaty of Amiens. Tobago became a British colony in 1814. The two islands became a joint British colony in 1899, gained independence in 1962, and became a republic in 1976. The republic has been politically stable since independence, power alternating between the two main political parties.

TUNISIA

Official name	Tunisian Republic
Local name	Tūnisiya; Al-Jumhūriyya at-Tunisiyya
Area	164 150 sq km (63 362 sq mi)
Capital	Tunis; Toûnis, Tunus
Chief towns	Bizerta, Sousse, Sfax, Gabes
Population	10 175 000 (2006e)
Nationality	Tunisian
Languages	Arabic; French is also spoken
Ethnic groups	Arab and Berber 98%, European 1%, Jewish and others 1%
Religions	Islam 98%, Christianity 1%, Judaism and others 1%
Time zone	GMT +1
Currency	1 Tunisian Dinar (TD, D) = 1000 millimes
Telephone	+216
Internet	.tn
Country code	TUN

Location

A north African republic, bounded to the west by Algeria; to the south-east by Libya; and to the north-east and north by the Mediterranean Sea.

Physical description

The Atlas Mountains in the north-west rise to 1544 m (5066 ft) at Djebel Chambi; the central depression runs west to east, containing several salty lakes; dry, sandy upland areas lie to the south.

Climate

Mediterranean climate on the coast, with hot, dry summers and wet winters; the daily maximum temperature is 14–33°C; the average annual rainfall is 420 mm at Tunis and more than twice this level in the Atlas Mountains; further south, rainfall decreases and temperatures can be extreme.

Economy

Diverse industrialized economy in transition from state to private ownership; main industries are oil production, mining (especially phosphates and iron ore), tourism, processing agricultural products, manufacturing (textiles, footwear, beverages, mechanical goods and chemicals); agriculture is of declining importance; the country is the world's fourth-largest producer of olive oil.

Government

Governed by an executive President, a Prime Minister and Council of Ministers, and a bicameral Parliament comprising a Chamber of Deputies and a Chamber of Councillors.

History

It was ruled at various times by Phoenicians, Carthaginians, Romans, Byzantines, Arabs, Spanish and Turks due to its situation at the hub of the Mediterranean. It became a French protectorate in 1883 and gained independence in 1956. The monarchy was abolished in 1957 and the country became a republic under one-party rule with Habib Bourguiba as president. The government's refusal to meet demands for the legalization of other political parties led to serious unrest in the 1970s; a multiparty system was introduced in 1981, although the ruling party has retained its grip on power and tolerates little dissent. Bourguiba was deposed in 1987 by Zine el-Abidine Ben Ali, who remains president.

TURKEY

Official name	Republic of Turkey
Local name	Türkiye; Türkiye Çumhuriyeti
Area	779 452 sq km (300 868 sq mi)
Capital	Ankara; Angora
Chief towns	Istanbul, İzmir, Adana, Bursa, Gaziantep
Population	70 414 000 (2006e)
Nationality	Turk, Turkish
Languages	Turkish
Ethnic groups	Turkish 80%, Kurdish 16%, others 4%
Religions	Islam 99% (mostly Sunni), others 1%
Time zone	GMT +2
Currency	1 Turkish Lira (TL) = 100 kurus
Telephone	+90
Internet	.tr
Country code	TUR

Location

A republic lying partly in Europe and partly in Asia. The western area (Thrace) is bounded by the Aegean Sea and Greece, and to the north by Bulgaria and the Black Sea; the eastern area (Anatolia) is bounded by Georgia, Armenia, Azerbaijan and Iran, and to the south by Iraq, Syria and the Mediterranean Sea.

Physical description

A mountainous country with ranges extending along the north and south coasts of Anatolia; average altitude of the high central plateau is 1000–2000 m (3281–6562 ft); the Taurus Mountains cover the entire southern part of Anatolia; east Anatolia is the highest region, and the highest peak is Mount Ararat (5165 m/16 945 ft); the alluvial coastal plains are 2030 km (1219 mi) wide; chief rivers include the Kizil Irmak, Sakarya and Seyhan; the Tigris and the Euphrates rivers have their origins in Turkey; the Turkish Straits (the Dardanelles, Sea of Marmara and Bosporus), which connect the Black Sea and the Mediterranean Sea, separate the European and Asian parts of Turkey.

Climate

Mediterranean climate on the Aegean and Mediterranean coasts, with hot, dry summers and warm, wet winters; on the Black Sea coast, rainfall becomes heavy in summer and autumn; rainfall is low on the interior plateau, with cold winters, hot summers and occasional thunderstorms, susceptible to severe earthquakes, especially in the north.

Economy

Developing, industrialized economy, although many emigrant workers; main industries are textiles and clothing manufacture, vehicle assembly, iron and steel, electrical machinery, food processing, mining (coal, iron ore, chromium, copper and boron), steel-making, metal manufactures, forestry, paper, tourism; transhipment point for oil and gas from Central Asian countries; agriculture employs 36% of the workforce; the chief cash crops are tobacco, cotton, cereals, olives, sugar beet, citrus and other fruits, mohair, wool and hides.

Government

Governed by a President, a Prime Minister and Cabinet, and a unicameral Grand National Assembly.

History

Modern Turkey developed out of the Ottoman Empire and includes the area known as Asia Minor. It was formerly part of the empire of Alexander the Great, and of the Byzantine Empire. In the 13th century the Seljuk Sultanate was replaced by the Ottoman Sultanate in north-west Asia Minor. The Turkish invasion of Europe began with the Balkans in 1375, and in 1453 Constantinople fell to the Turks. The empire was at its peak in the 16th century, but in the 17th century began a slow decline; it lost most of its European territory in the 19th and early 20th centuries. Turkey allied with Germany during World War I, and its remaining territory was partitioned after the defeat. Following a revolution, the sultanate was abolished and the Republic of Turkey was proclaimed in 1923. It was led by Kemal Atatürk, who introduced policies of westernization, economic development and secularism. Turkey was neutral

roughout most of World War II, before siding with the Allies in 1945. It joined NATO
1952. There were military coups in 1960, 1971, 1980 and 1997; the military's
olitical influence remains considerable, although measures to reduce this have been
troduced to satisfy European Union requirements since Turkey became a candidate
r membership in 1999. Relations with Greece have been strained since 1974, when
urkey invaded northern Cyprus in support of Turkish Cypriots and subsequently
cognized the regime established there. Since the 1980s the south-east of Anatolia
as suffered fierce fighting between government forces and Kurdish separatists,
specially the Kurdish Workers' Party (PKK), who want to establish an independent
tate for Turkey's 12 million Kurds. A number of political parties have been banned
nce 1998 for anti-secular activities. A number of bombings, attributed to Muslim
xtremists, occurred in 2003 and 2004.

URKMENISTAN

Official name	Turkmenistan
Local name	Turkmenostan; Turkmenostan Respublikasy
Former name	Turkmen Soviet Socialist Republic (1924–91), within the Union of Soviet Socialist Republics (USSR; 1925–91)
Area	488 100 sq km (188 400 sq mi)
Capital	Ashgabat; Ašgabat, Ašhabad
Chief towns	Chardzhou, Mary, Türkmenbashi, Nebit-Dag
Population	5 043 000 (1999e)
Nationality	Turkmens
Languages	Turkmen, Russian, Uzbek
Ethnic groups	Turkmen 85%, Uzbek 5%, Russian 4%, others 6%
Religions	Islam 89% (mostly Sunni), Christianity 9% (Orthodox), others 2%
Time zone	GMT +5
Currency	1 Manat (TMM) = 100 tenesi
Telephone	+993
Internet	.tm
Country code	TKM

Location

republic in south-west Central Asia, bounded to the north by Kazakhstan and
zbekistan; to the south by Iran and Afghanistan; and to the west by the Caspian
ea.

Physical description

ow-lying with hills and mountains in the south; the highest point is Ayrybaba
139 m/10 298 ft); there are some areas below sea level by the Caspian Sea; mainly
esert; the chief river is the Amudarya.

Climate

Continental; hot and arid in the large desert areas.

Economy

State-controlled and inefficient; hydrocarbon exports restricted by lack of pipelines, now under construction; agriculture employs 48% of workforce; chief crops are cotton, silk, cereals and livestock; main industries are oil and gas production, oil refining, petrochemicals, mining, processing agricultural products and textiles.

Government

Governed by an executive President, a Council of Ministers and a bicameral legislature consisting of an elected Parliament and a largely appointed People's Council, which is the supreme representative and legislative body.

History

The area was invaded and occupied by many empires, including the Persian, Greek (under Alexander the Great), Parthian and Mongol empires. In the 19th century it was incorporated into the Russian Empire. A brief period of autonomy ended in 1921, when it became part of the Union of Soviet Socialist Republics (USSR). In 1991 it gained its independence and became a member of the Commonwealth of Independent States (CIS). Saparmurad Niyazov became leader of the Turkmen Communist Party in 1985 and was elected president in 1990. He remained in power until his death in 2006, his autocratic regime preventing the development of political pluralism or press freedom and promoting a personality cult. Kurbanguly Berdymukhamedov became acting president until elections in 2007.

TUVALU

Official name	Tuvalu
Local name	Tuvalu; Fakavae Aliki-Malo I Tuvalu
Former name	Ellice Islands, as part of the Gilbert and Ellice Islands (until 1975)
Area	26 sq km (10 sq mi)
Capital	Funafuti (in Vaiaku village on Fongafale islet)
Population	11800 (2006e)
Nationality	Tuvaluan
Languages	Tuvaluan, English
Ethnic groups	Polynesia 96%, others 4%
Religions	Christianity 97%, Baha'i 1%, others 2%
Time zone	GMT +12
Currency	1 Australian Dollar (A$) = 100 cents
Telephone	+688
Internet	.tv
Country code	TUV

Location

An independent island group in the south-west Pacific, 1050 km (650 mi) north of Fiji.

Physical description

Comprises nine low-lying coral atolls, rising no higher than 5 m (16 ft), running north-west to south-east in a chain 580 km (360 mi) long.

Climate

Tropical; the average annual temperature is 30°C and the average annual rainfall is 3535 mm.

Economy

Undeveloped, with few resources; revenues from government investments, expatriates' remittances, sale of fishing licences, postage stamps and coins, leasing its international telephone code and internet suffix, fishing and subsistence agriculture; only cash crop is coconuts (copra); small-scale tourism exists.

Government

Governed by a Governor-General (representing the British monarch, who is head of state), a Prime Minister and Cabinet, and a unicameral Parliament.

History

Settled by Polynesians in the 16th century, the islands became a British protectorate as the Ellice Islands in 1877, were part of the British Protectorate of the Gilbert and Ellice Islands from 1892, and were annexed as the Gilbert and Ellice Islands Colony in 1916. The colonies were separated following a 1974 referendum, and the Ellice Islands gained independence as Tuvalu in 1978. Tuvalu is threatened by rising sea levels, which have already damaged its agriculture. In 2002, with Kiribati and the Maldives, it began legal action against the USA over its refusal to sign the Kyoto Protocol.

Internet Income

Until recently, Tuvalu had few ways of making money – the land supports only subsistence farming, leaving fishing as the country's main means of income. They had better fortune, however, when country internet suffixes were handed out. Tuvalu was assigned .tv and has been able to raise around $50 million by leasing the suffix to television and media companies over a ten-year period. The money has been used to pave roads, build schools and provide electricity; it also funds the country's membership of the United Nations.

UGANDA

Official name	Republic of Uganda
Local name	Uganda
Area	238 461 sq km (92 069 sq mi)
Capital	Kampala
Chief towns	Jinja, Mbale, Tororo, Soroti, Entebbe
Population	28 196 000 (2006e)
Nationality	Ugandan
Languages	English; Ganda/Luganda, Swahili and other languages are also spoken
Ethnic groups	Baganda 17%, Banyankole 8%, Basoga 8%, Iteso 8%, Bakiga 7%, Langi 6%, Rwanda 6%, Bagisu 5%, Acholi 4%, Lugbara 4%, non-African (European, Asian, Arab) 1%, others 26%
Religions	Christianity 66% (RC 33%, Prot 33%), traditional beliefs 18%, Islam 16%
Time zone	GMT +3
Currency	1 Uganda Shilling (USh) = 100 cents
Telephone	+256
Internet	.ug
Country code	UGA

Location

A landlocked east African republic, bounded to the south by Rwanda, Tanzania and Lake Victoria; to the east by Kenya; to the north by Sudan; and to the west by the Democratic Republic of the Congo.

Physical description

Mainly on a plateau with an elevation of 900–1000 m (2953–3281 ft); dry savanna or semi-desert north of Lake Kyoga; the population is concentrated in the fertile Lake Victoria basin; the Western Rift Valley runs along Uganda's frontier with the Democratic Republic of the Congo; straddling the frontier is the Mount Stanley massif, including Margherita Peak (5110 m/16 765 ft), the highest point in Uganda; c.20% of the country is lakes, rivers and wetlands; contains half of Lakes Victoria, Edward and Albert as well as Lakes Kwania, Kyoga, George and Bisina (formerly Lake Salisbury); the two main rivers are the upper reaches of the River Nile (the Victoria Nile and the Albert Nile).

Climate

Tropical; the highest rainfall is in the mountains to the west and south-west and along the shores of Lake Victoria, exceeding 1500 mm per year; daily temperatures at Entebbe on the north shore of the lake are 24–8°C; central and north-eastern areas receive less than 1000 mm of rain annually.

Economy

Poor, and dependent on international aid; agriculture and fishing are the economic mainstays, supporting 80% of the population and providing the main exports; chief cash crops are coffee, tea, cotton, tobacco and fresh flowers; other activities include mining, manufacturing (cotton textiles) and hydroelectric power generation.

Government

Governed by a President, a Prime Minister and Cabinet, and a unicameral Parliament. The first multiparty elections since 1980 were held in 2006. The National Resistance Movement has dominated politics since 1986.

History

Bantu-speaking peoples migrated into south-west Uganda in around 500 BC, and by the 14th century were organized into several kingdoms. Uganda was discovered by Arab traders and British explorers in the 19th century and granted to the Imperial British East Africa Company in 1888. The Kingdom of Buganda became a British protectorate in 1893, and other territory was included by 1903. Uganda gained its independence in 1962 as a federation of the kingdoms of Ankole, Buganda, Bunyoro, Busoga and Toro. It became a federal republic in 1963 but the federal status was dropped in 1966 after a coup by the prime minister, Dr Milton Obote, who became president. He was deposed in a 1971 military coup led by General Idi Amin Dada, whose repressive regime was overthrown in 1979. Obote returned to power but failed to restore stability and another military coup took place in 1985 in the midst of a civil war with rebels led by Yoweri Museveni. The rebels took control of the country in 1986 and Museveni became president, beginning a process of reconstruction that has resulted in relative peace and stability for the past 20 years. Museveni and his National Resistance Movement have retained power in subsequent elections. The ban on political parties was lifted in 1995 and they were allowed to contest elections for the first time in 2006. The Lord's Resistance Army (LRA) has conducted an insurgency in the north since the late 1980s, massacring or mutilating thousands, abducting over 20000 children to serve in its forces and displacing over 1.6 million people. A ceasefire began in 2006.

Uganda's Mountain Gorillas

Mountain Gorillas are the most endangered subspecies of gorilla, with only about 700 left in the wild. Nearly half of the world's Mountain Gorillas live in Uganda's Bwindi Impenetrable Forest Gorilla Sanctuary; the rest reside in the nearby Virunga mountains, which Uganda shares with Rwanda and the Democratic Republic of Congo. The gorillas are shy and gentle herbivores threatened mostly by forest clearance due to an expanding human population in the area. Although not proactively violent, the male Silverback gorilla will protect his group from humans or predators when threatened, giving his life for the sake of the others if necessary.

UKRAINE

Official name	Ukraine
Local name	Ukraïna
Former name	Ukrainian Soviet Socialist Republic (1919–91), within the Union of Soviet Socialist Republics (USSR; 1922–91)
Area	603 700 sq km (233 028 sq mi)
Capital	Kiev; Kyïv
Chief towns	Kharkov, Donetsk, Odessa, Dnepropetrovsk, Lvov, Zaporozhye, Krivoy Rog
Population	46 711 000 (2006e)
Nationality	Ukrainian
Languages	Ukrainian, Russian
Ethnic groups	Ukrainian 78%, Russian 17%, others (including Tatar) 5%
Religions	Christianity 75% (Orthodox), unaffiliated 22%, others 1%
Time zone	GMT +2
Currency	1 Hryvnia = 100 kopiykas
Telephone	+380
Internet	.ua
Country code	UKR

Location

A republic in eastern Europe, bounded to the south-west by Moldova and Romania; to the west by Hungary, Slovakia and Poland; to the north by Belarus; to the east by Russia; and to the south by the Black Sea.

Physical description

Most of the country lies in a plain, rising to plateaux in the west, south and south-east; the Ukrainian Carpathian Mountains in the west rise to 2061 m (6762 ft) at Hora Hoverla; the Crimean Peninsula separates the Black Sea from the Sea of Azov; the Crimean Mountains lie along the south coast of the peninsula; chief rivers are the Dnieper, Dniester, Severskiy Donets and Prut; there are many reservoirs and lakes.

Climate

Temperate continental, with cold winters and warm summers; Mediterranean on the south Crimean coast, with cool winters and hot summers.

Economy

Industrialized economy; growth inhibited by slow pace of economic reform; agriculture employs c.25% of the workforce; chief crops are wheat, sugar beet, sunflowers, vegetables and livestock; main industry is mining (coal, iron ore and non-ferrous minerals) and metallurgy, providing over 40% of export earnings; other industries are electricity generation, petrochemicals, chemicals, machinery and transport equipment, shipbuilding, engineering and food processing (especially sugar).

Government

Governed by a President, a Prime Minister and Council of Ministers, and a unicameral legislature, the Supreme Council.

History

Inhabited by Scythians in ancient times, the country was then invaded by Goths, Huns and Khazars. Kiev became the centre of power of a Slavic state in the 9th century, but it was overrun by the Golden Horde in the 14th century. Ruled by Lithuania in the 14th and 15th centuries, Ukraine came under Polish rule in the 16th century, when many people fled and formed resistance movements (Cossacks). It gradually became part of Russia in the 17th and 18th centuries. Ukraine declared its independence in 1918, but Kiev was occupied by Soviet troops and the country became a Soviet Socialist Republic in 1922. Ukraine gained territory in the west after World War II, and in 1954 the largely Russian-populated Crimea was transferred from Russia to Ukraine. In 1986 the Chernobyl nuclear disaster occurred, leaving around 8 per cent of the country contaminated. Ukraine became independent in 1991 and was a founding member of the Commonwealth of Independent States (CIS). There is a marked divide between the Russian-influenced east and the European-influenced west, which is reflected in political divisions. These came to a head after the presidential election in 2004, when mass demonstrations and civil disobedience greeted the announcement of the Russian-backed Viktor Yanukovych's victory; the result was eventually overturned because of voting irregularities and the rerun election was won by pro-European Viktor Yushchenko. Yanukovych became prime minister after the 2006 legislative election. Ukraine accepted the Crimea's declaration of autonomy in 1991, but rejected its 1992 vote for independence, imposing direct rule in 1994–5; considerable autonomy was granted in 1999.

Ukrainian Easter Eggs

The tradition of making decorative Easter eggs, called *Pysanka* or *Pysanky*, started in the Ukraine, where the origins of this art can be traced back 5,000 years – long before the appearance of Christianity. The egg was part of many ceremonies and rituals before Easter came about, because it was seen as a symbol of life and renewal just as the spring brings life and renewal to the Earth. The colours and symbols used in Pysanky have various symbolistic meanings relating to stages and events in life. Ukrainians saw the egg as a talisman and Pysanky was a way to protect them from the evils in the world.

Complicated Pysanky designs can take hours to complete. The patterns are often very ornate and contain many different colours from pastel to bold. Designs are drawn on eggs with wax and dye is added, much like the Batik wax-resist method of dying cloth; this method is repeated over and over again with different colours of dye until the egg is complete.

UNITED ARAB EMIRATES

Official name	United Arab Emirates (UAE)
Local name	Ittihād al-imārāt al-'Arabīyah
Former name	Trucial States (until 1968), Federation of Arab Emirates (1968–71)
Area	83 600 sq km (32 300 sq mi)
Capital	Abu Dhabi; Abū Zhaby
Chief towns	Dubai, Sharjah, Ras al-Khaimah
Population	2 603 000 (2006e)
Nationality	Emirati
Languages	Arabic; English, Persian, Hindi and Urdu are also spoken
Ethnic groups	Emirati 19%, other Arab and Iranian 23%, South Asian 50%, other expatriates (including Western and East Asian) 8%; fewer than 20% are UAE citizens
Religions	Islam 96% (Sunni 80%, Shia 16%), others 4%
Time zone	GMT +4
Currency	1 Dirham (DH) = 100 fils
Telephone	+971
Internet	.ae
Country code	ARE

Location

A federation of seven autonomous emirates in the eastern-central Arabian Peninsula. It is bounded to the north by the Arabian Gulf; to the east by Oman; and to the south and west by Saudi Arabia.

Physical description

Comprises the emirates of Abu Dhabi, Ajman, Dubai, Fujairah, Ras al-Khaimah, Sharjah and Umm al-Qaiwan; located along the southern shore (Trucial Coast) of the Arabian Gulf; Fujairah has a coastline along the Gulf of Oman; salt marshes predominate on the coast; there is a barren desert and gravel plain inland; the Hajar Mountains in Fujairah rise to more than 1000 m (3281 ft); the highest point is Jabal Yibir (1527 m/5010 ft).

Climate

Dry subtropical, hot with limited rainfall; winter temperatures average 21°C, with high humidity (in excess of 70%); less humid in summer, with maximum temperatures rising to 45°C; sandstorms are common; the average annual rainfall in Abu Dhabi is 32 mm.

Economy

Prosperity is based on oil and gas production; diversified into petrochemicals, construction and manufacturing (aluminium, cement, chemicals, fertilizer, pharmaceuticals, construction materials, handicrafts and textiles); fishing, ship repair, boat-building, financial services, tourism and agriculture (dates, vegetables and fruit); Abu Dhabi is a main hydrocarbon producer; Dubai is a regional entrepôt, tourist centre and free-trade zone; other emirates are dependent on Abu Dhabi and the federal government, although Sharjah is a manufacturing base.

Government

Governed by a Supreme Council comprising the hereditary rulers of the seven emirates. The Council elects a President and Vice-President from among its number, and the President appoints the Prime Minister and Council of Ministers; an appointed Federal National Council, which has an advisory role, became partially elected in 2006. Each emirate has its own government.

History

As early as the third millennium bc the area was crossed by many Sumerian trade routes. It came under Muslim influence from the 6th century and was visited by the Portuguese in the 16th century. The British East India Company arrived in the 17th century. Various peace treaties with Britain were signed from 1820 by the ruling sheikhs of what became known as the Trucial States, which accepted British protection in 1892. Abu Dhabi's huge oilfields were discovered in 1958. A federal state was formed by six emirates on independence in 1971; the emirate of Ras al Khaimah joined the following year. Sheik Zayed of Abu Dhabi was president from independence until his death in 2004. He was succeeded as Sultan of Abu Dhabi by his son, Sheikh Khalifa, who was also elected president of the UAE. A limited degree of democracy was introduced with elections to the consultative Federal National Council in 2006.

UNITED KINGDOM

Official name	United Kingdom of Great Britain and Northern Ireland (UK)
Local name	United Kingdom
Area	242 495 sq km (93 627 sq mi)
Capital	London
Chief towns	Belfast, Birmingham, Bradford, Cardiff, Edinburgh, Glasgow, Leeds, Liverpool, Manchester, Newcastle upon Tyne, Sheffield
Population[1]	60 210 000 (2005e)
Nationality	British, Briton
Languages	English; Welsh and Gaelic are spoken by minorities
Ethnic groups	White 94%, Asian 1%, West Indian 1%, Indian 1%, others 3%
Religions	Christianity 72%, none/unaffiliated 16%, Islam 3%, Hinduism 1%, others 2%, unknown 8%
Time zone	GMT
Currency	1 Pound Sterling (£) = 100 pence
Telephone	+44
Internet	.uk
Country code	GBR

[1] *Source: UK Office for National Statistics*

Location

A kingdom in western Europe, comprising England, Scotland, Wales and Northern Ireland.

Physical description

See England, Northern Ireland, Scotland and Wales below.

Climate

Temperate maritime climate, moderated by prevailing south-west winds; generally wetter and warmer in the west.

Economy

Highly developed and technologically advanced economy, now based on services and trade; first industrialized economy, in 19c; heavy industry and manufacturing declined in late 20c; services (especially banking, insurance and business services; electronics; telecommunications; and tourism) now form the largest economic sector, contributing 75% of GDP and employing c.80% of the workforce; industry is declining in importance, contributing 24% of GDP and employing 19% of the workforce; industrial output is predominantly of manufactured goods (machine tools; electronics, communications, automation, transport and electric power equipment; motor vehicles and parts; chemicals; paper and paper products; textiles; garments; other consumer goods), the rest being fuels (coal, North Sea oil and natural gas), processed food and agricultural raw materials, ores and metals; intensive, highly mechanized agricultural sector produces 60% of food needs with less than 2% of the workforce, contributing 1% of GDP.

Government

A hereditary constitutional monarchy with a Queen as head of state; governed by a Prime Minister and Cabinet, and a bicameral Parliament comprising an elected House of Commons and an appointed House of Lords.

History

Wales was effectively joined to England in 1301, then Scotland was joined under one crown in 1603 (and by legislative union in 1707) and Ireland in 1801 (the United Kingdom of Great Britain and Ireland). The present name dates from 1922, following the establishment of the Irish Free State. There was major colonial expansion in the 18th and 19th centuries; most colonies were granted independence in the 20th century. The UK joined the European Community in 1973.

England

Area	130 279 sq km (50 301 sq mi)
Capital	London
Chief towns	Birmingham, Bradford, Liverpool, Leeds, Manchester, Newcastle upon Tyne, Sheffield
Population[1]	50 431 831 (2005e)
Nationality	English

[1] *Source: UK Office for National Statistics*

Physical description

Largely undulating lowland, rising in the south to the Mendips, Cotswolds, Chilterns and North Downs, in the north to the north–south ridge of the Pennines and in the north-west to the Cumbria Mountains; the highest point is Scafell Pike at 978 m (3209 ft); drained in the east by the Tyne, Tees, Humber, Ouse and Thames rivers, and in the west by the Eden, Ribble, Mersey and Severn rivers; the Lake District in the north-west includes Derwent Water, Ullswater, Windermere and Bassenthwaite.

History

England was conquered by the Roman Empire in the 1st century ad. From the 4th century Germanic tribes raided and then occupied the country, forcing many of the Romano-British inhabitants westwards into Cornwall and Wales. Various kingdoms were established, coming under attack and eventual occupation by the Vikings in the 9th century. England was retaken in the 10th century and unified under the kings of Wessex, although it was conquered and ruled by Danish kings in the early 11th century. English rule was restored in 1042, but the country was conquered by William I, the Conqueror, in 1066. The Magna Carta, which began the nation's constitutional development, was signed during the reign of King John in 1215. Under Edward I, England succeeded in conquering Wales by 1283. The Wars of the Roses from 1455 until 1485 resulted in the House of Tudor becoming the ruling family until 1603. There was major colonial expansion in the 16th century. In the 17th century there was a seven-year war between Royalists and Parliamentarians (the English Civil Wars), at the end of which Charles I was executed (1649). The first Act of Union was signed in 1707, joining England in legislative union with Scotland; the second, which was signed in 1800, joined England and Scotland with Ireland, creating the United Kingdom (UK).

Northern Ireland

Area	13 576 sq km (5 242 sq mi)
Capital	Belfast
Chief towns	Armagh, Londonderry
Population[1]	1 724 400 (2005e)
Nationality	Northern Irish

[1] *Source: UK Office for National Statistics*

Physical description

Northern Ireland occupies the north-eastern part of Ireland, and is centred on Lough Neagh; to the north and east are the Antrim Mountains; the Mourne Mountains are in the south-east; the highest point is Slieve Donard at 852 m (2795 ft).

History

A separate parliament to the rest of Ireland (Stormont) was established in 1920, with a House of Commons and a Senate. There is a Protestant majority in the population, generally supporting political union with Great Britain; many of the Roman Catholic minority look for union with the Republic of Ireland. Violent conflict between the communities broke out in 1968 (the Ulster 'Troubles'), leading to the establishment of a British Army peacekeeping force. Sectarian murders and bombings continued both within and outside the province; as a result of the disturbances the Northern Irish parliament was abolished in 1972. Legislative and executive powers were vested in the UK Secretary of State for Northern Ireland from 1972 to 1999 and since 2002. Negotiations between the political parties took place in Belfast in 1991 and 1992, leading to the Downing Street Declaration by UK and Irish governments in 1993. An IRA ceasefire was announced in 1994–6, but there was renewed violence in 1996–7 until the ceasefire recommenced in 1997. Further cross-party talks resulted in the Good Friday Agreement in 1998, under which the Northern Ireland Assembly with devolved powers was established in 1999. Devolved government was suspended in late 2002 after the Unionists refused to work with Sinn Fein following the discovery of its apparent involvement in intelligence gathering for terrorist purposes. Talks on the restoration of devolved government have been unsuccessful so far.

Scotland

Area	77 907 sq km (30 080 sq mi)
Capital	Edinburgh
Chief towns	Aberdeen, Dundee, Glasgow, Inverness, Perth
Population[1]	5 094 800 (2005e)
Nationality	Scot, Scottish

[1] *Source: UK Office for National Statistics*

Physical description

Divided into the Southern Uplands (rising to 843 m/2766 ft at Merrick), the Central Lowlands (formed by the valleys of the Clyde, Forth and Tay rivers, and the most densely populated area) and the Northern Highlands (divided by the fault line following the Great Glen, and rising to 1344 m/4406 ft at Ben Nevis); there are 787 islands, most of which lie off the heavily indented west coast and only c.60 exceed 8 sq km (3 sq mi); there are several wide estuaries on the east coast, primarily the Firths of Forth, Tay and Moray; the interior has many freshwater lochs, the largest being Loch Lomond (70 sq km/27 sq mi) and the deepest Loch Morar (310 m/1017 ft); the major rivers are the Clyde, Tay (the longest, at 192 km/119 mi), Dee, Spey and Tweed.

History

Roman attempts to limit incursions of northern tribes were marked by the building of the Antonine Wall (AD 142), which extended from the Forth estuary to the Clyde, and Hadrian's Wall (AD 122–8), which extended from the Solway Firth to the River Tyne and was the principal northern frontier of the Roman province of Britain. The unification of the area now comprising Scotland began in the 9th century and was completed in the 12th century, with the Norse-controlled islands being added between the 13th and 16th centuries. From the 11th century there were frequent wars with England over territory and the extent of English influence, which amounted to overlordship in the late 13th century. Scottish independence was restored by Robert Bruce, and recognized by England in 1328. The Stuarts succeeded to the throne in the 14th century and united the crowns of Scotland and England in 1603; the parliaments were united under the Act of Union in 1707 although Scotland has always retained separate legal and educational systems. There were unsuccessful Jacobite rebellions in 1715 and 1745. A proposal for devolution failed in a referendum in 1979, but another in 1997 gave it overwhelming approval and a Scottish parliament with tax-raising powers was elected, officially opening in 1999.

Wales

Area	20 733 sq km (8 055 sq mi)
Capital	Cardiff
Chief towns	Swansea, Wrexham
Population[1]	2 958 600 (2005e)
Nationality	Welsh

[1] Source: UK Office for National Statistics

Physical description

Mostly high plateaux with short mountain ranges divided by deep river valleys; rises in the north-west to 1085 m (3560 ft) at Snowdon in the Snowdonia range (the highest point); the Cambrian Mountains rise in the centre, and the Brecon Beacons in the south; drained by the Severn, Clwyd, Conwy, Dee, Dovey, Taff, Tawe, Teifi, Towy, Usk and Wye rivers.

History

The Celtic peoples of Wales resisted the Roman invasion but were subjugated in around AD 78. With the retreat of the Romans, Wales became a refuge for the Romano-British inhabitants driven westwards by Germanic invaders of southern Britain from the 4th century. In the 8th century Welsh territory was lost to Offa, King of Mercia, who built a frontier dyke from the Dee to the Wye. Although in the 9th century Rhodri Mawr united Wales against the Saxons, Norse and Danes, union was never maintained permanently, weakening resistance to English incursions. Edward I of England established authority over Wales, building several castles in the 12 and 13th centuries, and his son was created the first Prince of Wales (1301). Nationalist feeling remained strong; a revolt against Henry IV was led by Owen Glendower in the early 15th century, although it was tempered by the accession of the Tudors to the English throne in 1485. Wales was politically united with England at the Act of Union in 1535, which extended English laws to Wales and gave it parliamentary representation for the first time. Wales became the centre of Nonconformist religion in the 18th century. A political nationalist movement developed; this was embodied in Plaid Cymru, which returned its first MP in 1966. A referendum in 1979 opposed devolution, but another in 1997 narrowly approved it; the opening session of the Welsh Assembly was held in June 1999.

British islands[1]

Channel Islands

Location	An island group of the British Isles in the English Channel, west of the Cotentin Peninsula of Normandy. A dependent territory of the British Crown, it has individual legislative assemblies and legal system and is divided into the Bailiwicks of Jersey and of Guernsey. Main islands: Guernsey, Jersey, Alderney, Sark; other islands include Herm, Jethou, Brechou, the Caskets, the Minquiers and the Chauseys.		
Area	194 sq km (75 sq mi)	Language	Both English and Norman-French *patois* are spoken
Capital	St Helier (Jersey); St Peter Port (Guernsey)	Internet	.gg (Guernsey), .je (Jersey)
Population	65 400 (Bailiwick of Guernsey; 2006e)	Country code	GGY (Guernsey), JEY (Jersey)
	91 000 (Bailiwick of Jersey; 2006e)		

Government

There are legislative assemblies in Jersey, Guernsey, Alderney (the States) and Sark (the Chief Pleas), and each Bailiwick has its own legal system and Royal Court. A Crown-appointed Bailiff presides over the States and the Royal Court of each Bailiwick.

Economy

Financial services (used as a tax haven); agriculture and horticulture (fruit, vegetables; flowers; dairy produce, Jersey and Guernsey cattle); tourism.

History

The islands were granted to the Dukes of Normandy in the 10th century, and were the only part of Normandy remaining with the English Crown after 1204. They were occupied by Germany in World War II.

Isle of Man

Location	A British Crown Dependency in the Irish Sea, west of England and east of Northern Ireland.		
Area	572 sq km (221 sq mi)	Languages	English; Manx is also spoken
Capital	Douglas	Internet	.im
Population	75 400 (2006e)	Country code	IMN
Nationality	Manx		

[1] *Part of the British Isles but not included in the United Kingdom.*

Government

The island has its own parliamentary, legal and administrative systems. The legislature, the bicameral Court of Tynwald, consists of the elected House of Keys and the Legislative Council (composed of the the President of Tynwald, the Bishop of Sodor and Man, the Attorney-General and eight members elected by the House of Keys). Acts of the British Parliament do not generally apply to the Isle of Man.

Economy

Financial services (used as a tax haven); tourism; light manufacturing; agriculture.

History

Ruled by the Welsh between the 6th and 9th centuries, then by the Scandinavians, Scots and English. The island was purchased by the British government partly in 1765 and wholly in 1828. Manx survived as an everyday language until the 19th century.

UK dependent territories

Anguilla

Location	The most northerly of the Leeward Islands in the east Caribbean Sea.		
Area	90 sq km/35 sq mi	**Nationality**	Anguillan
Capital	The Valley	**Internet**	.ai
Population	13 500 (2006e)	**Country code**	AIA

Government

Internally self-governing; the British monarch is represented by a Governor, assisted by an Executive Council and a unicameral House of Assembly.

Economy

Tourism, fishing; boatbuilding; offshore financial services, agriculture (peas, corn, sweet potatoes, cattle, tobacco).

History

Colonized by English settlers in 1650, Anguilla was linked administratively with St Christopher and Nevis for most of its history until 1980.

Bermuda

Location	A group of c.138 low-lying, coral islands and islets situated in the west Atlantic Ocean c.900 km (560 mi) east of Cape Hatteras, North Carolina (USA).		
Area	53 sq km (20 sq mi)	**Nationality**	Bermudian
Capital	Hamilton	**Internet**	.bm
Population	65 700 (2006e)	**Country code**	BMU

Government

Internally self-governing; the British monarch is represented by a Governor-General, assisted by a Cabinet and a bicameral assembly (Senate and House of Assembly).

Economy

Financial and business services (especially insurance and as a corporate business centre); tourism; manufacturing (petroleum products, pharmaceuticals, perfumes), boatbuilding, ship repair; vegetables; citrus and banana plantations; flowers; fish processing.

History

The island was discovered by a Spanish mariner, Juan Bermudez, in the early 16th century. It was colonized by English settlers in 1612, becoming an important naval station and (until 1862) penal settlement. Internal self-government was granted in 1968. A movement for independence caused tension in the 1970s, including the assassination of the Governor-General in 1973, but a referendum rejected independence in 1995.

British Antarctic Territory

Location	A United Kingdom Overseas Territory which includes the South Orkney Islands, the South Shetland Islands, the Graham Land Peninsula in Antarctica, and the Antarctic land mass extending to the South Pole.
Area	1 709 400 sq km (666 000 sq mi) **Population** Populated solely by scientists of the British Antarctic Survey.

Government

Administered by a Commissioner based at the Foreign and Commonwealth Office in London.

Economy

Some tourism; postage stamps.

History

It was first sighted by explorers in the early 19th century. It was part of the Falkland Islands Dependencies when the British Antarctic Survey arrived in 1943–4, and became the British Antarctic Territory in 1962.

British Indian Ocean Territory

Location	A British territory consisting of the Chagos Archipelago in the Indian Ocean, covering 54 400 sq km (21 003 sq mi) of ocean and lying 1900 km (1180 mi) north-east of Mauritius.		
Area	60 sq km (23 sq mi)	**Internet**	.io
Population	Indigenous population relocated; military personnel and civilian support staff only.	**Country code**	IOT

Government

Administered by a Commissioner based at the Foreign and Commonwealth Office in London.

Economy

Construction projects and services in support of the military base on Diego Garcia.

History

Acquired by France in the 18th century, the islands were annexed by Britain in 1814 and administered as dependencies of Mauritius and the Seychelles until 1965. The Territory was established to meet UK and US defence requirements in the Indian Ocean; Diego Garcia was evacuated in 1967–73 to allow the construction of a UK–US naval support facility.

British Virgin Islands

Location	A group of over 40 islands, islets and cays at the north-western end of the Lesser Antilles chain in the east Caribbean Sea.		
Area	153 sq km (59 sq mi)	**Nationality**	British Virgin Islander
Capital	Road Town	**Internet**	.vg
Population	23 100 (2006e)	**Country code**	VGB

Government

Internally self-governing; the British monarch is represented by a Governor, assisted by an Executive Council and a unicameral Legislative Council.

Economy

Tourism; financial services; rum; gravel and stone extraction; manufacturing (concrete, paint); livestock; coconuts; sugar cane; fruit; vegetables; fish.

History

Tortola, the largest of the islands, was colonized by British planters in 1666, and a constitutional government was granted in 1774. The islands became part of the Leeward Islands in 1872 and a separate Crown Colony in 1956. They gained internal self-government in 1977.

Cayman Islands

Location	An island group in the west Caribbean Sea, comprising the islands of Grand Cayman, Cayman Brac and Little Cayman, c.240 km (150 mi) south of Cuba.		
Area	260 sq km (100 sq mi)	**Nationality**	Caymanian
Capital	George Town	**Internet**	.ky
Population	45 400 (2006e)	**Country code**	CYM

Government

Mainly internally self-governing; the British monarch is represented by a Governor, assisted by a Cabinet and a unicameral Legislative Assembly.

Economy

Financial services; tourism (including cruise ship traffic); property development; oil transhipment; crafts, jewellery; cattle, poultry; vegetables; tropical fish; turtle products.

History

The islands were discovered by Christopher Columbus in 1503. They were ceded to Britain in 1670 and colonized by British settlers from Jamaica in the 18th century. They became part of a federal territory in 1959 and a separate colony in 1962.

Falkland Islands (Malvinas)

Location	An archipelago of around 700 islands situated in the South Atlantic Ocean, c.650 km (400 mi) north-east of the Magellan Strait.		
Area	12 173 sq km (4 700 sq mi)	**Nationality**	Falkland Islander
Capital	Stanley	**Internet**	.fk
Population	3 000 (2006e)	**Country code**	FLK

Government

Internally self-governing; the British monarch is represented by a Governor, assisted by an Executive Council and a unicameral Legislative Council.

Economy

Fishing; tourism; agriculture (oats, sheep); service industries to the continuing military presence in the islands.

History

The islands were seen by several early navigators, including Captain John Strong in 1689–90 who named them. There is a long history of occupation by European countries, including France, Spain and Britain, which established its first settlement in 1765. Argentina occupied the islands in 1820 but the settlement was destroyed in 1831. Britain asserted possession in 1833 and the islands were permanently colonized. Argentina's claims to sovereignty over the whole area resulted in invasion by its military forces in 1982; a British naval and military task force recaptured the islands two months later.

Gibraltar

Location	A narrow peninsula rising steeply from the low-lying coast of south-west Spain at the eastern end of the Strait of Gibraltar, which is an important strategic point of control for the western Mediterranean Sea.		
Area	6.5 sq km (2.5 sq mi)	**Nationality**	Gibraltarian
Capital	Gibraltar	**Internet**	.gi
Population	27 900 (2006e)	**Country code**	GIB

Government

Internally self-governing; the British monarch is represented by a Governor, assisted by a government and a unicameral House of Assembly.

Economy

Financial services; transhipment trade; shipping services; tourism; retail; manufacturing. The economy has adapted to reduction of British military activities since 1978.

History

Settled by the Moors in 711, Gibraltar was taken by Spain in 1462 and ceded to Britain in 1713. It became a British Crown Colony in 1830 and, as such, it played a key role in Allied naval operations during both world wars. A proposal to end British rule was defeated by a referendum in 1967 and a joint sovereignty arrangement with Spain was rejected in 2002. Since then, Spain has moderated its claims to sovereignty and the bilateral Anglo-Spanish talks about the territory became tripartite with the inclusion of the Gibraltarian government from 2003.

Montserrat

Location	A volcanic island in the Leeward Islands in the Lesser Antilles, east Caribbean Sea.		
Area	102 sq km (39 sq mi)	**Nationality**	Montserratian
Capital	Brades[1]	**Internet**	.ms
Population	9400 (2006e)[2]	**Country code**	MSR

[1] *The original capital, Plymouth, lies within the Exclusion Zone, an area into which entry is prohibited since the devastating volcanic eruption from the Soufrière Hills volcano in 1997 made it uninhabitable.*

[2] *Population decreased dramatically after the 1997 volcanic activity but has started to recover.*

Government

Internally self-governing; the British monarch is represented by a Governor; assisted by an Executive Council and a unicameral Legislative Council.

Economy

Before the 1997 volcanic eruption the main activity was tourism, with small-scale manufacturing and agriculture. The burial of over half the island in 1997 and continuing volcanic activity has left the economy largely moribund.

History

The island was visited by Christopher Columbus in 1493 and was colonized by English and Irish settlers in 1632. Possession was disputed between the French and British in the 17th and 18th centuries but the island was assigned to Britain in 1783 and became a Crown Colony in 1871. It was part of the Federation of the West Indies in 1958–62. Activity by the Chances Peak and Soufrière Hills volcanoes, especially in 1997, led to the evacuation of many residents and has made much of the island uninhabitable.

Pitcairn Islands

Location	An island group in the south-east Pacific Ocean, east of French Polynesia, comprising Pitcairn Island and the uninhabited islands of Duce, Henderson and Oeno.		
Area	4.5 sq km (2 sq mi)	**Nationality**	Pitcairn Islander
Capital	Adamstown	**Internet**	.pn
Population	45 (2006e)	**Country code**	PLN

Government

Internal affairs managed through a unicameral Island Council; the British High Commissioner to New Zealand is non-resident Governor.

Economy

Sales of postage stamps, internet domain names and handicrafts; subsistence fishing and horticulture.

History

The island was visited by the British in 1767 and settled by mutineers from HMS *Bounty* in 1790. Overpopulation led to emigration to Norfolk Island in 1856 but some islanders returned in 1859 and 1864. The settlement was administered from Fiji between 1952 and 1970, when responsibility was transferred to the British High Commissioner to New Zealand.

St Helena and Dependencies

Location	The territory comprises the islands of St Helena, Ascension and Tristan da Cunha, all volcanic, lying in the South Atlantic Ocean. St Helena is 1920 km (1200 mi) from the south-west coast of Africa; Ascension lies 1200 km (745 mi) north-west of St Helena and Tristan da Cunha 2333 km (1449 mi) south-west of St Helena.		
Area	122 sq km (47 sq mi)	**Nationality**	St Helenian.
Capital	Jamestown	**Internet**	.sh
Population	St Helena 7400; Ascension 1000; Tristan da Cunha 275 (2006e)	**Country code**	SHN

Government

St Helena has an Executive Council and a unicameral Legislative Council. Ascension and Tristan da Cunha both have an Island Council, chaired by the island's Administrator; the Administrators are the local representatives of the Governor of St Helena, who is the Crown's representative.

Economy

Fishing and fish processing; sales of postage stamps; Ascension provides services for RAF aircraft in transit to the Falkland Islands.

History

St Helena was discovered by the Portuguese in 1502. It was annexed by the Dutch in 1633 but not occupied by them, and the British East India Company seized it in 1659. It was lent to the British government as a place of exile for Napoleon Bonaparte from 1815 until 1821, and became a Crown Colony in 1834. Ascension Island (discovered in around 1501 but uninhabited until 1815) and Tristan da Cunha (discovered in 1506; annexed by Britain in 1816; evacuated in 1963 because of volcanic activity) were made dependencies of St Helena in 1922 and 1938 respectively.

South Georgia

Location	A barren, mountainous snow-covered uninhabited island in the South Atlantic Ocean, about 500 km (300 mi) east of the Falkland Islands.		
Area	c.3750 sq km (1450 sq mi)	**Internet**	.gs

South Sandwich Islands

Location	A group of small uninhabited islands in the South Atlantic Ocean, lying c.720 km (450 mi) south-east of South Georgia.		
Area	1152 sq km (445 sq mi)	**Internet**	.gs

Government

Administered by a Commissioner, who is the Governor of the Falkland Islands.

Economy

Sale of fishing licences, postage stamps and commemorative coins; customs and harbour dues.

History

Captain Cook landed on the islands in 1775. They were annexed by Britain in 1908 and 1917, and were a sealing and whaling centre until 1965. In 1982 they were invaded by Argentina and recaptured by Britain. The explorer Ernest Shackleton is buried on South Georgia.

Turks and Caicos Islands

Location	A pair of island groups which lie c.80 km (50 mi) south-east of the Bahamas, of which they form the south-eastern part of the archipelago; they lie 920 km (570 mi) south-east of Miami (USA).

Area	430 sq km (166 sq mi)	**Internet**	.tc
Capital	Cockburn Town	**Country code**	TCA
Population	32 000 (2006e)		

Government
Internally self-governing; the British monarch is represented by a Governor, assisted by an Executive Council and a unicameral Legislative Council.

Economy
Tourism; property development; financial services; fishing and fish-processing.

History
Sighted by the Spanish in 1512, the islands were linked formally to the Bahamas in 1799 and then annexed by Jamaica in 1872. They became a British Crown colony in 1962, were administered from the Bahamas in 1965–73, and achieved internal self-government in 1976.

UNITED STATES OF AMERICA

Official name	United States of America (USA)
Local name	United States
Area	9 160 454 sq km (3 535 935 sq mi)
Capital	Washington, DC (District of Columbia)
Chief towns	New York, Los Angeles, Chicago, Houston, Philadelphia, Phoenix, San Diego, Dallas, San Antonio, Detroit
Population	298 444 000 (2006e)
Nationality	American
Languages	English; there is a sizeable Spanish-speaking minority
Ethnic groups	white (including Hispanic) 82%, black 13%, Asian 4%, Amerindian, Alaskan native and native Hawaiian or Pacific Islander 1%
Religions	Christianity 76% (Prot 52%, RC 24%), Mormon 2%, Judaism 1%, Islam 1%, others 10%, none 10%
Time zone	GMT −5/10
Currency	1 US Dollar ($, US$) = 100 cents
Telephone	+1
Internet	.us
Country code	USA

Location

A federal republic in North America and the fourth-largest country in the world. It includes the non-contiguous states of Alaska and Hawaii. The mainland is bounded to the north by Canada; to the east by the Atlantic Ocean; to the south by the Gulf of Mexico; and to the west by the Pacific Ocean.

Physical description

The East Atlantic coastal plain is backed by the Appalachian Mountains from the Great Lakes in the north to Alabama in the south; this series of parallel ranges includes the Allegheny, Blue Ridge and Catskill mountains; to the south the plain broadens out towards the Gulf of Mexico and into the Florida peninsula; to the west, the Gulf Plains stretch north to meet the higher Great Plains from which they are separated by the Ozark Mountains; further west, the Rocky Mountains rise to more than 4500 m (14 760 ft); the highest point is Mount McKinley, Alaska, at 6194 m (20 322 ft); the lowest point is in Death Valley (−86 m/−282 ft); drainage in the north is into the St Lawrence River or the Great Lakes; in the east, the Hudson, Delaware, Potomac and other rivers flow east into the Atlantic Ocean; the central plains of the United States are drained by the great Red River–Missouri–Mississippi River system and by other rivers flowing into the Gulf of Mexico; in the west the main rivers are the Columbia and Colorado.

Climate

Temperate in most parts, but tropical in Florida and Hawaii, arctic in Alaska, semi-arid in the Great Plains and arid in the deserts of the south-west; most regions are affected by westerly depressions that can bring changeable weather; rainfall is heaviest in the Pacific north-west, lightest in the south-west; in the Great Plains, wide temperature variation is the result of cold air from the Arctic as well as warm tropical air from the Gulf of Mexico; on the west coast the influence of the Pacific Ocean results in a smaller range of temperatures between summer and winter; on the east coast there is a gradual increase in winter temperatures southwards; the states bordering the Gulf of Mexico and the Atlantic Ocean are subject to hurricanes moving north-east from the Caribbean Sea; tornadoes occur in the Midwest and south-east; states bordering the Pacific and Hawaii are affected by earthquakes and volcanic activity.

Economy

Highly diversified and technologically advanced economy, becoming in the 20c the leading industrial nation in the world; despite prosperity has large budget and trade deficits, with increasingly uneven distribution of wealth; vast mineral and agricultural resources; service sector (banking, financial and corporate services; real estate; tourism, etc) accounts for 78% of GDP and 76% of employment; main industries are oil and natural gas production, oil refining, manufacturing (steel, motor vehicles, aircraft and aerospace equipment, telecommunications equipment, chemicals, pharmaceuticals, electronic equipment and consumer goods), food processing, forestry, mining (iron ore, phosphates, copper, zinc and lead); agriculture and fisheries produce wheat, maize, other cereals, fruit, vegetables, cotton, soy beans, fish, meat and dairy products, contributing 1% to GDP.

Government

Governed by a President, who is elected every four years by a college of state representatives and appoints a Cabinet, subject to the confirmation by the Senate. The legislature, the Congress, comprises a House of Representatives, elected for two-year terms, and the Senate, elected for six-year terms. Each of the 50 states has a governor, executive and legislature; the District of Columbia has a Mayor.

History

The country was first settled by migrant groups from Asia over 25 000 years ago. These Native Americans remained undisturbed until the country was explored by the Norse (9th century) and the Spanish (16th century), who settled in Florida and Mexico. In the 17th century there were settlements by the British, French, Dutch, Germans and Swedish. Many black Africans were introduced as slaves to work on the plantations. In the following century, British control grew throughout the area. A revolt of the English-speaking colonies in the American Revolution (1775–83) led to the creation of the United States of America, which then lay between the Great Lakes, the Mississippi and Florida; the Declaration of Independence was made on 4 July 1776. Louisiana was sold to the USA by France in 1803 (the Louisiana Purchase) and the westward movement of settlers began. Florida was ceded by Spain in 1819, and further Spanish states joined the Union between 1821 and 1853. In 1860–1, eleven Southern states left the Union over the slavery issue, and formed the Confederacy; the Civil War (1861–5) ended in victory for the North, and the Southern states later rejoined the Union. As a result of the North's victory, slavery was abolished in 1865. In 1867 Alaska was purchased from Russia, and the Hawaiian Islands were annexed in 1898 (both admitted as states in 1959). The USA entered World War I on the side of the Allies in 1917. Native Americans were given the right to become US citizens in 1924. In 1929 the stockmarket on Wall Street crashed, resulting in the Great Depression. After the Japanese attack on Pearl Harbor in 1941, the USA entered World War II. The campaign for black civil rights developed in the 1960s, accompanied by much civil disturbance. From 1964 to 1975 the USA intervened in the Vietnam War, supporting non-communist South Vietnam. The USA led the space exploration programme of the 1960s and 1970s (in 1969 US astronaut Neil Armstrong was the first person on the moon). The Watergate scandal (1972–4) forced President Nixon to resign; there was further scandal in 1986 over arms sales to Iran to fund Contra rebels in Nicaragua. The Cold War between the USA and the Union of Soviet Socialist Republics (USSR) came to an end in 1990; since then US military force has been deployed in UN peacekeeping missions in countries such as Bosnia. In the 1991 Gulf War, US troops led the assault against Saddam Hussein following Iraq's invasion of Kuwait. In 1992 there was rioting in Los Angeles and other cities over racial issues. After Democratic President Bill Clinton came to power in 1993, the White House was dogged by financial and sexual scandals such as the Whitewater affair of 1994 and the Monica Lewinsky affair. On 11 September 2001, terrorists crashed one passenger plane into the Pentagon and two into the World Trade Center in New York, leading to the collapse of both towers and the loss of thousands of lives; a fourth plane also crashed without survivors. The Al Qaeda organization led by Osama bin Laden was blamed and President Bush declared a 'war on terror'. As part of this, the USA led multinational forces in wars on Afghanistan in 2001 and Iraq in 2003. US troops remain in both countries to stabilize internal security.

THE AUTOMOBILE REVOLUTION IN THE USA

Around 100 years ago the automobile arrived to claim its irrepressible place in US society. Many people initially thought of the motor car as an idea that would fail to catch on, but they quickly caught the motoring bug.

The birth of the motor industry

In 1908 Henry Ford released his Model T (the 'Tin Lizzie'), the first mass-produced motor car to be affordable by more than just the very rich. It initially cost approximately $800 (roughly 6 months' wages for a tradesman at the time) but the price fell to $355 (around 2 months' wages) by 1921. The Model T therefore promised mobility on a scale previously unimaginable. Americans took little convincing of the freedoms they could enjoy, and more than 15 million Model Ts were produced in a little under 20 years. 1908 also saw the founding of the world's most productive car manufacturer, General Motors, which has produced such iconic brands as Buick, Cadillac, Oldsmobile and Pontiac. The prosperity of the motor industry encouraged workers to move to cities such as Detroit, Michigan (home to both General Motors and Ford), and the building of cars and roads brought industry, construction and commerce.

Road culture

The automobile revolution also had an extraordinary impact on rural areas. Long highways were built to link major cities – the most famous highway, Route 66 (1926–85), crossed the country from Chicago to Los Angeles, passing through eight states and covering approximately 3,800 km (2,400 mi). Highways had to be serviced by garages, filling stations and diners, and therefore became economic lifelines to many small settlements along the way. As motorists began to travel further afield, they needed places to rest for the night. In December 1925 the first motel, or *mo*torist ho*tel*, was opened by James Vail in San Luis Obispo, California; each chalet had its own bathroom, telephone and garage. Before long the motel became a familiar feature of the physical and cultural landscape, appearing in many *films noirs* of the 1930s and 40s and in road movies of the 1960s and 70s. The best-known motel on screen is probably the one in the horror film *Psycho* (1960), set in the infamous Bates Motel.

Driving in and hanging out

The car craze continued to grow as commuting became popular and out-of-town shopping malls sprang up. Then, in 1932, the drive-in movie theatre was born. The trend spread rapidly, especially in the warmer southern states, and peaked in the 1950s and 1960s before being superseded by television. The car gave people freedom and became an important part of the sexual revolution: young people could meet and hang out together away from the prying eyes of their parents. Car culture was everywhere, and it was cool. Cinematic icons of the age, such as James Dean in *Rebel Without a Cause* (1955) and Steve McQueen in *Bullitt* (1968), were seen driving fast cars; even Dean's death in a crash failed to dampen the allure.

Today in the USA there isn't much you can't do from the comfort of your car. The drive-in convenience of movies, fast-food stores, launderettes, banks and even wedding chapels means that, despite worldwide concern about carbon emissions and climate change, the relationship between US residents and their automobiles will be a tough one to break up.

States of the USA

State (abbrev; ZIP)	Entry to Union	Population (2006e)[1]	Area	Capital	Inhabitant	Nickname
Alabama (Ala; AL)	1819 (22nd)	4 599 000	131 443 sq km (50 750 sq mi)	Montgomery	Alabamian	Camellia State, Heart of Dixie
Alaska (Alaska; AK)	1959 (49th)	670 000	1 477 268 sq km (570 373 sq mi)	Juneau	Alaskan	Mainland State, The Last Frontier
Arizona (Ariz; AZ)	1912 (48th)	6 166 000	295 276 sq km (114 006 sq mi)	Phoenix	Arizonan	Apache State, Grand Canyon State
Arkansas (Ark; AR)	1836 (25th)	2 811 000	137 754 sq km (53 187 sq mi)	Little Rock	Arkansan	Bear State, Land of Opportunity
California (Calif; CA)	1850 (31st)	36 458 000	403 971 sq km (155 973 sq mi)	Sacramento	Californian	Golden State
Colorado (Colo; CO)	1876 (38th)	4 753 000	268 658 sq km (103 729 sq mi)	Denver	Coloradan	Centennial State
Connecticut (Conn; CT)	1788 (5th)	3 505 000	12 547 sq km (4844 sq mi)	Hartford	Nutmegger	Nutmeg State, Constitution State
Delaware (Del; DE)	1787 (1st)	853 000	5133 sq km (1985 sq mi)	Dover	Delawarean	Diamond State, First State
District of Columbia* (DC; DC)	Established 1791	582 000	159 sq km (61 sq mi)	Washington	Washingtonian	—
Florida (Fla; FL)	1845 (27th)	18 090 000	139 697 sq km (53 937 sq mi)	Tallahassee	Floridian	Everglade State, Sunshine State
Georgia (Ga; GA)	1788 (4th)	9 364 000	152 571 sq km (58 908 sq mi)	Atlanta	Georgian	Empire State of the South, Peach State

* Not counted as one of the 50 states but included for reference

State (abbrev; ZIP)	Entry to Union	Population (2006e)[1]	Area	Capital	Inhabitant	Nickname
Hawaii (Hawaii; HI)	1959 (50th)	1285000	16636 sq km (6423 sq mi)	Honolulu	Hawaiian	Aloha State
Idaho (Idaho; ID)	1890 (43rd)	1466000	214325 sq km (82751 sq mi)	Boise	Idahoan	Gem State
Illinois (Ill; IL)	1818 (21st)	12832000	144123 sq km (55646 sq mi)	Springfield	Illinoisan	Prairie State, Land of Lincoln
Indiana (Ind; IN)	1816 (19th)	6314000	92903 sq km (35870 sq mi)	Indianapolis	Hoosier	Hoosier State
Iowa (Iowa; IA)	1846 (29th)	2982000	144716 sq km (55875 sq mi)	Des Moines	Iowan	Hawkeye State, Corn State
Kansas (Kans; KS)	1861 (34th)	2764000	211922 sq km (81823 sq mi)	Topeka	Kansan	Sunflower State, Jayhawker State
Kentucky (Ky; KY)	1792 (15th)	4206000	102907 sq km (39732 sq mi)	Frankfort	Kentuckian	Bluegrass State
Louisiana (La; LA)	1812 (18th)	4288000	112836 sq km (43566 sq mi)	Baton Rouge	Louisianian	Pelican State, Sugar State, Creole State
Maine (Maine, ME)	1820 (23rd)	1322000	79931 sq km (30861 sq mi)	Augusta	Downeaster	Pine Tree State
Maryland (Md; MD)	1788 (7th)	5616000	25316 sq km (9775 sq mi)	Annapolis	Marylander	Old Line State, Free State
Massachusetts (Mass; MA)	1788 (6th)	6437000	20300 sq km (7838 sq mi)	Boston	Bay Stater	Bay State, Old Colony
Michigan (Mich; MI)	1837 (26th)	10096000	150544 sq km (58125 sq mi)	Lansing	Michigander	Wolverine State, Great Lake State
Minnesota (Minn; MN)	1858 (32nd)	5167000	206207 sq km (79617 sq mi)	St Paul	Minnesotan	Gopher State, North Star State
Mississippi (Miss; MS)	1817 (20th)	2911000	123510 sq km (47687 sq mi)	Jackson	Mississippian	Magnolia State

State (abbrev; ZIP)	Entry to Union	Population (2006e)[1]	Area	Capital	Inhabitant	Nickname
Missouri (Mo; MO)	1821 (24th)	5 843 000	178 446 sq km (68 898 sq mi)	Jefferson City	Missourian	Bullion State, Show Me State
Montana (Mont; MT)	1889 (41st)	945 000	376 991 sq km (145 556 sq mi)	Helena	Montanan	Treasure State, Big Sky Country
Nebraska (Nebr; NE)	1867 (37th)	1 768 000	199 113 sq km (76 878 sq mi)	Lincoln	Nebraskan	Cornhusker State, Beef State
Nevada (Nev; NV)	1864 (36th)	2 496 000	273 349 sq km (105 540 sq mi)	Carson City	Nevadan	Silver State, Sagebrush State
New Hampshire (NH; NH)	1788 (9th)	1 315 000	23 292 sq km (8993 sq mi)	Concord	New Hampshirite	Granite State
New Jersey (NJ; NJ)	1787 (3rd)	8 725 000	19 210 sq km (7417 sq mi)	Trenton	New Jerseyite	Garden State
New Mexico (N Mex; NM)	1912 (47th)	1 955 000	314 334 sq km (121 364 sq mi)	Santa Fe	New Mexican	Sunshine State, Land of Enchantment
New York (NY; NY)	1788 (11th)	19 306 000	122 310 sq km (47 224 sq mi)	Albany	New Yorker	Empire State
North Carolina (NC; NC)	1789 (12th)	8 857 000	126 180 sq km (48 718 sq mi)	Raleigh	North Carolinian	Old North State, Tar Heel State
North Dakota (N Dak; ND)	1889 (39th)	636 000	178 695 sq km (68 994 sq mi)	Bismarck	North Dakotan	Flickertail State, Sioux State, Peace Garden State
Ohio (Ohio; OH)	1803 (17th)	11 478 000	106 067 sq km (40 952 sq mi)	Columbus	Ohioan	Buckeye State
Oklahoma (Okla; OK)	1907 (46th)	3 579 000	177 877 sq km (68 678 sq mi)	Oklahoma City	Oklahoman	Sooner State
Oregon (Oreg; OR)	1859 (33rd)	3 701 000	251 385 sq km (97 060 sq mi)	Salem	Oregonian	Sunset State, Beaver State

State (abbrev; ZIP)	Entry to Union	Population (2006e)[1]	Area	Capital	Inhabitant	Nickname
Pennsylvania (Pa; PA)	1787 (2nd)	12 441 000	116 083 sq km (44 820 sq mi)	Harrisburg	Pennsylvanian	Keystone State
Rhode Island (RI; RI)	1790 (13th)	1 068 000	2707 sq km (1045 sq mi)	Providence	Rhode Islander	Little Rhody, Plantation State
South Carolina (SC; SC)	1788 (8th)	4 321 000	77 988 sq km (30 111 sq mi)	Columbia	South Carolinian	Palmetto State
South Dakota (S Dak; SD)	1889 (40th)	782 000	196 576 sq km (75 898 sq mi)	Pierre	South Dakotan	Sunshine State, Coyote State
Tennessee (Tenn; TN)	1796 (16th)	6 039 000	106 759 sq km (41 220 sq mi)	Nashville	Tennessean	Volunteer State
Texas (Tex; TX)	1845 (28th)	23 508 000	678 358 sq km (261 914 sq mi)	Austin	Texan	Lone Star State
Utah (Utah; UT)	1896 (45th)	2 550 000	212 816 sq km (82 168 sq mi)	Salt Lake City	Utahn	Mormon State, Beehive State
Vermont (Vt; VT)	1791 (14th)	624 000	23 955 sq km (9249 sq mi)	Montpelier	Vermonter	Green Mountain State
Virginia (Va; VA)	1788 (10th)	7 643 000	102 558 sq km (39 598 sq mi)	Richmond	Virginian	Old Dominion State, Mother of Presidents
Washington (Wash; WA)	1889 (42nd)	6 396 000	172 447 sq km (66 582 sq mi)	Olympia	Washingtonian	Evergreen State, Chinook State
West Virginia (W Va; WV)	1863 (35th)	1 818 000	62 758 sq km (24 231 sq mi)	Charleston	West Virginian	Panhandle State, Mountain State
Wisconsin (Wis; WI)	1848 (30th)	5 557 000	145 431 sq km (56 151 sq mi)	Madison	Wisconsinite	Badger State, America's Dairyland
Wyoming (Wyo; WY)	1890 (44th)	515 000	251 501 sq km (97 105 sq mi)	Cheyenne	Wyomingite	Equality State

[1] Source: US Census Bureau

US territories and departments

American Samoa (AS)

Location	A group of islands in the South Pacific Ocean, some 3500 km (2175 mi) north-east of New Zealand.		
Area	199 sq km (77 sq mi)	**Nationality**	American Samoan
Capital	Pago Pago	**Internet**	.as
Population	57 800 (2006e)	**Country code**	ASM

Government

Has a measure of self-government, with a bicameral legislature (the *Fono*) that comprises the Senate (elected every four years from among the traditional chiefs) and the House of Representatives (popularly elected every two years); the directly elected Governor is the head of the executive branch.

Economy

Principal activities are fish processing and canning; tuna fishing; small-scale agriculture (taro, breadfruit, yams, bananas, coconuts); handicrafts.

History

The USA acquired rights to American Samoa in 1899, and the islands were ceded by their chiefs in 1900–25. It is now an unincorporated and unorganized Territory of the USA, administered by the Department of the Interior.

Guam

Location	The largest and southernmost of the Mariana Islands, in the north-west Pacific Ocean.		
Area	541 sq km (209 sq mi)	**Nationality**	Guamanian
Capital	Agaña	**Internet**	.gu
Population	171 000 (2006e)	**Country code**	GUM

Government

Has a measure of internal self-government, with a unicameral legislature directly elected every two years; the directly elected Governor is head of the executive.

Economy

Highly dependent on US defence expenditure (military installations cover 35 per cent of the island) and tourism; diversifying industrial and commercial projects include transhipment services, construction, printing, food processing and textiles.

History

A Spanish colony for centuries, it was ceded to the USA in 1898; it was occupied by Japan from 1941 to 1944.

Mariana Islands, Northern

Location	A territory comprising 14 islands in the north-west Pacific Ocean, c.2400 km (1500 mi) to the east of the Philippines.		
Area	471 sq km (182 sq mi)	**Internet**	.mp
Capital	Saipan	**Country code**	MNP
Population	82 500 (2006e)		

Government

Internally self-governing, with a directly elected bicameral legislature (Senate and House of Representatives); a directly elected Governor presides over the executive.

Economy

Tourism; garment manufacture; agriculture (cattle, coconuts, fruit, vegetables), handicrafts.

History

From 1947 to 1986 the islands were administered by the USA under UN mandate as part of the US Trust Territory of the Pacific Islands. They became a self-governing commonwealth of the USA in 1978.

Puerto Rico

Location	The easternmost island of the Greater Antilles, situated between the Dominican Republic in the west and the US Virgin Islands in the east, c.1600 km (1000 mi) south-east of Miami.		
Area	8870 sq km (3424 sq mi)	**Nationality**	Puerto Rican, American
Capital	San Juan	**Internet**	.pr
Population	3 927 000 (2006e)	**Country code**	PRI

Government

Internally self-governing, with a directly elected bicameral legislature consisting of a Senate and a House of Representatives; a directly elected Governor is head of the executive; a Resident Commissioner is elected every four years to represent the territory in the US House of Representatives.

Economy

Manufacturing (textiles, clothing, electrical and electronic equipment, food processing, petrochemicals); agriculture (dairy farming, livestock, sugar cane, coffee, tropical fruits); tourism; US trade and investment are important.

History

Originally occupied by Carib and Arawaks, the island was visited by Christopher Columbus in 1493. It remained a Spanish colony until ceded to the USA in 1898, and became a semi-autonomous commonwealth in association with the USA in 1952.

US Virgin Islands

Location	A group of more than 50 islands in the south and west of the Virgin Islands group of the Lesser Antilles in the Caribbean Sea, 64 km (40 mi) east of Puerto Rico (USA). There are three main islands: St Thomas, St Croix and St John.		
Area	342 sq km (132 sq mi)	Nationality	Virgin Islander
Capital	Charlotte Amalie	Internet	.vi
Population	108 600 (2006e)	Country code	VIR

Government
Internally self-governing, with a directly elected unicameral Senate; a directly elected Governor heads the executive.

Economy
Tourism; manufacturing (oil refining, watch assembly, rum distilling, construction, pharmaceuticals, textiles, electronics); small-scale agriculture (vegetables, fruit, sorghum, cattle); St Croix has one of the largest oil refineries in the world; there is a growing business and financial services sector.

History
Denmark colonized St Thomas and St John in 1671, and bought St Croix from France in 1733. The islands were purchased by the USA in 1917.

URUGUAY

Official name	Eastern Republic of Uruguay
Local name	Uruguay; República Oriental del Uruguay
Area	176 215 sq km (68 018 sq mi)
Capital	Montevideo
Chief towns	Salto, Paysandú, Mercedes, Las Piedras
Population	3 432 000 (2006e)
Nationality	Uruguayan
Language	Spanish
Ethnic groups	white 88%, Mestizo 8%, black 4%
Religions	Christianity 68% (RC 66%, Prot 2%), Judaism 1%, others/ unaffiliated 31%
Time zone	GMT −3
Currency	1 Uruguayan Peso (Ur$, UrugN$) = 100 centésimos
Telephone	+598
Internet	.uy
Country code	URY

Location

republic in eastern South America, bounded to the east and south-east by the Atlantic Ocean; to the north and north-east by Brazil; and to the west by the River Uruguay and Argentina.

Physical description

grass-covered plains in the south rise northwards to a high sandy plateau; the River Negro flows south to west to meet the River Uruguay on the Argentine frontier; the highest point is Cerro Catedral (514 m/1686 ft).

Climate

temperate, with warm summers and mild winters; the average annual rainfall at Montevideo is 978 mm, with an average temperature of 16°C.

Economy

developing economy, based on agriculture, especially ranching and livestock products; main exports are meat, wool, hides, skins and rice; other activities include tourism, offshore financial services, food processing, brewing and wine-making, fishing, forestry, manufacturing (electrical machinery, transport equipment, petroleum products, textiles and chemicals) and mining.

Government

governed by an executive President, a Council of Ministers and a bicameral General Assembly consisting of a Chamber of Representatives and a Chamber of Senators.

History

originally occupied by various Indian tribes known collectively as the Charrúas people, the area was discovered by the Spanish in 1515 and became part of the Spanish Viceroyalty of Río de la Plata in 1726. Between 1814 and 1825 it was a province of Brazil, and it gained independence in 1828. During the 19th century there was a struggle for political control between the liberals (the 'redshirts', or *Colorados*) and the conservatives (the 'whites', or *Blancos*), which was resolved when the former took office for 86 years (1872–1958). Unrest caused by the Marxist Tupamaros guerrillas lasted from 1962 to 1973, and military rule prevailed from 1973 until civilian rule was restored in 1985 after violent demonstrations. The Colorado and National (*Blanco*) parties' dominance of politics has been eroded in recent years by left-wing parties and coalitions such as the Progressive Encounter–Broad Front (EP-FA), which won the 2004 election and whose candidate won the presidency in 2004.

A FIFA First

The first ever FIFA World Cup was held in Uruguay in July 1930. Due to the arduous three-week sea voyage involved, very few European teams entered the competition; those that did so were only persuaded at the last minute by the Uruguayan government, which agreed to pay all travel expenses. The host nation, which also held the Olympic title, became the first winner of the trophy, a feat which it repeated in 1950.

UZBEKISTAN

Official name	Republic of Uzbekistan
Local name	Özbekiston; Özbekiston Respublikasia
Former name	Uzbek Soviet Socialist Republic (1924–91), within the Union of Soviet Socialist Republics (USSR; 1924–91)
Area	447 400 sq km (172 696 sq mi)
Capital	Tashkent; Toškent, Taškent
Chief towns	Samarkand, Andizhan, Namangan
Population	27 307 000 (2006e)
Nationality	Uzbek
Languages	Uzbek; Russian and Tajik are also spoken
Ethnic groups	Uzbek 71%, Russian 8%, Tajik 5%, Kazakh 4%, Tatar 3%, others 9%
Religions	Islam 88% (mostly Sunni), Christianity 9% (Orthodox), others/ unaffiliated 3%
Time zone	GMT +5
Currency	1 Sum = 100 tiyin
Telephone	+998
Internet	.uz
Country code	UZB

Location

A landlocked republic in central and northern Central Asia, bounded to the south by Afghanistan; to the south-west by Turkmenistan; to the west and north-east by Kazakhstan; to the north-west by the Aral Sea; and to the east by Kyrgyzstan and Tajikistan.

Physical description

The Tien Shan and Pamir mountains in the east and south-east drop through foothills to the fertile Fergana Valley and the Kyzyl-Kum desert, east of the Aral Sea; west of the desert is the Ustyurt Plateau and the delta of the Amudarya river; the highest point is Beshtor Peak (4299 m/14 104 ft).

Climate

Long, hot summers, mild winters; temperatures are lower in the mountains; low rainfall.

Economy

Centrally planned and state-controlled economy; intensive agriculture produces cotton, vegetables, fruit, cereals and livestock; main industries are mining (especially for gold and coal), oil and natural gas production (exports restricted by lack of pipelines at present), hydroelectric power generation, textiles and food processing.

Government

Governed by an executive President, a Prime Minister and Cabinet, and a bicameral Supreme Assembly consisting of a Legislative Chamber and a Senate. The (former communist) People's Democratic Party and its allies have dominated politics since independence.

History

The area formed part of the 'silk road' trade route linking China with Asia Minor and Europe in the 1st century bc. Islam was introduced by Arab invaders in the 7th and 8th centuries. In the 12th and 13th centuries it was the centre of Genghis Khan's empire, and its cities of Samarkand and Tashkent grew rich from the silk caravan trade. It later divided into the khanates of Bukhara, Khiva and Kokand, which were subjected to attacks by Russia from the early 18th century until they were annexed in 1876. The Uzbeks rebelled against Russian rule in 1918 but were suppressed, and the country was proclaimed a Soviet Socialist Republic in 1924. It declared its independence from the Union of Soviet Socialist Republics (USSR) in 1991, and became a member of the Commonwealth of Independent States (CIS). Post-independence politics is still dominated by the former communists; opposition parties are barred from participation in elections, the two main opposition parties are banned, and other forms of dissent are suppressed. The former communist leader Islam Karimov was elected president in 1991 and has retained the office since. The government has used a Muslim insurgency, which began in 1996 and is largely confined to the Fergana valley, as an excuse to curtail human rights and suppress political opposition and protests such as those in Andijan in 2005, in which around 200 protesters were killed by troops.

VANUATU

Official name	Republic of Vanuatu
Local name	Vanuatu; Ripablik Blong Vanuatu, République de Vanuatu
Former name	New Hebrides (until 1980)
Area	12336 sq km (4763 sq mi)
Capital	Port Vila
Population	209000 (2006e)
Nationality	Ni-Vanuatu
Languages	Over 100 local languages; Bislama (pidgin), English, French
Ethnic groups	Melanesian 95%, others 5%
Religions	Christianity 83% (Prot 70%, RC 13%), traditional beliefs 5%, unaffiliated 7%, others 5%
Time zone	GMT +11
Currency	1 Vatu (V, VT) = 100 centimes
Telephone	+678
Internet	.vu
Country code	VUT

Location

An independent republic comprising an irregular Y-shaped island chain scattered over 860 000 sq km (332 046 sq mi) of the south-west Pacific Ocean, 400 km (250 mi) north-east of the French islands of New Caledonia.

Physical description

Mainly volcanic and rugged, with raised coral beaches fringed by reefs; the highest peak (Tabwemasana on Espiritu Santo) rises to 1888 m (6194 ft); there are several active volcanoes; densely forested, with narrow strips of cultivated land on the coast.

Climate

Tropical, with a hot and rainy season in November–April when cyclones may occur; annual temperatures at Port Vila are 16–33°C, and the average annual rainfall is 2310 mm.

Economy

Poor country, dependent on international aid; agriculture, largely at subsistence level, engages 80% of the population; chief cash crops are coconuts (yielding copra and oil), beef, cocoa, kava and coffee; other activities include forestry, food processing, tourism and offshore financial services.

Government

Governed by a President, a Prime Minister and Council of Ministers, and a unicameral Parliament.

History

Visited by the Portuguese in 1606, the islands were named the New Hebrides in 1775 by Captain Cook. They were settled in the 19th century by the British and French, who established plantations, and from 1906 they were jointly administered as the Condominium of the New Hebrides. This gained independence as the Republic of Vanuatu in 1980.

Duke or Deity?

For more than 50 years, the Yaohnanen tribespeople on the island of Tanna have worshipped Prince Philip, Duke of Edinburgh, as their spiritual leader. The British Royal is believed to be the human incarnation of a mountain spirit who left the island many years ago in search of a powerful bride.

VATICAN

Official name	State of the Vatican City; the Holy See
Local name	Città del Vaticano; Stato della Città del Vaticano; Santa Sede
Area	0.4 sq km (0.2 sq mi)
Capital	Vatican City
Population	932 (2006e)
Languages	Latin; Italian is widely spoken
Ethnic groups	predominantly European, especially Italian
Religion	Christianity 100% (RC)
Time zone	GMT +1
Currency	1 Euro (€) = 100 cents
Telephone	+39
Internet	.va
Country code	VAT

Location

A papal sovereign state, and the smallest independent state in the world. Surrounded on all sides by Rome, Italy, it is a World Heritage Site and includes St Peter's Basilica, the Vatican Palace and Museum, several buildings in Rome, and the Pope's summer villa at Castel Gandolfo.

Physical description

Landlocked, urban and entirely enclosed within the Italian city of Rome; highest point is 75 m (246 ft).

Climate

Mediterranean; hot summers and mild winters.

Economy

Unique, predominantly non-commercial economy; supported by financial contributions (known as *Peter's Pence*) from Roman Catholics around the world; some sales of postage stamps, tourist items, publications and museum fees.

Government

The head of state is the Supreme Pontiff of the Roman Catholic Church, the Pope, who is elected for life by a conclave of members of the Sacred College of Cardinals. Administration of the Vatican City is carried out by the Secretariat of State and the Pontifical Commission, appointed by the Pope. There is no legislature.

History

The Vatican City State was created in 1929 by the Lateran Pacts signed by Pope Pius XI and Mussolini. In these pacts or treaties Italy recognized the Pope's sovereignty over the city of the Vatican and declared the state to be neutral and inviolable territory. The treaties resolved the dispute arising from the newly unified Italy's annexation of the Papal States in 1860 and capture of Rome in 1870; the papacy had always refused to recognize the loss of the Papal States and their incorporation into Italy. The Vatican is now protected by the 1954 La Haye Convention. In 2002 the Italian lira was replaced by the euro as the official currency.

VENEZUELA

Official name	Bolivarian Republic of Venezuela
Local name	Venezuela; República Bolivariana de Venezuela
Area	912 050 sq km (352 051 sq mi)
Capital	Caracas
Chief towns	Maracaibo, Ciudad Guayana, Valencia, Barquisimeto
Population	25 730 000 (2006e)
Nationality	Venezuelan
Languages	Spanish; local dialects are also spoken
Ethnic groups	Mestizo 67%, white 21%, black 10%, Amerindian 2%
Religions	Christianity 98% (RC 96%, Prot 2%), others/unaffiliated 2%
Time zone	GMT −4
Currency	1 Bolívar (Bs) = 100 centesimi
Telephone	+58
Internet	.ve
Country code	VEN

Location
The most northerly country in South America, bounded to the north by the Caribbean Sea; to the east by Guyana; to the south by Brazil; and to the south-west and west by Colombia.

Physical description
The Guiana Highlands in the south-east cover over half the country; the Venezuelan Highlands, part of the Andes, lie in the west and separate the coast from the interior, reaching heights of more than 5000 m (16 400 ft); the highest point is Pico Bolívar (5007 m/16 427 ft); there are lowlands around Lake Maracaibo and in the valley of the Orinoco River (the *Llanos*), which runs through the centre of the country between the two mountain ranges.

Climate
Tropical, though temperatures and humidity are lower at altitude; generally hot and humid in the lowlands; one rainy season (April–October); annual temperatures at Caracas are 13–27°C; monthly rainfall between 10 mm and 109 mm; annual rainfall on the coast increases from very low amounts around Lake Maracaibo to 1000 mm in the east; in the Guiana Highlands to the south-east, annual rainfall is c.1500 mm.

Economy
Developing, largely state-owned economy, based on oil and gas (70% of exports); other industries include telecommunications, mining (bauxite, coal, iron ore and gold), construction materials, textiles, metals (steel and aluminium), food processing

vehicle assembly and forestry; agriculture produces cereals, sugar cane, rice, bananas, vegetables, coffee, beef and dairy products.

Government

Governed by an executive President, a Council of Ministers and a unicameral National Assembly.

History

Originally inhabited by Caribs and Arawaks, it was seen by Christopher Columbus in 1498, and settled by the Spanish from 1520. There were frequent revolts against Spanish colonial rule, and in the early 19th century an independence movement arose under Simón Bolívar; this led to the formal establishment of the state of Gran Colombia (Colombia, Ecuador and Venezuela) in 1821. Following the collapse of Gran Colombia in 1829, Venezuela became an independent republic in 1830 under the first of a series of *caudillos* (military leaders). The first truly democratic elections were held in 1947 but the government was overthrown by the military within months. An enduring civilian democracy was established in 1958; since the 1960s there has been relative political stability, with power alternating between the two major parties, the Democratic Action and the Christian Democrats. President Carlos Andrés Pérez, who came to power in 1989 soon faced rioting in response to his austerity measures. He survived two attempted coups in 1992, but was removed from office charged with corruption in 1993 (and imprisoned in 1996). He was succeeded in 1994 by Rafael Caldera. In 1998 Hugo Chávez, imprisoned for his part in one of the 1992 coups, became president. He introduced unpopular economic reforms that provoked strikes and demonstrations. However, he survived an attempted coup in 2002 and a national referendum on his tenure of office in 2004 to win a third term in 2006.

> ### Little Venice
>
> The origins of the name Venezuela are widely believed to date from the expedition of Amerigo Vespucci and Alonso de Ojeda to the area in 1499. On seeing the stilted houses that the indigenous peoples had built around Lake Maracaibo, the explorers named the area Venezuela, meaning 'little Venice'.

VIETNAM

Official name	Socialist Republic of Vietnam (SRV)
Local name	Viêt Nam; Công-Hòa Xã-Hôi Chu-Ngh Viêt Nam
Former name	Formerly part of French Indochina (until 1945); Democratic Republic of Vietnam (North Vietnam; 1945–76), and State of Vietnam and Republic of Vietnam (South Vietnam; 1949–55 and 1955–76 respectively); the two Vietnams reunited as Socialist Republic of Vietnam in 1976
Area	329 566 sq km (127 213 sq mi)
Capital	Hanoi; Hà Nội
Chief towns	Ho Chi Minh City (formerly Saigon), Haiphong, Da Nang, Nha Trang
Population	84 403 000 (2006e)
Nationality	Vietnamese
Language	Vietnamese
Ethnic groups	Kinh Vietnamese 86%, others (52 ethnic groups) 14%
Religions	Buddhism 12%, Christianity 8%, Cao Dai 3%, Hao Hao 1%, others/unaffiliated/none 76%
Time zone	GMT +7
Currency	1 Dông (D) = 10 hào = 100 xu
Telephone	+84
Internet	.vn
Country code	VNM

Location

An independent socialist state in South-East Asia, bounded to the east by the South China Sea (including the Gulf of Tongking in the north); to the west by Laos and Cambodia; and to the north by China.

Physical description

Occupies a narrow mountainous strip along the coast of the Gulf of Tongking and the South China Sea, 1600 km (994 mi) long but only 40 km (25 mi) at its widest; broader and lower-lying at the Mekong River Delta in the south and along the Red River Valley in the north; mountains in the north-west; the highest peak is Fan si Pan at 3143 m (10 312 ft); a limestone plateau in the south stretches west into Cambodia.

Climate

Tropical monsoon, dominated by south to south-east winds during May–September and north to north-east winds during October–April; the rainy season (May–September) causes high humidity; the average annual rainfall is 1000 mm in the lowlands, 2500 mm in the uplands; temperatures are high in the south, cooler in the north during October–April.

Economy

Poor but developing; in receipt of international aid; agriculture and fishing, largely at subsistence level, employ 57% of the workforce; chief cash crops are fish, seafood, rice, coffee, rubber, cotton and tea; industries are food processing, machine building, coal-mining, forestry, manufacturing (garments, footwear, steel, cement, fertilizer, glass, tyres and paper) and offshore oil and gas production.

Government

Governed by a President, a Prime Minister and Council of Ministers, and a unicameral National Assembly (*Quoc-Hoi*). The Communist Party of Vietnam has dominated politics since independence; its Politburo and the Secretariat of the Central Committee, elected by the Party Congress every five years, exercise the real power.

History

The area was under the influence of China for many centuries and was visited by the Portuguese in 1535. Dutch, French and English traders arrived in the 17th century, along with missionaries. In 1802 the regions of Tongking in the north, Annam in the centre, and Cochin-China in the south united as the Vietnamese Empire, which was conquered by the French from the 1860s. French protectorates were established in Cochin-China in 1867, and in Annam and Tongking in 1884, and the French Indo-Chinese Union with Cambodia and Laos was formed in 1887. Vietnam was occupied during World War II by the Japanese, who were resisted by the communist Viet Minh League under Ho Chi Minh. The Viet Minh declared independence in 1945; however, this was not recognized by France, which attempted to reassert its control. The Indo-China War (1946–54) resulted in the withdrawal of the French and an armistice that divided the country between the communist 'Democratic Republic' in the north and the 'State' of Vietnam in the south. In 1957 a communist insurgency in South Vietnam escalated into a civil war between communist North Vietnam and US-backed South Vietnam, which broadened to involve the USA directly from 1964 until US troops were withdrawn in 1973 following a peace agreement with North Vietnam. North Vietnam violated the peace agreement to capture Saigon (now Ho Chi Minh City) and took control of the south in 1975. The country was reunified as the Socialist Republic of Vietnam in 1976. Large numbers of refugees tried to find homes in the West in the late 1970s; the number of 'boat people' attempting to leave the country by sea increased greatly in 1979, following China's invasion of Vietnam in response to Vietnam's intervention in Cambodia to oust the Khmer Rouge regime. After the collapse of the Union of Soviet Socialist Republics (USSR) in 1991, Vietnam improved its relations with China and the USA. A new constitution was adopted in 1992, which approved many economic and political reforms. Although power remains with the ruling Communist Party, in 2006 the party leadership requested comments on its political platform, prompting an open debate on the party's role, criticism of the government and some calls for political pluralism.

YEMEN

Official name	Republic of Yemen
Local name	Al-Yamaniyya; Al-Jumhūriyya Al-Yamaniyya
Former name	Yemen Arab Republic (North Yemen; 1918–90); People's Democratic Republic of Yemen (South Yemen; 1967–90); both Yemens reunited in 1990 as Republic of Yemen
Area	531 570 sq km (205 186 sq mi)
Capital	Sana'a; San'ā', Sanaa
Chief town	Ta'iz
Population	21 456 000 (2006e)
Nationality	Yemeni
Language	Arabic
Ethnic groups	Arab 96%, others 4%
Religion	Islam 100% (Sunni 70%, Shia 30%)
Time zone	GMT +3
Currency	1 Yemeni Riyal (YR, YRI) = 100 fils
Telephone	+967
Internet	.ye
Country code	YEM

Location

A republic in the south of the Arabian Peninsula, bounded to the north by Saudi Arabia; to the west by the Red Sea; to the south by the Gulf of Aden; and to the east by Oman.

Physical description

A narrow desert plain bordering the Red Sea rises abruptly to mountains at 3000–3700 m (9840–12 140 ft); the highest point is Jabalan Nabi Shu'ayb (3760 m/12 336 ft); a flat, narrow coastal plain in the south is backed by mountains rising to almost 2500 m (8202 ft); to the north, a plateau merges with the gravel plains and sand wastes of the Rub' al Khali Basin.

Climate

Hot and humid on the coastal strip in the west, with an annual temperature of 29°C; milder in the highlands, where winters can be cold; annual rainfall is higher in the north and west than in the east and south; hot all year round in the south, with maximum temperatures more than 40°C in July and August; very high humidity in this area; average temperatures at Aden are 24°C in January, 32°C in July.

Economy

Poorest country in the Middle East, despite oil resources; agriculture and fishing, largely at subsistence level, engage 75% of the population; chief cash crops are coffee and fish; main industries are oil production and refining, manufacturing (textiles, leather goods, aluminium products), food processing and ship repair.

Government

Governed by a President, a Prime Minister and Council of Ministers, and a unicameral House of Representatives.

History

From around 750 BC there were advanced civilizations in southern Arabia. The area came under the control of the Muslim caliphate in the 7th century ad, and was ruled by Egyptian caliphs from around 1000. North Yemen was part of the Ottoman Empire from the 16th century until 1918; it was then ruled by the Hamid al-Din Dynasty until a revolution in 1962, when the Yemen Arab Republic (North Yemen) was proclaimed by the army. Fighting between royalists and republicans continued until 1967, when the republican regime was recognized. Aden was under British occupation from 1839, and a protectorate over the neighbouring emirates of the southern hinterland was gradually established in the late 19th century. A rebellion against British rule began in 1963; after British troops withdrew in 1967, power was seized by the National Liberation Front, which established the People's Republic of Yemen (South Yemen). The country was renamed the People's Democratic Republic of Yemen in 1970. Following negotiations, which began in 1979, the two countries united in 1990 as the Republic of Yemen. The first free, multiparty elections took place in 1993. There was a brief civil war between the north and south of the country in 1994 after the south attempted to secede, and tensions remain. There was a religious uprising in the north-west in 2004–5, and rioting in 2005 over the economic situation. Ali Abdullah Saleh, president of North Yemen from 1978, became president of the united country in 1990 and has retained the office at each election.

Arabia Felix

The lands of the southern Arabian peninsular were known to the ancient Romans as *Arabia Felix* or 'Happy Arabia'. The fabled home of the Queen of Sheba, the area was shrouded in mystery, with travellers telling of a blessed land of enormous wealth and indescribable beauty. As the controlling centre of the early trade and cultivation of incense and spices, the area enjoyed an extended period of prosperity until the increasing presence of Roman traders began to break up its monopoly and spark a gradual decline.

YUGOSLAVIA ▸MONTENEGRO, SERBIA
ZAÏRE ▸CONGO, DEMOCRATIC REPUBLIC OF THE

ZAMBIA

Official name	Republic of Zambia
Local name	Zambia
Former name	Northern Rhodesia (1911–64), which formed part of the Federation of Rhodesia and Nyasaland (1953–63)
Area	752 613 sq km (290 509 sq mi)
Capital	Lusaka
Chief towns	Ndola, Kitwe, Kabwe, Livingstone
Population	11 502 000 (2006e)
Nationality	Zambian
Languages	English; local languages are also spoken
Ethnic groups	African 99% (over 70 ethnic groups, including Bemba, Maravi, Tonga and Lozi), European and others 1%
Religions	Christianity 50–75%, Islam and Hinduism 24–49%, others 1%
Time zone	GMT +2
Currency	1 Kwacha (K) = 100 ngwee
Telephone	+260
Internet	.zm
Country code	ZMB

Location

A landlocked republic in southern Africa, bounded to the west by Angola; to the south by Namibia; to the south-east by Zimbabwe and Mozambique; to the east by Malawi; to the north-east by Tanzania; and to the north-west by the Democratic Republic of the Congo.

Physical description

Occupies a high plateau at an altitude of 1000–1400 m (3281–4590 ft); the highest point is 2067 m (6781 ft), south-east of Mbala; the Zambezi River rises in the northern extremity of North-West Province; includes parts of Lakes Tanganyika, Mweru and Kariba.

Climate

Temperate on upland plateau; tropical in low-lying areas; rainy season is October–March; at Lusaka the average rainfall is 840 mm and the maximum average daily temperatures range between 23 and 35°C.

Economy

Very poor, and receiving international aid; dependent on copper mining and processing (64% of export earnings); agriculture, mostly at subsistence level, and horticulture engage 85% of the workforce; chief cash crops are tobacco, cut flowers and cotton; other activities are electricity generation, food processing, manufacturing (beverages, chemicals, textiles and fertilizer) and tourism.

Government

Governed by an executive President, a Cabinet and a unicameral National Assembly.

History

Most ethnic groups in Zambia at present arrived there between the 16th and the 18th centuries. Arab slave-traders arrived in the 19th century, as did European settlers. The country was administered by the British South Africa Company under Cecil Rhodes. Known as Barotseland, it was declared a British sphere of influence in 1888 and named Northern Rhodesia in 1911. It became a British protectorate in 1924. Massive copper deposits were discovered in the late 1920s. Between 1953 and 1963 Northern Rhodesia was joined with Southern Rhodesia (now Zimbabwe) and Nyasaland (now Malawi) as the Federation of Rhodesia and Nyasaland. Northern Rhodesia gained its independence in 1964 as the Republic of Zambia. Kenneth Kaunda became president at independence and remained in power until 1991. Zambia was a one-party state from 1972 until 1991, when the first multiparty elections since independence were held. These resulted in victory for a pro-democracy party and its candidate, Frederick Chiluba, became president. He was re-elected in 1996, surviving coup attempts in 1993 and 1997. Levy Mwanawasa became president in 2002 and initiated an anti-corruption campaign; he was re-elected in 2006.

ZIMBABWE

Official name	Republic of Zimbabwe
Local name	Zimbabwe
Former name	Southern Rhodesia (until 1965), which formed part of the Federation of Rhodesia and Nyasaland (1953–63); Rhodesia (1965–80)
Area	391 090 sq km (150 961 sq mi)
Capital	Harare
Chief towns	Bulawayo, Gweru, Mutare
Population	12 237 000 (2006e)
Nationality	Zimbabwean
Languages	English; Shona, Sindebele and other local languages are also spoken
Ethnic groups	African 98% (Shona 82%, Ndebele 14%, other 2%), mixed and Asian 1%, white less than 1%
Religions	Mixture of Christian and traditional beliefs 50%, Christianity 25%, traditional beliefs 24%, Islam and others 1%
Time zone	GMT +2
Currency	1 Zimbabwe Dollar (Z$) = 100 cents
Telephone	+263
Internet	.zw
Country code	ZWE

Location

A landlocked republic in southern Africa, bounded to the south by South Africa; to the south-west by Botswana; to the north-west by Zambia; and to the north-east, east and south-east by Mozambique.

Physical description

High plateau country with the Middleveld at 900–1200 m (2950–3940 ft) and the Highveld running south-west to north-east, with an altitude of 1200–1500 m (3940–4920 ft); the land dips towards the Zambezi River in the north and the Limpopo River in the south; the mountains on the eastern frontier rise to 2592 m (8504 ft) at Mount Inyangani.

Climate

Generally subtropical, strongly influenced by altitude; warm and dry in the lowlands, with an annual rainfall of between 400 and 600 mm; the mountains in the east receive 1500–2000 mm of rain annually; the average maximum daily temperatures at Harare, in the Highveld, range between 21 and 29°C.

Economy

Once-flourishing economy close to collapse; many people dependent on food aid; agriculture severely disrupted by seizure of white-owned farms (2000–1); main cash crops are cotton, tobacco and maize; other activities include mining (gold, coal, platinum, copper, nickel, tin and iron ore), metal processing and manufacturing (garments, footwear and food processing).

Government

Governed by an executive President, a Cabinet and a bicameral Parliament consisting of a House of Assembly and a Senate. The ZANU-PF party has dominated politics since independence.

History

From the 12th to the 16th centuries the country was a medieval Bantu kingdom, with its capital at Great Zimbabwe. In the 19th century it was taken over by the Ndebele people and named the Kingdom of Matabeleland; this was often in dispute with the Shona people of Mashonaland to the north. It came under British influence in the 1880s, when the British South Africa Company under Cecil Rhodes began its exploitation of the rich mineral resources of the area. The Company invaded Mashonaland in 1890 and by 1900 controlled much of Central Africa. Its area was divided into Northern and Southern Rhodesia in 1911. Southern Rhodesia became a self-governing British colony in 1923, and formed part of the Central African Federation with Northern Rhodesia (Zambia) and Nyasaland (Malawi) from 1953 to 1963. Opposition to the independence of Southern Rhodesia under African rule resulted in a unilateral declaration of independence by the white-dominated government of Prime Minister Ian Smith in 1965. Economic sanctions and internal guerrilla activity forced the government to negotiate with the main African groups of the Patriotic Front. Power transferred to the African majority and the country gained its independence as Zimbabwe in 1980. Robert Mugabe became prime minister on independence, and president in 1987. His regime has become increasingly autocratic; it suppresses internal dissent, especially by the opposition Movement for

Democratic Change and the media, and rejects international criticism of human rights and other abuses. Zimbabwe withdrew from the Commonwealth in 2003 because its membership had been suspended indefinitely over the political situation. The agricultural collapse following the appropriation of white-owned farms from 2000 has resulted in widespread food shortages since 2001; international food aid has not always been distributed equitably. Anti-government protests in 2003 were brutally suppressed, and around 700000 shanty dwellers were left homeless in 2005 after government demolition of urban shanty towns and street markets.

LARGEST COUNTRIES

The ten largest countries in the world by area.

Country	Area
Russia	17075400 sq km (6591104 sq mi)
Canada	9970610 sq km (3848655 sq mi)
China	9597000 sq km (3704000 sq mi)
United States of America	9160454 sq km (3535935 sq mi)
Brazil	8511965 sq km (3285618 sq mi)
Australia	7692300 sq km (2969228 sq mi)
Argentina	3761274 sq km (1451852 sq mi)
India	3166829 sq km (1222396 sq mi)
Kazakhstan	2717300 sq km (1048878 sq mi)
Sudan	2504530 sq km (966749 sq mi)

SMALLEST COUNTRIES

The ten smallest countries in the world by area.

Country	Area
Vatican	0.4 sq km (0.2 sq mi)
Monaco	1.9 sq km (0.75 sq mi)
Nauru	21 sq km (8 sq mi)
Tuvalu	26 sq km (10 sq mi)
San Marino	61 sq km (24 sq mi)
Liechtenstein	160 sq km (62 sq mi)
Marshall Islands	180 sq km (70 sq mi)
St Kitts and Nevis	269 sq km (104 sq mi)
Maldives	300 sq km (120 sq mi)
Malta	316 sq km (122 sq mi)

MOST POPULOUS COUNTRIES

The ten most populous countries in the world.

Country	Population estimate[1]
China	1 313 974 000
India	1 095 352 000
United States of America	298 444 000
Indonesia	245 453 000
Brazil	188 078 000
Pakistan	165 804 000
Bangladesh	147 365 000
Russia	142 894 000
Nigeria	131 860 000
Japan	127 464 000

[1] *Population figures are 2006 estimates rounded to the nearest 1,000. Data source: CIA World Factbook*

LEAST POPULOUS COUNTRIES

The ten least populous countries in the world.

Country	Population estimate[1]
Vatican	900
Tuvalu	11 800
Nauru	13 300
Palau	20 600
San Marino	29 300
Monaco	32 500
Liechtenstein	34 000
St Kitts and Nevis	39 100
Marshall Islands	60 400
Dominica	68 900

[1] *Population figures are 2006 estimates rounded to the nearest 100. Data source: CIA World Factbook*

COUNTRY POPULATION ESTIMATES

The six most populous countries in the world

	1950 Country	Population estimate[1]	2000 Country	Population estimate[1]	2050 Country	Population estimate[1]
1	China	554 760 000	China	1 275 133 000	India	1 592 704 000
2	India	357 561 000	India	1 008 937 000	China	1 392 307 000
3	USA	157 813 000	USA	283 230 000	USA	394 976 000
4	Russia	102 702 000	Indonesia	212 092 000	Pakistan	304 700 000
5	Japan	83 625 000	Brazil	170 406 000	Indonesia	284 640 000
6	Indonesia	79 538 000	Russia	145 491 000	Nigeria	258 108 000

[1] *Population figures are rounded to the nearest 1,000. Data source: United Nations Population Division, 'World Population Prospects: The 2004 Revision'.*

WORLD POPULATION

World population estimates (medium variant predictions) published by the UN in 2002. In 2005 the estimated world population in 2050 was revised to 9,076 million.

Date (AD)	Millions[1]	Date (AD)	Millions[1]	Date (AD)	Millions[1]
1	300	1900	1650	2000	6071
1000	310	1950	2519	2010	6830
1250	400	1960	3021	2020	7540
1500	500	1970	3692	2030	8130
1750	790	1980	4435	2040	8594
1800	980	1990	5264	2050	8919
1850	1260				

Population figures are rounded to the nearest 1,000,000. Data source: United Nations Population Division.

LIFE EXPECTANCY

Highest life expectancy at birth		Lowest life expectancy at birth	
Country	**Years**[1]	**Country**	**Years**[1]
Japan	81.9	Swaziland	32.9
Hong Kong, China	81.5	Botswana	36.6
Iceland	80.6	Lesotho	36.7
Switzerland	80.4	Zimbabwe	37.2
Australia	80.2	Zambia	37.4
Sweden	80.1	Central African Republic	39.4
Italy	80.0	Malawi	39.6
Macao, China	80.0	Sierra Leone	40.6
Canada	79.9	Angola	40.7
Israel	79.6	Mozambique	41.9

[1] *Figures are 2005 estimates. Data source: United Nations Population Division, 'World Population Prospects: The 2004 Revision'.*

Oldest and Youngest

Japan has the oldest overall population in the world, with a median average age in 2005 estimated to be 42.9 years. The youngest population is that of Uganda, where the median average age in 2005 was estimated to be 14.8 years.

CAPITAL CITIES

The principal English names of capital cities are listed. For local names, names in other languages and alternative spellings, see the entry for the individual country in the A–Z listings. Capitals of states, provinces, dependencies, overseas possessions and other territories are not listed.

Capital city	Country	Capital city	Country
Abidjan	Côte d'Ivoire (administrative and economic capital)	Andorra la Vella	Andorra
		Ankara	Turkey
		Antananarivo	Madagascar
		Apia	Samoa
Abu Dhabi	United Arab Emirates	Ashgabat	Turkmenistan
		Asmara	Eritrea
Abuja	Nigeria	Astana	Kazakhstan
Accra	Ghana	Asunción	Paraguay
Addis Ababa	Ethiopia	Athens	Greece
Algiers	Algeria	Baghdad	Iraq
Amman	Jordan	Baku	Azerbaijan
Amsterdam	The Netherlands (official capital)	Bamako	Mali

Capital city	Country	Capital city	Country
Bandar Seri	Brunei Darussalam	Cotonou	Benin (seat of
Bangkok	Thailand		government and
Bangui	Central African		economic capital)
	Republic	Dakar	Senegal
Banjul	The Gambia	Damascus	Syria
Basseterre	St Kitts and Nevis	Dar es Salaam	Tanzania
Beijing	China		(commercial
Beirut	Lebanon		capital)
Belgrade	Serbia	Dhaka	Bangladesh
Belmopan	Belize	Dili	East Timor
Berlin	Germany	Djibouti	Djibouti
Berne	Switzerland	Dodoma	Tanzania (political
Bishkek	Kyrgyzstan		capital)
Bissau	Guinea-Bissau	Doha	Qatar
Bloemfontein	South Africa	Dublin	Ireland
	(judicial capital)	Dushanbe	Tajikistan
Bogotá	Colombia	Freetown	Sierra Leone
Brasília	Brazil	Funafuti	Tuvalu
Bratislava	Slovakia	Gaborone	Botswana
Brazzaville	Congo	Georgetown	Guyana
Bridgetown	Barbados	Guatemala City	Guatemala
Brussels	Belgium	Hanoi	Vietnam
Bucharest	Romania	Harare	Zimbabwe
Budapest	Hungary	Havana	Cuba
Buenos Aires	Argentina	Helsinki	Finland
Bujumbura	Burundi	Honiara	Solomon Islands
Cairo	Egypt	Islamabad	Pakistan
Canberra	Australia	Jakarta	Indonesia
Cape Town	South Africa	Kabul	Afghanistan
	(legislative capital)	Kampala	Uganda
Caracas	Venezuela	Kathmandu	Nepal
Castries	St Lucia	Khartoum	Sudan
Cetinje	Montenegro	Kiev	Ukraine
	(historic and	Kigali	Rwanda
	cultural capital)	Kingston	Jamaica
Chisinau	Moldova	Kingstown	St Vincent and the
Colombo	Sri Lanka		Grenadines
	(commercial	Kinshasa	Democratic
	capital)		Republic of the
Conakry	Guinea		Congo
Copenhagen	Denmark	Kuala Lumpur	Malaysia (official
			capital)

Capital city	Country	Capital city	Country
Kuwait City	Kuwait	N'Djamena	Chad
La Paz	Bolivia (administrative capital)	New Delhi	India
		Niamey	Niger
		Nicosia	Cyprus
Libreville	Gabon	Nouakchott	Mauritania
Lilongwe	Malawi	Nuku'alofa	Tonga
Lima	Peru	Oslo	Norway
Lisbon	Portugal	Ottawa	Canada
Ljubljana	Slovenia	Ouagadougou	Burkina Faso
Lobamba	Swaziland (legislative capital)	Palikir	Micronesia
		Panama City	Panama
Lomé	Togo	Paramaribo	Suriname
London	United Kingdom	Paris	France
Luanda	Angola	Phnom Penh	Cambodia
Lusaka	Zambia	Podgorica	Montenegro (administrative centre)
Luxembourg	Luxembourg		
Madrid	Spain		
Majuro	Marshall Islands	Port-au-Prince	Haiti
Malabo	Equatorial Guinea	Port Louis	Mauritius
Malé	Maldives	Port Moresby	Papua New Guinea
Managua	Nicaragua	Port of Spain	Trinidad and Tobago
Manama	Bahrain		
Manila	Philippines	Porto Novo	Benin (administrative and constitutional capital)
Maputo	Mozambique		
Maseru	Lesotho		
Mbabane	Swaziland (administrative capital)		
		Port Vila	Vanuatu
		Prague	Czech Republic
Melekeok	Palau	Praia	Cape Verde
Mexico City	Mexico	Pretoria	South Africa (administrative capital)
Minsk	Belarus		
Mogadishu	Somalia		
Monaco	Monaco	Putrajaya	Malaysia (seat of government and administrative capital)
Monrovia	Liberia		
Montevideo	Uruguay		
Moroni	Comoros		
Moscow	Russia	Pyongyang	Korea, North
Muscat	Oman	Quito	Ecuador
Nairobi	Kenya	Rabat	Morocco
Nassau	The Bahamas	Rangoon	Myanmar (Burma) (historic capital)
Naypyidaw	Myanmar (Burma) (administrative capital)		
		Reykjavík	Iceland
		Riga	Latvia

Capital city	Country	Capital city	Country
Riyadh	Saudi Arabia	T'bilisi	Georgia
Rome	Italy	Tegucigalpa	Honduras
Roseau	Dominica	Tehran	Iran
St George's	Grenada	Tel Aviv-Jaffa[1]	Israel
St John's	Antigua and Barbuda	The Hague	The Netherlands (seat of government)
San José	Costa Rica		
San Marino	San Marino	Thimphu	Bhutan
San Salvador	El Salvador	Tirana	Albania
Sana'a	Yemen	Tokyo	Japan
Santiago	Chile	Tripoli	Libya
Santo Domingo	Dominican Republic	Tunis	Tunisia
		Ulan Bator	Mongolia
São Tomé	São Tomé and Príncipe	Vaduz	Liechtenstein
		Valletta	Malta
Sarajevo	Bosnia and Herzegovina	Vatican City	Vatican
		Victoria	Seychelles
Seoul	Korea, South	Vienna	Austria
Singapore	Singapore	Vientiane	Laos
Skopje	Macedonia	Vilnius	Lithuania
Sofia	Bulgaria	Warsaw	Poland
Sri Jayawardenepura Kotte	Sri Lanka (administrative capital)	Washington, DC	United States of America
		Wellington	New Zealand
Stockholm	Sweden	Windhoek	Namibia
Sucre	Bolivia (official and legislative capital)	Yamoussoukro	Côte d'Ivoire (official capital)
Suva	Fiji		
T'aipei	Taiwan	Yaoundé	Cameroon
Tallinn	Estonia	Yaren District[2]	Nauru
Tarawa	Kiribati	Yerevan	Armenia
Tashkent	Uzbekistan	Zagreb	Croatia

Israel claims Jerusalem as its capital, but this is not recognized internationally.
There is no capital as such, but government offices are situated in this area.

CAPITAL CITIES ON RIVERS

Information for selected major capital cities is given. Capital cities that are sea ports or that lie on bays, estuaries, lakes or other water expanses are not included.

Capital city	Country	River
Amman	Jordan	Zarqa
Amsterdam	The Netherlands	Amstel (and the IJsselmeer)
Ankara	Turkey	a tributary of the Ova
Baghdad	Iraq	Tigris
Bangkok	Thailand	Chao Phraya
Belgrade	Serbia	Danube, Sava
Berlin	Germany	Spree, Havel (and others)
Bratislava	Slovakia	Danube
Brussels	Belgium	Senne
Bucharest	Romania	Dambovit
Budapest	Hungary	Danube
Buenos Aires	Argentina	Plate
Cairo	Egypt	Nile
Canberra	Australia	Molonglo
Damascus	Syria	Barada
Dhaka	Bangladesh	Meghna
Dublin	Ireland	Liffey
Hanoi	Vietnam	Red
Islamabad	Pakistan	Jhelum
Jakarta	Indonesia	Liwung
Kiev	Ukraine	Dnieper
Lima	Peru	Rímac
Lisbon	Portugal	Tagus
Ljubljana	Slovenia	Sava, Ljubljanica
London	United Kingdom	Thames
Luxembourg	Luxembourg	Alzette, Petrusse
Madrid	Spain	Manzanares
Manila	Philippines	Pasig
Minsk	Belarus	Svisloch
Moscow	Russia	Moskva
New Delhi	India	Yamuna (Old Delhi)
Ottawa	Canada	Ottawa, Rideau
Paris	France	Seine
Phnom Penh	Cambodia	Mekong (at confluence with the Tonlé Sap lake)
Podgorica	Montenegro	Morača
Prague	Czech Republic	Vltava

Capital city	Country	River
Pyongyang	North Korea	Taedong
Rabat	Morocco	Bou Regreg
Riga	Latvia	Daugava
Rome	Italy	Tiber
Santiago	Chile	Mapocho
Sarajevo	Bosnia and Herzegovina	Miljacka
Seoul	South Korea	Han
Skopje	Macedonia	Vardar
Tokyo	Japan	Sumida
Vienna	Austria	Danube
Vilnius	Lithuania	Vilnya
Warsaw	Poland	Vistula
Washington, DC	United States of America	Potomac, Anacostia
Zagreb	Croatia	Sava

CAPITAL CITY POPULATIONS

As far as possible, population figures are for the city proper rather than the metropolitan area.

Capital city	Population[1]	Capital city	Population[1]
Abidjan	3 577 000 (2005e)	Bandar Seri Begawan	70 000 (2007e)
Abu Dhabi	1 850 000 (2006e)		
Abuja	1 405 000 (2006)	Bangkok	6 593 000 (2005e)
Accra	2 981 000 (2005e)	Bangui	735 000 (2006e)
Addis Ababa	2 893 000 (2005e)	Banjul	34 000 (2006e)
Algiers	3 221 000 (2006e)	Basseterre	13 000 (2007e)
Amman	1 292 000 (2005e)	Beijing	7 725 000 (2007e)
Amsterdam	1 147 000 (2005e)	Beirut	1 777 000 (2005e)
Andorra la Vella	20 000 (2007e)	Belgrade	1 106 000 (2005e)
Ankara	3 573 000 (2005e)	Belmopan	16 000 (2007e)
Antananarivo	1 585 000 (2005e)	Berlin	3 400 000 (2006e)
Apia	41 000 (2007e)	Berne	957 000 (2006e)
Ashgabat	848 000 (2007e)	Bishkek	934 000 (2007e)
Asmara	594 000 (2007e)	Bissau	404 000 (2006e)
Astana	357 000 (2007e)	Bloemfontein	498 000 (2007e)
Asunción	1 858 000 (2005e)	Bogotá	7 235 000 (2006e)
Athens	3 131 000 (2005e)	Brasília	2 384 000 (2006e)
Baghdad	5 904 000 (2005e)	Bratislava	422 000 (2006e)
Baku	1 856 000 (2005e)	Brazzaville	1 327 000 (2006e)
Bamako	1 368 000 (2005e)	Bridgetown	99 000 (2007e)

Capital city	Population[1]	Capital city	Population[1]
Brussels	1 012 000 (2005e)	Jakarta	8 569 000 (2006e)
Bucharest	1 934 000 (2005e)	Kabul	2 994 000 (2005e)
Budapest	1 693 000 (2005e)	Kampala	1 319 000 (2005e)
Buenos Aires	11 612 000 (2006e)	Kathmandu	815 000 (2005e)
Bujumbura	342 000 (2007e)	Khartoum	4 518 000 (2005e)
Cairo	7 438 000 (2005e)	Kiev	2 470 000 (2007e)
Canberra	325 000 (2005e)	Kigali	779 000 (2005e)
Cape Town	3 083 000 (2005e)	Kingston	585 000 (2006e)
Caracas	2 913 000 (2005e)	Kingstown	18 000 (2007e)
Castries	13 000 (2007e)	Kinshasa	8 419 000 (2007e)
Cetinje	15 000 (2003)	Kuala Lumpur[2]	1 405 000 (2005e)
Chisinau	611 000 (2007e)	Kuwait City	32 000 (2005)
Colombo	649 000 (2006e)	La Paz	1 527 000 (2005e)
Conakry	1 425 000 (2005e)	Libreville	591 000 (2006e)
Copenhagen	1 088 000 (2005e)	Lilongwe	722 000 (2007e)
Cotonou	761 000 (2006)	Lima	7 186 000 (2005e)
Dakar	2 159 000 (2005e)	Lisbon	499 000 (2007e)
Damascus	2 272 000 (2005e)	Ljubljana	254 000 (2006e)
Dar es Salaam	2 676 000 (2005e)	Lobamba	5 000 (2007e)
Dhaka	6 725 000 (2005e)	Lomé	1 337 000 (2005e)
Dili	167 000 (2007e)	London	464 000 (2005e)
Djibouti	643 000 (2007e)	London (Greater)	7 518 000 (2005e)
Dodoma	196 000 (2007e)	Luanda	2 766 000 (2005e)
Doha	351 000 (2006e)	Lusaka	1 260 000 (2005e)
Dublin	1 037 000 (2005e)	Luxembourg	76 000 (2006e)
Dushanbe	538 000 (2006e)	Madrid	3 155 000 (2005e)
Freetown	799 000 (2005e)	Majuro	28 000 (2006e)
Funafuti	4 500 (2002)	Malabo	167 000 (2007e)
Gaborone	221 000 (2007e)	Malé	89 000 (2007e)
Georgetown	237 000 (2006e)	Managua	1 165 000 (2005e)
Guatemala City	1 024 000 (2006e)	Manama	149 000 (2007e)
Hanoi	4 164 000 (2005e)	Manila	1 581 000 (2000e)
Harare	1 515 000 (2005e)	Maputo	1 320 000 (2005e)
Havana	2 189 000 (2005e)	Maseru	116 000 (2007e)
Helsinki	1 091 000 (2005e)	Mbabane	81 000 (2007e)
Honiara	58 000 (2007e)	Mexico City	8 659 000 (2006e)
Islamabad	834 000 (2007e)	Minsk	1 778 000 (2005e)
Jabalpur	1 213 000 (2005e)	Mogadishu	1 320 000 (2005e)
Jaboatão	651 000 (2006e)	Monaco City	1 000 (2007e)
Jacksonville	783 000 (2005e)	Monrovia	936 000 (2005e)
Jaipur	2 747 000 (2005e)	Montevideo	1 264 000 (2005e)

Capital city	Population[1]	Capital city	Population[1]
Moroni	45 000 (2007e)	San José	912 000 (2005e)
Moscow	10 568 000 (2007e)	San Marino	4 500 (2007e)
Muscat	24 000 (2007e)	San Salvador	1 517 000 (2005e)
Nairobi	2 773 000 (2005e)	Santiago	5 683 000 (2005e)
Nassau	232 000 (2006e)	Santo Domingo	2 022 000 (2005e)
N'Djamena	888 000 (2005e)	São Tomé	65 000 (2007e)
New Delhi	322 000 (2006e)	Sarajevo	737 000 (2006e)
Niamey	850 000 (2005e)	Seoul	10 297 000 (2005e)
Nicosia	202 000 (2006e)	Singapore	4 326 000 (2005e)
Nouakchott	753 000 (2007e)	Skopje	582 000 (2006e)
Nuku'alofa	24 000 (2007e)	Sofia	1 093 000 (2005e)
Oslo	802 000 (2005e)	Sri Jayewardenepura Kotte	119 000 (2007e)
Ottawa	1 149 000 (2005e)		
Ouagadougou	1 152 000 (2007e)		
Palikir	4 500 (2007e)	Stockholm	1 708 000 (2005e)
Panama City	404 000 (2007e)	Sucre	241 000 (2007e)
Paramaribo	226 000 (2007e)	Suva	203 000 (2006e)
Paris	2 154 000 (2006e)	T'aipei	2 492 000 (2006e)
Phnom Penh	1 364 000 (2005e)	Tallinn	392 000 (2006e)
Podgorica	163 000 (2007e)	Tarawa	47 000 (2007e)
Port-au-Prince	2 129 000 (2005e)	Tashkent	2 181 000 (2005e)
Port Louis	134 000 (2006e)	T'bilisi	1 047 000 (2005e)
Port Moresby	290 000 (2006e)	Tegucigalpa	927 000 (2005e)
Port of Spain	50 000 (2006e)	Tehran	7 314 000 (2005e)
Porto Novo	242 000 (2007e)	Tel Aviv-Jaffa	388 000 (2006e)
Port Vila	38 000 (2007e)	Thimphu	79 000 (2007e)
Prague	1 171 000 (2005e)	Tirana	380 000 (2006e)
Praia	121 000 (2007e)	Tokyo	8 404 000 (2006e)
Pretoria	1 271 000 (2005e)	Tripoli	2 098 000 (2005e)
Pyongyang	3 351 000 (2005e)	Tunis	941 000 (2006e)
Quito	1 514 000 (2005e)	Ulan Bator	863 000 (2005e)
Rabat	1 647 000 (2005e)	Vaduz	5 000 (2007e)
Rangoon[3]	4 574 000 (2006e)	Valletta	7 000 (2007e)
Reykjavik	195 000 (2006e)	Vatican City	750 (2007e)
Riga	738 000 (2006e)	Victoria	23 000 (2006e)
Riyadh	4 193 000 (2005e)	Vienna	1 651 000 (2005e)
Rome	2 817 000 (2005e)	Vientiane	698 000 (2006e)
Roseau	17 000 (2007e)	Vilnius	542 000 (2006e)
St John's	25 000 (2007e)	Warsaw	1 680 000 (2005e)
Sana'a	1 801 000 (2005e)	Washington, DC	544 000 (2007e)

Capital city	Population[1]	Capital city	Population
Wellington	179 000 (2006)	Yaren[4]	5 000 (2007e)
Windhoek	277 000 (2006e)	Yerevan	1 103 000 (2005e)
Yamoussoukro	206 000 (2007e)	Zagreb	701 000 (2006e)
Yaoundé	1 391 000 (2007e)		

[1] Population figures are generally rounded to the nearest 1,000.

[2] No accurate figure available for Putrajaya, Malaysia's administrative capital.

[3] No accurate figure available for Naypyidaw, Myanmar's administrative capital.

[4] Nauru has no official capital but the government offices are located in Yaren.

CONNECTING THE WORLD

INTERNATIONAL TIME DIFFERENCES

Hours ahead of GMT are indicated with a + symbol and hours behind GMT with a – symbol. Daylight saving time is not taken into account.

Afghanistan	+4½	Chad	+1	Gibraltar	+1
Albania	+1	Chile	−4	Greece	+2
Algeria	+1	China	+8	Greenland	−3
Andorra	+1	Colombia	−5	Grenada	−4
Angola	+1	Comoros	+3	Guatemala	−6
Antigua and	−4	Congo	+1	Guinea	0
Barbuda		Congo, DR	+1/2	Guinea-Bissau	0
Argentina	−3	Costa Rica	−6	Guyana	−4
Armenia	+4	Côte d'Ivoire	0	Haiti	−5
Australia	+8/10	Croatia	+1	Honduras	−6
Austria	+1	Cuba	−5	Hong Kong	+8
Azerbaijan	+4	Cyprus	+2	Hungary	+1
Bahamas, The	−5	Czech	+1	Iceland	0
Bahrain	+3	Republic		India	+5½
Bangladesh	+6	Denmark	+1	Indonesia	+7/9
Barbados	−4	Djibouti	+3	Iran	+3½
Belarus	+2	Dominica	−4	Iraq	+3
Belgium	+1	Dominican	−4	Ireland	0
Belize	−6	Republic		Israel	+2
Benin	+1	East Timor	+8	Italy	+1
Bermuda	−4	Ecuador	−5	Jamaica	−5
Bhutan	+6	Egypt	+2	Japan	+9
Bolivia	−4	El Salvador	−6	Jordan	+2
Bosnia and	+1	Equatorial	+1	Kazakhstan	+4/6
Herzegovina		Guinea		Kenya	+3
Botswana	+2	Eritrea	+3	Kiribati	+12/14
Brazil	−2/5	Estonia	+2	Korea, North	+9
Brunei	+8	Ethiopia	+3	Korea, South	+9
Bulgaria	+2	Falkland Is	−4	Kuwait	+3
Burkina Faso	0	Fiji	+12	Kyrgyzstan	+6
Burundi	+2	Finland	+2	Laos	+7
Cambodia	+7	France	+1	Latvia	+2
Cameroon	+1	Gabon	+1	Lebanon	+2
Canada	−3½/8	Gambia, The	0	Lesotho	+2
Cape Verde	−1	Georgia	+4	Liberia	0
Central African	+1	Germany	+1	Libya	+2
Republic		Ghana	0	Liechtenstein	+1

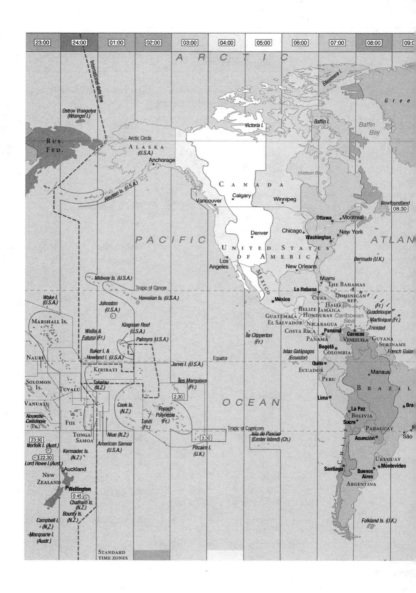

Lithuania	+2	Panama	−5	Sudan	+3
Luxembourg	+1	Papua New Guinea	+10	Suriname	−3
Macedonia	+1			Swaziland	+2
Madagascar	+3	Paraguay	−4	Sweden	+1
Malawi	+2	Peru	−5	Switzerland	+1
Malaysia	+8	Philippines	+8	Syria	+2
Maldives	+5	Poland	+1	Taiwan	+8
Mali	0	Portugal	0	Tajikistan	+5
Malta	+1	Qatar	+3	Tanzania	+3
Marshall Is	+12	Romania	+2	Thailand	+7
Mauritania	0	Russia	+2/12	Togo	0
Mauritius	+4	Rwanda	+2	Tonga	+13
Mexico	−6/8	St Kitts and Nevis	−4	Trinidad and Tobago	−4
Micronesia	+10/11				
Moldova	+2	St Lucia	−4	Tunisia	+1
Monaco	+1	St Vincent and the Grenadines	−4	Turkey	+2
Mongolia	+7/8			Turkmenistan	+5
Montenegro	+1			Tuvalu	+12
Morocco	0	Samoa	−11	Uganda	+3
Mozambique	+2	San Marino	+1	Ukraine	+2
Myanmar (Burma)	+6½	São Tomé and Príncipe	0	United Arab Emirates	+4
Namibia	+1	Saudi Arabia	+3	United Kingdom	0
Nauru	+12	Senegal	0		
Nepal	+5¾	Serbia	+1	United States of America	−5/10
Netherlands, The	+1	Seychelles	+4		
		Sierra Leone	0	Uruguay	−3
New Zealand	+12	Singapore	+8	Uzbekistan	+5
Nicaragua	−6	Slovakia	+1	Vanuatu	+11
Niger	+1	Slovenia	+1	Vatican	+1
Nigeria	+1	Solomon Is	+11	Venezuela	−4
Norway	+1	Somalia	+3	Vietnam	+7
Oman	+4	South Africa	+2	Yemen	+3
Pakistan	+5	Spain	+1	Zambia	+2
Palau	+9	Sri Lanka	+5½	Zimbabwe	+2

ALPHABETS

Various alphabets are used throughout the world for written communication; four of the most widely used are shown. The Cyrillic and Greek alphabets are 'true alphabets' that represent both vowels and consonants, while Arabic and Hebrew only depict consonants and are known as 'abjads'. Some other languages, including Chinese, do not have an alphabet; they instead use symbols to represent syllables and words.

Arabic

Letter	Name	Transliteration
	'alif	'
ب	ba	b
ت	ta	t
ث	tha	th
	jim	j
	ha	h
	kha	kh
	dal	d
	dha	th
	ra	r
	za	z
س	sin	s
ش	shin	sh
ص	sad	s
ض	dad	d
	ta	t
	za	z
	'ain	'
	ghain	gh
ف	fa	f
	qaf	q
	kaf	k
	lam	l
	min	m
	nun	n
	ha	h
	waw	w
ي	ya	y

Cyrillic

Letter		Transliteration
А	а	a
Б	б	b
В	в	v
Г	г	g
Д	д	d
Е	е	e
Ё	ё	ë
Ж	ж	zh
З	з	z
И	и	i
Й	й	ĭ
К	к	k
Л	л	l
М	м	m
Н	н	n
О	о	o
П	п	p
Р	р	r
С	с	s
Т	т	t
У	у	u
Ф	ф	f
Х	х	h, kh
Ц	ц	ts
Ч	ч	ch
Ш	ш	sh
Щ	щ	shch
Ы	ы	y
Ь	ь	'
Ъ	ъ	"
Э	э	é
Ю	ю	yu
Я	я	ya

Greek

Letter	Name	Transliteration
A α	alpha	a
B β	beta	b
Γ γ	gamma	g
Δ δ	delta	d
E ε	epsilon	e
Z ζ	zeta	z
H η	eta	e, ē
Θ θ	theta	th
I ι	iota	i
K κ	kappa	k
Λ λ	lambda	l
M μ	mu	m
N ν	nu	n
Ξ ξ	xi	x
O o	omicron	o
Π π	pi	p
P ρ	rho	r, rh
Σ σ, ς	sigma	s
T τ	tau	t
Y υ	upsilon	u, y
Φ φ	phi	ph
X χ	chi	kh
Ψ ψ	psi	ps
Ω ω	omega	ō

Hebrew

Letter	Name	Transliteration
א	'alef	'
ב	bet	b, v
ג	gimel	g
ד	daleth	d
ה	he	h
ו	vav	v, o, u
ז	zayin	z
ח	chet	ch, ch
ט	tet	t
י	yod	y, i
כ ך	kaph	k, kh
ל	lamed	l
מ ם	mem	m
נ ן	nun	n
ס	samekh	s
ע	ayin	'
פ ף	pe	p, f
צ ץ	tzade	s
ק	kof	k
ר	resh	r
ש	shin	sh
שׂ	sin	s
ת	tav	t

The Long and the Short of It

The smallest alphabet in use today is the alphabet of Rotokas, a language used on the Papua New Guinean island of Bougainville. It has only twelve letters: A, E, G, I, K, O, P, R, S, T, U and V. The Georgian alphabet, on the other hand, has a lengthy 41 letters.

LANGUAGES: NUMBERS OF SPEAKERS

Language families

The figures shown are estimates of the numbers of speakers in the main language families of the world in the early 1980s. The list includes Japanese and Korean, which are not clearly related to any other languages.

Language family	Description/examples	No. of speakers
Indo-European	Languages from Europe, North and South America, the Indian subcontinent and central Asia, including English, French, Russian, Greek, Hindi and Bengali	2 000 000 000
Sino-Tibetan	Languages from east Asia, including Mandarin, Cantonese, Taiwanese, Tibetan and Karen	1 040 000 000
Niger-Congo	Languages from southern Africa, including Swahili, Swazi, Zulu, Fulani, Yoruba and Malinke	260 000 000
Afro-Asiatic	Languages from northern Africa, the Middle East and south-east Asia, including Arabic, Hebrew, Aramaic, Tuareg, Somali and Hausa	230 000 000
Austronesian	Languages mostly from the islands of south-east Asia and the Pacific, including Malay, Javanese, Tagalog, Malagasy, Maori and Hawaiian	200 000 000
Dravidian	Languages from the Indian subcontinent, including Tamil, Malayalam, Kannada, Telugu, Gondi and Brahui	140 000 000
Japanese	—	120 000 000
Altaic	Languages mostly from central and north-east Asia, including Turkish, Azeri, Kazakh, Uzbek, Mongolian and Manchu	90 000 000
Austro-Asiatic	Languages mostly from south-east Asia, including Vietnamese, Muong, Khmer, Palaung, Nicobarese and Mundari	60 000 000
Korean	—	60 000 000
Tai	Languages from south-east Asia and China, including Thai, Lao, Shan and Zhuang	50 000 000
Nilo-Saharan	Languages from central and east Africa, including Masai and Nubian	30 000 000
Amerindian	Indigenous languages of North, Central and South America	25 000 000
Uralic	Languages from the Ural mountains and surrounding area, including Finnish, Hungarian, Estonian and Mordvin	23 000 000
Miao-Yao (Hmong-Mien)	Various languages from China and south-east Asia	7 000 000
Caucasian	Languages from eastern Europe and western Asia, including Georgian and Chechen	6 000 000
Indo-Pacific	Over 700 languages, mostly from New Guinea	3 000 000

Language family	Description/examples	No. of speakers
Khoisan	Languages from southern Africa, including San and Bushmen	50 000
Australian aboriginal	Indigenous languages of Australia	50 000
Palaeosiberian	Languages spoken in remote parts of Siberia	25 000

Specific languages

The figures shown are estimates for mother-tongue speakers of the 20 most widely used languages.

Language	Mother-tongue speakers (millions)
1 Chinese	1 000
2 English	350
3 Spanish	250
4 Hindi	200
5 Arabic	150
6 Bengali	150
7 Russian	150
8 Portuguese	135
9 Japanese	120
10 German	100
11 French	70
12 Punjabi	70
13 Javanese	65
14 Bihari	65
15 Italian	60
16 Korean	60
17 Telugu	55
18 Tamil	55
19 Marathi	50
20 Vietnamese	50

The figures shown are estimates of the total population of all countries where the language has official or semi-official status. These totals are often overestimates, as only a minority of people in countries where a second language is recognized may actually be fluent in it.

Language	Official language populations (millions)
1 English	1 400
2 Chinese	1 000
3 Hindi	700
4 Spanish	280
5 Russian	270
6 French	220

Language	Official language populations (millions)
7 Arabic	170
8 Portuguese	160
9 Malay	160
10 Bengali	150
11 Japanese	120
12 German	100
13 Urdu	85
14 Italian	60
15 Korean	60
16 Vietnamese	60
17 Persian	55
18 Tagalog	50
19 Thai	50
20 Turkish	50

COUNTRY INTERNET SUFFIXES

For suffixes listed by country see the individual country entries in the Nations of the World section.

.ac	Ascension Island	.bb	Barbados
.ad	Andorra	.bd	Bangladesh
.ae	United Arab Emirates	.be	Belgium
.af	Afghanistan	.bf	Burkina Faso
.ag	Antigua and Barbuda	.bg	Bulgaria
.ai	Anguilla	.bh	Bahrain
.al	Albania	.bi	Burundi
.am	Armenia	.bj	Benin
.an	Netherlands Antilles	.bm	Bermuda
.ao	Angola	.bn	Brunei Darussalam
.aq	Antarctica	.bo	Bolivia
.ar	Argentina	.br	Brazil
.as	American Samoa	.bs	The Bahamas
.at	Austria	.bt	Bhutan
.au	Australia	.bv	Bouvet Island
.aw	Aruba	.bw	Botswana
.az	Azerbaijan	.by	Belarus
.ba	Bosnia and Herzegovina	.bz	Belize

.ac Ascension Island
.ad Andorra
.ae United Arab Emirates
.af Afghanistan
.ag Antigua and Barbuda
.ai Anguilla
.al Albania
.am Armenia
.an Netherlands Antilles
.ao Angola
.aq Antarctica
.ar Argentina
.as American Samoa
.at Austria
.au Australia
.aw Aruba
.az Azerbaijan
.ba Bosnia and Herzegovina

.bb Barbados
.bd Bangladesh
.be Belgium
.bf Burkina Faso
.bg Bulgaria
.bh Bahrain
.bi Burundi
.bj Benin
.bm Bermuda
.bn Brunei Darussalam
.bo Bolivia
.br Brazil
.bs The Bahamas
.bt Bhutan
.bv Bouvet Island
.bw Botswana
.by Belarus
.bz Belize
.ca Canada
.cc Cocos (Keeling) Islands

.cd Congo, Democratic Republic of the
.cf Central African Republic
.cg Congo, Republic of
.ch Switzerland
.ci Côte d'Ivoire
.ck Cook Islands
.cl Chile
.cm Cameroon
.cn China
.co Colombia
.cr Costa Rica
.cu Cuba
.cv Cape Verde
.cx Christmas Island
.cy Cyprus
.cz Czech Republic
.de Germany

.dj Djibouti
.dk Denmark
.dm Dominica
.do Dominican Republic
.dz Algeria
.ec Ecuador
.ee Estonia
.eg Egypt
.eh Western Sahara
.er Eritrea
.es Spain
.et Ethiopia
.eu European Union (proposed)
.fi Finland
.fj Fiji
.fk Falkland Islands
.fm Micronesia
.fo Faroe Islands
.fr France

.ga	Gabon	.jp	Japan	.mw	Malawi	.sc	Seychelles
.gd	Grenada	.ke	Kenya	.mx	Mexico	.sd	Sudan
.ge	Georgia	.kg	Kyrgyzstan	.my	Malaysia	.se	Sweden
.gf	French Guiana	.kh	Cambodia	.mz	Mozambique	.sg	Singapore
		.ki	Kiribati	.na	Namibia	.sh	St Helena
.gg	Guernsey	.km	Comoros	.nc	New Caledonia	.si	Slovenia
.gh	Ghana	.kn	St Kitts and Nevis			.sj	Svalbard and Jan Meyen Islands
.gi	Gibraltar			.ne	Niger		
.gl	Greenland	.kp	Korea, North	.nf	Norfolk Island		
.gm	The Gambia	.kr	Korea, South	.ng	Nigeria	.sk	Slovakia
.gn	Guinea	.kw	Kuwait	.ni	Nicaragua	.sl	Sierra Leone
.gp	Guadeloupe	.ky	Cayman Islands	.nl	The Netherlands	.sm	San Marino
.gq	Equatorial Guinea					.sn	Senegal
		.kz	Kazakhstan	.no	Norway	.so	Somalia
.gr	Greece	.la	Laos	.np	Nepal	.sr	Suriname
.gs	Georgia and the South Sandwich Islands	.lb	Lebanon	.nr	Nauru	.st	São Tomé and Príncipe
		.lc	St Lucia	.nu	Niue		
		.li	Liechtenstein	.nz	New Zealand	.sv	El Salvador
		.lk	Sri Lanka	.om	Oman	.sy	Syria
.gt	Guatemala	.lr	Liberia	.pa	Panama	.sz	Swaziland
.gu	Guam	.ls	Lesotho	.pe	Peru	.tc	Turks and Caicos Islands
.gw	Guinea-Bissau	.lt	Lithuania	.pf	French Polynesia		
.gy	Guyana	.lu	Luxembourg				
.hk	Hong Kong	.lv	Latvia	.pg	Papua New Guinea	.td	Chad
.hm	Heard and McDonald Islands	.ly	Libya			.tf	French Southern and Antarctic Territories
		.ma	Morocco	.ph	Philippines		
		.mc	Monaco	.pk	Pakistan		
.hn	Honduras	.md	Moldova	.pl	Poland		
.hr	Croatia	.mg	Madagascar	.pm	St Pierre and Miquelon	.tg	Togo
.ht	Haiti	.mh	Marshall Islands			.th	Thailand
.hu	Hungary			.pn	Pitcairn Islands	.tj	Tajikistan
.id	Indonesia	.mk	Macedonia			.tk	Tokelau
.ie	Ireland	.ml	Mali	.pr	Puerto Rico	.tm	Turkmenistan
.il	Israel	.mm	Myanmar (Burma)	.ps	Palestinian Territories	.tn	Tunisia
.im	Isle of Man					.to	Tonga
.in	India	.mn	Mongolia	.pt	Portugal	.tp	East Timor
.io	British Indian Ocean Territory	.mo	Macau	.pw	Palau	.tr	Turkey
		.mp	Northern Mariana Islands	.py	Paraguay	.tt	Trinidad and Tobago
				.qa	Qatar		
.iq	Iraq	.mq	Martinique	.re	Réunion	.tv	Tuvalu
.ir	Iran	.mr	Mauritania	.ro	Romania	.tw	Taiwan
.is	Iceland	.ms	Montserrat	.ru	Russia	.tz	Tanzania
.it	Italy	.mt	Malta	.rw	Rwanda	.ua	Ukraine
.je	Jersey	.mu	Mauritius	.sa	Saudi Arabia	.ug	Uganda
.jm	Jamaica	.mv	Maldives	.sb	Solomon Islands	.uk	United Kingdom
.jo	Jordan						

.um	US Minor Outlying Islands	.vc	St Vincent and the Grenadines	.vn	Vietnam	.yt	Mayotte
.us	United States	.ve	Venezuela	.vu	Vanuatu	.yu	Serbia; Montenegro
.uy	Uruguay	.vg	Virgin Islands (British)	.wf	Wallis and Futuna Islands	.za	South Africa
.uz	Uzbekistan			.ws	Samoa	.zm	Zambia
.va	Vatican	.vi	Virgin Islands (US)	.ye	Yemen	.zw	Zimbabwe

ISO COUNTRY CODES

The International Organization for Standardization (ISO) has assigned three codes to each country and territory as recognized by the United Nations: a two-letter code, a three-letter code and a three-digit code. The two-letter codes correspond for the most part to the country internet suffixes, although there are exceptions (eg the United Kingdom's code is GB but its internet suffix is .uk). The three-letter codes are used in machine-readable passports, again with a few exceptions (eg German passports have D rather than DEU). The three-digit codes have the advantage of not being based on one particular alphabet.

Country	2-letter code	3-letter code	3-digit code	Country	2-letter code	3-letter code	3-digit code
Afghanistan	AF	AFG	004	Belize	BZ	BLZ	084
Åland Islands	AX	ALA	248	Benin	BJ	BEN	204
Albania	AL	ALB	008	Bermuda	BM	BMU	060
Algeria	DZ	DZA	012	Bhutan	BT	BTN	064
American Samoa	AS	ASM	016	Bolivia	BO	BOL	068
Andorra	AD	AND	020	Bosnia and Herzegovina	BA	BIH	070
Angola	AO	AGO	024	Botswana	BW	BWA	072
Anguilla	AI	AIA	660	Bouvet Island	BV	BVT	074
Antarctica	AQ	ATA	010	Brazil	BR	BRA	076
Antigua and Barbuda	AG	ATG	028	British Indian Ocean Territory	IO	IOT	086
Argentina	AR	ARG	032	Brunei Darussalam	BN	BRN	096
Armenia	AM	ARM	051				
Aruba	AW	ABW	533	Bulgaria	BG	BGR	100
Australia	AU	AUS	036	Burkina Faso	BF	BFA	854
Austria	AT	AUT	040	Burundi	BI	BDI	108
Azerbaijan	AZ	AZE	031	Cambodia	KH	KHM	116
Bahamas	BS	BHS	044	Cameroon	CM	CMR	120
Bahrain	BH	BHR	048	Canada	CA	CAN	124
Bangladesh	BD	BGD	050	Cape Verde	CV	CPV	132
Barbados	BB	BRB	052	Cayman Islands	KY	CYM	136
Belarus	BY	BLR	112				
Belgium	BE	BEL	056				

Country	2-letter code	3-letter code	3-digit code	Country	2-letter code	3-letter code	3-digit code
Central African Republic	CF	CAF	140	Fiji	FJ	FJI	242
				Finland	FI	FIN	246
				France	FR	FRA	250
Chad	TD	TCD	148	French Guiana	GF	GUF	254
Chile	CL	CHL	152	French Polynesia	PF	PYF	258
China	CN	CHN	156				
Christmas Island	CX	CXR	162	French Southern Territories	TF	ATF	260
Cocos (Keeling) Islands	CC	CCK	166				
				Gabon	GA	GAB	266
				Gambia	GM	GMB	270
Colombia	CO	COL	170	Georgia	GE	GEO	268
Comoros	KM	COM	174	Germany	DE	DEU	276
Congo, Republic of	CG	COG	178	Ghana	GH	GHA	288
				Gibraltar	GI	GIB	292
Congo, Democratic Republic of the	CD	COD	180	Greece	GR	GRC	300
				Greenland	GL	GRL	304
				Grenada	GD	GRD	308
				Guadeloupe	GP	GLP	312
Cook Islands	CK	COK	184	Guam	GU	GUM	316
Costa Rica	CR	CRI	188	Guatemala	GT	GTM	320
Côte d'Ivoire	CI	CIV	384	Guernsey	GG	GGY	831
Croatia	HR	HRV	191	Guinea	GN	GIN	324
Cuba	CU	CUB	192	Guinea-Bissau	GW	GNB	624
Cyprus	CY	CYP	196	Guyana	GY	GUY	328
Czech Republic	CZ	CZE	203	Haiti	HT	HTI	332
Denmark	DK	DNK	208	Heard and McDonald Islands	HM	HMD	334
Djibouti	DJ	DJI	262				
Dominica	DM	DMA	212	Holy See (Vatican City State)	VA	VAT	336
Dominican Republic	DO	DOM	214				
Ecuador	EC	ECU	218	Honduras	HN	HND	340
Egypt	EG	EGY	818	Hong Kong	HK	HKG	344
El Salvador	SV	SLV	222	Hungary	HU	HUN	348
Equatorial Guinea	GQ	GNQ	226	Iceland	IS	ISL	352
				India	IN	IND	356
Eritrea	ER	ERI	232	Indonesia	ID	IDN	360
Estonia	EE	EST	233	Iran, Islamic Republic of	IR	IRN	364
Ethiopia	ET	ETH	231				
Falkland Islands (Malvinas)	FK	FLK	238	Iraq	IQ	IRQ	368
				Ireland	IE	IRL	372
				Isle of Man	IM	IMN	833
Faroe Islands	FO	FRO	234	Israel	IL	ISR	376

Country	2-letter code	3-letter code	3-digit code	Country	2-letter code	3-letter code	3-digit code
Italy	IT	ITA	380	Micronesia, Federated States of	FM	FSM	583
Jamaica	JM	JAM	388				
Japan	JP	JPN	392				
Jersey	JE	JEY	832	Moldova, Republic of	MD	MDA	498
Jordan	JO	JOR	400				
Kazakhstan	KZ	KAZ	398	Monaco	MC	MCO	492
Kenya	KE	KEN	404	Mongolia	MN	MNG	496
Kiribati	KI	KIR	296	Montenegro	ME	MNE	499
Korea, North	KP	PRK	408	Montserrat	MS	MSR	500
Korea, South	KR	KOR	410	Morocco	MA	MAR	504
Kuwait	KW	KWT	414	Mozambique	MZ	MOZ	508
Kyrgyzstan	KG	KGZ	417	Myanmar	MM	MMR	104
Lao People's Democratic Republic	LA	LAO	418	Namibia	NA	NAM	516
				Nauru	NR	NRU	520
				Nepal	NP	NPL	524
Latvia	LV	LVA	428	Netherlands	NL	NLD	528
Lebanon	LB	LBN	422	Netherlands Antilles	AN	ANT	530
Lesotho	LS	LSO	426				
Liberia	LR	LBR	430	New Caledonia	NC	NCL	540
Libyan Arab Jamahiriya	LY	LBY	434				
				New Zealand	NZ	NZL	554
Liechtenstein	LI	LIE	438	Nicaragua	NI	NIC	558
Lithuania	LT	LTU	440	Niger	NE	NER	562
Luxembourg	LU	LUX	442	Nigeria	NG	NGA	566
Macao	MO	MAC	446	Niue	NU	NIU	570
Macedonia, the Former Yugoslav Republic of	MK	MKD	807	Norfolk Islands	NF	NFK	574
				Northern Mariana Islands	MP	MNP	580
Madagascar	MG	MDG	450				
Malawi	MW	MWI	454	Norway	NO	NOR	578
Malaysia	MY	MYS	458	Oman	OM	OMN	512
Maldives	MV	MDV	462	Pakistan	PK	PAK	586
Mali	ML	MLI	466	Palau	PW	PLW	585
Malta	MT	MLT	470	Palestinian Territory, Occupied	PS	PSE	275
Marshall Islands	MH	MHL	584				
Martinique	MQ	MTQ	474	Panama	PA	PAN	591
Mauritania	MR	MRT	478	Papua New Guinea	PG	PNG	598
Mauritius	MU	MUS	480				
Mayotte	YT	MYT	175	Paraguay	PY	PRY	600
Mexico	MX	MEX	484	Peru	PE	PER	604
				Philippines	PH	PHL	608
				Pitcairn	PN	PCN	612

Country	2-letter code	3-letter code	3-digit code	Country	2-letter code	3-letter code	3-digit code
Poland	PL	POL	616	Swaziland	SZ	SWZ	748
Portugal	PT	PRT	620	Sweden	SE	SWE	752
Puerto Rico	PR	PRI	630	Switzerland	CH	CHE	756
Qatar	QA	QAT	634	Syrian Arab Republic	SY	SYR	760
Réunion	RE	REU	638				
Romania	RO	ROU	642	Taiwan, Province of China	TW	TWN	158
Russian Federation	RU	RUS	643				
Rwanda	RW	RWA	646	Tajikistan	TJ	TJK	762
Saint Helena	SH	SHN	654	Tanzania, United Republic of	TZ	TZA	834
Saint Kitts and Nevis	KN	KNA	659				
Saint Lucia	LC	LCA	662	Thailand	TH	THA	764
Saint Pierre and Miquelon	PM	SPM	666	Timor-Leste	TL	TLS	626
				Togo	TG	TGO	768
Saint Vincent and the Grenadines	VC	VCT	670	Tokelau	TK	TKL	772
				Tonga	TO	TON	776
Samoa	WS	WSM	882	Trinidad and Tobago	TT	TTO	780
San Marino	SM	SMR	674				
Sao Tome and Principe	ST	STP	678	Tunisia	TN	TUN	788
				Turkey	TR	TUR	792
Saudi Arabia	SA	SAU	682	Turkmenistan	TM	TKM	795
Senegal	SN	SEN	686	Turks and Caicos Islands	TC	TCA	796
Serbia	RS	SRB	688				
Seychelles	SC	SYC	690	Tuvalu	TV	TUV	798
Sierra Leone	SL	SLE	694	Uganda	UG	UGA	800
Singapore	SG	SGP	702	Ukraine	UA	UKR	804
Slovakia	SK	SVK	703	United Arab Emirates	AE	ARE	784
Slovenia	SI	SVN	705				
Solomon Islands	SB	SLB	090	United Kingdom	GB	GBR	826
Somalia	SO	SOM	706	United States	US	USA	840
South Africa	ZA	ZAF	710	United States Minor Outlying Islands	UM	UMI	581
South Georgia and the South Sandwich Islands	GS	SGS	239				
				Uruguay	UY	URY	858
				Uzbekistan	UZ	UZB	860
Spain	ES	ESP	724	Vanuatu	VU	VUT	548
Sri Lanka	LK	LKA	144	Venezuela	VE	VEN	862
Sudan	SD	SDN	736	Vietnam	VN	VNM	704
Suriname	SR	SUR	740	Virgin Islands, British	VG	VGB	092
Svalbard and Jan Mayen	SJ	SJM	744				

Country	2-letter code	3-letter code	3-digit code	Country	2-letter code	3-letter code	3-digit code
Virgin Islands, US	VI	VIR	850	Yemen	YE	YEM	887
				Zambia	ZM	ZMB	894
Wallis and Futuna	WF	WLF	876	Zimbabwe	ZW	ZWE	716
Western Sahara	EH	ESH	732				

INTERNATIONAL VEHICLE REGISTRATION (IVR) CODES

IVR codes indicate the country of origin of road vehicles, and are displayed on an oval disc.

A	Austria
AFG	Afghanistan
AL	Albania
AM	Armenia
AND	Andorra
AUS	Australia[1]
AZ	Azerbaijan
B	Belgium
BD	Bangladesh[1]
BDS	Barbados[1]
BF	Burkina Faso
BG	Bulgaria
BIH	Bosnia and Herzegovina
BOL	Bolivia
BR	Brazil
BRN	Bahrain
BRU	Brunei Darussalam[1]
BS	The Bahamas[1]
BUR	Myanmar (Burma)
BW	Botswana[1]
BY	Belarus
BZ	Belize
C	Cuba
CAM	Cameroon
CDN	Canada
CH	Switzerland
CI	Côte d'Ivoire
CL	Sri Lanka[1]
CO	Colombia
CR	Costa Rica

CY	Cyprus[1]
CZ	Czech Republic
D	Germany
DK	Denmark
DOM	Dominican Republic
DY	Benin
DZ	Algeria
E	Spain
EAK	Kenya[1]
EAT	Tanzania[1]
EAU	Uganda[1]
EC	Ecuador
ES	El Salvador
EST	Estonia
ET	Egypt
ETH	Ethiopia
F	France
FIN	Finland
FJI	Fiji[1]
FL	Liechtenstein
G	Gabon
GB	United Kingdom[1]
GBA	Alderney[1]
GBG	Guernsey[1]
GBJ	Jersey[1]
GBM	Isle of Man[1]
GBZ	Gibraltar
GCA	Guatemala
GE	Georgia
GH	Ghana
GR	Greece

GUY	Guyana[1]
H	Hungary
HKJ	Jordan
HR	Croatia
I	Italy
IL	Israel
IND	India[1]
IR	Iran
IRL	Ireland[1]
IRQ	Iraq
IS	Iceland
J	Japan[1]
JA	Jamaica[1]
K	Cambodia
KS	Kyrgyzstan
KWT	Kuwait
KZ	Kazakhstan
L	Luxembourg
LAO	Laos
LAR	Libya
LB	Liberia
LS	Lesotho[1]
LT	Lithuania
LV	Latvia
M	Malta[1]
MA	Morocco
MAL	Malaysia[1]
MC	Monaco
MD	Moldova
MEX	Mexico
MGL	Mongolia
MK	Macedonia

MNE	Montenegro	RH	Haiti	TCH	Chad
MOC	Mozambique[1]	RI	Indonesia[1]	TG	Togo
MS	Mauritius[1]	RIM	Mauritania	TJ	Tajikistan
MW	Malawi[1]	RL	Lebanon	TM	Turkmenistan
N	Norway	RM	Madagascar	TN	Tunisia
NAM	Namibia[1]	RMM	Mali	TR	Turkey
NAU	Nauru[1]	RN	Niger	TT	Trinidad and
NEP	Nepal[1]	RO	Romania		Tobago[1]
NGR	Nigeria	ROK	South Korea	UA	Ukraine
NIC	Nicaragua	ROU	Uruguay	USA	United States of
NL	The Netherlands	RP	Philippines		America
NZ	New Zealand[1]	RSM	San Marino	UZ	Uzbekistan
P	Portugal	RU	Burundi	V	Vatican
PA	Panama	RUS	Russia	VN	Vietnam
PE	Peru	RWA	Rwanda	WAG	The Gambia
PK	Pakistan[1]	S	Sweden	WAL	Sierra Leone
PL	Poland	SA	Saudi Arabia	WD	Dominica[1]
PNG	Papua New	SRB	Serbia	WG	Grenada[1]
	Guinea[1]	SD	Swaziland[1]	WL	St Lucia[1]
PY	Paraguay	SGP	Singapore[1]	WS	Samoa
Q	Qatar	SK	Slovakia	WV	St Vincent and
RA	Argentina	SLO	Slovenia		the Grenadines[1]
RC	Taiwan	SME	Suriname[1]	YAR	Yemen
RCA	Central African	SN	Senegal	YV	Venezuela
	Republic	SO	Somalia	Z	Zambia[1]
RCB	Congo	SUD	Sudan	ZA	South Africa[1]
RCH	Chile	SY	Seychelles[1]	ZRE	Congo,
RG	Guinea	SYR	Syria		Democratic
RGB	Guinea-Bissau	T	Thailand[1]		Republic of the
				ZW	Zimbabwe[1]

[1]In countries so marked, the rule of the road is to drive on the left; in others, vehicles drive on the right.

AIR DISTANCES

Air distances between some major cities, given in statute miles. To convert to kilometres, multiply number given by 1.6093.

* Shortest route

	Amsterdam	Beijing	Buenos Aires	Cairo	Chicago	Delhi	Hong Kong	Honolulu	Istanbul	Johannesburg	Lagos	London	Los Angeles	Mexico City	Montreal	Moscow	Nairobi	Paris	Perth	Rome	Santiago	Sydney	Tokyo
Beijing	6566																						
Buenos Aires	7153	12000																					
Cairo	2042	6685	7468																				
Chicago	4109	7599	5587	6135																			
Delhi	3985	2368	8340	2753	8119																		
Hong Kong	5926	1235	3124	5098	7827	2345																	
Honolulu	8368	6778	8693	9439	4246	7888	5543																
Istanbul	1373	4763	7783	764	5502	2833	5998	9547															
Johannesburg	5606	10108	5725	4012	8705	6765	6728	12892	4776														
Lagos	3161	8030	4832	2443	7065	5196	7541	10367	3207	2854													
London	217	5054	8985	2187	3956	4169	5979	7252	1552	5640	3115												
Los Angeles	5559	6349	6140	7589	1746	8717	7231	2553	6994	10443	7716	5442											
Mexico City	5724	7912	4592	7730	1687	9806	8794	4116	7255	10070	7343	5703	1563										
Montreal	3422	7557	5640	5431	737	7421	8564	4923	4795	8322	5595	3252	2482	2307									
Moscow	1338	3604	8382	1790	5500	2698	4839	8802	1089	6280	4462	1550	6992	6700	4393								
Nairobi	4148	8888	7427	2203	8177	4956	7301	11498	2967	1809	2377	4246	9688	9949	7498	3951							
Paris	261	5108	6892	1995	4140	4089	5987	7463	1394	5422	2922	220	5633	5714	3434	1540	4031						
Perth	9118	4987	9734	7766	11281	5013	3752	7115	7846	5564	10209	9246	9535	11098	12402	8355	7373	12587					
Rome	809	5306	6931	1329	4828	3679	5773	8150	852	4802	2497	898	6340	6601	5431	1478	3349	688	8309				
Santiago	7714	13622	710	8029	5328	12715	3733	8147	10109	5738	6042	8568	5594	4168	5551	10118	7547	461	15129	7548			
Sydney	1039	5689	7760	9196	9324	6495	4586	5078	9883	7601	11700	10565	7498	9061	9980	9425	9410	10150	2037	10149	13092		
Tokyo	6006¹	1313	13100	6362	6286	3656	1807	3831	5757	8535	9130¹	6218	5451	7014	6913	4688	8565	6208¹	4925	6146	11049	4640	
Washington	3854	7930	6097	5859	590	7841	8385	4822	5347	8199	5472	3672	2294	1871	493	4884	7918	3843	11829	4495	5061	9792	6763

AIRLINE DESIGNATORS

Airline designators, or reservation codes, issued by the International Air Transport Association (IATA) consist of two letters or digits. They are used at the beginning of flight numbers and for other purposes including ticketing and reservations. Three-letter codes are issued by the International Civil Aviation Organization (ICAO). They are currently used mainly for communications purposes but it is planned that they will replace the two-character codes in the future.

IATA code	Airline	Country	ICAO code
AA	American Airlines	USA	AAL
AC	Air Canada	Canada	ACA
AF	Air France	France	AFR
AH	Air Algérie	Algeria	DAH
AI	Air India	India	AIC
AM	Aeromexico	Mexico	AMX
AQ	Aloha Airlines	Hawaii	AAH
AR	Aerolineas Argentinas	Argentina	ARG
AS	Alaska Airlines	USA	ASA
AT	Royal Air Maroc	Morocco	RAM
AV	Avianca	Colombia	AVA
AY	Finnair	Finland	FIN
AZ	Alitalia	Italy	AZA
A9	Georgian Airways	Georgia	TGZ
BA	British Airways	UK	BAW

IATA code	Airline	Country	ICAO code
BD	British Midland	UK	BMA
BE	Flybe	Channel Is	BEE
BG	Biman Bangladesh Airlines	Bangladesh	BBC
BI	Royal Brunei Airlines	Brunei	RBA
BL	Pacific Airlines	Vietnam	PIC
BO	Bouraq Indonesia Airlines	Indonesia	BOU
BP	Air Botswana	Botswana	BOT
BT	Air Baltic	Latvia	BTI
BU	SAS Braathens	Norway	CNO
BW	BWIA International Trinidad and Tobago Airways	Trinidad	BWA
BY	Britannia Airways	UK	BAL
CA	Air China	China	CCA
CB	ScotAirways	UK	SAY
CI	China Airlines	Taiwan	CAL
CJ	China North Airlines	Taiwan	CBF
CK	China Cargo Airlines	China	CKK
CM	COPA (Compania Panamena de Aviación)	Panama	CMP
CO	Continental Airlines	USA	COA
CS	Micronesia Continental	Mariana Is	CMI
CT	Air Sofia	Bulgaria	SFB
CU	Cubana	Cuba	CUB
CW	Air Marshall Islands	Marshall Is	CWM
CX	Cathay Pacific Airways	Hong Kong	CPA
CY	Cyprus Airways	Cyprus	CYP
CZ	China Southern Airlines	China	CSN
DI	dba	Germany	BAG
DL	Delta Air Lines	USA	DAL
DT	TAAG-Angola Airlines	Angola	DTA
DX	Danish Air Transport	Denmark	DTR
EI	Aer Lingus	Ireland	EIN
EK	Emirates	United Arab Emirates	UAE
ET	Ethiopian Airlines	Ethiopia	ETH
EU	Ecuatoriana	Ecuador	EEA
FE	Royal Khmer Airlines	Cambodia	RKH
FF	Tower Air	USA	TOW
FG	Ariana Afghan Airlines	Afghanistan	AFG
FM	Shanghai Airlines	China	CSH
FI	Icelandair	Iceland	ICE
FJ	Air Pacific	Fiji	FJI
FR	Ryanair	Ireland	RYR
GA	Garuda Indonesia	Indonesia	GIA

IATA code	Airline	Country	ICAO code
GF	Gulf Air	Bahrain	GFA
GH	Ghana Airways	Ghana	GHA
GL	Air Greenland	Greenland	GRL
GM	Air Slovakia	Slovakia	SVK
GR	Aurigny Air Services	Channel Is	AUR
GT	GB Airways	Gibraltar	GBL
G6	Angkor Airways	Cambodia	AKW
HA	Hawaiian Airlines	USA	HAL
HM	Air Seychelles	Seychelles	SEY
HP	America West Airlines	USA	AWE
HV	Transavia Airlines	Netherlands	TRA
HY	Uzbekistan Airlines	Uzbekistan	UZB
IB	Iberia	Spain	IBE
IC	Indian Airlines	India	IAC
IE	Solomon Airlines	Solomon Is	SOL
IL	Istanbul Airways	Turkey	IST
IN	Macedonian Airlines	Macedonia	MCS
IP	Airlines of Tasmania	Australia	ATM
IR	Iran Air	Iran	IRA
IV	Fujian Airlines	China	CFJ
IY	Yemenia Airways	Yemen	IYE
JA	B&H Airlines (Air Bosna)	Bosnia and Herzegovina	BON
JE	Manx Airlines	Isle of Man	MNX
JL	Japan Airlines	Japan	JAL
JM	Air Jamaica	Jamaica	AJM
JP	Adria Airways	Slovenia	ADR
JQ	Air Jamaica Express	Jamaica	JMX
JS	Air Koryo	North Korea	KOR
JU	JAT Airways	Serbia and Montenegro	JAT
KA	Dragonair	Hong Kong	HDA
KE	Korean Air Lines	South Korea	KAL
KL	KLM	Netherlands	KLM
KM	Air Malta	Malta	AMC
KP	Kiwi International Airlines	USA	KIA
KQ	Kenya Airways	Kenya	KQA
KT	Kampuchea Airlines	Cambodia	KMP
KU	Kuwait Airways	Kuwait	KAC
KV	Kavminvodyavia	Russia	MVD
KX	Cayman Airways	Cayman Is	CAY
KZ	Nippon Cargo Airlines	Japan	NCA
LA	LAN Airlines	Chile	LAN
LG	Luxair	Luxembourg	LGL

IATA code	Airline	Country	ICAO code
LH	Lufthansa	Germany	DLH
LJ	Sierra National Airlines	Sierra Leone	SLA
LN	Jamahiriya Libyan Arab Airlines	Libya	LAA
LO	LOT-Polish Airlines	Poland	LOT
LR	LACSA	Costa Rica	LRC
LT	LTU International Airways	Germany	LTU
LV	Albanian Airlines	Albania	LBC
LX	Swiss International Airlines	Switzerland	SWR
LY	El Al Israel Airlines	Israel	ELY
MA	Malev	Hungary	MAH
MD	Air Madagascar	Madagascar	NDG
MH	Malaysian Airlines	Malaysia	MAS
MK	Air Mauritius	Mauritius	MAU
MN	Comair	South Africa	CAW
MR	Air Mauritanie	Mauritania	MRT
MS	Egyptair	Egypt	MSR
MX	Mexicana	Mexico	MXA
NF	Air Vanuatu	Vanuatu	AVN
NG	Lauda Air	Austria	LDA
NH	All Nippon Airways	Japan	ANA
NM	Mount Cook Airlines	New Zealand	NZM
NU	Japan Transocean Air	Japan	JTA
NW	Northwest Airlines	USA	NWA
NY	Air Iceland (Flugfélag Íslands)	Iceland	FXI
NZ	Air New Zealand	New Zealand	ANZ
OA	Olympic Airways	Greece	OAL
OK	Czech Airlines	Czech Republic	CSA
OM	MIAT-Mongolian Airlines	Mongolia	MGL
ON	Air Nauru	Australia	RON
OO	Skywest Airlines	Australia	SKW
OS	Austrian Airlines	Austria	AUA
OU	Croatia Airlines	Croatia	CTN
OV	Estonian Air	Estonia	ELL
PC	Air Fiji	Fiji	FAJ
PE	Air Europe	Italy	AEL
PF	Palestinian Airlines	Israel	PNW
PG	Bangkok Airways	Thailand	BKP
PH	Polynesian Airlines	Samoa	PAO
PK	Pakistan International Airlines	Pakistan	PIA
PR	Philippine Airlines	Philippines	PAL
PS	Ukraine International Airlines	Ukraine	AUI
PU	Pluna Lineas Aereas Urugauyas	Uruguay	PUA
PX	Air Niugini	Papua New Guinea	ANG

IATA code	Airline	Country	ICAO code
PY	Surinam Airways	Suriname	SLM
PZ	TAM (Transportes Aereos del Mercosur)	Paraguay	LAP
QF	Qantas Airways	Australia	QFA
QM	Air Malawi	Malawi	AML
QR	Qatar Airways	Qatar	QTR
QU	Uganda Airlines	Uganda	UGX
QV	Lao Aviation	Laos	LAO
QW	Turks and Caicos Airways	Turks and Caicos	TCI
QX	Horizon Air	USA	QXE
Q3	Zambia Airways	Zambia	MBN
RA	Royal Nepal Airlines	Nepal	RNA
RB	Syrian Arab Airlines	Syria	SYR
RG	Varig	Brazil	VRG
RJ	Royal Jordanian	Jordan	RJA
RK	Air Afrique	Côte d'Ivoire	RKH
RO	Tarom	Romania	ROT
RR	Royal Air Force	UK	RFR
SA	South African Airways	South Africa	SAA
SB	Air Caledonie International	New Caledonia	ACI
SD	Sudan Airways	Sudan	SUD
SK	SAS (Scandinavian Airlines)	Sweden	SAS
SN	SN Brussels Airlines	Belgium	DAT
SQ	Singapore Airlines	Singapore	SIA
SU	Aeroflot	Russia	AFL
SV	Saudia (Saudi Arabian Airlines)	Saudi Arabia	SVA
SW	Air Namibia	Namibia	NMB
TC	Air Tanzania	Tanzania	ATC
TE	Lithuanian Airlines	Lithuania	LIL
TG	Thai Airways International	Thailand	THA
TK	Turkish Airlines	Turkey	THY
TM	LAM (Linhas Aereas de Moçambique)	Mozambique	LAM
TN	Air Tahiti Nui	Tahiti	THT
TP	TAP Air Portugal	Portugal	TAP
TU	Tunis Air	Tunisia	TAR
TV	Virgin Express	Belgium	VEX
UA	United Airlines	USA	UAL
UB	Myanmar Airlines	Myanmar (Burma)	UBA
UL	Sri Lankan Airlines	Sri Lanka	ALK
UM	Air Zimbabwe	Zimbabwe	AZW
UN	Transaero Airlines	Russia	TSO
UP	Bahamasair	The Bahamas	BHS

IATA code	Airline	Country	ICAO code
US	US Airways	USA	USA
UY	Cameroon Airlines	Cameroon	UYC
VE	Avensa	Venezuela	AVE
VN	Vietnam Airlines	Vietnam	HVN
VO	Tyrolean Airways	Austria	TYR
VP	VASP (Viação Aèrea São Paulo)	Brazil	VSP
VR	Transportes Aereos de Cabo Verde	Cape Verde	TCV
VS	Virgin Atlantic Airways	UK	VIR
VT	Air Tahiti	Tahiti	VTA
VV	Aeorosvit Airlines	Ukraine	AEW
WA	KLM Cityhopper	UK	KLC
WH	China Northwest Airlines	China	CNW
WJ	Labrador Airways	Canada	LAL
WM	Windward Islands Airways	Canada	WIA
WN	Southwest Airlines	USA	SWA
WT	Nigeria Airways	Nigeria	NGA
WX	Cityjet	Ireland	BCY
WY	Oman Aviation Services	Oman	OMA
YJ	National Airlines	South Africa	NTN
YK	Cyprus Turkish Airlines	Cyprus	KYV
YN	Air Creebec	Canada	CRQ
YU	Dominair	Dominican Republic	ADM
ZB	Monarch Airlines	UK	MON
ZC	Royal Swazi National Airways	Swaziland	RSN
ZP	Air St Thomas	Virgin Is	STT
2J	Air Burkina	Burkina Faso	VBW
3D	Denim Air	Netherlands	DNM
9U	Air Moldova	Moldova	MLD

Airlines in a Word

Airlines are issued with a call sign by the International Civil Aviation Organization (ICAO); this is used together with the flight number to identify aircraft to air traffic control. Some of these are just part of the airline's name, such as 'AMERICAN' for American Airlines. However, some are more evocative: planes from Aer Lingus use 'SHAMROCK', British Airways use 'SPEEDBIRD' and flights run by the British Antarctic Survey use the call sign 'PENGUIN'.

THE PHYSICAL WORLD

EARTH FACTS

There are no universally agreed figures for many of the measurements given below. Surveys make use of different criteria for identifying natural boundaries, and use different techniques of measurement. The estimated sizes of continents, oceans, seas, deserts and rivers are particularly subject to variation.

Age	4.6 billion years
Period of axial rotation	23 hours 56 minutes 4.0966 seconds
Distance from Sun (mean)	150 million km (93 million mi)
Aphelion: greatest distance from Sun	152.1 million km (94.5 million mi)
Perihelion: smallest distance from Sun	147.1 million km (91.4 million mi)
Surface area	510 million km^2 (196 million sq mi)
Mass	5976×10^{24} kg (13175×10^{24} lb)
Land surface area	Approx 148 million km^2 (57 million sq mi)
Land surface as percentage of total surface area	Approx 29%
Water surface area	Approx 361.6 million km^2 (140 million sq mi)
Water surface as percentage of total surface area	Approx 71%
Circumference (equator)	40076 km (24902 mi)
Circumference (meridian)	40000 km (24860 mi)
Diameter (equator)	12757 km (7927 mi)
Diameter (meridian)	12714 km (7900 mi)
Temperature at core	4500°C (8100°F)
Surface gravity	9.81 m/s^2 (32 ft/s^2)

> " Now there is one outstandingly important fact regarding Spaceship Earth, and that is that no instruction book came with it.
>
> —US architect, inventor, engineer and philosopher R Buckminster Fuller (1895–1983), *Operating Manual for Spaceship Earth* (1969). "

HOW THE EARTH HAS BEEN MEASURED

The Earth is spherical, but not a perfect sphere. This is because the rotation of the Earth causes the globe to bulge slightly around the equator. This bulge is only small: the diameter through the equator is 43 km longer than the diameter through the North and South poles, which is a tiny difference considering that the average diameter of the Earth is 12,742 km (7,918 mi). Various people have tried to determine the size of the Earth throughout history.

Aristotle

The Greek philosopher Aristotle realized that the eclipse of the Moon proved that the Earth was a sphere. He estimated that the Earth had a circumference of 74,000 km (46,000 mi) by making observations of a star from two places on the Earth at different degrees of latitude.

Aristotle's Academy

Aristotle was a highly important and influential figure in the history of Western thought. In 335 BC he founded a school, known as the Lyceum because of its proximity to the temple of Apollo Lyceius. Aristotle's followers became known as 'peripatetics', supposedly from his restless habit of walking up and down while lecturing.

Eratosthenes

The first person to make an accurate estimate of the size of the Earth was Eratosthenes, who lived in the ancient Greek city of Cyrene (now in Libya) between 275 and 194 BC. He realized that he could calculate the size of the Earth by placing two sticks vertically in the ground in different places and then simultaneously measuring the angles made by the shadows they cast . Using this method he estimated that the Earth had a circumference of 46,000 km (28,600 mi), which was amazingly accurate. With modern data collected using satellite technology we now know the Earth is, in fact, 40,000 km (24,900 mi) around its circumference.

Jean Picard

In 1671 the French scientist Jean Picard made new measurements based on the classical ideas of Aristotle and Eratosthenes. He realized that the accuracy of any measurement of the Earth depended on being able to measure distances accurately between two places on the same line of longitude. He attempted to make an accurate measurement of one degree of latitude in order to work out the Earth's radius. He decided to do this using a pendulum; unfortunately, he was unaware that pendulums swing at slightly different speeds at different latitudes. Despite this error, he calculated that one degree of latitude had a surface measurement of between 111 and 112 km. From this he calculated that the Earth's radius must be 6,372 km: a measurement exceptionally close to the average measurement of 6,371 km that is accepted today.

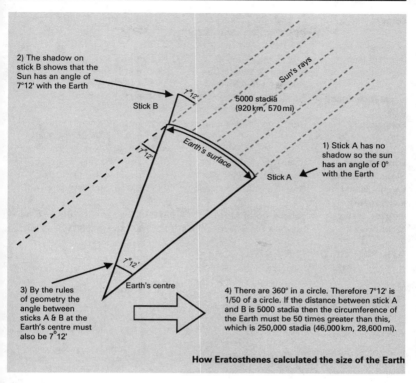

How Eratosthenes calculated the size of the Earth

2) The shadow on stick B shows that the Sun has an angle of 7°12' with the Earth

Stick B

7°12'

5000 stadia (920 km, 570 mi)

Sun's rays

Earth's surface

7°12'

1) Stick A has no shadow so the sun has an angle of 0° with the Earth

Stick A

3) By the rules of geometry the angle between sticks A & B at the Earth's centre must also be 7°12'

7°12'

Earth's centre

4) There are 360° in a circle. Therefore 7°12' is 1/50 of a circle. If the distance between stick A and B is 5000 stadia then the circumference of the Earth must be 50 times greater than this, which is 250,000 stadia (46,000 km, 28,600 mi).

PHYSICAL EXTREMES

Highest mountain	Mt Everest, China/Nepal	8 850 m (29 035 ft)
Longest mountain range	Andes, South America	7 200 km (4 500 mi)
Highest cliffs	Near Molokai, Hawaii, USA	1 010 m (3 300 ft)
Lowest point on Earth	Dead Sea, Israel/Jordan/West Bank	400 m (1 312 ft) below sea level
Deepest cave	Jean Bernard, France	1 494 m (4 902 ft)
Largest cave	Sarawak Chamber (Lubang Nasib Bagus), Malaysia	700 m (2 300 ft) long by 70 m (230 ft) high by average 300 m (985 ft) wide
Largest ocean	Pacific Ocean	155 557 000 sq km (60 060 557 sq mi)
Deepest point in the ocean	Challenger Deep, Mariana Trench, Pacific Ocean	11 040 m (36 220 ft)
Highest tides	Minas Basin, Bay of Fundy, Canada	16 m (53 ft) difference between high and low tide
Largest sea	Coral Sea	4 791 000 sq km (1 850 000 sq mi)

Largest lake	Caspian Sea, Iran/Russia/ Turkmenistan/Kazakhstan/ Azerbaijan	371 000 sq km (143 240 sq mi)
Deepest lake	Lake Baikal, Russia	1 637 m (5 371 ft)
Highest lake	In crater of Licancábur volcano, Chile/Bolivia	5 930 m (19 455 ft)
Highest navigable lake	Titicaca, Peru/Bolivia	3 810 m (12 500 ft)
Saltiest lake	Don Juan Pond, Antarctica	40.2% salt by weight *(for reference, the Dead Sea has 23.1%)*
Longest river	River Nile, Africa	6 690 km (4 160 mi)
Highest waterfall	Angel Falls, Venezuela	Total height 979 m (3 212 ft)
Largest island (not a continent)	Greenland, Arctic Ocean	2 175 500 sq km (840 000 sq mi)
Largest desert	Sahara, north Africa	8 600 000 sq km (3 320 000 sq mi)
Largest glacier	Lambert Glacier, Antarctica	1 000 000 sq km (386 102 sq mi)

STRUCTURE OF THE EARTH

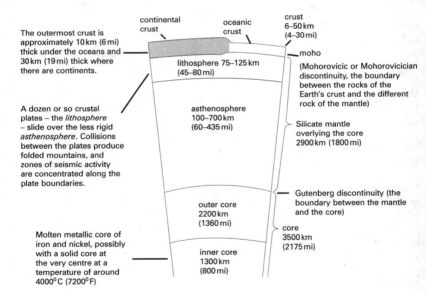

The outermost crust is approximately 10 km (6 mi) thick under the oceans and 30 km (19 mi) thick where there are continents.

A dozen or so crustal plates – the *lithosphere* – slide over the less rigid *asthenosphere*. Collisions between the plates produce folded mountains, and zones of seismic activity are concentrated along the plate boundaries.

Molten metallic core of iron and nickel, possibly with a solid core at the very centre at a temperature of around 4000°C (7200°F)

continental crust

oceanic crust

crust 6–50 km (4–30 mi)

lithosphere 75–125 km (45–80 mi)

moho

(Mohorovicic or Mohorovicician discontinuity, the boundary between the rocks of the Earth's crust and the different rock of the mantle)

asthenosphere 100–700 km (60–435 mi)

Silicate mantle overlying the core 2900 km (1800 mi)

outer core 2200 km (1360 mi)

Gutenberg discontinuity (the boundary between the mantle and the core)

core 3500 km (2175 mi)

inner core 1300 km (800 mi)

COMPOSITION OF THE EARTH'S CRUST

Element	% weight
Oxygen	46.60
Silicon	27.72
Aluminium	8.13
Iron	5.00
Calcium	3.63
Sodium	2.83
Potassium	2.59
Magnesium	2.09
Others	1.41

Legend: ☐ Oxygen ■ Silicon ☐ Aluminium ☐ Iron ■ Calcium ☐ Sodium ■ Potassium ☐ Magnesium ■ Other elements

HIGHEST MOUNTAINS

Mountain[1]	Location	Height[2]
Everest	China/Nepal	8850 m (29040 ft)
K2 (Qogir)	Jammu-Kashmir[3]/China	8610 m (28250 ft)
Kanchenjunga	India/Nepal	8590 m (28170 ft)
Lhotse	China/Nepal	8500 m (27890 ft)
Kanchenjunga South Peak	India/Nepal	8470 m (27800 ft)
Makalu I	China/Nepal	8470 m (27800 ft)
Kanchenjunga West Peak	India/Nepal	8420 m (27620 ft)
Lhotse East Peak	China/Nepal	8380 m (27500 ft)
Dhaulagiri	Nepal	8170 m (26810 ft)
Cho Oyu	China/Nepal	8150 m (26750 ft)
Manaslu	Nepal	8130 m (26660 ft)
Nanga Parbat	Kashmir-Jammu[3]	8130 m (26660 ft)
Annapurna I	Nepal	8080 m (26500 ft)
Gasherbrum I	Kashmir-Jammu[3]	8070 m (26470 ft)
Broad Peak I	Kashmir-Jammu[3]	8050 m (26400 ft)
Gasherbrum II	Kashmir-Jammu[3]	8030 m (26360 ft)
Gosainthan	China	8010 m (26290 ft)
Broad Peak Central	Kashmir-Jammu[3]	8000 m (26250 ft)
Gasherbrum III	Kashmir-Jammu[3]	7950 m (26090 ft)
Annapurna II	Nepal	7940 m (26040 ft)
Nanda Devi	India	7820 m (25660 ft)
Rakaposhi	Kashmir[3]	7790 m (25560 ft)
Kamet	India	7760 m (25450 ft)
Ulugh Muztagh	China (Tibet)	7720 m (25340 ft)
Tirichmir	Pakistan	7690 m (25230 ft)

[1] *Mt and similar designations have not been included in the name.*
[2] *Heights are given to the nearest 10 metres or feet.*
[3] *Kashmir-Jammu is a disputed region on the border of India and Pakistan.*
[4] *Ojos del Salado is the world's highest volcano.*

LONGEST MOUNTAIN RANGES

Mountain ranges of 3,000 km (1,900 mi) and longer are given to the nearest 100 km or mi.

Mountain range	Location	Length
Andes	South America	7 200 km (4 500 mi)
Rocky Mountains	North America	4 800 km (3 000 mi)
Himalaya–Karakoram–Hindu Kush	Asia	3 800 km (2 400 mi)
Great Dividing Range	Australia	3 600 km (2 250 mi)
Trans-Antarctic Mountains	Antarctica	3 500 km (2 200 mi)
Atlantic Coast Range South	America	3 000 km (1 900 mi)

THE CONTINENTS

A continent is any of the seven main land masses of the world. Areas also include the submerged continental shelf around the edge of the exposed land mass.

Continent	Area	% of total land mass	Lowest point below sea level	Highest elevation
Africa	30 293 000 sq km (11 696 000 sq mi)	20.2%	Lake Assal, Djibouti −156 m (−512 ft)	Mt Kilimanjaro, Tanzania 5 895 m (19 340 ft)
Antarctica	13 975 000 sq km (5 396 000 sq mi)	9.3%	Bently sub-glacial trench −2 538 m (−8 327 ft)	Vinson Massif 5 140 m (16 864 ft)
Asia	44 493 000 sq km (17 179 000 sq mi)	29.6%	Dead Sea, Israel/ Jordan/West Bank −400 m (−1 312 ft)	Mt Everest, China/Nepal 8 850 m (29 035 ft)
Australia and Oceania[1]	8 945 000 sq km (3 454 000 sq mi)	5.9%	Lake Eyre, Australia −15 m (−49 ft)	Puncak Jaya, Indonesia 5 030 m (16 503 ft)
Europe[2]	10 245 000 sq km (3 956 000 sq mi)	6.8%	Caspian Sea, Iran/Russia/ Turkmenistan/ Kazakhstan/ Azerbaijan −29 m (−94 ft)	Mt Elbrus, Russia 5 642 m (18 510 ft)
North America	24 454 000 sq km (9 442 000 sq mi)	16.3%	Death Valley, California, USA −86 m (−282 ft)	Mt McKinley, Alaska, USA 6 194 m (20 322 ft)
South America	17 838 000 sq km (6 887 000 sq mi)	11.9%	Península Valdés, Argentina −40 m (−131 ft)	Aconcagua, Argentina 6 960 m (22 835 ft)

[1] *The land mass of Australia plus the wider continental area.*
[2] *Including the former western USSR.*

CONTINENTAL DRIFT

Continental drift is a theory, proposed by the German geophysicist Alfred Wegener (1880–1930), that all the Earth's continents were originally one vast land mass that has broken up and drifted apart into separate continents over time. The single land mass is often referred to as Pangaea, from the Greek for 'all Earth'. Evidence supporting the theory includes fossil records showing that the same organisms lived in continents that are now separate. The more recent theory of plate tectonics provides a mechanism for the movement of continents.

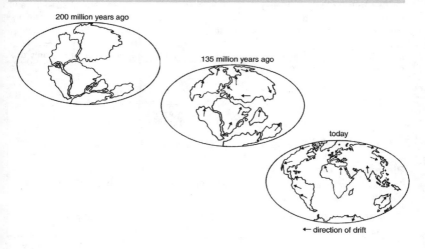

200 million years ago

135 million years ago

today

← direction of drift

> *I may be gullible. I may be gullible! But I am not gullible enough to swallow this poppycock.*
>
> —Andrew Lawson (1861–1952), professor of geology and discoverer of the San Andreas fault, in response to a demonstration in 1939 of the principles behind plate tectonics (quoted in *Challenger at Sea: A Ship That Revolutionized Earth Science* by Kenneth J Hsü, 1992). Many other geologists were also initially unconvinced by the theory.

PLATE TECTONICS

The theory of plate tectonics is a development of the older theory of continental drift. It proposes a feasible mechanism for the movement of the continents, and also explains the tectonic hazards (volcanoes and earthquakes) that are concentrated around the edges of each plate.

Theory of plate tectonics

The theory says that the lithosphere (the outer shell of the Earth's crust) is broken into a number of large, shifting plates, which are rather like irregularly shaped jigsaw pieces. Some plates drift apart, dividing the land masses: this is currently happening in east Africa. Other plates collide, creating larger land masses: this kind of collision created the Himalaya when the Indian subcontinent collided into the rest of Asia about 50 million years ago. Over millions of years, these processes alter not only the position but also the size of the continents and oceans.

> *Like Watching Fingernails Grow*
>
> Continental drift is an extremely slow process. The continents move at a rate of only a few centimetres per year – a speed similar to that at which fingernails grow.

Plate boundaries

The plates meet each other along plate boundaries. There are three different types of plate boundary.

Type of plate boundary	Description	Main tectonic features and hazards	Example
Divergent	Two plates move away from each other, creating more land.	Volcanic eruptions.	Mid-Atlantic Ridge and Iceland.
Convergent (collision)	Two continental plates collide; the plates are folded into huge mountain chains.	Collision can create powerful earthquakes.	The Himalaya.
Convergent (subduction)	An oceanic plate is dragged beneath either a continental plate or another oceanic plate.	Violent volcanic eruptions.	West coast of South America.
Conservative	Two plates slide past each other.	High magnitude earthquakes.	San Andreas fault in California; Anatolian fault in Turkey.

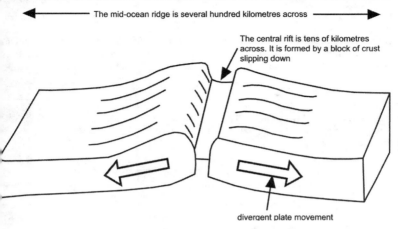

The mid-ocean ridge is several hundred kilometres across

The central rift is tens of kilometres across. It is formed by a block of crust slipping down

divergent plate movement

Divergent plate boundary

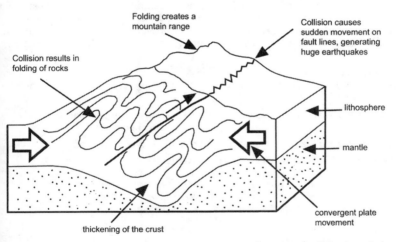

Folding creates a mountain range

Collision causes sudden movement on fault lines, generating huge earthquakes

Collision results in folding of rocks

lithosphere

mantle

convergent plate movement

thickening of the crust

Convergent collision boundaries

Mechanism for plate movement

During the 1960s it was thought that plate movement was driven by giant convection currents in the mantle (the hot layer beneath the crust), which pushed the plates apart. Nowadays, however, **slab-pull** is recognized as the mechanism for plate movement. Slab-pull occurs when one plate is subducted (pulled down) beneath another and bends down into the mantle. Rocks are poor conductors of heat, so the subducting plate remains colder and denser than the surrounding rock. Gravity makes it sink further into the mantle, dragging the rest of the plate behind it. This theory is supported by the fact that oceanic plates with long subduction boundaries move more quickly than other plates. The slower moving plates are the thicker continental plates; the main resistance to their movement comes from the mountain roots, which thicken these plates and protrude deep down into the asthenosphere, acting as a brake and making it much harder for the plates to move.

VOLCANOES

Between 30 and 60 volcanoes erupt every year, and over 500 volcanoes have erupted in recorded history. There are more than 10,000 volcanoes that are capable of erupting some time in the future.

The God of Fire

The word 'volcano' comes from the name Vulcan, the Roman god of fire. It was first used by the Romans to describe Mt Etna (now in Italy), under which Vulcan's forge was believed to be situated.

Distribution of volcanoes

Volcanoes are not distributed randomly over the Earth; instead, most are clustered in long lines close to the tectonic plate boundaries. A few others occur away from the plate boundaries where there are plumes of heat rising through the mantle below the crust. These are known as **hot spot volcanoes**.

Key to map on next page:

(1) Mt St Helens is one of several volcanoes in the range known as the Cascades. It is located on a subduction zone.

(2) Iceland has at least 120 volcanoes. It is located on a divergent plate boundary where the two plates below the Atlantic Ocean are tearing apart.

(3) The volcanic islands of Hawaii have been formed over a hot spot.

White arrows indicate direction of plate movement.

Mountains of Fire

The Chinese word for a volcano is *huoshan*, while the Japanese word is *kazan*. Both of these words mean 'fire mountain'.

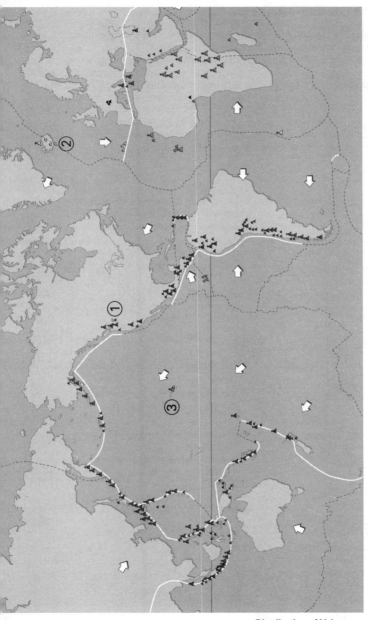

Distribution of Volcanoes

Subduction zone volcanoes

These volcanoes are formed when one tectonic plate is dragged beneath another, forcing sea-water and volatile chemicals downwards. The water lowers the melting point of the rock, and the overlying plate begins to melt, forming **magma**. The eruptions are very violent, owing to volatile gases in the magma, which expand and tear apart rock and partially solidified magma to form volcanic debris known as **tephra**. This is hurled out of the volcano in a cloud of rock and ash, which can cause devastating **pyroclastic flows**. The volcanoes are steep sided and are composed of alternating layers of tephra and lava, which build up over a number of eruptions; hence the alternative names **strata volcanoes** and **composite volcanoes**. The lava is fairly thick and viscous, and moves slowly.

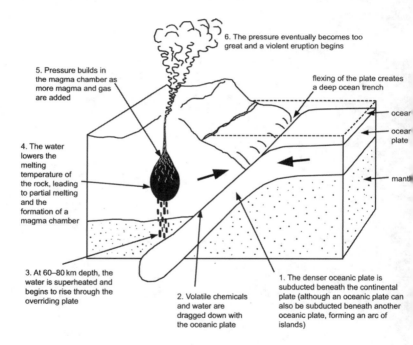

6. The pressure eventually becomes too great and a violent eruption begins

5. Pressure builds in the magma chamber as more magma and gas are added

flexing of the plate creates a deep ocean trench

ocean

ocean plate

4. The water lowers the melting temperature of the rock, leading to partial melting and the formation of a magma chamber

mantle

3. At 60–80 km depth, the water is superheated and begins to rise through the overriding plate

2. Volatile chemicals and water are dragged down with the oceanic plate

1. The denser oceanic plate is subducted beneath the continental plate (although an oceanic plate can also be subducted beneath another oceanic plate, forming an arc of islands)

Divergent plate boundary volcanoes

These volcanoes are formed when two plates pull apart, causing the pressure to drop within the mantle. This lowers the melting temperature, and rock begins to melt at a depth of about 40 km, forming **magma**. The pressure builds up until an eruption occurs. The rising magma usually contains only a few volatile gases, so most eruptions are much less violent and explosive than those on subduction zones. Some volcanoes erupt a mixture of **lava** and **tephra**; the tephra piles up in small cones whilst the lava runs a long way from the vent making an almost flat **lava field**.

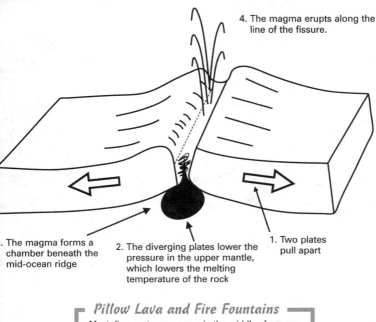

4. The magma erupts along the line of the fissure.

3. The magma forms a chamber beneath the mid-ocean ridge

2. The diverging plates lower the pressure in the upper mantle, which lowers the melting temperature of the rock

1. Two plates pull apart

Pillow Lava and Fire Fountains

Most divergent zones occur in the middle of oceans, so the eruptions are underwater. The magma therefore cools very quickly, forming large blobs of lava known as 'pillow lava'. In Iceland, however, the lava erupts on land; red hot lava can erupt from a long crack in the ground known as a fissure, making a spectacular 'fire fountain'.

Hot spot volcanoes

These volcanoes are commonly described as **shield volcanoes**. They occur on both continental and oceanic plates, and erupt above plumes of heat that rise through the mantle beneath the plate. The magma contains few gases, but often reaches the surface at temperatures of 1,200°C. At these high temperatures, the lava is fully molten and bright red, so the volcanoes are sometimes called **red volcanoes**. They have a gently curved profile and the slopes have gentle gradients of between 2 and 10°. The hot lava is runny and flows quickly away from the vent; it cools on the surface while remaining molten underneath. This creates a ropy-textured lava called **pahoehoe lava**.

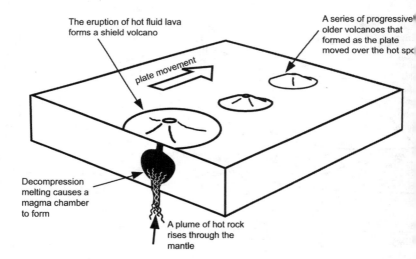

The eruption of hot fluid lava forms a shield volcano

A series of progressive older volcanoes that formed as the plate moved over the hot spot

plate movement

Decompression melting causes a magma chamber to form

A plume of hot rock rises through the mantle

EARTHQUAKES

An earthquake occurs when the rigid rocks of the Earth's lithosphere (crust) are subjected to strain in opposing directions. At first the rock will deform in response to the forces but eventually it will rupture, releasing a large amount of energy. The lithosphere shifts to a new equilibrium in which the rock on either side of the fault is offset slightly. The sudden displacement and release of energy causes the surrounding ground to shake in what is known as an earthquake.

Parts of an earthquake

Fault line	The line of rupture along which an earthquake occurs
Focus	The exact location at which the rupture starts
Epicentre	The point on the Earth's surface that lies directly over the focus

Earthquake intensity

The intensity of ground shaking tends to decrease with distance away from the epicentre, because the ground absorbs some of the energy. However, this is not always the case. For example, where the ground is saturated with water, it can behave like a liquid and make the shaking more intense. This phenomenon, known as **liquefaction**, occurred during an earthquake in Kobe, Japan, in 1995, when ground reclaimed from the sea continued to shake for several minutes after the main shock had ended.

Seismic wave groups

Seismic waves can be classified into two groups; body waves and surface waves. Body waves are faster than surface waves; however, surface waves do more damage to buildings and infrastructure during an earthquake.

Group	Source	Mode of travel	Range
Body waves	Focus	Through the Earth's interior	Detectable on the other side of the world
Surface waves	Epicentre	Through the Earth's surface	Shorter range

Types of seismic wave

The two types of surface wave are called Love waves and Rayleigh waves. The two types of body wave are described below.

Name	Type	Relative speed	Travels through
P-waves	Compression (longitudinal)	Faster	All materials
S-waves	Shear (transverse)	Not so fast	Only solids

Earthquake detection and protection

Earthquakes are detected using **seismographs,** which record the seismic waves created by an earthquake. At the moment, there is no way to predict where and when an earthquake is going to happen so it is impossible to warn people in advance. It is therefore very important to be prepared and to have well-rehearsed emergency plans. For example, families living in earthquake zones in Japan and the USA are encouraged to practise procedures such as 'drop, cover and hold on'. It is also very important to have strict building codes and not to build vulnerable structures in particularly hazardous areas.

Earthquake Legends

Various myths have become associated with earthquakes as different people have tried to understand them over the centuries. Earthquakes have often been attributed to animals that hold up the Earth. The Tongva, a Native American people of southern California, believed the Earth to be carried on the backs of several turtles, with earthquakes resulting from tussles between them. A Hindu legend had the Earth being borne by eight elephants, an earthquake occuring when one grew weary and lowered its head. Mongolian folklore held a twitching frog responsible, while Chinese mythology blamed restless dragons.

Richter scale

The Richter scale measures earthquake magnitude in terms of seismic energy released. It is logarithmic; a quake of magnitude 2 is barely perceptible, 5 is rather strong, and those over 7 are very strong. The scale was devised by US seismologist Dr Charles F Richter (1900–85).

Magnitude	Relative amount of energy released
1	1
2	31
3	960
4	30 000
5	920 000
6	29 million
7	890 million
8	28 billion
9	850 billion

Modified Mercalli intensity scale

The Mercalli scale, named after the Italian geologist Giuseppe Mercalli (1850–1914), measures earthquake intensity in terms of the damage caused. The 1956 revision is given below; it has twelve intensity values.

I   Not felt; marginal and long-period effects of large earthquakes.

II Felt by persons at rest, on upper floors or favourably placed.

III Felt indoors; hanging objects swing; vibration like passing of light trucks; duration estimated; may not be recognized as an earthquake.

IV Hanging objects swing; vibration like passing of heavy trucks, or sensation of a jolt like a heavy ball striking the walls; standing cars rock; windows, dishes, doors rattle; glasses clink; crockery clashes; in the upper range of IV, wooden walls and frames creak.

V   Felt outdoors; direction estimated; sleepers awoken; liquids disturbed, some spilled; small unstable objects displaced or upset; doors swing, close, open; shutters, pictures move; pendulum clocks stop, start, change rate.

VI Felt by all; many frightened and run outdoors; persons walk unsteadily; windows, dishes, glassware break; knick-knacks, books, etc, fall off shelves; pictures fall off walls; furniture moves or overturns; weak plaster and masonry D crack; small bells ring (church, school); trees, bushes shake visibly, or heard to rustle.

VII Difficult to stand; noticed by drivers; hanging objects quiver; furniture breaks; damage to masonry D, including cracks; weak chimneys broken at roof line; fall of plaster, loose bricks, stones, tiles, cornices, also unbraced parapets and architectural ornaments; some cracks in masonry C; waves on ponds, water turbid with mud; small slides and caving in along sand or gravel banks; large bells ring; concrete irrigation ditches damaged.

VIII Steering of cars affected; damage to masonry C and partial collapse; some damage to masonry B; none to masonry A; fall of stucco and some masonry walls; twisting, fall of chimneys, factory stacks, monuments, towers, elevated tanks; frame houses move on foundations if not bolted down; loose panel walls thrown out; decayed piling broken off; branches broken from trees; changes in flow or temperature of springs and wells; cracks in wet ground and on steep slopes.

IX General panic; masonry D destroyed; masonry C heavily damaged, sometimes with complete collapse; masonry B seriously damaged; general damage to foundations; frame structures, if not bolted, shift off foundations; frames racked; serious damage to reservoirs; underground pipes break; conspicuous cracks in ground; in alluviated areas sand and mud ejected, earthquake fountains, sand craters.

X   Most masonry and frame structures destroyed with their foundations; some well-built wooden structures and bridges destroyed; serious damage to dams, dykes, embankments; large landslides; water thrown on banks of canals, rivers, lakes, etc; sand and mud shifted horizontally on beaches and flat land; rails bent slightly.

XI Rails bent greatly; underground pipelines completely out of service.

XII Damage nearly total; large rock masses displaced; lines of sight and level distorted; objects thrown into the air.

Notes: Masonry types

A   Good workmanship, mortar and design; reinforced, especially laterally, and bound together using steel, concrete, etc; designed to resist lateral forces.

B   Good workmanship and mortar; reinforced, but not designed in detail to resist lateral forces.

C   Ordinary workmanship and mortar; no extreme weakness like failing to tie in at corners, but neither reinforced nor designed against horizontal forces.

D   Weak materials, such as adobe; poor mortar; low standards of workmanship; weak horizontally.

Where do earthquakes occur?

Earthquakes can occur absolutely anywhere, but they are most frequent and most severe at places of tectonic or volcanic activity. High magnitude earthquakes are often recorded where two continental plates are colliding, such as in the Himalaya. Conservative plate boundaries are particularly destructive because the crust is rigid and moves in a very jerky way. This creates friction, resulting in a large and sudden displacement and a shallow, high magnitude earthquake. Unfortunately, many conservative boundaries run through densely populated areas; for example, the San Andreas Fault runs through large cities such as San Francisco and Los Angeles.

The Wadati–Benioff zone

The American scientist Hugo Benioff (1899–1968) plotted the locations of earthquake foci in regions where slabs of oceanic crust are moving under a continental plate, a process called **subduction**. The earthquakes all occur in a slightly curving line which dips down deep into the Earth, travelling under the overlying slab. The earthquake foci are effectively mapping out the location of the subducting slab. The same phenomenon was observed independently by the Japanese seismologist Kiyoo Wadati (1902–95).

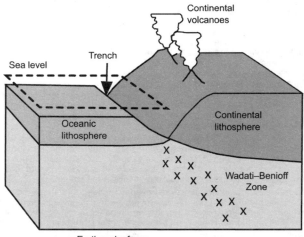

X Earthquake focus

TSUNAMIS

Where earthquakes occur in the sea bed or coastal regions, they can trigger a fast-moving wave known as a tsunami. Tsunamis can create devastating surges of water that flood coastal areas, as happened during the Indonesian tsunami of 26 December 2004. This tsunami is believed to have caused the deaths of over 300,000 people. Tsunamis are relatively rare events; they are usually triggered by high magnitude earthquakes caused by crustal movement in subduction zones.

GEOLOGICAL TIMESCALE

The various stages of the history of life on Earth are divided into **aeons**, based on fossil evidence and changes in climate. The aeons are further divided into **eras**, **periods**, **series** and sometimes **stages**. Three eras make up the most recent aeon, known as the **Phanerozoic aeon**. The most recent of these is the **Cenozoic**; further back in time are the eras known as **Mesozoic** and **Palaeozoic**. The period of time before the Phanerozoic aeon is called the **Precambrian aeon**, so named because it occurred before the earliest (Cambrian) period of the Palaeozoic era.

Precambrian aeon

The rocks that were formed during the Precambrian consisted of two divisions: the **Archaean** and the **Proterozoic**. Primitive plant life existed well back into the Archaean, and bacteria may have existed as early as 3,800 million years ago. In the most recent Proterozoic rocks there are impressions of soft-bodied animals and trace fossils (burrows and tracks) indicating a long period of earlier evolution.

Division	Era	Age (mya)[1]
Archaean		4600–2500
Proterozoic	Aphebian	2500–1650
	Riphean	1650–610
	Vendian	610–570

[1] *mya = million years ago*

> ### Hidden Life
> The Precambrian aeon is also known as the
> Cryptozoic, meaning 'hidden life'.

Palaeozoic era

The Palaeozoic is the oldest of the Phanerozoic eras. Until this time, only primitive life forms such as bacteria, algae and sponges existed. However, there was a sudden great expansion of animal life at the start of the Palaeozoic, known as the **Cambrian explosion**. Creatures included molluscs and small marine organisms called trilobites; early plant life was also present. The **Ordovician** was a time of diverse sea life, including the first coral reefs, and amphibians evolved by the end of the **Devonian**. During the **Carboniferous** there was rich plant life in parts of the world, but a glacial climate existed in other regions known as the Gondwana continents. The trilobites died out in the **Permian**, a period of desert conditions in Britain.

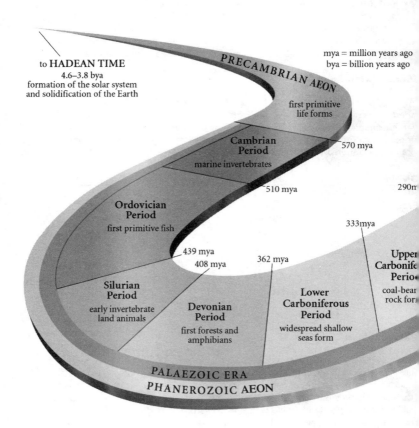

to **HADEAN TIME**
4.6–3.8 bya
formation of the solar system
and solidification of the Earth

PRECAMBRIAN AEON

mya = million years ago
bya = billion years ago

first primitive
life forms

**Cambrian
Period**

marine invertebrates

570 mya

510 mya

290m

**Ordovician
Period**

first primitive fish

333mya

439 mya

362 mya

**Upper
Carbonife
Perio**

408 mya

coal-bear
rock for

**Silurian
Period**

early invertebrate
land animals

**Devonian
Period**

first forests and
amphibians

**Lower
Carboniferous
Period**

widespread shallow
seas form

PALAEZOIC ERA

PHANEROZOIC AEON

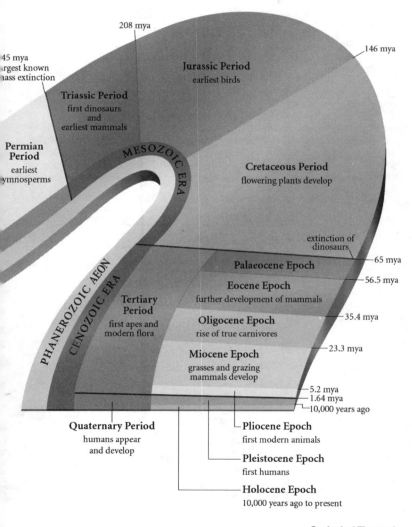

245 mya
largest known
mass extinction

208 mya

146 mya

Jurassic Period
earliest birds

Triassic Period
first dinosaurs
and
earliest mammals

**Permian
Period**
earliest
gymnosperms

MESOZOIC ERA

Cretaceous Period
flowering plants develop

extinction of
dinosaurs

Palaeocene Epoch — 65 mya

— 56.5 mya

Eocene Epoch
further development of mammals

PHANEROZOIC AEON

CENOZOIC ERA

**Tertiary
Period**
first apes and
modern flora

Oligocene Epoch
rise of true carnivores — 35.4 mya

— 23.3 mya

Miocene Epoch
grasses and grazing
mammals develop

— 5.2 mya
— 1.64 mya
— 10,000 years ago

Quaternary Period
humans appear
and develop

Pliocene Epoch
first modern animals

Pleistocene Epoch
first humans

Holocene Epoch
10,000 years ago to present

Geological Timescale

Period	Age (mya)[1]
Cambrian	570–510
Ordovician	510–439
Silurian	439–408
Devonian	408–362
Lower Carboniferous	362–333
Upper Carboniferous	333–290
Permian	290–245

[1] mya = million years ago

Mesozoic era

Animals present during the Mesozoic era included spiral-shaped molluscs called ammonites, as well as reptiles and corals. The earliest period, the **Triassic**, had an impoverished range of animals and plants that followed the extinctions at the end of the Palaeozoic era. However, during the middle period, the **Jurassic**, there was diverse plant life in the warm climate and reptiles, notably dinosaurs, were dominant on land. The first flowering plants developed and spread during the **Cretaceous** period. A mass extinction occurred at the end of the Cretaceous, which marked the extinction of most birds, a large proportion of marine life and all remaining dinosaurs.

Period	Series	Age (mya)[1]
Triassic	Lower	245–241
	Middle	241–210
	Upper	210–208
Jurassic	Lower (Lias)	208–178
	Middle (Dogger)	178–161
	Upper (Malm)	161–146
Cretaceous	Lower	146–97
	Upper	97–65

[1] mya = million years ago

Cenozoic era

The Cenozoic era (also Cainozoic or Kainozoic) is divided into two sub-eras, **Tertiary** and **Quaternary**. In the early part of the Tertiary sub-era, the plants and animals of the Cretaceous (see **Mesozoic era**) gave way to more modern forms, with mammals replacing reptiles as the dominant animals. Later, in the **Miocene**, large-scale earth movements built many of the mountain ranges of the world, and provoked wide-scale volcanic activity. Modern landscape and geography were laid down in the Quaternary. Large mammals such as mastodons and woolly mammoths were present at the start of the Quaternary but became extinct during the late **Pleistocene** and early **Holocene**, when humans appeared and developed.

Sub-era[1]	Period	Series[2]	Age[3]
Tertiary	Palaeogene	Palaeocene	65–56.5 mya
		Eocene	56.5–35.4 mya
		Oligocene	35.4–23.3 mya
	Neogene	Miocene	23.3–5.2 mya
		Pliocene	5.2–1.64 mya
Quaternary		Pleistocene	1.64 mya to 10 000 years ago
		Holocene (recent)	10 000 years ago to present day

[1] *Also known as Period* [2] *Also known as Epoch* [3] *mya = million years ago*

FOSSILS

Fossils are produced when animals and plants decompose and become preserved within sedimentary rock. Some examples of fossils are given below, together with an indication of the types of fossils that are representative of different time periods.

Echinoderms
Marsupites

Trilobites
Ogygiocaris

Ammonites
Echioceras

Corals
Syringopora

Period	Fossil type
Cambrian	Trilobites and brachiopods
Ordovician	Graptolites, trilobites (small crustacea)
Silurian	Graptolites (thin, branching, free-swimming, coral-like)
Devonian	Goniatites, fish and plants
Lower Carboniferous	Corals and brachiopods
Upper Carboniferous	Foraminifera, goniatites, freshwater bivalves and plants
Permian	Foraminifera, ammonites and goniatites (ammonite ancestors)
Triassic	Ammonites
Jurassic	Ammonites plus ostracods (tiny crustacea) and bivalves

Lower Cretaceous	Ammonites
Upper Cretaceous	Foraminifera, echinoderms, bivalves and belemnites
Cenozoic	Foraminifera (plankton)

ICE AGES

An ice age is a period during which areas of the Earth's surface are covered by ice sheets. We are technically still living in the tail end of 'The Ice Age' (the most recent ice age) – over 99% of Antarctica is covered in snow and ice, and in some places the ice is over 4,500 metres thick. Antarctica contains an estimated 29 million cubic kilometres of ice, which is 90% of all ice on the planet. There is also a significant volume of ice in the Arctic region with a large ice cap in Greenland, and permanent sea ice on parts of the Arctic Ocean.

The Earth's previous ice ages

Type	Time of ice age[1]	Geological time period	Part of time period
Hypothetical	2.7 bya–2.3 bya	Precambrian aeon	Early Proterozoic
Major	800 mya–600 mya	Precambrian aeon	Late Proterozoic
Minor	460 mya–430 mya	Palaeozoic era	Ordovician
Major	350 mya–260 mya	Palaeozoic era	Upper Carboniferous
Major	40 mya–present	Cenozoic era	Pleistocene (and Holocene)

[1] mya = million years ago; bya = billion years ago

> ### Snowball Earth
> The time period from 800 million to 600 million years ago was known as the Cryogenian period, which comes from the Greek for 'the birth of ice'. This ice age was so severe that it has been nicknamed 'Snowball Earth'.

Glacial and interglacial periods

In between ice ages, the world has been warmer and the polar regions have been free of permanent ice. However, even within each ice age there have been periods of relative warmth when the ice has retreated back towards the poles. These warm periods within an ice age are known as **interglacial periods**, while the colder periods are known as **glacial periods**.

> ### The Warm and the Cold
> There has been a succession of glacial and interglacial periods during the Ice Age. By the end of the last glacial period, 12,000 years ago, the ice had advanced into northern Europe. All Scotland, most of Wales and the northern part of England were covered in ice. Soon after this the climate began to warm and the ice retreated, so we are now living in an interglacial period.

Causes of the glacial–interglacial cycle

Milutin Milankovic (1879–1958) was an engineer and scientist who recognized that there were slight variations in the orbital pattern of the Earth around the Sun. These periodic variations would affect the amount of solar radiation reaching Earth, and could therefore possibly change the climate and trigger glacial periods, possibly by causing long cool summers in which the previous winter's snow and ice cannot melt. The cycle lengths of these patterns roughly correspond to the pattern of glacial and interglacial periods. The three types of orbital variation are explained below.

Orbital variation	Explanation	Approximate length of cycle
Eccentricity	The Earth's orbit is elliptical (oval) rather than circular, so the distance between the Earth and the Sun changes. This alters the total amount of solar energy received by the Earth.	100 000 years
Obliquity	The Earth's axis is tilted, and the amount of tilt varies by almost 2.5°. The greater the tilt, the greater the variation between summer and winter temperatures.	41 000 years
Precession	Because the Earth's axis is tilted, the axis itself rotates as if the Earth is a spinning top. This affects the timing and length of the seasons.	20 000–25 000 years

Factors causing an ice age

A number of factors, known as **forcing mechanisms**, can trigger an ice age. A forcing mechanism works by knocking the world's atmosphere, ocean and climate systems out of balance (see **World in the Balance: Gaia hypothesis**). This triggers a series of events that shift the Earth to a new equilibrium (state of balance) with new climatic conditions. This new climate could be the beginning or the end of an ice age. It seems likely that ice ages are triggered by a combination of forcing mechanisms.

The effect of continental drift and ocean currents on ice ages

One of the main forcing mechanisms is likely to be continental drift, which causes the size of the continents, and their relative positions to the poles, to change. This in turn affects the world's oceans, which are one of the main ways in which the world's heat balance is kept in order. Warm ocean currents or **gyres** can carry energy from the sun-warmed tropical and equatorial regions to the cooler polar regions, preventing these regions from getting extremely cold. Over millions of years the gradual movement of the continents can affect the routes of these ocean currents.

Before the present Ice Age, South America was much closer to Antarctica than it is today. Warm equatorial water was able to travel right down the west coast of South America and warm the continent of Antarctica, preventing it from freezing up. However, by the time the Ice Age started, South America drifted northwards and became separated from Antarctica. A powerful and cold circumpolar ocean current began to flow, preventing the warm water from reaching Antarctica and warming it.

The effect of continental drift and land masses on ice ages

When continents drift together to form massive land masses, this may also act as a forcing mechanism. The climate in the interior of massive land masses is not warmed or moderated by the warmer oceans and consequently becomes very cold in winter. It is believed that the continents go through periods of coming together and pulling apart. This is known as the **Wilson cycle** and results in the formation of a supercontinent roughly once every 600 million years. The last two of these supercontinents coincided with ice ages.

Supercontinent	Time period	Coinciding ice age
Pangaea	300 mya–200 mya	Carboniferous
Rodinia	1100 mya–750 mya	Late Proterozoic ('Snowball Earth')

The effect of the atmosphere on ice ages

Evidence shows that, over the last 160,000 years, abnormally high atmospheric levels of greenhouse gases such as carbon dioxide have occurred at the same time as a relatively warm climate. Cold periods are associated with low levels of carbon dioxide. Most scientists believe that human activity, such as burning fossil fuels, is accelerating the greenhouse effect. However, high levels of carbon dioxide can also occur naturally due to processes such as high levels of volcanic and biological activity, triggering natural global warming.

GLACIERS

A glacier is a slowly moving large body of permanent ice. About 10% of the Earth's land mass today is covered in glacial ice. Two or three million years ago, however, 30% of the Earth's land was ice-covered.

Formation of glaciers

Glaciers are formed over hundreds or thousands of years in regions where snow falls and accumulates at a faster rate than it melts. As new snow falls, it compacts the older layers of snow beneath it causing the snow to re-crystallize and turn to ice. With new snow constantly being layered on top, the ice crystals become more interlocked and the air spaces and voids are squeezed out. The resultant dense mass of glacial ice begins to move slowly under gravity, driven by its own sheer weight. Once the ice is moving, it can be called a glacier.

Types of glacier

There are several different names that can be given to glaciers depending on their characteristics.

Unconstrained by landscape
- Ice sheet (bigger than 50 000 sq km/ 19 300 sq mi)
- Ice cap (smaller than 50 000 sq km/ 19 300 sq mi)
- Ice shelf (a large sheet of ice floating on the sea)

Constrained by landscape
- Icefield (on a level area)
- Cirque glacier (within a hollow on a mountain)
- Valley glacier (within a valley)

Factors affecting glacier formation

Glaciers require two basic things to form: low temperatures and high precipitation (falling as snow). There are many factors that control this, which are described below. The overall effect is that glaciers occur in one of two places: in polar regions, eg Greenland and Antarctica, where they are called **polar glaciers**; and in high mountainous regions, eg the Alps, where they are called **Alpine glaciers**.

Factor	Optimal conditions for glacial growth	Reason
Latitude	High (near the poles)	Temperature decreases with distance from the equator
Altitude	High	Temperature decreases with height
Aspect	North-facing in the northern hemisphere, south-facing in the southern hemisphere	These directions receive the least sunshine
Continentality	In the middle of large land masses	Away from the moderating effect of the sea

Movement of glaciers

There are two ways in which a glacier can flow, depending on whether the base is warm or cold. A **warm-based glacier** has a base that is close to 0°C and is therefore partially liquid. There are a number of potential causes of this liquid layer, but the most common is melting due to friction. The liquid layer means that the whole glacier can easily slide on the lubricated surface. A **cold-based glacier**, on the other hand, has a base that is much lower than 0°C. The ice remains solid and, because of friction, there is no basal sliding. However, gravity is still applying a downward force on the glacier, which causes the ice within to deform. There is some internal fracturing and slippage between the ice crystals and, within the glacier, ice slides over ice. For these reasons the fastest moving part of a cold-based glacier is usually that nearest to the surface.

Glacial erosion

Glaciers break up and erode the bedrock over which they move. Erosion can occur when the underlying rock is crushed under the sheer weight of the glacier, or when the glacier freezes to the bedrock and then plucks the rock away as the glacier moves forward. A third process known as **frost-wedging** occurs when water seeps into cracks and then freezes, expands and forces the rock apart. The debris created by erosion, plus any other loose rocks, is picked up by the moving glacier, so the sheet of ice becomes like a giant sheet of sand paper which then scratches and scours the bedrock underneath it. This erosion process is called **abrasion**. Everything that is in the path of the glacier is destroyed and the debris becomes incorporated into the glacier.

Glacial features

Many features of past glaciation can be seen today, and provide evidence that many parts of North America, Europe and Asia were covered in ice during the last glacial period 117,000 to 11,000 years ago. This period is known by several names, including the Devensian (UK), Wisconsin (USA) or Würm (the Alps). It had its peak at about 18,000 years ago, at which time the ice sheets extended far into northern Europe and North America.

Feature	Description	Explanation
U-shaped valley	A valley with steep sides and a flat valley floor.	The glacier scours out the bedrock as it flows, deepening and widening an existing narrow valley into a smooth U-shape.
Till	Sediment which is unsorted and unstratified (with no distinct layers). It contains fragments of different rock types, sizes, shapes and angularity.	Glaciers pick up and erode everything in their path. When the glacier retreats, the debris is deposited rapidly without sorting by size or shape and without the formation of distinctive layers or strata.
Moraine	Piles or ridges of till. End moraines form a low ridge across the valley, while lateral moraines run down the length of the valley on either side.	Moraine is debris that is left behind by the glacier when it retreats. The end moraine represents debris that has been pushed in front of the glacier like a bulldozer, while lateral moraine is formed along the edges of the glacier by erosion of the valley sides.
Drumlin	A large mound of till that is very streamlined and is tear-shaped when viewed from above.	Drumlins are glacial deposits that have been shaped by the ice flowing over them. The drumlins are elongated in the direction of the ice flow, and are often formed in the end moraine.
Kettle hole	A depression or hole within a till deposit, roughly circular in shape.	As the glacier retreats, chunks of ice break off and melt, leaving a circular depression in the till. This may then fill with water to form a small lake.

Feature	Description	Explanation
Erratic	Pieces of rock that are different from the native rock and therefore have not come from the area.	Glaciers can transport rock fragments over large distances.
Cirque (corrie, cwm)	A steep-sided round hollow, which may contain a lake known as a **tarn** or **corrie loch**.	Cirques are formed by erosion at the head of a glacier.
Arête	A thin ridge of rock between two cirques.	Arêtes result from the formation of two cirques close together.
Pyramidal peak or glacial horn	A sharp mountain peak with flat sides and sharp ridges.	Pyramidal peaks result from the joining together of three or more cirques. Those with particularly steep sides are known as glacial horns.
Paternoster lakes	A chain of lakes connected by a stream along a valley.	As a glacier advances up a valley and then retreats, a series of terminal moraines are laid down. These act as dams to form the chain of lakes.

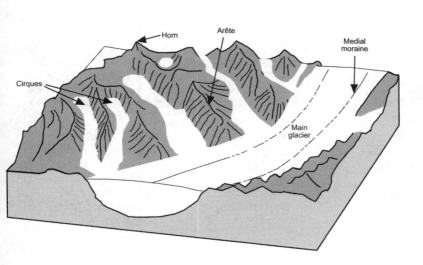

Landscape during a period of maximum glaciation

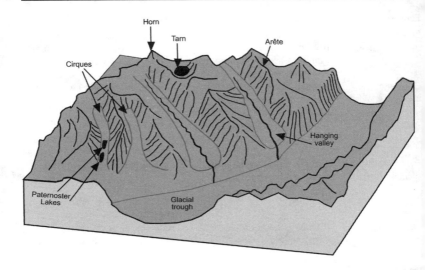

Horn

Tarn

Arête

Cirques

Hanging valley

Paternoster Lakes

Glacial trough

Landscape after retreat of a glacier

ICEBERGS

An iceberg is a mass of freshwater ice that has broken off an ice sheet or glacier. Icebergs can pose a significant hazard to shipping and as a result are reported, tracked and monitored. They are divided into two shape categories: **tabular icebergs,** which have a flat top and steep vertical sides, and **non-tabular icebergs.** The latter are further divided into groups including **pinnacled, domed, drydocked** and **wedged.**

Iceberg	Height above water	Approximate length
growler	<1 m (3 ft)	<5 m (15 ft)
bergybit	1–4 m (3–13 ft)	5–14 m (15–46 ft)
small	5–15 m (14–50 ft)	15–60 m (47–200 ft)
medium	16–45 m (51–150 ft)	61–120 m (201–400 ft)
large	46–75 m (151–240 ft)	121–200 m (401–670 ft)
very large	>75 m (240 ft)	>200 m (670 ft)

OCEANS

Four oceans were traditionally recognized, with the International Hydrographic Organization (IHO) officially delimiting a fifth, the Southern Ocean, in 2000. However, the Atlantic Ocean and the Pacific Ocean are often divided (by the equator) into the North Atlantic and South Atlantic, and the North Pacific and South Pacific, leading to the recognition of seven oceans.

Ocean	Area[1]	Average depth	Greatest depth
Arctic	14 056 000 sq km (5 427 000 sq mi)	1 330 m (4 400 ft)	Molloy Deep 5 680 m (18 635 ft)
Atlantic	76 762 000 sq km (29 638 000 sq mi)	3 700 m (12 100 ft)	Puerto Rico Trench 8 648 m (28 372 ft)
Indian	68 556 000 sq km (26 469 000 sq mi)	3 900 m (12 800 ft)	Java Trench 7 725 m (25 344 ft)
Pacific	155 557 000 sq km (60 061 000 sq mi)	4 300 m (14 100 ft)	Mariana Trench 11 040 m (36 220 ft)
Southern	20 327 000 sq km (7 848 000 sq mi)	4 500 m (14 800 ft)	South Sandwich Trench 7 235 m (23 737 ft)

[1] *Areas are rounded to the nearest 1 000 square kilometres or square miles.*

OCEAN TRENCHES

Ocean trenches are long, narrow steep-sided depressions in an ocean floor. They are commonly found running parallel to a continent. There are more than 20 in total; the majority are found in the Pacific Ocean.

Trench	Ocean	Greatest depth
Cayman	Atlantic	7 686 m (25 216 ft)
Japan	Pacific	8 513 m (27 929 ft)
Java	Indian	7 725 m (25 344 ft)
Kermadec	Pacific	10 047 m (32 962 ft)
Kuril	Pacific	10 542 m (34 587 ft)
Mariana (Marianas)	Pacific	11 040 m (36 220 ft)
Middle America	Pacific	6 669 m (21 880 ft)
Nansei Shoto (Ryukyu)	Pacific	7 507 m (24 629 ft)
Palau	Pacific	7 986 m (26 200 ft)
Peru–Chile (Atacama)	Pacific	8 065 m (26 460 ft)
Philippine (Mindanao)	Pacific	10 539 m (34 578 ft)
Puerto Rico	Atlantic	8 648 m (28 372 ft)
Romanche	Atlantic	7 758 m (25 453 ft)
South Sandwich	Southern	7 235 m (23 737 ft)
Tonga	Pacific	10 882 m (35 702 ft)
Yap (West Caroline)	Pacific	8 527 m (27 976 ft)

Note: Other major trenches include the Aleutian, the Izu Bonin and the Bougainville, all in the Pacific Ocean.

> ## Water, Water, Everywhere
> The Pacific Ocean makes up half of the planet's surface water. It covers approximately 28% of the Earth's surface, making this single ocean bigger than all the landmass of the Earth.

LARGEST SEAS

Oceans are excluded.

Sea	Area[1]
Coral Sea	4 791 000 sq km (1 850 000 sq mi)
Arabian Sea	3 863 000 sq km (1 492 000 sq mi)
South China (Nan) Sea	3 685 000 sq km (1 423 000 sq mi)
Caribbean Sea	2 718 000 sq km (1 050 000 sq mi)
Mediterranean Sea	2 516 000 sq km (971 000 sq mi)
Bering Sea	2 304 000 sq km (890 000 sq mi)
Bay of Bengal	2 172 000 sq km (839 000 sq mi)
Sea of Okhotsk	1 590 000 sq km (614 000 sq mi)
Gulf of Mexico	1 543 000 sq km (596 000 sq mi)
Gulf of Guinea	1 533 000 sq km (592 000 sq mi)
Barents Sea	1 405 000 sq km (542 000 sq mi)
Norwegian Sea	1 383 000 sq km (534 000 sq mi)
Gulf of Alaska	1 327 000 sq km (512 000 sq mi)
Hudson Bay	1 232 000 sq km (476 000 sq mi)
Greenland Sea	1 205 000 sq km (465 000 sq mi)
Arafura Sea	1 037 000 sq km (400 000 sq mi)
Philippine Sea	1 036 000 sq km (400 000 sq mi)
Sea of Japan (East Sea)	978 000 sq km (378 000 sq mi)
East Siberian Sea	901 000 sq km (348 000 sq mi)
Kara Sea	883 000 sq km (341 000 sq mi)
East China Sea	664 000 sq km (256 000 sq mi)
Andaman Sea	565 000 sq km (218 000 sq mi)
North Sea	520 000 sq km (201 000 sq mi)
Black Sea	508 000 sq km (196 000 sq mi)
Red Sea	453 000 sq km (175 000 sq mi)
Baltic Sea	414 000 sq km (160 000 sq mi)
Arabian Gulf	239 000 sq km (92 000 sq mi)
St Lawrence Gulf	238 000 sq km (92 000 sq mi)

[1] *Areas are rounded to the nearest 1 000 square kilometres or square miles.*

TIDES

Gravitational forces between the Earth and the Moon pull the Earth's seas and oceans towards the Moon. This creates tides as the Moon moves round the Earth. Gravitational forces between the Sun and the Earth also contribute towards tides, but they have less of an effect. When the Moon and the Sun are lined up (1 and 3 below), the tides are at their strongest and are called **spring tides**. This happens during a new Moon or a full Moon. During the first and last quarter, the Sun and the Moon pull the sea at right angles to each other (2 below), so the effect is much smaller. These tides are called **neap tides**.

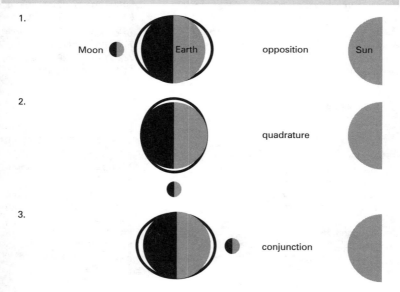

1.

Moon   Earth   opposition   Sun

2.

quadrature

3.

conjunction

LARGEST ISLANDS

Island	Area[1]
Australia[2]	7 692 300 sq km (2 970 000 sq mi)
Greenland	2 175 600 sq km (840 000 sq mi)
New Guinea	790 000 sq km (305 000 sq mi)
Borneo	737 000 sq km (285 000 sq mi)
Madagascar	587 000 sq km (226 600 sq mi)
Baffin	507 000 sq km (195 800 sq mi)
Sumatra	425 000 sq km (164 100 sq mi)
Honshu (Hondo)	228 000 sq km (88 000 sq mi)
Great Britain	219 000 sq km (84 600 sq mi)
Victoria, Canada	217 300 sq km (83 900 sq mi)
Ellesmere, Canada	196 000 sq km (75 700 sq mi)
Celebes	174 000 sq km (67 200 sq mi)

Island	Area[1]
South Island, New Zealand	151 000 sq km (58 300 sq mi)
Java	129 000 sq km (49 800 sq mi)
North Island, New Zealand	114 000 sq km (44 000 sq mi)
Cuba	110 900 sq km (42 800 sq mi)
Newfoundland	109 000 sq km (42 100 sq mi)
Luzon	105 000 sq km (40 500 sq mi)
Iceland	103 000 sq km (39 800 sq mi)
Mindanao	94 600 sq km (36 500 sq mi)
Novaya Zemlya (two islands)	90 600 sq km (35 000 sq mi)
Ireland	84 100 sq km (32 500 sq mi)
Hokkaido	78 500 sq km (30 300 sq mi)
Hispaniola	77 200 sq km (29 800 sq mi)
Sakhalin	75 100 sq km (29 000 sq mi)
Tierra del Fuego	71 200 sq km (27 500 sq mi)

[1] *Areas are rounded to the nearest 100 square kilometres or square miles.*
[2] *Sometimes discounted, as a continent.*

RIVERS

Rivers are an important part of the water cycle, helping to return the flow of precipitation that falls on the land back into the oceans. They are also important sculptors of the landscape, constantly changing the shape of landforms through a combination of **erosion** and **deposition** processes. Erosion – the wearing away of the landscape – occurs when the water has plenty of energy, especially when the river is in flood. The material is carried downstream until the river no longer has enough energy to transport it, at which point the sediment is deposited. This complex relationship between the amount of energy in the river and the processes of erosion, transport and deposition means that rivers can create a wide variety of landforms.

Erosional processes

Hydraulic Action The force of the flowing water can dislodge loose material on the river bed and in its banks. The water also forces air into cracks; this can weaken the river bank and cause it to collapse.

Solution (Corrosion) River water can dissolve minerals in some rocks, eg calcium carbonate in limestone. The rate of reaction depends on the temperature and acidity of the water.

Abrasion (Corasion) Sediment that is being carried by the river water crashes into the bottom and sides of the river channel, causing it to be worn away.

Attrition Pieces of sediment in the river bump into one another, making the pieces smaller, rounder and smoother. The longer they are in the river, the greater the effect.

Types of sediment transport

Solution	Soluble minerals such as calcium carbonate are carried in solution in river water.
Suspension	The smallest particles of sediment, such as clay or silt, are held in the flowing water for long distances.
Saltation	Sand bounces along the river bed in a hopping motion.
Traction	Pebbles, cobbles and sometimes boulders can roll down a river bed if the river is flowing fast enough.

River meanders and ox-bow lakes

A meander is a sweeping bend in the course of a river. Although they occur along the entire length of most rivers, the largest meanders occur where the river's channel is widest, usually in the middle and lower course of the river. Meanders are formed by variations in friction on the river bed, which cause the river water to flow from side to side within the channel in a corkscrew motion known as **helicoidal flow**. This side-to-side motion causes the erosion of alternate sides of the river channel, creating gentle bends. As the erosion continues, the bends become wider and slowly migrate downstream.

Meanders can eventually create such broad horseshoe-shaped curves that they begin to double back on themselves, leaving a very narrow strip of land at the neck of the meander. This neck may be breached during a flood and eroded right through. The main flow of water continues through the newly eroded neck; the water in the old meander stops flowing and an **ox-bow lake** is formed.

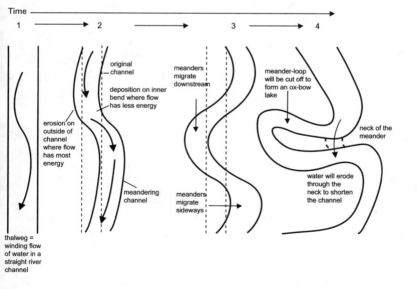

Longest rivers

River	Outflow	Length[1]
Nile–Kagera–Ruvuvu–Ruvusu–Luvironza	Mediterranean Sea (Egypt)	6690 km (4160 mi)
Amazon–Ucayali–Tambo–Ene–Apurimac	Atlantic Ocean (Brazil)	6570 km (4080 mi)
Mississippi–Missouri–Jefferson–Beaverhead–Red Rock	Gulf of Mexico (USA)	6020 km (3740 mi)
Chang Jiang (Yangtze)	East China Sea (China)	5980 km (3720 mi)
Yenisey–Angara–Selenga–Ider	Kara Sea (Russia)	5870 km (3650 mi)
Amur–Argun–Kerulen	Tartar Strait (Russia)	5780 km (3590 mi)
Ob–Irtysh	Gulf of Ob, Kara Sea (Russia)	5410 km (3360 mi)
Plata–Parana–Grande	Atlantic Ocean (Argentina/Uruguay)	4880 km (3030 mi)
Huang He (Yellow)	Yellow Sea (China)	4840 km (3010 mi)
Congo–Lualaba	South Atlantic Ocean (Angola/Democratic Republic of the Congo)	4630 km (2880 mi)
Lena	Laptev Sea (Russia)	4400 km (2730 mi)
Mackenzie–Slave–Peace–Finlay	Beaufort Sea (Canada)	4240 km (2630 mi)
Mekong	South China Sea (Vietnam)	4180 km (2600 mi)
Niger	Gulf of Guinea (Nigeria)	4100 km (2550 mi)

[1] *Lengths are given to the nearest 10 kilometres or miles, and include the river plus tributaries comprising the longest watercourse.*

Peak Flow

The River Amazon in South America may not be the longest in the world, but it is the largest in terms of its volume and flow rate. It discharges roughly 220,000 m^3 of water per second into the Atlantic Ocean, and accounts for a staggering 20% of all the fresh water that flows into the Earth's seas and oceans.

WATERFALLS

Where rivers fall over steep gradients, they create a series of rapids or waterfalls. Waterfalls commonly occur where a river has to flow across an existing step in the landscape. This might be because past glaciation of the landscape has created a steep U-shaped valley. As a river flows from the slopes above this valley, it plummets over the steep side into the valley below as a tall waterfall.

Waterfalls are also formed where a river crosses from a harder rock type to rock that is much softer and more susceptible to erosion. As the water plunges on to the less resistant rock it erodes a large plunge pool. The harder rock is eventually undercut by the erosion of the plunge pool and collapses under its own weight. In this way, the waterfall gradually retreats upstream, leaving a steep sided **gorge** below the waterfall. The Victoria Falls on the River Zambezi, Zimbabwe, and Gullfoss (the Golden Falls) on the River Hvítá, Iceland, are two examples of this type of waterfall.

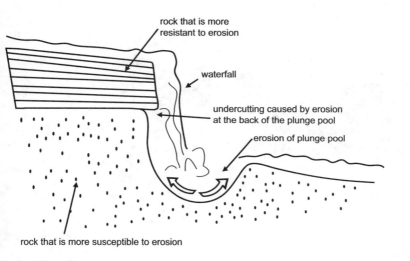

rock that is more resistant to erosion

waterfall

undercutting caused by erosion at the back of the plunge pool

erosion of plunge pool

rock that is more susceptible to erosion

Formation of a waterfall

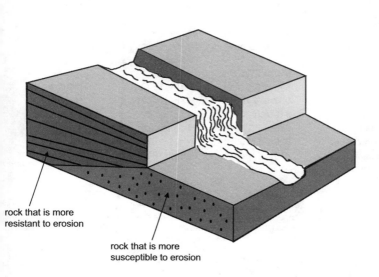

rock that is more resistant to erosion

rock that is more susceptible to erosion

Waterfall before gorge formation (continued overleaf)

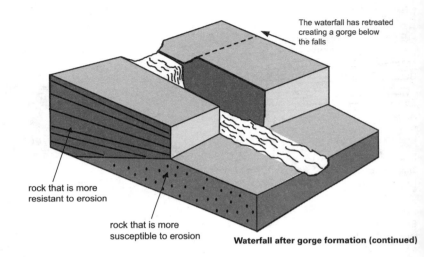

The waterfall has retreated creating a gorge below the falls

rock that is more resistant to erosion

rock that is more susceptible to erosion

Waterfall after gorge formation (continued)

Highest waterfalls

The ten waterfalls with the greatest total height are listed below.

Waterfall	Total height	Height of tallest drop	Location
Angel Falls	979 m (3 212 ft)	807 m (2 648 ft)	Venezuela
Tugela Falls	948 m (3 110 ft)	411 m (1 350 ft)	South Africa
Tres Hermanas (Three Sisters)	914 m (3 000 ft)	—	Peru
Olo'upena Falls	900 m (2 953 ft)	—	Hawaii, USA
Vinnufossen	860 m (2 822 ft)	420 m (1 378 ft)	Norway
Baläifossen	850 m (2 788 ft)	452 m (1 482 ft)	Norway
Pu'uka'oku Falls	840 m (2 756 ft)	—	Hawaii, USA
Browne Falls	836 m (2 744 ft)	244 m (800 ft)	New Zealand
Strupenfossen	820 m (2 690 ft)	—	Norway
Ramnefjellsfossen (Utigardsfossen)	818 m (2 685 ft)	600 m (1 968 ft)	Norway

Dramatic Drops

As well as being the world's tallest waterfall overall, Angel Falls also has the tallest single drop of any waterfall in the world. However, Inga Falls in Nigeria is the largest in the world by volume. Although this waterfall is only a paltry 96 metres (315 feet) tall, an average of 42,476 cubic metres (1,500,000 cubic feet) of water pass over it each second.

LAKES

The world's 20 largest lakes are listed below.

Lake	Location	Area[2]
Caspian Sea[1]	Iran/Russia/Turkmenistan/ Kazakhstan/Azerbaijan	371 000 sq km (143 240 sq mi)[3]
Superior	USA/Canada	82 260 sq km (31 760 sq mi)[4]
Aral Sea[1]	Uzbekistan/Kazakhstan	64 500 sq km (24 900 sq mi)[3]
Victoria	East Africa	62 940 sq km (24 300 sq mi)
Huron	USA/Canada	59 580 sq km (23 000 sq mi)[4]
Michigan	USA	58 020 sq km (22 400 sq mi)
Tanganyika	East Africa	32 000 sq km (12 360 sq mi)
Baikal	Russia	31 500 sq km (12 160 sq mi)
Great Bear	Canada	31 330 sq km (12 100 sq mi)
Great Slave	Canada	28 570 sq km (11 030 sq mi)
Erie	USA/Canada	25 710 sq km (9 930 sq mi)[4]
Winnipeg	Canada	24 390 sq km (9 420 sq mi)
Malawi/Nyasa	East Africa	22 490 sq km (8 680 sq mi)
Ontario	USA/Canada	19 270 sq km (7 440 sq mi)[4]
Ladoga	Russia	18 130 sq km (7 000 sq mi)
Balkhash	Kazakhstan	17 000–22 000 sq km (6 560–8 490 sq mi)[2]
Maracaibo	Venezuela	13 010 sq km (5 020 sq mi)[5]
Patos	Brazil	10 140 sq km (3 920 sq mi)[5]
Chad	Western Africa	10 000–26 000 sq km (3 860–10 040 sq mi)
Onega	Russia	9 800 sq km (3 780 sq mi)

[1] *The Caspian and Aral Seas, being entirely surrounded by land, are classified as lakes.*
[2] *Areas are rounded to the nearest 10 square kilometres or square miles.* [3] *Salt lakes.*
[4] *Average of areas given by Canada and USA.* [5] *Salt lagoons.*

CAVES

The world's ten largest caves are listed below.

Cave	Location	Depth
Jean Bernard	France	1 494 m (4 902 ft)
Snezhnaya	Georgia	1 340 m (4 396 ft)
Puertas de Illamina	Spain	1 338 m (4 390 ft)
Pierre-Saint-Martin	France	1 321 m (4 334 ft)
Sistema Huautla	Mexico	1 240 m (4 068 ft)
Berger	France	1 198 m (3 930 ft)
Vqerdi	Spain	1 195 m (3 921 ft)
Dachstein-Mammuthöhle	Austria	1 174 m (3 852 ft)
Zitu	Spain	1 139 m (3 737 ft)
Badalona	Spain	1 130 m (3 707 ft)

Gateway to the Underworld

Caves are extremely important in the mythology of the Maya, an ancient South American civilization that still exists today. The Mayans see caves as being a gateway to the underworld they call *Xibalbá* ('Place of Fear'), dwelling-place of the dead and home to the gods of rain and fertility as well as to more terrifying deities. It is thought that Mayan rituals have been performed in caves for thousands of years.

DESERTS

Some of the world's largest deserts are listed below.

Desert	Location	Area[1]
Sahara	north Africa	8 600 000 sq km (3 320 000 sq mi)
Arabian	South-west Asia	2 330 000 sq km (900 000 sq mi)
Gobi	Mongolia and north-east China	1 166 000 sq km (450 000 sq mi)
Patagonian	Argentina	673 000 sq km (260 000 sq mi)
Great Victoria	South-west Australia	647 000 sq km (250 000 sq mi)
Great Basin	South-west USA	492 000 sq km (190 000 sq mi)
Chihuahuan	Mexico	450 000 sq km (174 000 sq mi)
Great Sandy	North-west Australia	400 000 sq km (154 000 sq mi)
Sonoran	South-west USA	310 000 sq km (120 000 sq mi)
Kyzyl Kum	Kazakhstan	300 000 sq km (116 000 sq mi)
Takla Makan	North-west China	270 000 sq km (104 000 sq mi)
Kalahari	South-west Africa	260 000 sq km (100 000 sq mi)
Kara Kum	Turkmenistan	260 000 sq km (100 000 sq mi)
Kavir	Iran	260 000 sq km (100 000 sq mi)
Syrian	Saudi Arabia/Jordan/Syria/Iraq	260 000 sq km (100 000 sq mi)
Nubian	Sudan	260 000 sq km (100 000 sq mi)
Thar	India/Pakistan	200 000 sq km (77 000 sq mi)
Ust'-Urt	Kazakhstan	160 000 sq km (62 000 sq mi)
Bet-Pak-Dala	Southern Kazakhstan	155 000 sq km (60 000 sq mi)
Simpson	Central Australia	145 000 sq km (56 000 sq mi)
Dzungaria	China	142 000 sq km (55 000 sq mi)
Atacama	Chile	140 000 sq km (54 000 sq mi)
Namib	South-east Africa	134 000 sq km (52 000 sq mi)
Sturt	South-east Australia	130 000 sq km (50 000 sq mi)
Bolson de Mapimi	Mexico	130 000 sq km (50 000 sq mi)
Ordos	China	130 000 sq km (50 000 sq mi)
Alashan	China	116 000 sq km (45 000 sq mi)

[1] *Desert areas are very approximate, because clear physical boundaries may not occur.*

THE ATMOSPHERE

Layers of the atmosphere

Thermosphere

Uppermost layer, in which the air is very 'thin' (at low density) and atmospheric pressure is only a millionth of a billionth of that at sea level. Temperature increases with height, and may reach 2000°C (3600°F). Composed of the *ionosphere*, which reflects radio waves back to Earth enabling signals to be transmitted around the curved surface of the Earth, the *ionopause* transitional layer, and the *exosphere*, the outermost layer of the Earth's atmosphere, approximately 500km (300mi) above the surface, from which light gases can escape into space.

Mesopause

Transitional layer between the mesosphere and the thermosphere, approximately 80–85km (50–55mi) above the surface. The minimum atmospheric temperature of approximately –100°C (–150°F) occurs in this layer, and atmospheric pressure is a hundred thousand times lower than at sea level.

Mesosphere

Middle atmosphere, up to approximately 85km (55mi) above the surface. Temperature decreases with height.

Stratopause

Transitional layer, approximately 50–55km (30–35mi) above the surface. The temperature is approximately 0°C (32°F).

Stratosphere

Contains very few clouds. Aircraft usually fly in this layer above the weather disturbances in the troposphere. Temperatures increase with height, and typical pressure is only a hundredth of that on the surface. Also includes the ozone layer, approximately 20–40km (12–25mi) above the surface.

Tropopause

Transitional layer, approximately 10km (6mi) above the surface. The temperature is approximately –60°C (–80°F).

Troposphere

Lower part of the atmosphere, from the surface up to a height varying from approximately 9km (5mi) at the poles to 17km (10mi) at the equator. Contains almost all of the clouds. Temperature decreases with height.

Note: diagram is not to scale

Composition of the atmosphere

A number of different gases, together with water vapour, make up the air in the Earth's atmosphere. The amount of water vapour present depends on the temperature and humidity. The list and pie chart below show the composition of dry air.

Gas	% volume
Nitrogen	78.1
Oxygen	20.95
Argon	0.934
Carbon dioxide	0.031
Neon	0.00182
Helium	0.00052
Methane	0.0002
Krypton	0.00011
Hydrogen	0.00005
Nitrous oxide	0.00005
Ozone	0.00004
Xenon	0.000009

Legend:
- Nitrogen
- Oxygen
- Argon
- Carbon dioxide
- Others

WEATHER AND CLIMATE EXTREMES

Hottest place	Dallol, Ethiopia, with an annual mean temperature of 34.4°C (93.9°F).
Highest recorded temperature in the shade	58°C (136.4°F), at Al'Aziziyah, Libya, on 13 Sep 1922.
Coldest place	Plateau Station, Antarctica, with an annual mean temperature of −56.6°C (−69.8°F).
Coldest recorded temperature	−89.2°C (−128.6°F), at Vostok, Antarctica, on 21 Jul 1983.
Greatest temperature range	Verkhoyansk, Siberia, Russia, where temperatures can range from −68°C (−90.4°F) to 37°C (98°F), a difference of 105°C (189°F).
Driest place	Atacama desert near Calama, Chile, where no rainfall was recorded in over 400 years to 1972. Today, the desert's average annual rainfall is just 0.1 mm (0.0039 in).
Most rain to fall in 24 hours	1870 mm (74 in), which fell over Cilaos, Réunion, in the Indian Ocean, on 15–16 Mar 1952.
Most intense rainfall	38.1 mm (1.8 in), which fell in one minute at Basse Terre, Guadeloupe, Caribbean, on 26 Nov 1970.
Most rainy days in a year	Mt Wai'ale'ale, Kauai, Hawaii, USA, with an average of 350 days of rain each year.
Wettest place	Mawsynram, Meghalaya State, India, where the annual average rainfall is 11 870 mm (467 in).

Least amount of sunshine	The North and South Poles, where the Sun does not rise for 182 days of winter.
Greatest amount of sunshine	Yuma, Arizona, USA, with a mean average of 4055 hours of sun per year, or 91% of the possible hours of sunshine.
Greatest amount of snow to fall in a year	31102mm (1225in), at Paradise, Mt Rainier, Washington, USA, in 1971–2.
Greatest amount of snow to fall in a day	193cm (76in), at Silver Lake, Colorado, on 14 Apr 1921.
Highest recorded surface wind speed	371.75kph (231mph), at Mt Washington, New Hampshire, USA, on 12 Apr 1934.
Most days of thunder in a year	Tororo, Uganda, had an average of 251 days of thunder per year between 1967 and 1976.
Most hail in a year	Keriche, Kenya, has an average of 132 days of hail each year.
Heaviest hailstones	On 14 Apr 1986, hailstones weighing up to 1kg (2.2lb) fell in Gopalganj, Bangladesh, killing 92 people.

CLIMATE ZONES

The earth can be divided into zones, approximating to zones of latitude, with each zone having a distinct type of climate.

Zone type	Description	Examples
Tropics	Single zone of wet climate near the equator. May be constantly wet, or monsoonal (with wet and dry seasons). The tropical savanna has dry winters. Average temperature is not below 18°C (65°F).	Amazon forest, Congo Basin, Malaysia, Indonesia, South Vietnam, South-East Asia, India, Australia, Africa
Subtropical zones	Two zones of steppe and desert climate (transition through semi-arid to arid). Summers are generally hot; although winters are cooler, the temperature usually remains above 0°C.	Sahara, Australia, Central Asia, Kalahari, Mexico
Mediterranean zones	Areas with a rainy climate with mild winters; the coolest month has temperatures above 0°C (32°F) but below 18°C (65°F).	California, parts of Chile, South Africa, South-west Australia, Southern Europe
Temperate zones	Areas with a rainy climate, including areas of temperate woodland, mountain forests, and plains with no dry season. Influenced by seas; rainfall all year with only small changes in temperature. Average temperature is between 3°C (37°F) and 18°C (65°F).	Most of Europe, New Zealand, Asia, parts of Chile, north-west and north-east USA

Zone type	Description	Examples
Boreal zones	Areas in the northern hemisphere that experience a great range in temperature; precipitation varies by a factor of ten during the year. May be wet in summer and dry in winter or vice versa. In the coldest period, temperatures do not exceed 3°C (37°F); in the hottest period, temperatures do not drop below 10°C (50°F).	Prairies of USA, parts of Russia, parts of South Africa, parts of Australia
Polar caps	Areas consisting of tundra and ice-cap. The climate is snowy with little or no precipitation. There is permafrost in the tundra; vegetation includes lichen and moss all year and grass in the summer. The highest annual temperature in the polar regions is below 0°C (32°F), while in the tundra the average temperature is 10°C (50°F).	Arctic regions of Russia and North America, Antarctica

AIR PRESSURE

The atmosphere is made up of molecules of nitrogen, oxygen, carbon dioxide and other rarer gases. Despite their tiny size, these molecules have mass and exert a downward force. This is what is meant by **air pressure**. Air pressure is measured in units called millibars; the name comes from the Greek word baros, meaning 'pressure'.

Cyclones and anticyclones

When the Sun heats the Earth, it does not heat up all parts evenly. At the global scale, the equatorial and tropical regions are heated strongly whilst the polar regions remain cold. At the local scale, a hillside facing the Sun in the middle of the day (a south-facing slope in the northern hemisphere) will be warmed much more than a hillside that faces away from the Sun. Where the ground is warmed strongly by the Sun it transfers some of this heat to the air above. The warm air rises and expands and the molecules are further apart. This means that low air pressure, known as a **depression** or **cyclone**, is recorded at ground level. The opposite is true where the ground and air are cool: the cold air sinks and creates an area of high pressure – an **anticyclone** – at the Earth's surface.

WIND

Air flows across the Earth from regions of high pressure to regions of lower pressure, creating wind. The difference in pressure is known as a **pressure gradient**. The greater the pressure gradient, the stronger the wind.

Onshore and offshore breezes

During the day, the land heats up more quickly than the sea. Air rises over the land, creating a local area of low pressure, and sinks over the cooler sea, creating a region of lower pressure. A sea breeze blows onshore across this pressure gradient. During the night, however, the land loses heat rapidly but the sea retains heat it has stored. Air sinks over the cool land, creating a high pressure region, and rises over the warmer ocean, creating a lower pressure area. In this case, an offshore breeze blows.

Notable winds

Some parts of the world experience strong wind patterns that are caused by air movement over mountains. These are caused by two main processes. **Adiabatic winds** are warm, dry winds produced when descending air is compressed, causing it to warm up. These winds are also known as Föhn-type winds, after climbers who first described them when climbing in the Alps. **Katabatic winds** are cold winds produced when cold air flows down a mountainside. The cold night air from the mountain-tops is denser than the surrounding air, so it sinks under gravity. The air is funnelled into valleys where it creates cold winds. In addition, North Africa and Southern Europe experience notable winds when low pressure systems cross North Africa.

Wind	Country affected	Source	Description	Mechanism
Bora, Borino	Italy (Adriatic coast)	The mountains of central Europe	Cold, dry and violent. Can bring rain and snow. Strongest in winter (Bora) and weaker in summer (Borino).	Katabatic
Chinook	USA	Rocky Mountains	Warm and dry. A south-westerly wind blowing down the eastern side of the Rocky Mountains.	Adiabatic
Föhn	Germany (blows down the leeward side of mountains eg the Alps)	Mountain tops, eg the Alps	Warm and dry.	Adiabatic

Wind	Country affected	Source	Description	Mechanism
Mistral	France (Mediterranean coast)	The Alps	Cold, dry, powerful. A northerly wind that blows down the Rhone valley. Mainly occurs in winter.	Katabatic
Northwester, Nor'wester	New Zealand (South Island)	The New Zealand Alps	Powerful, gale-like, warm and dry. Mainly occurs in spring.	Adiabatic
Samun, Samoon	Iran	Descends from the mountains of Kurdistan	Warm and dry.	Adiabatic
Santa Ana, Santa Anna	USA (California)	The desert plateaus in Utah and Nevada	Hot and dry. Often carries a lot of dust. Mainly occurs in winter.	Adiabatic
Simoom, Simoon	North Africa (northern Sahara)	The deserts of Africa and Arabia	Very hot swirling wind that carries a lot of dust. Usually in spring or summer.	Low pressure system in the atmosphere
Sirocco	North Africa, Italy	Sahara	A southerly wind which is very hot. Dry over Africa but often humid by the time it reaches Italy. Strongest in late winter.	Low pressure system in the atmosphere

Poisonous Wind

The Simoom or Simoon wind is short-lived, but can be deadly. Its Arabic name reflects this – it means 'poison'.

BEAUFORT SCALE

Beaufort number	Wind name	Wind speed kph (mph)	Observable wind characteristics	Sea disturbance number	Average wave height m (ft)	Observable sea characteristics
0	Calm	<1 (<1)	Smoke rises vertically	0	0 (0)	Sea like a mirror
1	Light air	1–5 (1–3)	Wind direction shown by smoke drift but not by wind vanes	0	0 (0)	Ripples like scales, without foam crests
2	Light breeze	6–11 (4–7)	Wind felt on face; leaves rustle; vanes moved by wind	1	0.3 (0–1)	More definite wavelets, but crests do not break
3	Gentle breeze	12–19 (8–12)	Leaves and small twigs in constant motion; wind extends light flag	2	0.3–0.6 (1–2)	Large wavelets; crests begin to break; scattered white horses
4	Moderate breeze	20–28 (13–18)	Raises dust, loose paper; small branches moved	3	0.6–1.2 (2–4)	Small waves become longer; fairly frequent white horses
5	Fresh breeze	29–38 (19–24)	Small trees in leaf begin to sway; crested wavelets on inland waters	4	1.2–2.4 (4–8)	Moderate waves with a more definite long form; many white horses; some spray possible
6	Strong breeze	39–49 (25–31)	Large branches in motion; difficult to use umbrellas; whistling heard in telegraph wires	5	2.4–4 (8–13)	Large waves form; more extensive white foam crests; some spray probable
7	Near gale	50–61 (32–38)	Whole trees in motion; inconvenience walking against wind	6	4–6 (13–20)	Sea heaps up; streaks of white foam blown along
8	Gale	62–74 (39–46)	Breaks twigs off trees; impedes progress	6	4–6 (13–20)	Moderately high waves of greater length; well-marked streaks of foam
9	Strong gale	75–8 (47–54)	Slight structural damage occurs	6	4–6 (13–20)	High waves; dense streaks of foam; sea begins to roll; spray affects visibility
10	Storm	89–102 (55–63)	Trees uprooted; considerable damage occurs	7	6–9 (20–30)	Very high waves with long overhanging crests; dense streaks of foam blown along; generally white appearance of surface; heavy rolling
11	Violent storm	103–117 (64–72)	Widespread damage	8	9–14 (30–45)	Exceptionally high waves; long white patches of foam; poor visibility; ships lost to view behind waves
12–17	Hurricane	>118 (>73)		9	14 (>45)	Air filled with foam and spray; sea completely white; very poor visibility

WEATHER FRONTS

An air mass is an area of the atmosphere where atmospheric conditions such as air temperature and moisture content are more or less the same for hundreds of kilometres. The meeting of two air masses is called a weather front; the three main types are given below. The diagrams show the development of an occluded front.

Type	Description	Symbol on weather map
Warm front	A warm air mass meets a cold air mass. The warm air is more buoyant than the cold air and rises up and over it.	▲▲▲▲
Cold front	A cold air mass meets a warm air mass. The cold air is denser and clings to the ground, driving a wedge under the warm air mass.	●●●●
Occluded front or occlusion	A cold air mass overtakes a warm air mass, pushing the warm air mass upwards and cutting it off from the earth's surface.	●▲●▲

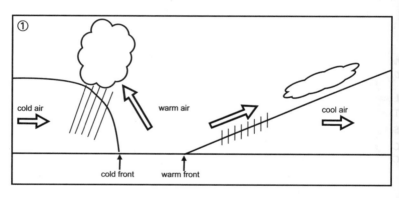

① cold air warm air cool air
cold front warm front

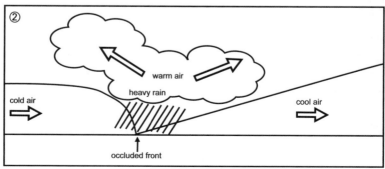

② cold air warm air heavy rain cool air
occluded front

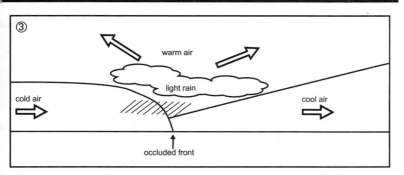

warm air

light rain

cold air

cool air

occluded front

CLOUDS

At any one time about half of the globe is covered in cloud. Clouds are formed by the condensation or freezing of water vapour on minute particles in the atmosphere. They play an important role in regulating climate, by absorbing and reflecting certain parts of the Sun's radiation. Cloud formation occurs when air masses move upward as a result of convection currents, unstable conditions, etc, and cool rapidly. Clouds are usually classified into ten main types according to their height and shape.

Meteorologists use feet to measure cloud height; to convert to metres, multiply by 0.3048.

Low clouds

The base of low clouds is usually surface–7 000ft.

Stratus (St)

Cloud base: usually surface–1 500ft.
Colour: usually grey.

Cumulonimbus (Cb)

Cloud base: usually 1 000–5 000ft.
Colour: white above with dark underside.

Cumulus (Cu)

Cloud base: usually 1 200–6 000ft.
Colour: white in sunlight but dark underside.

Stratocumulus (Sc)

Cloud base: usually 1 200–7 000ft.
Colour: grey or white, with shading.

Medium clouds

The base of medium clouds is usually 7 000–17 000ft, although nimbostratus may be much lower.

Nimbostratus (Ns)

Cloud base: usually 1 500–10 000ft.
Colour: dark grey.

Altocumulus (Ac)

Cloud base: usually 7 000–17 000ft.
Colour: grey or white, with shading.

Altostratus (As)

Cloud base: usually 8 000–17 000ft.
Colour: greyish or bluish.

High clouds

The base of high clouds is usually 17 000–35 000ft. High clouds are composed of ice crystals.

Cirrus (Ci)

Cloud base: usually 17 000–35 000ft.
Colour: white.

Cirrocumulus (Cc)

Cloud base: usually 17 000–35 000ft.
Colour: white.

Cirrostratus (Cs)

Cloud base: usually 17 000–35 000ft.
Colour: white.

Clouds and temperature

Low cumulus and cumulonimbus clouds reflect the Sun's heat and light radiation – that is why they are bright on top but dark underneath. Their reflection of heat reduces the temperature at the Earth's surface. High cirrus clouds trap radiation that is reflected from the Earth's surface, so they keep the surface warm.

Global dimming

Global dimming describes a reduction in the amount of light that reaches the Earth's surface. It is thought to occur due to pollutant particles such as soot, which can reduce the size of water droplets in clouds. Clouds that contain a larger number of smaller droplets can reflect a greater proportion of sunlight, reducing the amount that reaches the Earth.

PRECIPITATION

Precipitation is the falling of water, in various forms, from clouds in the atmosphere. The process starts when warm moist air rises into the atmosphere, forming clouds. The air cools as it rises, and water vapour carried in the air condenses to form tiny water droplets. These droplets usually form around a tiny particle of soot or dust. When two or more tiny droplets collide with each other within the cloud, they combine to make a bigger droplet. Eventually the droplets become so big that they can no longer be suspended in the air; instead, they fall under gravity as precipitation.

Types of precipitation

After the water vapour has condensed to form droplets, it can fall as rain, black ice, snow, hail, or sleet, depending on both the temperature of the cloud and the air temperature at ground level. There are three ways in which the cooling and condensation of water in the atmosphere can occur: **convectional rainfall**, **relief rainfall** and **frontal rainfall**.

Convectional rainfall

Convectional rainfall occurs when the Sun's energy heats up the Earth, which in turn heats up the air directly above the ground. The warm air rises, carrying with it moisture from the ground and vegetation. The warm moist air expands as it rises, causing the air to cool and the moisture to condense to form clouds and, eventually precipitation. This process is particularly common over tropical rainforests because they are hot and full of moisture. (See overleaf for diagram.)

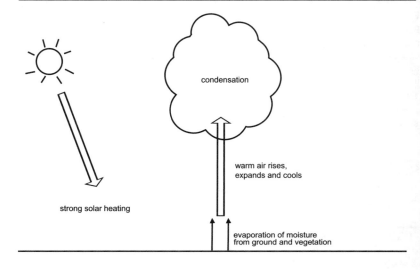

Relief rainfall

Relief rainfall occurs over mountainous areas. Air approaching a mountain or high ridge is forced to rise, causing it to expand and cool. The decrease in temperature causes water vapour to condense into droplets, forming clouds. The precipitation tends to fall over the higher ground, using up most of the cloud's water droplets. As the air descends on the other side of the ridge, the air warms and condensation stops. This means that the leeward side of a mountain has a **rain-shadow** effect with much lower rainfall totals.

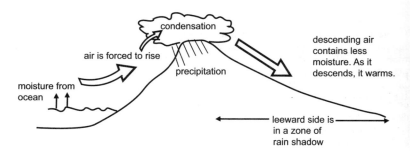

Professional Precipitation

The technical term for relief rainfall is **orographic precipitation**, from the Greek word *oros* meaning 'mountain'.

Frontal rainfall

Rainfall is often associated with weather fronts, which occur when two air masses meet. Warm moist air is always forced to rise over the colder dense air, causing it to cool and form a cloud. Rain tends to precede a warm front but follows a cold front, as shown in the diagram below. The rainfall from the cold front tends to be more intense than that from the warm front.

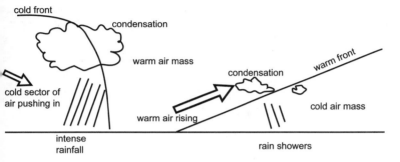

Precipitation by Numbers

There are nearly 13,000 km³ of water in the atmosphere at any one time. If this all fell at the same time on the USA, it would cover it to a depth of 1.3 m; if it all fell at the same time on the UK, it would cover it to a depth of 53 m. In total, 578,000 km³ of precipitation falls onto the earth each year – this is equal to 8.3 billion litres of precipitation per second.

THUNDERSTORMS

There are an estimated 40 million thunderstorms every year, and about 1,800 thunderstorms happen at any one time – the equivalent of 100 lightning strikes every second. The temperature of lightning is about 30,000°C, which is about five times hotter than the surface of the Sun.

Formation of storm clouds

Thunderstorms are created by huge quantities of rising warm moist air. The moisture condenses as the storm cloud grows in height, releasing heat and making the cloud rise further. This draws even more warm moist air upwards to fill the gap – thunderstorms are most common at sea and over tropical rainforests where there is a plentiful supply of water vapour.

The top of a thundercloud can reach heights of 12,000 m in equatorial regions and up to 18,000 m in higher latitudes. At these altitudes it is very cold (about −40°C) and ice crystals form in the top of the cloud. At the bottom of the cloud the water droplets become larger and heavier until eventually they fall as rain, causing the surrounding air to be sucked into the cloud. This causes water to evaporate, which uses up heat and cools the cloud around the edges so that it becomes dense and begins to sink.

The cloud is now a giant cell with warm air rising through its centre and cool air descending around its edges.

Thunder and lightning

The movement of moisture and ice crystals up and down within the thundercloud creates a negative electrical charge at the base of the cloud, and a positive charge at the top. The charge builds up to a critical point, at which point negative ions rush down through the base of the cloud at about 220,000 km/hour. This triggers positive ions to rush up from the ground. When the two sets of ions meet, a strong electrical current is created, which draws positive ions up from the Earth's surface into the cloud. This glows and is what we call a lightning strike. The heat of the lightning causes the air to expand incredibly quickly, which sends out shockwaves that we hear as thunder.

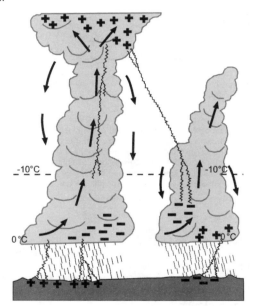

How Far Away Is That Thunderstorm?

A lightning strike creates both light and sound simultaneously. However, light travels much faster than sound, so you can always see lightning before hearing the thunder. The further you are from the storm, the bigger the delay will be, so the time difference between seeing the lightning and hearing the thunder indicates how far away the storm is. Roughly speaking, for every 3-second delay between the lightning and the thunder, the storm is 1 kilometre away; a 5-second delay is equal to 1 mile.

WORLD IN THE BALANCE

ENDANGERED SPECIES

The world's animal and plant species are increasingly under threat of extinction. Although the threats are varied, human activities are now the main cause of extinctions, putting 99% of threatened species at risk. The acronym HIPPO is sometimes used to summarize the threats to species and ecosystems.

H Habitat destruction and degradation; this also includes human-induced climate change, which is an increasing problem; these factors affect 86% of threatened birds and mammals and 88% of threatened amphibians

I Invasive species; this refers to non-native species (eg cats, rats, zebra mussels) that might be introduced to a place either deliberately or unintentionally and then start to destroy native species

P Pollution

P Population growth

O Over-harvesting/hunting; this refers to unsustainable levels of harvesting, hunting or fishing bringing species to the brink of extinction

Categories of threatened species

IUCN, the World Conservation Union, produces a list of the conservation status of animal and plant species. This is known as the Red List of Threatened Species and is updated every year. Experts assess species for the Red List against five criteria: rate of decline, population size, area of geographic distribution, degree of population, and distribution fragmentation. They then classify species into one of the following nine categories.

Category	Abbreviation	Description
Extinct	EX	Used when there is no doubt that the last individual in a taxon (any taxonomic group, eg subspecies, species, genus) has died; it is presumed extinct when exhaustive surveys in known or expected habitat throughout its range have failed to record an individual.
Extinct in the Wild	EW	Used when a taxon is known to survive only in cultivation, in captivity or as a naturalized population outside the historic range.
Critically Endangered	CR	Used when a taxon is facing an extremely high risk of extinction in the wild.
Endangered	EN	Used when a taxon is facing a very high risk of extinction in the wild.
Vulnerable	VU	Used when a taxon is facing a high risk of extinction in the wild.

Category	Abbreviation	Description
Near Threatened	NT	Used when a taxon is close to qualifying for, or is likely to qualify for, a threatened category in the near future unless conservation measures are taken.
Least Concern	LC	Used when a taxon does not qualify for the previous categories; includes widespread and abundant taxa.
Data Deficient	DD	Used when there is inadequate information to make an assessment of a taxon's risk of extinction based on its distribution and/or population status.
Not Evaluated	NE	Used when a taxon has not yet been evaluated against the criteria.

Numbers of extinct and threatened species

The IUCN 2006 Red List contains data for 40,177 species assessed against the criteria. The following data represent the situation as at May 2006.

Number of species officially declared extinct	784
Number of species found only in cultivation or captivity	65
Number of species threatened with extinction in one of the three threatened categories[1]	16 119
Number of species improved in status since last assessment	139
Number of species declined in status since last assessment	172

[1] *Critically Endangered, Endangered or Vulnerable; this includes 25% of the world's coniferous trees, 32% of amphibians, 12% of birds and 23% of mammals.*

Changes in the numbers of threatened species

The IUCN Red List Indices, which measure trends in extinction risk by comparing the status of specific groups over time, show that the status of birds and amphibians in particular has been declining steadily since before the 1990s. A comparison of data from 1996/98 and 2006 is given below.

Group	Critically endangered		Endangered		Vulnerable	
	1996/98	2006	1996/98	2006	1996/98	2006
Mammals	169	162	315	348	612	583
Birds	168	181	235	351	704	674
Reptiles	41	73	59	101	153	167
Amphibians	18	442	31	738	75	631
Fishes	157	253	134	238	443	682
Insects	44	68	116	129	377	426
Molluscs	257	265	212	222	451	488
Plants	909	1541	1197	2258	3222	4591

Examples of species under threat

Examples of endangered and vulnerable species are given for selected causes.

Habitat destruction or degradation	Invasive species	Pollution or climate change	Over-harvesting or hunting
Pygmy hippopotamus (West Africa)	Pritchardia palm (Hawaii)	Polar bear (Arctic)	Sturgeon (Central Asia)
Sri Lankan dragonflies (20 endemic species)	Tiger chameleon (Seychelles)	*Naufraga balearica* (plant endemic to Majorca)	Gulper shark (Atlantic)
Golden-rumped sengi (elephant shrew; Kenya)	Giant bronze gecko (Seychelles)	*Squalius keadicus* (fish endemic to Greece)	Common hippopotamus (Central Africa)
Mount Nimba toad (West Africa)	Campbell Island teal (New Zealand)		Pygmy sloth (Panama)
Aran rock lizard (Spain)			Asian yew (Asia)

Conservation programmes

Threatened species often require a combination of conservation measures to ensure their survival, such as research, species-specific actions, site- and habitat-based actions, policy responses, and communication and education. Some examples of current conservation programmes are given below.

Location	Focus of concern
India	Asian elephant, Bengal tiger
Africa	European bison, southern white rhinoceros
Mauritius	Asian vultures, grouse, pink pigeon
Russia	Siberian crane
South-east Asia	Marine and freshwater turtles, the western grey whale; ecosystems such as coral reefs and mangrove forests

Regulation of trade in endangered species

The Convention on International Trade in Endangered Species of Wild Fauna and Flora (CITES) was set up to ensure that trade in wild species does not threaten their survival. It protects about 5,000 species of animals and 28,000 species of plants against over-exploitation. It lists species in three Appendices, grouped according to how threatened they are by international trade.

Appendix I Species that are threatened with extinction (eg Asian elephants, gorillas, humpback whales, Brazilian rosewood, some orchid species); trade in these species is prohibited for commercial purposes; some non-commercial trade (eg for educational facilities) is allowed.

Appendix II Species that may become threatened unless trade is regulated (eg American black bears, common iguanas, southern fur seals, American mahogany); trade is allowed if it is not detrimental to the survival of the species, but it is strictly regulated.

Appendix III Species that any signatory of the Convention has identified as being exploited in its country and in need of the help of other signatory countries to regulate international trade in it (eg Hoffmann's two-toed sloths from Costa Rica; African civets from Botswana).

BIODIVERSITY

Biodiversity is a term used to describe the variety of life found in any one ecosystem. The biodiversity of an ecosystem is measured by counting two things: the total number of living things and the number of different species present. Scientists have identified around 1.5 million different species in the world, but the total is likely to be much greater because many species are still being discovered.

We know that human actions threaten many species with extinction. Pollution and poaching are two threats, but habitat destruction and climate change are the biggest threats to plants and wildlife. We need to protect habitats and their wildlife because we have a duty to conserve them for future generations: a concept known as stewardship.

Biodiversity needs protection for practical reasons too. Ecosystems contain complex relationships between the living things within them. Some species have essential roles within the ecosystem; these include acting as a critical food supply for others, pollinating plants or dispersing seeds. For example, research in the rainforests of Central America has shown that birds in the trogon family (such as the very colourful quetzal) and the toucan family are essential for the spreading of seeds. Such species are known as keystone species: without them the complex web of relationships within the ecosystem could fail and many species could quickly face extinction. Sadly, the quetzal is severely endangered – for many years it has been hunted for its brightly coloured feathers.

Conservationists believe that we should protect biodiversity by protecting and managing habitats. But, with so many habitats being destroyed around the world, where should we concentrate our efforts? One way is to map biodiversity. By protecting the places that have the highest biodiversities we can focus on saving as many species as possible. Scientists have recently identified 25 biodiversity hotspots around the world. These hotspots not only contain great biodiversities, they also contain many species that only live in one place. These are known as endemic species. An example would be the various species of lemur that only live in Madagascar – if we don't protect the lemurs there, then they will become extinct globally.

This website has an interactive map that allows you to examine each of the world's most important sites of plant and animal diversity:

http://www.biodiversityhotspots.org/xp/Hotspots

(Website addresses were correct at the time of publication.)

DEFORESTATION

Deforestation has taken place largely as a result of economic pressures for more agricultural land. Deforestation has serious implications for the environment (as carbon dioxide is released into the atmosphere) and can also cause the degradation of topsoil, increasing the risk of rivers silting up and flooding. Rainforests, which are home to half the world's plant and animal species, are in particular danger. The following data are taken from *State of the World's Forests 2005*, published by the Food and Agricultural Organization (FAO) of the United Nations.

| Country/ Area | Forest area 2000 | | Forest cover change 1990–2000 | |
	Total forest (1000 ha[1])	% of land area	Annual change (1000 ha[1])	Annual rate of change (%)
Africa	649 866	21.8	−5 262	−0.8
Asia	547 796	17.8	−364	−0.1
Europe	1 039 251	46.0	881	0.1
North and Central America	549 304	25.7	−570	−0.1
Oceania	197 623	23.3	−365	−0.2
South America	885 618	50.5	−3 711	−0.4
World	**3 869 455**	**29.6**	**−9 391**	**−0.2**

[1] *One hectare (ha) = 10 000 sq m. To convert ha to sq km, divide by 100; to convert ha to sq mi, divide by 259.*

NATURAL WORLD HERITAGE SITES

The United Nations Educational, Scientific and Cultural Organization (UNESCO) selects properties that make a unique cultural or natural contribution to the world to be World Heritage Sites. By 2006 a total of 830 sites were designated, 162 of which are natural properties. A further 24 properties (marked *) have mixed cultural and natural status.

Algeria

Tassili N'Ajjer National Park*

Argentina

Los Glaciares National Park
Iguazú National Park
Ischigualasto/Talampaya Natural Parks
Península Valdés

Australia

Central Eastern Rainforest Reserves
Fraser Island
Great Barrier Reef
Greater Blue Mountains Area
Heard and McDonald Islands
Kakadu National Park*
Lord Howe Island Group

Macquarie Island
Purnululu National Park
Queensland (wet tropics)
Riversleigh/Naracoorte (Australian fossil mammal sites)
Shark Bay
Tasmanian Wilderness*
Uluru-Kata Tjuta National Park*
Willandra Lakes region*

Bangladesh

Sundarbans (mangrove forest)

Belarus

Belovezhskaya Pushcha/Białowieża Forest (shared with Poland)

Belize

Barrier Reef Reserve System

Bolivia

Noel Kempff Mercado National Park

Brazil

Central Amazon conservation complex
Chapada dos Veadeiros and Emas
  National Parks
Discovery Coast Atlantic Forest Reserves
Fernando de Noronha and Atol das
  Rocas Reserves
Iguaçu National Park
Pantanal conservation area
South-East Atlantic Forest Reserves

Bulgaria

Pirin National Park
Srebarna Nature Reserve

Cameroon

Dja Faunal Reserve

Canada

Canadian Rocky Mountain Parks
Dinosaur Provincial Park
Gros Morne National Park
Miguasha National Park
Nahanni National Park
Tatshenshini-Alsek, Kluane National Park,
  Wrangell St Elias National Park and
  Reserve, and Glacier Bay National Park
  (shared with USA)
Waterton Glacier International Peace Park
  (shared with USA)
Wood Buffalo National Park

Central African Republic

Manovo-Gounda St Floris National Park

China

Huanglong area
Jiuzhaigou Valley area
Mount Emei scenic area, including
  Leshan giant Buddha scenic area*
Mount Huangshan*
Mount Taishan*
Mount Wuyi*
Wulingyuan area
Three Parallel Rivers of Yunnan
  protected areas

Sichuan giant panda sanctuaries

Colombia

Los Katíos National Park
Malpelo Fauna and Flora Sanctuary

Congo, Democratic Republic of the

Garamba National Park
Kahuzi–Biega National Park
Okapi Wildlife Reserve
Salonga National Park
Virunga National Park

Costa Rica

Cocos Island National Park
Guanacaste conservation area
Talamanca Range–La Amistad Reserves/
  La Amistad National Park (shared with
  Panama)

Côte d'Ivoire

Comoé National Park
Mount Nimba Strict Nature Reserve
  (shared with Guinea)
Taï National Park

Croatia

Plitvice Lakes National Park

Cuba

Alejandro de Humboldt National Park
Desembarco del Granma National Park

Denmark

Ilulissat Icefjord

Dominica

Morne Trois Pitons National Park

Ecuador

Galápagos Islands
Sangay National Park

Egypt

Wadi Al-Hitan (Whale Valley)

Ethiopia

Simien National Park

Finland

Kvarken Archipelago/High Coast (shared
  with Sweden)

France

Corsica (Cape Girolata, Cape Porto,

Scandola Natural Reserve and the Piana
  Calanches)
Pyrénées–Mont Perdu (shared with
  Spain)*

Germany

Messel Pit (fossil site)

Greece

Meteora*
Mount Athos*

Guatemala

Tikal National Park*

Guinea

Mount Nimba Strict Nature Reserve
  (shared with Côte d'Ivoire)

Honduras

Río Plátano Biosphere Reserve

Hungary

Aggtelek caves and the Slovak Karst
  (shared with Slovakia)

India

Kaziranga National Park
Keoladeo National Park
Manas Wildlife Sanctuary
Nanda Devi and Valley of Flowers
  National Parks
Sundarbans National Park

Indonesia

Komodo National Park
Lorentz National Park
Sumatra tropical rainforest heritage
Ujung Kulon National Park

Italy

Isole Eolie (Aeolian Islands)

Japan

Shirakami-Sanchi
Yakushima
Shiretoko

Kenya

Lake Turkana National Parks
Mount Kenya National Park

Macedonia

Ohrid region*

Madagascar

Tsingy de Bemaraha Strict Nature
  Reserve

Malawi

Lake Malawi National Park

Mali

Cliffs of Bandiagara (Land of the
  Dogons)*

Malaysia

Gunung Mulu National Park
Kinabalu Park

Mauritania

Banc d'Arguin National Park

Mexico

El Vizcaino Whale Sanctuary
Sian Ka'an (biosphere reserve)

Gulf of California islands and protected
  areas

Mongolia

Uvs Nuur basin (shared with Russia)

Montenegro

Durmitor National Park

Nepal

Royal Chitwan National Park
Sagarmatha National Park

New Zealand

New Zealand Sub-Antarctic Islands
Te Wahipounamu (south-west New
  Zealand)
Tongariro National Park*

Niger

Air and Ténéré Natural Reserves
W National Park

Winding like a 'W'

The W National Park, which is known
for its large animals such as warthogs,
elephants and buffalo, is situated around
a meander in the River Niger. The
meander is shaped like the letter 'W',
hence the park's unusual name.

Norway

West Norwegian Fjords (Geirangerfjord
and Nærøyfjord)

Oman

Arabian Oryx Sanctuary

Panama

Coiba National Park and marine
protection zone
Darien National Park
Talamanca Range–La Amistad Reserves/
La Amistad National Park (shared with
Costa Rica)

Peru

Huascarán National Park
Machu Picchu (historic sanctuary)*
Manú National Park
Río Abiseo National Park*

Philippines

Puerto-Princesa Subterranean River
National Park
Tubbataha Reef Marine Park

Poland

Belovezhskaya Pushcha/Białowieża
Forest (shared with Belarus)

Portugal

Laurisilva of Madeira (laurel forest)

Romania

Danube Delta

Russia

Altai (Golden Mountains)
Central Sikhote-Alin
Lake Baikal
Kamchatka volcanic region
Uvs Nuur basin (shared with Mongolia)
Virgin Komì Forests
Western Caucasus
Wrangel Island Reserve

Saint Lucia

Pitons Management Area

Senegal

Djoudj National Bird Sanctuary
Niokolo-Koba National Park

Seychelles

Aldabra Atoll
Vallée de Mai Nature Reserve

Slovakia

Aggtelek caves and the Slovak Karst
(shared with Hungary)

Slovenia

Škocjan caves

Solomon Islands

East Rennell

South Africa

Cape Floral Region protected areas
Greater St Lucia Wetland Park
uKhahlamba/Drakensberg Park*
Vredefort Dome

Spain

Doñana National Park
Garajonay National Park (Canary Islands)
Ibiza (biodiversity and culture)*
Pyrénées–Mont Perdu (shared with
France)*

Sri Lanka

Sinharaja Forest Reserve

Suriname

Central Suriname Nature Reserve

Sweden

Kvarken Archipelago/High Coast (shared
with Finland)
Laponian area*

Switzerland

Jungfrau-Aletsch-Bietschhorn
Monte San Giorgio

Tanzania

Kilimanjaro National Park
Ngorongoro conservation area
Selous Game Reserve
Serengeti National Park

Thailand

Dong Phayayen-Khao Yai forest complex
Thungyai-Huai Kha Khaeng wildlife
sanctuaries

Tunisia

Ichkeul National Park

Turkey

Göreme National Park and the rock sites
 of Cappadocia*
Hierapolis-Pamukkale*

Uganda

Bwindi Impenetrable National Park
Rwenzori Mountains National Park

UK

Dorset and East Devon coast
Giant's Causeway and its coast
Gough and Inaccessible Islands (South
 Atlantic Ocean)
Henderson Island (Pacific Ocean)
St Kilda*

USA

Everglades National Park
Carlsbad Caverns National Park
Grand Canyon National Park
Great Smoky Mountains National Park
Hawaii Volcanoes National Park
Mammoth Cave National Park

Olympic National Park
Redwood National and State Parks
Tatshenshini-Alsek, Kluane National Park,
 Wrangell St Elias National Park and
 Reserve, and Glacier Bay National Park
 (shared with Canada)
Waterton Glacier International Peace Park
 (shared with Canada)
Yellowstone National Park
Yosemite National Park

Venezuela

Canaima National Park

Vietnam

Ha Long Bay
Phong Nha-Ke Bang National Park

Zambia

Victoria Falls/Mosi-oa-Tunya (shared with
 Zimbabwe)

Zimbabwe

Mana Pools National Park and Sapi and
 Chewore safari areas
Victoria Falls/Mosi-oa-Tunya (shared with
 Zambia)

NATIONAL PARKS AND NATURE RESERVES

The first national park was Yellowstone, Wyoming, which was obtained by the US
government during the 1870s for the use and enjoyment of the people. By the late
1980s there were more than 3,000 national parks and wildlife reserves scattered
around the world, covering approximately 4 million square kilometres (1.5 million
square miles). Below is a selection of the best known.

Name	Country	Area (sq km)	Special features
Altos de Campana	Panama	48	Great variety of plant zones
Amazonia	Brazil	9940	Rainforest
Arctic National Wildlife Refuge	USA (Alaska)	79318	Centre of oil exploration controversy
Badlands	USA	985	Prehistoric fossils; dramatically eroded hills
Banff	Canada	6640	Spectacular glaciated scenery; hot springs
Beinn Eighe	UK	48	Original Scottish pine forest
Bialowieski	Poland	53	Largest remnant of primeval forest; European bison
Burren	Ireland	15	Limestone pavement with remarkable plants

Name	Country	Area (sq km)	Special features
Camargue	France	131	Wetland; many rare birds, especially flamingos
Canaima	Venezuela	30 000	World's highest waterfall, Angel Falls
Canyonlands	USA	1 365	Deep gorges, colourful rock, spectacular landforms
Carlsbad Caverns	USA	189	Huge limestone caverns with millions of bats
Carnarvon	Australia	2 980	Bush-tailed rock wallabies; aboriginal cave paintings
Chitwan	Nepal	932	Bengal tigers, gavials (type of Indian crocodile) and Gangetic dolphins
Corbett	India	520	Indian tigers; gavials and muggers (both types of Indian crocodile)
Dartmoor	UK	954	Wild ponies
Death Valley	USA	8 368	Lowest point in Western hemisphere; unique flora and fauna
Doñana	Spain	507	Wetland; rare birds and mammals; Spanish lynx
Everglades	USA	5 929	Swamp and mangrove; subtropical wildlife refuge
Etosha	Namibia	22 270	Swampland and bush; rare and abundant wildlife
Fiordland	New Zealand	12 570	Kiwis, keas, wekas, takahe and kakapo (all flightless birds, except for the kea)
Fuji-Hakone-Izu	Japan	1 232	Mount Fuji; varied animal and plant life
Galapagos Islands	Ecuador	6 937	Giant iguanas and giant tortoises
Gemsbok	Botswana	24 305	Desert, grassland; lions and large herds of game
Gir	India	258	Asiatic lions
Glacier	USA	4 102	Virgin coniferous forest; glaciers
Gran Paradiso	Italy	702	Alpine scenery; chamois and ibex
Grand Canyon	USA	4 834	Mile-deep canyon, colourful walls; many life zones
Great Smoky Mountains	USA	2 094	Varied wildlife including wild turkey and black bear
Hardangervidda	Norway	3 422	Plateau of ancient rock; large wild reindeer herd
Hawaii Volcanoes	USA	920	Active volcanoes, rare plants and animals and animals
Heron Island	Australia	0.17	Part of Great Barrier Reef; corals, invertebrates and fish

Name	Country	Area (sq km)	Special features
Hoge Veluwe	Netherlands	54	Largely stabilized dunes; wet and dry heath
Iguazú/Iguaçu	Argentina/ Brazil	6900	Iguazú/Iguaçu Falls
Ixtacihuatl-Popocatépetl	Mexico	257	Snow-capped volcanoes
Kafue	Zambia	22400	Numerous animals and birds; black rhinoceros refuge
Kakadu	Australia	20277	Aboriginal rock art; crocodiles and water birds
Kaziranga	India	430	Indian one-horned rhinoceros, swamp deer
Khao Yai	Thailand	2169	Large caves and waterfalls; many bird species
Kilimanjaro	Tanzania	756	Africa's highest peak, Mt Kilimanjaro; colobus monkeys
Kinabalu	Malaysia	754	Orchids; South-East Asia's highest peak, Mt Kinabalu
Kosciusko	Australia	6469	Australia's highest peak, Mt Kosciusko; mountain pygmy possum
Kruger	South Africa	19485	Wide range of animals and birds; rare white rhinoceros
Lainzer Tiergarten	Austria	25	Ancient forest and meadow; wild boar, deer and moufflon (wild sheep)
Lake District	UK	2292	Lake and mountain scenery
Los Glaciares	Argentina/ Chile	1618	Glacial landforms
Manu	Peru	15328	Small mammals, birds; Amazon/ Andean ecosystems
Mercantour	France	685	Alpine scenery and flora
Mt Apo	Philippines	728	Volcanoes; monkey-eating eagles
Mt Cook	New Zealand	699	New Zealand's highest peak, Mt Cook
Mt Olympus	Greece	40	Maquis and forest; wild mountain goats
Muddus	Sweden	493	Glaciated area with forest and tundra; Lapp pasture
Namib Desert/ Naukluft	Namibia	23400	Only true desert in southern Africa
Ngorongoro	Tanzania	21475	Huge volcanic crater
North East Greenland	Greenland (Denmark)	972000	Largest national park in the world
Olympic	USA	3712	Rugged peaks, glaciers, dense forest; Roosevelt elk

Name	Country	Area (sq km)	Special features
Petrified Forest	USA	379	Tree-trunks millions of years old; colourful sands
Pfälzerwald	Germany	1 793	Forest; European bison, moufflon (wild sheep) and mountain goats
Phu Rua	Thailand	120	Mountain forest zones from tropical to pine
Redwood	USA	442	Virgin redwood; Roosevelt elk
Royal	Australia	150	World's second-oldest national park (1879)
Ruwenzori	Uganda	995	Hippopotamuses, chimpanzees, baboons, colobus monkeys
Sagarmatha	Nepal	1 148	Mt Everest; impeyan pheasant and Himalayan tahr (wild goat)
Sarek	Sweden	1 970	Lapland; herds of reindeer
Sequoia and Kings Canyon	USA	1 635	The General Sherman Tree, the largest tree on earth
Serengeti	Tanzania	14 763	Huge animal migrations at start of dry season
Snowdonia	UK	2 142	Glaciated mountain scenery; varied flora and fauna
Swiss	Switzerland	169	Alpine forests and flora; reintroduced ibex
Tatra	Czech Republic/ Poland	712	Bears, lynxes and marmots; mountain scenery
Tikal	Guatemala	574	Mayan ruins; rainforest animals
Toubkal	Morocco	360	Barbary apes, porcupines, hyenas and bald ibis
Tsavo	Kenya	20 812	Vast range of wildlife
Ujung-Kulon	Indonesia	1 229	Low-relief forest; Javan tiger and Javan rhinoceros
Uluru	Australia	1 326	Desert; Uluru (Ayers Rock) and the Olgas
Victoria Falls	Zimbabwe/ Zambia	190	Spectacular waterfall
Virunga	Congo, Democratic Republic of the	7 800	Mountain gorillas; active volcanoes
Waterton Lakes	Canada	526	Varied flora and fauna
Waza	Cameroon	1 700	Giraffes, elephants, ostriches and waterbuck
Wolong	China	2 000	Giant pandas; also golden langurs and snow leopards
Wood Buffalo	Canada	44 800	Refuge for American buffalo (bison), whooping crane

Name	Country	Area (sq km)	Special features
Yellowstone	USA	8991	World's greatest geyser area; bears, deer, elk, bison
Yosemite	USA	3080	High waterfalls; varied flora and fauna; giant sequoias

Uninvited Guests

Visitors to Yosemite and Yellowstone National Parks occasionally find they have an extra dinner guest – in the form of a bear. Yosemite is famous for its black bears and Yellowstone is home to grizzlies; both these species are partial to picnics and will even break into cars to get their paws on provisions. The increased contact between bears and humans was proving to be so detrimental at Yosemite that bear-proof food lockers are now provided, in which food, waste and even fragranced toiletries must be stored.

ENVIRONMENTAL DISASTERS ON LAND

Many human activities can have disastrous consequences for the environment. Some major environmental disasters that have occurred on land are listed below.

Location	Event	Date	Consequence
Baia Mare, Romania	Cyanide leak from gold mine.	Jan 2000	Rivers and water supplies contaminated, fish stocks severely depleted.
Basle, Switzerland	Fire in Sandoz factory warehouse resulted in major chemical spill.	Nov 1980	River Rhine rendered lifeless for 200 km (124 mi).
Beirut	Toxic waste dumped by Italian company.	Jul–Sep 1988	Italy forced to take back its poison drums.
Bhopal, India	Toxic gas leaked from a Union Carbide pesticide plant and enveloped a nearby slum area housing 200 000 people.	Dec 1984	Possibly 10 000 people died (officially 2 352). Survivors suffer ravaged lungs and/or blindness. 100 sq km (39 sq mi) affected by the gas.
Camelford, Cornwall	20 tonnes of aluminium sulphate were flushed down local rivers after an accident at a water treatment works.	Jul 1988	60 000 fish killed. Local people suffered from vomiting, diarrhoea, blisters, mouth ulcers, rashes and memory loss.

Location	Event	Date	Consequence
Chernobyl, Ukraine	Nuclear reactor exploded, releasing a radioactive cloud over Europe.	Apr 1986	Fewer than 50 people were killed, but the radioactive cloud spread as far as Britain, contaminating farmland. 100 000 Soviet citizens may die of radiation-induced cancer, a further 30 000 fatalities are possible worldwide. 250 000 people evacuated from the area in five years.
Cubatão, Brazil	Uncontrolled pollution from nuclear industry.	1980s	Local population suffer serious ailments and genetic deformities. 30% of deaths are caused by pollution-related diseases and damage to respiratory systems.
Cumbria, England	Fire in Windscale plutonium production reactor burned for 24 hours and ignited 3 tonnes of uranium.	Oct 1957	Radioactive material spread throughout the countryside. In 1983 the British government said 39 people probably died of cancer as a result. Unofficial sources say 1 000.
Decatur, Alabama, USA	Fire at Browns Ferry reactor caused by a technician checking for air leaks with a lighted candle.	Mar 1975	$100 million damage. Electrical controls burned out, lowering cooling water to dangerous levels.
Detroit, Michigan, USA	Malfunction in sodium cooling system at the Enrico Fermi demonstration breeder reactor.	Oct 1966	Partial core meltdown. Radiation was contained.
Erwin, Tennessee, USA	Highly enriched uranium released from top-secret nuclear fuel plant.	Aug 1979	1 000 people contaminated (with up to 5 times as much radiation as would normally be received in a year).
Flixborough, England	Container of cyclohexane exploded.	June 1974	28 people died.
Goiânia, Brazil	Major radioactive contamination incident involving an abandoned radiotherapy unit containing radioactive caesium chloride salts.	Sep–Oct 1987	People evacuated; homes demolished; 249 people affected by sickness or death.

Location	Event	Date	Consequence
Gore, Oklahoma, USA	Cylinder of nuclear material burst after being improperly heated at Kerr-McGee plant.	Jan 1986	1 worker died, 100 hospitalized.
Idaho Falls, Idaho, USA	Accident at experiment reactor.	Jan 1961	3 workers killed. Damage contained, despite high radiation levels at the plant.
Jilin, China	Chemical plant explosion.	Nov 2005	Five people killed and around 70 injured. Explosion caused a toxic slick covering 80 km of the Songhua River.
Jiyyeh, Lebanon	Power station hit by Israeli bombing.	July 2006	Caused an oil spill affecting the Lebanese and Syrian coastlines.
Kasli, Russia	Chemical explosion in tanks containing nuclear waste.	Sep 1957	Radioactive material spread. Major evacuation of area.
Kuwait	Iraqi forces set alight 600 oil wells.	Feb 1991	Air pollution consisted of clouds of soot and oil particles which obscured the sun and fell as 'black rain'. Threat that it would turn into sulphur dioxide and fall as acid rain. Incidence of fatal bronchitis expected to increase. Possible serious contamination of agricultural land and water supplies particularly in Iraq's Tigris and Euphrates valleys.
Love Canal, near Niagara Falls, New York, USA	Dumping of drums containing hazardous waste at Love Canal, which by the 1970s were leaking toxic chemicals.	1940s to 1952	More than 240 families evacuated, countryside contaminated.
Lucens Vad, Switzerland	Coolant malfunction in an experimental underground reactor.	Jan 1969	Large amount of radiation released into cavern, which was then sealed.
Minimata Bay, Japan	Dumping of chemicals, including methyl mercury.	1953	Minimata disease, characterized by cerebral palsy, had killed more than 300 people by 1983. Thousands more suffered genetic abnormalities, brain disease and nervous disorders.

Location	Event	Date	Consequence
Monongahela River, Pennsylvania, USA	Storage tank ruptured and spilled 3 800 000 gallons of diesel oil into the Monongahela River.	Jan 1988	Water supply to 23 000 residents of Pittsburgh cut off. Oil slick spread into West Virginia, growing to 77 km (48 mi) and reached Steubenville, Ohio.
Monticello, Minnesota, USA	Water-storage space at Northern States Power Company's reactor overflowed.	Nov 1971	50 000 gallons of radioactive waste water dumped in Mississippi River. St Paul water system contaminated.
Rochester, New York, USA	Steam-generator pipe broke at the Rochester Gas & Electric Company's plant.	Jan 1982	Small amounts of radioactive steam escaped.
Seveso, N Italy	Leak of toxic TCDD gas containing the poison dioxin.	Jul 1976	Local population still suffering; in worst contaminated area, topsoil had to be removed and buried in a giant plastic-coated pit.
Sihanoukville, Cambodia	Around 3 000 tons of Taiwanese toxic waste dumped in a field.	Nov 1998	Reports of illness and death amongst scavengers who handled the waste.
Tennessee, USA	100 000 gallons of radioactive coolant leaked into the containment building of the TVA's Sequoyah 1 plant.	Feb 1981	8 workers contaminated.
Three Mile Island, Harrisburg, Pennsylvania, USA	Water pump broke down releasing radioactive steam.	Mar 1979	Pollution by radioactive gases. Some authorities claimed regional cancer, child deformity. Massive clean-up operation resulted in 150 tonnes of radioactive rubble and 250 000 gallons of radioactive water.
Tokaimura, Japan	Fire and explosion at power reactor and nuclear reprocessing plant.	Mar 1997	At least 35 workers contaminated.
Toulouse, France	AZF chemical factory exploded due to improper handling of ammonium nitrate.	Sept 2001	29 people killed, 2 500 seriously injured; 40 000 made temporarily homeless and several schools and hospitals evacuated.
Tsuruga, Japan	Accident during repairs of a nuclear plant.	Apr 1981	100 workers exposed to radioactive material.

MAJOR OIL SPILLS AT SEA

Some major oil spillages are listed below. Oil is generally measured by volume in barrels or by mass in tonnes (metric tons); for comparison, an offshore oil platform will typically produce between 40,000 and 400,000 barrels of crude oil per day. One barrel is equivalent to 42 US gallons, 35 imperial gallons or 159 litres. Conversion between volume and mass of oil varies depending on the density of the oil but is generally between 6 and 8 barrels per tonne.

Incident	Location	Date	Consequences
Aegean Sea tanker grounded, spilled approximately 500 000 barrels or 80 000 tonnes of light crude oil and caught fire.	La Coruña, Spain	Dec 1992	Marine pollution; 80 km (50 mi) of Spanish coast polluted.
Amoco Cadiz, Cyprus-registered tanker, grounded and spilled approximately1.6 million barrels or 220 000 tonnes of light crude oil.	off Portsall, France	Mar 1978	Marine pollution; 160 km (99 mi) of French coast polluted.
Aragon tanker; the hull ruptured and spilled approximately 175 000 barrels or 25 000 tonnes of crude oil.	off Madeira Is	Dec 1989– Jan 1990	Marine pollution.
Atlantic Empress and *Aegean Captain*; collision between the two tankers caused spillage of approximately 1.1 million barrels or 160 000 tonnes of crude oil. *Atlantic Empress* spilled a further 1 million barrels or 140 000 tonnes while being towed.	off Trinidad and Tobago	Jul 1979	Marine pollution.
Braer tanker ran aground and spilled approximately 600 000 barrels or 84 500 tonnes of crude oil.	Shetland, Scotland	Jan 1993	Marine pollution.
Burmah Agate collided with a freighter and spilled approximately 250 000 barrels or 36 500 tonnes of light crude oil.	Galveston Bay, Texas	Nov 1979	Marine pollution.
Castillo de Bellver tanker caught fire, causing spillage of approximately 1.85 million barrels or 252 000 tonnes of crude oil.	off Cape Town, South Africa	Aug 1983	Marine pollution.
Diamond Grace, Panamanian-registered tanker, grounded and spilled 9 700 barrels or 1 300 tonnes of light crude oil.	off Yokohama, Japan	Jul 1997	Marine pollution.
Ekofisk oil field; a blow-out caused spillage of 195 000 barrels of crude oil.	North Sea	Apr 1977	Marine pollution.

Incident	Location	Date	Consequences
Exxon Valdez, US tanker, grounded on Bligh Reef and spilled approximately 240 000 barrels or 38 500 tonnes of crude oil.	Prince William Sound, Alaska	Mar 1989	1770 km (1 162 mi) of Alaskan coastline polluted. More than 3600 sq km (1 390 sq mi) of water fouled. Thousands of animals killed.
Gulf War; Iraqi army sabotaged Kuwaiti oil wells and tankers as they left Kuwait. Crude oil entered the sea at a rate of approximately 1 million barrels or 130 000 tonnes per day; approximately 6 million barrels or 800 000 tonnes were released in total.	16 km/10 mi off coast near Kuwait City	Jan– Feb 1991	Threat to desalination plants and therefore to water supply; marine pollution.
Hawaiian Patriot tanker developed a leak and caught fire, causing spillage of approximately 700 000 barrels or 100 000 tonnes of crude oil.	North Pacific	Feb 1977	Marine pollution.
Ixtoc oil well; a blow-out caused spillage of approximately 3.5 million barrels or 470 000 tonnes of crude oil.	Gulf of Mexico	Jun 1979	Marine pollution.
Keo; hull failure caused spillage of approximately 210 000 barrels or 29 932 tonnes of crude oil.	off Massachusetts, USA	Nov 1969	Marine pollution.
Khark 5, Iranian supertanker, spilled approximately 480 000 barrels or 68 000 tonnes of heavy crude oil after an explosion in its hull.	700 km/435 mi north of the Canary Islands, Atlantic Ocean	Dec 1989	370 km (230 mi) oil slick, which almost reached Morocco. About 40% evaporated and much sank to ocean floor, endangering fish and oysters.
Kirki, Greek tanker, broke up; approximately 135 000 barrels or 17 000 tonnes of light crude oil were spilled during the incident and the subsequent towing of the vessel.	off Cervantes, Western Australia	Jul 1991	Pollution of conservation zones and lobster fishery.
Nowruz oil field; a blow-out caused the spillage of approximately 1.9 million barrels or 270 000 tonnes of crude oil as an indirect result of a tanker colliding with a platform. The ongoing Iran–Iraq war delayed the capping of the well and caused further damage and oil spillage.	Persian Gulf	Feb 1983	Marine pollution.

Incident	Location	Date	Consequences
thello tanker collided and spilled a large amount of crude oil; the total amount is controversial but was probably over 430 000 barrels or 0 000 tonnes.	Tralhavet Bay, Sweden	Mar 1970	Marine pollution.
restige tanker; hull cracked during storm, causing the vessel to sink and leak its cargo of 490 000 barrels or 77 000 tonnes of heavy fuel oil at a rate of approximately 800 barrels or 25 tonnes per day.	off north-western Spain	Dec 2002	Marine pollution; Spanish coast polluted as well as the coasts of five other countries.
ea Empress, Liberian-registered tanker, grounded and spilled approximately 500 000 barrels or 3 000 tonnes of light crude oil.	Milford Haven, Wales	Feb 1996	Marine pollution.
ea Star collided and spilled approximately 937 000 barrels or 30 000 tonnes of crude oil.	Gulf of Oman	Dec 1972	Marine pollution.
elendang Ayu cargo ship ran aground and spilled approximately 000 barrels or 1 600 tonnes of heavy fuel oil as well as large quantities of diesel.	Unalaska Island, Alaska	Dec 2004	6 crew members killed when a rescue helicopter crashed. Over 700 birds coated in oil.
olar I tanker sank; an initial spillage of approximately 1 400 barrels or 200 tonnes of fuel oil into the Guimaras trait was followed by further leakage once the vessel had sunk.	off Guimaras and Negros Occidental provinces of the Philippines	Aug 2006	Marine pollution, particularly affecting the Visayas Sea.
asman Spirit tanker ran aground and spilled 30 000 tonnes of crude oil.	Karachi, Arabian Sea	Aug 2003	Marine pollution.
orrey Canyon tanker grounded and spilled 860 000 barrels or 120 000 tonnes of crude oil.	off Land's End, England	Mar 1967	Marine pollution.
rquiola tanker grounded and spilled 40 000 barrels or 100 000 tonnes of crude oil.	La Coruña, Spain	May 1976	Marine pollution.
World Glory tanker; a freak wave caused hull failure and spillage of 34 000 barrels or 48 000 tonnes of crude oil.	off South Africa	Jun 1968	Marine pollution.

BIOSPHERE

The whole of the environment in which life can flourish is known as the biosphere. It consists of three main parts: the atmosphere, the hydrosphere and the lithosphere.

atmosphere   the air surrounding the Earth
hydrosphere   all the water on the surface of the Earth
lithosphere   the crust of the Earth, including the surface and deeper down

BIOMES, ECOREGIONS AND HABITATS

Biomes and ecoregions are terms used to describe regions of the biosphere that are characterized by their physical features and the species that live there. The use of these classifications varies, but some broad categories are listed. Each species has a particular habitat, a place that meets its environmental requirements, which i found within a biome or an ecoregion.

Desert

Deserts are extremely dry, harsh environments and only well-adapted plants and animals are able to flourish there. They are covered with sand, stones or rocks. Hot dry deserts, such as the Sahara (North Africa) and the Kalahari (south-western Afric have infrequent rainfall. Cold deserts, such as the Gobi (Mongolia and China) and th Atacama (Chile), experience their precipitation as snow rather than rainfall.

Tundra

Tundra describes vast, relatively flat zones, with permanently frozen subsoil. Its vegetation consists of dwarf trees and shrubs, grasses, sedges, mosses and lichens Areas of tundra are found mainly in the Arctic regions of Alaska, northern Canada, and Siberia, but also on the fringes of the Antarctic region.

Taiga

Taiga describes areas of pine forest that spread across much of subarctic North America and Eurasia, with tundra to the north and steppe to the south. It is also known as Boreal forest or coniferous forest.

Broad-leaf and mixed forest

Broad-leaf and mixed forests occur in temperate areas of the world, such as Europe, North America and parts of Russia, China and Japan. Many of the trees are deciduous, dropping their leaves as they become dormant for the winter. The forest floor is mainly covered in undergrowth.

Temperate rainforest

Some areas of the world have temperate rainforests, which occur in mountainous land near the coast. These have a higher rainfall than other temperate forests. Temperate rainforests are found in South America, the Pacific coast of North Americ eastern Europe, Australia, New Zealand and Japan.

Tropical rainforest

Tropical rainforests contain very tall trees that form a dense canopy. This blocks most light from reaching the forest floor, so tropical rainforests have very little undergrowth. They support an incredible diversity of plant and animal species. Tropical rainforests are mainly found in tropical Asia, Africa and South America.

Scrublands

Scrublands are covered with low-growing shrubs and stunted trees. The land can be flat or mountainous. Scrublands are known by different names in different parts of the world.

Name	Location
Chaparral	North America
Fynbos	South Africa
Mallee	Australia
Maquis	Europe
Matorral	Chile

Grasslands

Grasslands can be found in many parts of the world, and have different names. They are found in both temperate and tropical climates.

Name	Location
Pampas	South America
Prairie	North America
Savanna	Africa
Steppe	Asia and central Europe
Veld or veldt	South Africa

Wetlands

Wetlands are waterlogged spongy areas of land. Some wetlands are permanent, while others are seasonal. They include bogs, marshes, moors, fenland and swamps.

Aquatic ecoregions

Aquatic ecoregions include both marine (saltwater) and freshwater areas. There is variation in how aquatic ecoregions are described: some people consider that there is an aquatic biome, while others divide this into a marine biome and a freshwater biome. Yet another group of people have the view that biomes are land-based zones and that aquatic zones should not be described in terms of biomes.

Marine ecoregions

Marine ecoregions include coral reefs, where the water is warm and shallow, river estuaries, and oceans. The open ocean can be divided into three main zones: pelagic, benthic and abyssal. The parts where there is enough light for photosynthesis are described as photic or euphotic, while the deeper, darker parts are described as aphotic.

Ecoregion	Description	Examples of organisms
Coral reef	Warm shallow sea surrounding the reef	Coral, fish, molluscs, sea stars
Estuary	Brackish water at the mouth of a river	Wading birds, small fish, plants, molluscs and crustaceans
Ocean – Pelagic	Open ocean, near the surface; the upper part includes the photic zone	Fish, marine mammals, seaweed, plankton
Ocean – Benthic	Deep sea and ocean floor	Sponges, sea stars, anenomes, microorganisms
Ocean – Abyssal	Ocean trenches	Invertebrates, ancient fish, sulphur-metabolizing bacteria

Freshwater ecoregions

Freshwater ecoregions include lakes and rivers. Xeric (dry) basins do not have much permanent surface freshwater but tend to have freshwater springs. Many types of organism live in freshwater ecoregions, including plants, mammals, birds, amphibians and fish.

Endolithic ecoregion

The endolithic ecoregion has only recently been discovered. It consists of cracks in the rock deep down in the Earth's crust, where specialized microorganisms can live. These include bacteria and algae.

HYDROLOGICAL CYCLE

The hydrological cycle is the circulation of water between the Earth's surface and the atmosphere. Water moves from mountain streams to the sea, travelling along rivers. Evaporation from seas and lakes moves water into the atmosphere, where it condenses to form clouds. Plants also lose water to the atmosphere; this is known as transpiration. Water falls as precipitation, and either percolates into the ground or flows directly into the sea as run-off.

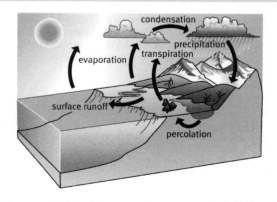

NITROGEN CYCLE

The nitrogen cycle is the continuous circulation of nitrogen and its compounds between the Earth and its atmosphere, resulting from the activity of living organisms. The uptake of nitrogen by plants, the consumption of plants by animals and the decay of waste products and dead organisms form important parts of the cycle. Various types of bacteria are essential throughout the cycle, for breaking down organic matter and for converting nitrogen compounds from one form into another.

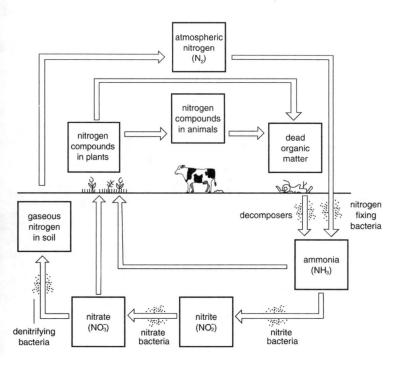

CARBON CYCLE

Carbon is one of the most common elements in the environment. It is present in all living things, in gases such as carbon dioxide (CO_2) in the atmosphere, and in the hydrocarbon compounds that make up fossil fuels. The carbon cycle is the transfer of carbon from the atmosphere into living organisms and, after their death, back again. Plants acquire carbon from the atmosphere by photosynthesis, while plants and animals release carbon back to the atmosphere by respiration. The consumption of plants by animals and the decay of dead organisms are important parts of the cycle; bacteria are important for this latter process. The parts of the environment that release carbon are known as carbon sources, while those that absorb carbon over long periods of time are known as carbon sinks.

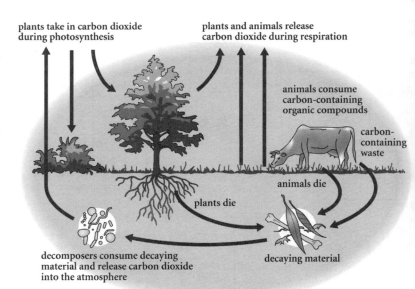

plants take in carbon dioxide during photosynthesis

plants and animals release carbon dioxide during respiration

animals consume carbon-containing organic compounds

carbon-containing waste

animals die

plants die

decomposers consume decaying material and release carbon dioxide into the atmosphere

decaying material

ROLE OF THE OCEANS IN REGULATING TEMPERATURE

The oceans and their living creatures play an essential part in regulating the temperature of the Earth.

Mechanisms of temperature regulation

Energy from the Sun strikes the equatorial regions at almost 90°. It is therefore more concentrated in these regions than it is near the poles, where the Sun's rays reach the Earth at a shallower angle. The oceans absorb some of the excess heat from the equatorial regions and move it towards the poles in a series of warm ocean currents called **gyres**, thus helping to regulate the Earth's temperature. Gyres are part of a massive system of water, the **thermohaline conveyor,** that circulates around the world's oceans. This is driven partly by the excess heat in the tropics and partly by the sinking of particularly salty water in the Southern and Arctic Oceans.

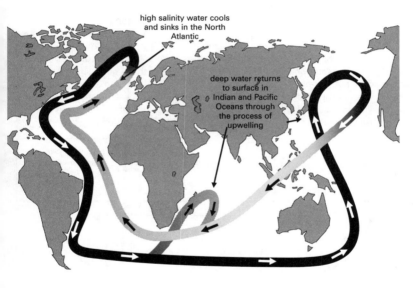

high salinity water cools and sinks in the North Atlantic

deep water returns to surface in Indian and Pacific Oceans through the process of upwelling

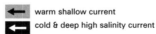

warm shallow current
cold & deep high salinity current

Consequences of global warming

Without the gyres, the equatorial and tropical regions would gradually get hotter and hotter. Scientists are concerned that global warming may switch off parts of this circulation system; if this were to happen then western and northern Europe would no longer be warmed by the Gulf Stream and could be plunged into a new glacial episode.

ROLE OF THE OCEANS IN REGULATING THE CARBON CYCLE

The world's oceans play a crucial part in regulating the carbon cycle.

Mechanisms of carbon cycle regulation

The oceans can absorb atmospheric carbon dioxide (CO_2) and store it, and then they can release it back into the atmosphere. This dual role means that they can be thought of as a **carbon dioxide pump**. The Arctic and Southern Oceans act as an effective **carbon dioxide sink**, as the cold water can efficiently absorb CO_2 from the atmosphere and store it. These regions also have abundant algae, which take up CO_2 during photosynthesis; when the algae die, their bodies sink to the sea floor and act as a long-term carbon store. Warmer oceans act as a **carbon dioxide source**, releasing CO_2 from their surface in a process known as **degassing**.

Consequences of global warming

On balance, the oceans absorb 100 billion tonnes (100 gigatonnes) more CO_2 from the atmosphere than they release. However, global warming may interfere with the carbon dioxide pump. As the oceans warm, they are likely to become less efficient at absorbing CO_2, and there will be less mixing between the warm surface water and the cooler water beneath. This means that more of the ocean's surface will be covered by nutrient-poor warm water, and there will be less food available for algae. The resultant drop in algae population means that less CO_2 will be absorbed by photosynthesis, so less will enter the carbon sink of sediment on the ocean floor. This positive feedback mechanism is illustrated in the diagram below.

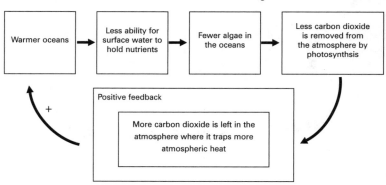

GAIA THEORY

The Gaia theory is a scientific view of the Earth in which the living and non-living parts of the Earth, oceans and atmosphere interact with each other in such a way as to regulate the environment. The goal of this complex system is the maintenance of environmental conditions that best favour the living things within the environment.

The geologist James Hutton was the first scientist to suggest that the Earth was a self-regulating system in 1785. However, it was not until 1972, with the publication by James Lovelock and Lynn Margulis of a controversial paper describing what was then called the Gaia hypothesis, that the scientific community began a serious debate of these ideas. Darwin's theory of evolution, published in 1859, had already proposed that living things adapt, through the process of natural selection, to suit their environmental conditions. Lovelock was now suggesting that life on Earth is able to regulate the non-living parts of the environment so that conditions are favourable for life. Whilst the Gaia hypothesis was initially hugely contentious, it is now supported by many scientists and is known as the Gaia theory.

The term 'Gaia' comes from Greek philosophy. The ancient Greek civilization believed that planet Earth was in some sense alive, and used the term to describe the personification of the Earth – the mother figure that supported all other life. But Lovelock's ideas are not based on those of the ancient Greeks. He developed them during the 1960s when he worked for the NASA space programme, devising techniques for analysing the atmosphere of Mars. His data about the chemical composition of the Martian atmosphere, together with his understanding of biological processes, enabled him to deduce that the planet had no life. It was this interest in the interrelationship between living things and the chemical composition of the atmosphere that made Lovelock begin to think about Gaia and how the biological, geological and atmospheric processes are all connected. Lovelock continues to write about the 'living Earth' as a way of explaining these complex relationships. However, he does not support the philosophical point of view that the planet is, as the Greeks believed, actually alive and self-aware.

The Gaia theory suggests that the function of the complex relationships that exist between the living and non-living parts of the environment is to maintain favourable environmental conditions for life. Many regulation mechanisms that maintain favourable conditions for life on Earth have now been identified. These mechanisms are not simple cause and effect; rather, they follow complex circular routes known as feedback mechanisms. Negative feedback mechanisms return the system to a state of balance or equilibrium, while positive feedback mechanisms change environmental conditions to a new state. An example of negative feedback is shown overleaf. Notice how this system involves both living parts (the plants) and non-living parts (the atmosphere).

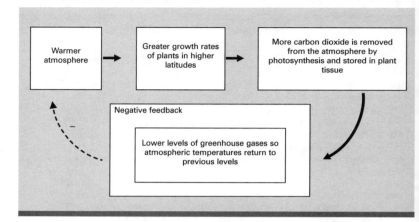

CHEMICAL IMBALANCES

Human activities can cause an imbalance in the amounts of naturally occurring substances.

Damage to the ozone layer

The ozone layer is a region of the atmosphere where ozone, a triangular molecule consisting of three oxygen atoms, makes up a greater proportion of the air than at any other height. It is located in the stratosphere, between about 20 and 40 km (12 and 25 mi) above the Earth's surface. Although the proportion of ozone in the ozone layer is still only a few parts per million, it is extremely important for the environment. It absorbs much of the ultraviolet radiation in sunlight, preventing it from reaching the Earth's surface and damaging living organisms.

Release of certain man-made pollutants has increased the atmospheric levels of molecules called free radicals. Each free radical can trigger thousands of ozone-destroying chain reactions before itself being destroyed. Pollutants of this type include the refrigerants and aerosol propellants known as CFCs (chlorofluorocarbons). The imbalance between formation and destruction of ozone that these pollutants have caused has contributed to the development of a hole in the ozone layer over Antarctica.

Increased carbon dioxide in the atmosphere

Carbon dioxide occurs naturally – it is a product of respiration. The level of carbon dioxide should be kept in balance, as plants and trees take it up through photosynthesis. However, the burning of fossil fuels, which are formed from fossilized plants and animals, alters this balance because carbon that has been stored for a long time is released as carbon dioxide in a short time, increasing the amount present in the atmosphere. Deforestation also reduces the amount of carbon dioxide removed from the air and thus increases the atmospheric levels.

Increased greenhouse effect

A layer of carbon dioxide, water vapour and other gases in the atmosphere acts somewhat like a greenhouse, trapping heat from the Sun near the Earth's surface. An increase in this greenhouse effect, due mainly to increased carbon dioxide release, is thought to be an important factor in global warming – the gradual rise in temperature of the atmosphere and oceans. CFCs and methane also act as 'greenhouse gases'.

Acid rain

Nitrogen oxides and sulphur dioxide occur naturally in small quantities due to lightning and volcanic activity. However, levels have increased substantially due to emissions from the burning of fossil fuels. These oxides dissolve in water, leading to increased acidity in rainwater. Acid rain is implicated in damage to forests and the stonework of buildings, and increases the acid content of soils and lakes, harming crops and fish.

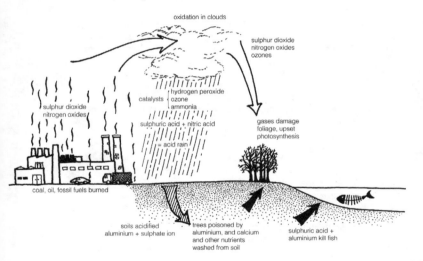

GLOBAL WARMING AND CLIMATE CHANGE

Global warming and climate change are both phrases used to describe the changes to the Earth's climate that are caused by human activity. The Earth's climate can change as a result of natural processes such as the forcing mechanisms that trigger ice ages. However, the current period of climate change is widely accepted by the scientific community to be a result of human actions. These include the burning of fossil fuels and the clearance of forests – both activities that enhance the greenhouse effect and lead to global warming of the atmosphere.

What is the evidence for climate change?

The evidence for human-induced climate change is plentiful, with contributions from very many different sources. Not one single piece of evidence can be taken as positive proof on its own; rather, the evidence needs to be added together like the pieces of a jigsaw.

Some evidence, such as the thinning of the ice in the Arctic, is so widespread and confirmed by so many sources that it is described as a fingerprint of climate change (rather like a fingerprint left at a crime scene). Other events, such as floods, hurricanes and other freak weather events, are described as harbingers: events that provide us with warning signs of the kinds of impacts that are likely to become more common in the future if global warming continues. For example, the record hurricane seasons in the Gulf of Mexico in 2004 and 2005 may be evidence of this change. Examples of climate change fingerprints and harbingers are shown below.

Fingerprints
- Warmer surface ocean temperatures.
- Glaciers in the Alps and Andes melting.
- Sea ice in the Arctic thinning.
- Ice sheets and glaciers melting in Greenland and Antarctica.

Harbingers
- The spread of the *Anopheles* mosquito (carrying malaria) into new regions.
- Earlier arrival of spring, eg swallows arriving earlier in Europe.
- Bleaching of coral reefs caused by excessive heat.
- Droughts and forest fires.
- Hurricanes and floods.

Wildlife appears to be responding to subtle changes in climate, and many populations are in decline because they can't adapt quickly enough to the changing environment. One example of this effect is the reduction in the polar bear population in Hudson Bay, Canada. There is strong evidence that polar bears are unable to hunt successfully because the Arctic sea ice is breaking up earlier than usual. As a result, polar bear pups are underweight and fewer are surviving the summer season when food is scarce.

What is causing climate change?

Climate change is caused by the emission of the so-called greenhouse gases, including carbon dioxide, methane, CFCs, nitrous oxides and ozone, into the Earth's atmosphere. The atmosphere acts rather like a filter, allowing energy in the form of sunlight to reach the Earth and then trapping some of the energy as it is given off again by the Earth as infrared radiation ('heat'). This is the greenhouse effect and is a natural process of our atmosphere. However, by burning fossil fuels for energy and transport, and various industrial processes, humans have significantly increased the concentration of greenhouse gases in the atmosphere over the last 200 years. With more gases able to absorb and trap heat, the greenhouse effect has become stronger, and this is what we call the enhanced greenhouse effect.

There is much evidence that the enhanced greenhouse effect is responsible for global warming. Ice cores drilled into the Greenland and Antarctic ice sheets prove that there is a close correlation between the amount of carbon dioxide (CO_2) in the atmosphere and atmospheric temperature. Levels of CO_2, which are measured at an observatory in Hawaii, have been rising steadily since records began in the 1950s and are far higher now than they have been in the last 300,000 years. The graph showing this increase is known as the Keeling Curve. Increasingly sophisticated computer models are also being built to simulate the complex relationship between atmosphere, oceans and life on Earth, allowing future conditions to be predicted.

James Lovelock, proposer of the **Gaia theory,** believes that we are reaching a tipping point: a point at which the climate will suddenly change. Climate is affected by both negative and positive feedback mechanisms; negative feedback mechanisms regulate the Earth's environmental conditions and keep them in a steady state, whereas positive feedback mechanisms push the system out of balance. Lovelock argues in his 2006 book *The Revenge of Gaia* that the positive feedback mechanisms are currently dominant and that the resulting instability is what is bringing the Earth to a tipping point. An example of a positive feedback mechanism that affects climate is given below.

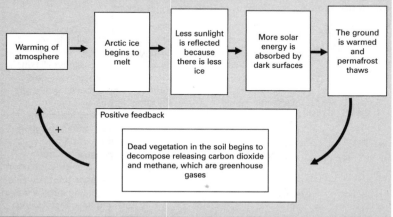

ENERGY AND THE ENVIRONMENT

We need energy for heat, light, transport and the electrical processes we use in our homes, offices, factories and farms. One of the biggest current challenges is finding ways of harnessing energy that do not harm the environment.

Types of energy sources

We can broadly divide energy sources into **renewables** and **non-renewables**. **Nuclear energy** uses uranium, which is a non-renewable resource. However, the rate of use of uranium is extremely slow, making nuclear energy unlike the other non-renewable sources.

Category	Resources	How they are harnessed
Non-renewable	Fuels that are a finite resource, eg the 'fossil fuels' (sources of fossilized carbon such as coal, oil, gas).	Burning fossil fuels generates heat, which turns water to steam to drive turbines. Also burned in vehicle engines.
Renewable	Resources with unlimited supply; eg Sun (eg solar panels), Moon (eg tidal power), Earth (eg geothermal energy).	See separate table below for the main types. Use varies hugely between countries; eg provide 2% of UK electricity but 100% of Iceland's electricity.
Nuclear	Uranium-235.	Nuclear fission (splitting apart) of fuel rods in a chain reaction produces heat, which turns water to steam to drive turbines.

Advantages and disadvantages of energy sources

Energy source	Advantages	Disadvantages
Fossil fuels	Power stations and engines fuelled by fossil fuels are relatively cheap to build and run. Have until now been cheap and reliable resources.	The burning of fossil fuels releases harmful gases such as carbon dioxide (CO_2) and sulphur dioxide (SO_2) into the atmosphere – the former is a greenhouse gas, while the latter causes acid rain pollution. Oil and gas supplies are running low, which is starting to lead to supply problems and rising prices.
Renewables	Produce energy that is either clean or carbon neutral, so their use does not contribute to global warming. Lack of pollutants means fewer environmental and health problems. Unlimited supply.	Relatively expensive; produce comparatively less energy than non-renewables. Reliance on renewable sources would require a reduction in energy consumption. Factors such as weather conditions cause supply to fluctuate.

Energy source	Advantages	Disadvantages
Nuclear	Clean, reliable source of cheap energy. Produces no CO_2 or SO_2, so does not contribute to global warming or acid rain. Produces little waste.	Radioactive waste is a huge health risk; disposal very difficult and expensive. Inefficient: only 1% of the uranium is used. High waste-handling and decommissioning costs mean that overall cost of nuclear power is high.

Types of renewable energy

Energy type	Description	Advantages	Disadvantages
Bioenergy (biofuels)	The production of fuels from plant material or animal waste. Includes production of bioethanol by fermentation of crops, biogas from the anaerobic respiration of slurry (from eg manure or grass clippings) by bacteria, and biodiesel from plant oils.	'Carbon neutral' – any CO_2 released when the fuels are burned is balanced by the CO_2 absorbed when the plants were alive. Compost or fertilizers can be produced as by-products from biogas production. Biodiesel can also be made from used cooking oil.	Planting appropriate crops can endanger natural habitats. Planting and harvesting appropriate crops for bioethanol and biodiesel can use a large amount of energy; fertilizing them can cause environmental problems.
Bioenergy (combustion)	The burning of fast-growing plant materials such as wood or straw.	'Carbon neutral' – any CO_2 produced by burning is balanced by the CO_2 absorbed when the plants were alive.	Requires a sustainable source (eg trees have to be replanted). Burning produces some pollution, eg particulates, dioxin and other harmful substances. Planting such crops can endanger natural habitats.
Geothermal	Superheated steam from within the earth is used to drive turbines.	Very reliable – can give a constant stable supply.	Can only be used in certain geological conditions that only exist in a few places.

Energy type	Description	Advantages	Disadvantages
Hydroelectric	River water flows through turbines, which generate electricity.	Very efficient, gives a good steady and reliable source. Reservoirs can be used as water supplies and dams can control flooding.	Causes extensive flooding when commissioned. Affects the flow regime of the river. These consequences can be detrimental to the environment and people living nearby.
Hydrogen	Hydrogen and oxygen are supplied to a fuel cell, where they react to form water. The resulting spare electrons flow out of the cell, generating an electric current.	The only by-product is water. Could be used to store energy like a battery, solving intermittence problems with other types of renewable energy.	Very expensive. Requires hydrogen but this is usually produced in ways that produce some greenhouse gases.
Solar	The Sun's energy is used either to heat up water or to produce an electric current in photovoltaic cells. These technologies are sometimes referred to as solar panels.	Electricity/heat is created at source, without the need to transport it. No mechanical parts, so no noise.	Expensive, dependent on the weather, and must be replaced every 15–20 years.
Tidal	A barrage retains the water of high tide; at low tide it is released through a turbine, generating electricity.	Reliable and predictable. Potentially could contribute 15% of the UK's energy.	Requires a 5 m head of water, which exists in few places around the world. Can damage aquatic and shoreline ecosystems. Can trap pollution and sediment.
Wave	The motion of the water is used to move parts of a machine or to force air through a turbine, generating electricity.	Low visual impact, creates calm water, provides coastal protection and attracts some marine wildlife.	Difficult to maintain in the harsh conditions of the sea.
Wind	The wind forces the blades of a turbine to rotate generating electricity	Countless potential sites, especially with offshore wind farms. Leave very little trace on countryside after decommission.	Some people believe them to be noisy and ugly. They depend on the weather.

PICTURING THE WORLD

WORLD POLITICAL MAP

RUS. FED.

Beaufort Sea

Alaska (U.S.A.)

Yukon

Great Bear Lake

Gulf of Alaska

Great Slave Lake

CANADA

Hudson Bay

Baffin Bay

Greenland (Den.)

Greenland St

Jan Mayen (Norw.)

Arctic Circle

ICELAND

Reykjavik

Labrador Sea

Faroe Is. (Den.)

NORW

Oslo

North Sea

DENMAR

København

UNITED KINGDOM

IRELAND

Berl

London

NETH.

GERMA

BELG.

LUX.

Paris

FRANCE

SWITZ. A

M.

ITA

Madrid

Roma

Nelson

Saskatchewan

Missouri

L. Winnipeg

L. Superior

L. Michigan

L. Huron

Montréal

Chicago

Ottawa

St-Lawrence

L. Erie

L. Ontario

New York

Washington

UNITED STATES

OF AMERICA

Colorado

Los Angeles

Rio Grande

Mississippi

St-Pierre-et-Miquelon (Fr.)

Bermuda (U.K.)

Azores (Port.)

PORTUGAL

SPAIN

Lisboa

Madeira (Port.)

Rabat

MOROCCO

Alger

Tunis

TUNISIA

T

Tropic of Cancer

MEXICO

Gulf of Mexico

México

La Habana

CUBA

Nassau

THE BAHAMAS

Atlantic Ocean

Islas Canarias (Sp.)

WESTERN SAHARA

Sahar

ALGERIA

DOMINICAN REP.

Puerto Rico (U.S.A.)

BELIZE

GUATEMALA

Guatemala

San Salvador

EL SALVADOR

JAMAICA

HAITI

Port-au-Prince

Santo Domingo

ST KITTS & NEVIS

ANTIGUA & BARBUDA

Guadeloupe (Fr.)

DOMINICA

Martinique (Fr.)

ST LUCIA

BARBADOS

Nouakchott

MAURITANIA

MALI

NIGER

e

HONDURAS

NICARAGUA

Managua

Caribbean Sea

ST VINCENT &

THE GRENADINES

GRENADA

TRINIDAD & TOBAGO

Port of Spain

CAPE VERDE

Dakar

SENEGAL

THE GAMBIA

Banjul

Bissau

GUINEA BIS.

Bamako

BURKINA

Niamey

NIGERIA

Île Clipperton (Fr.)

San José

COSTA RICA

Panamá

PANAMA

VENEZUELA

Georgetown

GUYANA

Paramaribo

SURINAME

Conakry

GUINEA

Freetown

SIERRA LEONE

CÔTE D'IVOIRE

Abuja

BENIN

TOGO

GHANA

Porto-Novo

Bogotá

COLOMBIA

Caracas

Fr. Guiana

Monrovia

LIBERIA

Yamoussoukro

Accra

Lomé

CAMEROON

Yaoundé

EQ. G.

Equator

Islas Galápagos (Ec.)

Quito

EQUADOR

Amazonas

Amazonia

SÃO TOMÉ & PRÍNCIPE

Libreville

GABON

CON

Brazzaville

PERU

Lima

BRAZIL

Brasília

Ascension (U.K.)

Luanda

AN

Pacific Ocean

La Paz

BOLIVIA

Sucre

St Helena (U.K.)

NA

Windho

PARAGUAY

Asunción

Rio de Janeiro

São Paulo

Tropic of Capricorn

Isla Sala y Gómez (Chile)

Isla de Pascua (Easter Island) (Chile)

CHILE

Paraná

Atlantic Ocean

Cape T

Archipiélago Juan Fernández (Chile)

Santiago

URUGUAY

Montevideo

Buenos Aires

Tristan da Cunha (U.K.)

ARGENTINA

Falkland Is. (U.K.)

South Georgia (U.K.)

Bouvetø (Norw.)

• capital city

• other major city

Antarctic Circle

120°

60°

120°

60°

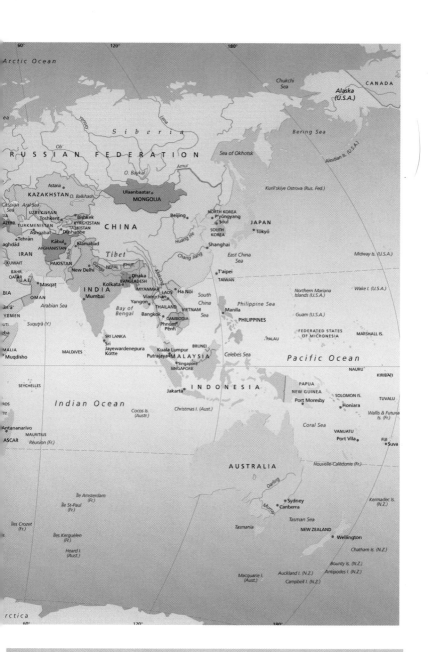

Arctic Ocean

60°　　　　120°　　　　180°

CANADA

Chukchi
Sea

Alaska
(U.S.A.)

ea

Siberia

Ob'　　　Yenisey

Bering Sea

RUSSIAN FEDERATION

Sea of Okhotsk

Aleutian Is. (U.S.A.)

O. Baykal

Amur

Lena

Astana

KAZAKHSTAN

O. Balkhash

Ulaanbaatar
MONGOLIA

Kuril'skiye Ostrova (Rus. Fed.)

Caspian
Sea

Aral Sea

UZBEKISTAN

Toshkent

Bishkek

KYRGYZSTAN

Beijing

NORTH KOREA
P'yōngyang
Sŏul

JAPAN

AZERB.

TURKMENISTAN

TAJIKISTAN

CHINA

SOUTH
KOREA

Tōkyō

Tehrān

Ashgabat

Dushanbe

Huang He

aghdād

Kābul

Islamabad

Shanghai

East China
Sea

Midway Is. (U.S.A.)

IRAN

AFGHANISTAN

Tibet

Chang Jiang

KUWAIT

PAKISTAN

NEPAL

BHUT.

New Delhi

Ganges

T'aipei

BAHR.

Kolkata

Dhaka

TAIWAN

QATAR

Mekong

U.A.E.

Masqaṭ

INDIA

BANGLADESH

MYANMAR

LAOS

Ha Nôi

BIA

OMAN

Mumbai

Viangchan

South
China

Philippine Sea

Wake I. (U.S.A.)

Northern Mariana
Islands (U.S.A.)

an'a'

Arabian Sea

THAILAND

VIETNAM

Sea

Manila

Guam (U.S.A.)

YEMEN

Bay of
Bengal

Bangkok

CAMBODIA

Phnúm
Pénh

PHILIPPINES

UTI

Suquṭrā (Y.)

ba

SRI LANKA

PALAU

FEDERATED STATES
OF MICRONESIA

MARSHALL IS.

MALIA

Muqdisho

MALDIVES

Sri
Jayewardenepura
Kotte

BRUNEI

Kuala Lumpur

MALAYSIA

Celebes Sea

Pacific Ocean

Putrajaya

SEYCHELLES

Singapore

SINGAPORE

NAURU

KIRIBATI

INDONESIA

PAPUA
NEW GUINEA

Jakarta

Indian Ocean

Cocos Is.
(Austr.)

Christmas I. (Aust.)

Port Moresby

SOLOMON IS.

Honiara

TUVALU

Wallis & Futuna
Is. (Fr.)

ROS

Antananarivo

MAURITIUS

Coral Sea

VANUATU

Port Vila

FIJI

ntarivo

Réunion (Fr.)

Suva

ASCAR

Nouvelle-Calédonie (Fr.)

Île Amsterdam
(Fr.)

Île St-Paul
(Fr.)

AUSTRALIA

Kermadec Is.
(N.Z.)

Darling

Sydney

Canberra

Îles Crozet
(Fr.)

s

Îles Kerguélen
(Fr.)

Murray

Tasman Sea

Heard I.
(Aust.)

Tasmania

NEW ZEALAND

Wellington

Chatham Is. (N.Z.)

Bounty Is. (N.Z.)

rctica

Macquarie I.
(Aust.)

Auckland I. (N.Z.)

Antipodes I. (N.Z.)

Campbell I. (N.Z.)

60°　　　　120°　　　　180°

RELIEF MAPS
Europe

70°N

GREENLAND (DEN.)

Denmark Strait

Lofoten

NORWEGIAN SEA

ICELAND
Reykjavík ▲ *Hvannadalshnúkur 2 119 m*

Faroe Islands (DEN.)

Shetland Is Bergen ● **Oslo** ● St

NORWAY Göte

Orkney Is

Outer Hebrides UNITED KINGDOM *NORTH*

BRITISH ISLES ● Glasgow **København (Copenhagen)** DENMARK

Belfast ● *SEA*

Liverpool

Dublin ● **Amsterdam** **Berlin**

IRELAND

Birmingham NETH. GERMANY

London ● Lille ● **Bruxelles** Frankfur BELG.

ATLANTIC

50°

ENGLISH CHANNEL LUX.

Paris München (Munich)

Nantes *Loire* FRANCE SWITZ. AUS

OCEAN

Bay of Biscay Lyon **Bern** **Ljublja**

Bordeaux *Mt Blanc 4 808 m* Milano (Milan) SL

Toulouse ITALY

Cabo Fisterra Marseille **R**

Bilbao *Pyrenees* Corse

ANDORRA

40°

Porto ● **Madrid** Barcelona Nap

PORTUGAL *Tajo* Valencia Sardegna (Nap

Azores (PORT.)

Lisboa (Lisbon) SPAIN *TYRRH SE*

Islas Baleares

Cabo de São Vicente Sevilla ● *Mulhacén ▲ 3 478 m* Palerm

Gibraltar (U.K.) Sic.

Tanger *Alger*

Oran

Casablanca ● **Rabat** TUNISIA T

Madeira (PORT.) MOROCCO ALGERIA

30°

Europe

200 500 1000 2000 4000 m

● population over 5,000,000
● population 1,000,000 to 5,00

BARENTS SEA

O. Kolguyev

Arctic Circle

Kol'skiy
Poluostrov
(Kola Peninsula)

*Beloye
More*

Arkhangel'sk

Z a p a d n o
(W e s t)

S i b i r s k a y a
(S i b e r i a n)

R a v n i n a
(P l a i n)

R U S S I A N

O. Onezhskoye
(L. Onega)

Ladozhskoye O.
(L. Ladoga)

F E D E R A T I O N

Irtysh

Tallinn

Sankt-Peterburg
(St Petersburg)

ONIA

Rīga

Volga

Nizhniy
Novgorod

Chelyabinsk

Omsk

Moskva
(Moscow)

Minsk

*Sredne-Russkaya
Vozvyshennost'*

KAZAKHSTAN

BELARUS

Don

Ural

Kyiv
(Kiev)

Dnipro

Volgograd

*Prikaspiyskaya
Nizmennost'
(Caspian Lowland)*

UKRAINE

Volga

Dnipropetrov'sk

Rostov-
na-Donu

MOLDOVA

est

Chişinău

SEA
OF AZOV

Crimea

*ARAL
SEA*

Syrdar'ya

UZBEKISTAN

ANIA

grad

Danube

București

Caucasus

CASPIAN

CASPIAN

SEA

Amudar'ya

BULGARIA

BLACK

Elbrus
5 642 m

Sofiya

SEA

kopje

İstanbul

GEORGIA

Tbilisi

Baki

TURKMENISTAN

Olympos 2 917 m

Ankara

Yerevan

AZERBAIJAN

Ashgabat

*AEGEAN
SEA*

Mt Ararat
5 165 m

ARMENIA

İzmir

Athina (Athens)

T U R K E Y

Adana

Lefkosia

SYRIA

IRAQ

Tehrān

AFGHANISTAN

Kriti

CYPRUS

Beirut

Damascus

LEBANON

ISRAEL

Baghdād

Nahr Dijlah

Esfahān

Kandahār

I R A N

EAN SEA

Jerusalem

'Ammān

Al Furāt

JORDAN

Cairo

KUWAIT
Kuwait

500 km

PAKISTAN

EGYPT

SAUDI
ARABIA

oulation 100,000 to 1,000,000

oulation less than 100,000

RELIEF MAPS
United Kingdom

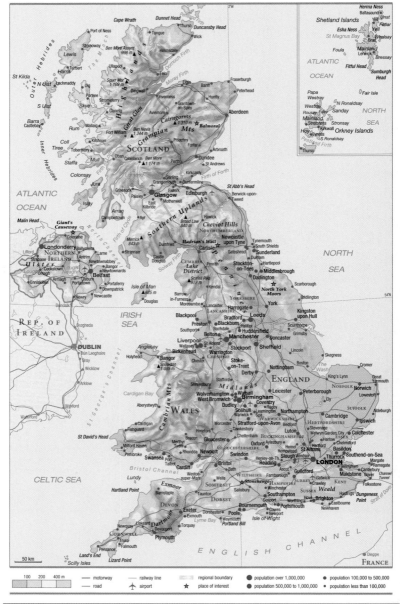

100 200 400 m   — motorway   — railway line   regional boundary   ● population over 1,000,000   ● population 100,000 to 500,000

— road   ✈ airport   ★ place of interest   ● population 500,000 to 1,000,000   • population less than 100,000

50 km

RELIEF MAPS
Republic of Ireland

Ireland

★ place of interest

100   200 m

— road
— railway line
✈ airport
▓ provincial boundary

● population over 500,000
● population 100,000 to 500,000
● population 50,000 to 100,000
• population less than 50,000

RELIEF MAPS
United States of America

HAWAIIAN ISLANDS

Kauai Hanalei
  Kapaa
Lehua   Lihue
Niihau   Waialua   Oahu
Kaula   Wahiawa Kaneohe
        Pearl Honolulu Molokai
        Harbor Hoolehua Halawa
              Lanai Wailuku Maui
        Kahoolawe   Channel
                Upolu   Hawi
                Point   Honokaa
            Kiholo Waimea
            Makena Area Hilo
            Kealakekua ▲ 4 205 m
            Bay   Captain Kilauea Crater
                  Cook Pahala
                  Ka Lae

PACIFIC

OCEAN

100 km

Gulf of
St Lawrence

Île d' Anticosti

Prince Edward
Island

Saint John   Halifax
MAINE
Bangor
Québec   Augusta
Montreal   Montpelier   Portland
Lake   Burlington NEW   Gulf
Placid ☆   VERMONT HAMPSHIRE of Maine
Adirondack   Concord
Mountains   MASSACHUSETTS
Saratoga Springs ☆ Worcester Boston
Syracuse   Albany Springfield Providence
Rochester   Hartford RHODE ISLAND
Niagara Falls Buffalo NEW YORK CONNECTICUT
              Scranton Long Island
Erie   PENNSYLVANIA Paterson New Haven
            Bethlehem Newark Bridgeport
Cleveland   Allentown New York NEW JERSEY
Akron Pittsburgh Harrisburg Trenton
OHIO   Philadelphia
        Gettysburg Atlantic City
Columbus   Dover
Dayton   Baltimore DELAWARE
Cincinnati WEST   Annapolis
          VIRGINIA WASHINGTON D.C.
Charleston   Richmond MARYLAND
        Appomattox Chesapeake Bay
Louisville Frankfort Norfolk
  Lexington Yorktown ☆ Virginia Beach
KENTUCKY Newport News Portsmouth
Owensboro VIRGINIA
        Greensboro Durham Cape Hatteras
Mammoth Mt Mitchell Raleigh
Cave ▲ 2 037 m Winston-Salem NORTH
Nashville Knoxville Fayetteville CAROLINA
TENNESSEE Charlotte Wilmington
Chattanooga Greenville
          Columbia SOUTH Cape Fear
Huntsville   CAROLINA
        Atlanta Augusta
          Charleston

WISCONSIN
Thunder Bay
Superior
Marquette Sault
Ste Marie Sudbury
Georgian
Bay OTTAWA
St Paul Green Bay
Eau Appleton MICHIGAN
Claire Saginaw Toronto
Madison Grand Lake
  Milwaukee Rapids Flint Ontario
Rockford Racine Lansing Warren Detroit
Cedar Ann Arbor
Rapids   South Bend Toledo
Davenport Chicago Gary
ILLINOIS Fort Wayne
Peoria Champaign Indianapolis
City   Springfield INDIANA
St Louis
SSOURI Evansville
Ozark Memphis
Plateau
KANSAS
ock
Pine Bluff West
      Point Birmingham Macon Savannah
MISSISSIPPI   ALABAMA GEORGIA Brunswick
eport Vicksburg Montgomery Columbus
Monroe Jackson
UISIANA   Pensacola
      Mobile Tallahassee
Baton Rouge   Jacksonville
Lafayette Metairie FLORIDA Daytona Beach
hur New Orleans Cape San Blas
Mississippi Delta   Orlando Cape Canaveral
        St Petersburg Tampa Grand
            Sarasota Palm Bahama Great
                  Beach   Abaco
        Cape Sable Fort Lauderdale
        Key West Miami Miami Beach Eleuthera
        Florida Keys Everglades NASSAU
              National Park Andros
GULF OF   Straits of Florida
MEXICO   LA HABANA Matanzas
        Pinar del Río Santa Clara BAHAMAS
        Cienfuegos Tropic of Cancer
            CUBA
        Isla de la Juventud
Yucatán Channel   Cayman
Mérida Cancún   Islands
                (U.K.)
Yucatán

CARIBBEAN SEA

ICO GUATEMALA BELIZE BELMOPAN

Lake Superior
Lake Michigan
Lake Huron
Lake Erie

ATLANTIC

OCEAN

Allegheny Mts
Cumberland Plateau
Appalachian Mountains

150 km

● population over 5,000,000
● population 1,000,000 to 5,000,000
● population 100,000 to 1,000,000
• population less than 100,000

— road   —— international
                  boundary
--- railway line --- state boundary
✈ airport   Denver state capital

★ place of interest

0   200   500   1000   2000 m

RELIEF MAPS
North America

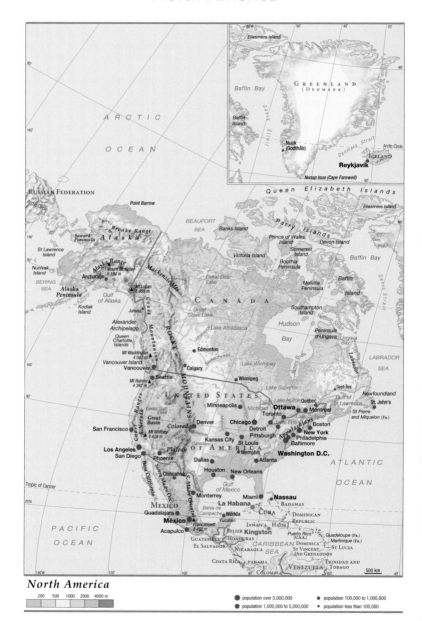

North America

RELIEF MAPS
Central and South America

Central and South America

200 500 1000 2000 4000 m

● population over 5,000,000   ● population 100,000 to 1,000,000
● population 1,000,000 to 5,000,000   · population less than 100,000

Africa

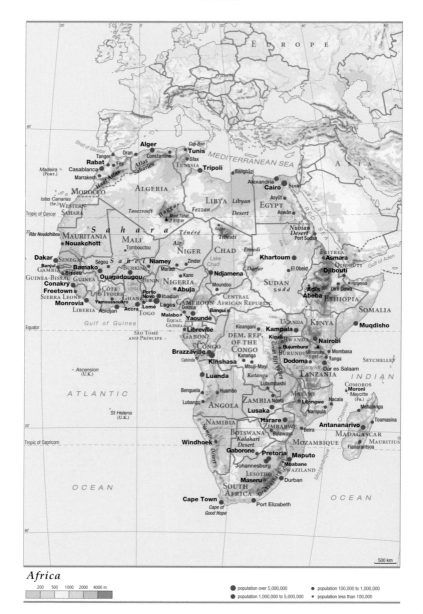

EUROPE

ASIA

Strait of Gibraltar

Madeira (Port.)

Alger
Tanger
Oran
Constantine
Tunis
Cap Bon
Sfax
TUNISIA
Tripoli
Banghāzī

MEDITERRANEAN SEA

Rabat
Fès
Casablanca
Atlas Saharien
Marrakech
MOROCCO
Atlas
Alexandria
Cairo
Sinai

Islas Canarias (Sp.)
WESTERN
SAHARA

Tropic of Cancer

ALGERIA
LIBYA
Asyūt
EGYPT
Aswān

Tanezrouft
Fezzan
Libyan Desert

Hassar
▲ Mont Tahat 2 918 m

Nubian Desert
Port Sudan

RED SEA

Rās Nouâdhibou
MAURITANIA
Nouakchott
MALI
Tombouctou
Air
NIGER
CHAD
Emedi
Tibesti

S a h a r a
Ténéré

Aozou

Khartoum
ERITREA
Asmara
DJIBOUTI
Gulf of Aden

Dakar
SENEGAL
Séguú
S a h e l
Niamey
Zinder
Maradi
Lake Chad
Darfur
El Obeid
Djibouti

Banjul
GAMBIA
Bissau
GUINEA-BISSAU
Bamako
BURKINA
Ouagadougou
BENIN
NIGERIA
Kano
Ndjamena
Moundou
SUDAN
Sudd
Ādīs Ābeba
Dirē Dawa
Hargeysa

Conakry
GUINEA
Freetown
SIERRA LEONE
Monrovia
LIBERIA
CÔTE D'IVOIRE
Yamoussoukro
Abidjan
GHANA
Accra
Lake Volta
Porto Novo
Abuja
Ibadan
Lagos
TOGO
Lomé
Malabo
EQUAT. GUINEA
Douala
CAMEROON
Bangui
CENTRAL AFRICAN REPUBLIC
Ethiopia
SOMALIA

Gulf of Guinea
SÃO TOMÉ AND PRÍNCIPE
Yaoundé
Libreville
GABON
Kisangani
Uele
UGANDA
Kampala
KENYA
Muqdisho

Equator
Congo
DEM. REP. OF THE CONGO
RWANDA
Kigali
Bujumbura
BURUNDI
Kilimanjaro 5 895 m
Nairobi
Mombasa

Brazzaville
Cabinda
Kinshasa
Kananga
Mbuji-Mayi
Katanga
Dodoma
TANZANIA
Tanga
Dar es Salaam
SEYCHELLES

Luanda
Benguela
Huambo
Lubumbashi
Lake Tanganyika
INDIAN

ATLANTIC
Lubango
ANGOLA
ZAMBIA
Ndola
Lusaka
MALAWI
Lilongwe
Nacala
Nampula
COMOROS
Moroni
Mayotte (Fr.)
Mahajanga
Toamasina

St Helena (U.K.)
Harare
ZIMBABWE
Bulawayo
Beira
Antananarivo

Ascension (U.K.)

20°
NAMIBIA
BOTSWANA
Kalahari Desert
MOZAMBIQUE
MADAGASCAR
MAURITIUS

Tropic of Capricorn
Windhoek
Gaborone
Pretoria
Maputo
Fianarantsoa

Johannesburg
Mbabane
SWAZILAND

OCEAN
Maseru
LESOTHO
Durban
SOUTH AFRICA

Cape Town
Cape of Good Hope
Port Elizabeth

OCEAN

500 km

Africa

200 500 1000 2000 4000 m

● population over 5,000,000   ● population 100,000 to 1,000,000
● population 1,000,000 to 5,000,000   · population less than 100,000

RELIEF MAPS
Asia

Asia

200 500 1000 2000 4000 m

● population over 5,000,000
● population 1,000,000 to 5,000,000
● population 100,000 to 1,000,000
· population less than 100,000

RELIEF MAPS
Australia and New Zealand

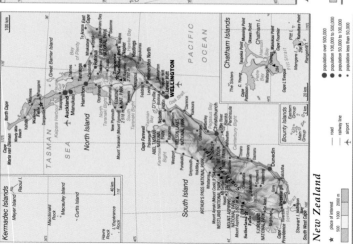

Australia

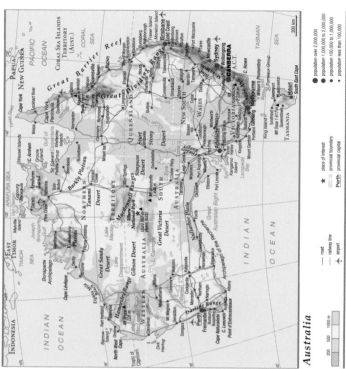

New Zealand

RELIEF MAPS
Oceania and Melanesia

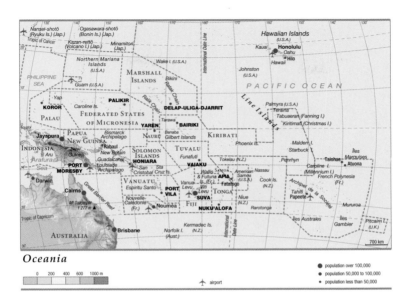

Oceania

0 200 400 600 1000 m

✈ airport

● population over 100,000
● population 50,000 to 100,000
• population less than 50,000

700 km

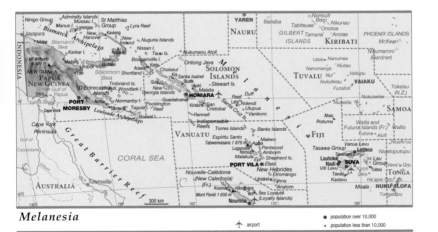

Melanesia

✈ airport

● population over 10,000
• population less than 10,000

300 km

RELIEF MAPS
Arctic and Antarctic

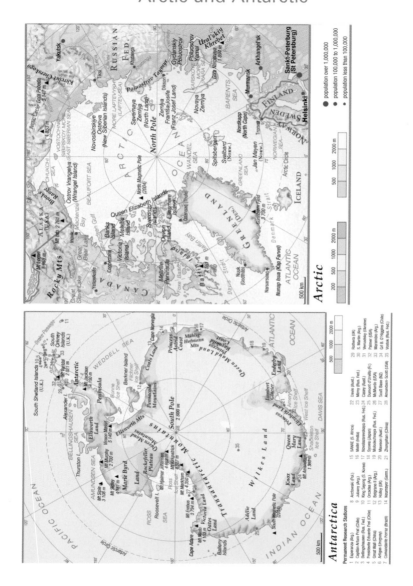

● population over 1,000,000
● population 100,000 to 1,000,000
• population less than 100,000

Arctic

Antarctica

Permanent Research Stations

1 Esperanza (Arg.)	8 Arctowski (Pol.)	15 SANAE (S. Africa)	22 Davis (Aust.)	29 Rothera (UK)
2 Capitán Arturo Prat (Chile)	9 Jubany (Arg.)	16 Maitri (India)	23 Mirny (Rus. Fed.)	30 S. Martin (Arg.)
3 Bellingshausen (Rus. Fed.)	10 King Sejong (S. Korea)	17 Novolazarevskaya (Rus. Fed.)	24 Casey (Aust.)	31 Vernadsky (Ukraine)
4 Presidente Eduardo Frei (Chile)	11 Orcadas (Arg.)	18 Syowa (Japan)	25 Dumont d'Urville (Fr.)	32 Palmer (USA)
5 Great Wall (China)	12 Belgrano II (Arg.)	19 Molodezhnaya (Rus. Fed.)	26 McMurdo (USA)	33 Marambio (Arg.)
6 Jinnah (Pak.)	13 Halley (UK)	20 Mawson (Aust.)	27 Scott Base (NZ)	34 Gral. B. O'Higgins (Chile)
7 Comandante Ferraz (Brazil)	14 Neumayer (Germ.)	21 Zhongshan (China)	28 Amundsen-Scott (USA)	35 Vostok (Rus. Fed.)

562

THEMATIC MAPS
Predominant languages and religions

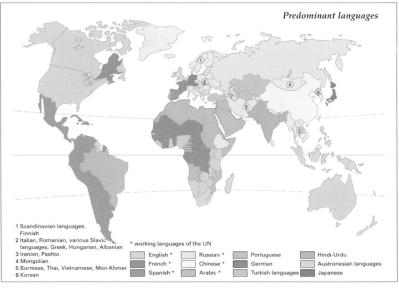

Predominant languages

1 Scandinavian languages,
  Finnish
2 Italian, Romanian, various Slavic
  languages, Greek, Hungarian, Albanian
3 Iranian, Pashto
4 Mongolian
5 Burmese, Thai, Vietnamese, Mon-Khmer
6 Korean

* working languages of the UN

English *	Russian *
French *	Chinese *
Spanish *	Arabic *

Portuguese	Hindi-Urdu
German	Austronesian languages
Turkish languages	Japanese

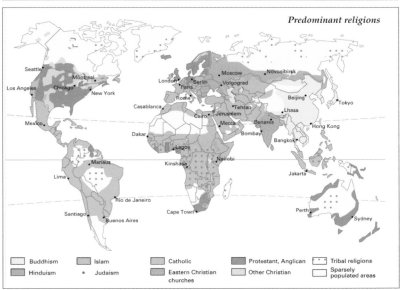

Predominant religions

Buddhism	Islam	Catholic
Hinduism	• Judaism	Eastern Christian churches

Protestant, Anglican	Tribal religions
Other Christian	Sparsely populated areas

THEMATIC MAPS
Population density and growth

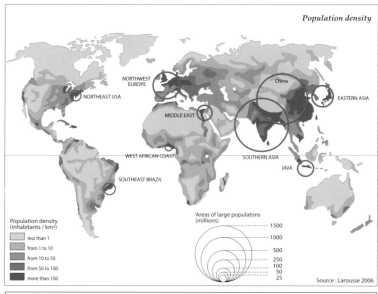

Population density

NORTHWEST
EUROPE

China

NORTHEAST USA

EASTERN ASIA

MIDDLE EAST

WEST AFRICAN COAST

SOUTHERN ASIA

JAVA

SOUTHEAST BRAZIL

Population density
(inhabitants / km²)

- less than 1
- from 1 to 10
- from 10 to 50
- from 50 to 100
- more than 100

Areas of large populatons
(millions)

1500
1000
500
250
100
50
25

Source : Larousse 2006

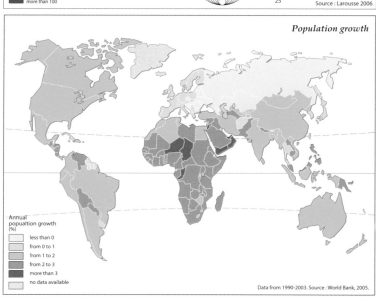

Population growth

Annual
popualtion growth
(%)

- less than 0
- from 0 to 1
- from 1 to 2
- from 2 to 3
- more than 3
- no data available

Data from 1990-2003. Source : World Bank, 2005.

THEMATIC MAPS
Birth and mortality rates

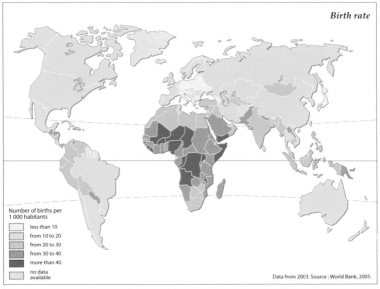

Birth rate

Number of births per
1 000 habitants

- less than 10
- from 10 to 20
- from 20 to 30
- from 30 to 40
- more than 40
- no data available

Data from 2003. Source : World Bank, 2005.

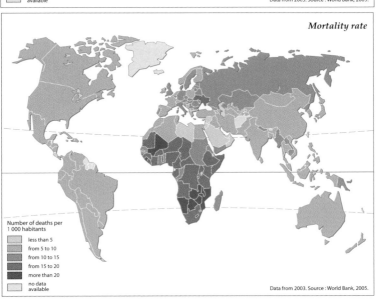

Mortality rate

Number of deaths per
1 000 habitants

- less than 5
- from 5 to 10
- from 10 to 15
- from 15 to 20
- more than 20
- no data available

Data from 2003. Source : World Bank, 2005.

THEMATIC MAPS
Life expectancy and available food supplies

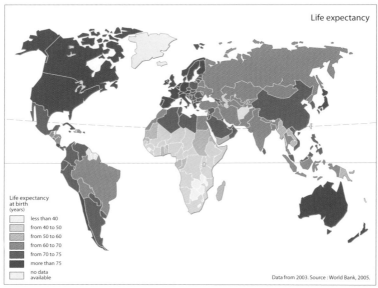

Life expectancy

Life expectancy
at birth
(years)

less than 40
from 40 to 50
from 50 to 60
from 60 to 70
from 70 to 75
more than 75
no data
available

Data from 2003. Source : World Bank, 2005.

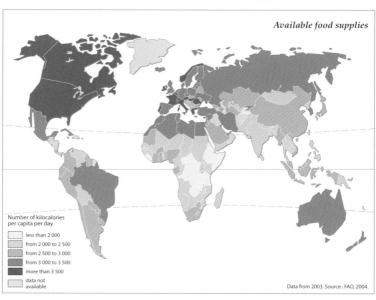

Available food supplies

Number of kilocalories
per capita per day

less than 2 000
from 2 000 to 2 500
from 2 500 to 3 000
from 3 000 to 3 500
more than 3 500
data not
available

Data from 2003. Source : FAO, 2004.

THEMATIC MAPS
Healthcare spending and access to medicines

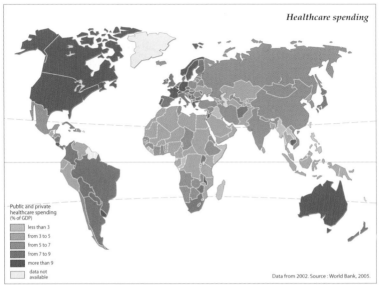

Healthcare spending

Public and private
healthcare spending
(% of GDP)

- less than 3
- from 3 to 5
- from 5 to 7
- from 7 to 9
- more than 9
- data not available

Data from 2002. Source : World Bank, 2005.

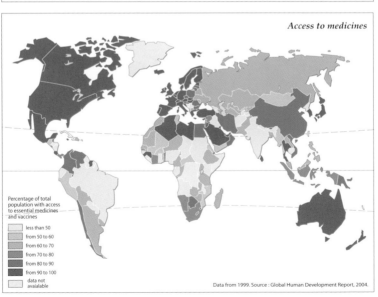

Access to medicines

Percentage of total
population with access
to essential medicines
and vaccines

- less than 50
- from 50 to 60
- from 60 to 70
- from 70 to 80
- from 80 to 90
- from 90 to 100
- data not avaialable

Data from 1999. Source : Global Human Development Report, 2004.

THEMATIC MAPS
Availability of doctors and school enrolment

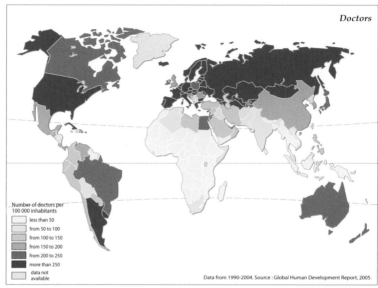

Doctors

Number of doctors per
100 000 inhabitants

- less than 50
- from 50 to 100
- from 100 to 150
- from 150 to 200
- from 200 to 250
- more than 250
- data not available

Data from 1990-2004. Source : Global Human Development Report, 2005.

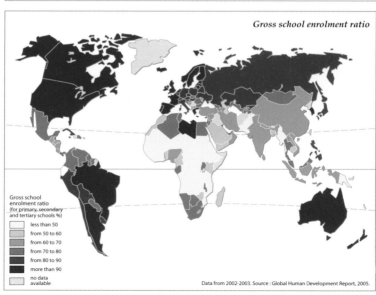

Gross school enrolment ratio

Gross school
enrolment ratio
(for primary, secondary
and tertiary schools %)

- less than 50
- from 50 to 60
- from 60 to 70
- from 70 to 80
- from 80 to 90
- more than 90
- no data available

Data from 2002-2003. Source : Global Human Development Report, 2005.

THEMATIC MAPS
Access to clean water and carbon dioxide emissions

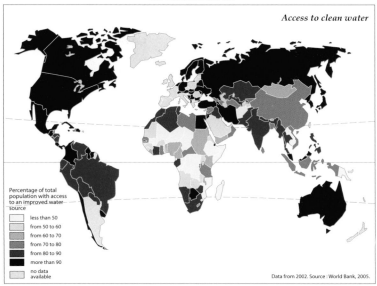

Access to clean water

Percentage of total
population with access
to an improved water
source

- less than 50
- from 50 to 60
- from 60 to 70
- from 70 to 80
- from 80 to 90
- more than 90
- no data available

Data from 2002. Source : World Bank, 2005.

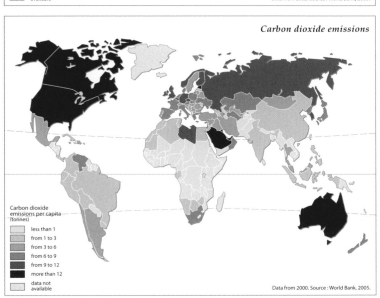

Carbon dioxide emissions

Carbon dioxide
emissions per capita
(tonnes)

- less than 1
- from 1 to 3
- from 3 to 6
- from 6 to 9
- from 9 to 12
- more than 12
- data not available

Data from 2000. Source : World Bank, 2005.

THEMATIC MAPS
Energy production and consumption

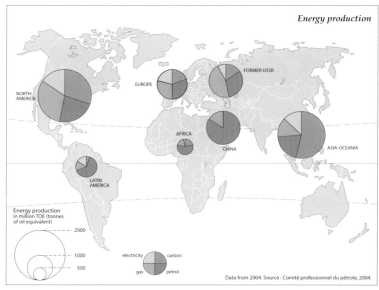

Energy production

NORTH
AMERICA

EUROPE

FORMER USSR

AFRICA

CHINA

ASIA-OCEANIA

LATIN
AMERICA

Energy production
in million TOE (tonnes
of oil equivalent)

- 2000
- 1000
- 500

electricity — carbon
gas — petrol

Data from 2004. Source : Comité professionnel du pétrole, 2004.

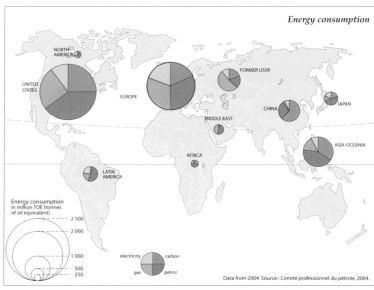

Energy consumption

NORTH
AMERICA

UNITED
STATES

EUROPE

FORMER USSR

MIDDLE EAST

CHINA

JAPAN

AFRICA

LATIN
AMERICA

ASIA-OCEANIA

Energy consumption
in million TOE (tonnes
of oil equivalent)

- 2 500
- 2 000
- 1 000
- 500
- 250

electricity — carbon
gas — petrol

Data from 2004. Source : Comité professionnel du pétrole, 2004.

THEMATIC MAPS
Forests and deforestation

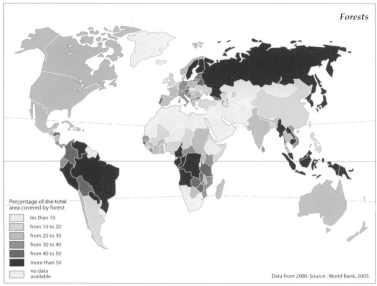

Forests

Percentage of the total area covered by forest

- les than 10
- from 10 to 20
- from 20 to 30
- from 30 to 40
- from 40 to 50
- more than 50
- no data available

Data from 2000. Source : World Bank, 2005.

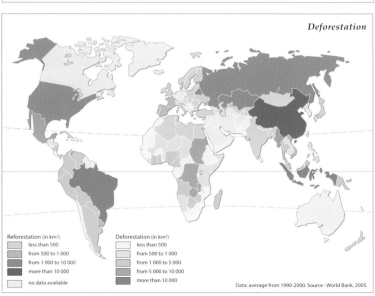

Deforestation

Reforestation (in km²)
- less than 500
- from 500 to 1 000
- from 1 000 to 10 000
- more than 10 000
- no data available

Deforestation (in km²)
- less than 500
- from 500 to 1 000
- from 1 000 to 5 000
- from 5 000 to 10 000
- more than 10 000

Data: average from 1990-2000. Source : World Bank, 2005.

THEMATIC MAPS
Freshwater resources and usage

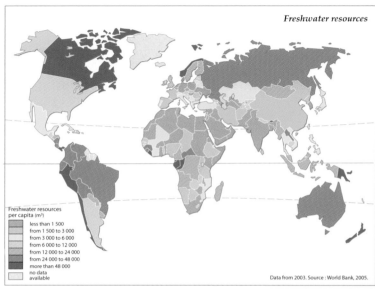

Freshwater resources

Freshwater resources
per capita (m³)

- less than 1 500
- from 1 500 to 3 000
- from 3 000 to 6 000
- from 6 000 to 12 000
- from 12 000 to 24 000
- from 24 000 to 48 000
- more than 48 000
- no data available

Data from 2003. Source : World Bank, 2005.

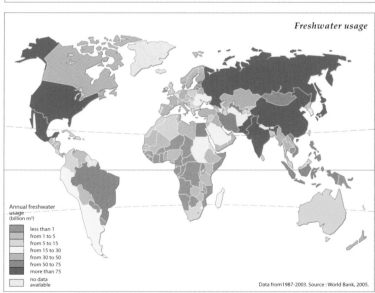

Freshwater usage

Annual freshwater
usage
(billion m³)

- less than 1
- from 1 to 5
- from 5 to 15
- from 15 to 30
- from 30 to 50
- from 50 to 75
- more than 75
- no data available

Data from 1987-2003. Source : World Bank, 2005.

THEMATIC MAPS
Climate and vegetation

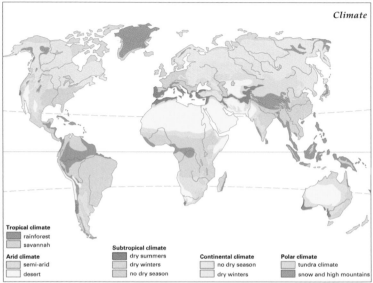

Climate

Tropical climate
- rainforest
- savannah

Arid climate
- semi-arid
- desert

Subtropical climate
- dry summers
- dry winters
- no dry season

Continental climate
- no dry season
- dry winters

Polar climate
- tundra climate
- snow and high mountains

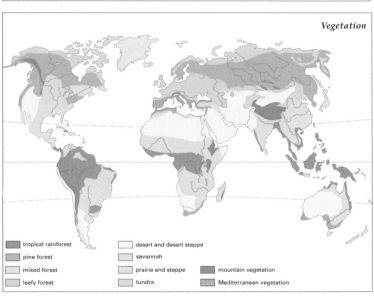

Vegetation

- tropical rainforest
- pine forest
- mixed forest
- leafy forest
- desert and desert steppe
- savannah
- prairie and steppe
- tundra
- mountain vegetation
- Mediterranean vegetation

WORLD FLAGS

Afghanistan

Albania

Algeria

Andorra

Angola

Antigua and
Barbuda

Argentina

Armenia

Australia

Austria

Azerbaijan

The Bahamas

Bahrain

Bangladesh

Barbados

Belarus

Belgium

Belize

Benin

Bhutan

Bolivia

Bosnia and
Herzegovina

Botswana

Brazil

Brunei

Bulgaria

Burkina Faso

Burundi

Cambodia

Cameroon

Canada

Cape Verde

Central African
Republic

Chad

Chile

China

WORLD FLAGS

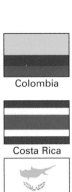
Colombia

Comoros

Congo

Congo, Democratic Republic of the

Costa Rica

Côte d'Ivoire

Croatia

Cuba

Cyprus

Czech Republic

Denmark

Djibouti

Dominica

Dominican Republic

East Timor

Ecuador

Egypt

El Salvador

Equatorial Guinea

Eritrea

Estonia

Ethiopia

Fiji

Finland

France

Gabon

The Gambia

Georgia

Germany

Ghana

Greece

Grenada

Guatemala

Guinea

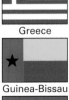
Guinea-Bissau

Guyana

Haiti

Honduras

Hungary

Iceland

WORLD FLAGS

India

Indonesia

Iran

Iraq

Ireland

Israel

Italy

Jamaica

Japan

Jordan

Kazakhstan

Kenya

Kiribati

Korea, North

Korea, South

Kuwait

Kyrgyzstan

Laos

Latvia

Lebanon

Lesotho

Liberia

Libya

Liechtenstein

Lithuania

Luxembourg

Macedonia

Madagascar

Malawi

Malaysia

Maldives

Mali

Malta

Marshall Islands

Mauritania

Mauritius

Mexico

Micronesia

Moldova

Monaco

WORLD FLAGS

Mongolia

Montenegro

Morocco

Mozambique

Myanmar (Burma)

Namibia

Nauru

Nepal

The Netherlands

New Zealand

Nicaragua

Niger

Nigeria

Norway

Oman

Pakistan

Palau

Panama

Papua New Guinea

Paraguay

Peru

Philippines

Poland

Portugal

Qatar

Romania

Russia

Rwanda

St Kitts and Nevis

St Lucia

St Vincent and the Grenadines

Samoa

San Marino

São Tomé and Príncipe

Saudi Arabia

Senegal

Serbia

Seychelles

Sierra Leone

Singapore

WORLD FLAGS

Slovakia

Slovenia

Solomon Islands

Somalia

South Africa

Spain

Sri Lanka

Sudan

Suriname

Swaziland

Sweden

Switzerland

Syria

Taiwan

Tajikistan

Tanzania

Thailand

Togo

Tonga

Trinidad and Tobago

Tunisia

Turkey

Turkmenistan

Tuvalu

Uganda

Ukraine

United Arab Emirates

United Kingdom

United States of America

Uruguay

Uzbekistan

Vanuatu

Vatican

Venezuela

Vietnam

Yemen

Zambia

Zimbabwe

INDEX

NOTE: Locators in **bold type** denote main references; those in *italics* denote maps or
Ilustrations of flags.

D

G

Ga-Adangame people 188
Gabon 34, **180–1**, 333, 448, 451, *548*, *558*, *575*
Gaborone 109, 429, 434, *548*, *558*
Gaddafi, Muammar 248
Gaelic languages and peoples 215, 387
Gagauzi people 272, 273
Gaia theory 55–6, **539–40**
Gairy, Eric 193
Galápagos Islands 160, 160, 518, 522, *548*, *557*
Galápagos Rift 32
gales 12, 20, 26, 29, 44
Galician language and people 352
Galveston Bay 529
Gama, Vasco da 41, 46, 339
Gambia, The 59–60, **181–2**, 448, 452, *548*, *558*, *575*
Gamsakhurdia, Zviad 184
Ganda/Luganda languages 382
Gandhi family 208
Ganges (Padma) River 96, 207
Gan language 132
Gardel, Carlos 83
gardens
    Persian walled 213
    physic 67
Garibaldi, Giuseppe 221
Garifuna people 102
Garnier, Francis (Marie Joseph François) 46
gas
    Bhopal leak of toxic 208, 525
    as energy source 544
Gaudí, Antonio 354
Gaulle, Charles de 177
Gauls, ancient 177
Gayoom, Maumoon Abdul 261
Gaza Strip 219
Gbagbo, Laurent 145
gecko, giant bronze 515
Geer, Baron Gerhard de 46
Gehry, Frank 354
General Motors 403
General Sherman Tree 524
genes, natural selection and individual 40
Genghis Khan 133, 276, 368, 413
gentrification 12
genus, in taxonomy 12
geochronology 12, 22, 50, 52–3, **477–82**
geodesy 12
geographers
    ancient 60, 62, 66
    medieval 42, 52
    early modern 48, 62
geology 13
    surveys and maps 37, 41, 48, 49, 57, 63

timescale 22, **477–82**
uniformitarian principle 56
see also fossils; *and individual geologists on pages 30–70*
geomorphology 13
geophysicists, leading 30, 33, 35, 69, 70
Georgetown 198, 199, 429, 434, *548*, *557*
George Tupou I, King of Tonga 375
Georgia, Republic of **183–4**, 448, 451, 497, *549*, *551*, *559*, *575*
Georgia, USA 64, **404**, *555*
Georgian language 183, 442
geothermal activity 13, 156
    power from 205, 544, 545
German Confederation 185, 250
German Democratic Republic 184, 185, 186
German East Africa 119, 370
German Federal Republic 184, 185, 186
German as official language 444, 445, *563*
    Austria 90
    Liechtenstein 249
    Luxembourg 251
    Switzerland 363
German people abroad 100, 101, 176, 184, 229, 251, 314, 363
Germany **184–7**, *548*, *550*
    African colonies 119, 122, 285, 326, 370, 373
    Anschluss with Austria 91
    Antarctic expedition 43
    in EEC 186
    flag *575*
    ISO codes 448
    IVR code 451
    natural heritage 519, 524
    Pacific colonies and protectorates 265, 272, 287, 306, 309, 331
    and Schleswig-Holstein 153
    reunification 185, 186
    settlers in North America 402
    Weimar Republic 186, 187
    in World War I 186, 251, 252
    in World War II 91, 153, 169, 177, **186**, 192, 252, 300, 315
geysers 205
Ghana (*formerly* Gold Coast) 36, **188–9**, 373, 448, 451, *548*, *558*, *575*
Ghibellines 221
Ghiberti, Lorenzo 222
Gibraltar **397**, 448, 451, *550*
Gibson Desert 47, 86, *560*
Gilaki people 212
Gilbert, Sir Humphrey 46, 48
Gilbert and Ellice Islands *see* Kiribati; Tuvalu
Giles, Ernest 47
Gio people 245
Giotto (di Bondone) 222

N